The Battle for Corporate Control

THE BATTLE FOR CORPORATE CONTROL

Shareholder Rights, Stakeholder Interests, and Managerial Responsibilities

Arnold W. Sametz, Editor
in collaboration with
James L. Bicksler

Salomon Brothers Center
for the Study of
Financial Institutions

Leonard N. Stern
School of Business
New York University

BUSINESS ONE IRWIN
Homewood, Illinois 60430

Project editor: Karen Nelson
Production manager: Carma W. Fazio
Jacket Design: Sam Concialdi
Printer: Arcata Graphics/Kingsport

Library of Congress Cataloging-in-Publication Data

The Battle for corporate control : shareholder rights, stakeholder
  interests, and managerial responsibilities / edited by A. W. Sametz.
    p.   cm.
  "Salomon Brothers Center for the Study of Financial Institutions.
  Leonard N. Stern School of Business. New York University."
  Includes index.
  ISBN 1–55623–305–1
    1. Corporate governance—United States—Congresses.
  2. Corporation law—United States—Congresses. 3. Institutional
  investments—United States—Congresses. 4. Consolidation and merger
  of corporations—United States—Congresses. 5. Stockholders—United
  States—Congresses. I. Sametz, Arnold. II. Salomon Brothers
  Center for the Study of Financial Institutions.
  HD2746.5.B37   1991
  658.4—dc20   90–15053

Printed in the United States of America

1 2 3 4 5 6 7 8 9 0 AGK 7 6 5 4 3 2 1 0

CONTENTS

PREFACE

This is the fifth volume in the on-going BUSINESS ONE IRWIN series of conference proceedings of the Salomon Brothers Center for the Study of Financial Institutions in the Stern School of Business of New York University. Like the first four proceedings volumes—Amihud's *Leveraged Management Buyouts,* White's *Crashes and Panics: The Lessons from History,* Altman's *The High-Yield Debt Market,* Figlewski's *Financial Options: From Theory to Practice*—this volume on *The Battle for Corporate Control* deals with an important current issue analyzed in depth and subjected to cogent criticism by top-notch specialists in finance: academics, practitioners, regulators, and also, in this case, legal experts.

From the 1930s to the 1960s, the separation of ownership from control centered on its economic implications for both shareholders and a presumed dominant incumbent management. Proxies were automatically ceded to the extant Board and Officers. This delegation of power was generally presumed to be in the public interest, largely based on the benefits of specialization: the public specialized in savings and putting them out at risk while management specialized in investing those funds at high average returns. The *financial* efficiencies of this corporate structure prevailed so long as the economy was expanding rapidly and institutionalization of finance was relatively small. But during the 1970s, the onset of a decade of inflation and economic stagnation (stagflation) uncovered the weakness of "tenured" management and the lack of managerial incentives to perform effectively.

Reexamination of corporate management not subject to discipline by its stockholders (owners) intensified as the surge of pension funding and its investment in stock shifted stock ownership from individual to institutional hands. By 1980, the needs for revitalized business management and the rise of block stock trading and ownership set the stage for the revolution in corporate control. Then the stock market upturn and boom and the surge of financial innovations, such as derivative securities and junk bonds, made for rapid implementation of a new pattern of corporate control. These developments could not have been so rapid and decisive in the absence of supporting judicial case law for new, nonpassive stockholder activities.

The new academic models of managerial economics and finance as implemented by the business and financial communities, established the new paradigm of corporate control, just as the new models of portfolio management required change in established legal "prudent man" doctrine. Today, after a decade of rapid development, the market for corporate control is still witnessing a number of dramatic changes in organizational form, financing arrangements, managerial incentives, and consideration of stakeholders other than shareholders. If we are to understand the cost/benefits of the evolving complex system of corporate governance, we must bring to bear the analytical tools and focus of a variety of disciplines. This is precisely the job done for us by the financial economists, the lawyers and judges, and the financial and managerial executives who authored the papers and critiques that compose this volume.

In addition to a many-sided approach to complex issues, such proceedings require dedicated, expert, and objective organization to assure a balanced and judicious overall approach to what in most cases are hotly debated issues. Jim Bicksler, Finance Professor at Rutgers University, was co-director of this conference with me, but, in particular, was the principal "casting director" who "signed up" the stellar speakers and discussants.

All in all, this volume has precisely the high quality and clear relevance that the Salomon Center series of books promised to deliver. It was a serendipitous meeting of minds and we are grateful for the participants' energy and enthusiasm as well as for their demonstrated expertise.

Preparation and delivery of this manuscript to the publisher, like the other volumes in the series, were in the capable hands of Jim Cozby.

Arnold W. Sametz

Professor of Finance,
New York University and
the Sidney Homer and Charles
Simon Director of NYU's
Salomon Brothers Center

INTRODUCTION

Progress, far from consisting in change, depends on retentiveness...
Those who cannot remember the past are condemned to fulfill it.
—George Santayana

When Berle and Means published their classic study in 1933, *The Modern Corporation and Private Property,* they focused on the fact, long recognized by those in business and the law, that a change had occurred in the nature of the corporate enterprise. They pointed to a distinction between stockholders, who played no direct role in corporate management, and the managers, whose ownership generally was insignificant. Federal intervention and guidance were the proposed solutions. In the abyss of the Great Depression, those ideas struck a responsive chord in academia and government. It was as if a blazing discovery had occurred. Yet, the changes observed by Berle and Means were not new. They had existed for many years, and by the 1920s were immutable.

One can speculate on the various factors that gave the Berle and Means' analysis the appearance of novelty. Whatever the reasons, it is probably safe to say that until then there was little discourse of any import, except perhaps the most formal kind, between financial economists, corporate executives, financiers, and the lawyers and judges who addressed their problems.

Fifty-six years after the Berle and Means work, the Conference on Corporate Governance, Restructuring, and the Market for Corporate Control brought these diverse groups together. It was a remarkable program. The expression of ideas, the clash of views, exposed all of us to some very provocative notions of differing disciplines. From free market economists there were a few idiosyncratic thoughts—companies should be sold every five years to maximize stockholders' value; tender offers should be restructured, giving the first bidder priority. Corporate managers expressed frustration at the perceived overzealous intervention by courts and others into the business and affairs entrusted to them. Law professors spoke of the need for new principles of corporate governance. Practicing lawyers discussed the business judgment rule, and the emerging powers and responsibilities of various corporate constituencies, while judges expressed skepticism of certain activities that have emerged in contests for corporate control. Each discipline challenged the other.

These open exchanges were fascinating, indeed memorable. But what brought such diverse groups together for this stimulating debate? One hopes that the force of history played a part.

John Brooks' *Once In Golconda* details the rampant self-indulgences of Wall Street in the 1920s, the stock market crash of 1929, followed by the Great Depression. Many of those events are said to have frightening portents for the 1990s. Like the '20s, the '80s were a time of prosperity, but did the activities on Wall Street at either time represent real economic growth or only wealth shifting? Are there troubling similarities between those two eras? Some, unhesitatingly, say "yes."

What parallels can be drawn from the failures of the conglomerate fad of the 1960s, thought at the time, with unremitting encouragement from Wall Street, to be smart? Where else could one so easily make two plus two equal five? Have the frenzies of the '70s and '80s been justified by productive economic achievement, or merely fueled by greed and ego without regard for potentially disastrous consequences? There are no easy answers to such queries, but the need to pose them is itself a disturbing comment on the period.

While hostile takeovers once were not done by "nice" people, that notion had almost evaporated in the '70s, and was totally repudiated in the '80s by the haste of the financial community and its customers to achieve staggering wealth. The era of junk bonds, those high-yield, highly subordinated securities, made companies thought to be untouchable vulnerable to a hostile bid. Imagine the profound changes that have occurred in our attitudes when a one- or two-billion dollar deal now is considered small. Examine the irony of companies endangering their very existence by deliberately incurring huge debts, depleting their assets with stockholder distributions, or being sold to self-interested management in a leveraged buyout—all in the name of *saving* the corporation.

Has the intense focus on next quarter's earnings, at the expense of management's attention to meeting competition and selling a product, so diverted American business that it has suffered a disastrous decline in world markets? Is the theory of an efficient market really valid, or is it the old, discredited, pre-Depression concept of laissez-faire trooped out in new colors?

From the law's perspective, these questions cannot be ignored. Lawyers and judges have had to confront them, often with sparse legal authority for guidance. New concepts of the business judgement rule, the enhanced role of independent directors, and a clearer focus by management upon their fiduciary duties have evolved from court decisions of the last five years. The clublike attitude in the board room has given way, without becoming unsupportive, to a searching, questioning concern for the merits of corporate actions. Have courts lent balance to an otherwise runaway situation, or, according to their critics, abandoned restraint to interfere either with the operation of a free market or the proper business decisions of corporate management?

It was in pursuit of such questions, their elusive answers, and the provocative ideas they generate that the Salomon Brothers Center for the Study of Financial Institutions brought these diverse interests and disciplines together. If the results of this and similar conferences can free us from tragic repetitions of the past, we will owe those responsible a debt of historic dimensions.

Andrew G. T. Moore II

Justice of the Delaware
Supreme Court

PART 1

THE INCREASINGLY COMPETITIVE MARKET FOR CORPORATE CONTROL

CHAPTER 1

UNSTABLE COALITIONS: CORPORATE GOVERNANCE AS A MULTIPLAYER GAME

John C. Coffee, Jr.

INTRODUCTION

Both law and economics have tended to view corporate governance as simply a principal/agent relationship. Under this view, shareholders are the principals; management, the agents. From such a starting point, lawyers and economists have still found much to dispute about the relative roles of legal and market forces in minimizing the "agency costs"[1] that shareholders must incur to hold their agents accountable, but in common both have conceived of corporate governance as basically the study of how legal and market forces combine to enable shareholders to hold management faithful to their interests. Unfortunately, this bilateral model of corporate governance oversimplifies because it leaves out an essential third player: stakeholders. Once we recognize that there are at least three essential players in the game—management, shareholders, and stakeholders—then the simple principal/agent model becomes inadequate at least as a descriptive or "positive" model of corporate governance. Put simply, if

John C. Coffee, Jr., is the Adolf A. Berle Professor of Law at Columbia Law School. He formerly practiced corporate law with Cravath, Swain & Moore. The author wishes to acknowledge the helpful comments of his colleague, Prof. Bernard Black.

a third player is introduced into the game, the "agent" may find ways to avoid being accountable to its nominal principal, the shareholders, by entering into contractual arrangements with stakeholders that effectively shelter it. Such arrangements may represent simple collusion by which the agent bribes the stakeholder (with the shareholders' funds) to support it against the principal; alternatively, they may represent an efficient, if implicit, system for protecting stakeholders against risks where contracting is too costly. In any event, what is clear is that in a three-sided game, any two players can form a coalition against the third, and outcomes thus become indeterminate.[2]

This triangular description of corporate governance will sound fanciful to some, and as recently as a decade ago, actual examples of coalitional bargaining would be difficult to find. Yet, as the takeover market has changed, stakeholders have begun to participate in corporate control contests, and seem likely to do so with even greater frequency in the future. Accordingly, this essay will seek to consider the different ways in which such bargaining could play out. Necessarily involved in this evaluation is an assessment of the judicial role: To what extent are courts competent to resolve or monitor these disputes? What new problems will they face? Still, it cannot simply be assumed that legal forces will be decisive. New market forces and mechanisms are also emerging, and the growing "institutionalization" of the stock market may prove to be the critical force that profoundly changes the nature of the bargaining within the firm. In assessing the interplay of these forces, this essay basically intends only a "positive" account and not a normative theory of the firm. Yet, while our focus will be descriptive rather than prescriptive, the recognition that changes are occurring in what "is" happening inevitably sets the stage to reconsider what "ought" to happen.

TAKEOVERS AND THE MODERN HISTORY OF THE FIRM

Before proceeding further, some terms need to be defined. "Stakeholder" is a deliberately ambiguous term, which includes a variety of subgroups whose own interests can often conflict. Clearly, however, the two largest constituents in this amorphous category are creditors and employees. Although stakeholders may or may not have formal or implicit contractual relationships with the firm, the one common factor that does unite them is a long-term interest in the firm's solvency. This in turn implies a preference that the firm retain or re-invest much of its "free cash flow." *Free cash flow* is a term coined by Professor Michael Jensen to refer to those discretionary cash flows that remain once the required payments to creditors and other fixed interest claimants are made.[3] In contrast to stakeholders, shareholders regard free cash flow as suboptimally invested capital, which they wish to have returned to them. Of course, this is exactly what restructurings, leveraged buyouts, and bust-up takeovers in fact do, thus explaining why stakeholders and shareholders view such transactions from opposing perspectives.

Jensen's focus on free cash flow and his concomitant recognition that there could be a significant divergence between the interests of shareholders and managers over its use are a significant concession that shows a new consensus developing among theorists of the firm. In a sense, it brings us full circle. For a generation, a number of economic and business scholars—including William Baumol, Robin Marris, Oliver Williamson, and Merritt Fox—have expressed the view that management had an innate preference for empire building, asset retention, and cash hoarding.[4] These writers—often called the "Managerialists"—tended to disagree with more neoclassical economists (such as Michael Jensen) who believed that either the market or internal contracting within the firm would suffice to discipline any such frolics and detours by management. Today, virtually all close observers of the takeover scene recognize that takeovers have spurred a massive "deconglomeration" movement that is pruning overgrown corporate empires and reshaping the size and scope of the American industrial corporation. The appearance of the "bust-up" takeover in the 1980s has demonstrated that many, if not most, publicly held firms trade in the stock market at a significant discount off their break-up or liquidation values. In effect, bust-up takeovers arbitrage this spread between stock market and break-up values.[5]

But what explains this spread between these two values? While there are various explanations,[6] free cash flow theory hypothesizes that this discount is explained by management's tendency to hoard discretionary (or free) cash flows, reinvesting them in unprofitable acquisitions or internal expansion, instead of paying them of out to shareholders in the form of dividends or other distributions. In this light, the free cash flow theory is only a reinterpretation of the Managerialists' original view that corporate managements were biased toward empire-building; as a theory, it at once concedes the accuracy of the Managerialists' diagnosis but then pronounces the problem largely solved by the advent of the bust-up take-over.

Still, this theory never answers the key question: Why is management so biased toward inefficient growth and retention of cash flows? Originally, the Managerialists focused on the psychic income and security that growth and large size afforded management. Professor Williamson also theorized that management had an "expense preference."[7] More recently, Professor Jensen may have come closer to the mark by focusing on problems in executive compensation that may give executives inadequate incentive to accept risk or to maximize the return on assets (instead of seeking to maximize corporate size).[8] Still, neither hypothesis explains why the discount between "going concern" and "bust-up" values can reach the magnitude sufficient to justify takeover premiums that now average nearly 50 percent. Thus, let me introduce a third possibility: The much discussed managerial preference for earnings retention and growth may be partially explained as the product of an implicit bargain with stakeholders. Just as aberrations in the planetary orbit of a distant planet may be explained by the weak gravitational force of a still remoter, hidden planet, so may the seeming infidelity of management to the goal of shareholder wealth maximization be explained to some degree by the hidden pull exerted on management by stakeholders. To be sure, stakeholders may not have approved of the waste and expense preference behavior that the Managerialists saw in corporate behavior during this pre-takeover era, but they did find common ground with management over a policy of earnings reinvestment.

Why were stakeholders this interested in free cash flow? In common, creditors and employees have reasons to resist the shareholders' desire to drain the firm of its free cash flow. Employees have specific human capital invested in the firm, and a policy of expansion through acquisitions and internal growth (even if inefficient) increased their opportunities for promotion and advancement within the firm. For creditors, any increase in the firm's debt/equity ratio reduces their security but, in contrast, acquisitions often have a co-insurance effect that decreases the variability of the firm's cash flow and thereby creates value for bondholders, even if the acquisition is debt-financed.[9]

The problem with this simple story is, however, that stakeholders could have protected themselves contractually. In principle, employees could have negotiated employment contracts (or "golden parachutes") that promised them employment security; similarly, creditors could have negotiated negative covenants in their loan agreements that restricted the firm's ability to increase leverage through acquisitions, financial restructuring, or large-scale dividends. Why didn't they secure contractual protections? Neoclassical financial economists have a simple answer to this question: Stakeholders in effect accepted the risk in return for a higher return. In the case of creditors, for example, they would argue that bondholders, being rational actors, discounted the risk of expropriation through wealth-transferring restructurings and accepted a higher interest rate to compensate them for bearing this risk. Hence, this argument concludes, bondholders cannot complain of unfairness when a firm later restructures in a manner that adversely affects them, because precisely this right was bargained for.

This answer is neat, tidy, and simplistic. The critical issue involves whether the right to expropriate (i.e., to make wealth transfers through restructurings) was truly bargained for or whether such expropriations instead reflect an omission in the contract that management is now exploiting opportunistically. This idea of contractual omissions is a familiar one to lawyers,[10] and indeed is at the heart of the "law and economics" approach to contract law.[11] Yet, it seems to have escaped the attention of finance theorists. Recognition that there may be risks that the parties did not anticipate and that the law will allocate by attempting to recreate the bargaining process does not, however, necessarily imply that bondholders win and shareholders lose. The "hypothetical bargaining" in which courts can engage is more open-ended, and different approaches exist. Before examining possible outcomes, it is useful to examine in more detail why the simple neoclassical story omits much of the relevant institutional detail from the contracting process between stakeholders and the corporation.

First, a more institutionally sensitive approach to economics begins with the recognition of "bounded rationality."[12] Put simply, parties do not anticipate all future contingencies, particularly in long-term contracting, because there are inevitable cognitive limitations on the human mind's information processing abilities. Indeed, the modern economic approach to contracts recognizes the inevitability of omissions in contracts and recommends that the court fill in missing terms by specifying the term that it believes rational parties would have specified had they focused on the issues.[13] But what contingencies could have been ignored by the creditors? The short answer is that, prior to 1985, the financial marketplace had never seen firms suddenly restructure themselves in the aggressively leveraged manner that Unocal and Phillips Petroleum both did in that watershed year. These two transactions each resulted in their companies' debt ratings falling from AA to BB, that is, to a level below investment grade.[14] Nor are these cases simply anecdotes. By a year later, in 1986, the pattern had begun to generalize, as debt downgradings by Standard & Poors in that year exceeded upgradings by a 2:1 margin.[15]

But why wasn't this risk that management would restructure so as to "leverage the firm to the eyeballs" perceived earlier? Beyond the simple answer that no one had ever seen a firm do this, it is historically important to recognize that new takeover defenses were continually being discovered during this period (1985 was also the year in which the poison pill was perfected and upheld by the Delaware courts).[16] Also, the general observation must be made that contracting for remote contingencies is costly. To begin with, the ability of lawyers to find techniques to outflank even the most seemingly ironclad set of debt covenants calls into doubt the efficacy of such financial contracting. Even if lawyers cannot find a loophole for every occasion, the market may be uncertain about such hard-to-price contingencies, and uncertainty destroys the value of the covenant to the investor. Equilibrium in an unsettled market does not arrive overnight. In theory, investors should accept a discount off the market rate if they receive "event risk" protection, but if they doubt the secondary market will price bonds as fully protected then they will not pay such a discount; nor will management rationally accept a lesser discount if it believes the covenants offer full protection. In short, so long as some traders in the market doubt that full protection has been given, an equilibrium position that properly discounts the risk will remain elusive.[17]

Special institutional factors further complicate the internal contracting process, so much so that the parties must inevitably rely on implicit arrangements and reputational capital. In the past, contracting over debt covenants was carefully conducted between the issuer and the underwriters (and counsel for each) over the extended period provided by SEC registration requirements and the relatively slow marketing process by which bonds were then sold. In the modern era of simplified SEC procedures and shelf registration, time is not available for the traditional "due diligence" review, and negotiation over remote contingencies is also infeasible. Today, a mature corporation can publicly issue debt within a few days of the time at which the financing decision is made. In such a compressed time span, close monitoring of the indenture's terms is less likely. In fact, the indenture and its covenants may not even be fully drafted at the time that oral commitments to purchase the debt securities are made by investors prior to the registration statement's effectiveness, and almost never will the investors have time today to review the documents with counsel. To be sure, the investment banker's reputational capital will be potentially at stake (to some degree), but this may not be an adequate protection in many cases.[18]

There is also an agency problem that complicates matters further: In the past, underwriters or bond purchasers hired their own counsel to examine and test the bond's covenants and other contractual protections (along with the adequacy of the prospectus's disclosures). Today, in an intensely competitive and time constrained market, more of the work and responsibility has shifted to the issuer's counsel and its agents.

Securitization of debt is still another factor. No longer do investors expect to hold debt for the duration of the investment contract. Rather, the initial purchasers may expect to sell their investments within a relatively short time horizon. In overview, the growth of the secondary market has provided an exit option that reduces the incentive to invest in information or monitoring costs. For example, if these purchasers expect (or hope) that they can liquidate their position well before the issuer nears insolvency, they may not expend the resources necessary to acquire and process even publicly available information. Moreover, the technological nature of trading has changed in a way that encourages some information to be slighted. Today, the screen trader buying debt securities in the secondary market may have little understanding about, or access to information concerning, the applicable negative covenants, and in any event is unsure about their efficacy. Although this trader's Quotran screen can tell him the security's interest rate and firm's credit rating, information about ambiguities in the firm's covenants does not reduce well to the kind of symbols that can appear on a computer screen. Ultimately, this is simply another example of information technology's tendency to squeeze out the softer variables in favor of those more easily quantified.

In principle, financial intermediaries—here, the credit rating agencies—could solve many of these problems of information costs, but the best empirical evidence is that they do not. Bond rating agencies are paid (a modest amount) by the issuer to review their securities, and typically the review process is cursory. Only the ratings of two agencies—Moody's and Standard & Poors—truly count, and such an oligopolistic market structure falls far short of perfect competition. In particular, bond rating agencies are thought to be slow in responding to new information and in changing ratings. Often, a rating change is an event that follows, rather than precedes, the market's adverse reaction to a change in the company's financial position. Such delayed rating changes are of more interest to historians than security analysts. Finally, the reviewers who rate bonds at these agencies are usually modestly paid clerks, who seldom have the skills of highly trained and compensated corporate attorneys.[19]

As a result, "contract term" information is not priced as efficiently as information about interest rates or firm-specific creditworthiness. Traders may therefore place little value on "strong" negative covenants (or place an excessive premium on "weak" ones), and management gets little value for binding its own hands against further issuances effectively. In such an active trading environment, where the individual firm cannot credibly signal that its covenants are effective restraints, a "market for lemons" may develop.[20] That is, to the extent that issuers cannot convince the market that their covenants are more effective than the "weak" covenants of other issuers, it becomes inefficient to include truly restrictive covenants in the trust indenture. Ultimately, the result will be that little effort will be made to write meaningful debt restrictions if the firm receives little in return for doing so. No doubt, improvements can and are being made in the structure of the information market for debt securities, but these improvements themselves imply a past failure.[21]

Beyond the fact that contracting is both costly and imprecise when remote contingencies must be provided for, and the tendency of the market to perceive such information noisily, additional problems complicate the problem of contracting with stakeholders. Even among neoclassical economists, it is recognized that long-term contracting within the corporation—whether over debt relationships, employment terms, or between classes of shareholders—falls into the special category of "relational contracts."[22] Focusing on the creditor/debtor relationship within the corporate nexus of contracts, Professor Scott has suggested that this relationship is "much more complex and refractory than that conceived by conventional analysis":

> Because peculiar stresses may undermine the efforts of both debtor and creditor to exploit [a firm's prospects]..., the parties will predictably agree in the credit contract to forego any actions that threaten the relationship. But the manifestations of self-interested behavior are difficult to anticipate, and their interaction with other variables is often complex and unpredictable. In such an environment, the parties frequently are unable to achieve their mutually beneficial objectives through conventional contractual arrangements.[23]

This is a description either of contractual failure or of a contractual system that anticipates broad-ranging judicial interpretation of the parties' intent (or, more accurately, of what their intent would have been had they focused on the problem). To give a relevant example of the stresses that prevent complete contractual specification, suppose it were simple to write an ironclad covenant that protected against opportunistic financial restructurings that transferred wealth from bondholders to stockholders. To work, such a provision would almost certainly have to be over-broad, and thus would also restrict mutually beneficial increases in corporate leverage. But, if it were over-broad, why wouldn't bondholders agree to waive their rights in any case where waiver was mutually beneficial? The problem is that the information and transaction costs of securing such waivers from widely dispersed bondholders are prohibitive, and in any event there is a holdout problem. Thus, perfect protections would in Professor Scott's phrase "threaten the relationship" and are therefore forgone. But if the market cannot adequately price the risk of future expropriation through wealth-transferring restructurings, then bondholders are contractually exposed without having received any compensating premium.

Similar problems confound the achievement of optimal contractual provision between the firm and its employees. For example, guaranteeing severance compensation to employees (or at least to managers) may have adverse incentive effects for the firm; or, it may force the firm to pick and choose among managers in a way that adversely affects employee morale.

The foregoing review of the institutional shortcomings in the market for debt securities contrasts sharply with the standard, static story told by financial economists.[24] Under the conventional neoclassical account, creditors and stockholders reach an equilibrium position, with management retaining some flexibility and creditors being compensated therefor through higher interest. This account assumes that anything not forbidden to management in the financial contract is permitted, and this assumption is simply at odds with the basic concept of relational contracting and with the law's general hostility to opportunism.[25] Another problem with the conventional account is its myopia to the dynamic changes occurring in the debt market. The equilibrium it assumes may have historically been a brief moment during the 1960s and 1970s when creditors had learned, based on their experience during the conglomerate acquisition waves of the 1950s and 1960s, that they need not fear managerial discretion in the large publicly held corporation. Even when conglomerate acquisitions increased leverage significantly, debt investors may have found that this impact was typically offset by a co-insurance effect, at least if the combining firms' cash flows were partially co-variant. Also, creditors observed over time that management had its own incentives to pursue growth and expansion and to avoid excess leverage. To sum up: Stability and the avoidance of risk were the common goals of management and bondholders during this era, with the result that most negative covenants seemed superfluous (or at least not worth the interest rate penalty that the issuer would demand). Here, my hypothesis encounters, and can explain, one important empirical finding: Although once common, negative covenants restricting the issuance of additional debt had become uncommon, particularly in the case of publicly issued debt instruments, by the early 1980s.[26]

Financial economists have placed little emphasis on this transition, but it is striking. The Smith and Warner study, which examined 87 public issues between 1974 and 1975, found that over 90 percent contained a negative covenant restricting the issuance of additional debt.[27] Examining 92 companies in the 1980s, McDaniel found that only 28 percent of issuers then included a similar covenant (and only 16% of newer issues did). [28] Reflecting and possibly encouraging this shift, the American Bar Association adopted a new streamlined model indenture in the early 1980s that largely dispensed with business covenants on the assumption that investors did not care about them.[29] Interestingly, the disappearance of negative covenants was not limited to publicly issued debt. A 1987 study of leveraged buyouts by Marais, Schipper, and Smith found that "more than 80 percent of [the] private long-term debt" in their sample lacked "covenants restricting the issuance of additional debt of equal or higher seniority."[30] Moreover, such debt without covenants represented, they found, the largest single category of noncommon stock security in their survey.[31] Here, neither the conventional view that covenants are dispensed with when the credit is sufficiently strong or my revisionist account that creditors no longer feared managerial discretion seems adequate to account adequately for this finding. Securitization and the growth of the secondary debt market may have simply created an audience of investors who believed it unnecessary to focus on covenants because they now had an easy exit option. Still, the basic picture as of the early 1980s is one of understandable complacency on the part of bondholders, not contractual acceptance of the risk of wealth transfers.

This capsule history is undoubtedly incomplete, but it sets the stage for the major changes in the early 1980s. With little warning, takeovers changed in the 1980s from a force that produced expansion in firm size to one that, at least frequently, produced contraction. With the appearance of junk bond financing, takeovers became a disciplinary force that contributed to the downsizing of the conglomerate form of business organization. Diversification became a vice, not a virtue, and a host of corporations in the early 1980s undertook voluntary divestiture programs under the threat of a hostile takeover.[32] Spinoffs, restructurings, and assets sales also became commonplace. Finally, as private markets developed in which corporate acquisitions could be quickly financed, the LBO matured into a force by which virtually any corporate management could take virtually any company private. The symbolically culminating event in this transition was, of course, the 1988 RJR-Nabisco leveraged buyout.

The full extent of the wealth transfers that have occurred from bondholders to shareholders in the 1980s is not yet known, because most studies have submerged the post-1985 data within a longer-term longitudinal study and also have not measured the impact on debt securities of potential targets in the period before a takeover or restructuring was announced. Still, it probably is the case that these losses to bondholders are but a fraction of the total takeover gains received by shareholders over the same period.[33]

THE STAKEHOLDERS STRIKE BACK: NEW DEFENSES FOR THE CONTRACTUALLY EXPOSED

Creditors

It seems a fair generalization that this sudden increase in event risk took bondholders by surprise, and Metropolitan Life's outraged reaction to the sudden losses it incurred in the RJR-Nabisco transaction is by now old news.[34] But how exposed are stakeholders? For some time, many financial economists refused to concede that there was any problem. For example, as late as 1988, Jarrell, Brickley, and Netter rejected out-of-hand the possibility that stockholders' gains in takeovers came at least partially at bondholders' expense:

> In sum, the evidence provides no support for the hypothesis that the supposed gains from acquisitions are actually transfers from the holders of senior securities to the holders of common stock.[35]

But is the matter this simple? More recent evidence suggests that it is not. First, the amount of leverage involved in more recent transactions is unprecedented. Studying leveraged buyouts even before the RJR-Nabisco buyout, Marais, Schipper, and Smith report that the median debt-equity ratio shifted from .263 before the buyout to .845 after.[36] In their sample of 113 firms, no firm had a debt/equity ratio exceeding .90 before the buyout (and only 22 had a ratio over .50), but afterwards 43 firms had a ratio over .90. The median firm in their sample increased its debt/equity ratio by nearly .50, and over one fifth of their sample increased leverage by at least .70. In over two thirds of the securities that they surveyed, no redemption, or other revision in the securities' terms, was undertaken in connection with the buyout to compensate bondholders.

Thus, it seems clear that at least some debt holders have been subjected to a substantial increase in risk. But how much of a loss is typically experienced? Although some studies have not found statistically significant losses, they are subject to various methodological problems. For example, in principle, an efficient market responds only to unexpected news. Thus, if a corporation gradually becomes perceived to be a potential target, its bonds may slowly decline in value and not show any abrupt, significant change that fulfills the market's prophecy when the actual merger or other transaction is announced. To correct for this problem of slow information leakage, Marais, Schipper, and Smith studied a subsample of firms where (1) the buyout proposal resulted in either a downgrading in the Moody's debt rating of the security or a significant increase in leverage, and (2) the buyout was a "nondefensive" one, which thus was more likely to take the market by relative surprise. By excluding defensive proposals where the market may have anticipated the adverse change in default risk, they were able to find significant losses in the remaining cases (at least when the increase in leverage was significant). Their results seem to suggest that downgradings by bond rating agencies are in fact associated with real losses to bondholders, although the loss may typically precede the downgrading.

Another finding in their study underlines the pervasiveness of debt rating downgradings. In 83 percent of the cases in their sample, the ratings of nonconvertible debt securities declined following successful management buyouts; in no case, did the rating improve.[37] In 61 percent of these cases, the debt security had an investment grade rating before the buyout; in no case did an investment grade rating survive a successful buyout. The message seems simple: For the bondholder seeking low-risk, investment grade debt investments, LBOs are usually always fatal.

A different study by Cook and Martin reveals another dimension of

the bondholders' dilemma. Studying corporate takeovers, they initially
found that the average effect of a takeover on target firms' bondholders
was not "significantly different from zero," but that when the leverage
increase was greater than 50 percent, there was a significant wealth loss.[38]
That is, once the takeover phenomenon is unpacked, some effects are
beneficial to bondholders, and some are very adverse. In their view, a co-
insurance effect, which benefits bondholders in most takeover transactions, is overcome by an adverse leverage effect in transactions involving
"very large increases in financial leverage." By their estimates, the positive
coinsurance effect was dominant when the leverage increase was less than
30 percent (in the ratio of debt to total assets), but the negative leverage
effect was clearly dominant when the increase exceeded 50 percent. If so,
the future is hardly reassuring for bondholders because the scale of leverage increases—measured either in percentage or absolute terms—continues
to grow.

Still, it would be a mistake to read this evidence as implying that
bondholders will remain exposed to loss (or "event risk") for long. Sudden transitions always prejudice some. The real issue is: What happens
next? How do intelligent and sophisticated institutions protect themselves
for the future? Already, the outlines of the predictable defensive response
of bondholders have emerged: New investor safeguards are appearing. Of
these, the most controversial is the "poison put." In brief outline, the
poison put is a right given in the debt instrument to bondholders at their
option to demand repayment of the full principal amount of the indebtedness (plus possibly a premium) in the event of certain occurrences, such
as a takeover, restructuring, recapitalization, or merger. To date, "poison
puts" have been used to compensate bondholders against "event risk"
more than to deter hostile takeovers. Generally, poison puts (or "super
poison puts" in the more extravagant language of the financial press) are
triggered if a "designated event" (as defined below) occurs and a specified
decline also takes place in the debt's rating by either Standard & Poors'
Corporation or Moody's Investors Services, Inc. Sometimes, a decline in
the rating of both rating agencies is required. *Designated events* are typically defined as (1) a change in control, as usually demonstrated by the
acquisition of either 20 percent or 30 percent by a person or group; (2) a
merger or acquisition of the issuer, including a sale of substantially all its
assets; (3) a buyback by the issuer of some percentage (usually 30 percent)
of its stock within a defined period (usually a 365-day period); (4) a
recapitalization that, either through repurchases or dividends, meets the

same criteria as in the preceding clause (30 percent in a 365-day period); or sometimes (5) a change in continuing directors—that is, a failure of a majority of the directors to remain in office.[39]

Poison put bonds first appeared in early 1986 (probably in direct response to the Revlon takeover the preceding fall).[40] However, the event that brought fear and loathing to the creditors' camp was the RJR-Nabisco buyout in 1988. Immediately, the popular financial press reported that the bond market has been seized by hysteria. Unable otherwise to offer long-term debt, several firms—including Harris Corp., Williams Cos.'s Northwest Pipeline Unit, Becton, Dickinson & Co., and Grumman Corp.—adopted poison put provisions in 1988.[41] Typically, a poison put would, for example, entitle the holders of $50,000,000 in face amount of debentures due in the year 2010 to be immediately paid this amount if a tender offer were made or if any person or group acquired more than 20 percent of the voting shares of the company. Particularly if interest rates had risen after the time of the debentures' issuance, the result could be a considerable windfall, as debt securities trading in the market for, say, $40,000,000 could suddenly become worth $50,000,0000 on their tender to the issuer. In addition, one could imagine an aggressively drafted poison put could entitle the holders to a call premium of, say, 10 percent (or $5,000,000 on these facts). The result then is two-fold: (1) Creditors are more than amply protected against event risk[42]; and (2) management has created a new defensive weapon against takeovers, one which I will shortly suggest is less vulnerable to judicial invalidation than the now familiar poison pill. Accordingly, the poison put represents an initial example of a coalitional strategy of the kind that I suggest may become a much more prevalent in future years. Here, bondholders and management link arms to re-establish their relative control over the firm's free cash flow, which the appearance of the bust-up takeover disrupted.

The defensive utility of the poison put as an antitakeover device is, to be sure, only marginal; it will not block those takeovers where the bidder is willing to pay off the debt. Yet, its defensive impact is hardly accidental. This becomes clearer once one recognizes that the most obvious protection for bondholders from event risk is not a put, but an upward interest rate shift in the event of a rating downgrading. Given an active secondary market, such a provision adequately compensates diversified bondholders, and permits nondiversified holders to sell into the market. Moreover, such contingent rate shifting bonds, which first appeared in 1989, also permit the issuer to reduce the interest rate slightly if the bond rating is upgraded.[43]   Today, issuers are choosing between the two formats. Given this choice (and the fact that the issuer benefits under the shifting rate formula if there is a credit upgrading), those issuers choosing the poison put format seem to be exploiting the bondholders' anxiety for their own self-protective ends. In short, a coalition is formed, and stockholders are the parties left out.

Employees
Employees have obvious reasons to fear that bust-up takeovers may result in staff reductions, pension plan terminations, and attempts by a new employer to breach old implicit contracts and negotiate give-backs.   The actual extent of employee losses from takeovers may be more debatable, but the phenomenon of a coalition forming between management and stakeholders to resist a takeover is, if anything, even more evident in the case of employees.   Indeed, 1989 has witnessed some notable illustration of this pattern.   In the recent control contest over NWA Inc. (the parent of a Northwest Airlines), NWA's pilots and machinists unions initially asked for job protection covenants in their collective bargaining agreements, which were explicitly intended to bar a hostile takeover by, or a sale of assets to, any person unacceptable to the unions.[44] When the pilots' collective bargaining agreement expired, both sides agreed to proceed slowly in renegotiating it, believing that its expiration served as a source of sufficient uncertainty to deter potential bidders.   Some commentators compared the use of an expired labor contract to a poison pill in that management could agree to significant salary increases if a bidder bought control in a hostile raid;[45] in effect, the raid would trigger a windfall for stakeholders. Midway in this takeover battle, the union representing NWA's 20,000 machinists submitted its own recapitalization proposal in order to oppose bids submitted by Pan Am and Marvin Davis.[46] Finally, the unions supported the winning bidder, Alfred Checchi, over several rival offerors, largely on his representation that he would avoid extreme leverage. Still, even then, the unions forced the NWA board to approve contingently a fall-back recapitalization proposal if the winning bidder was unable to finance and consummate his proposal within a defined period.

The NWA story is by no means unique. Also in 1989, the unions representing workers in the Chicago and Northwestern rail system submitted a proposal for an employee buyout of the system's parent, CNW Corp.[47] Similarly, the unions at Eastern Airlines searched for a takeover bidder in order to wrest control from Frank Lorenzo and eventually formed an unusual (and ultimately unsuccessful) alliance with a Chicago commodities broker to structure a takeover deal.[48]   Finally, in 1989, the Amalgamated Clothing and Textile Workers Union has proposed employee buyouts of both Cluett Peabody & Co. and Health-tex.[49]

The tactics in these union buyout initiatives have gone beyond simple threats of strikes and have begun to resemble the proposals submitted by other third party bidders. For example, both Eastern's unions and the Amalgamated Clothing and Textile Workers Union found independent businessmen to serve as their partners—in effect, to demonstrate their credibility as serious investors. In addition, Amalgamated threatened to strike if the Health-tex board accepted the buyout proposal of any other bidder—an unusual, but potentially effective, tactic by which to preclude an auction. In the case of NWA, although the pilots and machinists unions supported one bidder and opposed others, their basic demand was to restrict any financial restructuring that would result in high leverage; in short, the unions wanted free cash flow kept within the firm. In return, NWA's unions offered somewhat vague productivity savings as their quid pro quo for job protection.[50] Eastern's unions appear to have engaged in the most explicit bargaining, offering "to sacrifice as much as 35% of their wages to help [their preferred bidder] stem losses during a revamping of the airline."[51]

In one sense, these proposals by unions of financially distressed companies are not entirely new. Carl Icahn used a similar package of union concessions to take over and turn around TWA several years ago.[52] The pilots union at United Airlines offered to buy the company from its corporate parent in 1987 and at least succeeded in thereby sacking the parent's CEO, who had been their antagonist in a bitter strike.[53] But the idea of a formal partnership between a union and an equity investor, cemented by the use of a ESOP or similar employee ownership device, is a new twist. In one sense, the appearance of unions as bidders marks the logical culmination of the trend throughout the 1980s toward smaller and smaller bidders putting larger and larger companies into play. Ultimately, anyone can be a bidder—if they can obtain financing. The use of an equity partner may be a way of providing a "front man" whose presence assures those providing the debt financing that there is a logical scenario underlying the bid whereby gains will accrue; if so, the lender does not care how these gains are shared among the unions and their joint venturer.

The more puzzling question is why unions believe a change in ownership matters to them. In terms of classical economic theory, businesses do not shut down so long as average variable costs are being recovered. Even if a new owner finds it expedient to sell divisions or liquidate the company, viable operations do not disappear into a black hole. Losing operations may well be terminated, but in theory the old owner would do so also. Why then the union concern? One empirical fact stands out that may shed some light on this question: To date, the unions that have become "players" in corporate control contests have only sought troubled companies. Jack Sheinkman, the president of the clothing union seeking to buy Health-tex, has been particularly candid:

> We're doing this so that we'll have some say in the future outcome of the firm.... It's a very troubled company. If we're successful, we plan to bring in management.[54]

Apparently, unions bid for failing or distressed firms. Arguably, the unions have an irrational fear: namely, that the bidder will liquidate divisions or operations that other owners would not. On the hand, unions may more realistically fear that new bidders can exploit the uncertainty surrounding a financially distressed company in order to negotiate opportunistically for wage or other concessions that are not truly cost justified. That is, if workers are risk averse, they many not be willing to call the bidder's bluff when it threatens to close plants or operations. Indeed, the unions that have made bids are precisely those most likely to be risk adverse, because they have already suffered significant declines in membership and would not remain viable if such losses continued.[55] Of course, it is not apparent why the former owners could not also exploit these same fears or why a takeover is necessary before coercive pressure is brought to bear. Possibly, because the old owners made the implicit contract between management and stakeholders, they are more likely to respect it, whereas new owners do not feel themselves similarly constrained. Thus, if one posits that the new bidder is someone seeking a wealth transfer from stakeholders by disrupting implicit contracts, the unions' fear becomes comprehensible.

The sudden spurt in union activity in takeovers seems likely to grow. Once unions learn that takeovers are a game that anyone can play and that may have the potential power to scare off disfavored rival bidders, they have little reason not to use this leverage—unless they find that union-managed companies present them with more problems and conflicts than they wish to face. The factor most likely to increase stakeholder participation in takeovers is the new popularity of ESOPs as a takeover defense. Following the Polaroid decision, ESOPs have become the new takeover defense of 1989.[56] Moreover, new tax rulings now make it possible for ESOPs to issue debt publicly to the market. In short, given the tax advantages of ESOPs, they present the easiest of all strategies by which a coalition can form between management and stakeholders to block a takeover. Poison puts, ESOPs, collective bargaining agreements—all have this same potential for two sides in the three-sided game of corporate governance to conspire against the third.

THE JUDICIAL ROLE

With increasing, if still sporadic, frequency, courts have invalidated a broad range of antitakeover tactics as a breach of fiduciary duty: poison pills, lock-ups, recapitalizations, etc. What then is distinctive about stakeholder agreements as a takeover defense? The short answer is that there is truly bargained-for consideration in these cases. In contrast, a poison *pill* is a gratuitous transfer of warrants, issued by management in theory to protect shareholders from coercive offers. Yet, a poison *put* (or a similar provision in a collective bargaining agreement) was bargained for between parties who are normally at arm's length. Because management is a fiduciary for its shareholders (and must thus act out of undivided loyalty with respect to them), it is easier for a court to review this relationship than that between parties that are normally economic adversaries. Also, there is the factor of detrimental reliance. When the bondholder negotiates for a poison put, it presumably gives up something in the form of higher interest rates that it might otherwise have received in the absence of such a provision. Similarly, when a labor union negotiates for job security or makes its collective bargaining agreement automatically terminate on the occurrence of a takeover or a defined share acquisition, it may be foregoing higher wages. Conversely, when a board adopts a poison pill to block a potentially coercive takeover, the board is, and can be, acting only to benefit one party in interest, the shareholders. Hence, judicial review can be more searching (as Delaware's Unocal standard certainly is)[57] because the court only has to consider the impact of the board's action on one constituency, the shareholders. In contrast, in these bilateral agreements between unions or bondholders and management, the court cannot ignore that something was given up for the rights that the shareholder now wishes the court to invalidate. In general, absent proof of a conspiracy to defraud, contracts are not invalidated because one side gave up too much, and courts do not claim the competence to decide how much consideration is too much. Nor can it be denied that these new players in the takeover game have legitimate interests. Job security, for example, has always been a union goal in collective bargaining negotiations.

Nonetheless, the prospect of collusion is present, as stakeholders and management unite to lock free cash flow into the firm. How well will courts be able to do in distinguishing collusion from legitimate contractual measures to protect stakeholders? The few relevant cases to date provide mixed signals.

Perhaps the clearest illustration of a case where the concessions made by management to stakeholders appear to have been deliberately excessive is Gearhart Industries, Inc. v. Smith Intern., Inc.,[58] where the target responded to a creeping open market acquisition by the bidder by issuing a package of debentures and warrants to a group of institutional investors. Specifically, nearly $100,000,000 of subordinated debentures and accompanying warrants to purchase nearly 3,000,000 shares of the target's stock were issued by the target several days after a bidder had accumulated over 33 percent of its stock. Under a "springing" provision in the warrants, their exercise price declined from $33 per share to $24.60 per share if a tender offer were made without the target board's approval. Because the tender offer made by the bidder in Gearhart was at $31 per share, the impact of these warrants, suddenly exercisable at $24.60, was basically as dilutive as is the typical "flip-in" poison pill—with the one critical difference that the windfall gain here would go to the holders of the subordinated debentures. Finding that the debentures bore interest at an effective rate of 14 7/8 percent (on a yield to maturity basis) and that this rate was not disproportionate to prevailing rates, the court declined to enjoin the issuance of these securities. The court also emphasized that, prior to the open market buying campaign of the bidder, the target's stock had traded below the exercise price of the warrants, thus showing that their reduced strike price was not irrational.[59]

Still, the considerations cited by the court miss the point by a wide margin. The "springing warrants" issued by the bidder had value only to the extent that a hostile tender offer was made for the target. The greater their value as a deterrent, the lesser their value as a free-standing warrant. By analogy, they were very similar to a poison put that entitled bondholders to a call premium of 100 percent in addition to the full principal amount of their debentures—but only if a hostile tender offer was made for the target. Both such securities—the hypothetical poison put bond and

the "springing warrants" in Gearhart—respond to the exposed position of
the debt holders, but both respond excessively and in a manner that obviously
protects management. Today, the more proportional and appropriate remedy would be the poison put that entitled the debtholder only to be redeemed at face value (plus possibly some call premium).

If Gearhart suggests that courts will defer to the board when it offers
a collusive "bribe" to bondholders, a more recent case suggests a different
approach, at least when the transaction seems to reflect the board's lar-
gess, rather than hard bargaining. In Air Line Pilots Association v. UAL
Corp.,[60] the only case to date to deal with a "labor contract poison pill,"
the UAL board inserted in the machinists' collective bargaining agreement two provisions, which were ironically intended to deter a threatened
takeover by UAL's pilots' union. The first provision entitled the machinists union unilaterally to begin a new round of collective bargaining negotiations; in effect, this provision told the lenders to the pilots' buyout
proposal that they would be "lending into a strike." The second provision
established a "most favored union" rule with respect to ESOPs and similar employee ownership plans, entitling all unions to equivalent treatment
with respect to such equity ownership plans, but prescribing a curious rule
of equality: All stock to be issued under such plans had to be allocated not
on the basis of employee salaries but on the basis of the wage concessions
they were willing to make from the "market wages" that a to-be-appointed
arbitration panel found would prevail in a free and open (i.e., nonunion)
market. Although the uncertainty created by this proposal was itself a
deterrent, it was clear, as Judge Posner found for the Seventh Circuit, that
the effect of the provision would "be to dilute the pilots' ownership and
control."

The pilots' union claimed that these provisions violated Delaware
corporation law, but the district court found Delaware law preempted by
the federal Railway Labor Act. It then further held that the same federal
statute required the invalidation of the "most favored union" clause because the pilots had not had an opportunity to collectively bargain over
it.[61] On appeal, the Seventh Circuit overruled the finding that Delaware's
corporation law was preempted, but upheld the finding that the "most
favored union" provision violated the federal statute. While the Seventh
Circuit remanded to the trial court for further findings as to Delaware law,
the clear import of the decision is that a corporate board must comply
with relevant state takeover and fiduciary duty standards in including
provisions in its collective bargaining decisions that may have a chilling

effect on takeovers. Still, what probably most distinguishes the two cases is that in Gearhart the special provision—the "springing warrants"—was bargained for, while in the Air Line Pilots Association case it was not; the two labor contract provisions were the result of a gratuitous change offered by the board to one union in order, ironically, to block a bid proposed by another union.

The Air Line Pilots Association case ultimately suggests that the law is still at an early and formative point in this area. Courts have decided only that stakeholder agreements are reviewable under fiduciary standards, but not how to apply fiduciary criteria to them. Accordingly, it may be more useful to hold aside the possible judicial responses for the remainder of this essay and focus instead on how the parties are likely to behave in this new triangular bargaining game.

THE BARGAINING DYNAMICS

Two polar opposite scenarios can be envisioned:

SCENARIO ONE:

Shifting Coalitions. The prediction made to this point about collusion between management and stakeholders to lock free cash flow into the firm is subject to one major caveat: Because the gains (over the short-run at least) from LBOs appear to be very high, management may prefer to unite with stockholders rather than stakeholders. That is, whatever the psychic income and security from empire building, the possibility of owning a significant share of a *Fortune* 500 corporation on almost no equity investment may dwarf these less quantifiable gains. Put differently, the gains and losses are asymmetric, with stockholders winning more from takeovers than bondholders and employees lose. All the empirical evidence points to, and indeed compels, this conclusion.[62] Thus, in a perfect Coasean world, one would expect that stakeholders and stockholders would strike a bargain in order to realize these net gains, but obviously transaction costs interfere in the real world (particularly in the case of publicly held debt).

Given the asymmetry between the gains and losses in takeovers, stockholders can offer more than stakeholders to secure management's loyalty. Indeed, the process could resemble an auction as both stakeholders and stockholders (through LBO firms) compete for management's favor. Yet, there is an additional complication here: Once the company is put in play, management cannot know that it will be on the winning side. In fact, the law restricts a management LBO much more than any other bidder. Hence, management may fear putting the company in play and prefer to side with stakeholders.

Still, there is a probable answer to this problem that the outcome of an auction cannot be predicted with certainty: once the firm is in play, stakeholders may be able to determine the winning bidder and, as recently shown, unions can certainly deter some potential bidders. Arguably, they can also oust a winning bidder who, they believe, has opportunistically breached their implicit contract. Here, the name Frank Lorenzo bears obvious mention, but the same process played out in Carl Icahn's take-over of TWA and the break-up of Allegis (as the TWA and United unions in both cases exercised substantial influence over the selection of the winning bidder). More importantly, all three groups may want to form a coalition to make certain that they can manage events and not allow an unwanted third party hostile bidder to seize control. This brings us to Scenario Two.

SCENARIO TWO:

The Evolution of Cooperation.   In his now famous book, *The Evolution of Cooperation,* Robert Axelrod concludes that in actual practice the players in prisoners' dilemma type games quickly learn to cooperate. The strategy he termed "Tit for Tat" seemed regularly to dominate. The persuasive force of his book lay particularly in the real world examples he gave of reciprocity and cooperation in the business world, even where opportunism was possible. In effect, his message was that cooperative behavior was efficient, and rational parties would come to learn this and thus, through a survival-of-the-fittest type competition, come to dominate the field over those who did not.

Does this scenario apply to the triangular game of corporate governance that I have been describing? The problem is that we may always be at the end stage (the final move) where it is rational to depart from a tit-for-tat strategy. That is, the bidder may believe that it can break the prior implicit contract that management struck with stakeholders and then bustup the firm, quickly liquidating its assets and not having to manage them for long. Such a strategy makes sense if you are not a repeat player and do not need to be trusted in the future by others. Certainly, some bidders— the Irving Jacobs, Paul Bilzerians, and Victor Posners of this world—

seem to be following such a strategy of opportunism, by in effect violating the prior tradition of tit-for-tat. If they can quickly liquidate and move on, they may not need to be repeat players. Yet, the downside in this strategy is shown by the current predicament of Frank Lorenzo, who has united an alliance of stakeholders against him. Even more impor-tantly, institutional investors are repeat players. They do not "cut and run" with their takeover profits as small shareholders, who often spend their gains on personal consumption, seem to do. Rather, institutional investors reinvest their gains in the market. Also, they are bondholders as well as equity holders and thus do not want to encourage wealth transfers that merely transfer money from one pocket to another.

But what would an "evolution toward cooperation" mean in this context? A good example is supplied by Metropolitan Life's predicament in the RJR-Nabisco buyout. Metropolitan Life's staff has estimated that it would have cost Kohlberg, Kravis, Roberts & Co. only "about $4 per share to pay off bondholders" in the RJR buyout.[63] Instead of paying shareholders $109 per share for stock that had been trading at $55 a share at the time of the buyout's announcement, they could have paid $105 to stockholders and also redeemed the bonds. Should they have done so? The usual counterargument that bondholders accepted the risk of higher leverage because they did not contract against it seems particularly weak here, because investment grade securities are incompatible with the acceptance of a major risk. One cannot imagine Met Life rationally accepting the interest penalty on investment grade debt while also knowingly accepting a loophole through which a regiment of lawyers could march abreast to restructure the issuer. Thus, one has to assume that Met Life did not realize the extent to which it was contractually exposed. What really happened is that a new risk materialized.

Courts could, of course, respond to this circumstance by expanding the duty of good faith.[64] However, for the moment, let us focus on what the parties themselves would do in the absence of courts. In a world where tit-for-tat dominates as the most successful strategy, one would expect that new risks would be treated differently by the parties. Indeed, precisely because the gains to shareholders so vastly exceed the losses to bondholders, it is to be expected that stakeholders and stockholders would learn to cooperate. Also, to the extent that institutional investors are both bondholders and stockholders, it is in their interest to cooperate by reducing the extent of wealth transfers, because such transfers simply increase risk without creating real value. At present, however, the evidence is that bondholders are seldom compensated for their losses, unless the issuer is contractually required to do so.[65]

CONCLUSION

Economics has had trouble enough modeling games for two players, and no developed theory appears to exist for a three-player game. Still, speculative as it is to guess whether reciprocity will dominate opportunism, there is reason to believe that, as share ownership become more "institutionalized" (that is, as institutions continue to dominate the market and hold the majority of the stock in publicly held firms), institutional investors will unavoidably become repeat players. As recognizable repeat players, institutional investors could become more constrained than other stockholders in their ability to cooperate with opportunistic bidders. The key difference between their present position and that which they are likely to have in the near future is that they may soon lose their relative anonymity. Consider a hypothetical case where a bidder wishes to behave opportunistically by acquiring a firm in order to breach implicit contracts with its stakeholders. Today, such a bidder may incur some reputational loss (assuming that it has any reputational capital to lose), but the shareholders who tender to it do not—because they do so with relative anonymity. Arguably, however, they have aided and abetted the bidder's opportunism. In the future, however, it appears likely that 100 or fewer institutions will hold the majority of the stock in many publicly traded firms.[66] Perhaps, we will soon see the day when 25 or so large institutional investors, each holding 1 to 3 percent, will hold de facto working control among them and will be able easily to communicate and achieve a joint strategy. Such institutionally dominated firms will be the most susceptible firms to a takeover, because institutions can effectively resist anti-takeover measures and can solve the collective action problems that confound other shareholders. But, as the number of shareholders drops, so does their anonymity and thus also their ability to behave opportunistically by breaching implicit contracts. If such a small body of institutions can share de facto control, they will also become identifiable to the stakeholders and to some degree politically accountable. Indeed, to the extent that creditors are also institutions, greater direct communication seems inevitable. This prediction does not imply that there will not be more takeovers, but only that their wealth-transfer aspects will become more vulnerable. Tit-for-tat becomes more feasible as a game, and perhaps ultimately inevitable, when 25 shareholders are dealing with a dozen or so large creditors and unions. Of course, at this point, one is no longer describing a public corporation, but some new hybrid of public and institutional ownership. That day, however, appears to be gradually dawning.

Economists tend to look for equilibrium, even when it is not there. While markets do eventually re-equilibrate, the process by which they are surprised (and the judicial response during this interim) poses the more interesting phenomena for study. Ultimately, my long-run prediction then is that, while the game of corporate governance will remain unstable and indeterminate for an interim period, there is reason to believe that a trend toward cooperation may yet evolve here too. As investor anonymity is lost, repeat players should move in a direction away from opportunism and toward conventional and cooperative gaming strategies. Viewed from afar, this can be described as simply the attainment of a new equilibrium.

Notes

1. For the standard account, see Jensen and Meckling, "Theory of the Firm: Managerial Behavior, Agency Costs, and Ownership Structure," *Journal of Financial Economics, 3,* (1976), p. 305.
2. I recognize that there are also persons external to the corporate "nexus of contracts" with whom management may collude, such as the proverbial "white knight" or "white squire." For example, one can view the recent battle among Time, Warner, and Paramount as a case that at bottom involved a conflict between Time shareholders, who wished to accept a takeover premium, and its management, who wished to avoid ouster. From this perspective, Time's top-dollar offer for Warner plus its more than generous employment arrangements with Warner's senior executives can be viewed as collusion between management and an external ally. See Hilder, "Warner Employees to Get Record Total of $677 million if Time Deal is Approved," *Wall Street Journal,* (July 24, 1989) at A–4, cols. 2–3.
3. Jensen, "Agency Costs of Free Cash Flow, Corporate Finance, and Takeovers," *American Economic Review, 76,* (1986), p. 323.
4. For some of the better known works in this vein, see W. Baumol, *Business Behavior, Value and Growth* (1959); R. Marris, *The Economic Theory of "Managerial" Capitalism* (1964); Williamson, "Managerial Discretion and Business Behavior," *American Economic Review, 53,* (1963), p. 1032; M. Fox, *Finance and Industrial Performance in a Dynamic Economy: Theory, Practice, and*

Policy (1987). For an overview of this tradition, see Coffee, "Shareholders Versus Managers: The Strain in the Corporate Web," *Michigan Law Review, 85,* pp. 1, 20–24, 28–31.

5. I have discussed this theme at length elsewhere. See Coffee, loc. cit.

6. For an overview of the various theories that seek to explain the motives for takeovers, see Kraakman, "Taking Discounts Seriously: The Implications of 'Discounted' Share Prices as an Acquisition Motive," *Columbia Law Review, 88,* (1988), p. 981. Today, almost no theorists continue to subscribe to "information" theories under which the target company is seen as undervalued by the market.

7. See Williamson, "Managerial Discretion and Business Behavior," *American Economic Review, 53,* (1963), p. 1032.

8. See M. Jensen and K. Murphy, "Are Executive Compensation Contracts Structural Property?" MERC Working Paper No. 86-14 (1987); G. Baker, M. Jensen, and K. Murphy, "Compensation and Incentives: Practice vs. Theory, *Journal of Finance, 43,* (1988), p. 593; see also Note, "The Executive Compensation Contract: Creating Incentives to Reduce Agency Costs," *Stanford Law Review, 37,*(1985), p. 1147.

9. For a discussion of this point, see D. Cook and J. Martin, "The Co-insurance and Leverage Effects on Target-Firm Bondholder Wealth," working paper (November 1988).

10. See Farnsworth, "Disputes over Omissions in Contracts," *Columbia Law Review, 68,* (1968), p. 860. Lawyers also understand that the duty of good faith is a universal, nonwaivable element of contract law, which applies to bond indentures as to other contracts. See note 25 below. See also Burton, "Breach of Contract and the Common Law Duty to Perform in Good Faith," *Harvard Law Review, 94,* (1980), p. 369.

11. For a description of the "hypothetical bargaining" approach under which a court faced with an omission asks itself what term rational actors would have agreed upon, see R. Posner, *Economic Analysis of Law,* 3rd ed., (1986), pp. 79–85. See also, Jordon v. Duff & Phelps, 815 F.2d 429 (7th Cir. 1987).

12. This concept, which originates with Herbert Simon, has been most fully articulated by Oliver Williamson. See, e.g., Williamson, "Transaction-Cost Economics: The Governance of Contractual Relations," *Journal of Law and Economics, 22,* (1979), p. 233.

13. See note 11 above. Professors Easterbrook and Fischel argue that rational actors would agree upon that term which maximizes aggregate value for the parties, regardless of its distribution. See Easterbrook and Fischel, "Corporate Control Transaction," *Yale Law Journal, 91,*(1982), pp. 698, 702–04.

14. See Bratton, "Corporate Debt Relationships: Legal Theory in a Time of Restructuring," *Duke Law Journal, 92,* (1989), p. 138.

15. Ibid. at 138, note 196.

16. See Moran v. Household International, Inc., 500 A.2d 1346 (Del. 1985).

17. See Grossman and Stiglitz, "On the Impossibility of Informationally Efficient Markets," *American Economic Review, 70,* (1980), pp. 393–95.
18. For one anecdotal example of opportunism in the drafting of junk bonds, see Nulty, "Irwin Jacobs Stirs a Junk Bond Brawl," *Fortune,* (June 9, 1986), p. 104 (hidden provision allowed redemption of junk bonds at election of issuer to surprise of underwriters and purchasers).
19. For a critique of the performance of bond rating agencies, see J. Petersen, *The Rating Game: A Report to the Twentieth Century Fund Task Force on Municipal Bond Ratings* (1974); see also Coffee, "Market Failure and the Economic Case for a Mandatory Disclosure System," *Virginia Law Review, 70,* (1984), pp. 717, 745–46.
20. For the standard account of this phenomenon, see Akerlof, "The Market for Lemons: Quality Uncertainty and the Market Mechanism," *Quarterly Journal of Economics, 84,* (1970), p. 488.
21. The Standard & Poors Corporation announced in July 1989 that it would start a new rating service to evaluate takeover protection that issuers offered debt investors. A five-tier rating system (called "Event Risk Covenant Rankings") was developed and has been applied to 14 issues containing "poison puts." Interestingly, only one security of the 14 so rated was given the highest rating of E–1; this suggests that a poison put provision may also sometimes be ambiguous or illusory. See Gilpin, "S&P to Rate Protection on Takeovers," *New York Times* (July 22, 1989), p. 31.
22. The theory of relational contracts—long-term contracts that govern specialized relationships and thus necessarily anticipate future modification and do not attempt to provide fully for all contingencies—was originated by Ian Macneil. See I. Macneil, *The New Social Contract: An Inquiry into Modern Contractual Relations* (1980); and Goetz and Scott, "Principles of Relational Contracts," *Virginia Law Review, 67,* (1981), p. 1089.
23. See Scott, "A Relational Theory of Secured Financing," *Columbia Law Review, 86,* (1986), pp. 901–903; see also Klein, "The Modern Business Corporation," *Yale Law Journal, 91,* (1982), pp. 1521–1562 (as investment duration lengthens and number of contingencies increases, capacity to deal with them decreases, and governance mechanisms must be utilized in contracting).
24. For the standard neoclassical account, see Smith and Warner, "On Financial Contracting: An Analysis of Bond Covenants," *Journal of Financial Economics, 7,* (1979), p. 117.
25. For cases in which courts have refused to let issuers exploit bondholders even though the issuer's conduct conformed to the literal language of the bond indenture, see Van Gemert v. Boeing, 553 F.2d 812, 815 (2d Cir. 1977); Pittsburgh Terminal Corp. v. Baltimore & O.R. Co., 690 F.2d 933 (3d Cir. 1982); Sharon Steel Corp. v. Chase Manhattan Bank N.A., 691 F.2d 1039 (2d Cir. 1982). For an excellent review of the law in this area, see Bratton, "The Economics and

Jurisprudence of Convertible Bonds," *Wisconsin Law Review,* (1984), p. 667.

26. McDaniel, "Bondholders and Corporate Governance," *Business Lawyer, 41,* (1986), pp. 413, 425–26 (reporting survey of Fortune 100 corporations and finding that few had negative covenants in their indentures). Of course, negative covenants remain common in bank loan agreements, but these are easily renegotiated and banks can be more easily compensated on an *ex post* basis for accepting additional risk. Still common in bond indentures is the negative pledge clause and certain prohibitions on sale and leaseback transactions, but all other "business covenants" appear to be vanishing.

27. Smith and Warner, "On Financial Contracting: An Analysis of Bond Covenants," *Journal of Financial Economics, 7,* (1979), p. 117.

28. McDaniel, "Bondholders and Corporate Governance," *Business Lawyer, 41,* (1986), pp. 413, 425–26. For a fuller discussion of this transaction, see Bratton, "Corporate Debt Relationships: Legal Theory in a Time of Restruc-turing," *Duke Law Journal, 92,* (1989), p. 139–42.

29. ABA Section of Corporate, Banking and Business Law, "Model Simplified Indenture," *Business Lawyer, 38,* (1983), p. 741.

30. L. Marais, K. Schipper, and A. Smith, "Wealth Effects of Leveraged Buyouts for Senior Securities," *Journal of Financial Economics, 23,* (1989). This finding that privately placed debt also lacked such business covenants contradicts the traditional view, as set forth in Smith and Warner, op. cit., that privately placed debt, being riskier, had such covenants while purchasers of much less risky publicly held debt were willing to dispense with such covenants as superfluous.

31. Ibid., p. 14.

32. See Coffee, "Shareholders Versus Managers: The Strain in the Corporate Web," *Michigan Law Review, 85,* pp. 52–60.

33. See Lehn and Poulsen, "Leveraged Buyouts: Wealth Created or Wealth Redistributed?" In M. Weidenbaum and K. Chilton (eds.), *Public Policy Toward Corporate Takeovers,* (1988), pp. 46, 57–58.

34. Metropolitan Life held some $340 million in seven RJR investment-grade rated bonds at the time the RJR buyout was announced. See Franklin, "Met Life Looks for Help," *New York Law Journal,* (May 11, 1989), pp. 5–6, col. 5. A suit by Metropolitan Life alleging that RJR breached a duty of good faith and fiduciary duties owed to it is pending. See Metropolitan Life Insurance Co. v. RJR Nabisco Inc., Civ. 88-8148 (S.D.N.Y. 1988). For a discussion of these issues and the case law on the duty of good faith in this context, see Logan and Lamb, "Pending Bondholder Suits Could Have Broad Ramifications," *New York Law Journal,* (June 5, 1989), p. 37.

35. See Jarrell, Brickley, and Netter, "The Market for Corporate Control: The Empirical Evidence Since 1980," *Journal of Economic Perspectives, 49,* (winter 1988).

36. Marais, Schipper, and Smith, "Wealth Effects of Leveraged Buyouts for Senior

Securities," *Journal of Financial Economics, 23,* (1989), p. 12.
37. Ibid., p. 30.
38. D. Cook and J. Martin, "The Co-insurance and Leverage Effects on Target-Firm Bondholder Wealth," working paper (November 1988), pp. 1, 13–16.
39. See Heiberling, "Event Risk Provisions Protect Bondholders Against Take-overs," *National Law Journal,* (June 5, 1989), p. 22. Generally, these puts have had a five- or ten-year life, and thus do not last for the life of the bond. Sometimes, the issuer also has the option to override the put provision by increasing the interest rate to a level that in the judgment of a designated investment banking firm compensates the bondholders for the increase in event risk.
40. See "Poison Put Bonds," *Wall Street Journal,* (February 13, 1986), p. 5, (noting use by W.R. Grace and Co. and Sperry Corporation in January 1986). Moody's *Bond Survey* reported 46 related industrial downgradings for 1985, 1986, and 1987, which may also have spurred innovation in the bond market. See Cook and Martin, op. cit., p. 2.
41. See M. Winkler and J. White, "Shock Still Clouds Blue-Chip Corporate Bond Market," *Wall Street Journal,* (March 22, 1989), p. C–1, cols. 3–6.
42. Indeed, the early evidence suggests that bond purchasers have placed a high premium on these new put provisions. For example, the Harris debentures, which was one of the first debenture issues to contain this provision, traded at 120 basis points over U.S. Treasury securities, instead of the 160–190 basis points that other debentures of similar risk levels traded at. In short, the market valued this poison put at from 40–70 basis points. In addition, the market estimated the value of the ten-year term of the Harris put (as compared to the more typical five-year term) at 10–20 basis points. See Heiberling, "Event Risk Provisions Protect Bondholders Against Takeovers," *National Law Journal,* (June 5, 1989), p. 25. However, there is also evidence that on close inspection, many of these puts are not as protective as they initially seem. So far, Standard and Poors has given only one out of 14 issuers rated its highest special "event protection" rating. See note 21 above.
43. In June 1989, Enrop Corporation of Houston issued the first of these bonds, which peg the yield to the credit rating. Its bonds are rated BBB-, just above the floor in investment grade. Thus, investors had special reason to fear a rating decline, and Enrop responded to this need. Under its indenture, if the credit rating is moved up to A-, the interest rate moves from 9.5% to 9.4%, but if the rating falls one notch (to below investment grade), the rate goes from 9.5% to 12%. See "Investors Are Developing a Taste for Poison," *Business Week,* (July 10, 1989), p. 78. Such two-sided adjustments protect both sides.
44. See Valente, "NWA's Pilots and Machinists Indicate Willingness to Oppose a Hostile Bidder," *Wall Street Journal,* (May 8, 1989), p. A–4, cols. 2–3.
45. Valente and Smith, "Northwest Pilots Emerge as Critical Force in Determining if NWA Gets Taken Over," *Wall Street Journal,* (April 6, 1989), p. A–10.

46. See Berg, "2 More Bidders Enter NWA Contest," *New York Times,* (June 17, 1989), p. 33.

47. Marsh, "CNW Unions Submit Offer to Buy Stake," *Wall Street Journal,* (June 5, 1989), p. A–4.

48. Salpukas, "Eastern Union Set Back as Bid for Takeover Fails," *New York Times,* (June 6, 1989), p. D–1.

49. See, e.g., Trachtenberg, "Textile Union Discloses Hays as Partner in Its Attempts to Acquire Cluett Peabody," *Wall Street Journal,* (June 6, 1989), p. A–6.

50. Valente and Carey, "NWA Union's Restructuring Proposal Would Include Payout, Employee Stake," *Wall Street Journal,* (June 2, 1989), p. A–4.

51. Harlan, "Eastern's Creditors, Terming Ritchie Bid Unfeasible, to Renew Talks with Carrier," *Wall Street Journal,* (June 6, 1989), p. A–4.

52. See Salpukas, "The Long Fight for TWA: Unions Decided the Winner," *New York Times,* (August 31, 1985), p. 1, col. 5.

53. For a detailed account of this contest which nearly resulted in a formal tender offer by the union and did involve their hiring an investment banking firm, Lazard Frères and Co., see Hyde, "Employee Takeovers," *Rutgers Law Review, 41,* (1989).

54. Trachtenberg, "Clothing Union to Make Offer for Health-tex," *Wall Street Journal,* (June 13, 1989), p. A–6.

55. See Trachtenberg, "Clothing Union Enters the Buy-Out Fray," *Wall Street Journal,* (Amalgamated Clothing and Textile Workers Union declined from 325,000 to 274,000 members over past five years).

56. See Hilder and Smith, "ESOP Defenses Are Likely to Increase," *Wall Street Journal,* (April 6, 1989), discussing popularity of ESOPs after successful defense by Polaroid Corporation of 1989 takeover attempt by Shamrock Holding, Inc.

57. See Unocal Corp. v. Mesa Petroleum Co., 493 A.2d 946 (Del. 1985).

58. 592 F. Supp. 203 (N.D. Tex. 1984), *aff'd in part, mod'd in part,* 741 F.2d 707 (5th Cir. 1984).

59. 592 F.Supp. at 206–07.

60. Fed. Sec. L. Rep. (CCH), Para. 94, 419 (7th Cir. May 4, 1989).

61. 699 F. Supp. 1309 (N.D. Ill. 1989).

62. Indeed, one study finds that even if bondholders in leveraged buyouts lost the entire book value of their claims (an obviously unrealistic assumption), their losses would only amount to approximately 48% of shareholders' gains from the same transactions. See Marais, Schipper, and Smith, "Wealth Effects of Leveraged Buyouts for Senior Securities," *Journal of Financial Economics, 23,* (1989), p. 28.

63. See Franklin, "Met Life Looks for Help," *New York Law Journal,* (May 11, 1989), pp. 5–6, col. 5.

64. For a discussion of this theme, see Bratton, "Corporate Debt Relationships: Legal Theory in a Time of Restructuring," *Duke Law Journal, 92,* (1989), p. 138.

65. See Marais, Schipper, and Smith, op. cit., p. 16, (68% of 404 securities in their sample "remain outstanding without revisions in the explicit terms of the contract" following a buyout; of the remainder many had contractual rights to be redeemed).

66. A survey by the Investor Responsibility Research Center (IRRC) of actively traded firms on the New York Stock Exchange has found that nearly 40% today have institutions holding a majority of their shares. Nearly 60% have institutions holding more than 40% of their shares. In these institutionally dominated firms, a limited number of institutions may own a majority of the stock. In roughly 23% of the NYSE-listed firms that were majority owned by institutions, less than 100 institutions held a majority of the stock, and in another 33% of these firms, between 101 and 200 institutions held the majority. See A. Conard, "Fiduciary Obligations of the Asset Manager," in McGill (ed.), *Proxy Voting of Pension Plan Equity Securities,* (1989), The Wharton School. Hence, if these trends continue, it appears likely that there will be a significant population of publicly held corporations in which less than 100 institutions hold an absolute majority (and in which perhaps 20 hold a de facto working control). Of course, it is also possible that institutions will seek to avoid this structure of share ownership precisely because they do not wish to lose their anonymity (and perhaps wish to behave opportunistically). But that view filters out all that is interesting.

CHAPTER 2

THE BOARD OF DIRECTORS, MANAGEMENT, AND CORPORATE TAKEOVERS: OPPORTUNITIES AND PITFALLS

Elliott J. Weiss

When a corporation becomes the target of a takeover bid, its board of directors usually moves to center stage and begins to play a key decision-making role, one similar to the role played by management in most other corporate situations. Much has been written, and much will be said at this conference, about why the law assigns this role to boards of directors and what a board is obligated to do when its company becomes the target of a takeover bid.

This paper, too, discusses the responsibilities of a target company's board of directors. But our concern is broader than that. We are interested in, and offer some suggestions concerning, how boards of directors should deal with two other sets of takeover-related situations: those in which a board is asked to authorize a bid to acquire another company and those in which a board concludes that its company, while not yet a target, is likely to become one.

Elliott J. Weiss has an LL.B. degree from Yale and is currently Professor at Benjamin N. Cordozo School of Law, Yeshiva University. This chapter draws on ideas Professor Weiss has developed in the course of working with Harold M. Williams on a book concerning the responsibilities of corporate boards of directors. The chapter expresses the views of Professor Weiss, who wishes to acknowledge Mr. Williams's contribution to his thinking.

Our thesis, which relates both to those situations and to situations in which a company has become a target, can be stated briefly. It is that boards of directors realistically can be expected to exert a major, constructive influence on corporate decision-making in all three sets of takeover-related situations, and that boards' decisions should be guided by an understanding both of relevant legal requirements and of the massive economic literature that has developed relating to mergers and takeovers.

If widespread consensus existed as to how corporate boards of directors interact with corporate managements, we would turn immediately to a discussion of how boards of directors should deal with the unique problems posed by takeover-related situations. But no such consensus exists. Opinions differ sharply concerning the dynamics of board-management relationships. Consequently, we first outline the elements of this controversy and set forth the assumptions that underlie our analysis of board-management relationships. Then we suggest how boards of directors should approach the three sets of takeover-related problems: those faced by the boards of bidder firms; those to be considered by the boards of firms that are likely to become the targets of takeover bids; and those that arise after firms become targets.

We recognize that takeovers themselves are controversial, as are many related legislative and court-made rules. However, for purposes of this chapter, we largely accept those rules as a given and do not address, or suggest that boards of directors should address questions relating to how those rules might be improved.

THE DYNAMICS OF BOARD-MANAGEMENT RELATIONSHIPS

When we speak of boards of directors, we have in mind the nonmanagement, or outside, members of corporate boards. To be sure, virtually all boards include some of the company's senior executives and some boards include a majority of these inside directors. But nobody takes very seriously the notion that inside directors behave very differently when they are functioning as directors than they do when they are functioning as managers. Moreover, it is difficult to conceive what usefully could be said about how inside directors, when wearing their directors' hats, should deal with their other, managerial selves. Thus, when we speak about the relationship between corporate boards and management, we are referring to the relationship between outside directors and senior executives.

The received legal model of the corporation places the board at the pinnacle of the corporate structure, grants the board authority to manage the corporation's business, and, at least implicitly, holds the board responsible for the success or failure of the corporate enterprise. Nobody takes that model seriously, at least in the case of publicly held corporations. The universally held, modern view is that a company's senior executives, not its directors, have primary responsibility for the success or failure of the company's business. The board, in general, is expected only to oversee senior executives and to evaluate their performance.[1]

Most commentators agree that four factors constrain outside directors' ability to perform effectively even these oversight and evaluation functions. First, most directors hold very demanding, full-time jobs as senior officials of other organizations. Consequently, they have limited time available to devote to their secondary jobs as directors of other organizations. A recent survey found that during 1988, only 20 percent of outside directors devoted more than 10 hours a month to their directorial duties.[2]

Second, outside directors usually lack expertise in the business of the companies on whose boards they sit. Antitrust laws effectively prohibit companies from having on their boards directors employed by their competitors and, even absent legal prohibitions, few companies would want to invite into their boardrooms people whose primary loyalties ran to one of their competitors. But directors' awareness that they lack relevant expertise is an intimidating factor, making directors understandably reluctant to speak out at board meetings for fear that they will be perceived as naive or uninformed.

Third, directors depend upon a company's executives to supply them with information about the issues the board is to consider and about corporate performance in general; rarely do directors have access to reliable, independent sources of information about corporate activities or management's performance. Executives, of course, generally want the board to approve the proposals they make and to think well of their performance. Consequently, executives rarely are inclined to provide the board with information likely to lead it to reject their proposals or to focus on the negative aspects of their performance. But without such information—or sources from which it might readily be obtained—directors find it difficult to question meaningfully what executives propose to do or how well they have performed.

Finally, directors have little in the way of financial incentives and face little in the way of legal pressures to perform effectively. The fees most directors receive, while substantial if viewed in relation to average workers' salaries, usually represent only a minor portion of directors' income. Few directors own large enough stock positions in the firms on whose boards they sit to motivate them to work hard to ensure that those firms prosper.

The legal standards applicable to most board decisions are so imprecise and flexible that directors have little reason to believe that they must follow some procedure, make some inquiry, or reach some decision in order to comply with a legal requirement or to avoid the threat of financial liability. The business judgment rule is particularly significant; it requires courts to presume that most board decisions were reasonable and were made in good faith and allows courts to reject that presumption only where they are convinced that no rational person could have made a challenged decision. The rule has the sensible effect of allowing courts to avoid reviewing the merits of directors' business decisions, but the rule also effectively insulates directors from the threat that they will be held liable for having made an unwise or even a foolish decision.

The business judgment rule extends beyond transactions between a company and persons unrelated to that company's directors or senior executives; it protects many board decisions that affect a company's executives directly, including, most notably, decisions concerning executive compensation. Even when the business judgment rule does not apply, directors are not required to prove that the terms of transactions they have approved replicate those that would have been negotiated by strangers bargaining at arm's length. Rather, directors' decisions will be upheld unless a court is convinced that the terms of a challenged transaction are outside the bounds of what reasonably could be considered fair. Moreover, even if a transaction is proven to be unfair, the director or executive who benefited improperly from the transaction is much more likely to be held liable than are the directors who approved the transaction, thus further diminishing the prospect that fear of liability will motivate directors to perform effectively.

Many commentators believe these constraints limit the contribution directors can make, or can be expected to make, to a company's business success. They also are skeptical about whether directors can deal effectively with situations where managers' and shareholders' interests conflict. They point out that directors' concern about the former, promoting business success, often further impedes their inclination to deal with the latter, since directors, with considerable justification, believe that any effort on their part to limit managers' self-dealing is likely to jeopardize their ability to work effectively with those same managers on solving a company's business problems. Thus, Victor Brudney argues that "the ambiguity of the standards of fairness, the difficulty of ascertaining the relevant facts, the psychological and social pressures on independent directors, and the limited incentives and weak sanctions available suggest that to elicit disapproval from outside directors would make a transaction so grossly overreaching as not often to be proposed by management."[3] Similarly, Warren Buffet observes: "[M]y experience overwhelmingly has been that the boards of directors (there are exceptions) tend to go along with what management wants."[4] These and similar observations about board passivity[5] make it seem silly to believe that directors' concerns about their reputations are sufficiently strong to motivate them to perform effectively.

Other commentators, drawn mostly from the business community, do not deny the existence of the constraints noted above, but nonetheless contend that boards can be counted on both to help managers succeed and to protect shareholders' interests when they conflict with the interests of managers.[6] As to the former, these commentators argue that directors are successful people, committed to the success of any organization that they serve, and that they have the capacity and the will to provide much in the way of judgment, perspective, and advice to the managers of any company on whose board they sit. As to the latter, they emphasize that those asked to serve as outside directors typically are people of integrity and prominence who are acutely sensitive to the reputational price they will pay if they, or the companies on whose boards they serve, fail to perform properly. For example, Donald V. Siebert, former chairman of J.C. Penney Co., recently wrote:

> [O]utside directors serve primarily because they believe that they are performing a valuable public service which carries with it great responsibility for the success of our free enterprise system. I do not believe any of the many outside directors I have come to know would violate what they rightly perceive to be a public trust; nor would they put their reputations in jeopardy by condoning management misbehavior.[7]

Clearly, at the heart of these differing predictions about how effective boards of directors have been and are likely to be lie differences of opinion concerning directors' personal characteristics and inclinations. As Warren Buffet's comment makes clear, any generalization about individual directors or boards of directors is subject to numerous exceptions. With that caveat in mind, we are comfortable asserting that in most situations where managers' interests conflict with those of shareholders, directors are unlikely to effectively constrain managers' self-serving behavior, absent threats of litigation or regulation. At the same time, where managers' and shareholders' interests coincide, we believe directors have the ability to assist managers substantially and are likely to want to provide such assistance.

Our views about how directors can be expected to behave are influenced strongly by the fact that most directors are senior executives (usually chief executives) of other companies. As such, their socioeconomic status and outlook on the world is similar to that of the executives, especially the chief executives, of the companies on whose boards they sit. In addition, while acting in their primary occupational roles as chief or senior executives, these people have developed clear views about what constitutes desirable behavior by directors, views that shape their behavior when they act in their secondary occupational roles as corporate directors.[8] Specifically, when these people are operating as executives, they hope and expect that their boards will be sources of support and encouragement, not criticism or skepticism. Then, on the one or two days a month that these same people shift into their roles as directors of other companies, they similarly, and quite naturally, see their responsibility to be to support and encourage that company's managers, not to criticize their plans or question them sharply about what they are proposing or what they have done. In short, most directors observe what might be termed the Golden Rule of the Boardroom: "Do unto the managers of a company on whose board you sit only what you would have the directors of your company do unto you."

This attitude—combined with limited time, limited expertise, limited information, a noncritical mindset, and concerns about the possibility of disrupting collegial board-management relationships—leads most outside directors of American corporations to be very deferential to management. Moreover, in many companies, an additional obstacle confronts directors who are not inclined to observe the Golden Rule of the Boardroom. Many CEOs are not receptive to directorial interventions that involve even a hint of criticism or skepticism; they react to such interventions as if they represented threats to their authority or challenges to their business acumen. Directors of any company that has such a CEO may well conclude that any activism on their part, rather than promoting constructive dialogue or leading to desirable changes, will merely increase tensions in the boardroom. If that outcome seems likely, why bother taking the initiative, unless the board is dealing with a crisis.

These observations are not meant to suggest that most directors are venal, lazy, or uncaring. Most probably accept positions on corporate boards largely in a spirit of service. They want to contribute to the operation of the free market system; they want the companies on whose boards they sit to prosper; they want those companies to operate lawfully, ethically, and in a fashion that advances the public good. But the constraints under which directors operate, the attitude with which most directors enter the boardroom, and the social environment within many boardrooms combine to make it unlikely that even the most conscientious director will contribute as much as he or she might.

When it comes to takeover situations, many of the same factors influence board-management relations and affect directors' ability and desire to play a constructive role. But other aspects of takeover-related situations make it reasonable to expect directors to perform more effectively.

That a number of boards have dealt effectively and responsibly with a variety of takeover-related situations in recent years provides one indication that these expectations are not Panglossian. Probably the best publicized such incident involved the reaction of the RJR-Nabisco board to CEO Ross Johnson's proposal to take that company private in a leveraged buy-out. Rather than simply acquiescing to Johnson's proposal, as some boards have done in similar situations, the RJR-Nabisco board initiated a full-fledged auction for the company, a process that resulted in shareholders receiving about 50 percent more for their stock than the price Johnson originally proposed to pay. What is particularly striking about the RJR-Nabisco incident is that the very same board that adopted such an independent posture had, in the years prior to Johnson announcing his bid, regularly and seemingly unquestioningly supported virtually anything Johnson had wanted to do, including a number of decisions that, in retrospect, struck RJR-Nabisco's directors as unsound.[9]

Why have the RJR-Nabisco board and the boards of several other companies acted independently and forcefully in takeover-related situations? One part of the explanation, we believe, is that takeovers almost always involve a crisis of sorts. The financial stakes almost always are huge, and the decisions a board must make almost always will have a dramatic impact on the company involved, its managers, its shareholders, and all other parties with a stake in that company's operations. Because of the crisis atmosphere that surrounds most takeover bids, directors are likely to feel obligated to spend a good deal of time dealing with them, despite the pressure of their other obligations.

Secondly, the courts, especially the Delaware courts, have developed legal rules relating to certain aspects of takeover situations that provide directors with far more specific guidance than they usually receive. At the start of the current wave of takeovers, the courts generally held that board decisions concerning how to respond to a takeover bid were protected from judicial scrutiny by the business judgment rule.[10] But as target company boards, in case after case, appeared to go along with whatever actions management proposed, seemingly without paying much attention to how those actions affected shareholders' interests, the courts reacted by developing new rules that greatly limited boards' discretion.

Unocal v. Mesa Petroleum Co.[11] established a two-part test in terms of which defensive tactics are now reviewed. First, a company's board must establish that is has reasonable grounds for believing that a takeover bid jeopardizes corporate policy or legitimate shareholder interests, as might be the case if a bid is coercive in form or inadequate in price. Second, the board must demonstrate that the measures it employs in response to that bid are reasonable in relation to the danger posed. Moreover, Unocal emphasizes that defensive tactics will receive even the limited deference implicit in this two-part test only where a company's outside directors approve those tactics.

Revlon, Inc. v. MacAndrews & Forbes Holdings, Inc.[12] extended Unocal by holding that once a company's board of directors has decided that the company is to be sold (or inevitably will be sold), the board's obligation becomes solely to ensure that shareholders realize the highest possible price for their stock. Accordingly, once an auction has begun, the board cannot properly employ defensive tactics for any purpose other than advancing a fair auction. Subsequent Delaware decisions support the proposition that to qualify as reasonable, defensive actions must be directed at attracting other bids or restructuring a target company so that shareholders will receive more in value than is being offered by a hostile takeover bidder.[13]

The operation of these principles is illustrated by Moran v. Household Int'l, Inc.[14] and its progeny. Moran established that it was permissible for a company's board to adopt a poison pill, but also held that whether a board could use the pill to block a hostile takeover bid would be tested under the Unocal standard. Subsequent to Moran, many companies adopted poison pills. When some of those companies became targets of takeover bids, the courts allowed their boards to use their poison pills to buy time in which to shop for better bids or to negotiate financing for restructuring plans that arguably advanced shareholders' interests. But where a board attempted to rely on a pill to favor a management group over other bidders,[15] or to block an all cash offer that nobody was prepared to top and that most shareholders wanted to accept,[16] the courts held those actions to be improper.

A third reason why directors can be expected to perform more effectively in takeover-related situations is that much about the dynamics of those situations is now well understood. (The most notable exception relates to the question of whether takeovers create net social gains or only redistribute wealth. Consideration of that question is outside the scope of this chapter, but see "Problems of Target Firms," p. 57.) Economists, lawyers, and others have devoted an enormous amount of study to understanding takeovers. Directors, without too much effort, can familiarize themselves with the conclusions of those studies. As the following sections of this paper make clear, once they have done so, directors should not find it too difficult to identify many of the opportunities and pitfalls presented by takeover-related situations. Moreover, there is no reason why directors' understanding of those opportunities and pitfalls should not be at least comparable to that of the managers of the companies on whose boards they sit. Thus, when making takeover-related decisions, directors need not be constrained by the comparative lack of expertise that impairs their ability to deal with many other corporate problems.

PROBLEMS OF BIDDER FIRMS

Most legal writing about takeovers has focused on target companies and questions relating to the propriety of various takeover defenses. This may be a consequence of the fact that most litigation in this area has dealt with the efforts of target companies to resist takeover bids. But the neglect of issues relating to the behavior of bidder firms nonetheless is surprising, given the evidence that few companies benefit by making successful takeover bids.[17]

One group of studies, conducted by financial economists, measures the returns to shareholders of acquiring companies. These studies find small, but statistically significant, gains associated with announcements of takeover bids in the 1960s and 1970s, and small, statistically insignificant losses to bidders in the 1980s. This deterioration in the returns realized by the shareholders of bidder firms may be explained by the shift in the legal rules governing takeover defenses in the direction of requiring auctions. When a takeover target becomes the subject of an auction, a dynamic is created in which a bidder is likely to succeed only if it offers the shareholders of the target a premium that reflects the lion's share of the cash flows that the target seems to have the potential to generate. Any lesser bid probably will be topped by a competing bidder.

A second group of studies finds that acquiring firms have experienced negative abnormal returns in the period one to three years after successful takeover bids. The one-year studies found average abnormal negative returns of 5.5 percent, and a three-year study found average abnormal negative returns of 16 percent.[18] While these negative returns were not statistically significant, because of the larger variance expected when a market price study uses an extended time period, they still represent disquieting evidence that shareholders of acquiring firms are more likely to experience losses than gains.

Other studies, conducted by industrial organization economists, have found that takeovers generally have not resulted in improvements in the financial performance of acquired firms. As one might expect, given the view that takeovers serve to discipline inefficient managers, the profit performance of acquired companies was found to have been slightly inferior to that of other companies in their industries prior to takeover. But, adjusting for accounting revaluation effects, the cash flow/sales performance of acquired companies was comparably inferior after they were taken over. Thus, "operating performance neither improved nor deteriorated significantly following takeover."[19]

Other analysts, focussing on the dynamics of the takeover process, have concluded that bidders often overpay for target companies, in the sense that the risk-adjusted returns bidders realize often are lower than the returns they would have received had they, or their shareholders, invested comparable amounts in a diversified portfolio of marketable securities.[20] Several reasons may account for such overpayment. Managers of bidding companies may overestimate the value of targets or overestimate their ability to run other businesses as successfully as they have run their own. Investment bankers, on whom acquirors often rely for valuation advice, may be biased in favor of overestimating the value of targets, since investment bankers often receive much higher fees when their clients succeed in completing takeover bids.   Managers of acquiring firms may overpay because takeovers can provide a means of using shareholders' money to obtain nonfinancial benefits that are of interest to managers, but not shareholders—increased prestige and visibility, greater job security due to diversification of the acquiring firms' lines of business, protection from takeovers by dispersing cash that would have made an acquiring firm an attractive target, or simply avoiding being branded a "loser" by the financial press when a firm announces a takeover bid and then fails to acquire the target company.

Of course, not all takeovers produce negative returns. Even average returns of less than zero usually involve netting out some winners against a larger number of losers. Further analysis of the studies of the takeover process suggests which takeovers are likely to prove successful and which are not.

A takeover is most likely to produce net positive returns to an acquiring company where it increases the market power of that company. The Reagan administration allowed a number of companies to proceed with acquisitions of competitors that previous administrations probably would have challenged on antitrust grounds. Several of those acquisitions, such as those where airline companies obtained dominant positions in important markets or developed more attractive route structures, seem to be working out well for the acquiring companies.

The Bush administration, however, has signalled that it intends to enforce the antitrust laws more vigorously. Thus, while acquisitions that allow a company to substantially increase its market power continue to be potentially profitable for acquiring firms, the likelihood that the government will allow such acquisitions to occur probably is substantially less than it was during the Reagan years.

Other takeovers appear to produce positive returns largely by transferring wealth to shareholders from other parties. Some such transfers come from the U.S. Treasury, in the form of tax savings. Some come from labor or suppliers, in the form of lower costs that an acquired company's managers were not prepared to seek or were not able to negotiate. Some come from selling off businesses owned by acquired firms that those firms' managers were not prepared to divest (often businesses that incumbent managers had been responsible for acquiring). As noted above, if these transfers are identifiable in advance of a takeover, an acquiring firm probably will have to pay the lion's share of the anticipated gains to a target company's shareholders, in the form of a takeover premium. But to the extent that an acquiror has a comparative advantage, vis-à-vis other acquirors in transferring wealth to shareholders from the Treasury, labor, suppliers, or incumbent managers, it should be able to retain some portion of the benefits that it produces.[21]

Positive returns to an acquiring firm are much less likely where that firm pays a premium in the expectation that it will be able to operate more profitably the business or businesses previously operated by the target company, especially where the acquiring and acquired companies are engaged in different businesses. Acquiring company managers' generic skills usually have not proven adequate to improve the performance of acquired companies whose businesses those managers did not know or understand. Industry-specific expertise is important.

Finally, an acquisition probably is least likely to prove profitable for an acquiring firm where the primary motivation for the acquisition, expressly or implicitly, is to advance some private interest of the acquiring firm's management. As noted above, managers may be tempted to use shareholders' money to pursue acquisitions to obtain a variety of benefits that managers care about but shareholders do not. Few such acquisitions will prove beneficial to the acquiring firms, and one group of such acquisitions has the potential to be particularly harmful.

Managers of companies engaged primarily in stable, low-growth businesses that generate large cash flows have seemed more disposed than most to pursue acquisitions of firms engaged in unrelated lines of business that appear either to have greater growth potential or to be more glamorous than the business of the acquiring firm. Although these managers lack expertise in the businesses of the firms they acquire, they often devote much of their time and attention to the new, more glamorous businesses they now control. As a consequence, they tend to neglect their companies' core business—the "cash cow" that generated the funds that made the takeover possible—and to promote development of a corporate culture in which efforts to make marginal improvements in that core business are not valued. Experience demonstrates, though, that worldwide competition in most basic industries is quite intense. When the top managers of a company in a basic industry neglect their core business, the returns produced by that business are likely to decline. The value of most of the company's productive assets are placed in jeopardy. And, ironically, the acquiring company often becomes a takeover target itself, as the case of Goodyear amply illustrates.

Given the risks associated with "successful" takeover bids, one might expect that corporate law would impose numerous constraints on boards and managers before they can effectuate such a bid. It does not. Decisions to make a takeover bid or to acquire another company generally are insulated from judicial scrutiny by the business judgment rule. Moreover, if the managers of an acquiring company use cash or debt, rather than stock, to effectuate an acquisition, they can easily structure the transaction so that no vote by shareholders is required before they proceed.

State legislatures have sought to regulate takeovers almost entirely by adopting laws that increase the ability of target companies' managers to resist such bids. No effort has been made to amend state corporate laws to require bidding companies' shareholders to approve takeover bids, despite the fact that shareholders might realistically be expected to decline to grant such approvals. This dichotomy could be interpreted as additional evidence that state corporate laws are drafted to appeal primarily to managers, not shareholders.

However, managers must obtain board approval before making any significant takeover bid. The board thus has the authority to block an unwise bid. But if directors wish to maintain a constructive working relationship with management, they should be prepared to explain to management why they are questioning the rationale for a bid or why a bid should not be made.

This burden should not prove to be unmanageable. Several factors combine to strengthen directors' ability to react effectively and authoritatively to requests that they authorize takeover bids. On the most general level, directors can point to their fiduciary obligation to approve a takeover bid only where they conclude that making the bid and, presumably, acquiring the proposed target company will serve the best interests of the acquiring company and its shareholders. More specifically, in a market economy, the fact that the company almost certainly will have to pay a substantial premium over prevailing market prices to acquire the proposed target surely provides directors with an initial basis for questioning whether a proposed transaction is wise.

The studies of the takeover process, noted above, suggest additional questions that directors should be able to ask without creating an undue risk that management will suspect they have lost confidence in management's judgment:

- What is management's rationale for proposing the takeover bid?
- What basis does management have for believing that, after paying a

significant premium for the target, it will be able to generate gains that will adequately compensate the bidding company's shareholders for the risks involved in the acquisition?

- What will be the source of those gains?
- Would management be better off directing its time and energies to attempting to improve the competitive position of the company's existing business?
- Finally (and this is a question directors largely should ask themselves), is there anything in the company's situation, or in the nature of the proposed takeover, that leads directors to suspect it is designed to promote managers' interests at shareholders' expense?

Directors should only approve proposed acquisitions that make substantive, long-term business sense for the acquiring company. They should be wary of acquisitions that bear little relationship to the company's existing business and of general claims about synergy or how better management or improved financial controls will lead to marked improvements in a target's performance. Unless a company's management has established a track record of successfully evaluating other companies, integrating acquired companies with its existing business, and delivering the benefits it projected in connection with other acquisitions, a board may be well advised to eschew most or all acquisition "opportunities."

In those cases where a board makes a threshold determination that a proposed acquisition is strategically sound, it should next direct its attention to the proposed offering price. In the case of a hostile offer, making a judgment about the premium is apt to be particularly troublesome, because management will lack complete information about the target and because the problems involved in integrating the acquired company into the bidder's operations are apt to be more acute. Moreover, takeover bids in general, and especially contested bids, take on many aspects of the hunt. Those involved have been known to get so caught up in making sure that they prevail that they lose perspective on whether "winning" remains a desirable goal. A prudent board should guard against this phenomenon. It should make sure, when it first approves a takeover bid, that it retains enough control over the situation to prevent management, and the board itself, from getting so caught up in the excitement of the chase that it increases the price the company is offering above the level at which the acquisition is likely to be profitable.

In considering the potential profitability of an acquisition, a board need not disregard gains that may be available as a consequence of tax laws or other public policies. Those laws and policies may provide incentives for companies to pursue takeover bids of questionable social or economic merit, but a board has no obligation to deny its company's shareholders the financial benefits that they make available.[22] Dollars generated by tax savings buy just as many groceries as dollars generated by production efficiencies.

Nonetheless, a board should be wary of a proposed acquisition of which most of the projected benefits are attributable to tax or other financial—as opposed to economic—factors. The corporate landscape is littered with the wrecks of too many acquisitions that have failed to work out, in business terms, for a board to be very confident that its company's managers will be able to operate successfully an acquired company that they do not know and whose business they may not understand. We have tried to be careful, when discussing the responsibilities of boards of directors, to avoid assuming that directors are the Supermen or Superwomen of the business world, capable of understanding as well as full-time managers the nuances of every company's business. But directors should similarly be wary of assuming their company's managers are Supermen or Superwomen, capable of operating efficiently businesses in which they have no experience or of performing effectively in corporate cultures that differ markedly from those to which they are accustomed.

Especially where directors are told or suspect that a takeover bid is designed largely to prevent a bidding company from becoming a takeover target itself, they should consider carefully, before authorizing a takeover bid, whether some alternative would better serve shareholders' interests. Those alternatives, by and large, relate to the actions to be considered by the boards of potential takeover targets, which we discuss below.

PROBLEMS OF POTENTIAL TARGET FIRMS

A company's board of directors generally should have a pretty clear idea about whether the company is likely to become the target of a takeover bid. Some bids, to be sure, arrive like bolts from the blue, unanticipated and unanticipatable. But most companies that become targets of takeover bids have had, or could have obtained, some warning as to their probable status as targets.

Takeovers appear to be driven largely by financial considerations. A company is most likely to become a target when the market price of its stock does not reflect the present value of the cash flows that it is generating, or that could be generated by its business or assets. Many people—corporate planning officers, merger experts at investment banks, investment advisors, and others—maintain lists of likely target companies. A board should be able to obtain from either a company's planning staff or its investment banker ongoing readings as to the likelihood that the company will become a target.

Experience demonstrates that most companies that become targets of takeover bids do not succeed in remaining independent, even if that is what their management and board of directors would prefer. Consequently, the board and management of any company that is a likely target are well advised to direct their attention, first, to considering whether there are sensible steps that they can take to reduce or eliminate the prospect that the company will remain an attractive target. Of secondary importance are questions concerning how to react to possible takeover bids and what takeover defenses to adopt.

A company may become a takeover target because the stock market does not value it very accurately. Most observers agree that the stock market reacts rationally and reasonably to discrete bits of information—that is, that it deals with information efficiently. But substantial disagreement exists concerning the accuracy with which stock market prices reflect companies' fundamental value. Fischer Black recently offered the following description of an efficient market:

> [W]e might define an efficient market as one in which price is within a factor of 2 of value, i.e., the price is more than half of value and less than twice value. The factor of two is arbitrary, of course.... Intuitively, though it seems reasonable to me, in light of the sources of uncertainty about value and the strength of the forces tending to cause prices to return to value. By this definition, I think almost all markets are efficient almost all of the time. "Almost all" means at least 90 percent.[23]

Some economists believe the stock market is much more efficient than suggested by Black's statement; others do not. Frederick M. Scherer calculates that if Black's estimate applies to the stock market, at any given time the stocks of 16 percent of all public companies would be undervalued by 34 percent or more.[24] Takeover bidders, if they have the capacity to identify those undervalued companies, could earn substantial profits by acquiring those companies. More importantly for our purposes, if such structural deficiencies exist in the operation of the stock market, there is little if anything that the board or management of an undervalued company can do to remedy them.

Other studies suggest four company-specific reasons why the market price of a company's stock will not reflect the cash flows that company is capable of generating:

- The company's core business may be poorly managed.
- The company may be engaged in several lines of business, some of which may be poorly managed and some of which the market may undervalue.
- The company may be managing its business well but making inefficient use of the cash flows it does not need to maintain or improve the competitive position of its existing business.
- The company's capital structure may not maximize the after-tax cash flows retained by it or received by those who provide it with capital.

A board of directors concerned about a company's status as a potential takeover target should review with that company's management whether any of these four reasons seems to apply. The board should also consider involving the company's investment bankers in such a review, hoping that the bankers will bring to bear both their expertise in evaluating companies as acquisition targets and an independent point of view about the market's perception of the strengths and weaknesses of the company's operations.

A board of directors may find that the threat of an uninvited takeover bid can serve as a catalyst to stimulate management to consider courses of action that it previously was unprepared to pursue and that the directors were reluctant or unprepared to suggest. Put differently, a board may be able to employ the threat of a takeover to make the previously unmentionable seem reasonable and even constructive.

Consider, for example, a situation in which a company's board and management conclude that the company is a likely target because its profit margins are below industry norms and directors believe the company has too large an administrative staff. Whereas once management might have bridled at directors' suggestion that it cut back on staff, viewing it as implying that management was engaged in unnecessary "empire building," now directors can present the same idea as part of a strategy to increase profit margins so as to reduce the company's vulnerability as a target. Such a suggestion is likely to be especially effective in the case of a low margin business, where a small percentage reduction in costs can produce a much larger percentage increase in margins.

Similarly, directors might urge a management that has been reluctant to face up to the unpleasantness involved in asking workers to accept cuts

in pay or benefits to begin negotiating for such cuts, perhaps arguing that
if incumbent management does not do so, some outsider is likely to come
along, take over the company, and make the same or harsher demands.

Boards of undervalued diversified companies are likely to conclude
that somewhat different suggestions are in order. If a board decides that
managing many unrelated businesses is beyond the capability of the
company's managers, it might suggest that management sell off some of
those businesses. If the board believes the price of the company's stock is
depressed because the market anticipates that the company will use its
excess cash flows to acquire additional, unrelated businesses and perhaps
pay inflated prices when it does, the board and management might agree
on an announced policy of forgoing future acquisitions. Often, the credibility of either of these strategies will be enhanced if the company's
board and management commit themselves to distribute to shareholders
the proceeds of such divestitures or excess future cash flows. Here again,
without having to take a confrontational posture a board may well find
itself in a position where it can discreetly imply that if management does
not take the necessary action, somebody else is likely to take it for them.

One alternative that the board and management of any company with
excess cash, or excess borrowing capacity, may want to consider is a buy-
back of its own stock. Some people view buy-backs as reflecting adversely on the ability of a company's management to build the company,
as contrasted to liquidating it. They see buy-backs as creating no more
than an illusion of growth by reducing the number of shares outstanding
and thus allowing the company to report increased earnings per share.
However, a stock buy-back can be an economically attractive alternative
for a company that sees limited opportunities for additional investment in
its traditional lines of business.

Moreover, while a buy-back has the same economic impact on a
company and its creditors as does the payment of a dividend, the tax laws
provide tax-preferred treatment to buy-backs, at least where they are sufficiently disproportional not to qualify as de facto dividends.[25] Shareholders can treat the proceeds of a buy-back as a return of capital, up to the
amount they paid for their stock. In contrast, shareholders must treat as
ordinary income all payments they receive from a company in the form of
dividends.

Concern that management has not fully exploited potential tax advantages may lead a board to suggest management consider changes in
the company's capital structure. Interest payments are deductible from

taxable income, whereas dividends are not. Thus, in general, the greater the portion of a company's capital that is represented by debt, the greater the portion of its operating income that the company will be able to shield from taxes. The stock market's hospitable reaction to many companies' decisions to revise their capital structures, often by buying back stock with borrowed money, provides evidence that investors currently prefer to own more highly leveraged equity investments. A company can provide its shareholders with the benefits of added leverage, and can avoid the risk of entering unfamiliar lines of business and paying a premium for the privilege of doing so, by both forgoing diversification and borrowing money to repurchase its own shares. Directors should recognize this reality. They should be particularly alert to the need to bring it to the attention of management if and when management proposes making a takeover bid for another company primarily to use up the bidding company's cash reserves.

Management, of course, may not respond favorably to directors' suggestions that they forgo diversification, distribute more cash, and increase debt. Such actions tend to increase the risks associated with managers' jobs and to reduce the size of the organization managers control. A board may be able to alleviate these concerns, and also advance shareholders' interests, by suggesting that management investigate the possibility of a leveraged management buy out, or MBO. A properly structured MBO will give managers a much larger equity stake in the firm, which they may consider a reasonable trade-off for the additional risks managers will be required to incur. Such a transaction also can provide shareholders with a payment for their stock that reasonably reflects a firm's inherent value.

Moreover, an MBO may eliminate the pressure managers feel from worrying about whether their company will become the target of a takeover bid. No econometric studies corroborate the frequently made claim that companies that make significant investments in sound, long-range projects are particularly likely to become takeover targets, but many managers believe that claim and become preoccupied with short-term projects and results. Thus, it may be that MBOs have the potential to be both socially useful and profitable for a firm's managers and shareholders.[26]

The foregoing does not represent a universal endorsement of high leverage or of paying out as dividends most or all of every company's earnings. Capital structures and dividend policies clearly must be tailored to the needs of individual companies and, as Scholes and Wolfson make clear, the tax impact of particular transactions often is far from obvious.[27]

But, at least over the past decade, most takeover targets have been companies, engaged in relatively slow growth businesses, that have had substantial earnings, substantial assets, and relatively low debt. For such companies, changes in dividend policies, investment strategies and capital structure are particularly likely to prove to be the best takeover defenses.

Attempts to eliminate undervaluation problems are likely to serve both managers' and shareholders' interests. But boards of potential target companies also no doubt will want to consider, or will be urged by management to consider, adopting specific takeover defenses. Whether such defenses protect or injure shareholders' interests is far from clear. Perhaps for that reason, corporate law places some constraints on boards' decisions to adopt such defenses, although as a practical matter those constraints rarely have proven to be very significant.

Most defensive measures require shareholder approval, either of the actual defensive measure, as where a corporation amends its charter to provide that its board of directors shall be divided into three classes, each of which is elected to serve for a three-year term; or of some necessary condition precedent, such as the authorization of "blank check" preferred stock that can serve as the basis for a board decision to create a shareholder rights plan, or poison pill.

Increasing numbers of investors, especially institutional investors, appear to be hostile to any measure that reduces the likelihood a company will become the target of a takeover bid. Fear of negative shareholder votes no doubt has deterred some companies' boards or managements from proposing defensive measures that required shareholder approval. Nonetheless, large numbers of companies have proposed defensive measures for shareholder approval, and it has been a rare day indeed that shareholders have refused to go along.

Both theoretical and practical explanations exist for why shareholders tend to be so compliant. For present purposes, suffice it to say that the threat of shareholder disapproval of defensive measures, other than in situations where a takeover bid is on the table, may be no more than a toothless tiger.

Courts also review some board decisions to adopt defensive measures more closely than they do ordinary business decisions. However, except where a board acts to so entrench a company's management as to make a hostile takeover close to impossible, the courts generally will allow a board considerable freedom to adopt anticipatory defensive measures. Whether the courts will allow a board to fully exploit all available defenses once a takeover bid has been made presents a different question, but, in advance of any bid being made, the courts are reluctant to prevent boards from taking actions that, at least arguably, will allow them to better cope with a potentially coercive or inadequate bid.

Whether a corporation's shareholders are better served by deploying takeover defenses or by desisting from authorizing any anticipatory defensive measures poses an interesting theoretical question. All defensive measures make it at least somewhat more difficult to take over a company and, consequently, reduce somewhat the likelihood that the company will become the target of an uninvited takeover bid. At the same time, most, if not all, defensive measures can be waived by a company's board of directors, which means that they increase a board's ability to bargain with a potential acquiror on behalf of the company's shareholders. Thus, not authorizing any takeover defenses increases the likelihood of a company becoming the target of a takeover bid, while adopting such defenses probably will increase the premium shareholders receive if and when a bid is made. While directors should consider which choice best serves shareholders' interests, as a practical matter, given the courts' tolerant attitude, it seems clear most boards will resolve this issue by deciding to adopt some takeover defenses.

It seems clear that a board can adopt and rely upon takeover defenses for at least one purpose: to protect shareholders against structurally coercive takeover bids, such as front-end-loaded, two-tier bids. A number of techniques can be used to negate the coercive effects of such bids, but the most effective defense against coercion of this sort is the "flip-in" poison pill. Such a pill is activated when an acquiror purchases more than a set amount of a company's stock, usually 15 or 20 percent. It gives all shareholders other than the acquiror the right to purchase additional shares of the company's stock at a substantial discount, usually 50 percent. If activated, such a pill has the potential to so increase the price that a bidder will have to pay to gain control of a target company as to make an acquisition prohibitively expensive.

To our knowledge, no court has been called upon to approve activation of a flip-in poison pill in response to a structurally coercive takeover bid. However, the Delaware courts have approved use of other discriminatory defensive measures in response to such bids,[28] and it seems likely that they would allow a flip-in pill to be used to like effect. That being the case, for present purposes it suffices to note that other, less powerful antidotes to coercive bids also exist.

In addition to approving takeover defenses, a board should organize itself to be prepared to respond if and when a company becomes the target of an uninvited takeover bid. All too often, target company boards of directors have reacted to takeover bids much as a team of tennis players might react to the news that in a few days they must play a football game for high stakes. The first inclination of the tennis players might be to go it on their own. But, as the magnitude of the task they face and their lack of relevant skills become clear, the tennis players undoubtedly would recruit expert coaches to advise them. Eventually, given the limited time available to prepare, the tennis players probably would defer almost entirely to the coaches, letting them design and call the plays, decide which player should be in which position, and otherwise allowing them to assume complete control over the football game.

Similarly, many target company boards, having failed to prepare themselves to respond to possible takeover bids, have found themselves with little alternative but to rely heavily on "coaches"—generally lawyers and investment bankers—to tell them what to do when their companies became the targets of such bids. Moreover, the coaches they have relied on generally have been retained not by the board but by management, to whom those coaches have felt a certain loyalty. Often directors have felt overwhelmed by the urgency of the situation, the importance of the issues they had to decide with little notice and the complexity of the choices they were required to make. Understandably, they have relied heavily on their coaches to tell them what strategy the company should pursue. Those coaches, by and large, have not pushed directors very hard to give priority to protecting shareholders' interests. Rather, at least where management is so inclined, they have devoted their energies to developing strategies designed to increase management's chances of retaining control.

In Mills Acquisition Co. v. MacMillan, Inc.,[29] the board of MacMillan found itself in just such a position. The board allowed its advisors, all of whom management had suggested the board retain, to assume close to complete control over the company's response to a series of takeover bids and over the auction through which the company eventually was sold. These advisors, in turn, so favored a bidder affiliated with MacMillan's management that the court described their conduct as "fail[ing] all basic standards of fairness."[30] The court also observed that the "board's virtual abandonment of its oversight functions... was a breach of its fundamental duties of loyalty and care...."[31] Mills did not involve claims that MacMillan's directors should be held personally liable for their actions, but the court's observation clearly stands as a warning to other boards that if they so conduct themselves in the future, they run a significant risk of being held personally liable for any losses that such conduct causes shareholders to sustain.

Directors can avoid placing themselves in such a vulnerable position. If a board determines that a company is likely to become a takeover target, it should get prepared to respond to any takeover bid that might be made. In addition to conducting the sort of strategic review discussed above, the board should create a special committee, made up of all outside directors or some portion of that group, and charge it with coordinating the company's response to all takeover bids.

The special committee, as a first order of business, should retain investment bankers and lawyers to advise it. It should make clear to those specialists that if and when a bid eventuates, it is the committee, or the outside directors as a group, who will determine the tenor and thrust of the company's response. If management expresses concern about the board taking such action, the board should respond by pointing out that if an offer is made, the courts will focus on outside directors' decisions, not those of management, in determining the propriety of any corporate defensive actions. Therefore, directors need to protect themselves, and can best protect management, by putting into place a decision-making structure that will enhance the prospect that whatever the outside directors decide to do will withstand the close judicial scrutiny that it is likely to receive.

We consider in the next section questions relating to responses to takeover bids, including their propriety, their desirability, and their legality.

PROBLEMS OF TARGET FIRMS

Takeover bids can be hostile or friendly; they can be made by unrelated parties or by a company's own managers. No matter what the nature or what the source of a takeover bid, the first task of the target company's board should be the same. The board should ascertain the price, or range of prices, that a third party with full information about the company could be induced to pay to take the company over in a transaction negotiated at arm's length. That price should become the benchmark against which all takeover bids will be evaluated.

That a board should adopt the same approach to evaluating a company, no matter who is seeking to acquire it or whether the proposed transaction is hostile or friendly, bears emphasis. Experience demonstrates that most offerors' opening bids are significantly lower than the best prices those offerors are prepared to pay. Boards of target companies appear to appreciate this fact when a bid is hostile. They almost always resist such bids and usually are able to elicit a higher bid, either from a white knight or from the original offeror. But many boards adopt a different approach when management supports (or is making) a takeover bid.[32]   The board of J.P. Stevens, for example, recently recommended shareholders accept a management group's buy-out offer of $38 per share in cash and $5 per share in debentures, only to see a bidding contest erupt between West Point-Pepperell, one of Stevens's competitors, and Odyssey Partners, a leveraged buy-out firm. Eventually, Odyssey Partners acquired Stevens for $68.50 per share in cash, a price 60 percent greater than the management group's first bid. Similarly, the board of Roper Corporation endorsed management's recommendation that the company be sold to Whirlpool in a friendly transaction for $37.50 per share in cash. GE then entered the bidding and Whirlpool responded by increasing its offer to $50 per share, or one third more than the price Roper's management and board had been prepared to accept. (Ultimately, GE acquired Roper for $54 per share, or 44 percent more than the price Roper's board had accepted.)

Deciding how much a company is worth as a takeover target, of course, is far from simple. Directors usually will be well advised to retain an investment banker to help it decide what price to seek. They should make clear to the investment banker that they are interested in determining the highest price for which the company can be sold, rather than asking if the price is "fair," in the case of a friendly offer, or "adequate," in the case of a hostile bid—questions that, in the argot of the investment banking world, have distinctly different meanings.[33]

Moreover, directors should not accept unquestioningly an investment banker's assessment of the company's value. They should inquire about the key assumptions that underlie the banker's conclusion, including how the banker valued the company's assets, how rapidly the banker assumed the company's business was likely to grow in the future, and what discount rate the banker used to assign present values to future cash flows.

Directors then should scrutinize carefully those assumptions. In particular, they should be alert to projections of sales or earnings that deviate significantly from those used in recent corporate planning documents, and should question assertions concerning intrinsic values that investors in the company's stock appear not to have appreciated. If directors conclude that seemingly important assumptions are questionable, they should discuss their concerns with management and with the investment banker. Where directors continue to have doubts, they should ask the investment banker to prepare alternative valuations, using different assumptions, in order to appreciate how sensitive the banker's bottom line figure is to changes in assumptions. Scherer, for example, points out that changing the discount rate used to value Marathon Oil's interest in the Yates field, from the 16.04 percent prevailing at the time Marathon became a target to 10.39 percent beginning five years after that date, increases the estimated value of Marathon's Yates Field interest from $4.74 billion to $6.90 billion, or 46 percent more than the value assuming the 16.04 percent rate would have persisted indefinitely.[34]

While directors may want to defer until after a bid is on the table making a firm decision concerning what valuation figure, or range of figures, they believe is most accurate, they often will be well advised to begin the valuation process soon after they conclude the company is likely to become a target. Under current SEC rules, the board of a target company must respond to a takeover bid within 10 days. That gives directors and their advisors scant time to complete the complex task of valuing a company, especially if a board has not even retained an investment banker at the time the offer is made.

Directors also may find that there are litigation advantages to engaging in the valuation process in advance of a bid.[35] Bidders now regularly file suit as soon as their bids are announced, seeking to enjoin target companies from engaging in any defensive actions. All materials thereafter exchanged between the target and its investment bankers become subject to discovery, including preliminary analyses, drafts, and other "working" papers. Often these documents contain information or statements that a target may find awkward to explain, thus providing the bidder with litigation advantages. If the valuation process is completed in advance of a bid, the risks of a bidder obtaining such advantages can be reduced.

Once it completes the valuation process, the directors of a target company must make a fundamental decision: Should they attempt to sell the company, or should they seek to keep it independent? A decision to resist a takeover bid involves great risks, but nonetheless may be the right choice. If the bidder increases its bid, or if a white knight comes forward with a higher bid, shareholders are likely to benefit from the board's initial resistance.

Resistance that leads a bidder to withdraw also may work to shareholders' benefit. In the short run, the price of the target company's stock is almost sure to decline, but another bidder may then emerge, prepared to pay more than the initial bidder. Then shareholders gain. But if no other bidders emerge, shareholders are more likely than not to find themselves worse off than if the target's board had endorsed the initial bid. On average, post-withdrawal increases in the price of shares of companies that successfully resist bids, and do not thereafter become targets, fall short of making up post-withdrawal declines.[36]

In short, deciding to resist a takeover bid is a high-stakes gamble. Resistance remains an acceptable choice, as the Delaware Supreme Court recently recognized:

> Circumstances may dictate that an offer be rebuffed, given the nature and timing of the offer; its legality, feasibility and effect on the corporation and its stockholders; the alternatives available and their effect on the various constituencies, particularly the stockholders; the company's long-term strategic plans; and any special factors bearing on stockholder and public interests.[37]

But directors should give careful consideration both to the probable consequences of resisting and to the form their resistance should take. Rarely will it make sense for directors to signal that a company is not for sale at any price.

If directors decide that the company should be sold, or that an acquisition is inevitable, they are obliged to seek to obtain the highest available price for shareholders. To that end, directors should consider making available, on terms that protect the company's legitimate business interests, significant, nonpublic information that may lead a bidder to increase its bid or may induce a white knight to enter the bidding. In fact, since hostile bidders often discount their bids to take account of the risk that a target company has not disclosed significant, negative information, target company directors who possess significant positive information about the target, such as undisclosed projections or asset valuations, often will find that they can induce a bidder to increase its offer by giving the bidder access to such information.

The courts recognize that boards must make complex judgments concerning how best to conduct an auction and how to evaluate competing bids. The Delaware Supreme Court recently listed the following as factors that a board may properly consider:

> [T]he adequacy and terms of the offer; its fairness and feasibility; the proposed or actual financing for the offer and the consequences of that financing; questions

of illegality; the impact of both the bid and the potential acquisition on other constituencies, provided that it bears some reasonable relationship to general shareholder interests; the risk of nonconsummation; the basic stockholder interests at stake; the bidder's identity, prior background and other business venture experiences; and the bidder's business plans for the corporation and their effects on stockholder interests.[38]

As noted above, the courts have not allowed a board to use defensive measures, such as a poison pill, to coerce shareholders into accepting a bid or a restructuring proposal that the board favors. This does not mean that a board can never favor one bidder over another, but if a board decides to treat different bidders differently, it must be prepared to convince the court both that it acted to enhance the interests of all shareholders and that the actions it took were reasonable in relation to the advantages obtained.[39]

In fact, protecting shareholders' freedom to accept takeover bids is a pervasive theme in the courts' opinions. In contexts other than selling or voting shares, courts generally assume that shareholders should look to a company's board of directors to protect their interests, but that assumption does not hold with regard to voting shares or accepting takeover bids. Shareholders' rights to make those decisions are viewed as central to the integrity of the corporate governance system.

Blasius Industries, Inc. v. Atlas Corp.[40] contains a cogent explanation of the philosophy that governs the courts' (at least the Delaware courts') approach. Blasius, the holder of 9.1 percent of Atlas's stock, had begun to solicit shareholder consents to elect a majority of Atlas's directors, with a view to then restructuring Atlas. The incumbent Atlas board concluded in good faith that Blasius's restructuring proposal was unsound. The board, operating within its legal authority, then acted to effectively make it impossible for Blasius to elect a majority of the directors. Blasius sued. The court set aside the directors' action, explaining:

> The only justification that can, in such a situation, be offered for the action taken is that the board knows better than do the shareholders what is in the corporations' best interest. While that premise is no doubt true for any number of matters, it is irrelevant (except insofar as the shareholders wish to be guided by the board's recommendation) when the question is who should comprise the board of directors. The theory of our corporation law confers power upon directors as the agents of the shareholders; it does not create Platonic masters. It may be that the Blasius restructuring proposal was or is unrealistic and would lead to injury to the corporation and its shareholders if pursued.... I am inclined to think it was not a sound proposal. The board certainly viewed it that way, and that view, held in

good faith, entitled the board to take certain steps to evade the risk it perceived. It could, for example, expend corporate funds to inform shareholders and seek to bring them to a similar point of view.... But there is a vast difference between expending corporate funds to inform the electorate and exercising power for the primary purpose of foreclosing effective shareholder action. A majority of the shareholders, who were not dominated in any respect, could view the matter differently than did the board. If they do, or did, they are entitled to employ the mechanisms provided by the corporation law and the Atlas certificate of incorporation to advance that view. They are also entitled, in my opinion, to restrain their agents, the board, from acting for the principal purpose of thwarting that action.

Consistent with this statement, where a takeover bid is made subject to the approval of a target company's board of directors, the board is not obliged to give shareholders an opportunity to accept the bid, and need not do so where it believes the company would fare better by remaining independent or the bid is too low.[41] But where a bidder goes directly to a company's shareholders with an offer to purchase all of the company's shares, and where that offer is not contingent on the approval of the target's board of directors, the target company's board probably will find its options limited to trying to convince the company's shareholders not to accept the bid, to seeking to induce the bidder to increase its offer, to locating a white knight, or to developing a restructuring plan that shareholders will find more attractive than the hostile bid.

Some companies have reacted to this trend in the case law by undertaking to induce state legislatures to amend state corporate laws so as to make hostile takeovers more difficult. Most state legislatures have responded positively to corporations' pleas; some have adopted packages of antitakeover measures that appear to effectively empower the board of a target company to make discretionary judgments, on virtually any grounds it deems fit, to block any takeover bid that board opposes. How the courts will interpret these state laws remains an open question, but it seems likely that the very existence of these laws has deterred takeover bids for companies covered by them.

Delaware law, with its emphasis on auctions, represents a sounder approach to the problems takeover bids pose for corporate boards of directors. Moreover, beyond the question of the board's legal obligations, it is important for directors to consider the potential political consequences of sponsoring or relying upon "showstopper" provisions of state antitakeover laws. Those laws undermine one of the fundamental principles supporting our market-based economy: that society can rely on the discipline of the marketplace as an antidote to ineffective performance by corporate managers. Continuing corporate support for state legislation that insulates managers from marketplace forces may well increase support for an expansion of federal regulation to deal more directly with questions of corporate structure and governance now dealt with, indirectly, by marketplace forces and takeover bids.

CONCLUSION

Corporate boards of directors generally function more as advisors to management than as independent decision-making bodies. With regard to takeover transactions, though, the problems that often constrain directors from acting as independent decision-makers are not so salient. Information disparities are not as great, the crisis atmosphere surrounding takeover bids leaves directors with little choice but to devote substantial time to their directorial responsibilities, and the dynamics of takeover transactions provide directors with market-based benchmarks against which to evaluate alternative courses of action.

Corporate law continues to allow a board of directors great discretion with regard to the decision to authorize a takeover bid or to adopt defenses in anticipation of a takeover bid. Once a bid is made, though, the combination of corporate law rules and market forces increasingly limits a board to acting largely as an auctioneer.

A board of directors can best meet its responsibilities in connection with takeover bids not by becoming preoccupied with legal rules or by focussing on defensive tactics, but by gaining an understanding of why takeovers occur and then working with management to develop and implement business and financial strategies that will eliminate the attractiveness of the company as a takeover target. Within the context of existing tax laws and other public policies, such strategies also have the potential to help those companies become more efficient, more competitive, and more profitable.

Notes

1. American Law Institute, Principles of Corporate Governance: Analysis and Recommendations, §§ 3.01, 3.02 (tentative draft no. 2, April 13, 1984).
2. The Wyatt Company, Trends in Compensation and Policy Practices of Boards of Directors, 2 (1988).
3. Brudney, "The Independent Director—Heavenly City or Potemkin Village?" *Harvard Law Review, 95* (1982), pp. 597–616.
4. "Hostile Takeovers and Junk Bond Financing: A Panel Discussion (remarks of Warren Buffet)," in J. Coffee, L Lowenstein, and S. Rose-Ackerman (eds.), *Knights, Raiders and Targets*, p. 16.
5. M. Mace, *Directors: Myth and Reality* (rev. ed. 1986), pp. 182–18.
6. Pratt, "The ALI Corporate Governance Project: A Radical Cure for a Healthy Patient," (1989), mimeograph; Siebert, "The ALI and Its 'Litigation Model' of Corporate Governance," (1989), mimeograph.
7. Siebert, op. cit., p. 13.
8. Knowlton and Millstein, "Can the Board of Directors Help the American Corporation Earn the Immortality It Holds So Dear?" in J. Meyer, and J. Gustafson (eds.), *The U.S. Business Corporation: An Institution in Transition*, (1988), p. 183.
9. Sterngold, "Nabisco Battle Redefines Directors' Role," *The New York Times*, (December 5, 1988), p. 1, col. 3.
10. Treadway Cos. v. Care Corp., 638 F.2d 357 (2d Cir. 1980); Crouse-Hinds Co. v. Internorth, Inc., 634 F.2d 690 (2d Cir. 1980); and Panter v. Marshall Field & Co., 646 F.2d 271 (7th Cir. 1981), are typical.
11. 493 A.2d 946 (Del. 1985).
12. 506 A.2d 173 (Del. 1986).
13. Mills Acquisition Co. v. MacMillan, Inc., C.A. No. 10168 (Del. Sup. Ct. May 3, 1989); see also chapter 11, "Auction Law and Practice in Unsolicited Takeovers," this volume.
14. 500 A.2d 1346 (Del. 1985).
15. Capital City Assoc. Ltd. Partnership v. Interco, Inc., [CCH] Fed. Sec. L. Rep. Para. 94,084 (Del. Ch. 1988).
16. Grand Metropolitan PLC v. The Pillsbury Co., [1988–89 Transfer Binder] Fed. Sec. L. Rep. (CCH) ¶ 99, 104 (Del. Ch. 1988).
17. Jarrell, Brickley, and Netter, "The Market for Corporate Control: The Empirical Evidence Since 1980," *Journal of Economic Perspectives, 2*, 69 (1988); and Scherer, "Corporate Takeovers: The Efficiency Arguments, *Journal of Economic Perspectives, 2,* 69 (1988), survey the relevant literature. Bradley, Desai, and Kim, "Synergistic Gains from Corporate Acquisitions, and Their Division Between Stockholders of Target and Acquiring Firms," *Journal of Financial Economics, 21*, 3 (1988), report more recent results.

18. Scherer, op. cit., p. 71.
19. Ibid., p. 76.
20. Black, "Bidder Overpayment in Takeovers," *Stanford Law Review, 41*, 597 (1989); Roll, "The Hubris Theory of Corporate Takeovers," *Journal of Business, 59*, 197 (1986).
21. Schliefer and Vishny, "Value Maximization and the Acquisition Process," *Journal of Economic Perspective, 2*, 7 (1988).
22. Weiss, "Comment," in J. Coffee, L Lowenstein, and S. Rose-Ackerman (eds.), *Knights, Raiders and Targets*, p. 360 (see note 4 above).
23. Black, "Noise," *Journal of Finance, 41*, 533 (1988).
24. Scherer, "Corporate Takeovers: The Efficiency Arguments, *Journal of Economic Perspectives, 2*, 72–73 (1988).
25. Bagwell and Shoven, "Share Repurchases and Acquisitions: An Analysis of Which Firms Participate," in A. Auerbach (ed.), *Corporate Takeovers*, (1988), p. 191.
26. Jensen, "Takeovers: Their Causes and Consequences," *Journal of Economic Perspectives, 2*, 21 (1988); and Jensen, "The Takeover Controversy: Analysis and Evidence," in J. Coffee, L Lowenstein, and S. Rose-Ackerman (eds.), *Knights, Raiders and Targets*, p. 314.
27. Scholes and Wolfson, "Employee Stock Ownership Plans and Corporate Restructuring: Myths and Realities," chapter 18, this volume.
28. Unocal v. Mesa Petroleum Co., 493 A.2d 946 (Del. 1985).
29. C.A. No. 10168 (Del. Sup. Ct. May 3, 1989).
30. Op. cit., p. 44.
31. Id., p. 53, note 32.
32. Weiss, "A Proposal for a Federal Takeover Law," *Cardozo Law Review, 9*, 1699, 1718–19 (1988).
33. Weiss, "Balancing Interests in Cash-Out Mergers: The Promise of Weinberger v. UOP, Inc.," *Delaware Journal of Corporate Law, 8*, 1, 52–53 (1983).
34. Scherer, "Corporate Takeovers: The Efficiency Arguments," *Journal of Economic Perspectives, 2*, 73 (1988).
35. Shapiro, "Judicial Business Judgment: The Investment Banker's Role," chapter 6, this volume.
36. Ruback, "An Overview of Takeover Defenses," in A. Auerbach (ed.), *Mergers and Acquisitions*, (1988).
37. Mills Acquisition Co. v. MacMillan, Inc., slip op., p. 55, note 35.
38. Id., p. 48, note 29.
39. Id., p. 64.
40. [CCH] Fed. Sec. L. Rep. Para. 93, 965 (Del. Ch. 1988).
41. TW Services v. SWT Acquisition Corp., [CCH] Fed. Sec. L. Rep. Para. 94, 334 (Del. Ch. 1989).
42. Weiss, "A Proposal for a Federal Takeover Law," *Cardozo Law Review, 9*, 1699. 1718–19 (1988).

CHAPTER 3

THE RESPONSIBILITY OF THE INSTITUTIONAL INVESTOR IN CORPORATE MANAGEMENT

Ira M. Millstein

Corporate governance for all its lack of political charisma is of immense importance; its neglect is not benign.[1]

At the core of corporate governance is the accountability of management to the board, and of the board to its shareholders. The ultimate burden of credibility for this chain of accountability falls on the shareholder.

The market for corporate control is a perfect example—but only an example—of why this is so and, more importantly, of what may happen if the shareholder doesn't shoulder that burden.

Markets for corporate control, like other markets, operate value free and mindlessly. But markets are not ends in themselves: Policy makers have an obligation to observe them and a right to interfere when necessary. We encourage market results when they are consistent with a public good.

If a public good emanates from the market for corporate control, the policy makers should keep their hands off. If, on the other hand, a public bad emanates from the market for corporate control, then policy makers have an obligation to correct it—or stop it all together. If it is a mix of good and bad, policy makers will stymie, and that is exactly what has

Ira M. Millstein is a senior partner with Weil, Gotshal & Manges, New York City. He is a graduate of Columbia University School of Law (1949).

happened here. The results of the market for corporate control are neither bad enough to call a halt to that market, or good enough to forget about it. Hence, we worry a lot about that market, but policy makers, I think, will only in the end poke at it from the edges.

That means—for the moment and unless and until policy makers act—that corrections for what seems to be wrong with that market will have to be created by the participants in that market. Enter corporate governance. I believe that if our governance system works, the means for correcting whatever is wrong lie within the system. But neglecting to assure ourselves that our corporate paradigm works will not be benign.

Obviously the first question is, what may need fixing in the market for corporate control?

What is it that we all seem to want, and hence, what should be the public good emanating from the market for corporate control?

We all want the private sector to succeed in globally competitive markets. We need corporations that are efficient and productive and, at the same time, good citizens. To achieve that end, corporations need managements that are energetic, competent, and capable of planning for their long-term profitable growth, while meeting their short-term business requirements.

It is contended that the market for corporate control has an immensely beneficial effect: It either in fact removes and replaces incompetent managers or, just as a threat, has a beneficial effect upon managers by forcing them to re-evaluate what they are doing, so as to ward off takeovers.

Whether in fact there is such a therapeutic effect is largely debatable. After all, Germany and Japan don't have takeovers and yet seem to have the means to remove and replace managements—sufficient at least so as to keep their private sectors quite competitive in world markets. Furthermore, in our heated takeover world, my non-statistical eye judges that at least as many good companies and managements have become targets as have bad ones.

Moreover, and again from a non-empirical perch, the market for corporate control seems to have created sufficient uncertainty and instability in corporate managements. Sufficient, at least, to cause concern as to whether that market isn't force feeding a short-term management focus that is counter to competitiveness and long-term profitable growth.

I find a wide and deeply-felt perception amongst managers and credible academics that the market for corporate control has created an excessive instability. An instability which may well be working against managers' ability to plan sufficiently long-term to create the effective global competitors we want.

If competence and competitiveness are the goals, the jury is out on whether the market for corporate control works its wonders. I would tend to agree with Jonathan Charkham, who wrote:

> Takeovers in other words are the lazy way out. Even if, at the moment, they are often the only way, they are expensive and founded on a monstrous illogicality—that a change of ownership is necessary in order to change management.[2]

What may need fixing is managements—or their direction—when necessary. Not the very bad managements; they do get swept away by boards, but sometimes too late to avoid the clutches of chapter 11 and equity wipeouts. Not the very good ones either, obviously. But the range in between, where performance could be better, sometimes a lot better.

The issue is, then, whether we have the means within our existing corporate governance system to change managements that are not sufficiently competent and are not running sufficiently competitive enterprises, or, at least, to change management courses for the better. In my view, we don't have to change ownership to do it. But we do have to use the governance structures already in place to achieve real accountability and credible monitoring of managements. Enter the institutional shareholders.

Elliott Weiss has spelled out the role of the board in takeovers.[3] He does not focus, however, on replacing ineffective managements. Rather, he focuses on the questions boards ought to ask relating to takeovers. I subscribe to his questions and suggest further that these very same questions will enable boards to monitor the competitive competence and effectiveness of their managements—and to replace those managements found wanting or to change directions, when necessary.

What then is the role of the shareholder in this process of accountability? I believe it is to monitor and assure that the governance system works to achieve effective management and competitiveness, that the governance system works to replace the ineffective manager or to change the course of management, more surgically, more surely and more accurately than does the blunderbuss uncertain market for corporate control; and to assure that the governance system works to support and reward with loyalty those managements whose performance is good—performance not so much in the financial market place, as in the market for goods and services.

Who then are our shareholders today? And how can they monitor the process of accountability?

Pension funds are fast becoming the owners of corporate America. They are a dominant force in the securities markets and a major capital formation engine. They hold approximately two trillion dollars in assets, and ownership of an increasing percentage of U.S. public corporations. Pension funds' phenomenal growth in assets and power is brought home by the following statistics: According to a study undertaken by the Institutional Investor Project, pension fund assets have grown at a rate of about 14.6 percent per year, from $891 billion in 1981 to over two trillion dollars in 1987. As of 1987, pension funds comprised approximately 43.5 percent of all institutional investors and, as a group, institutional investors controlled about 49 percent of the shares in the top 50 U.S. corporations. By the year 2000, we project that pension funds will hold over two thirds of all shares in the large publicly traded corporations.

Pension funds are not only the primary source of funds to pay retirement benefits for millions of retirees, but are also a primary source of capital in the United States, and increasingly, in fact, an important influence on corporate management. After all, they elect the directors who watch the managers.

Because of their concentration of capital and corporate ownership, pension funds have an important role in the future of our economy: Pension funds control the capital necessary to promote U.S. global competitiveness and, through that capital, wield the power to ensure the stability and continuity of ownership essential to long-term corporate growth.

With power, however, must come responsibility. Pension funds have a disturbing history, however, of abdicating their ownership responsibilities by not participating in the corporate governance process—either by not voting proxies (as sometimes happens in the case of indexed investments), by always voting automatically with management or, on certain issues, by always voting against management without regard to the particular situation of the corporation involved.[4] Yet because of their growing corporate ownership, pension funds "are in an ideal position to help assure that American management takes a balanced time-horizon approach to running their companies."[5]

Granted, the funds could be a factor in correcting management directions so as to assure competence and competitiveness where there are deficiencies and thereby lessen the purported need to rely on the market for corporate control and its alleged resultant excessive instability. What could be the model for doing so?

Pension fund managers would have to change their focus and start paying attention to the goods and services market performance of the companies in which they invest. Bear in mind that, increasingly, pension funds are heavily invested in indexes—either in fact or in practice—which means that they cannot or will not practice the Wall Street Walk. Fund performance will increasingly be dependent on the performance of companies that they have chosen and actively monitor—and on companies they remain invested in because the companies are in an index. As to the latter, the funds should know more about them individually because the funds are tied to the successful performance of those companies as well.

At the outset, then, fund managers would have to start thinking company-specific. At the moment, their actions in governance are mostly generic and directed at maintaining their ability to "walk"—that is, fighting the poison pill and the staggered board and all other takeover defenses almost reflexively—or they concern social issues such as South Africa, Northern Ireland, and other causes. I repeat, regardless of the merits of these issues, they are not issues of product and service market performance to which the funds should turn their attention.

In the long run, the ability of pension funds to provide benefits depends on the strength of the corporations that the funds invest in, and the health of local and national economies.

When the funds move from generic to company-specific, based upon knowledge of the company, they need to broaden their horizons from simply making their pile bigger—pure maximization—to a concept of optimizing their investments. A more appropriate guide for our times would stress promoting real economic growth over the long term. This requires replacing the verb *to maximize* with the verb *to optimize* in the corporate lexicon.

I am not playing with semantics here. Traditionally we speak of the duty of management "to maximize shareholder value," and the duty of the pension fund trustee as a fiduciary "to maximize" returns for its beneficiaries. The dictionary defines that verb as "to increase or make as great as possible." *Optimize,* however, means "to make as good or as effective as possible."[6]

I posit that to enable the modern U.S. corporation to compete effectively in world markets and promote real economic growth over the long term, each level of the corporate governance structure should change its focus from the traditional model that strives to maximize value—a model too simple for the complexities of today's international markets—to a model that focuses on optimizing growth, productivity, efficiency, and, ultimately, competitiveness; a change from immediate profit-driven thinking to concern for the enhancement of the corporation as a provider of goods, services and profits over the long term. Optimization should be the top priority of the board and investors, so as to free managers of short-term pressures, thereby enabling them to plan for the long term.

The new amendment to New York's Business Corporation Law is a step in the right direction.[7] The amended section 717(b) allows directors, in determining what the long- and short-term interests of the corporation and its shareholders are, to consider the impact of the corporation's actions upon the corporation's current and retired employees, its consumers, suppliers, distributors, and creditors. Additionally, directors may factor in the ability of the corporation as a going concern to provide goods, services, employment, and other contributions to economic growth, in the communities in which the corporation does business. In essence, this law gives directors, and hence the corporation, the ability to optimize.

If the board can monitor in accordance with this standard, help management go in this direction, and oversee the communication of the corporation's plans and achievements, we'll have a good start. But the board has to be perceived as credibly willing and able to monitor. And, if the board can assist management in optimizing for the long term, shareholders must have similar goals and abilities—and not always sell out to the first bidder.

To repeat, pension funds need a new investment and ownership attitude: Our patient capital must adopt as its decision-making goal "the promotion of real economic growth over the long term." Real economic growth over the long term contemplates entrepreneurship, efficiency, productivity, and new and improved products and services achieved by R&D and internal growth; it will produce successful global competitors and at the same time achieve the pension funds' purposes and a variety of social goals—greater employment, consumption, and tax revenues—all leading to an improved economy.

Assuming then, our goal—which incorporates this new attitude—how would a fund implement it?

Fund managers, in a tender offer situation, would not make their decisions reflexively, but would consider and compare the premium to be paid today with the strength of the company over the long term. This is similar to the factors that Professor Weiss urges boards to consider.

Additionally, pension funds would actively participate in proxy voting and corporate governance matters, using real economic growth over the long term as the guide. Because a short-term orientation does little to improve an enterprise, the tendency for pension funds exclusively to "vote with their feet"—the exit model of corporate governance—would be complemented with a "voice" model. The voice model stresses the need to monitor the performance of corporations, and when performance lags, to communicate with that corporation the fund's concerns. The communication should be moderate, hopefully private, and supportive to be effective. It need not be public, loud, or hostile. Boards don't need to be threatened; they will hear the responsible voice of a large shareholder. For example, when a corporation in its portfolio attempts to acquire another corporation, the fund managers could voice their concerns about the prudence of the bid, assuming there are legitimate concerns, to the bidder corporation's board. Questions similar to those Professor Weiss suggests that boards ask management are equally relevant here. The voice model also dictates that pension funds similarly communicate their concerns to boards of undervalued corporations in their portfolios who may be potential takeover targets.

Generically, fund managers could articulate through proxy voting or other appropriate means their concerns about many of the issues that the market for corporate control is supposed to monitor: that is, assuring that the board is monitoring management so as to achieve the most efficient global competitors possible, replacing or supporting as appropriate.

But active pension fund management requires expertise, discipline, and continuity, and requires proper compensation and incentives to attract and keep professionals who are capable of handling enormous assets, and dealing with the responsibilities those assets create. This type of support would have to provided.

This, obviously, is not an exhaustive list of how pension funds could make the governance system function credibly to replace the excesses of the market for corporate control—just some of the steps to be taken. Nor is correcting the excesses of the market for corporate control the only reason for credible corporate governance.

Here, then, is the basic question we're going to study seriously at the Columbia University Institutional Investor Project:

Can the type of system and model I've outlined work? Can it deliver the accountability we seek? It is one thing to ask for it; it is another to see it happen.

The answer to the basic question breaks into some discrete pieces:

1. *Can the pension funds really act as the type of owner I've described? Is it legally and practically feasible?*

Take the legal issue. Pension funds continue to be governed by laws that reflect age-old policies. The traditional legal standards were not designed to guide investment managers in making complex ownership and investment decisions having a broad economic impact on our corporations and our society. Rather, they were intended to prevent thievery and self-dealing by fund trustees. To that end, the law imposes not only duties of strict loyalty and prudence on fiduciaries but also certain technical "exclusive benefit" requirements, all intended to ensure that fund assets are not misappropriated, diverted, or used in a manner that does not directly further the interests of the plan participants. As a result, investment decisions tend to be made solely on the basis of immediately quantifiable returns.

The regulatory requirements on pension fund investing, as they have been interpreted over time, have become encrusted and unwieldy; they contemplate neither the staggering size to which pension funds have grown, nor the concomitant ownership power that fund managers now wield over the economy as a whole. The law's focus on the duty owed to plan participants gives little guidance on the extent to which the health of the local or national economy, let alone the long-term success of the corporations invested in, may be factored into their decision-making.

Thus, the law does not explicitly recognize the wide range of people and organizations that have a stake in the investment and ownership decisions of pension funds—sponsors, other corporations and their constituents, taxpayers, and the government.[8] Nor does it explicitly recognize that the traditional and primary stakeholders—the plan participants—have a multiplicity of interests that may not be contemplated by a law widely perceived to permit investment managers to consider only the direct financial benefits to participants of pension fund investments.

2. *More importantly, do the fund managers perceive their wider responsibilities—and how to achieve them?*

Even this question breaks down into public and private pension funds. Public fund activity is visible and, in the best democratic sense, is subject to political direction from elected officials. Legislatures can give direction. But private funds—controlling two thirds of the two trillion dollars—are less visible. Will corporate sponsors insist that their corporate pension funds take a voice role in the affairs of other corporations? To state the question is to demonstrate its subtle complexity.

3. *Will companies welcome or resist pension fund voices?* At the moment, some public funds, have, because of the stridency of their voices, created resistance and concern. There needs to be dialogue and it is not yet happening.

4. *Assuming it is desirable for fund voices to be joined together in talking to corporations, are there technical legal impediments to such joinder?*

Those are the questions I hope you all work on, either with us at Columbia, or on your own.

I repeat Charkham's caveat:[9] Ignoring the governance system will not be benign. If it doesn't function to produce successful international competitors, either something else—more destabilizing and more unknown—will, or the country will lose out, long range, in a sea of complacency.

Notes

1. Charkham, Panel Paper No. 25, Bank of England, (March 1989), p. 14.
2. Id., p.11.
3. See Weiss, "The Board of Directors, Management, and Corporate Takeovers: Opportunities and Pitfalls," chapter 2, this volume.
4. It is now recognized that such practices are not in accord with existing legal standards. Proxies are viewed as plan assets under ERISA and the same fiduciary duties apply to proxy voting decisions as apply to investment decisions. The Department of Labor has recently emphasized this and instructed pension funds to either diligently review each proxy proposal or establish general proxy voting guidelines.
5. "U.S. Prods Pension Funds Toward Long-Term Planning," *The Washington Post*, (April 5, 1989), quoting Deputy Treasury Secretary M. Peter McPhearson.
6. *The American Heritage Dictionary*, (2d College Edition, 1985), pp. 774, 873.
7. Act of June 30, 1989, ch. 228, 1989, New York Laws.
8. As sponsors of the funds, employers are obligated to contribute to the funds for the purpose of satisfying long-term (indeed, intergenerational) liabilities and, therefore, the health of the fund is inextricably linked to the health of its corporate sponsor. Other corporations have an interest because of the impact that the pension fund's decision will have on their continuing economic health and on their constituencies—including their shareholders, employees, suppliers, customers, and the communities in which they operate.
    Taxpayers and the government also have an interest in how pension funds behave because of the government-sponsored pension benefit insurance program and the significant fiscal consequences of the funds' exemption from income taxation. The general public has an interest to the extent that pension funds play

an important role in the functioning of the capital markets and thereby impact the health of our economy and our standard of living.

Those impacted by pension fund decisions are beginning to seek a voice in the manner in which pension funds behave. Of course, one of the loudest voices—with a strong claim of interest—is organized labor. Union leaders are coming to realize that American workers, as the beneficiaries of pension funds, collectively own—but do not control—a large percentage of U.S. corporations. The trend among public pension funds, to give labor some representation on the funds' boards of trustees, will likely be urged on private funds as well.

9. See Charkham, Panel Paper No. 25, Bank of England, (March 1989), and accompanying test.

CHAPTER 4

COMMENTS ON
CHAPTER 1

Lemma W. Senbet

In preparing this discussion, I had an opportunity to take a look at Professor Coffee's previous work[1] on a related project. Frankly, I found his treatment of the issues in corporate governance and markets for corporate control rather provocative. Here are a few provocative examples:

1. The study of corporate governance should move beyond a two-party, management/shareholder game, to incorporate other stakeholders, such as creditors and employees. This three-party treatment may complicate things considerably.

2. Takeovers may disrupt implicit contracts with stakeholders. For instance, they may endanger employee security.

3. Professor Coffee has advocated that takeover premia should be shared among shareholders, stakeholders, and management on the basis of efficiency and equity. I found this proposition worrisome, of course, because its logical extension may be to require shareholders to share all the unexpected stock appreciation associated with major events even in the absence of takeovers.

4. Professor Coffee has also defended the role of state antitakeover legislation and golden parachutes on the ground of takeover disruption of stakeholder implicit contracts.

5. Professor Coffee has proposed a managerial compensation scheme analogous to a lawyer's contingent fee; that is, contingent on takeovers,

Lemma W. Senbet is Albright Professor of Finance, University of Wisconsin-Madison.

management obtains a certain fraction of the takeover premium. The worrisome aspect of this is, of course, the incentive for management to maximize the premium by maximizing inefficiency.

Professor Coffee's central concept is his triangular view of corporate governance which he explains in the context of markets for corporate control. He suggests the game is unstable and outcomes are indeterminate, because coalitions can be formed of any two groups.

Coalition between management and stakeholders, particularly creditors and employees, can exist so as to lock-in the firm's "free cash flow" in the sense of inefficient asset expansion and retention of cash flows. In this vein, creditors/employees were unconcerned about management takeovers during the conglomerate wave of the 1950s and 1960s. If anything, Professor Coffee suggests that these stakeholders had a free ride on managerial bias toward growth and retention. He goes on to say that this view accounted for the demise of negative bond covenants by the early 1980s.

However, the emergence of "bust-up" takeovers in the 1980s which yielded deconglomeration were negative surprises for stakeholders, and hence new forms of safeguards, particularly the poison put, have emerged. These safeguards have the effects of (a) providing excessive protection for bondholders/employees, and (b) serving as a deterrent to takeovers. Unfortunately, these conclusions are not substantiated by a coherent structure (or model) or by some available empirical evidence. Professor Coffee suggests some anecdotes, but they are not convincing at a serious level. For instance, one is never sure that the poison put provides an undue advantage to the creditors or provides them excessive protection without determining how the put option itself is factored into the puttable bond price ex ante. Indeed, if the put is efficiently priced, the issue of "excessive" protection is moot. Likewise, I am not totally convinced that such an option deters legitimate takeovers which result in efficiency gains. I just don't believe that the poison put is as poisonous as the poison pill! One needs to show that the discount in the breakup value versus the market value that motivates takeover, is affected materially by the issuance of a contingent claims contract issued as part of the financial contracting process.

Professor Coffee's conclusion regarding indeterminacy of the three-party outcome has to do with the possibility that coalitions could shift. For instance, management may collude with shareholders, or shareholders could collude with stakeholders. Actually, the earlier analysis of coalition between management and stakeholders must follow from inefficient managerial compensation schemes and inefficient private contracting involving stakeholders. Any three-party model must contend with the structure of compensation schemes and altering the debt claim itself into an alternative structure, such as convertible debt or debt with call provisions. Such complexities in financial contracts can greatly alter the degree to which parties are aligned with each other. Professor Coffee's approach does not address these issues; nor is it, I think, rich enough to handle these. For instance, in the limiting case, even the poison put may be rendered redundant in the context of complex debt contracts which align bond/stockholder interests.

In conclusion, I agree that the study of corporate governance and corporate control should accommodate stakeholders.[2] Professor Coffee has raised some interesting issues within this framework, but the predictions are premature. In particular, one needs a coherent model which can render testable restrictions. These testable restrictions are important in choosing between alternative views, because we could literally have a myriad of ex post rationalizations for unusual events in the area of corporate control. Moreover, I am not confident that the existing models are adequate enough in predicting major future developments or waves of the type that have occurred in the past, such as bust-up takeovers.

Notes

1. See, for instance, J. Coffee, "The Uncertain Case for Takeover Reform: An Essay on Stockholders, Stakeholders and Bust-Ups," *Wisconsin Law Review*, (1988), pp. 435–65.
2. There is now a growing recognition in corporate finance that multiple-party agency analysis provides considerable insights beyond the two-party agency tradition. See, for instance, K. John and L. Senbet, "Limited Liability, Corporate Leverage and Public Policy," working paper, December 1988.

CHAPTER 5

COMMENTS ON CHAPTERS 2 AND 3

Leo Herzel

I will begin with Ira Millstein's paper since he raises some of the most important issues we face in corporate law today. As I understand it, the main line of his argument is that the market for corporate control in the U.S. is causing an excessively short-term management outlook. That is bad, he says, because it undermines the ability of U.S. companies to compete internationally.

Part of Millstein's solution is to broaden the discretion of directors to allow them to consider the long run when dealing with takeovers. He cites as an illustration of how to do this, a New York bill that would give directors the legal power in takeover situations to consider factors other than immediate shareholder gains and losses. Some of these factors are the interests of employees, consumers, suppliers, distributors and creditors, and contributions to economic growth.

Several other states, for example, Indiana, New Jersey, and Ohio, have already passed statutes designed to achieve similar goals.[1] In fact, New York itself has already gone a large part of the way. It has a statute that permits directors to consider the long run interests of shareholders and the company in takeover situations.[2] I'm not sure whether the New York bill that Millstein mentions would be a big change in what New York already has.

Millstein understands that such a statute by itself isn't enough. Bidders usually don't care what target directors are considering, so long as

Leo Herzel is a partner at Mayer, Brown & Platt. His specialty is corporate and securities law which he teaches at the University of Chicago Law School.

they can make unimpeded bids directly to the targets' shareholders. The statutes that have been enacted so far attempt to solve this problem with another statutory provision that gives directors the legal power to issue and use flip-in poison pills. (Elliott Weiss's paper explains what a flip-in poison pill is and how it works.) New York has a temporary statute that legalizes flip-in poison pills which expires on July 1, 1989.[3] Probably, it will eventually become a permanent statute but there are political considerations involved that go beyond takeovers.

Millstein, however, doesn't suggest plugging this strategic gap with flip-in poison pills. His suggestion is far more ambitious. He wants to change the way institutional shareholders behave.

My reactions to Millstein's paper are as follows:

1. Like Millstein, I'm not persuaded that takeovers have improved the efficiency of U.S. industry. I agree with him that right now takeovers and the threat of takeovers are probably, on balance, a drain on the ability of U.S. companies to compete internationally. There are two reasons. First, a tremendous amount of resources are devoted to the takeover business itself—investment bankers, commercial bankers, lawyers and executive time. This is a drain on the U.S. economy unless takeovers on the average improve the efficiency of companies that are taken over. I don't know of any convincing evidence that they do. There is some evidence that they don't and some of it is mentioned by Weiss. If takeovers don't improve efficiency, all of that effort in moving the control of companies around is a waste, a social loss. (Those bankers, lawyers, and executives could be producing other goods and services instead of takeovers.)

Second, takeovers may be an important contributing factor to an excessive and harmful focus in U.S. companies on short-run considerations. This is Millstein's fundamental point. It is also an important point made in the 1989 book published by the MIT Commission on industrial productivity in the U.S., *Made in America, Regaining the Productive Edge,* Chapter 4, page 62 and Chapter 10, page 144.

2. Millstein's suggested solution is essentially to get institutional shareholders more involved in the companies that they invest in. They will solve the problem by adopting long-run investment goals. But in my opinion, institutional shareholders are the problem, and they are not likely to be the solution.

Millstein is right when he points out that, by and large, institutional shareholders have a short-run point of view.[4] So long as institutional investors are guided by economic considerations, their viewpoints will be short run. For them, the long run is a sequence of short runs.

However, one important advantage of a short run institutional investors' outlook is that it is easy for clients and the market to monitor their performance. If institutional investors change to a long run point of view, who will monitor their performance and how? The long run is by its nature only a guess, a hope. It is very difficult or impossible to monitor. If that weren't so, there wouldn't be a problem about the long run. We would all see it and agree on it.

Institutional investors are quasi-political institutions and their long run investment decisions are likely to be political decisions. We are beginning to see that already in public pension funds—issues like the environment and South Africa are concerns. The likely correction for that problem would be that the U.S. and state governments would have to provide the monitoring but that also would be political. In short, Millstein's suggestions, if adopted, would be likely to lead us down the path to a politicized economy. In my mind, not an improvement.

3. Is there any other solution to the problem Millstein poses? Yes, to increase the power of directors a little but not too much. In effect, that is the poison pill solution.

In theory, a combination of poison pills and the statutes that allow directors to consider long run factors could give directors an absolute power to veto takeovers. That, of course, could also have undesirable results. However, we know that the market and the courts closely monitor directors. For example, if 90 percent of the shareholders should tender their shares to a bidder in a bid that is conditional on board approval, it would be highly unlikely that many boards of directors would stand in the way of the bid or some higher priced immediate alternative. And, even with these new statutes, the courts are going to examine very carefully the reasons of directors who decide on long run grounds to stand in the way of tender offers that shareholders overwhelmingly want to accept.

Admittedly, this is a rickety solution but it appears to be much better than turning the economy over to the long run views of institutional shareholders.

***

Elliott Weiss's paper is a competent, conventional shareholder-oriented, efficient market theory-influenced treatment of the subject. There are no surprises in it. My comments on Millstein's paper reveal my bias. It's time for some surprises.

Like Weiss, I admire many of the effects of takeovers and the threat of takeovers on American business. Fear of takeovers has had a tremendously liberating effect on big business. It has helped to eliminate that complacent insularity that was such a discouraging characteristic of boards of directors and managements of big companies in America. But foreign competition in the product market has a similar effect and fear of takeovers may no longer be so important. There is plenty to fear in the product market.

Also, like Weiss, I enjoy and admire the intellectual backbone of the takeover movement, efficient market theory. But unfortunately, it doesn't tell the whole story. I wish it were otherwise—it's so easy and pleasant to think about the world in efficient market theory terms.

Within those limits, I have a few specific comments about Weiss's paper.

1. I have a higher opinion than Weiss of the effectiveness of boards of directors in noncrisis situations. The threat of takeovers and foreign competition have improved the quality of boards of directors enormously. Boards don't interfere more because it is unwise, not because they don't know enough about the company's business. It's not as hard as Weiss thinks for a director to understand a company's business quite well after several years on the board. The main problem with boards is that they are too big. You can see this particularly in banks and insurance companies. However, the widespread use of standing committees such as audit, compensation, and nominating reduces that problem substantially.

2. On the other hand, special board committees are very divisive. You end up with two groups running the same company which is an unstable situation. In my opinion, special committees should only be used sparingly and in very specific crisis situations, such as a management bid for the company. Weiss appears to expect more from them and to recommend that they should be used too soon and too often.

3. If I understand Weiss, I don't agree with his interpretation of the Revlon case and Delaware law on the subject of auctions: He says: "Once a bid is made, though, corporate law increasingly limits a board to acting largely as an auctioneer." How would Weiss deal with negotiated acquisitions? Are they bids and must there be an auction to have a legally binding acquisition agreement? Were the directors of Time and Warner acting illegally under Delaware law when they approved the Time/Warner merger without holding an auction? I don't think they were but I'm not sure what Weiss thinks.

4. I agree with Weiss that the law should pay more attention to the decisions of bidders. There is an odd lack of symmetry in the law's

suspicious treatment of target directors' takeover decisions and the paucity of legal restrictions on bidders' directors. One easy part of the solution would be to require bidders to obtain shareholder approval for large acquisitions. There already are stock exchange rules that do this, but for historical reasons they apply only when shares are being issued in an acquisition. Weiss says that a pro-management bias in corporation law explains the divergence in treatment of targets and bidders. If that is so, the threat of takeover has changed managements' views a long time ago. It shouldn't be difficult to get a change in stock exchange rules or state corporation laws.

5. I don't think Weiss is correct when he says that most defensive measures require shareholder approval. Flip-in poison pills, the most effective defensive measure, don't require shareholder approval. In fact, that is one of their most controversial characteristics. And, you don't need to have shareholders authorize blank check preferred stock to have a flip-in poison pill.

6. I don't agree with Weiss that pro-takeover federal legislation is an important issue at this time. Neither the Bush administration nor Congress is likely to view such an idea with enthusiasm. For one thing, both the administration and Congress are highly unlikely to do anything that makes foreign takeovers of U.S. companies easier. In fact, I think federal antitakeover legislation against foreign bidders is a much more likely possibility.

Notes

1. Ind. Code Ann., 23-1-35-1, 23-1-26-5(a)-(i) (1989); Ohio Rev. Code 1701.59(E) (1989); N.J. Senate, Nos. 3295 and 3296 (1989).
2. N.Y. Bus. Corp. Law, 717(b) (1987).
3. N.Y. Bus. Corp. Law, 505(a) (1989).
4. J. M. Keynes makes a similar point in *The General Theory of Employment Interest and Money,* chapter 12, pp.157–58 (1935):
   "Finally it is the long-term investor, he who most promotes the public interest, who will in practice come in for most criticism, wherever investment funds are managed by committees or boards or banks. For it is in the essence of his behavior that he should be eccentric, unconventional and rash in the eyes of average opinion. If he is successful, that will only confirm the general belief in his rashness; and if in the short run he is unsuccessful, which is very likely, he will not receive much mercy. Worldly wisdom teaches that it is better for reputation to fail conventionally than to succeed unconventionally."

PART 2

THE BUSINESS JUDGMENT RULE APPLIED TO TAKEOVER ACTIVITY

CHAPTER 6

JUDICIAL BUSINESS JUDGMENT: THE INVESTMENT BANKER'S ROLE

Stuart L. Shapiro

This chapter discusses the recent transmutation of the business judgment doctrine from one of judicial deference to, to one of active judicial review of, board decision when corporate control is implicated. This doctrine, first articulated explicitly in the landmark Unocal Corp. v. Mesa Petroleum Co. decision,[1] requires Delaware courts to evaluate the reasonableness of board decisions made by a disinterested and informed board in connection with takeover or control transactions. The chapter will examine the recent development of this doctrine by the Delaware courts and will discuss some of its practical implications for investment banks and other M&A professionals.

As an initial matter, it is important to note that it is the business judgment *doctrine*, which applies to the validity of board decisions, and not the business judgment rule, which involves personal liability of fiduciaries for their acts, which is at issue here.[2] How the courts will develop these principles in the context of director liability is not the subject of this chapter.

Historically, the business judgment doctrine developed as one of judicial deference to business decisions rendered by an informed and disinterested board. Courts declined to invalidate such business decisions

Stuart L. Shapiro, Partner, Skadden, Arps, Slate, Meagher & Flom; J.D., Georgetown University, 1969.

absent a finding to extreme behavior such as bad faith or "gross and palpable overreaching."[3]

The modern high-water mark for the doctrine is Sinclair Oil Corp. v. Levian:[4]

> *A board of directors enjoys a presumption of sound business judgment, and its decisions will not be disturbed if they can be attributed to any rational business purpose.* A court under such circumstances will not substitute its own notions of what is or is not sound business judgment.

Because the business judgment doctrine involves an evidentiary presumption in favor of the board, the party challenging the board decision bears the burden of proof.[5] Absent a showing of conflict or lack of due care, the complaining shareholder would have to show such "gross and palpable overreaching" as to preclude a finding of a rational business purpose.[6] The articulated standard is so demanding that its availability can be outcome determinative.[7]

As takeover activity accelerated in the 1970s and 1980s, the business judgment doctrine became the basis for judicial approval of a number of sophisticated defensive techniques employed by boards to fend off hostile takeovers.

> More recently, as the sophistication of both raiders and targets has developed, a host of other defensive measures to counter such ever mounting threats has evolved and received judicial sanction. These include defensive charter amendments and other devices bearing some rather exotic, but apt, names: Crown Jewel, White Knight, Pac Man, and Golden Parachute. Each has highly selective features, the object of which is to deter or defeat the raider.[8]

With judicial imprimatur there also came controversy. There were sharp debates between proponents of business judgment and free market economists and practitioners.[9] These debates to an increasing extent caught the attention of judges.[10] They focused to a large degree on the relative powers of boards versus stockholders to decide the outcome of tender offers. Put another way, the issue under debate was a board's entitlement to exercise its power over the corporation's assets, securities, or processes to defeat a tender offer.

Under the business judgement doctrine a disinterested, informed board which concluded an offer was inadequate or unlawful was free, indeed obligated, to oppose the offer and seek its defeat.[11] If the means used by the board were not themselves unlawful and its motivation was not solely or primarily entrenchment, the court was required to defer to the board's business judgment even if the net result was the offer's demise.

In 1985 that changed. The Delaware Supreme Court decided Unocal Corp. v. Mesa Petroleum Co. Unocal imposes a two-part threshold requirement which must be satisfied by a board of directors before the board is entitled to the evidentiary presumptions of the business judgment rule. That is, the burden of proof is shifted, as an initial matter, from the plaintiff to the board. As will be discussed later, this shifting of burdens has significant practical consequences.

In his recent Mills Acquisition Co. v. Macmillan, Inc. decision Justice Moore, also the Unocal author, described the Unocal standard as an "*enhanced* business judgment rule" pursuant to which the court exacts "an enhanced judicial scrutiny at the threshold."[12]

The rationale underlying enhanced judicial scrutiny is the inherent conflict directors have in dealing with a potential takeover of their corporation.

> Because of the omnipresent specter that a board may be acting primarily in its own interests, rather than those of the corporation and its shareholders, there is an enhanced duty which calls for judicial examination at the threshold before the protections of the business judgment rule may be conferred.[13]

The first branch of this enhanced duty is the traditional policy conflict standard found in Cheff v. Mathes.

> In the face of this inherent conflict directors must show that they had reasonable grounds for believing that a danger to corporate policy and effectiveness existed because of another person's stock ownership (pp. 554–55). However, they satisfy that burden "by showing good faith and reasonable investigation" (p. 555). Furthermore, such proof is materially enhanced, as here, by the approval of a board comprised of a majority of outside independent directors who have acted in accordance with the foregoing standards (p. 955).

As such, it represents no radical departure from the past.

The second branch of this threshold test does, however, constitute a radical change.[15]

A further aspect is the element of balance. *If a defensive measure is to come within the ambit of the business judgment rule, it must be reasonable in relation to the threat posed.* This entails an analysis by the directors of the nature of the takeover bid and its effect on the corporate enterprise. (Italics added.)[16]

Under this proportionality test, the board must know not only that its actions are ones a rational board could take but that they are *reasonable* in the circumstances. As Gilson and Kraakman put it, Unocal imposes "a reasonableness test that impliedly allows courts to identify and reject unreasonable tactics, whatever the motives of their authors."[17] The Court's focus on the *appropriateness* of defensive measures taken by a board appears to involve the Court in exercising its own business judgment.[18]

Delaware's Chancellor Allen recognized both the advantages and dangers posed by Unocal's invocation of judicial business judgment:

Delaware courts have employed the Unocal precedent cautiously. The promise of that innovation is the promise of a more realistic, flexible and, ultimately, more responsible corporation law. The danger that it poses is, of course, that courts—in exercising some element of substantive judgment— will too readily seek to assert the primacy of their own view on a question upon which reasonable, completely disinterested minds might differ.[19]

The Unocal case involved extreme facts. The offer, which was two-tier and front-end loaded, was found to be structurally coercive. Its price was held to be inadequate. The Court also concluded that the offeror had a history of greenmail. The defensive device, a self-tender which was selective in that it excluded the hostile offeror, was novel.[20]

The Unocal Court held that Unocal's board "consisting of a majority of independent directors has reasonably determined" that Mesa's offer was "contrary to the best interests of Unocal and its other shareholders."[21] The first branch of the test satisfied, the Court looked to the appropriateness of the means chosen:

Further, the selective stock repurchase plan chosen by Unocal is reasonable in relation to the threat that the board rationally and reasonably believed was posed by Mesa's inadequate and coercive two-tier tender offer.[22]

The Unocal Court, having determined that the board's actions had survived enhanced judicial scrutiny, declared the business judgment doctrine to be in effect and shifted the burden of proof to Mesa.

> Under the circumstances the board's action is entitled to be measured by
> the standards of the business judgment rule. Thus, unless it is shown by a
> preponderance of the evidence that the directors' decisions were primarily
> based on the perpetuating themselves in office, or some other breach of
> fiduciary duty such as fraud, overreaching, lack of good faith or being
> uninformed, a Court will not substitute its judgment for that of the board.[23]

Not surprisingly, Mesa was unable to carry its burden.[24]

What exactly this enhanced business judgment rule will become in
its application is far from clear. As Chancellor Allen observed, when
courts exercise "some element of substantive judgment," there is the risk
that the test of reasonableness will become what particular judges conclude is preferable, even though reasonable, disinterested directors might
disagree. At a minimum, it suggests that plaintiffs should have an easier
time in depriving boards, which engage in active wrongdoing, of business
judgment protections.[25]

The truest test of the viability of Unocal's enhanced business judgment standard is likely to come in a case where the board can show that it
is disinterested and fully informed and the tender offer is noncoercive,
fully financed, and in compliance with law. The only issue will be the
adequacy of the offering price and the reasonableness of the board's
response. That case will pose significant practical issues for investment
bankers and lawyers. Its resolution by the Delaware Supreme Court will
help define the practical impact of Unocal on takeover defenses.

At this writing, Chancery Court decisions since Unocal raise serious
doubts about a board's ability to sustain a determination to preclusively
oppose an inadequately priced tender offer. And even assuming a preclusive defense may be available in the face of a grossly inadequate offer,[26]
the quantum of proof which may be required under Unocal, in light of the
practical exigencies created by the federal tender offer timing rules and
the equitable processes of the court, places extraordinary demands on
investment bankers and M&A lawyers.

To be specific, Unocal requires that the board demonstrate that its
conclusion that a tender offer is inadequate is reasonable. Although boards
will likely have long-term and in-depth familiarity with the company's
businesses, directors are rarely trained valuation specialists. The Delaware Supreme Court has never held that boards must use investment

bankers in valuation situations, but the wisdom of so doing has been made clear.[27] For that reason boards can be expected to look to investment bankers to advise them concerning adequacy.

Investment bankers, however, work under enormous constraints in hostile tender offer situations. Under federal law, the board is required to announce its position on the offer within 10 business days of the offer's commencement (SEC Rule 14d–9). As a consequence, investment bankers must engage in intensive study of the company's businesses, historical performances and projections or business plans within that 10-business-days period. The work by necessity is done in conjunction with management, who understandably may be distracted by the pressure of imminent takeover and a myriad of other issues associated with that prospect.

Key to the banker's analyses are the company's past results and its business plans and projections. In the easy case, historical results will justify an inadequacy conclusion. In many cases, the company's projected results will play a material role in determining adequacy. In most instances, the company's business plans will have been made without regard to the necessity of defending against a premium tender offer. Once the offer is announced, management may be sufficiently galvanized to radically change its business plans to maximize near-term earnings and shareholder value. How should investment bankers evaluate the reality of these new plans? How credible will courts view them to be?

In these circumstances, it is not surprising that bankers have generally declined to give full-blown fairness opinions typical in friendly merger situations. Rather, they opine as to adequacy.

In performing their adequacy analyses, investment bankers utilize a number of different valuation techniques[28] to create a reference range of values. Bankers quite candidly acknowledge that no individual methodology will necessarily yield a precise calculation of fair value and that these various methodologies may do no more than provide directors with a context in which to come to an adequacy conclusion.[29]

In substance, an inadequacy opinion means that the banker believes that a price higher than the one being offered can be obtained, either from the offeror, a third party, or by remaining independent. In that sense the opinion is predictive and does not necessarily address intrinsic fairness. Thus, an offer made at a price which reflects the intrinsic value of the company's stock may be fair but still inadequate because the banker is convinced the offeror would pay more for a friendly transaction.

This type of opinion makes perfect sense given the time exigencies of tender offers. The investment bankers, after all, may be newly retained. It would be a daunting undertaking for an investment bank to render a formal opinion on the intrinsic value of a company in ten business days. Whether, however, an inadequacy opinion will be sufficient to justify preclusive board action under Unocal is by no means clear.[30]

The difficulty of building a credible record in 10 business days on these issues is obvious. Yet the board must announce its position in that period and, it must be assumed, that the offeror will be seeking a preliminary injunction to dismantle the target's poison pill or other defenses at the earliest possible moment.[31]

The additional pressure imposed by litigation is considerable. Unocal's burden shifting to the directors can create an exquisite pain. Not only must directors come to expedited decisions but they must garner their evidence and defend their decisions promptly.

Moreover, under Unocal the inadequacy determination is only the beginning of the analysis. The directors are required to show that an inadequate offer represents a danger to corporate policy and effectiveness or to stockholder interests.[32] The nature of that threat will, under Unocal, determine what the directors can do to respond. And the extent of the response may be limited to what the court ultimately believes its business judgment is reasonable in the circumstances.[33]

In most cases, a board should have little difficulty in demonstrating that an inadequate offer is reasonably perceived to be inadequate. But even assuming inadequacy, the difficult problem is demonstrating that an inadequate offer poses a sufficient threat that it is reasonable for a board to utilize a preclusive defensive device, such as a poison pill or a cram down restructuring, to defeat the tender offer. Two recent decisions illustrate the point.

In City Capital Associates Limited Partnership v. Interco, Inc.,[34] Chancellor Allen's landmark opinion, the issue posed was whether an informed, independent board could use a poison pill to stop an inadequate $74 cash offer for all shares (with a $74 cash back-end merger promised) while unilaterally effecting by dividend a restructuring, which the board reasonably concluded had a short-term trading value of $76 and might be worth substantially more in the future.

The court noted as significant the fact that the poison pill was being utilized solely to protect the restructuring—"that is, precluding the shareholders from choosing an alternative to the restructuring that the board finds less valuable to shareholders."[35]

The Interco court found it to be beyond dispute that:

> The value of the Interco restructuring is inherently a debatable proposition, most importantly (but not solely) because the future value of the stub share is unknowable with reasonable certainty.[36]

and that:

> A reasonable shareholder could prefer the restructuring to the sale of his stock for $74 in cash now, but a reasonable shareholder could prefer the reverse.[37]

The court held that the offer was not structurally coercive, that is, shareholders' freedom to exercise choice was not impinged upon by the structure of the offer.[38] The restructuring, being in the form of a dividend, arguably was but the court declined to enjoin it.[39]

The court stated that the only threat a financially inadequate offer posed was to shareholder economic interests. In this case the court viewed the threat as "mild," finding that, even if the restructuring were valued at $76, the $74 cash offer was only 3 percent lower.[40]

The court, applying the Unocal proportionality test, held that preclusive board action in the form of a poison pill could not be justified as a reasonable response to this "mild" threat.

> Without wishing to cast any shadows upon the subjective motivation of the individual defendants…, I conclude that reasonable minds not affected by an inherent, entrenched interest in the matter, could not reasonably differ with respect to the conclusion that the CCA $74 cash offer did not represent a threat to shareholder interests sufficient in the circumstances to justify, in effect, foreclosing shareholders from electing to accept the offer.[41]

Interco is significant in a number of respects. It seems to say that where shareholders, "depending upon one's liquidity preference, expectations about future events, etc." could reasonably choose either the hostile offer or management's alternative, the court should hold that shareholders must be permitted to make that choice and directors will not be permitted to take preclusive action.[42]

To be sure, the Interco court recognized that a preliminary injunction against a poison pill was tantamount to final relief. Consequently, the court treated the motion as if it were one for summary judgment. It relied only on undisputed facts and phrased its conclusion in terms of there being no reasonable dispute that the $74 offer was not a sufficient threat to justify a poison pill.

This articulation of the standard could be read to suggest that if reasonable minds could differ as to the seriousness of the threat posed by an inadequate offer, the court should defer to the board's decision to use a preclusive defense. That would sound suspiciously close to the Sinclair Oil v. Levien attributable "to any rational business purpose" test.

But the Interco court also seemed to be implying that absent extreme circumstances, reasonable minds would not in the future be found to differ over the proposition that price inadequacy alone would not justify the preclusive use of a poison pill.

> Our corporation law exists, not as an isolated body of rules and principles, but rather in a historical setting and as part of a larger body of law premised upon shared values. To acknowledge that directors may employ the recent innovation of "poison pills" to deprive shareholders of the ability effectively to choose to accept a noncoercive offer, after the board has had a reasonable opportunity to explore or create alternatives, or attempt to negotiate on the shareholders' behalf, would, it seems to me, be so inconsistent with widely shared notions of appropriate corporate governance as to threaten to diminish the legitimacy and authority of our corporation law.
>
> ***
>
> Our cases, however, also indicate that in the setting of a noncoercive offer, absent unusual facts, there may come a time when a board's fiduciary duty will require it to redeem the rights and permit the shareholders to choose.[43]

These expressions are reminiscent of Judge Weinfeld's oft-quoted comments in Conoco Inc. v. Seagram Co., Ltd.:

> What is sometimes lost sight of in these tender offer controversies is that the shareholders, not the directors, have the right of franchise with respect to shares owned by them; stockholders, once informed of the facts, have a right to make their own decisions in matters pertaining to their economic self-interest, whether consonant with or contrary to the advice of others, whether such advice is tendered by management or outsiders or those motivated by self-interest.[44]

In Grand Metropolitan PLC v. The Pillsbury Co.,[45] which was decided only a few weeks after Interco, the court was asked to order the

Pillsbury board to redeem its poison pill so that its stockholders could accept an all-cash $63 tender offer for all shares. The Pillsbury board had concluded the price was inadequate and refused to redeem its pill. The board's inadequacy conclusion was based on an intensive analysis of Pillsbury's business by its new chief executive officer, who had been hired several months before the tender offer to improve Pillsbury's recent disappointing financial results. The new chief executive was developing a plan to materially cut costs and improve profit margins when the offer was announced. At the time of the offer, Pillsbury's stock was trading around $39. The offer was made at $60 and later raised to $63 with a request by the offeror to negotiate a friendly merger at $65. At the time of decision, 87 percent of the shares had been tendered.

After reviewing management's new business plans in detail over several lengthy board meetings and receiving careful and detailed advice from Pillsbury's four investment banking firms as to Pillsbury's value, the board concluded that Pillsbury's minimum fair value was between $68 and $72 per Pillsbury share—or $5 to $9 higher than the offer price.[46] The board reached this conclusion based on its adoption of a plan to spin off certain assets and reorganize others to maximize the efficiency of their operations. The board was advised this restructuring would make both the remaining Pillsbury and the spun-off assets more attractive to potential buyers and that both could be sold in several years for a total consideration materially higher than $63 per share. The board discounted back the assumed sales prices to derive the present value range of $68–$72.

Having determined that the offeror's $63 offer and $65 merger proposal were inadequate in light of the company' future prospects based on its new business plan, the board declined to redeem its poison pill and voted to implement its spin-off of assets via a dividend, that is, without seeking stockholder approval. The spin-off, if implemented, would have created adverse tax consequences to Pillsbury and its shareholders for some period of time if there was a subsequent takeover of the company.

The Pillsbury court found that the board acted in good faith, made a reasonable investigation, and was composed of a majority of outside, independent directors, thereby materially enhancing its proof of good faith. The court also held that the only threat an inadequate price posed was to shareholder value and not to corporate policy or effectiveness.

In analyzing the balancing branch of the Unocal test, the court said:

> But the real threat to shareholder value, as I see it, is not the spread between

$63 and $68 per share.[†] It is, rather, what will probably happen if the Pill remains in place and Grand Met's offer is withdrawn. That threat of "loss" measured in dollars as to all Pillsbury shareholders could amount to $1.5 billion and perhaps as much as $1.9 billion (assuming the price of the stock returns to its September 1988 level).[47]

The court emphasized that Pillsbury's business plans, even if reasonable, "are subject to economic and competitive conditions which are beyond Pillsbury's control." In contrast, the offer was seen as a fully financed offer to pay $63 immediately upon the invalidation of the poison pill and the spin-off dividend.[48]

As the court put it:

> Certain it is that a Pillsbury shareholder, seeking to make a determination as to what is in his/her best interest, could conclude that $63 in present cash is preferable to the possibility of $68 if all of the "ifs" in Pillsbury's plan disappear and its hopes for the future become realities. But a stockholder in Pillsbury cannot make that choice unless the Rights are redeemed.[49]

The court, having concluded that a reasonable shareholder might well prefer to sell for $63 rather than hold, found that it was not reasonable for the Pillsbury board to deny shareholders the right to decide for themselves by refusing to redeem Pillsbury's poison pill.[50]

The Pillsbury court's test of reasonableness can be read as putting on the board the burden of showing that reasonable stockholders could not or should not prefer the hostile offer's price over the alternative the board was proposing. If the board cannot make such a showing, then according to Pillsbury, a preclusive defense cannot be justified. Shareholders must be permitted to decide for themselves.

Pillsbury and Interco were mooted while on appeal and the Delaware Supreme Court has not yet addressed the issue directly. There have been indications in the press that the fate of those decisions in the Supreme Court was far from clear.[51]

In Shamrock Holdings, Inc. v. Polaroid Corp., Vice-Chancellor Berger clearly echoed Interco and Pillsbury's rejection of the notion that an inadequate, noncoercive offer poses any Unocal threat:

[†]There were approximately 80 million fully diluted shares. The $5 spread thus represented almost $400 million.

However, where there has been sufficient time for any alternatives to be developed and presented and for the target corporation to inform its stockholders of the benefits of retaining their equity position, the "threat" to the stockholders of an inadequate, noncoercive offer seems, in most circumstances, to be without substance.[52]

The Polaroid court held, however, that there were special circumstances in that case and upheld the Polaroid board's defensive maneuvers (a $300 million preferred stock placement with a White Squire, a self-tender and market buy-back program and an ESOP). The special circumstances were Polaroid's unliquidated patent infringement judgment against Kodak, which "may exceed $5 billion." The court concluded that:

> there is a real possibility that the Polaroid stockholders will undervalue the Kodak judgment and it does not appear that the mere dissemination of information will cure this problem. Thus, I am satisfied that the Polaroid directors were entitled to treat the Shamrock tender offer as a threat.[53]

Despite validating Polaroid's self-tender and market purchase program (presumably as nonthreats or lesser threats), the court observed that:

> there is a valid basis for concern that the Polaroid stockholders will be unable to reach an accurate judgment as to intrinsic value of their stock in light of the current status of the Kodak litigation.[54]

Polaroid's value uncertainty principle suggests a somewhat different "reasonableness" than evidenced in Interco and Pillsbury. Management's self-tender seems to demonstrate that "reasonable stockholders" could differ as to whether it would be advisable to take money now or wait for a future bonanza. The court found that Polaroid's defenses were not preclusive and that may help explain the result. The court's holding on preclusiveness must have come as a surprise to the litigants. The marketplace had no doubt as to the preclusive nature of the defenses. Then the Delaware Supreme Court declined to stay these defenses pending appeal, and Shamrock immediately abandoned its efforts, demonstrating just how preclusive and successful Polaroid's multiple defenses were.

Where then does this leave the investment banker? It seems clear at a minimum that the banker's role in providing expert valuation advice in support of board decisions will remain crucial to the takeover defense process. Given the limitations the Unocal proportionality standard may imply for defensive tactics, the necessity of defining the threat of an inadequate price in the starkest terms possible will be paramount.

The first casualty may be the inadequacy opinion. Comfortable like a well-worn, old shoe for the bankers, its fuzziness will not serve well in the new Unocal world of precisely defined threats and responses. Chancellor Allen's discomfort with Interco's adequacy opinion based on an ever shifting reference range of values was apparent:

> This analysis generated a "reference range" for the Company of $68–$80 per share.
>
> ***
>
> Now the studies showed a "reference range" for the whole Company of $74–$87. The so-called reference ranges do not purport to be a range of fair value; but just what they purport to be is (deliberately, one imagines) rather unclear.[55]

The questions currently being heard in courtrooms are, if the offer is claimed to be inadequate, how inadequate is it? What is the fair or intrinsic value of the target company's shares? Given Interco and Pillsbury, target company boards may conclude that they need an investment bank or some other valuation expert willing to render fairness opinions in tender offer situations.

The Unocal burden shifting feature is also significant when viewed in the context of preliminary injunction litigation. It is now quite customary for an offeror to file suit in the Delaware Chancery Court immediately upon commencing its offer and to seek a prompt hearing on a preliminary injunction motion to compel the target board to redeem its poison pill. Expedited discovery will likely be sought and allowed.

The result will be that the investment bankers and the company will be subjected to discovery while they are in the process of doing their valuation work. Preliminary analyses, draft, erroneous computations, and the like all become available. Management's projections and business plan will likewise be grist for the litigation mill. And then there are depositions—an exercise much loathed by most investment bankers and often passed down to juniors by senior partners too busy to be available.

These kinds of circumstances make the compilation of a persuasive valuation record extremely difficult. If Gilson and Kraakman are right in predicting that it will be necessary for a target company board to prove that its projections and plans will produce share values that make reasonable a preclusive defense, either court practices will have to change or the preliminary injunction format will be unsuitable for the exercise.[56]

The Chancery Court, as a matter of long-standing practice, does not hold evidentiary hearings on preliminary injunction motions. Thus, there is no opportunity for the court to assess credibility or for the parties to explore the intricacies of valuation analyses with the court. In these circumstances it seems likely that the court will not be able to decide which experts to credit.[57]

It is these types of practical considerations which make the placement of burdens of proof and the delineations of what will be perceived as "reasonable" so crucial. Under the unenhanced business judgment rule, the board enjoyed an evidentiary presumption, which by itself was often sufficient to preclude preliminary relief. Under the Unocal-enhanced business judgment rule, it is not clear yet whether increased judicial scrutiny in the context of a truncated record may not work to the opposite effect.

Moreover, if the court is not convinced that the board's valuation conclusion is clearly right (and not just reasonable), there may be a tendency for the court to throw the decision to the stockholders. Because the directors bear the burden of showing both a reasonably perceived threat and that the preclusive response they have chosen is proportionate to the threat, such a conflict of evidence may be deemed fatal.

The board and its investment bankers face other strategic dangers as well. The poison pill may be the only obstacle to the offer's success. Yet to sustain the pill, the board may have to disclose its most intimate valuation information to the court and the offeror's lawyers. For litigation purposes, the board will be driven, as advised by its investment bankers, to fix a minimum fair price for the company.

The net result may well be that the hostile offeror will derive material strategic advantage in pricing its offer.[58] Conversely, the strategic advantage in the form of access to inside information a board heretofore has been able to offer prospective white knights, who sign standstill agreements, to induce them to consider bidding may be diluted or lost if the hostile offeror is perceived as having equal access through the litigation.

These results may appear quite reasonable, if one believes that a noncoercive offer once made inevitably should lead to the company being sold. If, however, independence is the board's preferred course, the Unocal standard, as interpreted in two recent Chancery Court decisions, may make that goal problematic. But then, we have yet to hear from the Delaware Supreme Court.

Notes

1. Del. Supr., 493 A.2d 946 (1985).
2. Mills Acquisition Co. v. Macmillan, Del. Supr., Nos. 415 and 416 1988 (consolidated, May 3, 1989) Slip op., p. 53, note 32. See J. Hinsey IV, "Duty of Care Business Judgment and the American Law Institute's Corporate Governance Project: The Doctrine, and the Reality," *George Washington Law Review, 52,* 609, 611–13 (1984).
3. Sinclair Oil Corp. v. Levien, Del. Supr., 280 A.2d 717, 720 (1971).
4. Id. (Italics added).
5. Warshaw v. Calhoun, Del. Supr., 221 A.2d 487, 492–3 (1966).
6. In the context of a sale of assets, Delaware courts have described the test as requiring the plaintiff to show "gross inadequacy." Board decisions to sell assets are to be upheld "so long as the inadequacy of price may reasonably be referred to an honest exercise of sound judgment" even though mistaken. Gimbel v. The Signal Cos., Inc., Del. Ch., 316 A.2d 599, 610 (1975).
7. Mills Acquisition Co. v. Macmillan, Inc., p. 40.
8. Unocal, 493 A.2d, p. 957.
9. R. J. Gilson and R. Kraakman, "Delaware's Intermediate Standard for Defensive Tactics: Is There Substance to Proportionality Review?," *Business Lawyer, 44,* 247, 249–50, notes 10, 11 (1989).
10. Unocal, p. 954, note 9.
11. See, e.g., Panter v. Marshall Field & Co., 646 F.2d 271, 298–99 (7th Cir.) cert. denied, 454 U.S. 1092 (1981); Northwest Industries v. B.F. Goodrich Co., 301 F. Supp. 706, 712 (no. Ill. 1969).
12. Mills Acquisition Co. v. Macmillan, Inc., p. 62–63.
13. Unocal, p. 954.
14. Del. Supr., 199 A.2d 548 (1964).
15. For a thoughtful analysis of this standard and proposals for its development, see Gilson and Kraakman, "Delaware's Intermediate Standard for Defensive Tactics: Is There Substance to Proportionality Review?," *Business Lawyer, 44,* 247, 249–50, (1989).
16. Id. (Italics added). In Macmillan the Court made clear that the Unocal-enhanced duty requires that "the board's action must be reasonable in relation to the advantage sought to be achieved" as well as to threats posed. (Mills Acquisition Co. v. Macmillan, Inc., p. 64).
17. Gilson and Kraakman, op. cit., p. 251, (1989).
18. See Zapata Corp. v. Maldonado, Del. Supr., 430 A.2d 779, 789 (1981), "The Court should determine, applying its own independent business judgment, whether the motion [to dismiss a derivative action] should be granted."
19. City Capital Associates Limited Partnership v. Interco, Inc. [1988–1989 Transfer Binder] Fed. Sec. L. Rep. (CCH) ¶94, 084 at p. 91, 070 (Del. Ch., 1988). Also

see generally, Gilson and Kraakman, loc. cit., note 8.

20. Shortly after Unocal was decided the Securities and Exchange Commission adopted a rule outlawing selective self-tenders. SEC Rule 14d–10.

21. Unocal, p. 958.

22. Id.

23. Id.

24. Id., pp. 958–59. It is unclear how a board could pass muster under this enhanced judicial scrutiny yet fail to be sustained under the ordinary business judgment rule analysis.

25. See, for example, Revlon, Inc. v. MacAndrews & Forbes Holdings, Inc., Del. Supr., 506 A.2d 173 (1986); Mill Acquisition Co. v. Macmillan, Inc., Del. Supr., Nos. 415 and 416 (1988) consolidated (May 3, 1989); In Re Holly Farms Corp. Shareholders Litigation, Del. Ch., C.A. No. 10340, consolidated (December 30, 1988); In Re Holly Farms Corp. Shareholders Litigation, Del. Ch., C.A. No. 10350, consolidated (May 18, 1989).

26. See Revlon, Inc. v. MacAndrews & Forbes Holding, Del. Supr., 506 A.2d 173, 180–81 (1985).

27. See Smith v. Van Gorkom, Del. Supr., 488 A.2d 858, 876–78 (1985); Gimbel v. The Signal Cos., Inc., Del. Ch., 316 A.2d 599, 612, 615 (1974).

28. The commonly used valuation methodologies include discounted cash flow analyses, comparable company or transaction analyses, leveraged buyout analyses, restructuring analyses, and liquidation or break-up analyses.

29. Not all courts have been comfortable with this reference range approach. See City Capital Associates Limited Partnership v. Interco, Inc., p. 91, 067.

30. See Interco, p. 91.

31. While there should be no problem in sustaining the use of a poison pill to run an auction or even search for alternatives, if the "just say no" defense is the board's preferred course, the time pressure will likely intensify. See CFRT v. Federated Department Stores, Inc., 683 F. Supp. 422 (S.D.N.Y., 1988); Grand Metropolitan PLC v. The Pillsbury Co., 5 Mergers and Acquisitions L. Rep. 1097 (C.A. Nos 10319, 10323, Del. Ch., November 22, 1988).

32. Revlon, 506 A.2d, p. 182.

33. Unocal, 493 A.2d, p. 955.

34. [1988–1989 Transfer Binder] Fed. Sec. L. Rep. (CCH) ¶ 94, 084 (Del. Ch., 1988).

35. Interco, p. 91, 065.

36. The proposed restructuring contemplated a sale of Interco assets (including its "Crown Jewel" Ethan Allen division) which generated half of Interco's gross revenues and borrowings of $2.025 billion. Interco proposed making two dividends with a stated value of $66, consisting of $38.15 in cash and $27.85 in debt and preferred securities. Its bankers opined the stub share would trade at a minimum value of $10.

37. Interco, p. 91, 069.
38. Examples of structurally coercive offers include two-tier, front-end loaded offers, partial offers or offers whose timing may serve to coerce. [Interco, p. 91, 070; AC Acquisition Corp. v. Anderson, Clayton & Co., Del Ch., 519 A.2d 103 (1986)].
39. Id., pp. 91, 073–75.
40. Id., p. 91, 072. On appeal, Interco argued that its restructuring did not cash stockholders out and, therefore, was not equivalent to a sale. Interco asserted it was improper to compare the immediate trading value of the restructuring with a cash out sale price. [*Mergers and Acquisitions Reporter, 4,* 921, 929 (1989)]. The appeal was mooted by events.
41. Id., p. 91, 072.
42. Id., p. 91, 073.
43. Id., p. 91, 071.
44. [1981–1982 Transfer Binder] Fed. Sec. L. Rep. (CCH) ¶98, 234 at p. 91, 556 (S.D.N.Y., 1981). See Shamrock Holdings, Inc. v. Polaroid Corp., [Current] Fed. Sec. L. Rep. ¶94, 340 at p. 92, 223 (Del. Ch., 1989).
45. [1988–1989 Transfer Binder] Fed. Sec. L. Rep. (CCH) ¶99, 104 (Del. Ch., 1988).
46. Immediately prior to argument of the case, the offeror had attempted to negotiate a merger at $65 per share. The management had set $66 as the minimum price it would recommend to the board.
47. Grand Metropolitan PLC v. The Pillsbury Co., 5 Mergers and Acquisitions L. Rep. 1097 (C.A. Nos 10319, 10323, Del. Ch., November 22, 1988), p. 91, 194. This "threat" is what Gilson and Kraakman call "agency cost." They posit that shareholder mistrust of management's claims that independence will produce a better share value may lead to heavy tendering to avoid this agency cost. They suggest that a court may be better equipped than shareholders to evaluate the reality of management's projections (Gilson and Kraakman, op. cit., p. 263).
48. Grand Metropolitan PLC v. The Pillsbury Co., 5 Mergers and Acquisitions L. Rep. 1097 (C.A. Nos 10319, 10323, Del. Ch., November 22, 1988), p. 91, 193–94.
49. Id.
50. The court was obviously influenced by the fact that 87 percent of Pillsbury's shares had been tendered. (Id., at p. 91, 194).
51. W. Meyers, "Showdown in Delaware: The Battle to Shape Takeover Law," *Institutional Investor, 64,* (February 1989).
52. Id., p. 92, 223.
53. Id., p. 92, 224.
54. Id.
55. Id., p. 91, 066–67.
56. Gilson and Kraakman, op. cit., p. 263.

57. See, e.g., Gimbel v. The Signal Cos., Inc., Del. Ch., 316 A.2d, 617. "Hence, even for preliminary injunction purposes, the Court is unable to properly judge the validity of the ultimate valuations which conflict so greatly."
58. See Shamrock Holdings, Inc. v. Polaroid Corp., [Current] Fed. Sec. L. Rep. ¶94, 340 at p. 92, 223 (Del. Ch., 1989).

CHAPTER 7

THE ECONOMIC IMPORTANCE OF THE BUSINESS JUDGMENT RULE: AN EMPIRICAL ANALYSIS OF THE TRANS UNION DECISION AND SUBSEQUENT DELAWARE LEGISLATION

Michael Bradley
Cindy A. Schipani

INTRODUCTION

The purpose of this chapter is to gain insight into the economic importance of liability rules for corporate officials. Specifically, how would a change in the liability rules for corporate managers affect social welfare?

There are at least two schools of thought regarding the welfare implications of imposing greater liability on corporate officers and directors.

Michael Bradley is the Everett E. Berg Professor of Business Administration, Professor of Finance, and Professor of Law at The University of Michigan. Professor Bradley received his Ph.D. in economics and finance from the University of Chicago in 1979.

Cindy A. Schipani is an Assistant Professor of Business Law at The University of Michigan. She received her Juris Doctor at the University of Chicago Law School in 1982.

The authors would like to thank Louis Columna, Andrew Terry, Daniel Schofield, and C. Thomas Ludden, Jr., for valuable research assistance.

There are those like the drafters of the American Law Institute Project on Corporate Governance who argue that the agency costs of the large-scale corporation are solved largely through the constraints imposed by liability rules and judicial review.[1] Citing the traditional arguments for the inefficiencies arising from absentee stockholders and unbridled corporate managers, they propose, *inter alia,* to strengthen the role of the legal rules in constraining corporate managerial behavior.[2] Those who hold this view and stress administrative solutions might be referred to as institutionalists.

There is an alternative view regarding the importance of mandated liability rules. This position, often referred to as the contractarian view of the corporation, recognizes that market forces act to discipline corporate managers and cause the managers to align their interests with those of the firm's security holders. These forces stem from competition in the factor and product markets, as well as competition in the market for corporate control. This view of the large-scale corporation follows from the works of Coase,[3] Manne,[4] Alchian and Demsetz,[5] Jensen and Meckling,[6] Fama,[7] and Fama and Jensen.[8]

The distinction between these two views is the mechanism believed to be primarily responsible for the continued existence of the public corporation. Institutionalists exalt the importance of legal rules and judicial review (the "legal constraint theory"); contractarians focus on voluntary contracting and the market forces that work to constrain the behavior of corporate managers (the "market constraint theory").

The legal constraint and market constraint theories generate drastically different implications for public policy. According to the market constraint theory, public policy should be directed toward facilitating contracting among self-interested individuals. Judicial or legislative constraints imposed on this contracting process disadvantage all corporate stakeholders.[9] In contrast, the legal constraint theory predicts that judicial and legislative intervention is needed to protect the interest of absentee owners.[10] According to this view, corporate managers are accountable to neither their stockholders nor to society in general. Their behavior must, therefore, be held in check by legal rules and judicial review.[11]

While the two schools of thought generate distinctly different predictions for public policy, subjecting these hypotheses to empirical tests is very difficult.[12] It is undoubtedly the case that both liability rules and market forces are important in constraining the behavior of corporate officials. The contractarian and institutionalist views are abstract, polar extremes. Reality lies somewhere in between.

Nevertheless, it is important to examine the relevance of each at the margin. Given a marginal change in the environment, which of the two is a better predictor of subsequent events and effects? A series of events between January of 1985 and July of 1986 affords a rare opportunity to examine one aspect of this debate.

On January 29, 1985, the Delaware Supreme Court in Smith v. Van Gorkom (the "Trans Union" case)[13] reversed a lower court decision and ruled that the directors of Trans Union Corporation violated their fiduciary duty by accepting a merger proposal after only two hours of deliberation and without review of the relevant documentation.[14] It was irrelevant to the court that the offer was at a substantial premium over market.[15] The court's analysis focused on the board's decision-making process as opposed to the outcome.[16] The court found that by making an important decision in such an impulsive fashion, and without ascertaining the intrinsic value of the corporation, the directors violated the duty of care owed the firm's security holders.[17] Eventually, the case was settled out of court reportedly for $23.5 million.[18] Trans Union came as a complete shock to the corporate community.[19] There was widespread concern that the decision undermined the business judgment rule and exposed corporate managers to intolerable levels of liability. Many predicted that the decision would adversely affect the ability of corporations to attract qualified individuals to serve on their boards of directors.[20]

In direct response to these concerns, the Delaware legislature enacted Senate Bill 533, effective July 1, 1986 [hereinafter "Section 102(b)(7)"], which allowed firms to "opt" out of the strengthened duty of care standard established by the Trans Union court. In fact the legislation went further. The statute allows Delaware firms to amend their articles of incorporation to eliminate monetary liability of directors to the corporation and its shareholders for breach of the duty of due care. In other words, the statute allows each firm to adopt its own (explicit) business judgement rule.

The two theories outlined above generate contrasting predictions regarding the economic effects of this chain of events. According to the contractarians, the corporation is nothing more than a nexus of contracts made between and among self-interested individuals. The agency costs of the corporate form are held in check through the workings of competitive markets. Within this context, the liberties afforded corporate managers by the business judgment rule represent a mutually advantageous relationship between stockholders and managers. Under the business judgment rule, courts generally will not second guess the business decisions of management, provided there is not evidence of bad faith, self-dealing, gross neglect, or intentional misconduct. To the extent the business judgment rule affords management the benefit of the presumption that its business decisions are in the corporation's best interests, it is in harmony with the market constraint theory.[21]

Consequently, Trans Union should have had a detrimental effect on the wealth of all corporate stakeholders, including the firm's equity holders. To the extent that the decision constrained the ability of corporate stockholders to contract freely, the agency costs of the corporate form would increase and the value of equity claims would decrease.

Since the Trans Union decision pertains exclusively to firms incorporated in the state of Delaware, the market constraint theory predicts that the decision would reduce the equity values of Delaware corporations relative to firms incorporated elsewhere. This effect may, however, be dampened by the tendency of courts in other jurisdictions to consider Delaware case law in interpreting their own corporate laws. The market may expect that other state courts will follow the Trans Union interpretation of the duty of care standard and the business judgment rule. Thus, Trans Union may not significantly affect the stock prices of Delaware corporations vis-à-vis other corporations. Yet, due to the controversy surrounding the decision, it is also plausible that some jurisdictions would take a wait-and-see attitude before adopting the Trans Union rule. Under this scenario, we expect to see a difference in the returns to Delaware firms relative to firms incorporated elsewhere.

In a similar vein, the market constraint theory predicts that this wealth loss would have been reversed with the passage of Section 102(b)(7). To the extent that the law unexpectedly negated the stricter and inefficient fiduciary standard articulated by the Trans Union court, the value of the equity of Delaware firms should have increased in the wake of the legislation.

In contrast, the legal constraint theory predicts just the opposite pattern in the relative value of Delaware firms. The theory holds that stronger liability rules favor (absentee) stockholders. Thus, the Trans Union decision should increase the relative value of Delaware firms and the subsequent legislation should have the opposite effect.

THE TRANS UNION DECISION AND SUBSEQUENT DELAWARE LEGISLATION

The Trans Union Decision

Facts and Holding
Trans Union involved a class action brought by shareholders of the Trans Union Corporation ("Trans Union" or the "Company") against its directors. These shareholders sought damages resulting from the cash-out merger of their corporation.[22]

Trans Union's earnings derived principally from its railcar leasing business. As such, the Company generated large investment tax credits ("ITCs"). Trans Union did not, however, generate sufficient taxable income to offset the ITCs. Jerome Van Gorkom, Trans Union's chairman and chief executive officer, met with senior management to discuss solutions to the ITC problem. In August 1980, the chief financial officer of Trans Union, Donald Romans, indicated that his department had done a little work on the possibility of a leveraged buyout. On September 5, 1980, Romans and Van Gorkom discussed the feasibility of a leveraged buyout based on the amount to be paid for the shares of stock and the cash flow necessary to service the debt. Based on rough calculations, Romans indicated that a leveraged buyout would be easy to do at $50 per share but would be difficult at $60 per share. Van Gorkom stated that he would accept $55 per share for his own shares but was opposed to a leveraged buyout.

On September 13, 1980, Van Gorkom approached Jay A. Pritzker with a proposed price and financing structure. Van Gorkom requested the company's controller to calculate the feasibility of a leveraged buyout at $55 per share. Van Gorkom then used the $55 per share figure in his discussions with Pritzker. On September 18, Pritzker made an offer at $55 per share (a 48 percent premium relative to market), requiring a decision by September 21. As part of the agreement, Trans Union would be free to accept any better offer during the following 90-day period, but could not solicit such offers. Pritzker, however, would be permitted to buy one million shares of treasury stock at $38 per share, 75 cents above the prevailing market price. Pritzker could than sell these shares to any higher bidder if a better offer were accepted.

Van Gorkom disclosed the Pritzker offer to senior management at a meeting on September 20. Only two persons in addition to Van Gorkom had prior knowledge of the offer. Management's reaction was negative. Romans criticized the $55 price as too low, criticized the timing and argued that the proposal was in reality "an agreed merger as opposed to an offer."[23]

Van Gorkom than met with the board at a special meeting. Copies of the proposal were not delivered to the board members in time to be studied before the meeting. Van Gorkom made a 20-minute presentation describing the company's ITC situation and the merger proposal, then asked the board to decide whether $55 was a fair price to be submitted to a vote of the stockholders. Van Gorkom felt that the 90-day market test would validate $55 as a fair price. The company's attorney advised that a fairness opinion was not legally required and that there was a potential for a lawsuit if the premium offer were not accepted. Romans told the board that his studies did not indicate a fair price but in his opinion $55 was at the beginning of a range for a fair price.

The board meeting lasted approximately two hours, with the board approving the merger agreement. The agreement was signed by Van Gorkom on September 20 at a formal social event he hosted for the Chicago Lyric Opera. Neither Van Gorkom nor any other director read the agreement before signing it. As a result of widespread dissent among senior management, Van Gorkom called another board meeting for October 8. At this meeting, the board approved amendments to the merger agreement and authorized the employment of Salomon Brothers to solicit other offers during the 90-day market test. The board members did not review the actual amendments.

Alden Smith, a shareholder, filed the lawsuit on December 19. On January 21, management mailed a proxy statement to the shareholders. On January 26, the board met and approved a supplement to the proxy statement setting forth information on the Pritzker Merger Agreement. At this meeting, the board reviewed the entire sequence of events from Van Gorkom's initiation of the negotiation forward. At this time, the board believed they could (1) continue to recommend the Pritzker merger, (2) recommend that the stockholders vote against the merger, or (3) take a noncommittal position on the merger and simply leave the decision to the stockholders. The board decided to continue to recommend the proposal. On February 10, the shareholders approved the merger agreement by a large majority.

The board of directors of Trans Union consisted of five inside and five outside directors. Of the five outside directors, four were chief executive officers of Chicago-based corporations at least as large as Trans Union. One director, Dr. Allan Wallis, a nationally renowned economist and math statistician, had been a professor of economics at Yale University, Dean of the Graduate School of Business at the University of Chicago, and Chancellor at the University of Rochester. He had also served on the boards of Bausch & Lomb, Kodak, Metropolitan Life Insurance Company, Standard Oil, and other companies. Another director, William B. Johnson, was a University of Pennsylvania law graduate, president of Railway Express, and chief executive of IC Industries Holding Company. John Lanterman was a certified public accountant and former chief executive of American Steel, serving on the boards of International Harvester, People's Energy, Illinois Bell Telephone, Harris Bank and Trust Company, and Kemper Insurance Company. Grant Morgan, a chemist and former chairman and chief executive officer of U.S. Gypsum, had been involved in an estimated 32 corporate takeovers prior to the Trans Union transaction. Robert Reneker attended the University of Chicago and the Harvard Business School, was president and chief executive of Swift and Company, and was a member of the boards of seven other corporations, including U.S. Gypsum and the Chicago Tribune.

The Delaware Supreme Court held that (1) the board's decision to approve the merger agreement was not a product of an informed business judgment; (2) the board's subsequent efforts to amend the merger agreement and other curative action were ineffectual; and (3) the board did not deal with complete candor with the stockholders. According to the court, the proxy statement should have stated that the board had not made any study of the intrinsic worth of the company. The court also found the statement in the proxy statement referring to a substantial premium offered by Pritzker to be misleading. The proxy statement should have told the stockholders that the $55 figure was chosen in the context of the feasibility of a leveraged buyout. The members of the Trans Union board thus breached their fiduciary duty to the stockholders by their failure to inform themselves of all reasonably available information and their failure to disclose all material information to the stockholders.

The court decided that the business judgment rule did not apply because the directors did not fully inform themselves before making the merger decision. The court was troubled by the process by which the board reached its decision. The board deliberated for only two hours after a 20-minute presentation given by Van Gorkom. Most of the directors had no prior knowledge of the purpose of the meeting nor did they have any documents before them concerning the proposed transaction. The board did not request an evaluation study or documentation justifying the $55 price. No one questioned the chief financial officer as to why he considered the $55 originally offered a fair price. Furthermore, the court found that "Van Gorkom was basically uninformed as to the essential provisions of the very document about which he was talking."[24]

That no better offers were obtained during the so-called 90-day market test did not validate the $55 price, according to the court. Rather, the court found that, as a factual matter, the merger agreement and the board's activities discouraged a better offer. The provision in the agreement granting Pritzker the right to buy one million shares at 75 cents over the market price discouraged the only serious suitor who came forward. There was no mention of the right to receive and accept higher offers in a press release issued on September 22.

In addition, the court gave no credence to the argument that counsel may have advised the directors that failure to accept Pritzker's offer could have resulted in litigation and that a fairness opinion was not legally required. The court stated that such advice was meaningless unless the directors had before them adequate information regarding the intrinsic value of the company.

The court then analyzed the conduct of the board after its September 20 approval of the Pritzker offer to determine whether the board was informed, and whether the board's later actions cured its prior misconduct. Again, the court found the board's actions to be grossly negligent. In the court's opinion, the amendments to the agreement made the agreement even more onerous. The merger documents, according to the court, could not be construed as incorporating either of the conditions the board members required at the first meeting.

The court then reviewed the board's conduct at the January 26 meeting. The defendants argued that the board's vote on January 26 to continue to recommend the proposal was an informed and deliberate decision. The court disagreed, finding that the board had no other feasible choice. The board could not remain committed to the merger and recommend that the stockholders veto it, nor could it take a neutral position and delegate the decision to the stockholders. The board could either recommend approval of the merger, or rescind its agreement with Pritzker, withdraw its approval of the merger, and notify the stockholders that the meeting was canceled. The second alternative, however, would subject the company to risk of a lawsuit for breach of contract. Thus, the court found that the defendants' later conduct did not cure the deficiencies of their September 20 conduct because they had no choice other than to continue to recommend the merger.

Implications

As noted above, the Trans Union decision came as a shock to the corporate community. The most troublesome feature of the decision appears to the court's ruling on the inapplicability of the business judgment rule. The business judgment rule generally affords directors the presumption that their actions have been made in good faith, on an informed basis, considering the best interests of the corporation.[25] Yet, the Trans Union court decided to scrutinize the process by which the board arrived at its decision, substituting its own judgment regarding the proper procedure for the judgment of the board.

The Trans Union board was comprised of sophisticated business people who had served the corporation for some time. The qualifications of the outside directors included significant business expertise. The five inside directors were collectively employed by the company for 116 years, with 68 years of combined experience as directors. The directors, already quite knowledgeable about corporate affairs, met and deliberated (albeit only two hours) over a business decision. One might have predicted that the business judgment rule would have protected these directors. As noted by a dissenting Justice in Trans Union, directors of the caliber of the directors of Trans Union "are not ordinarily taken by a 'fast shuffle.'"[26]

In reviewing the facts as presented by the dissenting opinion, one could conclude that the directors made an informed business decision and that the finding of gross negligence was unwarranted. The dissent found that the directors were more than well qualified to make an on-the-spot informed business judgment concerning the affairs of Trans Union, including a 100 percent sale of the corporation. The board had repeatedly discussed the problems created by the ITCs. At the meeting at which Van Gorkom presented the offer, the board heard from the company's counsel, who discussed the legal documents. The board then required certain changes in the documents to make it clear that a better offer could be accepted. One could thus conclude that the board did inform itself of the relevant and available facts before deciding in favor of the merger.[27]

The Court of Chancery, and two Delaware Supreme Court justices, all charged with applying the law of Delaware to the facts of this case, found that the business judgment rule protected the Trans Union directors. The Chancery Court, the dissenting justices, and the majority opinion all formulated the business judgment rule in the same fashion. All seemed to agree that the business judgment rule creates the presumption that in making a business decision, the directors of a corporation acted on an informed basis, in good faith, and in the honest belief that the action taken was in the best interest of the company. Yet, the majority of the Delaware Supreme Court held the directors liable for gross neglect, while the Court of Chancery and the dissenting justices would have applied the same business judgment rule to exonerate the directors.

Rather than permitting directors to decide how much time and attention need be given to any particular business decision, the Delaware Supreme Court has indicated that it will closely scrutinize the process utilized in reaching decisions before it will provide business judgment rule protection. Before the Trans Union decision, courts rarely found directors grossly negligent.[28] Gross negligence was found only in the case of absolute neglect.[29]

The Trans Union decision thus seems to evidence a change in Delaware law, tightening the legal constraints of directors. Accordingly, the legal constraint theory predicts that the decision should have a positive impact on the value of Delaware firms relative to firms incorporated elsewhere. The market constraint theory, on the other hand, predicts the opposite result. Trans Union, therefore, provides an opportunity to test these theories empirically. The results of the empirical study are described below.

The 1986 Delaware Legislation

Section 102(b)(7)
Effective July 1, 1986, Delaware law permitted corporations to include the following provision in their articles of incorporation:

> A provision eliminating or limiting the personal liability of a director to the corporation or its stockholders for monetary damages for breach of fiduciary duty as a director, provided that such provision shall not eliminate or limit the liability of a director (i) for any breach of the director's duty of loyalty to the corporation or its stockholders, (ii) for acts or omissions not in good faith or which involve intentional misconduct or a knowing violation of law, (iii) under section 174 of this Title, or (iv) for any transaction from which the

director derived an improper personal benefit. No such provision shall eliminate or limit the liability of a director for any act or omission occurring prior to the date when such provision becomes effective. All references in this subsection to a director shall also be deemed to refer to a member of the governing body of a corporation which is not authorized to issue capital stock.[30]

This law was proposed in Senate Bill 533 and is found in Section 102(b)(7) of Title 8 of the Delaware Code. It was enacted by the Delaware legislature after the Trans Union decision in response to the perceived crisis in the D&O liability insurance industry. The Synopsis to Senate Bill 533 refers to the legislators' concern regarding changes in the market for directors' liability insurance.[31] These changes resulted in the unavailability of D&O liability insurance in many cases.[32] Many persons were unwilling to serve as directors without the protection of insurance.[33]

Section 102(b)(7) permits the shareholders of a corporation to amend the articles of incorporation to exonerate the directors from monetary liability to the corporation or its shareholders for a breach of fiduciary duty of care not involving intentional misconduct, improper payments of dividends, improper stock purchases or redemptions, or a breach of the duty of loyalty. In Trans Union, the court found that the directors breached their fiduciary duty to the stockholders by failing to inform themselves of all information reasonably available to them and relevant to their decision. The Trans Union court did not make any finding of intentional misconduct, bad faith, or breach of the duty of loyalty. If the court were to decide Trans Union today, and if the company had amended its articles of incorporation to eliminate liability in accordance with Section 102(b)(7), it is likely the court would exonerate the directors from monetary liability to the shareholders.

Implications
To the extent that Trans Union can be interpreted as a movement of Delaware law in the direction of the legal constraint theory, Section 102(b)(7) appears to have reversed that trend. In strictly scrutinizing the process by which directors make decisions, the Trans Union court gave less deference to the good faith business decisions of directors than did other courts interpreting the ambit of the business judgment rule. While the Trans Union decision is in line with the legal constraint theory, using legal rules to monitor the activities of the board, Section 102(b)(7) evidences a movement

in line with the market constraint theory. Under Section 102(b)(7), Delaware corporations are permitted to eliminate monetary liability to the corporation and its shareholders for the breach of the fiduciary duty alleged in Trans Union, apparently even in the context of gross negligence.[34] The law now permits the corporation to contract freely with its directors regarding the scope of the directors' personal liability to the corporation. Stockholders are permitted to forgo legal protections available to them in favor of relying on the market to protect their interests.

The Trans Union decision and Delaware's subsequent enactment of Section 102(b)(7) thus provide an opportunity to study the economic effect of a jurisdiction's movement in both the direction of the legal constraint theory and the market constraint theory. This study is described below.

EMPIRICAL EVIDENCE

Trans Union

In order to measure the effects of Trans Union and Section 102(b)(7) on the equity values of firms incorporated in Delaware, we calculate a series of abnormal returns to Delaware firms. The daily abnormal return to Delaware firms is calculated using standard event study methodology.[35] Specifically, the following model was estimated using daily data from January 1981 through December 1984:

$$DEL,t = \alpha + \beta NDEL,t$$

where DEL,t is the daily return to an equally weighted portfolio of all firms incorporated in Delaware and $NDEL,t$ is the daily return to an equally weighted portfolio of firms incorporated elsewhere. α and β are market model parameters.

In order to be included in either sample, a firm had to be listed on either the NYSE or AMEX from January 1, 1981, through December 31, 1986. The Delaware portfolio consists of 593 firms and the non-Delaware portfolio contains 951 firms.

The regression analysis for the four years 1981 through 1984 yields the following estimates (t-statistics are reported in parentheses):

$$DEL,t = -0.0001 + 1.12\,NDEL,t$$
$$(-2.10) \qquad (123.82)$$

The R-squared of the regression is 95.3 and the Durbin-Watson statistic is 2.06.

Using the above predicting equation, we estimate the daily abnormal return to Delaware firms according to the formula:

$$AR\text{-}DEL,t = DEL,t - (0.0001 + 1.12\,NDEL,t)$$

where $AR\text{-}DEL,t$ is the estimated abnormal return to Delaware firms on day t.

Figure 7–1 presents the cumulative abnormal return (the "CAR") to Delaware firms from January 1, 1985, through December 31, 1986. The CAR is the summation of the daily abnormal return, which is defined above. The date of the decision (January 29, 1985) and the effective date of Section 102(b)(7) of the Delaware Code (July 1, 1986) are indicated on the graph.

The data reveal no significant change in the value of Delaware firms around the date of the Trans Union decision. This impression is confirmed by the statistics reported in Table 7–1. The 13-day CAR to Delaware firms around the court decision date is 0.26 percent, with a t-statistic of 0.42. These results suggest that Trans Union had no material effect on the relative values of Delaware firms.

Thus, contrary to either the market or the legal constraint theories, Trans Union does not appear to have had a significant effect on the stock price of Delaware corporations vis-à-vis corporations incorporated in other states. There are several possible explanations for this finding. One possible reason is the persuasive value of Delaware case law on the corporate law of other states. While Trans Union, a decision of the Delaware Supreme Court, is binding precedent only in Delaware, other state courts may follow the lead of Delaware in interpreting their rules of law regarding the duty of care and the business judgment rule. The market may have expected a general application of the Trans Union decision in other jurisdictions. Stock prices of corporations incorporated in states other than Delaware may therefore react in tandem with the prices of the shares of Delaware corporations, and, thus, no significant abnormal returns would be evidenced.

In addition, confounding events may well mask the effect of the

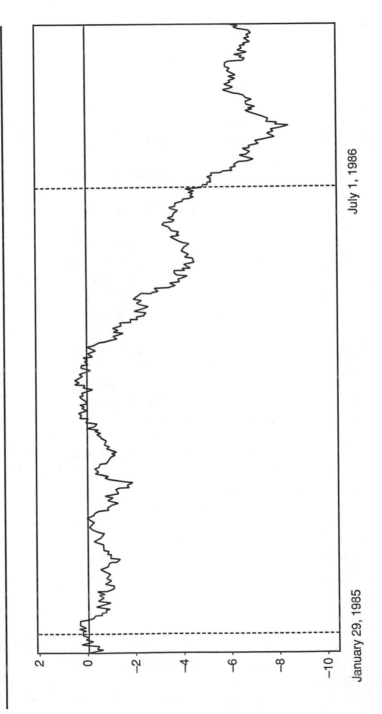

FIGURE 7–1
Cumulative Abnormal Return (CAR) to Delaware Firms (January 1, 1985–December 31, 1986)

TABLE 7–1
Abnormal Return (AR) and Cumulative Abnormal Return (CAR) to Delaware Corporations around the Trans Union Decision (January 29, 1985)

Trading Day	Event Day	AR (%)	T-Stat	CAR (%)	T-Stat
January 21	−6	−0.004	−0.03	−0.004	−0.03
January 22	−5	0.178	1.04	0.174	0.72
January 23	−4	−0.013	−0.07	0.161	0.54
January 24	−3	−0.005	−0.03	0.156	0.46
January 25	−2	−0.030	−0.17	0.126	0.33
January 28	−1	−0.058	−0.34	0.068	0.16
January 29	0	0.228	1.33	0.296	0.65
January 30	1	−0.244	−1.43	0.052	0.11
January 31	2	0.063	0.37	0.115	0.22
February 1	3	0.019	0.11	0.134	0.25
February 4	4	0.108	0.63	0.242	0.43
February 5	5	−0.024	−0.14	0.218	0.37
February 6	6	0.044	0.26	0.262	0.42

Trans Union decision. On the same day Trans Union was decided by the Delaware Supreme Court, the Delaware Court of Chancery upheld the poison pill defense erected by Household International in Moran v. Household International, Inc.[36] It is not at all clear how this decision would affect Delaware firms. We note, however, that the Household International decision was rendered by the Court of Chancery, a trial court in Delaware, and thus should have less impact than the decision of the Delaware Supreme Court in Trans Union.

Furthermore, it may be the case that the Trans Union decision did not increase the liability of corporate officials in general.[37] Rather, Trans Union could be narrowly interpreted as applicable only to directors contemplating a change in corporate control.[38]

Finally, event study methodology has been questioned as to whether it is an appropriate measure of the economic effects of court decisions. Since we find no abnormal stock returns, we need not debate this issue here.[39] We simply note that our finding that Trans Union had no material effect on the market value of Delaware firms may be due more to the ambiguous economic implications of court decisions and less to a serious shortcoming of event study methodology.

Section 102(b)(7)

In contrast to the absence of a market response to Trans Union, the CAR to Delaware firms dropped significantly around the enactment of Section 102(b)(7). Table 7–2 reports the market reaction around the effective date of the legislation. The CAR from six days before through one day after the date on which Section 102(b)(7) became effective is −0.98 percent, with a *t*-statistic of −2.02. The significant decrease in the value of Delaware firms around the effective date of the law is better reflected in the statistics reported in Table 7–3. The 21-day CAR over the month preceding the passage of the law is −1.39, with a *t*-statistic of −1.78. The 22-day CAR over the month following the enactment of the law is −1.28 percent, with a *t*-statis-tic of −1.59. For the entire two-month period, the CAR to the portfolio of Delaware firms is −2.67 percent, with a *t*-statistic of −2.38. Clearly, the passage of the law is associated with a significant decrease in the equity values of firms incorporated in Delaware relative to those of firms incorporated elsewhere.

The significant decrease in the relative values of Delaware firms in the wake of Section 102(b)(7) indicates that the relaxed liability exposure for violations of the duty of care standard allowed by this act is detrimen-

TABLE 7–2
Abnormal Return (AR) and Cumulative Abnormal Return (CAR) to Delaware Corporations around the Enactment of Section 102(b)(7) of the Delaware Code (July 1, 1986)

Trading Day	Event Day	AR (%)	T-Stat	CAR (%)	T-Stat
June 23	−6	−0.321	−1.87	−0.321	−1.87
June 24	−5	0.204	−1.19	−0.525	−2.17
June 25	−4	−0.258	−1.50	−0.783	−2.64
June 26	−3	0.053	0.31	−0.730	−2.13
June 27	−2	−0.131	−0.77	−0.861	−2.25
June 30	−1	−0.054	−0.31	−0.915	−2.18
July 1	0	−0.114	−0.66	−1.029	−2.27
July 2	1	0.054	0.32	−0.975	−2.02
July 3	2	0.016	0.09	−0.959	−1.87
July 7	3	−0.042	−0.25	−1.001	−1.85
July 8	4	0.177	1.03	−0.824	−1.45
July 9	5	−0.225	−1.31	−1.049	−1.77
July 10	6	0.031	0.18	−1.018	−1.65

TABLE 7–3
Cumulative Abnormal Return (CAR) to Delaware Corporations
Pre- and Post-Event (July 1, 1986)

	Holding Period	Trading Days	CAR (%)	T-Statistic
Pre-Event	860602–860630	21	−1.392	−1.78
Post-Event	860701–860731	22	−1.275	−1.59
Total	860602–860731	43	−2.667	−2.38

tal to the wealth of the stockholders of Delaware firms. The results are consistent with the view that the new regime established by Section 102(b)(7) allows corporate managers greater latitude in managing their firms, which in turn increases the agency costs of the corporate firm and reduces the value of the equity claims of these firms.

SUMMARY AND CONCLUSIONS

The objective of this chapter is to gain insight into the relative importance of legal rules and economic forces in explaining the existence of the public corporation. The Trans Union decision and subsequent enactment of Section 102(b)(7) provide an ideal opportunity to empirically study the relative importance of these two theories. If strong liability rules serve as necessary monitoring devices for efficient corporate governance, we expect that the strengthened liability rules pronounced by the Trans Union court will positively affect the wealth of shareholders of Delaware corporations and that the relaxation of such rules by Section 102(b)(7) have a negative effect. Conversely, if market forces sufficiently monitor the behavior of management, the stronger liability rules of Trans Union should decrease shareholder wealth whereas the relaxation of such rules by Section 102(b)(7) should increase shareholder wealth.

In this regard, we studied the effect of these changes in Delaware law on the market value of Delaware corporations. Our results can be summarized as follows.

The Trans Union Decision

We found no effect on the market value of Delaware corporations in the wake of the stronger liability rules espoused by the Trans Union court. This finding is consistent with the view that the decision had no real impact on the way U.S. corporations were managed or the way the common stock of these firms were being priced by the market. Apparently, investors believed that the decision would be applied very narrowly, perhaps only in the context of a takeover.[39]

Our empirical results cannot reject the hypothesis that the Trans Union decision had no real impact on the liability standards of corporate officials. However, this is not the case with the passage of Section 102(b)(7).

Section 102(b)(7)

Our most important results involve the effects of the passage of Section 102(b)(7) of the Delaware Code. We found that the relative value of Delaware firms fell significantly around the enactment of this legislation. Moreover, Delaware firms amending their articles of incorporation to take advantage of the provisions of Section 102(b)(7) suffered statistically significant abnormal losses at that time as well. We interpret these results as suggesting that the provisions of this legislation reduced the liability of corporate officials and that this resulted in a decrease in the value of Delaware corporations. Thus, we conclude that liability rules are a binding constraint on the behavior of corporate officials. Our results indicate that liability rules do matter.[40]

Notes

1. The American Law Institute ("ALI") was founded in 1923 for the purpose of remedying the "increasing uncertainty and complexity" of American law through the establishment of a "Restatement of the Law." The ALI has produced numerous restatements of the common law and has joined the Commissioners on Uniform State Laws in drafting the Uniform Commercial Code. See generally, The American Law Institute, *The American Law Institute 50th Anniversary*, (1973). See also, "Special Project Note, The Corporate Governance Debate and the ALI Proposals: Reform or Restatement?," *Vanderbilt Law Review, 40,* 693–694 (1987), suggesting that the ALI is reforming corporate law with respect to director liability rather than restating it; further suggesting that the ALI should

follow the lead of the courts which have clarified the duty of care and the duty of loyalty owed by directors and officers to the stockholders.

2. See Staff of Securities and Exchange Commission, Senate Committee on Banking, Housing & Urban Affairs, 96th Congress, 2d Session, *Report on Corporate Accountability*, (Comm. print 1980); Brudney, "Corporate Governance, Agency Costs, and the Rhetoric of Contract," *Columbia Law Review, 85*, 1403 (1985); Buxbaum, "Corporate Legitimacy, Economic Theory, and Legal Doctrine," *Ohio State Law Journal, 45*, 515 (1984); Blumberg, "A Need for Supplementary National Legislation," *Commentaries on Corporate Structure and Governance: The ALI-ABA Symposiums 1977–1978*, p. 343 (D. Schwartz, ed., 1979); Cary, "Federalism and Corporate Law: Reflections Upon Delaware," *Yale Law Journal, 83*, 663 (1974); Ratner, "Regulating Management Through Corporate Law," *Commentaries on Corporate Structure and Governance: The ALI-ABA Symposiums 1977–1978*, p. 138 (D. Schwartz, ed., 1979); Comment, "Law for Sale: A Study of the Delaware Corporate Law of 1967," *Pennsylvania Law Review, 117*, 861 (1969).

3. Coase, "The Nature of the Firm," *Economica, 4*, 386 (1937).

4. Manne, "Mergers and the Market for Corporate Control," *Journal of Political Economy, 73*, 110 (1965).

5. Alchian and Demsetz, "Production, Information Costs and Economic Organization," *American Economic Review, 62*, 777 (1972).

6. Jensen and Meckling, "Theory of the Firm: Managerial Behavior, Agency Costs and Ownership Structure," *Journal of Financial Economics, 3*, 305 (1976).

7. Fama, "Agency Problems and the Theory of the Firm," *Journal of Political Economy, 88*, 228 (1980).

8. Fama and Jensen, "Separation of Ownership and Control," *Journal of Law and Economics, 26*, 301 (1983).

9. See for example, Alchian and Demsetz, note 5 above; Fama, note 7 above; Fama and Jensen, note 8 above; Jensen and Meckling, note 6 above; and Manne, note 4 above.

10. See sources in note 1 and 2 above.

11. See sources in note 1 and 2 above.

12. See Fischel and Bradley, "The Role of Liability Rules and the Derivative Suit in Corporate Law: A Theoretical and Empirical Analysis," *Cornell Law Review, 71*, 261 (1986).

13. Smith v. Van Gorkom, 488 A.2d 858 (Del. 1985).

14. 488 A.2d at 874.

15. 488 A.2d at 875–76. The price obtained for the Trans Union stock constituted a 48 percent premium over its last available closing price and a 39 percent premium over the highest price at which the stock had traded during the preceding six years. (Id. at 869, note 9). The Trans Union court stated that "[t]he record is clear that before September 20, Van Gorkom and other members of Trans Union's Board

knew the market consistently undervalued the worth of Trans Union's stock…"
(Id. at 876). Existence of a premium alone was not sufficient evidence of an
informed decision. (Id. at 878).

16. 488 A.2d at 878. See, e.g., Burgman and Cox, "Corporate Directors, Corporate
Realities and Deliberative Process: An Analysis of the Trans Union Case,"
Journal of Corporate Law, 11, 311, 320, 329 (1986); Herzel and Katz, "Smith v.
Van Gorkom: The Business of Judging Business Judgment," *Business Lawyer,
41,* 1187, 1190 (1986); Lee, "Limiting Corporate Directors' Liability: Delaware's
Section 102(b)(7) and the Erosion of the Directors' Duty of Care," *University of
Pennsylvania Law Review, 136,* 239, 249 (1987); Manning, "Reflections and
Practical Tips on Life in the Boardroom After Van Gorkom," *Business Lawyer,
41,* 1, 4 (1985).

17. 488 A.2d at 874–75, 893.

18. Manning, "Reflections and Practical Tips on Life in the Boardroom After Van
Gorkom," *Business Lawyer, 41,* (1985) at Editor's Note: "[A]n agreement was
reached to settle the Van Gorkom litigation by the payment of $23.5 million to
the plaintiff class. Of that amount, a reported $10 million, the policy limit, is to
be provided by Trans Union's directors' and officers' liability insurance carrier.
Although the group which acquired Trans Union in the disputed acquisition was
not a defendant, according to a newspaper account nearly all of the $13.5 million
balance will be paid by the group on behalf of the Trans Union defendant
directors."

19. See, e.g., Burgman and Cox, "Corporate Directors, Corporate Realities and
Deliberative Process: An Analysis of the Trans Union Case," *Business Lawyer,
41,* 313 (1986); Chittur, "The Corporate Director's Standard of Care: Past,
Present, and Future," *Delaware Journal of Corporate Law, 10,* 505, 526–27 (1985);
Herzel, Shepro, and Katz, "From the Boardroom, Next-to-last Word on Endangered
Directors," *Harvard Business Review,* p. 39 (January/February 1987); Glaberson
and Powell, "A Landmark Ruling that Puts Board Members in Peril," *Business
Week,* p. 56 (March 18, 1985); Lee, "Limiting Corporate Directors' Liability:
Delaware's Section 102(b)(7) and the Erosion of the Directors' Duty of Care,"
University of Pennsylvania Law Review, 136, 247 (1987); Manning, "Reflections
and Practical Tips on Life in the Boardroom After Van Gorkom," *Business
Lawyer, 41,* 1 (1985); Comment, "Statutory Limitations on Directors' Liability
in Delaware: A New Look at Conflicts of Interest and the Business Judgment
Rule," *Harvard Journal on Legislation, 24,* 527 (1987); "Corporate Liability
Crisis," *Wall Street Journal,* (August 21, 1986), p. 22, col. 1. But see Altschul,
"Corporate Directors' Liability in the U.S.," *International Financial Law Review, 10,* 33 (1986), "The Smith case does not represent a significant change in
either the law itself or in its application, but it does constitute a novel interpretation
of the facts."

20. See, e.g., Balotti and Gentile, "Commentary from the Bar, Elimination or

Limitation of Director Liability for Delaware Corporations," *Delaware Journal of Corporate Law, 12,* 5, 9 (1987); Block, Barton, and Garfield, "Advising Directors on the D&O Insurance Crisis," *Sec. Reg. Law Journal, 14,* 130 (1986); Chapman, "Statutory Responses to Boardroom Fears," *Columbia Business Law Review, 3,* 749–50 (1987); Herzel, Shepro, and Katz, "From the Boardroom, Next-to-last Word on Endangered Directors," *Harvard Business Review,* p. 38 (January/February 1987); Veasey, Finkelstein, and Bigler, "Delaware Supports Directors with Three-Legged Stool of Limited Liability, Indemnification, and Insurance," *Business Lawyer, 42,* 399, 401 (1987); Borden, "First Thoughts on Decision in Delaware on Trans Union," *New York Law Journal,* (February 25, 1985), p. 1, col. 3; Baum and Byrne, "The Job Nobody Wants," *Business Week,* (September 8, 1986), p. 56; but see "Corporate Directors Stay On," *Management Review, 76,* (July 1987), p. 9, col. 2; Prickett, "An Explanation of Trans Union to 'Henny-Penny' and Her Friends," *Delaware Journal of Corporate Law, 10,* 451 (1985); Quillen, "Trans Union, Business Judgment, and Neutral Principles," *Delaware Journal of Corporate Law, 10,* 465 (1985).

21. See, for example, Easterbrook, "Managers' Discretion and Investors Welfare: Theories and Evidence," *Delaware Journal of Corporate Law, 9,* 540–45 (1984).

22. The original plaintiff, Alden Smith, sought to enjoin the merger. (488 A.2d at 864, note 1). However, after extensive discovery, Smith's motion for a preliminary injunction was denied by the trial court on February 3, 1981. The merger was approved by the Trans Union stockholders on February 10, 1981, and became effective at that time. Thereafter John Gosselin intervened as an additional plaintiff, and Smith and Gosselin were certified to represent the class of persons (excluding defendants) holding Trans Union stock on the relevant dates.

23. 488 A.2d at 867–68.

24. 488 A.2d at 875.

25. Aronson v. Lewis, 473 A.2d 805, 812 (1984). See also, Unocal Corp. v. Mesa Petroleum Co., 493 A.2d 946, 954 (Del. 1985), quoting Aronson v. Lewis; Sinclair Oil Corp. v. Levien, 280 A.2d 717, 720 (Del. 1971), "a court will not interfere with the judgment of a board of directors unless there is a showing of gross and palpable overreaching"; Beard v. Elster, 39 Del. Ch. 153, 165, 160 A.2d 731, 736–38 (1960), because stockholder ratification of a stock option plan for directors does not supply "the necessary element of good faith exercise of business judgment by directors," directors must prove that the plan was at least as favorable to the corporation as would have been required if the optionees were strangers); Auerbach v. Bennett, 47 N.Y.2d 619, 629, 393 N.E.2d 994, 419 N.Y.S.2d 920, 926 1979), business judgment rule "bars judicial inquiry into actions of corporate directors taken in good faith and in the exercise of honest judgment in the lawful and legitimate furtherance of corporate purposes." The directors in Trans Union were not afforded the protection of the business judgment rule because, in the opinion of the Delaware Supreme Court, they were

grossly negligent in ascertaining relevant information for their business decision. Smith v. Van Gorkom, 488 A.2d 858, 881 (Del. 1985). The business judgment rule is inoperative in cases of gross negligence. (Id. at 873). See also Balotti and Gentile, "Commentary from the Bar, Elimination or Limitation of Director Liability for Delaware Corporations," *Delaware Journal of Corporate Law, 12,* 7–9 (1987); Herzel and Katz, "Smith v. Van Gorkom: The Business of Judging Business Judgment," *Business Lawyer, 41,* 1187–88 (1986). The American Law Institute proposes the following formulation of the business judgment rule:

A director or officer does not violate his duty under this Section with respect to the consequences of a business judgment if he: (1) was informed with respect to the subject of the business judgment to the extent he reasonably believed to be appropriate under the circumstances; (2) was not interested in the subject of the business judgment and made the judgment in good faith; (3) had a rational basis for believing that the business judgment was in the best interests of the corporation. (*Principles of Corporate Governance: An Analysis and Recommendations,* Section 401(d)(Tent. Draft No. 3, 1984).

This formulation has been criticized by the Business Roundtable, an organization composed of chief executive officers of approximately 200 large U.S. corporations, as representing an overly narrow formulation of the business judgment rule. ["Pease, Aronson v. Lewis: When Demand Is Excused and Delaware's Business Judgment Rule," *Delaware Journal of Corporate Law, 9,* 39, 75 (1984).] In particular, the Business Roundtable objected to the requirements of reasonable inquiry and rational basics, arguing that they were not uniformly accepted in the law and vitiated the protection of the rule. (Id., citing Memorandum prepared by Counsel for the Roundtable 7–8, January 13, 1984).

26.   488 A.2d at 894 (McNeilly dissenting).

27.   For an account of the facts of Trans Union from the point of view of Trans Union's former chairman and chief executive officer, see "Van Gorkom, The 'Big Bang' for Director Liability: The Chairman's Report," *Directors and Boards, 12,* 17 (1987).

28.   See Chittur, "The Corporate Director's Standard of Care: Past, Present, and Future," *Delaware Journal of Corporate Law, 10,* 505, 521–22 (1985); see also Aronson v. Lewis, 473 A.2d 805, note 6 (Del. 1984), "a long line of Delaware cases holds that director liability is predicated on a standard which is less exacting than simple negligence"; Bishop, "Sitting Ducks and Decoy Ducks: New Trends in the Indemnification of Corporate Directors and Officers," *Yale Law Journal, 77,* 1078, 1099–1100 (1968).

29.   See note 28 above; see also Chittur, "The Corporate Director's Standard of Care: Past, Present, and Future," *Delaware Journal of Corporate Law, 10,* 505, 523–24 (1985), contrasting the qualifications and attentiveness of the Trans Union directors with that of the directors in earlier cases of director liability.

30.   Del. Code Ann. title 8 Section 102(b)(7) (1983 & Supp. 1986). Section 174

[referred to in Section 102(b)(7)(iii)] concerns proscriptions against the unlawful payment of dividends and unlawful stock purchases and redemptions.

31. *Synopsis,* S. 533, 133d Gen. Assembly (1986) at 2.
32. Id.; see, e.g., Hinsey, "Directors' and Officers' Insurance: A Status Report," *Inst. on Sec. Reg., 18–2,* 179 (1986); Taravella and Shapiro, "Psst... Do You Know a D&O Insurer?," *Business Insurance,* (October 20, 1986), p. 26; Veasey, Finkelstein, and Bigler, "Responses to the D&O Insurance Crisis," *Securities & Commercial Regulations, 19,* 263, 265 (1986); Note, "Delaware Amendment Relaxes Directors' Liability," *Washington and Lee Law Review, 44,* 111, 117–18 (1987); Lewin, "Director Insurance Drying Up," *New York Times,* (March 7, 1986), p. D1, col. 2; Hertzberg, "Insurers Beginning to Refuse Coverage on Directors Officers in Takeover Cases," *Wall Street Journal,* (January 21, 1986), p. 3, col. 2; Hilder, "Risky Business: Liability Insurance is Difficult to Find Now for Directors and Officers," *Wall Street Journal,* (July 10, 1985), p. 1, col. 6.
33. *Synopsis,* S. 533, 133d Gen. Assembly (1986) at 2; see Veasey, Finkelstein and Bigler, "Responses to the D&O Insurance Crisis," *Securities & Commercial Regulations, 19,* 263, 265 (1986); Block, Barton, and Garfield, "Advising Directors on the D&O Insurance Crisis," *Sec. Reg. Law Journal, 14,* 131, note 8 (1986); Baum and Byrne, "The Job Nobody Wants," *Business Week,* (September 8, 1986), p. 56–58; Farrel, Welch, Hamid, and Cahan, "The Insurance Crisis: Now Everyone in a Risky Business," *Business Week,* (March 10, 1986), p. 88; Lewin, "Director Insurance Drying Up," *New York Times,* (March 7, 1986), p. D1, col. 3; "Crutcher's Chairman and Three Directors Quit: Lack of Insurance Cited," *Wall Street Journal,* (February 12, 1986), p. 21, col. 2. There was clearly a panic in the boardroom. See also, Armstrong, "Is D&O Insurance Worth the Risk?," *ABA Banking Journal,* (January 1988), p. 36; "Financial Boards Say It's Harder to Attract Qualified Directors," *Journal of Accounting, 162,* 39 (1986); Foley, "The First Line of Defense," *Directors & Boards, 10,* (Spring 1986); Olson, "The D&O Insurance Gap: Strategies for Coping," *Legal Times,* (March 3, 1986), p. 25, col. 1; Honabach and Sargent, "Director Liability Statutes Placed in Perspective," *National Law Journal,* (July 4, 1988), p. 10, col. 1; Cheever, "Liability Fears Scaring Off Potential Board Directors," *New Jersey Law Journal,* (April 23, 1987), p. 1, col. 1; Taravella and Shapiro, "Psst... Do You Know a D&O Insurer?," *Business Insurance,* (October 20, 1986), p. 26; "Corporate Liability Crisis," *Wall Street Journal,* (August 21, 1986), p. 22, col.1; Galante, "The D&O Crisis: Corporate Boardroom Woes Grow," *National Law Journal, 8,* (August 4, 1986), p. 1, col. 3; Brenner, "Some Flaws in Alternative to Directors', Officers' Liability," *American Banker,* (May 16, 1986), p. 14, col. 3; Herzel and Harris, "Uninsured Boards Mount Weak Defense," *Nation Law Journal,* (April 21, 1986), p. 19, col. 1; Victor, "Statutory Response to D&O Crisis Studied," *Legal Times,* (March 31, 1986), p. 1, col. 2; "Businesses Struggling to Adapt as Insurance Crisis Spreads," *Wall Street Journal,* (January

21, 1986), p. 31, col. 1; Hertzberg, "Insurers Beginning to Refuse Coverage on Directors Officers in Takeover Cases," *Wall Street Journal,* (January 21, 1986), p. 3, col. 2; Fowler, "Scarce Corporate Directors," *New York Times,* (January 7, 1986), p. D20, col. 1; Royner, "D&O Indemnity: Discrete Contracts Seen as an Option," *Legal Times,* (November 25, 1985), p. 1, col. 3; Hilder, "Risky Business: Liability Insurance is Difficult to Find Now for Directors and Officers," *Wall Street Journal,* (July 10, 1985), p. 1, col. 6; Leisner, "Boardroom Jitters: A Landmark Decision Upsets Corporate Directors," *Barron's,* (April 22, 1985), p. 34, col. 1; but see, Hazen, "Corporate Directors' Accountability: The Race to the Bottom—The Second Lap," *North Carolina Law Review, 66,* 171, 174 (1987), the D&O insurance industry is merely perceived as being in a crisis, much of which may have been manufactured by insurance companies.

34. Schaffer, "Delaware's Limit on Director Liability: How the Market for Incorporation Shapes Corporate Law," *Harvard Journal of Law & Public Policy, 10,* 665, 668 (1987); Veasey, Finkelstein and Bigler, "Responses to the D&O Insurance Crisis," *Securities & Commercial Regulations, 19,* 267 (1986); Note, "Delaware Amendment Relaxes Directors' Liability," *Washington and Lee Law Review, 44,* 119 (1987).

35. The market model is used in event study methodology. For a detailed explanation of the market model, see E. Fama, *Foundations of Finance, Portfolio Decisions and Securities Prices,* (1976), pp. 66–77. For examples of the use of event studies in determining the economic effects of various laws, see, e.g., Weiss and White, "Of Econometrics and Indeterminancy: A Study of Investors' Reactions to 'Changes in Corporate Law,'" *California Law Review, 75,* 551 (1987); Bhagat, Brickley and Coles, "Managerial Indemnification and Liability Insurance: The Effect on Shareholder Wealth," *Journal of Risk and Insurance, 54,* 721 (1987); Romano, "Law as a Product: Some Pieces of the Incorporation Puzzle," *Journal of Law, Economics, and Organizations, 1,* 225 (1985); Schumann, "State Regulation of Takeovers and Shareholder Wealth: The Effects of New York's 1985 Takeover Statutes," *Bureau of Economics Staff Report to the Federal Trade Commission,* (March 1987).

36. 490 A.2d 1059 (Del. Ch.) *aff'd* 500 A.D. 1346 (Del. 1985).

37. See, e.g., Altschul, "Corporate Directors' Liability in the U.S.," *International Financial Law Review, 10,* 33 (1986); Prickett, "An Explanation of Trans Union to 'Henny-Penny' and Her Friends," *Delaware Journal of Corporate Law, 10,* 451 (1985); Quillen, "Trans Union, Business Judgment, and Neutral Principles," *Delaware Journal of Corporate Law, 10,* 465 (1985).

38. Thus, Trans Union may have been perceived by investors as simply requiring directors to obtain an opinion regarding the fairness of the proposed offer from one or more investment bankers before proceeding with a corporate merger or acquisition. See Macey and Miller, "Trans Union Reconsidered," *Yale Law Journal, 98,* 127 (1988).

39. See, e.g., Weiss and White, "Of Econometrics and Indeterminancy: A Study of Investors' Reactions to 'Changes in Corporate Law,'" *California Law Review, 75*, 589–90 (1987), discussion of limits of event study methodology and the market model; Fox, "The Role of the Market Model in Corporate Law Analysis: A Comment on Weiss and White," *California Law Review, 76*, 1047 (1988), Weiss and White's response to the criticisms of Fox, "A Response to Professor Fox," *California Law Review, 76*, 1047, 1054–55 (1988).

40. For further analysis of the issues raised in this article as well as their effects on the directors' and officers' liability insurance industry, corporations adopting the provisions of Section 102(b)(7), and corporations reincorporating into Delaware in the wake of the enactment of Section 102(b)(7), see Bradley and Schipani, "The Relevance of the Duty of Care Standard in Corporate Governance," *Iowa Law Review, 75*, (forthcoming).

CHAPTER 8

INVESTMENT BANKERS' AND JUDICIAL REVIEW OF CORPORATE ACTION TO DEFEAT HOSTILE TAKEOVERS: COMMENTS ON CHAPTER 6

William T. Allen

It falls to each generation to reinvent the law, to deal with recurring problems as they appear in a new guise, and to struggle to work out solutions to new problems. What judges do in courts is just a part, but it is a part of this process by which our history is refitted for present use. Recognition of this fact provides a helpful starting place for some comment on the subject of Stuart Shapiro's chapter on the business judgment rule and the job of investment bankers in change-in-control transactions. My comments on Mr. Shapiro's chapter fall under two headings.

In inverse order, my second point relates to the notion that I just introduced—that law in courts may sometimes helpfully be viewed through the glasses of a historian. My first comments, however, will be a little more specific in their relation to the responsibilities of investment bankers in contested takeovers and how courts asked to review defensive steps taken by boards of directors may be affected by some aspects of a banker's work.

William T. Allen is Chancellor (presiding judge) of the Delaware Court of Chancery which is a non-jury trial court that in effect is the nation's only specialized court of corporation law. He holds the J.D. 1972 - University of Texas.

THE BANKER'S ROLE IN TAKEOVER
TRANSACTIONS

First, it is the case that every board or special committee that is required to deal with a proposed change-in-control transaction will, these days, retain investment bankers, along with legal specialists, to advise it. Those advisors will be experienced in takeover fights, and the directors, if they have been lucky, will not be. The bankers and the lawyers will be invaluable and will be at the center of the process. But it is important for all participants to recall at all times that the duty to exercise corporate powers rests with the board or a duly constituted committee. While the board may retain advisors and may appropriately rely upon their advice, ordinarily the board may not delegate to its advisors ultimate responsibility for the transaction. This basic proposition is sometimes lost sight of. Too frequently it appears that, in the language of the Delaware Supreme Court in its recent Macmillan opinion,[1] the special committee appears "supine," a passive instrumentality whose actions appear frankly underserving of independent respect.[2] The RJR-Nabisco transaction appears (at least on the record created as an application for preliminary injunction) to have been a counter example in which active advisors (both lawyers and bankers) did not, in fact, supplant a special board committee that itself appeared active and well motivated.[3]

In all events, it is well to remind the legal advisors that it is the board and not its advisors that must be seen as exercising judgment if deference to that judgment is to be expected.

Second, courts who frequently see takeover litigation come quickly to realize that even in the instance in which the special committee appears energetic, well informed, and well motivated, the role of the committee's advisors will be critically important. Thus, if one advising on the transaction seeks to maximize the prospect for real judicial deference, he or she will attempt to assure that the advisors are and appear to be independent. Suspicions of bias can arise from a number of sources, and one may be unable to remove them completely in any particular instance. The firm's traditional banker may be in a position to give the best informed opinion in the limited time that Rule 14D–9 permits.[4] Yet, that firm, with its existing business relationship with current management, may seem subject to a certain influence, at least in a transaction in which management is a bidder for the company.

A source of apparent "interest" that will be less difficult to remove is that which may rise from the firm's compensation arrangement with the banker-advisor.   The courts have not as yet probed this subject very deeply, but it is plainly the case that some compensation arrangements do create in the banker a financial incentive to prefer one outcome rather than another.   In such circumstances, legal counsel experienced in litigation would rarely advise that his or her client could expect a court to be unaffected by that fact.   Indeed, in the Interco case to which Mr. Shapiro refers, the investment banker advising the board was seen as having a rather straightforward, garden-variety conflict of interest.[5]

Third, another area of judicial concern, and one that rarely works its way into opinion, is the reliability of the projections that the banker is given.   Projections, of course, form a critical source of information in arriving at an investment banker's opinion on adequacy or fairness.   It is, I submit, human nature to be somewhat suspicious of projections that are created after an unsolicited proposal to merge presents itself, particularly if they are materially more optimistic than earlier projections.   I suppose an investment banker can do little about the company's projections unless they appear unsupportable, in which event he can decline to use them, an unlikely response.   But when new projections that are materially more optimistic form an important part of the ground for an opinion, one might expect a court, unless persuaded otherwise on the particular facts, to show less deference to a board decision premised in part on such opinion than would otherwise be expected.

The fourth observation I make relates to the nature of the opinion itself.   I refer now to what I think of as the first substrate of the opinion that the proposed transaction is or is not fair or adequate.   Beneath such an opinion, so to speak, will be a lot of analytical work.   The first substrate beneath it is typically a determination by the banker of a range of values within which the fair value of the firm is seen as falling.   This range of fair value for the firm will, of course, represent a judgment derived from a number of other ranges of value derived from applying different methodologies to the firm's financial data.   Courts have, of course, taken note of the remarkable ability of bankers from time to time to shift this range upward very materially during a contest for control without a material change in the business of the firm for the larger financial context within which the firm exists.[6]   But I do not here refer to any such tendency, but rather to the rarer practice of not supporting an opinion with a supporting view as to a range of fair value at all.

For example, in In Re Trans World Airlines, Inc. Shareholders Litigation,[7] it appears that a very respected investment banking firm generated a number of "reference ranges" for the firm that, taken together, covered a huge range (on a per share basis from $14.50 to $66.29) and then, without going through the exercise of reducing these variously generated ranges to a single range of value, simply opined that the transaction, as finally proposed, was fair. Value is always a judgment; and in these circumstances, the best one can do is to come to a view, competently and in good faith, of a range within which that value is most likely to fall. But unless an investment banker is willing to try to reduce the several "reference ranges" it generates to a single range of fair value, as is customarily done, the board or committee may be left relying to a quite uncomfortable extent upon judgment that has not been sufficiently rationalized or explained. This was a concern at the preliminary injunction phase in the TWA case.

ADEQUACY OF THE BUSINESS JUDGMENT RULE TODAY

I pass beyond these specifics on the role of investment bankers in takeover contests to a more general thought inspired by Mr. Shapiro's chapter. It is with respect to this thought that I referred earlier to the work of each generation in refitting the law to meet current problems—for that is precisely what Unocal[8] and the cases applying its broad holding are doing.

In the field of corporation law, the dominant problems of this era are the problems that arise from the contest for control of publicly traded corporations. Prominent among them is the question: How should a court go about reviewing the validity of director action taken to defeat a proposed change-in-control transaction when shareholders complain? Does the business judgment rule provide the pertinent form of judicial review?

It is not self-evident that it should. The business judgment rule is a rule of judicial creation with its roots in the 19th century.[9] Most basically, that rule reflects the fact that ours is an economic order in which investment choices and implementing business decisions are chiefly made by private persons, not by government functionaries or judges. Thus, the business judgment rule is at once a reflection of our free market economy and one of those rules that help define and create that economy. Among the reasons that courts refrain under the business judgment rule from passing upon the wisdom of a business decision, when it has been made in good faith and with an appropriate level of consideration, is that in our social order courts are (correctly, I would say) not thought to be very good institutionally at making such judgments.

But a completely hands-off approach has not been thought appropriate either. Despite the literature to which Professors Bradley and Schipani point us, the law has generally assumed that, absent some legal controls, directors would have a tendency to expropriate corporate wealth. Thus, self-dealing transactions have generally not been subject to the limited review of other business transactions. Rather, directors have been required to establish the complete fairness of the terms of a transaction between themselves and the corporation.[10]

The paradigm case for application of the business judgment rule is a suit in which shareholders claim damages, on the part of the corporation, for loss arising from a transaction undertaken in the pursuit of the firm's ongoing business—a decision to launch a new product, for example, or build a new plant. The application of the rule to preclude liability for losses of this type is so well established today that suits of this nature are generally not brought.

Today, prototype corporation law litigation involves not a challenge to a board decision in pursuit of the firm's ordinary business, but to board action taken, allegedly, in an effort to defeat an attempted acquisition of control over the corporation.[11] One could have argued one way or the other whether board decisions made for this purpose should be subject to a business judgment form of analysis. But the courts presented with this issue did not hesitate to review questions concerning "defensive" corporate steps under the traditional business judgment rule.[12]

The Delaware Supreme Court was the first court to recognize that litigation arising from steps taken to defeat a proposed acquisition of corporate control involved considerations not present in the simpler cases involving board decisions concerning the business operations of the firm. In Unocal, which is nicely summarized by Shapiro, the court, speaking through Justice Moore, made a necessary and important innovation. I have elsewhere referred to Unocal as "the most innovative and promising case in our recent corporation law."[13] It is the first giant step in formulating a business judgment rule for our age.

The job is not complete. Unocal opens a field for careful new work. Macmillan appears to expand that field. The principal remaining job is the formulation or refinement of a legal test for deciding whether an act *is* reasonable in response to the legitimate corporate goal sought. The game is still afoot. For those who, like Professor Gilson, welcome the Unocal innovation,[14] as well as for those who regard it as a dangerous experiment, the prize is yet to be won or lost. But the forces to which the business judgment rule originally responded remain powerful and are deeply respected by courts. Those who publicly decry the dawn of a new age in which courts will freely reach out to second-guess business decisions reached in good faith have misread the stars or the opinions.

Notes

1. Mills Acquisition Co. v. Macmillan, Inc., Del. Supr., Nos. 415 and 416, 1988 (Cons.) (May 3, 1989).
2. Attached are excerpted portions of an apposite unreported Chancery Court opinion in litigation arising out of the transaction in which TWA was taken private. The facts are enlightening as to how a special committee can misunderstand, in my view at least, the responsibility of such a committee and the role of its banker-advisor.
3. In Re RJR-Nabisco, Inc. Shareholders Litigation, Del. Ch., C.A. No. 10389 (January 31, 1989); Freedman v. Restaurant Assoc., Del Ch., C.A. No. 9212 (October 16, 1987).
4. See 17 C.F.R. § 240.14d–9; that rule of the Securities Exchange Commission requires the board to communicate its recommendation, which may be favorable, unfavorable, or neutral, as to the acceptance or rejection of the offer to the company's shareholders within ten days of the commencement of a public tender offer for the company's shares.
5. City Capital Associates v. Interco Incorporated, Del. Ch., 551 A.2d 787 (1988). I say "was seen" to be historically accurate while acknowledging that some might disagree. There the banker had a financial interest (opportunity for additional compensation) in seeing the board's preferred outcome eventuate. Yet it was this advisor's opinion about future value that the board importantly relied upon in reaching a decision as to what was a preferred outcome.
6. Mills Acquisition Co. v. Macmillan, Inc., Del. Supr., Nos. 415 and 416, 1988 (consolidated), slip. op. pp. 20–21, 25; In Re Anderson Clayton Shareholders Litigation, Del. Ch., 519 A.2d 669, 674 (1986).
7. In Re Trans World Airlines, Inc. Shareholders Litigation, Del. Ch., Cons. C. A. No. 9844 (October 21, 1988), excerpts appended.
8. Unocal Corp. v. Mesa Petroleum Co., Del Supr. 493 A.2d 946 (1985).
9. See generally, Arsht, "The Business Judgment Rule Revisited," *Hofstra Law Review, 8,* 93 (1979); Block, *The Business Judgment Rule: Fiduciary Duties of Corporate Directors and Officers,* 2d edition, (1988).
10. Guth v. Loft, Del. Supr., 5 A.2d 503 (1939).

11. A list of such cases decided in just the last four years would be very lengthy. Such a list might include, for example:

    Revlon v. MacAndrews & Forbes Holdings, Inc., Del. Supr., 506 A.2d 173 (1986);

    Moran v. Household International, Inc., Del Supr., 500 A.2d 1346 (1985);

    Ivanhoe Partners v. Newmont Mining, Del. Supr., 535 A.2d 1334 (1987);

    Hanson Trust PLC v. ML SCM Acquisition, Inc., 781 F.2d 264 (2d Cir., 1986);

    Edelman v. Fruehauf, 798 F.2d 882 (6th Cir., 1986);

    CFRT v. Federated Department Stores, Inc., 683 F. Supp. 522 (S.D.N.Y., 1988);

    In Re J.P. Stevens & Co., Inc. Shareholders Litigation, Del. Ch., 542 A.2d 770 (1988);

    City Capital Associates Limited v. Interco Inc., Del. Ch., 551 A.2d 787 (1988);

    Shamrock Holdings, Inc. v. Polaroid Corp., Del Ch., C.A. Nos. 10075 and 10079, Berger, V.C. (January 6, 1989).

12. See, e.g., Johnson v. Trueblood, 629 F.2d 278 (3d Cir., 1980); Panter v. Marshall Field & Co., 646 F.2d 271 (7th Cir., 1981), but see Judge Cudahy's dissent at 646 F.2d 299.

13. City Capital Associates v. Interco Inc., Del. Ch., 551 A.2d 787 (1988).

14. Gilson and Kraakman, "Delaware's Intermediate Standard for Defensive Tactics," *Business Lawyer, 44,* 247 (1989).

APPENDIX TO CHAPTER 8

IN THE COURT OF CHANCERY OF THE STATE OF DELAWARE IN AND FOR NEW CASTLE COUNTY

In Re: }
                                          }
    Trans World Airlines, Inc.   }   Consolidated
    Shareholders Litigation   }   Civil Action No. 9844

[Excerpt from]

Memorandum Opinion

                 Date Submitted: September 20, 1988
                 Date Decided: October 21, 1988

On September 7, 1988, the minority shareholders of Trans World Airlines, Inc. ("TWA"), a Delaware corporation, voted by an overwhelming majority to approve a proposed merger transaction by which entities controlled by TWA's dominating shareholder, Carl C. Icahn, would acquire all of the voting stock of the Company (excepting 10% to be owned by an Employee Stock Ownership Plant). In the proposed merger, each share owned by the public shareholders would be converted into the right to receive $20 per share in cash and $30 in principal amount of a new 12% subordinated debenture due in 2008. The vote was pursuant to a commitment from Mr. Icahn, who controls 77% of TWA's common stock, to vote his shares in the same proportion as the public shares were voted. Over 96% of the public shares voting approved the transaction.

These consolidated class action cases seek to enjoin the effectuation of this going private transaction. Plaintiffs offer several theories to justify this strong medicine. Those theories may be divided into two classes: substantive fiduciary duty theories and adequacy of disclosure theories. As to the claim of substantive unfairness, plaintiffs claim, in summary, that (1) the price proposed is unfairly low; (2) that the transaction was timed to mask the upward trend of TWA's earnings; and (3) that a special two member committee of the TWA board that purported to represent the interests of the public shareholders in the negotiation process with Mr. Icahn, (a) misunderstood its responsibility to seek to negotiate the best available transactions, (b) as a result, was passive, and (c) relied entirely upon an investment banker who, as it knew, had a material conflict of interest, and who never proceeded with its own analysis of value far enough to reduce its view to a single range of fair value. The special committee, therefore, is said to have had no dependable basis to determine that the price offered was in the best interests of the minority shareholders and the members of the special committee knew or should have known that fact.

Plaintiffs' disclosure theories claim that the resounding approval of the proposed transaction is an undependable indicia of public shareholder preference because critical (or at least material) facts were not disclosed to the shareholders in the proxy solicitation materials. Five specific points are focused upon.

***

These matters, now consolidated, are before the court on plaintiffs' motion for a preliminary injunction. Such a motion, of course, presents no occasion to resolve finally the factual and legal issues raised by the pleadings. Rather, the court is required to make a preliminary assessment of the probability that plaintiffs will be able, at trial, to establish the wrongs alleged. More fundamentally, the court is required on such a motion to determine whether the act sought to be enjoined preliminarily will, if accomplished, result in an injury to plaintiffs that may not be adequately remedied thereafter, either through an award of money or a decree for equitable relief. In addition, in concluding that a situation is one in which preliminary equitable relief is appropriately granted, it is essential for the court to consider as well all of the circumstances of the case as they then appear, to balance the equities, as it is customarily said, in order that it be reasonably content that the risk of any harm its order may create does not outweigh the good that the remedy seeks to achicvc. The legal test is well settled and noncontroversial. See, e.g., Ivanhoe Partners v. Newmont Mining Corp., Del. Supr., 535 A.2d 1334 (1987).

***

I.

The background of the proposed merger begins in 1985 when Carl C. Icahn and entities controlled by him acquired a large block of stock in TWA. The incumbent board attempted to resist Mr. Icahn by arranging an alternative merger, but failed in this attempt. Once the TWA board's resistance was overcome, it was envisioned by all involved that the Icahn entities would arrange a merger transaction that would eliminate the public shareholders from TWA. Such a transaction was first proposed in the spring of 1985. Mr. Icahn proposed to pay the minority shareholders $19.50 in cash and $4.50 in face amount of a new series of preferred stock. This proposed merger was abandoned when TWA announced disappointing financial results in December 1985. It is said that Mr. Icahn's financing for the proposed merger was withdrawn by his investment banker necessitating his withdrawal of the proposal.

The merger was again proposed on July 22, 1987, when Mr. Icahn announced an offer to purchase shares of TWA common stock for $20 in cash and $20 in principal amount of a 20-year 12% subordinated debenture. In response, the TWA board established a special committee, comprising directors Edward Crane and Lester Cox, to review the terms of the proposal. Mr. Crane and Mr. Cox are former directors of Ozark Airlines and the only TWA directors that are arguably "outsiders." This committee retained the now defunct law firm of Finley, Kumble, etc., as its attorneys, and the investment banking firm of Dillon, Read & Co., Inc. ("Dillon Read"), as its financial advisor. Dillon Read was engaged to give financial advice to the committee and to render an opinion as to the fairness, from a financial point of view, of any offer extended. In carrying out that function, Dillon Read interviewed TWA's senior officers, as well as Mr. Icahn, and examined TWA's asset appraisals, historical financial results, operations and prospects. In connection with its review, Dillon Read gave the committee several written comparative analyses of various aspects of TWA's financial position.

After doing this work, Dillon Read concluded on September 10, 1987, that it was not in a position to opine that the offer of $20 cash and $20 face amount of debenture was fair.

At the special committee's request, Dillon Read commenced negotiations with Mr. Icahn and his representatives which took place by phone and in person during the course of the next month. It is said that the price offered by Mr. Icahn in mid-October—$20 in cash and $25 face amount of a 12% subordinated debenture—was the result of these negotiations. On October 15, Dillon Read announced its willingness to issue an opinion that that proposal was fair from a financial point of view. A press release announcing the approval of the revised proposal was issued the following day. The stock market break of October 19, 1987, however, intervened and Mr. Icahn terminated the second proposal on October 20. At the time the second proposal was withdrawn, Mr. Icahn owned 73% of TWA's stock.

Consideration of the Present Proposal

The proposal now under consideration was announced on April 22, 1988, the same day on which the Company announced very favorable financial results for the first quarter of 1988. The special committee, still comprising Messrs. Cox and Crane, was again asked to consider the proposal. It elected to retain Dillon Read as investment banker, and continued with its prior legal counsel, now associated with another firm. The latest proposal remained at $20 in cash but increased the face amount of the 12% subordinated debenture to $29.

The members of the special committee appear to have had a narrow view of the responsibilities they assumed in accepting service on that committee. Mr. Cox testified:

Q: My questions now refer to the independent committee.

Did you understand that, in negotiating with Mr. Icahn, it was your function, and the function of Dillon Read, to get the highest value within the range of fairness that you could in negotiations with Mr. Icahn?

***

A: Our function wasn't to deal with Mr. Icahn at all, the independent committee. That was Dillon Read's charge to do that. Their charge was to negotiate with Mr. Icahn until they felt they could render their fairness opinion, and whatever that range was, I don't know. (Cox Dep. at 127–128).

Mr. Crane had a similar perception of the duties of the committee:

Q: Was it your concern that, in negotiations, that you would be able to obtain the highest price that could be obtained?

***

A: No, it was not our intent to obtain the highest price possible.

Our charge was to determine whether the offer was fair to the minority shareholders, and we engaged investment bankers to determine whether it was fair from a financial standpoint.

I think we would have had an impossible charge to determine what is the highest value that could be achieved.

Further, our charge was to evaluate the offers that were on the table from Mr. Icahn.

Q: Did you instruct Dillon Read to attempt to get the highest possible value from Mr. Icahn?

***

A: No, we did not instruct them to get the highest price. In 1987, they indicated that they could not render an opinion based on the original offer, and they were asked to go back and negotiate the possibility of an increase in Mr. Icahn's offer.

Q: Was it your understanding that Dillon Read was attempting to negotiate the highest possible price within a range of fair value?

***

A: I think I have just answered the question. No, we did not tell Dillon Read to get the highest price.

> We asked, is the offer fair... (Crane Dep. at 113–115).

The committee appears to have relied almost completely upon the efforts of Dillon Read, both with respect to the evaluation of the fairness of the price offered and with respect to such negotiations as occurred. This is not itself unusual in concept, although a number of factors make this heavy reliance somewhat unusual in this instance. First, as pointed out above, the directors did not seem to understand that their duty was to strive to negotiate the highest or best available transaction for the shareholders whom they undertook to represent. Second, it is not clear that Dillon Read itself thought its responsibility was to push for the best available price rather than one it could regard as falling within a range of fairness. Dillon Read's Mr. Yancey, who was in charge of the assignment for the firm, testified as follows:

> [O]ur role was to provide the independent committee with our opinion with respect to the fairness of the consideration being offered by the Icahn entities to the minority interest of TWA... (Yancey Dep. at 14).

Third, Dillon Read never brought its various analyses down to a single range of values for TWA shares...and the special committee in this case, appearing to reflect a complacency referable to an imperfect appreciation of the proper scope and purpose of such a special committee, did not ask its advisor to express a view about a range of fair value for TWA shares held by the minority shareholders.

At a meeting on May 5 Dillon Read presented its various analyses to the special committee. The special committee then sought an indication of Dillon Read's view of the fairness of the $20/$29 offer then on the table. Plaintiffs assert that Dillon Read, in effect, there indicated that it found that offer to be unfair. While I cannot here finally resolve factual disputes, for purposes of this motion, I accept Dillon Read's testimony that it refrained from expressing an opinion because it felt the $20/$29 offer was fair and that to express such a view would diminish the opportunity for further improvement. The committee instructed Mr. Yancey of Dillon Read to attempt to increase consideration from Mr. Icahn. That was done the following day by telephone. In that exchange, Mr. Icahn—according to his testimony—asked Mr. Yancey:

> Are you telling me, in all honesty... I remember saying this to him... are you telling me in all honesty, you are telling me this is unfair or even inadequate? This offer is the right offer...

to which Yancey replied:

> I think you should go higher. (Icahn Dep. at 68).

Faced with this weak response, Mr. Icahn increased the paper part of this offer one dollar (about $.63 of cash value). He stated that this would be his last, his highest offer. Dillon Read did not press Mr. Icahn further, but agreed to issue its fairness opinion on the resulting price of $20 in cash and $20 face amount 12% debenture.

The board of TWA adopted the position that Dillon Read and the independent committee eventually reached. Following Mr. Icahn's offer, which Dillon Read accepted as having reached a level which could be called fair, the board unanimously approved and adopted the merger agreement. Messrs. Icahn, Kingsley, and Schnall abstained from voting on the decision.

A proxy statement was issued on August 12, 1988, and the transaction has since been approved by 95% of the minority stockholders.

***

II.

Consideration of the pending motion to preliminarily enjoin the effectuation of the merger authorized on September 7 entails consideration of the effect, in the circumstances presented, of two techniques of corporate governance, each of which is designed to assure nonjudicial protections to minority shareholders in the setting of an interested merger. Both the device of the special negotiating committee of disinterested directors and the device of a merger provision requiring approval by a majority of disinterested shareholders, when properly employed, have the judicial effect of making the substantive law aspect of the business judgment rule applicable and, procedurally, of shifting back to plaintiffs the burden of demonstrating that such a transaction infringes upon right of minority shareholders. By referring to the substantive aspects of the rule, I refer to the fact that the burden that is shifted back to plaintiffs by the proper use of these devices is a particular and a particularly difficult one. Both of these devices were treated by our Supreme Court in its well-noted opinion in Weinberger v. UOP, Inc., Del. Supr., 457 A.2d 701 (1983). Thus, to be seen now as having a reasonable probability of success on their claims, plaintiffs must, at the least, establish a substantial basis to doubt the effectiveness of both of these devices in this instance.

As to the special committee, plaintiffs claim, in brief, that it was so passive, ill-informed and confused as to its mission that its actions can be accorded no effect. It is claimed that the members of that committee never properly considered the value of TWA shares, indeed, had no view at all on the critical subject, were uninformed on material aspects of value, had a fundamental misunderstanding of their responsibilities, and were advised by an investment banker who itself never arrived at a view as to a range of value for the TWA minority shares (or the shares of the Company generally), and who had a conflict of interest.

If these allegations were ultimately sustained, the result would be, not as plaintiffs contend—that the transaction itself would be deemed to constitute a breach of duty—but that the burden shifting effect of the independent negotiating committee would not obtain and Mr. Icahn and his affiliates would, putting other matter to one side, be required to establish the entire fairness of the transaction at trial.

The majority of the minority voting provision, however, provides to defendants an alternative technique to avoid the heavy burden of establishing the entire fairness of this transaction, even if the special committee is found to be ineffective to shift the burden. With respect to that technique, defendants must show that the ratifying vote of the disinterested shareholders was on complete information. This, plaintiffs say, defendants cannot do. The proxy statement, plaintiffs contend, was materially misleading and deficient.

***

I have concluded that, in light of the record as it now appears, the current motion should be decided on the preliminary view that the special committee did not supply an acceptable surrogate for the energetic, informed, and aggressive negotiation that one would reasonably expect from an arm's-length adversary. Weinberger envisions that minority interests might be protected by a special committee that did emulate that arm's-length process. (See Weinberger, 457 A.2d 701, note 7.) Experience has shown that that procedure can work well. See, for example, Freedman v. Restaurant Associates, Inc., Del. Ch., C.A. No. 9212, Allen, C. (October 16, 1987). But the burden shifting effect will not occur where the special committee did not adequately understand its function—to aggressively seek to promote and protect minority interests— or was not adequately informed about the fair value of the firm and the minority shares in it. This motion does not occasion any final determination of the legal effect of the actions taken by the special committee. I am satisfied, however, that such substantial questions have been raised as to its effectiveness that, for these purposes, no weight may be accorded to its actions. Thus, so far as the special committee device is concerned, this case currently appears to be one in which defendants do bear the burden to establish the entire fairness of the transaction.

Turning to the majority of the minority voting provision, I also am left, having reviewed the limited record available, with a number of unresolved doubts concerning the adequacy of the proxy disclosures. Those matters are explained below. For that reason, I cannot regard the approving vote of a majority of disinterested shareholders as having a preclusive effect on the present motion, which it clearly would otherwise have as a practical matter.

Accordingly, I conclude for these purposes that defendants will bear the burden to show the entire fairness of the transaction at trial, even though plaintiffs continue on this application to bear the burden to establish their entitlement to the preliminary relief sought. See Joseph v. Shell Oil Co., Del. Ch., 482 A.2d 335 (1984). My assessment of the merits of plaintiffs' contentions—both with respect to the inadequacy of price and the inadequacy of disclosure—does not yield the degree of confidence that, in these circumstances, would justify enjoining the effectuation of the merger. A number of circumstances persuade me that more is needed than has here been shown.

First, although Mr. Icahn is a controlling shareholder who bears fiduciary obligations, he also has rights that may not be ignored. His rights include a right to effectuate a transaction of this kind so long as the terms are intrinsically fair. Since as a controlling shareholder he may do so for reasons unrelated to the corporation's business, his principal, but not sole, obligation as a controlling shareholder in a self-interested merger is to pay a price that is completely fair to the minority considering all relevant circumstances (including timing of the transaction). Thus, a central issue here, ultimately, is whether the price proposed and approved is fair considering all of the circumstances. The proposed merger *may*, in fact, offer such a price. Dillon Read apparently concluded that the price was fair. Plaintiffs' expert has reached a very different conclusion, but I can make no responsible choice between these two expert valuations now. Accordingly, to enjoin the transaction now would be plainly to injure the interests of (and perhaps infringe the right of) Mr. Icahn with no confidence that the price proposed is not entirely fair.

Secondly, a huge majority of class members have approved this transaction and expect the transaction to be closed shortly. While the record does not show the composition of the public shareholders, it is noteworthy that the market has known for about three years that this merger would be effectuated sooner or later, and the huge margin by which it was approved—when the minority knew that it alone had power to reject it—is not without significance in evaluating the interests of the class members.

Thirdly, if an injunction is denied on the assumption that the price is entirely fair, and that assumption is proven at trial to be incorrect, an award of damages to the class, with prejudgment interest, will be effective to compensate for any injury sustained. This is not an instance in which calculation of damages (i.e., an "entirely fair" price) would be more difficult or speculative later. We have no ongoing contest for control. Moreover, here an award of damages would not be so large in relation to the financial ability of the defendants to pay as to make resort to a damage alternative a formalistic fiction, as it may be in some instances in which enormous personal liability from individuals is the alternative to a transaction related preliminary remedy.

If an injunction were to be granted on the alternative assumption that the price is not completely fair, and that assumption were proven incorrect at trial, there would be no effective way to remedy any resulting loss to Mr. Icahn occasioned by the mistake. It would be difficult to prove a loss resulting from such an error. Moreover, even more practically, given the large amount that the Icahn entities will withdraw from the enterprise in connection with the merger and the relatively small number of shares in the class, the entry of an injunction would no doubt create a substantial pressure on defendants to settle this claim promptly by paying more money, even if the price already offered is entirely fair.

While this court does seek to protect the rights of minority shareholders who are subject to the power of a dominant shareholder, it does not seek to be a partisan on their behalf.

I therefore conclude that, even though plaintiffs have raised serious questions about the effectiveness of the special committee, and about the adequacy of the disclosure, they have not sufficiently demonstrated that it is likely that the price offered is not fair, that the transaction otherwise constitutes a breach of fiduciary duty, or that the disclosure is inadequate. The availability of an action for rescission or, more realistically, damages, and the inability effectively to protect the defendants from the consequences of an improvident grant of the remedy, in addition, lead me to decline to issue the remedy sought.

***

CHAPTER 9

LAW AND MARKETS AS SOCIAL PRODUCTS: COMMENTS ON CHAPTER 7

William T. Allen

Professors Bradley and Schipani saw in the juxtaposition of the opinion of the Supreme Court of Delaware in the Trans Union case,[1] and the enactment 18 months later by the Delaware General Corporation Law, a unique opportunity to test empirically what they understood to be two opposing theoretical explanations of why corporate managers have not regularly looted corporations to such an extent as to render the corporate form of organization unworkable. The premise that such a theory is called for is that Professors Berle and Means, in their famous study,[2] have shown that the shareholders of large-scale publicly traded corporate enterprise in this country do not exercise effective control over the management of the enterprise. Thus, the question: If shareholders do not control directors, what has prevented directors from simply expropriating much of a firm's capital?

Bradley and Schipani tell us that they seek to test two competing explanations why the corporate form continues as a vital—indeed, the dominant—form of economic organization despite the separation of ownership and control. Those theories are said to look, on the one hand, to

William T. Allen is Chancellor (presiding judge) of the Delaware Court of Chancery which is a non-jury trial court that in effect is the nation's only specialized court of corporation law. He holds the J.D. 1972 - University of Texas. The author's comments are addressed to the conference paper presented by Professors Bradley and Schipani and not necessarily to the revision presented as Chapter 7 of this volume.

147

legal rules as the effective constraint on corporate managers and, on the other hand, to the discipline of the various markets within which the corporation and its managers must function as supplying the significant (optimum) constraint on self-interest.[3]

Professors Bradley and Schipani were, in my view, incorrect in their imaginative insight that the Delaware Supreme Court's opinion in Trans Union and the later adoption of Section 102(b)(7) did provide an opportunity to test the validity of those competing views of the sources of effective social control of director conduct. Analysis of the relative stock price movement of Delaware corporations during periods coincident with these events does not permit the authors to satisfy their goal: "to gain insight into the importance of legal rules on the one hand and economic forces on the other in explaining the continued prosperity of the public corporation." Indeed, the study is not only inconclusive but is, in my opinion, not legitimately suggestive of the insight sought. This is in part a result of what the data simply fails to show, and in part it is because the inferences sought to be drawn from what the authors say their data show are infected by flawed theory, or so I believe.

My comments are broken down into two parts. First, I have a few remarks directed to the predicate findings of the Bradley and Schipani paper, touching upon the Trans Union aspect of the study and then turning to the Section 102 aspect. Second, I touch briefly upon the fundamental flaws, as I see them, in the premises from which the authors' larger conclusions are inferred.

BRADLEY AND SCHIPANI AND THE TRANS UNION DECISION

Turning first to the measurement of cumulative abnormal returns to Delaware corporations following the Trans Union opinion, my comments will necessarily be somewhat truncated. It is the case that the Trans Union decision was met with surprise and concern by those who sit on corporate boards or represent corporate directors. The authors of this study, however, are incorrect, in my opinion, in their premise that the Trans Union decision "appears to represent a change in Delaware law." Moreover, their assumption that Trans Union represents a "tightening" of "the legal constraints on directors" is a contestable proposition. That opinion did not purport to represent a formal or doctrinal change in Delaware corporation law. The more difficult question was whether it implied that the same formal law would be applied in a new fashion in the future. The question raised concern and confusion. It has not, I think, been laid to rest; but for a period there was uncertainty. The significant point, however, is that it was never plain that the Trans Union case represented a generalizable event.

Thus, while the Trans Union decision generated an enormous amount of discussion during the time the world was unsure what the opinion might imply, and while it apparently provided the D&O industry with an opportunity to raise its premiums, it did not plainly represent a tightening of existing rules of liability nor did it represent a change in the governing Delaware law.

It is not surprising that Bradley and Schipani find no significant "abnormal returns" to the hypothetical basket of common stock of Delaware corporations following the Trans Union decision. Experts had no confidence that one could generalize from the case; one would hope that a marginally rational market would not implicitly to do.

Moreover, the coincidence of the Chancery Court opinion in Moran v. Household Finance[4] being issued the same day as the Trans Union opinion cannot be ignored by one employing the methodology here used. Although Moran was, at that stage, a Chancery Court opinion and not an opinion of the Delaware Supreme Court, the subject with which it dealt— the validity of so-called poison pill stock rights plans—had, in an era in which takeover activity was coming to form an important source of upward pressure on stock markets, far greater significance for stock prices than one would intuitively expect Trans Union to have. In all events, without regard to the relative importance of the two cases for future stock prices of other firms, it is plain that Moran, being decided on the same day, muddles the Trans Union event beyond salvation for one employing this method.

SECTION 102 AND CUMULATIVE ABNORMAL RETURNS

The data with respect to the cumulative abnormal returns of Delaware stock around various Section 102-related events is not so compromised. Nor is it inconclusive in quite the same way as the Trans Union data. It is, nevertheless, inconclusive in my opinion.

The 43-trading-day data reflected on Table 7–3 of the Bradley and Schipani study (Chapter 7 this volume) does indicate, putting to one side questions of the appropriate period for measuring such an effect, that a loss in market capitalization was associated with enactment of Section 102(b)(7).[5] Does that association represent a causal relationship? Deducing causation from correlation is always problematic. Bradley and Schipani assume causation but their data does not offer compelling evidence to support such an account of events.

First, the longer term data disclosed in Figure 7–1 show that the 3.7 percent negative cumulative abnormal return ("CAR") experienced in the months of June and July by Delaware stocks was part of a secular trend of falling negative abnormal returns to Delaware stock. Indeed, the authors state that their –3.7 percent CAR finding for the period may be subject to serial correlation.

Second, and more importantly, the finding of association between decreased relative returns to the stock of Delaware companies and a liberal regime that includes the flexibility that Section 102(b)(7) provides, does not appear when the authors look at reincorporation data. It is, I think, an important fact that reincorporation data does not yield a correlation between subjecting a firm's governance to Section 102(b)(7) and any negative cumulative abnormal return. Bradley and Schipani state that:

> The significant increase in the value of the securities of firms that reincorporate into Delaware for the express purpose of seeking protection of Section 102(b)(7) is inconsistent with the conclusion that the statute operated to the detriment of the stockholders of Delaware firms.

This significant observation, however, is not sufficiently taken into account when the authors summarize their empirical findings and state their conclusion.[6]

Accordingly, I am not persuaded that the factual assertion that enactment of Section 102(b)(7) *caused* a decrease in wealth to the shareholders of Delaware corporations has been demonstrated.

Moving beyond that factual assertion, these scholars go on to deduce from it an important further conclusion: that "legal rules are important constraints on the behavior of corporate managers" or, stated differently, that "liability rules are important for efficient corporate governance." These large-scale inferences are, I suggest, not only not shown to be justified by the data, but are derived from premises that are deeply flawed, as I think can be shown rather quickly.

FLAWS IN THE PREMISES OF BRADLEY AND SCHIPANI

One in my professional position would almost certainly be driven by the psychic need to believe one's own life and work to be significant, to agree with the assertion that legal rules act as important constraints on the behavior of corporate managers. Moreover, aside from matters of psychic necessity, it has for more than a century been a presupposition of the American law that rules of liability do matter as a social control mechanism.[7] But despite the fact that I am firmly of the view that rules of liability do matter in shaping conduct, I cannot apprehend that this study lends support to that notion.

First, it is not the case that one who takes what the authors call the institutionalist perspective (that is, contending that the rules governing potential liability of corporate directors have a constructive role to play in the social management of our system of economic organization) needs to believe as Bradley and Schipani posit, that "relaxed liability exposure for duty of care violations is detrimental to shareholder wealth." Nor need one with such a view believe that a decision (such as Trans Union is said to be) that represents "tightening the legal constraints on directors" would necessarily "have a positive impact on the value of Delaware firms relative to firms incorporated elsewhere."

But no thoughtful "institutionalist" could really hold to the view that *all* tightening of liability rules with respect to standards of care will tend to be economically beneficial to share values or, conversely, that all loosening of such standards (such as Section 102 is said to permit) will logically tend to have a contrary effect. Consider, for example, the likely consequence of a rule change holding that a director will be personally liable for any loss suffered by the corporation as a consequence of a transaction that he has authorized. That would be a rule of very strict liability. Such a rule would no doubt constitute a tightening, admittedly an absurd tightening, of liability rules. What would be its expected result? First, under such a regime it would be more difficult (that is, expensive) to get directors to serve on boards of directors, or at least to get directors who are not judgment proof to do so. Second, putting incentive compensation and indemnification considerations to one side, one could expect a board operating in such a "tightened liability" regime to take as little risk as possible. Bank certificates of deposit or, better still, treasury obligations might seem like an appropriate degree of risk for directors to authorize in such a world.   The effect of such a rule of liability upon the operation of business corporations could be expected to be dramatic. Would any "institutionalist" suppose that the imposition of such a "tightened" rule of liability would likely increase the value of the stock of firms incorporated in the jurisdiction that adopted the rule? Or might not one holding such a position likely conclude that "tightening" to that extent would plainly tend to decrease such value relative to firms organized under a regime in which risk-taking is not so thoroughly discouraged?[8]

Have not Professors Bradley and Schipani in assuming an institutionalist theory which asserts unqualifiedly that "stronger liability rules... favor absentee stockholders" relied upon an obviously flawed perception of the view that legal rules may play a productive part in the social management of the economic order?

THE ALTERNATIVE MARKET/IMPLICIT CONTRACT THEORY OF CONTROL

Bradley and Schipani's rendition of the alternative market or implicit contract theory of control is, I suggest, subject to parallel criticism. As these scholars portray it, that alternative theory holds that "*market forces... cause the managers to align their interests with those of the firm's securities holders...*" (italics added).

The significant factor is here seen to be the market, and thus Bradley and Schipani's conception of the contractual theory of director control must in the end include a rather sharp distinction between constraints on director behavior imposed by legal rules and constraints imposed by various markets within which corporate enterprise functions.

But the distinction between the law as an instrument of social control and the market as a constraining force on behavior is not so clear as the juxtaposed hypothesis of this paper implies. Our "free market" is not a naturally occurring condition. It is a social creation supported by all manner of customs, habits, and beliefs generally shared.[9] The "free market" is most directly the product of legal rules themselves. If the market constraint theorists posit that "economic forces" independent of legal rules will control director discretion optimally (or at least better than legal rules are apt to do), they fail to understand this basic truth. It is legal rules that define certain claims to exercise dominion over property as legitimate; it is legal rules that define rights and enforce duties with respect to contracts; and legal rules proscribe as tortious or even criminal certain conduct closely relevant to the function of markets (e.g., unfair competition, misappropriation of trade secrets, fraud, theft, etc.).   It is the existence and enforcement of rules of this type that permit one to regard the market as an effective constraint of any sort at all.

But the property-creating and liability-defining legal rules that are basic to the existence of a functioning "free" market are not different in principle from the corporation law rules governing liability of directors. There is no technique to distinguish *a priori* or noncontroversially those rules that are necessary to bring the market to a condition of optimum functioning (somehow defined) from those rules that are cumbersome baggage, imposing costs without sufficient justification.   Thus, in an important sense, Bradley and Schipani's version of the contractualist theory they in part seek to test is premised on a false dichotomy.

Both markets and law *are social products* that importantly reflect value judgments.   To evaluate the wisdom or utility of a change in a legal rule relating to the organization or operation of the economic order, whether such rule is one impacting directly upon the operation of markets or one that impacts in the first instance upon internal firm governance, it is not helpful simply to characterize that rule as being either "corporation law" on the one hand governing the potential liability of a director to his corporation (and which is not seen as "the market"), or "elementary law" (i.e., those basic legal rules that permit a "free market" to function) on the other.[10]   Rather, a judgment concerning the wisdom of a specific legal rule requires "thick" substantive information about the systemwide operation of the rule under review and its alternatives and a clear understanding concerning the various ends (values) the system (and, thus, the rule) ought (normatively) to seek to promote.

Thus, the interesting questions that the Trans Union case and the enactment of Section 102(b)(7) raise to my mind begin with empirical, sociological questions.   Primarily among them is the question: Do boards of directors, when confronted with a merger proposal, in fact tend to behave differently after the Trans Union opinion (or after the enactment of Section 102(b)(7)) than they tended to act formerly?   Once one has an empirically grounded notion as to whether or not boards' conduct has tended to be different under one regime or the other, a host of further questions for the financial economist, the student of industrial organization, the psychologist, and other social scientists will arise concerning the significance and utility of those changes.

It is, of course, no criticism of Bradley and Schipani's methodology that it does not generate richer, more textured data. The technique of searching for short-run, abnormal returns to stock market investments presents a method capable of identifying stock market reaction to certain events from which some particular significance can sometimes be inferred.[11] This study, however, deepens the suspicion that the technique will typically be unable to detect *general* market reactions to judicial decisions. Moreover, this method of inquiry cannot, I submit, generate a meaningful answer to an inquiry into "the relative importance of legal rules, on the one hand, and economic forces on the other," in explaining the continued vitality of the corporate form of organization.

Notes

1.   Smith v. Van Gorkom, Del. Supr., 488 A.2d 858 (1985).
2.   A. Berle and G. Means, *The Modern Corporation and Private Property,* (1932).
3.   As formulated by Bradley and Schipani, neither of these theories of control recognize any restraint arising out of nonlegal or *supra*-legal cultural norms. It is, of course, the case that all persons who serve on boards of directors of publicly traded companies exist in a culture in which violation of norms (legal or otherwise) may be seen as shaming, and compliance with such norms may be seen as an indication of a valued personal character. Thus, as an aside, I would suggest "culture," including the ideology of shareholder democracy, as another source of "constraint" upon director conduct. See A. Etzioni, *The Moral Dimension: Towards a New Economics,* (1988), pp. 53–55.
4.   Moran v. Household International, Inc., Del. Ch. 490 A.2d 1059, *aff'd* Del. Supr., 500 A.2d 1346 (1985).
5.   The length of this period does, of course, present the risk that unrelated events have clouded the data. The shorter 12-day period data (Table 7–2), however, is subject to a more difficult problem. It takes as its event date the July 1 effective date of the statute. The effective date of the statute, however, is itself not a critical date for these purposes. The enactment was introduced on June 10, passed by both Houses of the Delaware General Assembly by June 17 and signed into law on June 18. Certainly no later than that time, the market knew that the law had been changed. Indeed, if in fact any investor truly regarded this matter as one of significance with respect to investment decisions, she could be expected to have begun to factor it into her market activities prior to June 18. Thus, market activity measured between June 23 and July 10 (Table 7–2) seems to focus on a suspect period. The 43-trading-day period, while lengthy, does cover the full month of June, during which time the statute was being considered and enacted, and the month of July.

6. Additionally, the finding that enactment of Section 102(b)(7) "caused" net selling pressure in Delaware shares, while not necessarily inconsistent with, is nevertheless curious in light of the findings of large-scale survey reports that show institutional investors voting favorably on charter amendments incorporating liability limiting provisions. See Investor Responsibility Research Center, "Voting by Institutional Investors on Corporate Governance Issues," (October 1987), pp. 32, 62 *et seq.*

7. It is not inevitably the case that a legal system must make this assumption. A legal order is imaginable in which backward-looking concepts of retribution and compensation predicated upon some given natural law predominate and forward-looking concepts of deterrence or incentives play little role in the justification of the law. It is extremely doubtful that our own legal system—even during the mid- to late 19th century when judges most regularly appeared to operate under the delusion that the decision of contested cases never called for more than deductive logic—ever failed to assume that rules of liability matter with respect to future actions. See generally M. Horwitz, *Transformation of American Law 1780–1860,* (1977), giving an instrumental interpretation to the evolution of early American law.

8. For purposes of completeness, one should note that where the board of a corporation could otherwise be expected to make poor business decisions and return less than the riskless rate of return, such a rule of liability, which encouraged the investment in treasury obligations, might actually increase the value of a company's shares. This, one could safely assume, would be a rare instance and surely not one that would otherwise last very long.

9. See, for example, K. Arrow, "Gifts and Exchanges," in E. Phelps (ed.), *Altruism, Morality and Economic Theory,* (1975), pp. 13–28.

10. This is what Bradley and Schipani imply that the contractualists do, although there is no indication that it is done consciously.

11. For example, the less complex inquiry into whether enactment of state tender offer regulations is correlated with a decrease in market capitalization of regulated firms would seem better suited to this technique. See, e.g., Romano, "The Political Economy of Takeover Statutes," *Virginia Law Review, 73,* 111 (1987); Schumann, "State Regulation of Takeovers and Shareholder Wealth," Federal Trade Commission, Bureau of Economics Staff Report (1987). So would an inquiry into the immediate (two-day) impact upon shareholder wealth of the adoption of so-called "poison pill" plans. See Ryngært, "The Effect of Poison Pill Securities on Shareholder Wealth," *Journal of Financial Economics,* (January 1988), 377–417; Malatesta and Walking, "Poison Pill Securities: Stockholder Wealth, Profitability and Ownership Structure," *Journal of Financial Economics,* (January 1988), 347–76.

CHAPTER 10

THE LAW AND FINANCE OF THE BUSINESS JUDGMENT RULE: COMMENTS ON CHAPTERS 6 AND 7

Ronald J. Gilson

Corporate governance lies at the intersection of law and finance. The wisdom of existing or proposed corporate governance rules is difficult to evaluate without applying the tools of modern finance to assess the rule's impact on the value of the firm.[1] Conversely, the likely success of strategies to enhance firm value is difficult to evaluate without understanding the legal rules that define both the range of the firm's alternatives and the potential responses available to other players in the firm's competitive environment.[2] For purposes of the study of corporate governance, the required discipline is "law and finance."[3]

The two chapters to which this comment is directed—Bradley and Schipani, "The Economic Importance of the Business Judgment Rule: An Empirical Analysis of the Trans Union Decision and Subsequent Delaware Legislation" (Chapter 7) and Shapiro, "Judicial Business Judgment: The Investment Banker's Role" (Chapter 6)—can be collectively described as law and finance. Michael Bradley, and Cindy Schipani, Professor of Finance and Assistant Professor of Business Law, respectively, at the University of Michigan Business School,[4] creatively apply the economet-

Ronald J. Gilson, a J.D. from Yale Law School, is Professor of Law at Stanford Law School, a Visiting Scholar at the Hoover Institution, and counsel to the San Francisco firm of Marron, Reid & Sheehy.

ric tools of financial economics to measure the impact of recent Delaware judicial and legislative action concerning the business judgment rule on the value of Delaware corporations. Stuart Shapiro, a prominent takeover lawyer, comes to the intersection of law and finance from the other direction. He evaluates the role of investment bankers' financial adequacy opinions in the structure of legal rules governing the target company's response to a hostile tender offer.

While the two studies can be collectively described as law and finance, individually they seem to me one finance paper that could be better informed by more detailed legal analysis and one legal paper that could be better informed by modern finance. Bradley and Schipani claim too much for their econometric tools, and miss the insights that more rigorous legal analysis could have added to the interpretation of their data. Shapiro, in turn, too narrowly focuses on legal analysis, thereby missing the challenge that finance poses for the structure of legal rules. The two studies are examples of good finance and good legal scholarship. What they lack is the sufficient emphasis on the conjunction in the phrase "law *and* finance."

BRADLEY AND SCHIPANI: THE ROLE OF DIRECTOR LIABILITY IN CORPORATE GOVERNANCE

The role of director personal liability in the structure of corporate governance has been the subject of vociferous debate in recent years. The argument in favor of director liability is straightforward. A general principle of the common law is that those who are negligent are liable for the consequences of their actions. The notion is simply that the potential for monetary damages provides an incentive to act carefully. Bradley and Schipani label those who believe that director liability is an important component of corporate governance as institutionalists.[5]

The argument against director liability is more complex. Outside directors occupy an unusual position. By definition, an outside directorship is only a part-time position for which the compensation is typically a fixed fee. As a result, outside directors receive little of the gain that results from their efforts and the corporation's activities. A liability rule means that, under specified circumstances, outside directors will be personally liable, for potentially enormous amounts, if the corporation's activities result in a loss. Option pricing theory (and common sense) teaches that if a decision maker shares only in the losses from risky projects, but not in the gains, the decision maker will behave more conservatively than would be preferred by those who also participate in the project's gains. As the opponents of personal liability for directors put it, the specter of liability discourages beneficial risk taking.

The most direct way to eliminate this conflict is for the decision maker to share in the gains as well as the losses. The problem is that outside directors typically lack a large ownership stake in the corporation; a reward structure that nonetheless allowed them to share in the gains would conflict with their independence.[6]

If the conflict cannot be eliminated by outside directors sharing in the corporation's gains, the alternative approach is to eliminate the directors' sharing in the corporation's losses. This is the concept on which the business judgment rule is built. In the absence of behavior so extreme that there is little danger of judicial mistake,[7] directors have no personal liability for their business decisions and therefore have no incentive to be excessively conservative. Bradley and Schipani label those who believe director liability is given too prominent a role in corporate governance as contractarians.

The major problem with the debate has been that it seemed incapable of resolution. Because both sides' arguments were internally consistent, logic chopping alone would not resolve it. Nor did it seem resolvable empirically. The only available empirical evidence fit within a lawyer's definition of data: the plural of anecdote. Examples were plentiful both of corporate failures that, at least in retrospect, might have been avoided if directors exercised greater care, and of loss of competitiveness that might be explained by directors having too little appetite for risk. However, there was no way to tell which anecdotes were more compelling.

In this setting, the Bradley and Schipani study aspired to provide reliable data concerning the existing balance between director liability and director protection. An event occurred—the Delaware Supreme Court's decision in Smith v. Van Gorkom[8]—that the corporate bar and business community seemed overwhelmingly to believe weakened the business judgment rule and thereby increased the role of director liability in corporate governance. Trans Union appeared to allow a natural experiment to determine whether the pre-decision balance—between director liability and director protection and, hence, between institutionalists and contractarians—was optimal.[9] Event study methodology measures the stock market's reaction to an occurrence that might have had an impact on the value of a corporation (or a portfolio of corporations), holding constant all other influences on stock value. If the market believed that there had been too little risk of director liability prior to Trans Union (the institutionalist position), the decision would have had a positive impact on the value of Delaware corporations. Their stock then would respond more favorably than otherwise would have been expected—in econometric terms, the stock would have earned positive abnormal returns.

Alternatively, if the market believed that there had been enough (or more than enough) risk of director liability prior to Trans Union (the contractarian position), the decision would have had a negative impact on the value of Delaware corporations. Their stock then would respond less favorably than otherwise would have been expected—in econometric terms, the stock would have earned negative abnormal returns.

Sometimes nature smiles on her experimenters. A second natural experiment testing the importance of duty of care liability in corporate governance followed on the heels of Trans Union. In response to Trans Union, the Delaware legislature amended Delaware General Corporation Law Sec. 102(b) to add subsection (7) to the litany of permissible provisions that may be placed in a corporation's certificate of incorporation. New Sec. 102(b)(7) authorized existing companies to adopt charter amendments that not only overturned Trans Union, but entirely eliminated director monetary liability for breach of the duty of care.

The natural experiment was straightforward. If Trans Union went too far in increasing director liability, the Delaware legislature's invitation to eliminate liability would result in positive abnormal returns. Alternatively, if increased liability was desirable, or if Sec. 102(b)(7) went too far by authorizing not only reversal of Trans Union, but wholesale elimination of duty of care liability, the legislature's response to Trans Union would result in negative abnormal returns.

Thus, the Bradley and Schipani study held out the promise of a substantial interdisciplinary contribution to our understanding of corporate governance. The accident of Trans Union and the Delaware legislature's response, combined with the power of econometrics, would provide a means to assess where we really stood concerning director liability before and after Trans Union.

Disappointingly, the study does not quite deliver on its promise. Two problems get in the way. First, the econometric technique employed may not be sufficiently sensitive to pick up any impact that Trans Union may have had. Second, even assuming that the econometrics are sensitive enough to measure the impact of the decision, significant problems of interpretation cloud assessment of the meaning of the results Bradley and Schipani report. With respect to Trans Union, an alternative legal analysis of what the case means suggests quite different interpretations of Bradley and Schipani's data. With respect to Sec. 102(b)(7), the measurement periods over which the study was conducted make one leery of the causal connection between the abnormal returns reported and the event to which they are ascribed.

THE TRANS UNION EXPERIMENT

The Sensitivity of Abnormal Return Methodology

Bradley and Schipani report that their sample of Delaware corporations experienced no statistically significant abnormal returns in connection with Trans Union. They treat this outcome as "consistent with the view that the decision had no real impact on the way U.S. corporations were managed." There is, however, an alternative explanation of the absence of statistically significant abnormal returns that has much less substantive significance. Abnormal return methodology may not be sufficiently sensitive to pick up the limited impact on firm value that one would expect from an event like Trans Union.[10] From this perspective, their data can tell us only that Trans Union did not have an impact large enough to measure.

The limits of abnormal return methodology follow from its underlying logic. The technique first predicts the way the stock of companies in the sample should have responded on a particular day given the response of a general market index. The sample's actual response is then compared to its predicted response. The difference, positive or negative, is the abnormal return.

The next step is interpreting the results, which is an analytical, not a statistical task.[11] The abnormal return can be interpreted as being the result of an unexpected event if the temporal relation between announcement of the event and the period over which the abnormal return was experienced is consistent with causation. Interpretation is complicated, however, because the stock prices of companies in the sample also are subject to change as a result of chance—the background noise of the stock market. So, a critical statistical step in an abnormal return study applies a test of statistical significance to determine the likelihood that the abnormal return observed could be the result of chance. If the expected impact of an event is smaller than the size necessary for statistical significance, abnormal return methodology is not suited to measuring its impact.

Merrit Fox provides a useful illustration of the problem.[12] Suppose that a court decision is expected to result in an increase of 0.1 percent in future shareholder returns to the average Delaware corporation. Assuming a standard error consistent with that found by Weiss and White in their study of 7 important Delaware Supreme Court corporate governance decisions, Fox concludes that the observed price change "would have to be at least 1.3 percent before we could reject the null hypothesis [that the true effect of the decision is zero] with 95 percent confidence. There is less than one chance in 20 that an increase of 0.1 percent in the actual value of a sample portfolio will be accompanied by an observed change in prices sufficiently large, that is 1.3 percent, to be considered statistically significant."[13]

Our confidence in Bradley and Schipani's interpretation of their data thus turns on our expectations of the likely magnitude of Trans Union's impact on the value of a Delaware corporation's stock, whatever the direction of the impact. If the likely impact is small relative to the background noise in stock market prices, the absence of abnormal returns reflects the limits of the methodology. The proper interpretation of that result is that it sets a boundary: The upper limit of the decision's impact is set by the lower limit of statistical significance.

There are two good reasons to believe that Trans Union's impact on share value would be below the limits of statistical significance. One concerns the difference between a judicial decision of general application and other kinds of events to which abnormal return methodology has been applied. The second concerns Trans Union itself.

Judicial decisions concerning the general rules of corporate governance are quite different from the kinds of events to which abnormal return methodology has most commonly been applied. At least in the corporate governance area, abnormal return studies largely have focused on events that could be expected to have a discernible impact on a specific company, for example, making or being the subject of a tender offer. In these studies, the sample portfolio is composed of all corporations that experienced such an event at any time over a fairly long period.[14] As Merritt Fox has pointed out, a judicial decision concerning a corporate governance rule of general application will affect a large number of corporations at one time in a manner that would affect operations only indirectly and over an extended period. Thus, one would expect that the impact on share prices would be much smaller.[15] To be sure, abnormal return methodology has also been used to study the impact of regulatory changes which also have a general, rather than firm-specific, impact. However, regulation typically is at least industry specific, thereby still affecting a more limited universe of companies than general corporate governance rules.[16]

Further, the expected size of a judicial decision's immediate impact on firm value depends on when (or over what period) the corporation's cash flow will be affected. The further in the future when (or the longer the period over which) cash flow is expected to be affected, the smaller the immediate impact of the decision on firm value. Thus, for purposes of evaluating the value of an abnormal return study, the critical point is not the identity of the party—judicial, legislative, or administrative—responsible for the event, but the breadth of the population which experiences the event and how far in the future its effect will be felt. The broader the population affected, and the further in the future that effect will be felt, the less appropriate will be abnormal return methodology.[17]

The particular aspect of corporate governance at issue in Trans Union—the extent of business judgment rule protection from liability—reinforces the expectation that, because of the decision's breadth of effect and the long period over which that effect would be felt, the decision's impact on share value would not be statistically significant. Any change Trans Union may have made in the role of director personal liability would have an impact on director conduct and, hence, on cash flows and firm value only at the margin.

First, even those Bradley and Schipani characterize as institutionalists acknowledge that liability is only one of the corporate governance techniques that influence mangerial conduct. Where product and reputation markets create an incentive for managers to exercise care, legal liability for failure to satisfy the duty of care likely adds only little additional incentive at the margin. As the Reporters of the American Law Institute state the point:

> The [governance] structure of the modern public corporation reflects the interaction of ... three types of techniques [for assuring management's adequate performance]—market forces, legal liability rules, and requirements for shareholder action. Because markets give both management and shareholders a common interest in profitable operations, the business judgment rule ... in large measure protects from judicial review management's exercise of its delegated discretion to operate the business.[18]

Second, the particular circumstances of Trans Union limit the decision's impact. Factually (and, as we will see, perhaps doctrinally as well), Trans Union is a takeover case.[19] What can outside directors learn about their obligations from it? Once past a hyperbolic reaction to the directors' personal liability, the corporate bar seems to read Trans Union as focusing on boiler plate procedures—the creation of a record establishing that directors carefully considered the value of the corporation and fairness of the price offered before agreeing to sell the company.[20] Trans Union's impact on a company's stock price then would be a function of the extent to which the new procedures adopted in response to the decision could be expected to have an impact, discounted by the likelihood that the company ever would be a takeover target, discounted further to reflect that, in any event, the effect on cash flow would occur only some time in the future. Treating Trans Union as a business judgment case, it seems unlikely that the case would have a large enough impact in either direction to generate statistically significant results. In short, the character of the case and the limits of the statistical technique combine to cause the data to tell us very little about the importance of director liability in the structure of corporate governance.[21]

INTERPRETING TRANS UNION AND THE DATA

The next step in assessing the Trans Union aspect of the Bradley and Schipani study is to assume that abnormal return methodology is appropriate to the study of judicial decisions, and turn to the problem of interpreting the abnormal returns reported in connection with Trans Union. Two levels of inquiry are necessary. First, the event itself must be understood. Where the object of study is a judicial decision, legal interpretation is called for: The event is defined by the decision's holding. What does Trans Union actually hold? Second, the relationship between the event and the abnormal returns observed must be understood: What explanation links the event and returns? Ambiguity about what Trans Union holds, together with ambiguity about how its holding might affect firm value, makes Bradley and Schipani's data very difficult to interpret.

Interpreting Trans Union: Is It a Takeover Case?
Together with most commentators, Bradley and Schipani treat Trans Union as a business judgment rule case. Viewed this way, the link between the event and the abnormal returns observed is the influence of an increased possibility of liability on general board behavior: Increased liability may make directors more careful; alternatively, increased liability may make directors too cautious. But Trans Union may have a less diffuse effect on

board conduct. Directors may more specifically alter their behavior in connection with the type of transaction that was involved in Trans Union. From this perspective, Trans Union is primarily a takeover case. And from this perspective, it may have significant implications for how such transactions are conducted.

One quite plausible reading of Trans Union is that it counsels directors about the safe way to sell the corporation.[22] Recall that the offerer had given the Trans Union board only three days to act and had demanded a stock lock up and a no shop clause.[23] The court held that by acceding to these demands, without seeking investment banking advice or otherwise determining the corporation's "intrinsic" value, the directors violated their duty of care. Thus, Trans Union may hold, in practical effect, that target directors will avoid liability if they act with deliberation, solicit competing bids, and sell the corporation to the highest bidder.[24]

Interpreting Trans Union as a pro-auction case creates a problem at the second level of interpretation—understanding the link between the event and firm value. A theoretical debate continues over whether encouraging auctions benefits or harms target company shareholders.[25] An auction will increase the price paid in a particular transaction, but may decrease the number of transactions. A large literature has yet to resolve the direction of the balance, in part because its resolution is likely to be fact dependent, the facts are difficult to determine, and, in all events, the balance may change over time with changes in the acquisition climate and in transaction and financing technology.[26] Understood this way, Bradley and Schipani test not the importance of director liability in corporate governance but, rather, the impact of a pro-auction rule on firm value.[27]

The Further Problem of Conflicting Effects

Understanding the empirical results Bradley and Schipani report is further complicated by the fact that the two interpretations of Trans Union— business judgment rule and pro-auction—are not mutually exclusive. The decision may generally increase the role of director liability in corporate governance and increase the likelihood of auctions.

In this case, the decision is really two different events. The abnormal returns associated with the decision then may be impossible to interpret because the two events may have offsetting effects.[28] Even if the effects reinforce rather than offset each other, it may be impossible without more to determine their relative importance.

The problem can be seen from the following matrix:

	Increased director liability	
	positive effect on firm value	negative effect on firm value
Pro-auction: positive effect on firm value	reinforce	offset
negative effect on firm value	offset	reinforce

Thus, because of the different interpretations of Trans Union—because Trans Union may be more than one event—any reported abnormal return is consistent with a number of interpretations. For example, no abnormal returns is consistent with either the northeast or southwest cells of the matrix. Alternatively, a positive or negative abnormal return may be consistent with any of the cells. In the end, it is very difficult to discriminate among competing interpretations.

CONCLUSION

The two levels of criticism that I have directed at the Trans Union aspect of the Bradley and Schipani study have quite different implications. Skepticism over whether abnormal return methodology is sufficiently sensitive to measure the impact on firm value of a judicial decision concerning a corporate governance rule of general application does not mean that we learn nothing from the study. From this perspective, Bradley and Schipani's finding of no significant abnormal returns associated with Trans Union tells us that the lower boundary of statistical significance sets the upper boundary of the decision's impact. Moreover, in light of Weiss and White's similar findings in connection with six other important Delaware Supreme Court decisions concerning corporate governance rules of general application,[29] this outcome seems to generalize: The impact on firm value of judicial corporate governance decisions is exceeded by market noise.

That is an interesting thing to know. However, it is important not to draw the wrong conclusion from the finding that judicial decisions are unlikely to cause statistically significant changes in firm value. The absence of statistical significance does not mean that liability rules or judicial decisions concerning them are unimportant. Precisely because legal rules are imbedded in a complex web of law, contract, and market components that comprise the governance structure of the public corporation, statistical significance is far too crude a measure of importance.[30]

There is a problem, however, in treating Bradley and Schipani's study as identifying the upper boundary of judicial decisions' impact on firm value. If my second criticism is correct, one or both of the two "events" I argue comprise Trans Union may have had a statistically significant impact which is masked by their combination. Thus, it would be useful to know whether it is my first or second criticism that is correct: Is the problem the size of Trans Union's impact in relation to market noise or the masking effect of the potentially conflicting events that make up Trans Union?

In an effort to be constructive as well as critical, I proffer an amateur's suggestion as to how one might approach distinguishing between the two criticisms. If the picture painted by the first criticism is correct and Trans Union has only an insignificant effect on firm value, investors would have little reason to adjust their portfolios in response to the decision. In contrast, if the picture painted by the second criticism is correct and the Trans Union decision has sizeable but potentially conficting impacts, investors may have reason to adjust their portfolios. Thus, the two criticisms predict different levels of trading volume in response to Trans Union. A finding that no unusual trading volume occurred following the decision would support the first criticism's view that the impact of Trans Union is small. In contrast, a finding that unusual trading volume did occur would support the second criticism.

The Sec. 102(b)(7) Experiment

Bradley and Schipani report an intriguing result with respect to their second natural experiment. Statistically significant negative abnormal returns appear to be associated with Delaware's enactment of Sec. 102(b)(7). This leads them to conclude that, contrary to the post-Trans Union doom sayers, "the relaxed liability exposure for violations of the duty of care standard allowed by this act is detrimental to the wealth of the stockholders of Delaware firms."[31]

Unfortunately, I find myself quite skeptical about the causal link they describe. The problem is a different kind of interpretive difficulty with abnormal return studies. While I have no quarrel with Bradley and Schipani's determination that their sample earned statistically significant negative abnormal returns over the periods studied, I am quite leery of the conclusion that they result from the enactment of Sec. 102(b)(7)

The interpretive problem that troubles this aspect of the study is the potential for conflicting events. Abnormal return studies conducted in "event time"[32] avoid this problem because each company in the sample will have experienced the event of interest at a different chronological time. Conflicting events with respect to any particular company then should randomize over the entire sample. In contrast, when a study is conducted in real time aggregating the experience of individual companies into a sample will not eliminate the impact of a conflicting event because that event may affect every company in the sample.

The result is that in a real time study of the type conducted with respect to Sec. 102(b)(7), much more so than in an event time study, statements about the relationship between the event and the abnormal returns discovered are a matter of interpretation, not econometric science. The discovery of abnormal returns is a matter of statistics; the linking of those returns to an assigned cause is a matter of logic. Bradley and Schipani argue that the discovery of abnormal returns over the periods they study is best explained by the enactment of Sec. 102(b)(7). Careful review of the periods studied, however, strongly suggests that the returns may well not be explained by the statute. Without more analysis, agnosticism seems in order.

Bradley and Schipani calculate abnormal returns (CAR) over four periods:

Period	CAR	T Statistic
−6 to +1	−0.98%	−2.02
−21 to 0	−1.39	−1.78
0 to +22	−1.28	−1.59
−21 to +22	−2.67	−2.38

Day 0 (event date) = Effective Date of Statute July 1, 1986

The problem is that the event date seems to be misspecified. The statute's effective date is probably too late to capture any abnormal returns Sec.

102(b)(7) may have caused. The chronology associated with the enactment of Sec. 102(b)(7) is as follows:[33]

Date	Event
June 10, 1986	Legislation introduced
June 17, 1986	Legislation passed by both houses
June 18, 1986	Governor signs legislation
July 1, 1986	Effective date

Given the assumption of semi-strong form market efficiency on which abnormal return methodology is based, and assuming with Bradley and Schipani that the statute's invitation to corporations to eliminate damages for violations of the duty of care would result in negative abnormal returns, when should these returns have occurred? I believe that no one familiar with the legislative process in Delaware had any doubt that the legislation, once introduced, would be enacted. On this analysis, the entire response should have occurred on June 10th. No abnormal returns would be expected on any later date because subsequent events, such as the actual passage of the legislation, conveyed no new information.

Even this analysis may place the critical event associated with the enactment of Sec. 102(b)(7) too late in time. The legislation was drafted by a Delaware bar committee, and it was hardly a secret in the legal community that an effort was under way to formulate a legislative response to Trans Union. Moreover, the approach being taken by the bar drafting committee also was not a secret. On this analysis all abnormal returns associated with a legislative response to Trans Union would have occurred prior to June 10th—the date the legislation was introduced and the earliest date considered by Bradley and Schipani.

My conclusion is that the abnormal returns reported by Bradley and Schipani cannot be ascribed to the enactment of Sec. 102(b)(7) in the absence of an explanation for why the returns occurred so long after knowledge of the legislation was public.

Here I have little constructive to offer other than a suggestion about how to go about formulating hypotheses. Bradley and Schipani's methodology compared the experience of Delaware and non-Delaware corporations because both Trans Union and Sec. 102(b)(7) presumptively affect only Delaware corporations. We know, however, that Delaware and non-Delaware corporations differ from each other in systematic ways.[34] What else was going on in the economy between mid-June and mid-July, 1986, that might affect the two categories of corporations differently? In a real time, as opposed to an event time, study, controlling for conflicting events is an analytic, not a statistical, exercise.

SHAPIRO: THE ROLE OF FINANCIAL OPINIONS IN CORPORATE GOVERNANCE

While Bradley and Schipani approach the intersection of law and finance by using econometrics to measure the impact of a judicial decision, Stuart Shapiro comes to the crossroad by focusing on the interaction of finance and legal rules in corporate governance litigation. He sets as his context a target company that wants to take an action—like declining to redeem a poison pill—to preclude its shareholders from accepting a hostile tender offer. Under Delaware law the target company bears the burden of proving that defensive action is reasonable in relation to the threat posed by the hostile offer.[35] From the target's perspective, the problem is identifying the threat. If the offer is all cash with a commitment to take out non-tendering shareholders at the same price, what threat does the offer pose?

Finance enters the picture through the Delaware Supreme Court's litany in Unocal, repeated in Ivanhoe Partners,[36] of the factors directors appropriately may consider in determining whether an offer poses a threat. In particular, directors are told that it would be appropriate to consider the "inadequacy of the price offered...."[37] A target board, then, has a number of reasons to secure the opinion of an investment banking firm that the price offered by a hostile bidder is inadequate.

First, a board acting in good faith genuinely will desire competent professional guidance concerning the adequacy of the offer. As Shapiro comments: "Although the boards will likely have long-term and in-depth familiarity with the company's businesses, directors are rarely trained valuation specialists."[38] Second, commentators have concluded that, under Trans Union, an investment banker's opinion concerning price may provide directors protection against personal liability even if a court ultimately concludes that the defensive action taken is not reasonably related to the hostile offer's threat.[39] Finally, the possibility remains that the gambit of securing an inadequacy opinion will work—the investment banker's opinion may persuade a court that the offer is so inadequate as to constitute a sufficient threat to justify preclusive action.

The difficulty Shapiro identifies with this intersection of law and finance is the double bind legal rules impose on the investment banker's financial analysis. Shapiro tells us that "an inadequacy opinion means that the banker believes that a price higher than the one being offered can be obtained, either from the offeror, a third party, or by remaining independent."[40] The opinion typically takes the form of a reference range of values—for example, $68–$80 per share in Interco[41]—because the Williams Act requirement that the target board announce its evaluation within 10 days following the offer gives the investment banker too little time to provide a "full blown fairness opinion."[42]

The investment banker's dilemma is completed by a second legal constraint—the Chancery Court's increasing skepticism that price inadequacy alone constitutes a threat under Unocal.[43] For price inadequacy to carry that burden, Shapiro tells us that courts will want to know just how inadequate is the offer and to what intrinsic value the offer is being compared. Thus, the investment bankers' double bind is that the federal Williams Act requires investment bankers to act with a speed that is inconsistent with the depth of analysis increasingly required by state courts.

I share Shapiro's view that legal rules and valuation practice seem to be in conflict in this area. I disagree, however, that the conflict is as broad as Shapiro argues and that, in this case, the problem is with the legal rules. Analysis of the operational difficulties Shapiro describes investment bankers as confronting suggests that the courts' increasing unwillingness to rely upon investment bankers' opinions that an offer is inadequate is movement in the right direction.

Shapiro describes the investment banker's inadequacy opinion as depending on the availability of a better price from another bidder, from the existing bidder, or by remaining independent.[44] But if the banker believes that the tender offer price is inadequate because a higher price can be obtained from a third party or because further negotiations with the bidder may increase the price, neither the target company nor the investment banker confronts a dilemma. The same cases that display skepticism of the reliability of investment banker adequacy opinions make clear that a target company may decline to redeem a poison pill for some period of time while a higher price is sought without a significant showing of price inadequacy.[45]

The investment banker's double bind thus seems to arise only when the banker's conclusion about price inadequacy rests on a belief about the projected value of the company if it remains independent. But the real problem is not whether investment bankers lack the time to render an opinion based on careful analysis of management's projections, but the extent to which even carefully constructed management projections, duly sanctified by an investment banker, can serve to justify preclusive defensive tactics. In a non-coercive offer, why should management's and their investment banker's beliefs about the corporation's future value prevent shareholders from acting on their own beliefs about value?

So understood, the issue is not the impact of legal rules on the preparation of investment banker opinions. Rather, we are back to the central issue on the legal side of corporate governance—that is, the respective roles of management and shareholders. Chancellor Allen put the matter well in Interco: "To acknowledge that directors may employ the recent innovation of 'poison pills' to deprive shareholders of the ability effectively to choose to accept a noncoercive offer, after the board has had a reasonable opportunity to explore or create alternatives, or attempt to negotiate on the shareholders' behalf, would, it seems to me, be so inconsistent with the widely shared notions of appropriate corporate governance as to threaten to diminish the legitimacy and authority of corporate law."[46]

One model of corporate governance contemplates that shareholders, with the benefit of whatever advice management and investment bankers may proffer, in the end determine the adequacy of the price offered. An alternative model contemplates that management, with the benefit of whatever advice investment bankers may proffer, in the end determines the adequacy of the price offered. Only in the management dominated model does judicial skepticism of the reliability of investment banker opinions make any difference.[47]

Thus, integrating investment bankers' valuation opinions into the legal rules governing the conduct of hostile tender offers requires that we first resolve the role management and shareholders are to play. To be sure, finance will illuminate our deliberation, but the issue is now the impact of preclusive actions on shareholders, not the mechanics of investment bankers' opinions.

On this issue, the empirical finance literature speaks with a single voice. As Judge Easterbrook recently summarized the evidence: "The best available data show that if a firm fends off a bid, its profits decline, and its stock price (adjusted for inflation and marketwide changes) never tops the initial bid, even if it is later acquired by another firm."[48] Thus, the question posed by the intersection of law and finance in this area is what would justify a rule that makes shareholders worse off.

Notes

1. A good example is the legal rule governing the right of a controlling shareholder to sell control at a premium in which minority stockholders are not allowed to share. Since Perlman v. Feldmann, 219 F.2d 173 (2nd Cir. 1954), lawyers have debated whether minority shareholders are injured by such a sale. See R. Gilson, *The Law and Finance of Corporate Acquisitions*, pp. 617–20 (summary of debate). Empirical evidence that the value of minority shares increases as a result of a sale of control has begun to appear. See Holderness and Sheehan, "The Role of Majority Shareholders in Publicly Held Corporations: An Exploratory Analysis," *Journal of Finance, 20*, 317 (1988). In turn, the data have begun to influence legal policymaking. See American Law Institute, *Principles of Corporate Governance: Analysis and Recommendations,* Tentative Draft No. 9, Reporters' Note to Sec 5.15, pp. 29–31 (April 14, 1989).
2. An example of how legal analysis can inform finance arises in connection with the Grossman and Hart argument that a tender offeror must have the ability to freeze out non-tendering shareholders to prevent free-riding. Grossman and Hart, "Takeover Bids, the Free Rider Problem, and the Theory of the Corporation," *Bell Journal of Economics, 11,* 42 (1980). The idea is that target shareholders will infer from the fact of the offer that the offeror believes the target is worth more than the tender offer price. If each shareholder believes that his decision not to tender will not affect the offer's likelihood of success, every shareholder will free-ride by not tendering. As a result, the argument goes, no offer will ever succeed unless the offeror can freeze out non-tendering shareholders at an unfavorable price to discourage free-riding.

    The problem with this analysis is its assumption that there is only a single way of discouraging free-riding. Suppose the offeror can allocate to itself a disproportionate share of post-acquisition transactions with its newly controlled subsidiary. The result is to discourage free-riding by reducing the value of the shares of non-tendering shareholders. Thus, free-riding is discouraged not by freezing out non-tendering shareholders, but by freezing them in. Legal analysis suggests that this alternative is not only available, but may be less costly. See R. Gilson, *The Law and Finance of Corporate Acquisitions*, 854–68 (summary of debate).
3. I have put my effort where my mouth is. Although my textbook on corporate acquisitions is designed in part for a legal audience, the first six chapters provide a survey of the areas of finance I believe necessary to sophisticated study of the legal rules governing corporate acquisitions. See R. Gilson, *The Law and Finance of Corporate Acquisitions*.
4. Professor Bradley is also Professor of Law at the University of Michigan Law School.
5. Bradley and Schipani are a little inaccurate in their labeling. The only example

of institutionalists they identify are the Reporters of the American Law Institute Corporate Governance Project: "There are those like the drafters of the American Law Institute Corporate Governance Project who argue that the agency costs of the large-scale corporation are solved largely through the constraints imposed by liability rules and judicial review…. Those who hold this view and stress administrative solutions might be referred to as institutionalists." The problem is that most people's positions (and the world) are a little more complicated. For example, Bradley and Schipani use Delaware Sec. 102(b)(7), allowing corporations by charter amendment to eliminate director liability for breach of the duty of care, as the antithesis of an institutional approach because it reduces reliance on liability rules and judicial review. In fact, the original proposal to limit director liability for duty of care violations was made by the Corporate Governance Project, not the Delaware Legislature. See, for example, American Law Institute, *Principles of Corporate Governance: Analysis and Recommendations,* Council Draft No. 4, Sec. 7.17 (January 13, 1984). Indeed, the Project's original proposal limited directors' duty of care liability even without charter amendment. The idea of limiting liability by charter amendment was put forward by the Reporters in 1984 and was communicated to the Delaware committee charged with drafting a legislative response to Trans Union. Delaware did not enact Sec. 102(b)(7) until mid-1986. To be sure, the American Law Institute proposal and the Delaware statute differ. Delaware allows liability to be eliminated completely while the American Law Institute proposal allows adoption of a ceiling on liability of one year's directors' fees. For purposes of Bradley and Schipani's categories, however, the difference is trivial.

I should note that my sensitivity on this point likely derives from the fact that I am one of the Reporters of the Corporate Governance Project.

6.   The alignment of the interests of the decision-maker and the residual owner has been treated as one of the benefits of a controlling shareholder in a public corporation. See, e.g., Shleifer and Vishny, "Large Shareholders and Corporate Control," *Journal of Political Economy, 94,* 461 (1986); Demsetz and Lehn, "The Structure of Corporate Ownership: Causes and Consequences," *Journal of Political Economy, 93,* 1155 (1985).

7.   In formulating the appropriate standard of behavior, one must also consider the relationship between the formulation and the probability of error. So long as there is a positive probability that a judge or jury will make a mistake—that is, find the directors liable when, in fact, their conduct did not warrant liability—the disincentive to risky decisions remains. The more extreme the standard, the less likely that a mistake by the decision-maker will result in liability.

8.   488 A.2d 858 (Del. S. Ct. 1985). Following Bradley and Schipani's custom, I will refer to this decision hereafter as Trans Union.

9.   A careful reader will note that I have restated Bradley and Schipani's hypothesis to solve the problem of the absence of a baseline. Bradley and Schipani

hypothesize that if the constraints imposed by the duty of care are important, shareholder wealth would increase following Trans Union but if market constraints are sufficient, shareholder wealth would decrease. As Chancellor Allen points out, however, both legal and market rules are important; the issue is the correct proportion. Allen, "Law and Markets as Social Products: Comments on Chapter 7," Chapter 9, this volume. As a result, we cannot predict whether more or less liability is a good or bad thing unless we know something about the balance at the starting point. How the market responded to Trans Union thus will tell us something about our starting point, not whether extreme versions of the institutionalist or contractarian positions are correct.

10. The question of whether abnormal return methodology is sufficiently sensitive to measure the impact of judicial decisions concerning corporate governance rules of general application has been most extensively considered in a thoughtful and illuminating exchange between Professors Elliott Weiss and Lawrence White on the one hand, and Professor Merrit Fox on the other. Weiss and White, "Of Econometrics and Indeterminacy: A Study of Investors' Reactions to Changes in Corporate Law," *California Law Review, 75,* 551, 589–90 (1987); Fox, "The Role of the Market Model in Corporate Law Analysis: A Comment on Weiss and White," *California Law Review, 76,* 1015, 1033–58 (1988); Weiss and White, "A Response to Professor Fox," *California Law Review, 76,* 1047, 1054–55 (1988).

11. For a discussion of the difficulties in interpreting abnormal return studies, see R. Gilson, *The Law and Finance of Corporate Acquisitions*, pp. 235–38, 432–45 (1986).

12. Fox, "The Role of the Market Model in Corporate Law Analysis: A Comment on Weiss and White," *California Law Review, 76,* 1036 (1988).

13. Ibid. Weiss and White point out that with the variability in their sample, a sample size of 8,500 Delaware corporations—much larger than the number of corporations listed on all United States stock exchanges—would be necessary to reject a possible effect of 0.1 percent. Weiss and White, "A Response to Professor Fox," *California Law Review, 76,* 1054, note 40 (1988).

14. Studies of this type calculate abnormal returns with reference to "event time," measured not by chronological dates, but in relation to the date on which knowledge of the event became public. Thus, the date of the event's announcement typically is set as day 0 for all companies, and abnormal returns computed with respect to an event time date—e.g., day 0, or period—e.g., day –5 through day +5 (from 5 days before the announcement through 5 days after the announcement).

15. Fox, "The Role of the Market Model in Corporate Law Analysis: A Comment on Weiss and White," *California Law Review, 76,* 1023 (1988). Litigation can also have firm-specific rather than general impact. For example, one approach to evaluating the efficiency of derivative litigation is to study the impact on firm

value of the filing of a derivative suit. Here the methodology precisely parallels a study of the impact of a tender offer on a target company. The difference between such a study and Bradley and Schipani's study of Trans Union is that the former aggregates the effect of many firm-specific events and the latter aggregates the effect of a single market-wide event on many companies.

16. Fox, "The Role of the Market Model in Corporate Law Analysis: A Comment on Weiss and White," *California Law Review, 76,* 1025, note 29 (1988).

17. Put differently, the difference is between the measurability of a single event (i.e., the change in the governance rule) which applied to a large number of objects and which was small in relation to each of the event's objects.

18. The American Law Institute, *Principles of Corporate Governance: Analysis and Recommendations,* Discussion Draft No. 2 (April 20, 1989), p. 5.

19. See note 24 below.

20. See the sources referred to in note 39 below.

21. Bradley and Schipani decline to enter the debate over whether cumulative abnormal return methodology is appropriate to studying the effects of judicial decisions concerning corporate governance rules of general application. The explanation for their abstention is puzzling in that it rests on the fact that they found no abnormal returns associated with Trans Union: "Since we find no abnormal stock returns, we need not debate this issue here." (See Bradley and Schipani, Chapter 7, this volume.) But it is precisely the fact that no abnormal stock returns were found that motivates the debate over the methodology's use in this context. Bradley and Schipani's finding, together with those of Weiss and White, indicate that of a sample of the Delaware Supreme Court's most important corporate law decisions, *not one* resulted in positive or negative abnormal returns. The test, following Weiss and White and Fox, suggests an explanation for the pattern: An abnormal return study is insufficiently sensitive to pick up the likely impact of a judicial decision. Simply noting the existence of the pattern—that no abnormal returns were found—is not a competing explanation.

22. See Macey and Miller, "Trans Union Reconsidered," *Yale Law Journal, 98,* 127 (1988).

23. 488 A.2d, p. 868.

24. It is quite likely that Trans Union would have been treated as an acquisition case if it had arisen after Mills Acquisition Co. v. Macmillan, C.A. No. 10168 (Del. Sup. Ct. May 3, 1989). Under Macmillan, when a company is for sale the standard of review of director conduct is an "enhanced business judgement test." Under this enhanced standard, to obtain the protections of the traditional business judgment rule target directors have the burden of showing that any favoritism granted a bidder was reasonable in relation to the advantage sought. Given the court's belief that Trans Union received nothing for the no shop clause and lock up given the offeror, that burden would not have been met, in which case the applicable standard of review would be the much more rigorous entire fairness

test. Application of the latter test should be perfunctory; if directors' conduct cannot meet the enhanced business judgment test, it could hardly meet the entire fairness test.

That Trans Union turns out to be an enhanced business judgement case, rather than a garden variety business judgment case, has one interesting consequence. If the directors fail the enhanced business judgment test, the entire fairness test—the measure of compliance with the duty of loyalty—applies. Violations of the duty of loyalty, however, are expressly excluded from the protection against liability offered by charter amendments adopted pursuant to Sec. 102(b)(7). Because the enhanced business judgment test applies under Unocal to defensive actions and under Macmillan to the target's sale, director personal liability remains applicable in all takeover cases. The personal liability remains applicable in all takeover cases. The irony is that, after Macmillan, the statute adopted to overrule Trans Union seems not to apply to the Trans Union facts.

It should be apparent that I am much more uncertain than Bradley and Schipani that "[i]f the court were to decide Trans Union today, and if the Company had amended its articles of incorporation to eliminate liability in accordance with Section 102(b)(7), it is likely the court would exonerate the directors from monetary liability to the shareholders." For an approach to reconciling Delaware takeover law and the duty of loyalty exclusion in Sec. 102(b)(7) in a fashion that would allow exoneration of the Trans Union directors, see R. Gilson and R. Kraakman, *1988 Supplement to The Law and Finance of Corporate Acquisitions*, pp. 234–36 (1988).

25. The early rounds of the debate are summarized in Easterbrook and Fischel, "Auctions and Sunk Costs in Tender Offers," *Stanford Law Review, 35,* 1 (1982); Bebchuk, "The Case for Facilitating Competing Tender Offers: A Reply and Extension," *Stanford Law Review, 35,* 23 (1982); and Gilson, "Seeking Competitive Bids Versus Pure Passivity in Tender Offer Defense," *Stanford Law Review, 35,* 51 (1982). The most recent exchange, which picks up contributions between 1982 and 1988, is found in Schwartz, "The Fairness of Tender Offer Prices in Utilitarian Theory," *Journal of Legal Studies, 17,* 165 (1988); Bebchuk, "The Sole Owner Standard for Takeover Policy," *Journal of Legal Studies, 17,* 197 (1988); and Schwartz, "The Sole Owner Standard Reviewed," *Journal of Legal Studies, 17,* 321 (1988).

26. See Gilson, "Seeking Competitive Bids Versus Pure Passivity in Tender Offer Defense," *Stanford Law Review, 35,* 51 (1982).

27. Bradley and Schipani do acknowledge the possibility that Trans Union is a takeover case. In canvassing the possible explanation for the absence of abnormal returns in response to Trans Union, they state: "Furthermore, it may be the case the Trans Union decision did not increase the liability of corporate officials in general. Rather, Trans Union could be narrowly interpreted as applicable only to directors contemplating a change in control." (Bradley and

Schipani, Chapter 7, this volume.) The problem, however, is their implicit prediction that if Trans Union were a takeover case, it would result in no abnormal returns. Because of the conflict in the auction literature, this prediction likely would be controversial.

28. This interpretive problem is not limited to studies of judicial decision. It was initially noted in connection with studies of shark repellant amendments. Abnormal return studies were undertaken to determine whether shark repellant amendments are bad for shareholders because they allow disloyal management to entrench themselves, in which event their proposal would result in negative abnormal returns, or whether they are good for shareholders because they allow loyal management to bargain effectively for a high price, in which event their proposal would result in positive abnormal returns. The problem was that shark repellant amendments also could have an information effect: Management's very proposal of the amendments may signal that management believes there is a significant risk of a hostile tender offer. If this information causes the market to increase its assessment of the likelihood of a tender offer, positive abnormal returns would result. The outcome actually reported by the studies—essentially no abnormal returns—could be explained by a number of different combinations of the information effect and either of the hypotheses concerning the amendments' impact on shareholders. See Gilson, *The Law and Finance of Corporate Acquisitions*, pp. 683–84.

29. The cases studied were Singer v. Magnavox, 380 A.2d 969 (Del. Supr., 1977); Lynch v. Vickers Energy Corp., 383 A.2d 278 (Del. Supr., 1977); Lynch v. Vickers Energy Corp., 429 A.2d 497 (Del. Supr., 1981); Weinberger v. UOP, 457 A.2d 701 (Del. Supr., 1983); Zapata Corp. v. Maldonado, 430 A.2d 779 (Del. Supt., 1981); Unocal v. Mesa Petroleum, 493 A.2d 946 (Del. Supr, 1985).

30. Weiss and White may disagree. They describe their abnormal study as having "tested directly whether investors reacted significantly to the seven decisions and thereby tested indirectly whether the seven decisions changed Delaware corporate law in ways that were economically significant." [Weiss and White, "A Response to Professor Fox," *California Law Review, 76,* 1048 (1988)]. My point is to distinguish between changes that are *econometrically* significant based on the particular statistical techniques applied and changes that are *economically* significant, a quite different concept.

31. Bradley and Schipani, Chapter 7, this volume.

32. See note 14 above.

33. See Allen, Chapter 9 (comments on Bradley & Schipani), this volume, note 5.

34. See, for example, Romano, "Law as a Product: Some Pieces of the Incorporation Puzzle," *Journal of Legal and Economic Organizations,* p. 225 (1985).

35. Unocal v. Mesa Petroleum, 493 A. 2d 946 (Del. Supr., 1985); see Gilson and Kraakman, "Delaware's Intermediate Standard for Defensive Tactics: Is There Substance to Proportionality Review?," *Business Lawyer, 44,* 247 (1989).

36. 493 A.2d at 955–56; Ivanhoe Partners v. Newmont Mining Corp., 535 A.2d 1334, 1341–42 (Del. Supr., 1987).

37. 493 A.2d at 955; 535 A.2d at 1341.

38. Shapiro, Chapter 6, this volume.

39. See, e.g., Fischel, "The Business Judgment Rule and the Trans Union Case," *Business Lawyer, 40,* 1437 (1985); Manning, "Reflections and Practical Tips on Life in the Boardroom after Van Gorkom," *Business Lawyer, 41,* 1 (1985). The Delaware Supreme Court's recent decision in Mills Acquisition Co. v. Macmillan, Inc., Nos. 415 and 416, 1988 (Cons.) (May 3, 1989), necessarily undercuts blanket confidence in the ability of a favorable investment banking opinion to provide complete liability protection to directors when they accept an offer to buy the company. Having concluded that the Macmillan directors violated their duties of care and loyalty in favoring acceptance of a management-affiliated offer, the court went out of its way to express its view that the directors *and* the investment bankers who provided management with the expected opinions would have personal liability.

40. Shapiro, Chapter 6, this volume.

41. Capital City Associates Limited Partnership v. Interco Inc., 551 A.2d 787, 792 (Del. Ch., 1988).

42. Shapiro, Chapter 6, this volume. The difficulty lawyers and courts seem to have in understanding what investment bankers actually mean by their various grades of valuation opinions highlights one of the real difficulties in undertaking interdisciplinary work: How can a practitioner of one discipline ever be sure that she really understands what the other discipline is talking about? The cultural anthropologist Clifford Geertz captures the dilemma:

> Whether it be mathematicians, discoursing, like so many wine-tasters, on the differences, apparently real to them and invisible to everybody else, between "deep," "elegant," "beautiful," "powerful," and "subtle" proofs; physicists invoking such peculiar words of praise and blame as "tact" or "skimming"; or literary critics invoking the relative presence of a mysterious property, to outsiders anyway, called "realization," the terms through which the devotees of a scholarly pursuit represent their aims, judgments, justifications, and so on seems to me to take one a long way, when properly understood, toward grasping what that pursuit is all about. [C. Geertz, *Local Knowledge: Further Essays in Interpretive Anthropology,* pp. 158–59 (1983)].

43. See Capital City Associates Limited Partnership v. Interco Inc., 551 A.2d 787, 792 (Del. Ch., 1988); Grand Metropolitan PLC v. The Pillsbury Co., [1988-1989 Transfer Binder] Fed. Sec. L. Rep. (CCH) par 99, 104 (Del. Ch., 1988); Shamrock Holdings, Inc. v. Polaroid Corp. [Current] Fed. Sec. L. Rep. (CCH) par. 94, 340 (Del. Ch., 1989).

44. Id. at 13.

45. See note 43 above.

46. Capital City Associates Limited Partnership v. Interco Inc., 551 A.2d 799–800 (Del. Ch., 1988).

47. Reiner Kraakman and I have elsewhere described the nature of judicial view of target management decisions to preclude a tender offer that would be appropriate if the courts should ultimately conclude that management's determination that the price offered is inadequate is to be treated as a sufficient threat to justify preclusive tactics. See Gilson and Kraakman, "Delaware's Intermediate Standard for Defensive Tactics: Is There Substance to Proportionality Review?," *Business Lawyer, 44,* 247 (1989).

48. Amanda Acquisition Corporation v. Universal Foods Corporation, No. 88-C-1296 (JPS) E.D. Wis. (7th Cir., 1989).

PART 3

AUCTION PRICING OF CORPORATE CONTROL AND SHAREHOLDER WELFARE

CHAPTER 11

AUCTION LAW AND PRACTICE IN UNSOLICITED TAKEOVERS (and in Other Corporate Control Transfer Cases)

Peter Allan Atkins
Blaine V. Fogg

PRELIMINARY STATEMENT

To coin a paraphrase: egregious facts can make confusing law. Such appears particularly to be true in the area of judicial review of the obligations of directors when selling a company. In response to a few cases in this area presenting rather egregious facts, we have seen a series of judicial opinions which have:

- Described the duty of directors as that of "auctioneers" whose focus should be on obtaining the "best price" for stockholders. (Revlon)
- Commanded "auctioneer"-directors to act as "fair and neutral auctioneer[s]" running a process "on an even and illuminated playing field.' (Fruehauf)

Peter Allan Atkins is a partner of the law firm of Skadden, Arps, Slate, Meagher & Flom.

Blaine V. Fogg, Partner, concentrates in Corporate Law at Skadden, Arps, Slate, Meagher & Flom. He holds the J.D., Harvard University, 1965.

All or part of this material has been, or may be, used in other materials published by the author or his colleagues.

- Described the "auction" process as requiring "the most scrupulous adherence to ordinary principles of fairness." (Macmillan)

These opinions have unleased enormous uncertainty in an arena of major import in America today—the sale of corporate control. Questions abound. When does the so-called "Revlon duty" arise? What is an "auction" in the sale of control context? Does Revlon literally require directors to be Sotheby-style "auctioneers"? Does the term imply legally required procedures? If so, what are they? Is price alone relevant, or may other factors be considered? Must directors be "fair" in an abstract sense in running an "auction"—even if they act on a disinterested, informed basis and in good faith?

The duty of directors under Revlon has become a fertile area of litigation. This litigation has focused as much on attempts to clarify the fundamental meaning of the duty as it has on determining whether specific conduct violates it.

This outline addresses key issues and developments relating to Revlon and its meaning. As a preamble, two points are worth noting. First, the central issue appears to be whether directors—in seeking to implement their duty of loyalty to shareholders in the sale of control context by attempting to maximize current value for the benefit of shareholders—will (a) be held to a business judgment standard (acting as disinterested directors on an informed basis and in good faith) or (b) have the burden of an additional higher, undefined standard ("fairness"). That question has recently been framed by a number of Delaware decisions and may soon be addressed more fully by the Delaware Supreme Court. See II.E. below.

Second, whatever standard ultimately is applied, it is evident that directorial conduct is being more carefully scrutinized than ever before in change in control situations. Even in cases not evincing egregious facts, courts are looking closely at whether the decision-making by directors in particular cases is truly informed, and whether their conduct reflects a lack of good faith by failing (at least in Delaware) honestly to look primarily to the interests of shareholders.

I.   When does Revlon "Auction" Duty Attach?

A. Revlon—Clear sale decision in face of unsolicited bid.
   1. *Key facts:* Pantry Pride initial friendly overtures to Revlon, offering $43 per share, were rebuffed. Revlon board determined that price up to $45 a share should be inadequate and adopted "back-end" poison pill. Pantry

Pride then commenced cash tender offer for any and all outstanding Revlon common shares at $47 per share (and for outstanding convertible preferred). Conditional bid to be financed by "high-yield" bonds, and Pantry Pride intended to sell certain Revlon assets to finance acquisition. Revlon recommended against offer and initiated self-tender for up to 10 million shares in exchange for $47 face amount per share of subordinated notes containing restrictive covenants, including incurrence of more debt, and 1/10 of a share of convertible preferred stock valued at $100 per preferred share. Exchange resulted in issuance of $475 million of notes and one million shares of preferred. Pantry Pride lowered tender offer price to $42 per share, reflecting exchange's dilutive effect. Revlon, meanwhile, began negotiating with Forstmann Little & Co., an LBO firm. Revlon board rejected Pantry Pride's pending offer, which then was increased in quick succession to $50 and then $53 per share. Revlon board again rejected offer. It approved proposed LBO in which management would participate and shareholders would receive $56 in cash per share. In connection with proposed LBO, Forstmann agreed to assume $475 million exchange notes and Revlon agreed to redeem "poison pill" rights and lift certain restrictive covenants in exchange notes, which resulted in a significant decline in market price of notes and litigation threats from noteholders. Pantry Pride thereafter increased offer to $56.25 per share, subject to redemption or voiding of "poison pill" rights, waiver of covenants in exchange notes and preferred, and placement of three Pantry Pride directors on Revlon board. Pantry Pride indicated it was prepared to bid further, and would top any Forstmann offer with slightly higher one. At subsequent Revlon board meeting, Forstmann raised its offer to $57.25 in cash per share, but in return demanded "no-shop" provision, cancellation fee and "lock-up" option to purchase two Revlon divisions for $525 million. "Lock-up" could be exercised by Forstmann when any person acquired 40 percent of Revlon's shares. Revlon board decided Forstmann's offer was more favorable to shareholders than Pantry Pride's, in part because it protected Revlon's noteholders and its financing was in place. Pantry Pride obtained temporary restraining order against transfer of "lock-up" option assets, then increased its offer to $58 per share, subject to withdrawal of "lock-up" option.

2. *Key judicial conclusion:* Delaware Supreme Court held:
   "[W]hen Pantry Pride increased its offer to $50 per share, and then to $53, it became apparent to all that *the break-up of the company was inevitable.* The Revlon board's authorization permitting management to negotiate a

merger or buyout with a third party was a recognition that *the company was for sale.* The duty of the board had thus changed from the preservation of Revlon as a corporate entity to the maximization of the company's value at a sale for the stockholders' benefit. This significantly altered the board's responsibilities under the Unocal standards. It no longer faced threats to corporate policy and effectiveness, or to the stockholders' interests, from a grossly inadequate bid. The whole question of defensive measures became moot. *The directors' role change from defenders of the corporate bastion to auctioneers charged with getting the best price for the stockholders at a sale of the company."* (Emphasis added.)

B. American Standard—Defensive recapitalization effecting change in majority ownership equals "sale."

  1. *Key facts:* Black & Decker Corp. (B&D) commenced all cash tender offer for all American Standard Inc. (ASI) shares. ASI adopted "interim rights plan" and proposed a recapitalization, subject to shareholder approval. Under recap, shareholders would receive cash dividend and debentures, and retain stub equity; part of funding for recap was to be provided by purchase by ESOP of $80 million of stub stock. Before recap, public shareholders held 92.6 percent, management held 4.8 percent, and ASI savings plan held 2.6 percent of ASI stock. Recap would have resulted in public holding 45.5 percent, management holding 23.9 percent, and savings plan plus ESOP holding 30.5 percent of ASI stock, on fully diluted basis giving effect to exercise of options granted to management in recap.

  2. *Key judicial conclusions:*

    a. A transaction which results in change in control, although not acquisition of entire equity of company, nonetheless results in "sale" under Revlon.

    "It seems unreasonable to conclude that the Delaware Supreme Court would limit the applicability of the duties of Revlon, Inc., to only those situations involving the complete sale of all shares of the company. Indeed, the Court of Chancery has recognized that the directors of a company have an obligation to maximize the amount received by shareholders once it is clear to them that the 'corporation is to be subject to a change in control.' (citation omitted]."

    b. Options granted to management in recap, and not conditioned so that exercise could not effect change in control, should be treated as exercised for purposes of determining whether public shareholders have given up control.

    "[M]anagement [through the exercise of its options] will receive the exclusive right to remove control from the public shareholders. Thus, while the Recapitalization Plan calls for a reduction in public ownership in American Standard to 55 percent [initially], it inherently effects the acquisition of control of the corporation."

c. By contrast with Newmont (see D. below), which involved pro rata dividend to shareholders, ASI shareholders were "selling" portion of their equity in exchange for distributed cash and debentures, management and ESOP were "buying" additional percentage of ASI for value, and recap plan "provide[d] for no mechanism to stop a change in control."

3. *Other similar cases with different result:*
   a. Gelco: Court found that no "irreversible" change of control would occur if Gelco's partial exchange offer and sale of preferred stock was successful, although Gelco's management and directors, together with company's financial advisor, would then control 53 percent of voting power of company. Court noted that preferred stock was likely to be redeemed in relatively near future and, in meantime, company's financial advisor who held the preferred stock was not bound to vote in any particular way.

   b. Harcourt Brace: Court found that proposed recapitalization would not prevent successful bid for control of HBJ, despite fact (not noted in opinion) that shares held by ESOP, by financial advisor, and by management as result of recap aggregated over 50 percent of voting shares outstanding. Court noted that although HBJ's financial advisor had been issued shares of exchangeable redeemable preferred stock carrying 8,160,000 votes that gave it "some voice in running the company," there was nothing that would compel it to favor management or reject attractive offer for its stock. Plan also called for contribution of new issue of convertible preferred stock to preexisting HBJ ESOP and offer to ESOP of HBJ common shares to be repurchased on open market. Court found that this feature of restructuring would not prevent a successful bid for control as well, since pass-through provisions (under which shares allocated to individual participants' accounts would be voted by participants) allowed shares allocated to ESOP to be voted by employees and not management; and trustees of ESOP had agreed to vote nonallocated shares in proportion to allocated shares.

C. Macmillan (Evans)—Defensive recapitalization effecting concentration of working control in insider group equals "sale."

1. *Key facts:* Over period of one year, in advance of any direct takeover threats, Macmillan management and financial advisors studied possible recaps, all of which had management "ending up owning absolute majority control of restructured company," which management would acquire "not by investing new capital at prevailing market prices, but by being granted several hundred thousand restricted Macmillan shares and stock options" which would be "'exchanged'... into several million shares of recapitalized company." Also, ESOP would purchase large block of stock with company-provided debt, and management would be installed as trustee, thus giving management control over unallocated shares. Management proposed and board approved certain elements (restricted shares and option grants, leveraged ESOP stock purchase and change of ESOP trustee) although not presented as part of overall restructuring. Design of restructuring approach shifted to split up of Macmillan into "Publishing" and "Information" companies, with management remaining with Information. While still under consideration, Bass Group filed Schedule 13D reflecting holdings of 7.5 percent of Macmillan stock. Management continued working on restructuring, creating charts continuing to show in all variations management ending up with over 50 percent of Information's shares. Bass Group submitted to board offer to acquire Macmillan for $64 per share cash, conditioned on board approval, and indicated possibility of bidding more if it could review nonpublic information. Management thereafter presented to special committee of board split-up restructuring proposal, which contemplated senior management owning more than 50 percent of Information (as a result of conversion of management's aggregate equity-based Macmillan compensation arrangements).

Proposal was revised to reduce management ownership in Information to 39 percent (based on certain valuations by financial advisors of *pro forma* equity of Publishing and Information), at suggestion of special committee's advisors so restructuring would not be regarded as transfer of corporate control. No negotiations were held with Bass Group. After advice that Bass Group $64 per share cash offer was inadequate and restructuring (valued at between $63 and $65 per share) was fair from financial point of view, and without any negotiations with management on any aspect of restructuring, including ownership levels in restructured companies, restructuring was approved by Macmillan special committee and board. Restructuring was not subject to shareholder approval.

As approved, restructuring provided following treatment: public shareholders to get, as dividend, for each Macmillan share: (i) $52.35 cash; (ii) $4.50 debenture, (iii) "stub" share of Publishing valued at $5.10, and (iv) one-half share of Information valued at $2.10. Management to be treated differently. Management to forgo cash and debenture part of dividend and exchange most of their restricted stock and unexercised option (representing 4.5 percent of Macmillan), for aggregate of 39.2 percent of Information, based on an "equivalent value" methodology designed by financial advisors.

Bass Group made revised, alternative proposals: (i) to acquire entire company for $73 cash per share or (ii) participate in restructuring very similar to one board approved, except (A) management would participate pro rata with other shareholders in dividend rather than increased percentage ownership in Information, (B) Bass Group would pay cash for Information stock otherwise to go to management, and (C) Macmillan shareholders would receive $5.65 more cash ($58 per share total).

Macmillan financial advisors concluded that revised $73 offer was inadequate, based on range of break up values for Macmillan, and that Bass Group alternative restructuring constituted a "sale of control" while management restructuring did not (although no opinion was given that Bass Group restructuring was "unfair"). Special committee and board rejected both Bass Group alternatives in favor of proceeding with management restructuring.

2. *Key judicial conclusion:* Delaware Chancery Court applies Unocal analysis. In considering whether Macmillan restructuring response was reasonable in relation to "threat" posed by Bass Group, Court, focuses on "cram down" nature of nonshareholder-approved dividend, and addresses comparative value of Bass Group $73 per share acquisition proposal and $64.15 per share management restructuring. In so doing, Court addresses whether restructuring fairly can be compared with acquisition proposal— i.e., whether restructuring constitutes a "sale." Court finds it does:

   "[T]he present record indicates that the restructuring, although not a sale of an absolute majority interest, does constitute a sale of effective control of Information that would warrant a control premium. Wasserstein Perella so recognized in its comparison of the management and restructuring proposals. Documents internally generated by Macmillan reported that the management group would have effective control over Information even with less than 50 percent of its stock. …That conclusion is consistent with decisions by the courts of this and other states.

Finally, the conclusion that effective control will pass to management is consistent with the intent and historical evolution of the restructuring which, in every proposed permutation, had management owning over 50 percent of Information. That was the plan up until the last moment, when counsel advised the Special Committee that the issuance to management of an absolute majority of Information stock could be interpreted as a sale of the company. ...Such a sale would arguably trigger duties under Revlon, which requires that the directors selling the company realize the highest available value for shareholders. By reducing management's equity percentage to below 50 percent, the risk of triggering Revlon duties would be reduced if not eliminated, yet the objective of giving management effective control would still be accomplished. The change, then, was one of form, not substance, a conclusion supported by charts prepared for the board on May 27, 1988, which stated that management would obtain "voting control" over Information even with a block of less than 50 percent...

To summarize: The Court finds (preliminarily) that the restructuring involves a transfer of effective control that under normal market conditions would command a control premium. However, the "fairness" opinions upon which the defendants rely to defend the restructuring are expressly grounded on the assumption that control will not pass. Accordingly, the $64.15 restructuring is inferior to the $73 Bass offer on that basis as well." (Footnotes omitted.)

D. Newmont Mining—Defensive recapitalization, and related third party purchases boosting ownership to 49 percent, not a "sale" where provisions of standstill agreement protected public shareholders from exercise of control by large third party shareholder.

1. *Key facts:* Newmont Mining became subject to unsolicited takeover interest from T. Boone Pickens. Newmont had resolved a prior takeover threat from Consolidated Gold Fields (CGF) by agreeing CGF could buy up to 33 1/3 percent of Newmont stock, but subject to long-term standstill agreement which, among other things, limited its ownership and board representation to that percentage. Standstill agreement was terminable by CGF if another party acquired 9.9 percent of Newmont. CGF acquired 26 percent of Newmont and held it under standstill arrangement for some years. Pickens' entities acquired 9.95 percent of Newmont, giving CGF right to terminate. Thereafter, Pickens' entities commenced unsolicited partial cash tender offer for 42 percent of Newmont shares. If successful, such entities would have held just over 50 percent of Newmont. In

response, Newmont (a) declared $33 per share extraordinary cash dividend to all shareholders (including CGF, which then owned 26 percent of Newmont) and (b) extended and amended existing standstill agreement with CGF to permit CGF to buy additional Newmont shares but limited CGF's ownership to 49.9 percent and restricted its Newmont board representation to 40 percent. Newmont's actions facilitated CGF engaging in "street sweep" which increased its Newmont holdings to 49.7 percent and defeated Pickens' offer. Such actions (particularly extraordinary dividend, which provided substantial financing for street sweep) helped avoid risk CGF would terminate standstill and itself engage in unfettered street sweep.

2. *Key judicial conclusions:* In rejecting claim that Newmont directors had breached Revlon duties, Delaware Supreme Court found that under Revlon the sale of Newmont was not "inevitable" because:

> "First, *Newmont was never for sale.* During the short period in which these events occurred, the *Newmont board held fast to its decision to keep the company independent.* ...Ultimately, *this goal was achieved by the standstill agreement and related defensive measure.*
>
> Second, there was neither a bidding contest, nor a sale. The only bidder for Newmont was Ivanhoe. Gold Fields was not a bidder, but wished only to protect its already substantial interest in the company. It did so through the street sweep. Thus, the *Newmont board did not 'sell' the company to Gold Fields. The latter's purchases were from private sellers.* While Gold Fields now owns 49.7 percent of the stock, its representation on the board is only 40 percent because of the restrictions of the standstill agreement. These facts do not strip the Newmont board of the presumptions of independence and good faith under the business judgment rule. ...*Even though Newmont's declaration of the dividend facilitated the street sweep, it did not constitute a 'sale' of the company by Newmont.*" (Emphasis added.)

E. Holly Farms—Contracts with, and receipt of bids from, prospective acquirors (including party initiating unsolicited tender offer) *prior to* board decision to sell target did not (in absence of demonstrable presale decision "auction" effort seeking to maximize value) satisfy Revlon duty which attaches *after* sale decision made.

1. *Key facts:* Holly Farms board, after rejecting prior acquisition overtures by Tyson Foods at lower price, was faced with all cash Tyson tender offer for all Holly shares at $52 per share. Board rejected offer, while its financial advisors explored alternatives, including seeking "white knights."

Thereafter, Holly advised Tyson that Holly's board would meet on November 16, 1988, to consider its alternatives, although no decision to sell company had been made, and entered into confidentiality agreement with Tyson pursuant to which Tyson was given confidential information which already had been provided to other interested parties. Holly's board met on November 16 and 17 and considered various alternatives (including recapitalization, which its financial advisors valued at $56–$57 per share; Tyson's cash offer which it raised to $54 per share; ConAgra's offer to acquire Holly in stock-for stock tax-free pooling transaction which Holly's financial advisors valued at $54 per share; and taking no action). During board's deliberations, it determined to sell company and that ConAgra's proposal was best financially for shareholders. Without advising any other parties (including Tyson) of sale decision and without seeking further bids, Holly's board authorized execution of, and Holly and ConAgra executed, merger agreement. Among other things, agreement provided for grant to ConAgra of option to purchase Holly's core poultry business, and $15 million termination fee as well as expense reimbursement, if merger not completed.

2. *Key judicial conclusion:* In preliminary enjoining asset "lock-up" option, termination fee and expense reimbursement provisions, Delaware Chancery Court stated it was doing so "because the board of Holly Farms did not utilize the proper procedures to maximize the value of the corporation *after* the board decided to sell it...." (Emphasis added.)

II. Directors Obligations as "Auctioneers."

A. Value maximization vs. best overall transaction.
   1. *Judicial formulations.* Have been various judicial formulations of duty of directors under Delaware law once they determine to sell company (or have concluded that sale is inevitable):
      a. Revlon: "The duty of the board had...changed...to the *maximization* of the company's *value* at a sale for the stockholders benefit." "The directors' role change...to auctioneers shareholders at a sale of the company." (Emphasis added.)
      b. Fruehauf: The directors' "cardinal fiduciary 'obligation to the corporation and its shareholders is to ensure *maximization of* the company's *value* at a sale for the stockholders benefit.'" (Emphasis added.)
      c. J. P. Stevens: Revlon recognizes that once a change in control is concededly in the works, the responsibility of the board is limited to

facilitating and achieving the *best possible transaction* for the share-holders." (Emphasis added.)

    d. Fairchild Camera: The board's obligation is "to try in good faith…to get the *best available transaction* for the shareholders." (Emphasis added.)

  2. *Analysis:* Are these formulations really different? A rationalizing—and rational—approach:

    a. Revlon's basic teaching is that, when faced with third party unsolicited bid, if target directors determine to take action which effectively constitutes sale of target, directors must attempt to follow a process which legitimately provides opportunity to develop maximum value for shareholders. If no such process honestly pursued, directors fail to satisfy Revlon duties.

    b. Assuming value-maximization process honestly undertaken and pursued, if multiple bids result, then directors should have freedom to exercise honest business judgment in choosing between or among them based on all relevant factors, not just nominal value, in light of directors good faith belief regarding what overall would best serve shareholder interests.

      (i)   Focus is still on delivering most valuable transaction to share-holders.

      (ii)   However, directors in many cases will be faced with difficult comparative issues of valuation, "doability" and timing—all of which may be legitimately relevant to assessing the overall best transaction for shareholders.

    c. Cases such as J.P. Stevens and Fairchild Camera, which express Revlon duty in broader terms than "value maximization" alone, can be explained on foregoing basis—i.e., directors functioning in good faith to maximize value are not stripped of right to evaluate all aspects of bids received in light of real world risks and issues affecting ability to achieve such result.

    d. Foregoing analysis supported by language in recent opinion of Chancellor Allen in TW Services. See C.2. below.

B. Factors to consider.

  1. *General.* Any number of factors may be relevant in given case to assessing which competing transaction is likely to produce best overall result for shareholders. Each situation must be judged on its own.

  2. *Relevant factors.* Relevant factors, in given case, may include:

    a. Valuation-related issues.

(i)   If securities to be received by target shareholders, important valuation issues can be presented by terms of securities, and by differences in terms of similar securities in competing bids. See RJR for noteworthy judicial appreciation of value implications of such features as presence or absence (and timing of implementation) of dividend and interest reset mechanisms in pay-in-kind and convertible securities, and presence or absence of call protection in convertible securities.

(ii)   Can be significant differences between nominal and "real" value. See RJR.

(iii) Important to recognize need for expert assistance in potentially difficult and unfamiliar territory of securities valuation, and ability of directors to rely on expert advice. See, e.g., Delaware General Corporation Law §141(e).

b. Timing-related issues/risk areas.

(i)   Differences in timing can involve:
- Differences in present value of bids.
- Differences in known risks to consummation.
- Differences in exposure to unknown risks.

(ii)   Antitrust risk can affect timing:
- Hart-Scott-Rodino clearance period.
- Substantive U.S. antitrust enforcement potential.
- Non-U.S. issues, if any.

(iii) Regulatory clearances, if any, can affect timing.

(iv)   Financing requirements can create timing issues/risks:
- Bridge financing technique often used as means of mitigating target's concerns.
- Credibility of financing sources a factor to assess.

c. Conditions to closing can have timing implications, e.g.:

(i)   Financing
(ii)   Litigation
(iii) Solvency opinion

3. *A case in point: Fairchild Camera.* In connection with bidding contest for Fairchild Camera, Delaware Chancery court held that Fairchild board had fulfilled its fiduciary duties of loyalty and care in conducting "auction" of company. Two proposals to acquire Fairchild were made by Gould. Fairchild board authorized its advisors to commence search for "white knight" after being advised that both offers were inadequate and that Fairchild-Gould combination would create antitrust problems. After

exhaustive search, potential bidder, Schlumberger, indicated interest in acquiring Fairchild. Both bidders were asked to make their best offer to board after it became evident that there were no other potential suitors for company.

Gould offered to make tender offer for slightly over 50 percent of outstanding stock of Fairchild at $70 per share in cash followed by merger in which each remaining share of Fairchild would receive new issue of Gould preferred stock (terms of which were not disclosed). When Gould's financial advisors were repeatedly asked to describe terms of preferred, they indicated that security would have market value of $70 but declined to provide its specific terms. Schlumberger proposed to purchase all of Fairchild's outstanding stock for $66 per share in cash conditioned upon, among other things, acceptance of transaction by board on day offer made.

Fairchild's financial advisors advised that $66 offer from Schlumberger was adequate, but were unable to value Gould offer because it did not contain terms of preferred to be issued in second step. Board accepted Schlumberger offer because (i) significant antitrust problems inherent in business combination with Gould were not present in similar transaction with Schlumberger, (ii) possible four-month delay in Gould transaction could, in opinion of management, adversely affect Fairchild's operations, (iii) uncertain value of preferred stock offered by Gould, and (iv) concern that Gould could not fully finance takeover (which was to be partially funded by refinancing of Gould subsidiary.)

In face of arguments that board improperly favored Schlumberger by accepting its lower-priced offer, Delaware Chancery Court held that board had acted in good faith. In responding to plaintiff shareholder's argument that only possible explanation for choosing lower-priced offer was bad faith, Court indicated that:

> "The Schlumberger offer was all cash and from a source that required no financing. It could be closed quickly. The Gould offer was in significant part paper and there had been no specifics given as to the terms of the paper. Moreover, the Gould offer, if accepted, would require some time to get cash into the shareholders' hands. Finally, there was some basis to suspect that Gould may have intentionally left itself some maneuvering room on the issue of the precise terms of its second step consideration."

C. Is there literal duty to "auction"—or even to "shop?": scope of Revlon "auctioneer's" process.

1. *General.* Cases exploring meaning of Revlon make clear that Revlon has not substituted simple set of Sotheby's auction rules for directorial judgment. Widely varying procedures have been adopted in particular cases—and have been judicially approved. See cases referenced below in this section and under IV. below. The key inquiry is whether "process," however structured, provides directors with sufficient information to make good faith judgment regarding what is highest value transaction for shareholders.

2. *Recent judicial statement: TW Services.* Observation of Chancellor Allen in recent TW Services opinion states this view succinctly:

   [I]n my opinion, the so-called Revlon duty is not necessarily a duty to conduct an "auction" or to keep "a level playing field" when a firm is for sale or, indeed, to proceed in any prescribed way; rather it is the duty to exercise judgment (in good faith and prudently) in an effort to maximize immediate shareholder value.

3. *A metaphorical device.* Under this view of Revlon, use of term "auctioneer" seems more a judicial/literary device to emphasize ultimate goal—maximization of immediate value of owners of property in question—rather than literal definition of process to be followed.

4. *An elaborated view: Interco.* In earlier Interco decision, Chancellor Allen provided more elaborate commentary:

   "[Revlon] does not require…that before every corporate merger agreement can validly be entered into, the constituent corporations must be shopped or, more radically, an auction process undertaken, even though a merger may be regarded as a sale of the Company. But mergers or recapitalizations or other important corporate transactions may be authorized by a board only advisedly. There must be a reasonable basis for the board of directors involved to conclude that the transaction involved is in the best interest of the shareholders. This involves having information about possible alternative… Indeed, the central obligation of a board (*assuming it acts in good faith*—an assumption that would not hold for Revlon) is to act in an *informed manner*. When the transaction is so fundamental as the restructuring here (or a sale or merger of the Company), the obligation to be informed would seem to require that reliable information about the value of alternative transactions be explored. When the transaction is a sale of the Company, in which the interest of current stockholders will be converted to cash or otherwise terminated, the requirement to be well informed would ordinarily mandate an appropriate probing of the market for alternatives (and a public auction, should interest be shown). Particularly is that true when a sale is to a management affiliated group (the ubiquitous management LBO transactions) for apparent reasons involving human frailty. But even in that setting, fiduciary obligations can be met in ways other than a traditional auction, if the procedure supplies the board with information from which it can conclude that it has arranged the best available transaction for shareholders." (Emphasis in original.)

5. *Scientific Leasing.* In Scientific Leasing, involving sale of company not in response to unsolicited bid, no auction was conducted (board determined "that to disclose prematurely the fact that SLI might be for sale, could adversely affect SLI's business and decrease, rather than enhance, SLI's value to particular acquirer"), although historically SLI was known in industry as willing acquisition candidate and in fact acquisition interest from other parties had surfaced and was entertained, including concurrently with deal ultimately approved. Delaware Chancery Court held that board had not breached fiduciary duty "by negotiating an acquisition agreement with only one bidder without having first conducted an auction calculated to elicit bids high than the...agreed to offering price." Court reached conclusion despite presence of negotiated stock option on 16 percent of SLI stock, "window shop" provision, expense reimbursement provision and management incentive arrangements, as to which Court found there was "no showing...that those arrangements constituted the type of provisions condemned as lock-up devices that improperly preclude competing in active auctions." Court stated that specific methods directors may use to elicit bids from potential acquirors is a matter within business judgment of board that necessarily must vary from case to case. Court's conclusion that challenge to directors' process not likely to prevail influenced by presence of 26 percent shareholder, with two board representatives and interests identical with other shareholders, which supported negotiated deal.

6. *Texas Air.* In Texas Air, District Court for the Southern District of Florida, applying Delaware law, stated that board had no duty to help arrange competing bid before entering into merger agreement that contained "lock-up" option and "no-shop" provision, even if board expected competing bid to materialize within few days. Court stated that plaintiff failed to cite "any legal authority that obligated a board to directors to jeopardize the bid in order to give a group of employees or anyone else an indefinite amount of time in which to develop and finance an acquisition proposal."

7. *KDI.* Delaware Chancery Court held directors entitled to protection of business judgment rule as evidence indicated special committee was adequately informed before approving acquisition by group including CEO. Court found that special committee knew its financial advisors were soliciting bids from other sources for almost three months. and rejected as having no precedent under Delaware law plaintiffs contention that this knowledge was insufficient and special committee was required to wait for at least one other bid to surface. Court also noted special committee received opinion of financial advisors that price was fair after unsuccessful attempts were made to solicit bids.

8. *Fort Howard.* Delaware Chancery Court (Chancellor Allen) upheld, as satisfying Revlon duties, action of special committee in responding to management group LBO proposal, where special committee, although it "did not conduct an action of any kind" "it did, however, negotiate provisions purportedly intended to permit an effective check of the market before the [management group's] offer could close." Court concluded "this approach was adopted in good faith and was effective to give the board an informed, dependable basis for the view that the [management group's] offer is the best available transaction from the point of view of the Fort Howard shareholders." Court found that rationale for keeping management group's interest secret—to complete negotiations before turning to the market—"makes sense." Court was also "particularly impressed" with announcement, made at time agreement on LBO transaction was announced, that board would entertain alternative bids. Court declined to find obligation to shop company prior to signing LBO transaction because it was satisfied that "the alternative course pursued [of a post-signing market check] was reasonably calculated to (and did) effectively probe the market for alternative possible transactions." See IV.B. below for more detailed statement of facts. (See also Van Gorkom, where Delaware Supreme Court (pre-Revlon) did not reject outright post-signing market test theory of value validation, although Court found facts did not support claim of unfettered market test.)

9. *Amstead.* Although approving settlement of shareholder litigation challenging failure to shop management sponsored LBO, Delaware Chancery Court (Chancellor Allen) reflected severe misgivings about process used. Court framed issue by asking "was the process one that adequately checked the appropriate market for alternatives." Court criticized procedures used by special committee, noting that "the record discloses no active effort...to attempt to shop the company or to engage

in an alternative form of proceeding designed to encourage the emergence of an offer that would compete with the management sponsored ESOP LBO transaction." Thrust of Court's concern was framed in traditional business judgment rule terms—whether special committee acted in good faith. Court stated:

> "[W]here the transaction is so important to shareholders as this one was, the question does arise, 'why did the independent committee of the board—if it was motivated in good faith to achieve the best transaction for the shareholders—not check that opinion by shopping the company, or at least negotiating for a period in which it could publicly encourage any information that a canvas of the relevant market could provide. Why did the committee not try to explore the alternatives actively?'"

Despite genuine misgivings, Court approved settlement in recognition of difficulty plaintiff would have in proving gross negligence or bad faith. Court also found "particularly important" that a substantial "sophisticated, self-interested" shareholder had accepted offer after negotiating a $.75 per share price increase.

D. Consideration of nonshareholder interests.
1. *Basic teaching of Revlon:* Directors, in fulfilling duty of loyalty by trying to obtain best available transaction for shareholders, may not consider nonshareholder interests unless "there are rationally related benefits accruing to the stockholders."
2. *Analysis.* Consistency of shareholder and other constituents' interest may exist—up to a point:
   a. Transactions where shareholders to get securities:
      (i)   Success of business, and therefore performance and treatment of various nonshareholder constituencies, relevant to shareholder value and realization.
   b. Transaction where shareholders to get all cash:
      (i)   More difficult to tie, at time of transaction, to shareholder interest.
      (ii) Retention of business relationships (e.g., employee population, customers, suppliers, financing sources) may still be important if transaction fails or as part of enterprise buyer is paying for.
3. *Recent judicial statement.* In recent TW Services opinion, Chancellor Allen observed in footnote:
   > "Even where the board has elected to pursue a sale for cash, however, several factors justify some board concern with long-term corporate

issues: first, the enterprise must be well maintained in order to attract the best price; second, a sale on acceptable terms might not be arranged; third, the best available sales transaction might entail a part of the sale price being paid in debt or equity in the corporation or the successor to its business...."

E. "Scrupulous adherence to... fairness."

　1. *Key open question: business judgment or "fairness" review standard?*
Delaware Supreme Court bench opinion in Macmillan, and cases following, have raised, but left unanswered, critical question regarding standard of judicial review of board conduct in conducting "auction" under Revlon. In essence, question is whether apart from the normal business judgement review of board decisions—which focuses on disinterested directors making adequately informed decisions in good faith—Revlon imposes some separate "fairness" standard for "auctions" involving sale of corporate enterprise.

　2. Macmillan Bench Opinion.

　　a. Delaware Supreme Court enjoined asset "lock-up" option granted to Kohlberg Kravis Roberts & Co., the bidding group with which management allied itself in responding to an unsolicited tender offer by Maxwell Communications. In reversing Chancery Court decision, Delaware Supreme Court adopted lower court findings that management favored KKR during the course of auction. Most significantly, management was found to have tipped KKR regarding bidding, without providing comparable information to Maxwell. Moreover, management, which had real role in conducting auction process despite its tie to one of bidding groups, failed to advise board of its lack of neutrality.

　　b. In brief bench opinion, Court stated:

　　　"While 8 Delaware Code, Section 141(e) permits a board of directors to rely in good faith upon information, opinions, reports or statements presented by corporate officers and employees and experts, the information which the board was furnished here at critical moments in the auction was neither accurate nor complete; if anything, it was misleading in its lack of candor. We consider such breaches of duty to be material to an informed decisional process under Revlon.

　　　When senior management is a party to such breaches and, as here, has a personal interest in the outcome of the board's action, the process is tainted. The business judgment rule has no application. Instead, the matter is governed by principles of intrinsic fairness. The trial court ignored this basic rule of law and reversal is mandated.

c. Importantly, bench opinion tied Macmillan ruling to Revlon. Court stated: "Our decision in Revlon...requires that there must be the most scrupulous adherence to ordinary principles of fairness in the conduct of an auction for the sale of a corporate enterprise.

d. Concept of "ordinary principles of fairness" as part of Revlon obligation of directors expected to be elaborated on in full opinion of Delaware Supreme Court.

e. In advance of such elaboration, two Chancery Court opinions have attempted to explore or apply Macmillan bench ruling in auction contexts, each applying different approach.

3. Holly Farms

a. See I.E.1. above for summary of key facts of case.

b. Tyson challenged Holly/ConAgra agreement on bases that (1) it was product of process that unfairly precluded active bidding for Holly (Tyson stated that it had been prepared all along to bid $57 per share) and (2) Holly's directors breached their fiduciary duty in not maximizing value for shareholders. As stated by Chancery Court, "essence of...claim is that the board did not conduct an auction...as mandated by Revlon...."

c. Vice Chancellor Hartnett observed: "While it is normally within the board's prerogative as [to] how to satisfy the Revlon mandate, the Delaware Supreme Court has recently reiterated that 'Our decision in Revlon...requires that there must be the most scrupulous adherence to ordinary principles of fairness....'" Hartnett further stated: "Even if the board thought it was acting in good faith, the sale process itself was so substantially flawed that the board's actions, considering all the facts and circumstances, were not likely to have maximized the value of the corporation for its shareholders and, therefore, its actions cannot be viewed as rational."

d. "Substantial flaws" found by Chancery Court were that, "once having decided to sell, and notwithstanding strenuous negotiations with ConAgra to get the best deal from it, Holly made no real effort to negotiate with Tyson, did not even tell Tyson of board's sale decision and did not respond in any meaningful way to Tyson's inquiries as to the adequacy of its price, much less encourage an improved Tyson bid."

e. Chancery Court enjoined ConAgra "lock-up" option on Tyson's primary poultry business as not only not necessary to enhance auction process but, in fact, as "a showstopper that effectively precluded the first act." Termination fee and expense reimbursement provisions also enjoined as "likely to have been part of the effort to preclude a genuine auction."

f. Despite some language of decision, outcome may be explainable on traditional business judgment analysis. Protection of business judgment rule requires board action to be made on informed basis. In context of Revlon duty of seeking to maximize shareholder value in sale of company in response to unsolicited bid, a critical element of information is: What will credible bidders who are on the scene be willing to pay if asked for their highest and best bid with knowledge that company is for sale (or at least based on an instruction to make that assumption for purposes of submitting bid)? Having never asked this question of Tyson, and having no legitimate explanation for not having done so, it appears that Holly Farm board did not meet informed decision-making requirement imposed as prerequisite to availability of business judgment rule defense to board action.

4. RJR

a. On October 19, 1988, group which included members of RJR Nabisco's senior management ("Management Group") indicated desire to formulate proposal to acquire company in leveraged buyout at price of about $75 per share cash. Independent directors permitted Management Group to proceed and publicly disclosed that, while no decision had been made to sell company, Management Group effort was under way, with special committee formed to deal with it and any other acquisition interest that might surface. Numerous events ensued, including: bid by Kohlberg Kravis Roberts & Co. to acquire RJR (initially at $90 per share in cash and unspecified securities); independent director's decision to conduct auction of RJR pursuant to published rules and procedures; receipt of three proposals at initial November 18 deadline, including ostensibly highest but incomplete and complex proposal from group including The First Boston Corporation ("First Boston Group"); extension of bidding process to November 29 in light of First Boston Group proposal; and receipt of new bids from Management Group, KKR and First Boston Group On November 29. Although First Boston Group's second proposal was more detailed than first and nominally still highest, it was subject to substantial risks and uncertainties, including significant risk of not closing by year end which was necessary to obtain critical value-enhancing tax treatment, and accordingly was not pursued.

As result, struggle for control of RJR over course of November 29 and November 30 became match between KKR and Management Group. KKR's November 29 bid had claimed value of $106; Management Group's bid at that deadline had claimed value of $101. Since it appeared that KKR had winning bid, RJR board instructed its advisors to proceed to negotiate terms of both merger agreement and securities comprising KKR's "package." Management Group learned of these negotiations and submitted additional bid with claimed value of $108 approximately midday on November 30. Various negotiations ensued during which both bidders raised their bids, culminating, in response to requests made of each party by special committee representatives for their highest and best bids, in final bids by both KKR and Management Group valued by bidders at $109 and $112 per share, respectively. These bids were valued by company's financial advisors at $108 to $108.50 and $108.50 to $109, respectively—amounts which, given unprecedented size of debt offering necessary to finance either bid and uncertainties inherent in valuation of securities, company's advisors deemed to be "substantially equivalent."

At this point, RJR's independent directors, after 24 hours of intense activity on part of their advisors and themselves aimed at evaluating and enhancing real value of bids submitted, including at special committee meeting which had been in continuous session about 12 hours, was confronted with final, one-half hour deadline from KKR coupled with stated intent by KKR to withdraw its bid if not acted on by then. Believing this threat to be real, and concerned about risks to shareholders if it were implemented, special committee and other independent directors evaluated a number of nonfinancial—but shareholder welfare-oriented considerations—and selected KKR bid.

b. In litigation commenced by RJR shareholders in Delaware Chancery Court, plaintiffs argued, among other things, that Revlon imposes upon board in auction sale of corporate control a duty to run fair or effective auction—without regard to board's good faith or due care—and that this "Revlon duty" was violated by special committee not seeking tie-breaking set of bids.

c. Chancellor Allen rejects this view of Revlon. Rather, he opines that traditional business judgment rule is appropriate standard for judicial review of director conduct in performing their so-called Revlon duties as "auctioneers"—that Revlon decision does not impose any special duty to conduct abstractly "fair" or "effective" auction process if directors otherwise are found to have acted on fully informed, disinterested basis and in good faith. He specifically finds that RJR board had no independent duty to seek "tie breaker" round of bids when presented with what, on basis of its financial advisors' opinions, were bids that were "substantially equivalent" from financial point of view.

d. Chancellor Allen does, however, engage in fairly thorough-going and instructive review of RJR directors' "auctioneer" conduct under traditional business judgment rule analysis—reviewing directors' independence, good faith and due care.

In assessing whether business judgment rule defense was available, Court first analyzed threshold question of board's independence. Court held that only type of interest which would deprive board's determination of protection of business judgment rule is financial interest in transaction adverse to that of corporation and its shareholders. Chancellor Allen found RJR board free of any such interests, including indirect financial interest alleged to be present due to increase potential of director liability to company's bondholders if Management Group's bid succeeded.

Turning to question of whether RJR board acted in good faith, Court accepted that, as matter of law, bad faith may be inferred from directors favoring one bidder over another for private nonfinancial reasons, including (if proved) one alleged by plaintiffs: importance to members of special committee to disassociate themselves from RJR's president and CEO, whose actions had been portrayed in press as being motivated by greed, and their desire to be viewed as being free from his influence. However, Court found no reasonable likelihood that plaintiffs would prove this claim at trial.

Further as to RJR board's good faith, Court held that special committee's decision to accept one of two "substantially equivalent" bids without seeking to break tie between them was reasonable and proper. Board's action in cutting off auction in light of perceived risk that KKR would withdraw from process and in favoring that bid based on nonfinancial—but shareholder-welfare oriented—considerations was bolstered by circumstances surrounding such action: board's permissible reliance on opinions of acknowledged experts that such bids were, in fact, substantially equivalent from financial point of view; reasonableness of those opinions in light of importance to value of securities in each bidder's package of interest rate resetting mechanism and plausibility of higher relative value of KKR's securities given their version of this mechanism; and, finally, severe time constraints placed on committee by KKR and perceived risk that KKR would withdraw its bid.

Finally, as to due care, in assessing process followed by special committee and RJR board, Court could find "no neglect of duty of any sort in this instance." Court noted that board has duty to be informed of all "reasonably available" material information relating to pending matter before making decision and that more information concerning bids (that is, whether either party would pay more) could have been available if committee had asked for tie-breaking bids. Court nonetheless held that it was appropriate for board to weigh advantages of obtaining such information against risk that asking for such information could be viewed as not "reasonably available."

5. What direction next?
   a. Difficult to believe Delaware Supreme Court will articulate supervening "fairness" standard as test for after-the-fact review of director "auctioneer" conduct under Revlon notwithstanding that business judgment rule predicates of independence, good faith, and due care met. (Of course, problem with predictions is that they can be wrong!)
   b. However, even if traditional business judgment rule review is applied, prerequisites of good faith and due care appear to provide ample room to test honesty (if not "fairness" or "effectiveness") of "auction" process in any given case. Chancellor Allen expressly recognizes in RJR that freedom of judgment afforded directors under business judgment rule may not be used "as a sham or pretext to prefer one bidder for inappropriate reasons...."
   c. Macmillan bench injunction may itself be explainable in traditional business judgment terms—on theory that when *board permits* management to have significant role in running auction process in which it also has an interest tied to one of competing parties, and if management use its position to tilt process in its favor, and breaches its duty of candor by not advising or misinforming board of such conduct, board's failure to be fully informed cannot be excused by normal right to rely on management (or alternatively, board could be found not to have acted in good faith in permitting management, as an interested party, to play role in running auction process). In any event Delaware Supreme Court should soon express its views more fully.

F. Role of lock-ups, leg-ups, etc.
1. Types of arrangements often involved.
    a. "Crown jewel" asset purchase option.
    b. Stock purchase option.
    c. "Topping" or "cancellation" fees.
    d. Expense reimbursement provisions.
    e. "No shop" or "window shop" provisions.
2. Basic attitude of courts.
    a. While not *per se* unlawful, arrangements designed to give some advantage to one bidder, or to preclude other bidders, generally viewed with suspicion. See, e.g.:
        (i) *Enstar*. Delaware Chancery Court noted that lock-up arrangements have been "justifiably criticized" in past because they often have effect of chilling potential for competing bids in corporate control struggles, and stated its view that lock-ups "must be given careful scrutiny by a court to see if under all the facts and circumstances existing in a particular case they are fair to the shareholders."
        (ii) *SCM*. Second Circuit Court of Appeals, in applying New York law, stressed that "lock-up" option in takeover context creates heightened duty of care, which is further accentuated when "white knight" takes form of defensive LBO in which management intends to participate.
    b. If such arrangement reasonably related to enhancing bidding, will be upheld; but if used to preclude or prematurely end bidding, will be invalidated. See, e.g.:
        (i) *Revlon*. In upholding injunction against asset "lock-up" option, "no-shop" provision and cancellation fee, Delaware Supreme Court stated: "[W]hile those lock-ups which draw bidders into the battle benefit shareholders, similar measures which end an active auction and foreclose further bidding operate to the shareholders detriment.... The Forstmann option had a ...destructive effect on the auction process. Forstmann had already been drawn into the contest on a preferred basis, so the result of the lock-up was not to foster bidding, but to destroy it."
        (ii) *Holly Farms*. In preliminarily enjoining asset "lock-up" option, termination fee and expense reimbursement provision, Delaware Chancery Court cited proposition that "lock-ups" which encourage further bidding are acceptable, but those which deter bidding

are invalid; held that "the record does not substantiate that the lock-up was necessary to obtain ConAgra's proposal. Under the circumstances present, the lock-up was nothing but a 'show stopper' that effectively precluded the opening act." Termination fee and reimbursement provisions found "likely to have been part of the effort to preclude a genuine auction."

(iii) *J. P. Stevens.* In upholding "topping fee" and break-up fee arrangements, Delaware Chancery Court stated: "Revlon recognizes that once a change in control is concededly in the works, the responsibility of the board is limited to facilitating and achieving the best possible transaction for the shareholders. Revlon, however, does not purport to restrict the powers of a disinterested board from entering into agreements of the kind here under attack if, in doing so, the board acts in good faith and with appropriate care. While it is true, that once agreements of this kind are in place, they do have the effect of tilting the playing field in favor of the holder of such rights, that fact alone does not establish that they necessarily are not in the best interest of shareholders. Furthermore, it is the shareholders to whom the board owes a duty of fairness, not to persons seeking to acquire the Company. To continue with the metaphor, the board may tilt the playing field if, and only if, it is in the shareholders' interest to do so." (In Fort Howard, Court stated in similar vein, that board may favor one bidder over another "if in good faith and advisedly it believes shareholder interest would be thereby advanced.")

(iv) *Burlington.* In upholding "break-up" fee (2 percent of transaction value) and "window shop" clause (which allows board to respond to other bids but not solicit them), U.S. District Court for Southern District of New York, citing Revlon, stated that "lock-up" agreements, "break-up" fees, and "no-shop" agreements granted to "white knight" were permissible if such strategies enhance bidding, noting that "such arrangements may also be legitimately necessary to convince a 'white knight' to enter the bidding by providing some form of compensation for the risks it is undertaking."

(v) *Compare Storer.* In upholding "crown jewel" asset options granted at end of auction, Eleventh Circuit Court of Appeals observed that generally "lock-ups" have been held enforceable if they draw new bidders or exclude hostile ones. Criticizing this

distinction as tenuous because "[a]ll auctions must end sometime, and lock-ups by definition must discourage other bidders,"
Court thought more relevant inquiry was "whether Storer conducted a fair auction and whether KKR made the best offer,"
which Court answered affirmatively.

3. *Need for case-by-case analysis.* Analysis in each situation is highly fact
sensitive. If, in particular case, target contemplates "unleveling" playing
field, should recognize potential for judicial second-guessing is significant. Important to fully understand implications of arrangements (including
as a totality, when more than one involved) and to make reasoned
judgment regarding bidding enhancing aspect of the arrangements in light
of relevant surrounding circumstances [such as stage in bidding process;
"spread" between bids and/or indicated willingness of competing party to
bid further; relative certainty of bids; deadline, if any, imposed; assessment of bid value level by target financial advisor; "height of barrier"
created by arrangement (e.g., percentage of deal price represented by
"topping"/"cancellation" fees/expense reimbursement)].

4. Some specific cases (auction/nonauction).

   a. Cases where arrangements have been upheld:

      (i)   *Enstar:* After selling effort, and in face of proxy contest by
            shareholder not bidding for company, board approved transac-
            tion with bidder making highest concrete offer and presenting
            risk of withdrawal, including assuring to bidder voting control
            over "crown jewel" subsidiary (in which bidder had interest)
            even if offer failed.

      (ii) *Sea-Land:* after extensive selling effort, and in face of presence
            of 39.5 percent stockholder, in exchange for obtaining "fair"
            cash bid for all shares, bidder was granted option on 21.7 percent
            (fully diluted) shares at deal price.

      (iii) *Storer:* see 2.b.(v) above.

      (iv) *Scientific Leasing:* see C.5. above.

      (v)   *Keyser:* in negotiated intrastate bank acquisition, target board
            acceded to demand for issuance to bidder of warrant to purchase 24.9
            percent of target stock as part of overall proposal; target had failed in
            active efforts to encourage bid from another interested bank.

      (vi) *Texas Air:* stock option and "no shop" provisions included in
            negotiated acquisition agreements to induce rescue of financially
            troubled target; complaining party was union wishing to make
            bid but with no viable proposal on table.

(vii) *J. P. Stevens:* see 2.b.(iii) above.

(viii) *Burlington:* see 2.b.(iv) above.

(ix) *Macmillan* (Chancery Court): "break-up" fee and expense reimbursement provisions seen as having "clear effect" of drawing second bidder into auction, and combined fees of 2.5 percent of deal value not excessive.

(x) *Federated:* "break-up" fee for expenses, "topping" fee, fair value asset "lock-up" options and "window shopping" provisions viewed, in active control contest auction, as enhancing bidding; recipient changed mix of consideration to more in cash and less in securities.

(xi) *Fort Howard:* see IV.B. below.

(xii) *Becor Western:* "no-shop" provision included in management LBO merger agreement after company extensively shopped.

  b. Cases where arrangements have been invalidated:

(i) *Revlon:* see 2.b.(i) above. Duty of loyalty breached.

(ii) *SCM:* in face of active "hostile" bidder, "crown jewel" option granted at below market value to LBO group with which management would participate. Duty of care breached.

(iii) *Fruehauf:* concurrently with approving management LBO, and in face of "hostile" third party tender offer, board acted to amend stock options and incentive awards to accelerate in event 40 percent of company acquired in hostile bid, amend retirement plan to preclude hostile acquiror access to $75–100 million excess funds in plan, and exempt management LBO from state takeover statute. Duties of loyalty and care breached.

(iv) *Macmillan:* see E.2. above.

(v) *Holly Farms:* see E.3. above.

5. Binding effect of strict "no-shop" provisions.

  a. *General.* Related to questions of whether, under particular circumstances, board is obligated to seek value maximizing transaction and whether it has acted properly during course of fulfilling such duty, is question of extent, if any, to which board can restrict itself in acquisition agreement from considering alternative transactions. Before entering into acquisition agreement "white knight" or other acquiror will often require provisions that limit, and in some cases strictly forbid, target consideration of third-party acquisition interest or proposal. Frequently, target will insist on express "fiduciary out" provision with respect to certain conduct, e.g., providing information to and/or negotiating with third party (but not soliciting third-party interest) or perhaps only withdrawing recommendation of agreed-upon transaction in face of unsolicited third-party bid. Generally this "out" is exercisable only if board concludes (or is expressly advised by counsel) that action to be taken is required by directors' fiduciary duty to shareholders. In case where no "fiduciary out" exists or where it is very limited, situation can arise where third-party interest does surface and target board wishes to pursue it. Difficult questions can be presented whether board entitled (or required) to do so not withstanding restrictions in acquisition agreement, and whether liability may exist if contract breached. Two cases have directly considered some of these issues.

b. *Jewel.* In Jewel Ninth Circuit addressed issue of whether board of directors could authorize exclusive merger agreement. Jewel Companies, would-be acquiror, and Pay Less Drug Stores (Pay Less), target, entered into merger agreement which purported to prohibit Pay Less from talking with, reaching an agreement with, or otherwise approving business combination proposed by, any third-party acquiror. Subsequent to execution of "exclusive" merger agreement, Pay Less Drug Stores, Northwest (Northwest), an unrelated company, announced tender offer for outstanding shares announced tender offer for outstanding shares of Pay Less, which offer ultimately was approved unanimously by Pay Less board. Jewel sued for breach of "no-shop" covenant and for Northwest's interference with "exclusive" merger agreement. Ninth Circuit confronted issue of whether, under California law, target's board could "lawfully agree in a merger agreement to forbear from entering into competing and inconsistent agreements until the shareholders' vote occurs." Ninth Circuit found that while directors could not divest themselves of their fiduciary obligations in a contract, they could agree to refrain from entering into competing contracts until stockholders considered initial proposal. Court rejected lower court's finding that "exclusive" merger agreements were anticompetitive and contrary to public policy. Circuit court held instead that decision was within the informed business judgment of the target's board.

Court made following observations: (i) an "exclusive" agreement could be in best interests of shareholders where it attracts a desirable merger partner who would not be interested without assurances of its likelihood for success; (ii) an "exclusive" agreement tends to decrease costs of merging by increasing likelihood that combination would be effected without lengthy and expensive litigation or proxy battles; (iii) while unanticipated business proposal may be more lucrative, decision to include a "no-shop" provision is made at finite point in time by directors who lack clairvoyance; and (iv) despite board's decision, target's shareholders still retain ultimate control over disposition of company's assets, since "no shop" clause extends only until shareholder vote.

c. *ConAgra.* After execution of definitive merger agreement between MBPXL Corporation and ConAgra, which contained provision requiring board and management of both companies to use their "best efforts" to ensure that their respective shareholders approve merger, Cargill commenced tender offer for MBPXL. Board of MBPXL, relying on another clause in merger agreement which provided that "nothing herein contained shall relieve either Board of Directors of their continuing fiduciary duties to their respective shareholders," declined to recommend merger agreement to its shareholders and instead chose to recommend Cargill's tender offer.

ConAgra brought action against Cargill alleging that it tortiously interfered with merger agreement. Nebraska Supreme Court determined that the "fiduciary out" in the merger agreement expressly permitted MBPXL's course of action. However, went on to indicate that, even absent "fiduciary out" provision, it would have imposed supervening obligation on board. Court stated that it would not approve of provisions such as "best efforts" clause if their effect was to restrict board's ability to use its own judgment on management matters. Court held that MBPXL's board could not pledge to use its best efforts to ensure that its shareholders approved merger agreement when to do so would violate its fiduciary duties to obtain highest value. Court stated that if MBPXL directors found subsequent offer to be superior, they were bound to recommend better offer to their shareholders. Finally, Court expressly did not answer question whether MBPXL directors would have personal liability resulting from breach of ConAgra merger agreement.

III. Board Process.

A. General.

1. *Conflicts review:* conduct conflicts/"relationships" review at outset. Even where management/other directors not actively participating in

acquisition proposal to be submitted to board, should focus on other arrangements/relationships that may exist. E.g., target director also on board of one or more prospective bidders or entity providing financing to one or more bidders; target director also investor in LBO fund that is participating as bidder. Should understand operation of existing compensation and benefit programs applicable to directors (management and non-management) in relation to alternatives that may be pursued, types of bids that may be requested or received.

2. *Advisors:* engage financial and legal advisors. Given complexity and pitfalls of financial, strategic, tactical, legal, as well as logistical and mechanical judgments and terrain, is practical necessity for board to have assistance of experienced financial and legal advisors with full range of potentially necessary capabilities. While courts have avoided mandating retention of financial advisors (see, e.g., Van Gorkom: "we do not imply that an outside valuation study is essential to support an informed business judgment; nor do we state that fairness opinions by independent investment bankers are required as a matter of law"), failure to do so meaningfully increases exposure to not being adequately informed and eliminates protection of reliance on expert advice. Process of selection sometimes involves interview of multiple candidates. Frequently, when "auction" is in response to unsolicited takeover attempt, "auction" response is arrived at after considerable time has passed and other efforts have been exhausted, while financial advisors engaged at outset. Accordingly, retention of financial advisor at outset involves broader inquiry into advisor's experience and capability, although credentials examined will include experience and capability in exploring and implementing sale alternative, including through "auction" process.

3. *Early stage advice:* receive advice at very beginning of process which focuses and educates directors regarding what is likely or possible to come. Should include: state law fiduciary obligations and standards of conduct applicable to directors; disclosure rules and considerations; general nature of process; approach to board participation; issues that may develop at various stages; potential timing; need for ongoing vigilance and flexibility. Can be very salutary in reducing risk of substantive and procedural missteps as process proceeds.

4. *Initial process with bidders:* design, with advisors, process for (a) qualifying bidders and (b) once qualified, providing information on company to bidders which is even-handed from standpoints of scope and timing. Be cognizant of confidentiality need, special risks (e.g., prospective

bidders or bidding groups which may present anti-trust concerns) and desire of board to control process. Use of appropriate confidentiality/ standstill agreement at outset will help achieve these goals (see V. below).

5. *Consideration of other strategies:* consider other strategies for current value maximization and strategies for long-term business development. In most cases where "auction" undertaken in response to unsolicited takeover effort, alternative strategies short of sale or breakup of target already will have been examined and found wanting. Is possible, however, to pursue parallel tracks, concurrently focusing two key questions: (a) should target seek to maximize current value for shareholders or pursue a longer-term development plan (a question which, to answer fairly, involves tying together critical judgments regarding target's business and other economic factors, and regarding legal posture of board and available techniques in seeking to pursue longer-term plan) and (b) if current shareholder-value maximizing program is goal, how is this best achieved (i.e., through sale, recapitalization or some other strategy). Compare RJR situation, where board, although authorizing auction process, made clear it had not decided to sell company, and specifically noted in communications to bidders that even at time final bids requested pursuant to auction procedures, recapitalization plan was actively under consideration by board as alternative to sale.

6. *Target valuation:* get educated on valuations of target. Valuations of businesses today involve applying range of methodologies and examining values derived from alternative possible transaction structures. Expert financial advisors can develop and present these. Board should be given not only bottom line numbers or ranges derived from each valuation methodology and structure; should also have, among other things, explanation of methodology and transaction structure itself, key assumptions made in applying methodology or implementing structure in target's case, and possibly sensitivity analyses based on variances in key assumption. From board process standpoint, frequently helpful to have this information delivered in stages: e.g., initial meeting generally to review basic methodologies and briefly outline structures; subsequent meeting to walk through valuation methodologies and structural alternatives on hypothetical basis; further meeting to review application of valuation methodologies and transaction structures specifically to target, based on target's own financial projections, business characteristics and requirements, and assumptions. Valuation of target apart from "auction" process will provide non-market test benchmark against which to gauge "auction"

results and bids, including basis for opinion from financial advisor—and judgment by directors—regarding fairness of bids presented.

7. *Special "auction" circumstances:* determine whether special circumstances exist relevant to shaping "auction" process or bids submitted. In RJR situation, e.g., decision to establish and publish formal bidding procedures and guidelines arose from concerns about need of special committee to take control of very unruly process. Also in RJR, e.g., request made to bidders that consideration offered to RJR shareholders include substantial common-stock-related equity interest in purchasing entity going forward, which stemmed from concern that, because of major risks and uncertainties associated with tobacco business generally, potential value of RJR's tobacco business would be substantially discounted and not fully recognized in bid with no residual equity component.

8. *Documents:* receive and review documents. As practicable, where review likely to be materially enhanced by doing so, key documents (or adequate summaries, or both) should be provided in advance of meeting at which they will be subject to primary review. Directors should read them. In any event, key documents should be available at such meetings. Careful presentations should be addressed to board regarding all key documents, explaining content and implications of key provisions.

9. *Expert advice:* request/receive expert advice on issues of special concern. Special issues may arise in context of sale of target, including in "auction." E.g., if shareholder or bondholder litigation develops, or issue of fraudulent conveyance is presented (as generally would be case in LBO, or highly leveraged recap alternative), board should receive expert advice regarding matter and how to handle it.

10. *Questions by directors:* directors should ask questions. Generally, directors should not simply be passive receivers of information. Especially true in "auction" setting which presents multiple and complex issues not ordinarily within directors' experience. Informed decision-making necessitates asking questions to try to understand and apply critical judgments to information provided to board. While directors not "experts" and should not be held to standard of knowledge and understanding as experts, due care requires reasonable effort to be informed, and questions regarding good faith also may be raised if directors mute when matters outside their normal experience are presented. (Of course, experts who present information to directors known not to be completely familiar, and perhaps very unfamiliar, with the information presented, will often "answer" many potential questions by anticipating them in presentation itself.)

11. *Time:* directors should take enough time—and use it. Neither the "auction process vis-à-vis bidders nor the board's education or deliberations in structuring, evaluating and making decisions throughout the process should be rushed or perfunctory. Due care requires adequate time—and taking adequate time is evidence of informed decision making. At certain stages in process, particularly at end if parties impose deadlines of their own, question of adequacy of time (in light of relevant benefits/risks involved) may present important issue for directors themselves to decide. Each timing decision should be addressed in a discreet, clear and rational manner from a shareholder cost/benefit analysis standpoint.

B. When management is competing bidder—role of disinterested directors/ special committee.

1. Benefits/impact of management as bidder. Frequently, in response to third party unsolicited bid, target's management (or group with which such management allies itself) will wish to present competing proposal (often LBO bid) to acquire target.

a. Is perfectly legitimate approach to developing maximum value for shareholders.

 (i) LBO, with current management participating, may in fact be transaction that will produce highest value.

 (ii) Fostering competition through presence of management-sponsored LBO may be important tactical tool for driving up price from other.

b. Once management determines to participate in bidding, relationship with board and "auction" process changes.

 (i) Fundamental—and classic—conflict of interest exists.

 (ii) "Disinterested" directors should assume responsibility for protecting and advancing shareholder interests, and assuring that board satisfies its Revlon duties.

 (iii) Traditional notion of "interested" director is director with personal financial interest in transaction adverse to interests of shareholders. See, e.g., discussion in RJR opinion.

 (iv) Some courts, perhaps aggravated by other facts and circumstances, have from time to time suggested that other types of relationships may constitute director "interest" in some sense. See, e.g., footnote 3 of Revlon opinion:

 "There were 14 directors on the Revlon board. Six of them held senior management positions with the company, and two others held significant blocks of its stock. Four of the remaining six directors were associated at some point with entities that had various business relationships with Revlon. On the basis of this limited record, however, we cannot conclude that this board is entitled to certain presumption that generally attach to the decisions of a board whose majority consists of truly outside directors."

(v)   Generally, existence of such other relationships should not disqualify directors as "interested." However, may well tend to produce even closer judicial scrutiny of director conduct, whether under rubric of a broader concept of director "interest" applied on a hindsight basis, or based on an analysis of the "good faith" of directors. See, e.g., discussion in RJR opinion.

(vi) Interested directors (including, as is sometimes the case, non-management directors who will or may be part of buyout group) generally should be asked to absent themselves from participation in board process relating to conduct of "auction" and consideration of alternatives.

(vii) Courts have recognized that, in change in control situations, presumptive legitimacy of process for dealing with change in control situation, and of outcome of such process, is enhanced when guided and recommended by a majority of disinterested directors. E.g., Unocal; Koppers: USG Corp.; Federated.

(viii) Disinterested directors also should be mindful of management's role, if any, on behalf of target vis-à-vis other bidders when management itself is allied with one bidding group. Of necessity, management will have certain functions it will continue to have to perform for target in "auction" process, e.g., arranging for gathering of information (financial and otherwise) to be made available to disinterested directors and their advisors, and to other bidders; and participating in due diligence interviews with such parties. To provide assurance to disinterested directors and third parties of integrity and uniformity of information flow, disinterested directors should consider use of participating and monitoring mechanisms (e.g., direct presence of disinterested directors' financial and/or legal advisors in target information gathering and communication process). In general, disinterested directors should be sensitive to need for them (including through their advisors) to be running sale process, including deciding who will participate; whether any limits should be imposed on access to information by particular parties; timing; whether formal rules are appropriate and, if so, what; communicating specific requirements and requests to bidders; and negotiating price/terms. In adverting to certain aspects of RJR auction process which underscored its neutrality, Court in RJR stated: "Nor did the board permit management to occupy an insider role in the auction process itself." Court specifically compared this to Macmillan situation, where company's CEO was heavily involved in such manner.

2. Use of special committees.
   a. Comprised of independent directors;may be comprised of all or only of some independent directors.
   b. Not a legal requirement; however, when management is competing bidder, delegating to specially constituted committee of independent directors the principal responsibility for dealing with matters relating to possible sale of company provides some real benefits.
      (i)   Underscores, and helps keep clear as matters proceed, that management (including interested directors who are part of management group) has its own interests to advance and is not functioning in context of sale process as guardian of shareholder interests. From disinterested directors' and shareholders' perspective, important to have this procedural recognition of conflict issue to, among other things, help combat fears of other parties and possible suspicion in courthouse of bias toward management. Courts have given special recognition to properly constituted, actively functioning special committees. E.g., J. P. Stevens; Restaurant Associates.
      (ii) If full complement of disinterested directors is "large," special committee comprised of smaller core group (e.g., 3–5) provides more sensible, workable vehicle for dealing with significant, ongoing demands of "auction" process. Special committee members should be available and willing to potentially devote significant time to process.
      (iii) Special committee should not usurp role of full group of disinterested directors. Although special committee may be "more involved," important that other disinterested directors not be "uninvolved." Procedures (e.g. inviting nonspecial committee disinterested directors to certain special committee meetings, of having briefing

sessions with such other directors, as process progresses) to accomplish this should be developed in given case.

    (iv)   Substantive selection of special committee best left to disinterested directors, not management. In Fort Howard, Court viewed management "preselection" of committee members with some suspicion and disfavor. In RJR, Court, in summarizing some of key elements of auction process involved stated: "Notably, the auction was conducted so that the Company's CEO had no role in the selection of the membership of the Special Committee or its legal or investment banking advisors."

c. Authority of special committee, if formed specifically to conduct "auction," should be broadly framed to encompass all actions deemed appropriate by committee to develop and make available transactions for the purpose of maximizing value of target on current basis for shareholders and to recommend to board whether to accept transaction resulting from such actions which, in special committee's judgment, constitutes best overall transaction for shareholders. Generally if special committee designated, also given authority to select financial advisors and legal counsel for committee and outside directors.

d. All processes, steps and guidelines noted in A. above also applicable to functioning of special committee. Committee should be active body, should consult closely and on continuing basis with financial and legal advisors engaged to advise them, and should be prepared to deal directly with bidders, including management group, on important issues.

    (i)   Special committee should have direct due diligence session with management regarding current and projected business and affairs of target and other matters, if relevant. In anticipation, and promptly after management interest surfaces, special committee should request all studies, reports, analysis, etc., prepared by or on behalf of management or target, within appropriate time period, relating to value of target or any of its assets or businesses, possible extraordinary transactions involving target (e.g., sale, split-up, recap, spin-off, LBO, subsidiary IPO, joint ventures); forward-looking business plans and projections for target on normal (non-LBO) basis and LBO basis also should be obtained.

    (ii)   Special committee should consider whether any specific instructions should be given to management group (and in what form). E.g., reinforcing obligation of management to: continue to operate business in ordinary course for benefit of shareholders; to provide information to other parties as directed by special committee or its advisors; to not disclose information in process of organizing its LBO beyond parameters, and only subject to appropriate confidentiality/standstill agreement, prescribed by committee; and to not engage in reselling of assets.

IV. "Auction" Procedures.

A. *General*. As discussed in II.C. above, Revlon has not mandated a single "auction" procedure—nor, indeed, any particular procedure—for selling company on basis which satisfies directors' fundamental Revlon duty. Substantial latitude appears to exist in structuring sales process in particular cases. Frequently, when sale decision affirmatively made by target board in response to publicly disclosed unsolicited takeover threat, process involves receipt of "white knight" interest proffered by "friendly" parties, and active solicitation by target of competing bids. Even in such situations, which are "public auctions" in some general sense, procedures for implementing "auction" may vary considerably from case to case.

Certain formal sale procedures have been subject to intense judicial scrutiny. Although not directly in response to unsolicited takeover threats, procedures used, and judicial responses to them, are instructive.

B. *Fort Howard:* post-signing market test opportunity procedure upheld.

Although not arising in unsolicited takeover context, Fort Howard provides useful insight into "auction" concept under Revlon. Key facts were: Buyout group composed of third party and senior management of Fort Howard advised board of group's desire to seek to organize LBO, and requested permission to do so. Disinterested directors gave permission. Neither buyout group nor disinterested directors wished to make public announcement at this point, and none made. Events proceeded almost to signing of acquisition agreement before brief public announcement made in response to substantial market activity. Agreement signed few days later, following: receipt of buyout group's initial proposal of $50 per share coupled with provisions severely limiting special committee's ability to "shop" company; rejection of such proposal as below low end of range of fair value in financial advisor's opinion and not providing for "market check"; discussions among management group, special committee and committee's advisors; and submission of revised management group bid at $53 per share and with provisions not precluding market check. In responding to insistence of Fort Howard disinterested directors that meaningful post-signing market test opportunity be provided, agreement provided that first-step tender offer would not close for minimum of 30 business days from signing; company could entertain third-party acquisition interest, including providing information to and negotiating with such parties, although could not solicit such interest; company had "fiduciary out" to terminate agreement in favor of better third-party transaction; LBO organizer (not management) entitled to "break-up" fee and expense reimbursement but, in contrast to original request, capped in aggregate at $1 per share (less than 2 percent of purchase price) and subject to more restrictive conditions for payment. No option to purchase Fort Howard shares provided (was requested and rejected). Importantly, when deal announced, Fort Howard directors insisted on statement in press release (which received widespread publicity) that notwithstanding signed agreement with buyout group, special committee and its financial advisor were prepared to receive and respond to third-party interest in acquiring Fort Howard, including by providing information to and negotiating with such parties. Within days, eight parties registered interest and certain of them requested and received confidential information, although none made a bid.

Procedure was challenged in Delaware Chancery Court as violative of Revlon. In denying preliminary injunction, Court upheld procedure, finding, among other things, that: (1) Revlon did not require a public announcement at time board gave permission to buyout group to seek to organize LBO (Court focused on fact that disinterested directors had own reasons in good faith for not making announcement then—obtaining certainty that management group's all cash bid for all shares at price approved by board would be available, before increasing risk, through premature disclosure, of possible takeover attempt at less than "fair" price or for less than all shares); (2) Revlon requirement of informed decision-making seeking to maximize value for shareholders satisfied by availability of legitimate market check opportunity post-execution of LBO acquisition agreement.

C. *RJR:* use of formal, written, publicly disclosed procedures and guidelines for submission of bids not itself challenged; outcome of process unsuccessfully challenged—court held that disinterested directors faced with "tie" bids from financial point of view, not automatically required by Revlon to seek tie-breaking bids.

See II.E.3. above for summary of key facts and discussion of Delaware Chancery Court decision.

RJR bidding procedures were aimed at creating one-round, sealed bid "auction," with each participant requested to submit highest and best bid on specified bid date. Bidding procedures explicitly mentioned factors special committee and board expected to consider in evaluation bids (beyond just nominal price), addressed range of mechanics for submission of bids, and expressed certain guidelines and preferences of special committee regarding form, structure, and composition of bids. Bidding procedures also reserved to RJR right to modify or terminate them and to negotiate with any party.

Because of special circumstances and concerns, bidding procedures also stated RJR board had not made a decision to sell company, and board did not intend to deal with any party which did not by a specified early date agree to abide by procedures.

Copy of RJR bidding procedures attached as Annex A hereto.

D. Other approaches; certain observations.

1. *Myriad possibilities.* Frequently, efforts to sell takeover target are conducted on considerably less formal basis than RJR procedures. Techniques vary considerably, but often involve identification of likely buyer candidates (including from parties indicating interest in light of publicly announced takeover threat); preparation by target and financial advisors of information book on target; distribution of book to likely buyer candidates; obtaining expressions of interest; providing "second round" information pursuant to confidentiality agreement; requesting bids; negotiating with parties once bids submitted. Key variations may involve whether any bidding deadline set, whether any guidance on bidding (price or other terms) provided; whether bids sealed or open; whether multiple rounds anticipated; whether "lock-ups," "leg-ups," etc. offered or permitted.

2. *Basic test to be applied.* Generally, when management not participating as (or with) bidder in process, and board has made decision to seek to maximize current shareholder value, little reason to suspect process actually followed not a good faith effort to accomplish goal. Nonetheless, and even absent some overriding "auction fairness" concept derived from Revlon (see II.E. above), requirement that directors exercise due care implementing Revlon duty imposes need to evaluate sale (or "auction") approach being used in specific case (including particular steps in process, and whether (in light of facts and circumstances of such case) approach will provide directors with all reasonably available information relevant to maximizing current shareholder value. In this regard, if more than one active, credible bidder involved, ordinarily (absent demonstrably special circumstances) each should have comparable opportunity to submit highest and best bid.

3. *Heightened scrutiny when management bids.* When management is participating as (or with) bidder in process, while directors' Revlon duty does not change, on practical level there is increase risk of shareholder litigation challenging, and judicial probing of, board conduct, including how process for sale of target was shaped and implemented. See II.F.2.a.(ii) above.

E. When to bring "auction" down; when is enough, enough?

1. *Legal analytical framework.* Touchstone is duty articulated in Revlon that, when target sale is inevitable, directors must seek to maximize shareholder value. Actions of directors throughout process, including when to bring it to close, should be judged by this standard.

Plaintiffs in RJR argued that Revlon requires auctioneer-directors to keep going back (at least in "tie" situation) until one party left. Plaintiffs argued that such procedures is required by Revlon because it is necessary to conduct of "fair" or "effective" auction—a supervening standard plaintiffs argued is imposed by Revlon. Chancellor Allen rejected any such mechanistic rule; rather, he applied business judgment analysis to determine if RJR disinterested directors acted on informed basis, in good faith, to fulfill basic Revlon duty, and found they had despite not seeking tie-breaking bid. (Chancellor Allen also observed that, even applying such a supervening standard—whatever it might mean—RJR auction satisfied test.) See II.E.3.above.

Under Chancellor Allen's approach in RJR, assuming disinterested directors who are acting in good faith, informed decision-making is key. Ultimate decision is whether shareholder value has been maximized. "Auction" process is tool for developing information relevant to that decision. Accordingly, "auction" may be terminated when it has functioned to best serve this purpose. Timing issue—when to terminate—is itself business judgment directors permitted to make, in light of surrounding facts and circumstances, on basis of cost/benefit assessment termination decision in terms of maximizing current shareholder value. Process of decision-making—explicitly focusing termination decision and articulating and considering factors relevant to it (including with help of advisors)—important litmus test of presence of information relevant to termination decision and, accordingly, to protection of such decision.

2. *Real world decision-making.* "Auction" termination decisions are made in real world context often involving deadlines (self-imposed or third-party imposed); demands by one or more parties for varying "lock-up" and/or related arrangements; bids not comparable on basis of form of

consideration, structure, timing, complexity, completeness and/or risk; and business risks to target arising from uncertainty regarding nature of, timing of, and parties to change in control transaction. Moreover, atmosphere can become tense and emotional at end of "auction" process.

Factors to be particularly alert to include:

a. have all bidders been provided with same target information (or, if not, is there good reason why not) and had sufficient time to absorb it;

b. have all biders been requested to submit highest and best bid (and have they responded);

c. has any bidder advised board of willingness to continued bidding (and what precisely was said);

d. what is value spread between/among bids.

e. has any bidder set a deadline or threatened to withdraw (and how credible is deadline/threat, and how important is that bidder);

f. where is value of preferred bid relative to financial advisors' valuation of target for sale and in other current value maximization strategies.

Substantial chance one or more other bidders or shareholder-plaintiffs may challenge "auction" termination decision.

3. Challenges made to "auction" close.

a. *"Lock-ups," etc.* "Lock-ups" and/or related arrangements have been challenged on variety of bases, e.g., preclusive of further bidding and granted prematurely; asset option granted at below market price; asset option/other arrangements granted in exchange for buyer's commitment to take action protective of directors; directors not informed of implications of arrangements. See II.F. above for review of cases dealing with "lock-ups" and related arrangements.

b. *Substantially equivalent bids.* In RJR, after extended auction process, last round of bids submitted were found by financial advisors to be "substantially equivalent" from financial point of view. In light of certain factors, particularly deadline set by KKR and statement it would withdraw if deadline not met, special committee and board looked to nonfinancial, but shareholder welfare-oriented factors, and chose KKR bid. Plaintiff shareholders argued Revlon required directors to seek tie-breaking bids. Preliminary injunction denied. See II.E.3., and see B., above.

c. *"Tipping" a bidder.* In Macmillan, Delaware Supreme Court effectively reopened "auction" based on competing bidder's claim that management had "tipped" its bidding group and failed to inform board, thus tainting process.

V. Use of Confidentiality/Standstill Agreements.

A. Treatment of unsolicited bidder.
  1. *Basic posture.* Once target responds to unsolicited bid by initiating an "auction" and providing confidential information to other potential bidders, unsolicited bidder often will request—or demand—access to same information. Generally information is provided to other parties, and offered to unsolicited bidder, pursuant to confidentiality agreement, which often contains other provisions (e.g., precluding recipient from buying target shares or making proposal for target without target board's consent). Unsolicited bidder likely to balk at signing such agreement, given constraints is may impose on unilateral action.
  2. *Court tests.* Courts addressing duty of target board in this situation have held target not automatically obligated to provide information to unsolicited bidder unwilling to sign confidentiality agreement.
    a. *Burlington.*   Unsolicited bidder, after being refused confidential information by target after auction started, challenged refusal decision. Court held that target could ask unsolicited bidder to sign confidentiality agreement, like all other prospective bidders were asked to do. Board's conditioning access to confidential information by unsolicited bidder on its signing confidentiality agreement did not constitute selective dealing with bidder.
    b. *J. P. Stevens.* Competing bidder, which appeared on scene after management LBO proposal announced, was offered opportunity to same confidential information as other bidders, subject to execution of confidentiality agreement with standstill provisions. Competing bidder objected to provisions and sought judicial relief.   Court held no equitable basis to complain that access to information unfairly denied. However, where information improperly withheld, Court may order that it be provided. In Fruehauf, see II.F.4.b.(ii) above, in order "to insure an open bidding process for Fruehauf," make available upon reasonable notice to any potential bidder...all information concerning Fruehauf's business and properties (subject to such bidder agreeing to reasonable provisions to keep such information confidential) and to meet on mutually agreeable and reasonable terms with any potential bidder in good faith."
  3. *Approach taken by some unsolicited bidders.* Unsolicited bidders sometimes seek to avoid justifiable refusal by agreeing to execute confidentiality agreement with certain modifications, e.g., agreement not to buy shares at lower price than currently offered, or pursuant to offer for

less than specified minimum. Approach is to emphasize board's Revlon duty to seek to maximize current shareholder value, present unsolicited bidder as credible party prepared to participate in "auction" process toward that end, and structure modifications to respond to target concerns without requiring termination of unsolicited tender offer and giving up ability to bid (and perhaps run proxy contest or consent solicitation) without target board consent. Board seeking to maximize current shareholder value may find it difficult to reject this approach.

B. Mechanism for controlling process/maximizing value.

1. *Target concerns.* Target may have number of legitimate concerns regarding conduct of "auction" participants during course of process. Concerns may include (a) risks to target's business (and value) if sensitive business information becomes too widely disseminated, particularly to competitors; (b) risk of antitrust law violation in providing certain information to competitors; (c) risk of disruption of process if participants seek, especially with target confidential information, to "presell" parts of target business; (d) risk that participant will bid at time and in manner disruptive of orderly bidding process and/or in violation of "auction" procedures and guidelines then, or thereafter, established; (e) risk of intervention with winning bid [e.g., by post-winning bid "street sweep" (assuming no "poison pill" rights plan in place)].

2. *Imposing constraints.* Carefully drafted confidentiality agreement can address and control these risks, if access to nonpublic target information conditioned on its execution and participants likely to want such information to proceed. (One potential problem may be that important prospective bidders unwilling to execute confidentiality agreement with many "bells and whistles." Judgment may be required as to tradeoff between loss of important competition and protection regarding certain risks.)

3. *Specific provisions.* Provisions sometimes incorporated (in addition to normal confidentiality provisions) include: (a) prohibition on providing information to third parties, other than to financial institutions providing debt financing which execute special form of confidentiality agreement made available; (b) prohibition on providing information to competitors in any target business; (c) prohibition on "preselling" target assets or businesses; (d) agreement participant will not make any bid (and will not make any other proposal to acquire, or actually acquire any securities of, target or any target business) unless invited by target to do so; (e) agreement participant will abide by any rules and procedures established by target from time to time.

VI. "Poison Pill" Protection.

A. Federated and progeny: while "auction" continuing.
  1. *Overview.* Shareholder rights plan (so-called "poison pill"), particularly "flip-in" discriminatory variety, can be very effective—and very necessary—tool for directors seeking to keep "auction" alive for sufficient time to maximize value for shareholders through "auction" process. This role of rights plans in assisting directors in performing their Revlon duties has been judicially recognized and sanctioned.
  2. *Federated.* In connection with widely publicized takeover contest for Federated Department Stores between R. H. Macy and Campeau Corporation, District Court of Southern District of New York denied Campeau's motion for preliminary injunction which sought to enjoin Federated's rights plan. Federated's rights plan contained both "flip-over" and "flip-in" provisions, latter triggered if, among other things, "Adverse Person" (as determined by Federated board), acquired 15 percent or more of shares of Federated's common stock. To be Adverse Person, majority of outside directors must determine (i) entity which owned 15 percent or more of Federated's common stock was entity which owned 15 percent or more of stock of a competitor, or (ii) 15 percent holder is either greenmailer or is causing or reasonably likely to cause "material adverse impact" on Federated's business or prospects. Plan's redemption provision allowed board to redeem rights at any time until tenth day (which date could be extended by board) following public announcement that (i) third party had acquired 20 percent of Federated's common stock, (ii) person holding 15 percent of outstanding stock had become materially adverse person," or (iii) entity which owned 15 percent or more of stock of competitor of Federated acquired 15 percent of Federated's common stock.

     Federated board agreed to redeem rights with respect to offer that Macy's would commence (pursuant to merger agreement that two companies had entered into), which board deemed superior to Campeau's then-pending offer, but to leave in place rights with respect to Campeau offer.

     In assessing Federated's rights plan, Court stated that plan was not "showstopper" and "provide[d] the directors with a *shield to fend off coercive offers, and with a gavel to run an auction.*" (Emphasis added.) Court found that the rights plan was clearly instrumental in achieving improvements in price and financing arrangements in Campeau's bid and in allowing Macy's to make bid.

With respect to board's selective agreement to redeem rights only with respect to Macy's offer, Court stated that "[a] board clearly has the right to use its powers to defeat a coercive, two-tiered, front-end loaded bid with a timing advantage, where the board believes the offer would not be in the interests of shareholders." Most significantly, Court specifically rejected Campeau's argument that Revlon required that once auction had been set in motion, Federated must drop all its defenses and redeem rights. To contrary, Court believed that "the teachings of Revlon require directors to enhance the bidding in an auction as best they can." Court found that compelling board to redeem rights plan would disrupt auction and observed that there was no evidence to suggest that board was acting to entrench itself. Court then declined to grant preliminary injunction, stating that to do so would make Federated vulnerable to street sweep, coercive offers, and to "a decrease in the existing offers."

Court specifically declined to overrule board's determination that auction was still in progress, especially in absence of representation by Campeau both that it believed its bid was higher, and that it had made its highest and final bid.

3. *Facet Enterprises.* In March 1988, Facet Enterprises adopted rights plan in response to all-cash tender offer by The Prospect Group. Delaware Chancery Court denied request by Prospect to enjoin Facet's rights plan. Court found that answer to one question would be dispositive of outcome: "Given the pendency of the proposed auction, should the directors be allowed to keep the rights in place until the auction process has reasonably run its course?" Relying in part on court's recognition in Federated that rights plan, if properly used, "provides the directors with a shield to fend off coercive offers and with a gavel to run an auction," court determined that judicial action as to rights as premature. Court also noted that rights plan "could benefit shareholders by deterring a street sweep or 'front-end loaded offer' by a bidder or a third party that could otherwise end the auction." Court denied request for injunction so that Facet would be given "a reasonable opportunity to conduct and complete auction," but "without prejudice to Prospect's right to renew [its motion] on the basis that changed circumstances require the directors to redeem the rights and they have refused to do so." Court was concerned that compelling board to redeem rights plan at preauction stage in the contest would deprive Facet shareholders of any increased returns to be reaped from that auction.

4. *Staley Continental.* In connection with its amended offer for all shares of Staley Continental, Tate & Lyle sought to enjoin implementation of

Staley's shareholder rights plan. In response to Tate & Lyle offer, Staley's board determined that it would not redeem rights and directed management to explore other financial alternatives. Delaware Chancery Court once again acknowledged that rights plan can promote an auction and, · noting that market price was above offer price, refused to grant plaintiff's motion for injunction. Court further suggested that redeeming rights "could conceivably subject the board of actions predicated upon their failure to earnestly seek the highest bidder." Plaintiffs also attacked Staley board's actions in reducing percentage flip-in trigger from 40 percent to 20 percent after Tate & Lyle had filed HSR report stating its intention to purchase additional shares. Court refused to review board's action, however, reasoning that since Tate & Lyle's offer was conditioned on majority of shares being tendered, there was no harm to Tate & Lyle.

5. *Moore McCormack.* In late February 1988, Southdown commenced an offer to purchase all shares of Moore McCormack for $31 a share. Southdown raised its offer to $35 per share after Moor McCormack rejected earlier offer and disclosed it was considering defensive measures. Moore McCormack then announced recapitalization plan while continuing its efforts to develop alternative that would be more favorable to shareholders than capitalization. In response to announced recapitalization, Moore McCormack's common stock began to trade above $35 per share. After bringing suit, Southdown raised its offer per share to $35 in cash plus $5 bond and then, responding to Moore McCormack's invitation to increase its bid, increased its offer to $40 in cash per share, an amount that court noted fell above mid-range of values as determined by Moore McCormack's financial advisors.

Court ordered Moore McCormack to redeem rights issued under its rights plan prior to consummation of Southdown tender offer and enjoined execution of its announced recapitalization plan. In enjoining rights plan, Court nonetheless noted that legitimate uses of rights plan include "driving a bidder to the negotiating table or preventing shareholders from being stampeded in a coercive offer in which later sellers receive an inadequate price for their stock."

In assessing board's refusal to redeem rights, Court articulated novel standard for judging director conduct: "the standard to be applied should be whether a fully informed, wholly disinterested, reasonably courageous director would dissent from the board's act in any material part." In applying this standard, Court determined that claimed benefits of plan were unrelated to plan itself but were rather result of market forces. Court distinguished Federated on basis that rights plan in that case was used as gavel in auction and that Federated was faced with two-tier offer. Court concluded that Moore McCormack was "no longer attempting to use its poison pill to increase the price of the stock." Court found that there was no valid business reason for rights plan except to defeat Southdown's offer because there was no evidence that plan would be used to achieve higher value for shareholders. Court, in contrast to decisions discussed above, ordered redemption of rights despite fact that Moore McCormack's efforts to develop higher value alternative were continuing.

6. *Doskocil.* On July, 27, 1988, Doskocil Companies and Doskocil Acquisition Corp. (collectively, "Doskocil") commenced tender offer for all common stock of Wilson Foods. In connection with control contest that then ensued between Doskocil and Soparind Meat Packing Corporation, Doskocil brought suit challenging decision by Wilson Foods board to redeem rights with respect to Soparind's $13.50 offer but to leave in place rights with respect to Doskocil's $14.50 offer (which was raised from its initial $12.50 offer in response to negotiated transaction with Soparind).

Court, after determining that Soparind was considering making higher offer and that board would consider higher offers, denied Doskocil's motion, concluding that injunctive relief was not then appropriate. "[T]here is evidence that the auction has not yet concluded and that the defendant directors intend to bring the process to a close on a reasonable schedule." Court reached its decision in face of arguments by Doskocil that (i) offering price could not be deemed inadequate because it was higher than Soparind's offer; (ii) majority of target's shareholders tendered into Doskocil's first (and lower) offer; and (iii) board was not acting in good faith because it repeatedly refused to meet with Doskocil representatives to discuss possible acquisition.

Court, however, indicated that at some point an obligation to redeem rights would arise: "[i]t is difficult to imagine that Wilson Foods will continue to block the Doskocil amended tender offer if no higher bid is forthcoming." Court gave a clear warning to Wilson Foods that it would consider appropriate action "if further developments indicate that Wilson Foods is not acting in accordance with its fiduciary duties." Eventually, after Soparind failed to make higher offer, Wilson Foods agreed to be acquired by Doskocil for $14.50 per share in cash.

B. When "auction" is over.

1. *Overview.* In context of "auctions," once "auction" process has run its course so, in most cases, has the need for retention of rights plan. Courts

addressing this situation have required board to make rights inapplicable to all bidders at auction's end.

2. *Macmillan.* During contest for control of Macmillan between Maxwell Communications Corp. (MCC) and Kohlberg Kravis Roberts & Co. (KKR), Delaware Chancery Court held that in light of fact that Macmillan advisors opined that $90.50 KKR bid was fair (and that *a fortiori* $90.25 MCC bid was fair) "keeping the rights in place will only cause the shareholders irreparable harm, since they will be deprived of the opportunity to consider, as an alternative to the KKR offer, MCC's higher bid." Rights plan was still in place at end of auction when there was no evidence that higher bid would emerge. Court accepted MCC's argument that there is "no longer any corporate purpose served by maintaining the rights in place, because the auction is over and the two highest bids are now on the table."

3. *Copeland Enterprises.* On October 25, 1988, A. Copeland Enterprises commenced a tender offer for all outstanding shares of Church's Fried Chicken at $8 per share in cash, with stated intention of effecting second-step merger in which shareholders who had not tendered would receive same $8 cash consideration paid in tender offer. Board voted to recommend rejection of offer on basis of advice from its financial advisors that offer was inadequate and that higher value could be realized in alternative transaction. Additionally, Church's adopted rights plan which contained both "flip-in" and "flip-over" provisions. On January 18, 1989, Church's board publicly announced its intention to "sell" company and conduct auction which was scheduled to end on day before schedule expiration date of tender offer.

Applying Texas law, Court first considered whether rights plan was valid on date of its adoption. Court held that "[a]lthough the defendant directors *may* have acted in their own interest in adopting the pill, hoping to entrench themselves as Church's directors, adoption of the pill was not unfair to the corporation." Even assuming entrenchment motive (which Court observed was not likely to be case), Court held that adoption of rights plan was fair because it (i) provided board with time to seek alternative transactions, (ii) provided board with negotiating leverage, and (iii) "propped up" price of Church's stock.

In deciding whether failure to redeem rights plan was breach of board's duty of loyalty on date that motion for a preliminary injunction was brought, court noted that since decisions was made to sell company, board became charged with Revlon duties to maximize shareholders' value.

Citing Federated, Court observed that after auction is concluded, however, there will be no reason to keep pill in place. Court noted that "allowing the pill to remain in place past the conclusion of the auction virtually insures that the auction will be unsuccessful and Church's board will remain in place." As result Court held that if rights plan was not redeemed by expiration of auction, board will be deemed to have breached its duty of loyalty.

APPENDIX A TO CHAPTER 11

RJR NABISCO, INC.

November 7, 1988

To: Potential Purchasers

Re: *Rules and Procedures for Submission of Proposals*

The Board of Directors of RJR Nabisco, Inc. ("RJR Nabisco" or "Company") is in the process of exploring alternatives for providing value to shareholders. As previously announced, no determination has been made to recommend the sale of the Company. However, the possibility of the sale of the Company is one alternative being considered. Accordingly, the Board of Directors is interested in receiving proposals to acquire the Company ("Proposals"), in order to determine which alternative would best serve the interests of the Company's shareholders. In this connection, please be advised that the Board of Directors is considering the possibility of the Company itself selling its food businesses, with the full after-tax net proceeds being for the account of the Company's shareholders prior to any acquisition of the Company. In view of this possibility, in addition to submitting Proposals to acquire the Company with all of its existing businesses, you are requested to submit Proposals which assume that the food businesses are sold separately on the basis indicated above. If a determination is made that a Proposal presented to the Company is the best alternative, the Board of Directors would be prepared to authorize pursuing such transaction.

The Board of Directors is mindful that the process of publicly considering alternatives, in which the Company is now engaged, while entirely voluntary on the part of the Board of Directors with a view toward benefiting shareholders, does present certain risks, particularly if the process is prolonged, including disruption to the Company's business and an overall uncertainty among the Company's constituencies as to the Company's future. In order to mitigate these risks, the Board of Directors believes that the most prudent course of action is to bring to a prompt and orderly close the process it has initiated for developing acquisition proposals for the Company.

Accordingly, the purpose of this letter is to invite all interested parties to submit, pursuant to the rules and procedures specified below, their final and best Proposals to acquire the Company. A Special Committee of the Board of Directors (the "Special Committee") has been appointed and is overseeing the process.

It is the strongly held view of the Special Committee and Board of Directors that this process must be conducted in a fair and orderly manner. The interests of our shareholders, employees, customers, suppliers, communities and the public generally can and will be best served by such an approach. Toward that end, we have developed the rules and procedures specified below. To date, each potential purchaser has either expressly agreed to abide by the rules and procedures promulgated by the Company or indicated a willingness to do so. Those potential purchasers which have not yet expressly agreed are being requested to do so by executing and returning a copy of this letter to the person designated in paragraph (A) below by Wednesday, November 9, 1988. The Board of Directors believes that such agreement is critical to assuring that each potential purchaser is acting and will continue to act responsibly. The acquisition interest expressed by potential purchasers who have agreed or confirm their agreement promptly is most welcome. A refusal by a potential purchaser to confirm its agreement by executing and returning the enclosed copy of this letter will be viewed by the Board of Directors as a hostile act inimical to the best interests of all concerned. Accordingly, the Special Committee does not intend to consider or recommend, and the Board of Directors does not intend to consider or approve, any Proposal made by any purchaser which has not agreed as provided in this paragraph to the rules and procedures specified below.

In connection with its consideration of Proposals from potential purchasers, the Special Committee and Board of Directors will, consistent with their fiduciary duties, consider such matter as they deem appropriate, including, without limitation, (1) the amount and form of consideration, including any continuing equity participation, (2) the timing of consummation of Proposals, (3) the risk of nonconsummation of Proposals, (4) the structure of Proposals, (5) certainty with respect to proposed financing arrangements and the sources for such financing, (6) antitrust and other relevant legal considerations, and (7) proposed changes to the Special Committee's form of the merger agreement submitted with a Proposal.

The following rules and procedures will govern the submission of Proposals:

(A)   Proposals should be addressed and delivered in a sealed envelope to the Special Committee of the Board of Directors of RJR Nabisco: c/o Peter Allan Atkins, Skadden, Arps, Slate, Meagher & Flom, 919 Third Avenue, New York, NY 10022. Proposals must be *received* on Friday, November 18, 1988, at 5:00 P.M. (the "Submission Date," unless extended by notice to potential purchasers). Potential purchasers may not make any offer or proposal (or modify or amend any pending Proposal) to purchase any or all of the securities or assets of the Company, whether before or after the Submission Date, except as prescribed herein, and in compliance with the confidentiality agreement executed by each potential purchaser.

(B)   Except as may be required by law, we will not publicly disclose the terms of Proposals or communicate them to any other potential purchaser until a Proposal has been accepted by the Company. We reserve the right, however, to discuss any Proposal with the party submitting it and to clarify the terms of any Proposal. It would facilitate consideration of any Proposal if as many of the terms thereof as the party submitting it deems appropriate could be communicated to our financial representative (Dillon, Read & Co. Inc. and Lazard Frères & Co.) prior to the Submission Date.

(C)   Each Proposal should include all the material terms on which the party submitting it is basing its bid, including any conditions relating to acceptance of the Proposal. The Special Committee has determined not to invite or accept any Proposal which is conditioned on the potential purchaser, its affiliates, agents or representative initiating, engaging or participating in or entering into any agreement or arrangement regarding the sale of any assets of the Company.

(D)   The form of the Agreement and Plan of Merger (the "Merger Agreement") to be furnished to potential purchasers will contain terms, other than the form or amount of consideration, which the Special Committee recommends be used in submitting Proposals. Proposals should be in the form of a completed, definitive Merger Agreement executed by the party submitting it, with a copy marked to show any changes to the form of the Merger Agreement. The extent and nature of any changes made by a potential purchaser to the form of the Merger Agreement provided will be taken into consideration by the Special Committee.

(E)   With regard to the form and amount of consideration offered in Proposals, the Special Committee is interested in the possibility of the Company's shareholders being provided with a substantial common stock-related interest in the purchasing entity, and encourages potential purchasers to consider providing for this in their Proposals.

(F)   The terms and present status of all financing arrangements should be detailed in the Proposal, including providing all commitment agreements and securities purchase agreements which have been obtained and the forms of all commitment agreements and securities purchase agreements anticipated to be obtained. In addition, to the extent that any element of the consideration to be offered to the Company's shareholders is not cash, any information or opinions which will assist the Special Committee and Board in valuing such consideration should be provided.

(G)   Any Proposal which contains provisions that would vary (including as to the consideration offered) depending upon the terms of another Proposal (including the consideration offered) will not be considered.

(H)   Each Proposal should indicate that it has been approved by the Board of Directors of the party submitting it (and of each investor whose Board of Directors' approval is required in connection with consummating the Proposal), and that the Proposal will be irrevocable until midnight on the fifteenth (15th) day after the Submission Date.

(I)   The rules and procedures outlined above are intended to constitute a single round of bidding. Any Proposal should reflect the potential purchaser's highest offer.

As soon as practicable following the submission of Proposals, the Special Committee, with the advice and assistance of its legal and financial advisors, will evaluate the Proposals and determine which Proposal, if any, will be recommended to the Board of Directors for acceptance. As soon as practicable thereafter, the Board of Directors will make a determination regarding any recommended Proposal.

(J)   The Special Committee and Board of Directors shall have no obligation to accept any Proposal whether or not such Proposal represents the highest proposed purchase price for the Company. An offer will only be deemed to be accepted upon the execution and delivery of a definitive Merger Agreement. Until such time, the Company will not have any obligation to any potential purchaser with respect to the sale of the Company, and following such time the Company's only obligations will be to the other party to the definitive Merger Agreement, and only as set forth in the definitive Merger Agreement.

(K)   A Proposal will be accepted only by a written acceptance signed by the Chairman of the Board, or other official of the Company specifically authorized by the Board of Directors.

The Board of Directors and Special Committee expressly reserve the right, in their sole discretion, consistent with their fiduciary duties and without stating a reason therefor, to amend or terminate any or all of the procedures set forth herein, to terminate discussions with any or all potential purchasers, to negotiate with any party with respect to a transaction and to reject any or all Proposals. The Special Committee and its financial and legal advisors are prepared to meet with each potential purchaser at any time to discuss these rules and procedures.

Very truly yours,
THE SPECIAL COMMITTEE OF
THE BOARD OF DIRECTORS

By: _____
Charles E. Hugel, Chairman

Agreed and Accepted:
Name of Potential Purchaser:

By: _____
Name:
Title:

APPENDIX B TO CHAPTER 11

TABLE OF CASES

American Standard: Black & Decker Corp. v. American Standard Inc., 682 F. Supp. 772 (D. Del. 1988)

Amstead: In re Amstead Industries Inc. Litigation, No. 8224 (Del. Ch. Aug. 24, 1988)

Becor Western: Rosenfeld v. Becor Western, Inc., No. 87–C–0988 (E. D. Wis. Nov. 5, 1987)

Burlington: Samjens Partners I v. Burlington Industries, Inc., 663 F. Supp. 614 (S.D.N.Y. 1987)

ConAgra: ConAgra, Inc. v. Cargill, Inc., 222 Neb. 136, 382 N.W.2d 576 (Neb. Sup. Ct. 1986)

Copeland Enterprises: A. Copeland Enterprises, Inc. v. Guste, No. SA-88-CA 1238 (W.D. Tex. Feb. 9, 1989)

Doskocil: Doskocil Companies v. Wilson Foods Corp., Nos. 10,095, 10,106-10, 108, 10,116 (Del. Ch. Aug. 4, 1988) (LEXIS, States library, Del. file)

Enstar: Huffington v. Enstar Corp., No. 7543 (Del. Ch. Apr. 25, 1984)

Facet Enterprises: Facet Enterprises, Inc. v. Prospect Group, Inc., No. 9746 (Del. Ch. Apr. 15, 1988)

Fairchild Camera: Citron v. Fairchild Camera and Instrument Corp., [1987–1988 Transfer Binder] Fed. Sec. L. Rep. (CCH) ¶ 93,915 (Del. Ch. 1988)

Federated: CRTF Corp. v. Federated Department Stores, Inc., 683 F. Supp. 422 (S.D.N.Y. 1988)

Fort Howard: In re Fort Howard Corp. Shareholders Litigation, No. 9991 (Del. Ch. Aug. 8, 1988)

Fruehauf: Edelman v. Fruehauf Corp., 798 F.2d 882 (6th Cir. 1986)

Gelco: Gelco Corp. v. Coniston Partners, 652 F. Supp. 829 (D. Minn. 1986), *aff'd in part, vacated in part,* 811 F.2d 414 (8th Cir. 1987)

Harcourt Brace: British Printing & Communications Corp. v. Harcourt Brace Jovanovich, Inc., 664 F. Supp. 1519 (S.D.N.Y. 1987)

Holly Farms: In re Holly Farms Corp. Shareholders Litigation, No. 10,350 (Del. Ch. Dec. 30, 1988)

Interco: City Capital Associates Limited Partnership v. Interco Inc., 696 F. Supp. 1551 (D. Del. 1988)

Jewel: Jewel Companies, Inc. v. Pay Less Drug Stores Northwest, Inc., 741 F.2d 1555 (9th Cir. 1984)

J. P. Stevens: In re J. P. Stevens & Co. Shareholders Litigation, 542 A.2d 770 (Del. Ch. 1988)

KDI: In re KDI Corp. Shareholders Litigation, No. 10,278 (Del. Ch. 1988) (LEXIS, States library, Del. file)

Keyser: Keyser v. Commonwealth National Financial Corp., 644 F. Supp. 1130 (M.D. Pa. 1986)

Koppers: BNS Inc. v. Koppers Co., 683 F. Supp. 458 (D. Del. 1988)

Macmillan: Mills Acquisition Co. v. Macmillan, Inc., [Current] Fed. Sec. L. Rep. (CCH) ¶ 94,072 (Del. Nov. 2, 1988)

Macmillan (Chancery Court): Mills Acquisition Co. v. Macmillan, Inc., [Current] Fed. Sec. L. Rep. (CCH) ¶ 94,071 (Del. Ch. Oct. 18, 1988)

Macmillan (Evans): Robert M. Bass Group, Inc. v. Evans, [Current] Fed. Sec. L. Rep. (CCH) ¶ 93,924 (Del. Ch. July 14, 1988)

Moore McCormack: Southdown, Inc. v. Moore McCormack Resources, Inc., 686 F. Supp. 595 (S.D. Tex. 1988)

Newmont Mining: Ivanhoe Partners v. Newmont Mining Corp., 535 A.2d 1334 (Del. 1987)

Revlon: Revlon, Inc. v. MacAndrews & Forbes Holdings, Inc., 506 A.2d 173 (Del. 1986)

Restaurant Associates: Freedman v. Restaurant Associates Industries, Inc., [1987–1988 Transfer Binder] Fed. Sec. L. Rep. (CCH) ¶ 93,502 (Del. Ch. Oct. 16, 1987)

RJR: In re RJR Nabisco, Inc. Shareholders Litigation, No. 10,389 (Del. Ch. Jan. 11, 1989)

Scientific Leasing: Yanow v. Scientific Leasing, Inc., [1987–1988 Transfer Binder] Fed. Sec. L. Rep. (CCH) ¶ 93,660 (Del. Ch. Feb. 8, 1988)

SCM: Hanson Trust PLC v. SCM Corp., 774 F.2d 47 (2d Cir. 1985)

Sea-Land: Hecco Ventures v. Sea-Land Corp., No. 8486 (Del. Ch. May 19, 1986)

Staley Continental: Tate & Lyle PLC v. Staley Continental, Inc., [1987–1988 Transfer Binder] Fed. Sec. L. Rep. (CCH) ¶ 93,764 (Del. Ch. May 9, 1988)

Storer: Cottle v. Storer Communications, Inc., 849 F.2d 570 (11th Cir. 1988)

Texas Air: Hasting-Murtagh v. Texas Air Corp., 649 F. Supp. 479 (S.D. Fla. 1986)

TW Services: TW Services v. SWT Acquisition Corp., No. 10427 (Del. Ch. Mar. 2, 1989)

Unocal: Unocal Corp. v. Mesa Petroleum Co., 493 A.2d 946 (Del. 1985)

USG: Desert Partners, L.P., v. USG Corp., 686 F. Supp. 1289 (N.D. Ill. 1988)

Van Gorkom: Smith v. Van Gorkom, 488 A.2d 858 (Del. 1985)

CHAPTER 12

THE DUTY TO AUCTION AND LOCK-UPS IN CONTESTED TAKEOVERS

Jesse A. Finkelstein
Kevin G. Abrams
David L. Finger

THE DUTY TO AUCTION

Introduction

In Revlon, Inc. v. MacAndrews & Forbes Holdings, Inc., 506 A.2d 173 (Del. 1986), the Delaware Supreme Court issued its seminal ruling that, once the target's board determines that a change in control of the corporation is inevitable and decides to put the corporation up for sale, the board is obliged to assume the role of an "auctioneer," charged with the duty of maximizing the amount to be received by the shareholders. This duty to conduct a so-called "Revlon-style auction" of a corporation has become one of the most important tenets of Delaware corporate law, and one of the most highly litigated issues in recent corporate control contests. The decision in Mills Acquisition Co. v. Macmillan, Inc., 559 A.2d 1261 (Del.

Jesse A. Finkelstein is a member of Richards, Layton & Finger, Wilmington, Delaware.
Kevin G. Abrams and David L. Finger are associates with Richards, Layton & Finger.

1989) (hereinafter "Macmillan"), sheds new light on the legal standards applied under Delaware law to assess board action during the sale of the corporation. In addition, given the underlying facts of the case, the Macmillan decision contains a prescription of the steps which should be taken—and avoided—by target directors, bidders, and their advisors in the midst of the sales process. Macmillan also is noteworthy in that it confirms a number of generally accepted notions, based on lower court decisions, regarding the use of particular devices in negotiating and finalizing acquisition agreements. Moreover, Macmillan sets forth a hybrid two-step test based on Unocal which will be employed under Delaware law to evaluate target directors' actions which "tilt the playing field" during the sale.

This outline attempts to synthesize the numerous decisions addressing the scope of target directors' duties under the Revlon doctrine. Particular attention will be devoted to Macmillan since the decision addresses a number of key questions which arise frequently in the context of corporate auctions. A review of prior decisions also demonstrates the generally consistent efforts made by the courts to deal with the complex legal issues surrounding corporate auctions which have occupied so much of the time of judges, practitioners, and commentators in recent years. However, given the ingenuity of the marketplace and the provocative factual twists which always emerge in this context, Macmillan undoubtedly will not be the final word on the scope of the various parties' duties and responsibilities in selling control of the corporation to one of several competing bidders.

Summary of Macmillan

On September 12, 1988, the directors of Macmillan decided that the company should be sold. This decision led to several rounds of bidding between Maxwell Communications and Kohlberg Kravis Roberts & Co. ("KKR"). By September 26, 1988, Maxwell's bid was $89 cash per share for all shares, while KKR's bid was $89.50 per share, consisting of $82 cash and the balance in debentures and warrants. The KKR bid, however, was subject to three conditions: an asset option, a definitive merger agreement, and a no-shop provision. Macmillan's advisors concluded that the bids were too close to recommend either bid to the board. Accordingly, Macmillan's advisors conducted a final round of bidding. Prior to the conclusion of the final bidding, the chief executive officer of Macmillan advised KKR of the value of Maxwell's bid in an unauthorized telephone call which was not disclosed to the public or to the board of Macmillan. Knowing the precise amount of the Maxwell bid, KKR submitted a revised bid for $90 per share payable in cash, debentures, and warrants, with the same three conditions (except that the exercise price for the optioned assets in the lock-up was increased). After a discount for the time delay inherent in the KKR bid and its non-cash components, the KKR bid was valued at between $89.67 and $89.80 per share. Maxwell, however, believed that it had already submitted the highest bid and, therefore, did not revise its $89.00 offer.

The Macmillan board considered both offers and decided to accept the higher KKR proposal. The Macmillan directors also refused to solicit a higher bid from Maxwell even after his representatives specifically inquired whether a higher bid would be necessary to "win" the auction contest. Previously, the Macmillan directors had acquiesced to a "no-shop" proposal from KKR which effectively prevented the board from disclosing information relating to KKR's bid. Although the Macmillan board recognized that there was a possibility that Maxwell might increase its bid if the company "shopped" the KKR bid, it concluded that the risks of doing so in the face of the no-shop demand of KKR outweighed the possible rewards. On learning of the KKR bid, Maxwell increased its pending tender offer to $90.25 per share cash for all Macmillan shares, conditioned upon the invalidation of the KKR asset option and upon Macmillan's shareholder rights being redeemed or otherwise made inapplicable to Maxwell's offer. Macmillan's board, however, considered that it was bound by the asset option with KKR and refused to accept the later Maxwell bid.

Maxwell argued that the auction was conducted in an inequitable manner and was fatally imbalanced in favor of KKR. This imbalance was said to result from: (1) the unauthorized telephone call to KKR "tipping" the amount of Maxwell's bid; (2) Macmillan's advisor, reading a specially prepared script to KKR (but not to Maxwell) that purportedly drew a road map for KKR to formulate its successful bid; (3) the refusal of a Macmillan advisor to tell Maxwell whether Macmillan had received a higher bid than the pending Maxwell bid; and (4) the omission to tell Maxwell in a pointed way that it would have to raise its bid in order to win. Maxwell contended that the Macmillan advisors were clearing the path for KKR by instructing it how to submit the lowest possible winning bid. Therefore, Maxwell argued that the asset option should be invalidated because the auction was corrupted.

On appeal, the Delaware Supreme Court enjoined the KKR transaction and reversed the decision of the Court of Chancery. The Delaware Supreme Court found that the legal conclusions of the Court of Chancery were inconsistent with the factual finding that the bidding process was neither "evenhanded nor neutral." Specifically, the Delaware Supreme Court found that actions by senior management were inconsistent with the Revlon requirement of "the most scrupulous adherence to ordinary principles of fairness...in the conduct of an auction for the sale of corporate control."[1] The Delaware Supreme Court held that the information furnished to the Macmillan board at critical moments in the auction was inaccurate, incomplete, and misleading. Furthermore, the Delaware Supreme Court stated that where senior management is a party to the breach and has an interest in the outcome of the board's action, the business judgment rule has no application and the matter is governed by principles of intrinsic fairness.

When Does the Duty to Conduct an Auction Arise?

The courts have held that a duty under Revlon arises once it is "inevitable" that the corporation will be subject to a change in control and the board has decided to put the company up for sale.[2] However, it is not always clear when the duty to conduct an auction is triggered, or indeed what transactions will trigger such a duty. Cases involving defensive restructurings and recapitalizations present some of the greatest uncertainty regarding whether a corporation is about to undergo a "change in control" or "sale" which triggers the Revlon duties.[3]

A number of courts have addressed such issues and subsequent case law indicates that the directors' duties under Revlon apply only where a sale of the company is inevitable. However, this in turn necessarily involves a fact intensive inquiry in each case. The difficulty of resolving the question was illustrated graphically in Ivanhoe Partners v. Newmont Mining Corp., 535 A.2d 1334 (Del. 1987), where the target corporation, Newmont, declared a $33.00 per share dividend in an attempt to block a hostile tender offer by Ivanhoe. The payment of this dividend allowed Newmont's largest shareholder, Gold Fields, to engage in a "street sweep" of Newmont stock, thereby increasing Gold Fields' ownership of Newmont from 25 percent to 49.9 percent. In addition, Gold Fields entered into a "standstill" agreement with Newmont which restricted Gold Fields' acquisition of Newmont stock to the 49.9 percent level and limited its voting power to elect only 40 percent of the directors of Newmont. Ivanhoe argued that the Newmont Board had breached its duties under Revlon by refusing to entertain Ivanhoe's bid. However, the Delaware Supreme Court found that, under the facts of the case, the Revlon principle was not implicated:

> Revlon applies here only if it was apparent that the sale of Newmont was 'inevitable.' The record, however, does not support such a finding for two reasons.
>
> First, Newmont was never for sale.... Newmont board held fast to its decision to keep the company independent....
>
> Second, there was neither a bidding contest, nor a sale. The only bidder for Newmont was Ivanhoe. Gold Fields was not a bidder, but wished only to protect its already substantial interest in the company. It did so through the street sweep.[4]

The difficulty of the analysis in Ivanhoe on the sale question may have led the Delaware Supreme Court to restate its rationale in a subsequent decision.[5]

In Buckhorn, Inc. v. Ropak Corp., 656 F. Supp. 209 (S.D. Ohio 1987), *aff'd* by sum. ord., 815 F.2d 76 (6th Cir. 1987), the Court, applying Delaware law, held that because the directors of Buckhorn, "did not inevitably commit themselves to selling any part or all of Buckhorn," and since the Buckhorn directors' "primary objective was to maintain Buckhorn as a going-concern," the duty to conduct a Revlon-style auction did not arise.[6] Thus, the Court concluded that the Buckhorn directors did not breach a fiduciary duty by refusing to negotiate with Ropak for the sale of Buckhorn.

In Black & Decker Corp. v. American Standard, Inc., 682 F. Supp. 772 (D. Del. 1988), the Court found that a proposed management-sponsored defensive recapitalization would have amounted to a sale and triggered the duty to conduct an auction. The restructuring contemplated a reduction in the public shareholders' ownership of the corporation from 92.6 percent to 45.5 percent, while management's share was to increase from 4.8 percent to 23.9 percent. The restructuring also included the transfer of 30.6 percent of the shares to an ESOP. The Court held that the surrender of majority control by the public stockholders constituted, in those circumstances, a sale of control that was equivalent to a "sale of the company" under Revlon.[7] Furthermore, the Court found that although management had said that the company wanted to remain independent, its actions revealed that, in fact, the company was for sale. The Court emphasized that the recapitalization transferred control from the public shareholders to management and employees.[8]

Similarly, in Robert M. Bass Group, Inc. v. Evans, 552 A.2d 1227 (Del. Ch. 1988), appeal dismissed sub nom., Macmillan, Inc. v. Robert M. Bass Group, Inc., 548 A.2d 498 (Del. 1988), the Court noted that a proposed restructuring that would increase management's equity participation from 4.5 percent to 39.2 percent in one of two corporations contemplated by the restructuring "could be interpreted as a sale of the company" and that "[s]uch a sale would arguably trigger duties under Revlon, which requires that the directors selling the company realize the highest available value for shareholders."[9] The Delaware Supreme Court in Macmillan resolved any uncertainty by recognizing that "[b]y any standards this company was for sale" at the time the recapitalization was proposed. 559 A.2d at 1285. Under Macmillan, it is arguable that a transfer of "effective control" over the corporation, even if less than a majority of the voting power, may trigger Revlon obligations.[9] Given the references in Macmillan and American Standard to the self-interest of management in the transfer of voting power, and the notation by the Delaware Supreme Court in Macmillan that the target directors in Newmont had no such interest, it appears that a transaction resulting in management significantly increasing its voting power will be closely scrutinized.

In City Capital Associates L.P. v. Interco Inc., 551 A.2d 787 (Del. Ch. 1988), the Court addressed plaintiff's argument that the implementation of a restructuring scheme in the face of plaintiff's all-cash tender offer violated the target board's fiduciary duty under Revlon. Plaintiff argued that the restructuring scheme—which involved the sale of assets generating about one half of Interco's sales, substantial borrowings, and distributions of cash and debt securities to shareholders equivalent to approximately 85 percent of the market value of Interco stock—in effect involved the break-up and sale of the company and, accordingly, implicated the Revlon duty to sell the company through an auction.[11] Interco argued that Revlon did not apply to the restructuring because the company was not for sale and no determination had ever been made that it was in the best interests of the shareholders to sell the company. The Court stated that the question as to whether a board has a duty to conduct an auction of the company is not "answered by merely referring to a board resolve to try to keep the Company independent."[12] The Court continued by recognizing that Revlon was not intended "to narrowly circumscribe the range of reactions that a board may make in good faith to an attempt to seize control of a corporation":

> Even when the corporation is clearly 'for sale,' a disinterested board or committee maintains the right and the obligation to exercise business judgment in pursuing the stockholders' interests. . . .
>
> ***
>
> *[F]iduciary obligations can be met in ways other than a traditional auction, if the procedure supplies the board with the information from which it can conclude that it has arranged the best available transaction for shareholders.*[13]

Thus, upon finding that the board proceeded prudently and in good faith in pursuing the restructuring as a financially attractive alternative to the plaintiffs' offer, the Court found that the board had not breached its fiduciary duties under Revlon.

In TW Services, Inc. v. SWT Acquisition Corp., C.A. Nos. 10427 & 10928 (Del. Ch. Mar. 2, 1989), the Court raised, but did not decide, the issue whether a board may find itself involuntarily placed in a Revlon mode:

> Many a board find itself thrust involuntarily into a Revlon mode in which it is required to take only steps designed to maximize current share value and in which it must desist from steps that would impede that goal, even if they might otherwise appear sustainable as an arguable step in the promotion of "long term" corporate or share values? Revlon did not address that subject but implied that a board might find itself in such a position when it said the duty it spoke of arose "when the break-up of the company is inevitable."[14]

The Delaware courts had the opportunity to confront this question head on in Paramount Communications Inc. v. Time Inc., C.A. No. 10866 (Del. Ch. July 14, 1989), *aff'd*, 565 A.2d 280 (Del. 1989). Upon the appearance of Paramount, Time and Warner rescinded the stock swap contemplated by their unconsummated merger agreement in favor of a tender offer by Time for the stock of Warner. One group of shareholders argued that the original merger agreement constituted a decision to transfer control of Time to Warner since the Warner stockholders would have received 62 percent of the stock in the combined entity. Thus, it was argued, the Time board's duty changed from long-term management of the corporation for the benefit of its shareholders to the narrower and specific goal of present maximization of share value.

The Court of Chancery began its analysis in Time by noting that the fact that the Time board did not expressly resolve to sell the company was not dispositive of anything. The Court held, however, that the initial merger agreement did not contemplate a change in the control of Time:

> If the appropriate inquiry is whether a change in control is contemplated, the answer must be sought in the specific circumstances surrounding the transaction. Surely under some circumstances a stock for stock merger could reflect a transfer of corporate control. That would, for example, plainly be the case here if Warner were a private company. But where, as here, the shares of both constituent corporations are widely held, corporate control can be expected to remain unaffected by a stock for stock merger. This in my judgment was the situation with respect to the original merger agreement. When the specifics of that situation are reviewed, it is seen that...neither corporation could be said to be acquiring the other. Control of both remained in a large, fluid, changeable and changing market.[15]

Another group of shareholders argued that the Time directors assumed Revlon duties because the original merger would have precluded Time shareholders from realizing a control premium for their shares for the foreseeable future. The merger implicitly would have represented the same loss of a control premium as would result in a change in control transaction with no premium. Plaintiffs argued that even if the stock-for-stock merger was not a change in control, the same duty to maximize current value should attach to it as to a sale. The Court found that the action of the Time board in approving the merger with Warner was a business decision which did not constitute a change-in-control, and so would be afforded the protection of the business judgment rule unless it were found to be a defensive measure. Thus, the Court of Chancery recognized that Unocal, and not Revlon, would be the appropriate standard of review.[16]

It is also arguable that Revlon duties can apply even when there is no competitive bidding. In Rand v. Western Airlines, Inc., C.A. No. 8632, slip op. at 7-8 (Del. Ch., Sept. 11, 1989), the Court held that a complaint stated a cause of action by alleging that the corporation agreed to merge on terms which limited the ability of potential acquirers to bid, even though there was no other bidder.

The Nature of the Auction Process

No Duty to Conduct an Auction or Solicit Bids
Delaware courts traditionally have recognized that, depending on the circumstances, the directors may not have an obligation to solicit competing bids or auction the company.[17] Other decisions suggest obliquely that directors might have some duty to undertake affirmative steps to obtain competing bids.[18]

In Macmillan, the Delaware Supreme Court distinguished between the responsibility of target directors and the steps which might be taken to comply with their fiduciary obligations:

> We stated in Revlon, and again here, that in a sale of corporate control the responsibility of the directors is to get the highest value reasonably attainable for the shareholders. Beyond that, there are no special and distinct "Revlon duties."[19]

Thus, the directors appear to have some flexibility in undertaking steps to secure "the highest value reasonably attainable for the shareholders."[20]

In Yanow v. Scientific Leasing, Inc., C.A. Nos. 9536 & 9561 (Del. Ch. Feb. 8, 1988), Scientific Leasing agreed to provide potential bidders with financial information, subject to the execution of a confidentiality and standstill agreement. The board of Scientific Leasing also appointed a negotiating committee to meet with any interested bidders. However, the board determined not to disclose that the corporation might be for sale, due to the concern that a "fire sale" auction would adversely affect the corporation. LINC was the only serious bidder to emerge. The parties agreed to an acquisition agreement in which LINC commenced a tender offer and received an option to purchase in excess of 16 percent of the stock of Scientific Leasing at the tender offer price. Provision was also made for reimbursement of LINC's expenses under certain circumstances. Scientific Leasing, however, refused a request to negotiate exclusively with LINC, and also refused to agree to a break-up fee or to a no-shop agreement. In addition, Scientific Leasing negotiated a "window shop clause" which allowed Scientific Leasing to provide financial information to other bidders if it appeared that such parties might make an economically superior offer.

Despite the existence of the window shop clause, certain shareholders of Scientific Leasing brought an action claiming that the directors had breached their fiduciary duties by negotiating an agreement with only one bidder without having conducted a true auction. The Court rejected the attack upon the auction process:

> [P]laintiffs argue that the directors employed an inadequate auction process in breach of their duties imposed by Revlon. They contend that, while it was not necessary to conduct a 'fire sale' auction directed to the public at large, the directors should have, at the very least, discreetly contacted all companies that had previously expressed an interest in SLI and invited them to submit bids. *The real dispute boils down to what specific methods corporate directors may use to elicit bids from potential acquirers. That issue would appear to be normally a matter of director judgment that necessarily must vary with each case.*[21]

Although the Court found that the record was not completely clear that the market was as fully informed as it might have been, the Court was satisfied that the "relevant 'players' in the industry" were aware that Scientific Leasing was for sale. In addition, the Court was satisfied that Scientific Leasing's directors had valid reasons to proceed discreetly in marketing the company and that they had no motive to obtain less than the best available price.

In *In re* Fort Howard, the board of directors, acting through a special committee, approved a merger agreement with a management-affiliated group which permitted an effective market test of the offer before the management offer could be completed. The merger agreement proscribed active solicitation of alternative bids by the company, but allowed the company to receive unsolicited bids, to provide information to unsolicited third parties, and to negotiate with such parties. Following the approval of the merger agreement, Fort Howard issued a press release announcing that the special committee's investment banker would provide information to interested third parties.

Plaintiffs in Fort Howard argued that Revlon required the directors to "search, in good faith and advisedly, for the best available alternative and to remain perfectly neutral as between competing potential buyers."[22] Plaintiffs also alleged that the decision made by the special committee not to make a public announcement of the possible buyout and the fact that the merger agreement precluded Fort Howard from actively "shopping" the company or from soliciting additional offers indicated that the board had breached its fiduciary duties by preventing an effective auction. The

Court acknowledged that "[t]he more significant the subject matter of the [directors'] decision, obviously, the greater will be the need to probe and consider alternatives,"[23] and the fact that certain aspects of the transaction could give rise to concern to a "suspicious mind." Despite this, the Court upheld the process by which Fort Howard was sold:

> [It was] reasonably calculated to (and did) effectively probe the market for alternative possible transactions [and that] [t]he alternative 'market check' that was achieved was not so hobbled by lock-ups, termination fees or topping fees; so constrained in time or so administered (with respect to access to pertinent information or manner of announcing 'window shopping' rights) as to permit the inference that this alternative was a sham designed from the outside to be ineffective or minimally effective.[24]

The Court also upheld the board's rationale for adopting this approach:

> Management had proposed to make an all cash bid for all shares if and only if the board endorsed it. The rest of the world was not bound by any of these three important qualifications. To start a bidding contest before it was known that an all cash bid for all shares could and would be made, would increase the risk of a possible takeover attempt at less than a 'fair' price or for less than all shares.[25]

The Chancellor apparently was persuaded that the market check provision had the legitimate effect of placing a floor beneath bids by any third parties.

It would seem, therefore, that Revlon does not necessarily impose a duty on a corporation to publicly solicit bids by announcing that it is for sale. The decision in City Capital v. Interco, supports this approach:

> Revlon should not, in my opinion, be interpreted as representing a sharp turn in our law. It does not require, for example, that before every corporate merger agreement can validly be entered into, the constituent corporations must be 'shopped' or, more radically, an auction process undertaken, even though a merger may be regarded as a sale of the Company.

The Court, however, continued by stating:

> When the transaction is so fundamental as the restructuring here (or a sale or merger of the Company), the obligation to be informed would seem to require that reliable information about the value of alternative transactions

be explored. *When the transaction is the sale of the Company, in which the interests of current stockholders will be converted to cash or otherwise terminated, the requirement to be well informed would ordinarily mandate an appropriate probing of the market for alternatives (and a public auction, should interest be shown).* Particularly is that true when a sale is to a management affiliated group (the ubiquitous management LBO transactions) for apparent reasons involving human frailty. *But even in that setting, fiduciary obligations can be met in ways other than a traditional auction, if the procedure supplies the board with information from which it can conclude that it has arranged the best available transaction for the shareholders.*[26]

In *In re* Amsted Industries, Inc., C.A. No. 8224 (Del. Ch., Aug. 24, 1988), a special committee was formed to evaluate a leveraged buyout by management. The board, however, prohibited the special committee from shopping the company. Although the Court noted that there were no compelling business reasons not to shop the company, it approved a class action settlement because the company's investment banker testified that the offer was high on the range of fairness and the special committee had no "economic reason to do less than its best."

In Holly Farms I, however, the Court found that the Holly Farms directors' actions were inconsistent with their duties under Revlon. The investment banker for Holly Farms had testified that he did not consider his role to be that of an auctioneer, and three Holly Farms directors testified that the board never conducted an auction of the company. While the Court found substantial evidence that Holly Farms had negotiated with ConAgra, the Court found that the board "did not make any serious effort to likewise negotiate with Tyson Foods nor encouraged Tyson Foods to put its best offer on the table." The Court also emphasized that Holly Farms refused to tell Tyson Foods whether the company was for sale and did not respond meaningfully to numerous inquiries from Tyson Foods about the adequacy of its bid.

In *In re* Envirodyne Industries, Inc. Shareholders Litigation, Cons. C.A. No. 10702 (Del. Ch. Apr. 20, 1989), the Court rejected an argument that the directors violated their Revlon duties by approving the merger agreement without conducting an auction of the corporation. Prior to the merger, Envirodyne's advisors had contacted 100 possible buyers. No serious proposals came forth. Several months thereafter, the negotiations leading to the proposed merger were publicly announced. The Court concluded that there was no evidence that efforts to sell the company, which produced no offers, did not constitute "a true market test of

Envirodyne's worth."[27] Moreover, the Court noted that the merger agreement did not foreclose discussions with other interested parties. The highly publicized negotiations put the financial community on notice that the company was for sale, and no bona fide offer had emerged. The Court also rejected arguments that the special negotiating committee did not negotiate in good faith or contrary to the best interest of the shareholders, holding that there was no showing that the 9.2 percent negotiating shareholder "had any other motivation than to secure the highest price for his and his fellow shareholders' stock."

In Edelman v. Fruehauf Corp., 798 F.2d 882 (6th Cir. 1986), the Court disapproved of the board's actions, which showed favoritism to a management buyout team. The board had accepted a no-shop provision, agreed to pay inducement fees, amended a stock option plan to trigger the options in the event of a hostile offer, and amended a pension plan to give advance board approval to any 40 percent acquirer who offered at least $48.50 per share. The court concluded that "the Board simply decided to make a deal with management no matter what other bidders might offer." The court stated that once the target is to be sold, the directors have a duty to auction the corporation and to get the best price possible.[28]

The Duty to Obtain the Highest Value for the Stockholders' Benefit

The Delaware courts have been cognizant of the fact that the presence of competing bids may complicate the directors' decisions.[29]

The traditional principle of Delaware law is that, once it becomes clear that an asset will be sold, fiduciaries faced with two competing bids on essentially identical terms (other than price) for an asset normally must accept the higher bid.[30] The Delaware courts also have recognized that directors remain free to reject the apparently higher bid if it is conditional or otherwise indefinite.[31]

In Revlon, the Delaware Supreme Court recognized that directors acting as the "auctioneers" of a target corporation were under a duty to obtain "the best *price* for the stockholders at a sale of the company."[32] However, as the Macmillan decision confirmed, the directors' duty is something different than merely obtaining the best possible price *per se*.

The Delaware Supreme Court in Macmillan stated that the "proper objective" of target directors in the auction process is "to obtain the highest price reasonably available for the company, provided it was offered by a reputable and responsible bidder." The Delaware Supreme Court proceeded to elaborate on the factors which may be considered in determining whether a particular bid is the "highest price reasonably available":

> In assessing the bid and the bidder's responsibility, a board may consider, among various proper factors, the adequacy and terms of the offer; its fairness and feasibility; the proposed or actual financing for the offer, and the consequences of that financing; questions of illegality; the impact of both the bid and the potential acquisition on other constituencies, provided that it bears some reasonable relationship to general shareholder interests; the risk of nonconsummation; the basic stockholder interests at stake; the bidder's identity, prior background and other business venture experiences; and the bidder's business plans for the corporation and their effects on stockholder interest.[33]

Macmillan raises a number of questions insofar as it leaves unresolved how the courts are supposed to apply "enhanced scrutiny" to the business decisions of directors in evaluating such inherently judgmental factors in connection with the decision to grant a "lock-up" or some other form of favorable treatment to one bidder. Nevertheless, the Delaware Supreme Court expressly tempered its highest price directive with the declaration that the target board may choose the best offer which is "reasonably available" and "provided it was offered by a reputable and responsible bidder." To the extent Macmillan will be interpreted as authorizing judicial deference to certain board decisions in the auction process, it is consistent with the prevailing view of the decisions in other cases.

In Freedman v. Restaurant Associates Industries, Inc., C.A. No. 9212 (Del. Ch. Oct. 16, 1987), the court found that the Restaurant Associates directors did not breach their duty of loyalty by rejecting a high-priced tender offer in favor of its own tender offer in order to take the corporation private. Plaintiff argued that Revlon established the directors' affirmative duty to maximize the price received by stockholders in the sale of the company. The special committee of disinterested directors who evaluated the board's and the outside offeror's (AWR) proposals recommended against accepting AWR's highest offer, and the board rejected it. Plaintiffs asserted that the board breached its duty of loyalty by placing their own interests as buyers over the interest of the shareholders to get the highest price. The court distinguished this case from those in which a fiduciary chooses the lower of two cash offers for the corporation, and recognized that a fiduciary must consider all of the relevant factors and alternative possibilities. The court found the special committee's rejection of the AWR offer to be reasonable since the proposal contained numerous conditions and "outs" under which AWR could withdraw. After scrutinizing the special committee's handling of the offers, the court found nothing improper and deferred to the committee's business decision.

In In re J.P. Stevens & Co. Shareholders' Litigation, 542 A.2d 770 (Del. Ch. 1988), the Court stated that in an "auction" context the directors should achieve "the best possible transaction for the shareholders."[34] The Chancellor elaborated by stating that this did "not mean that other material factors other than 'price' ought not to be considered and, where appropriate, acted upon by the board. Such consideration might include form of consideration, timing of the transaction or risk of nonconsummation."[35] Therefore, the Court found that the special committee of the J.P. Stevens's board was "entirely justified in considering any legitimate threat that the antitrust laws posed to the consummation of any West Point proposal."

Similarly, in Citron v. Fairchild Camera and Instrument Corp., C.A. No. 6085, (Del. Ch. May 19, 1988), the Court held that Revlon did not recognize "a duty on the part of directors when a corporation is 'for sale,' to get the highest available price. Rather, the duty can only be to try in good faith, in such a setting, to get the best available transaction for the shareholders. Directors are not insurers."[36] In Citron, the Court upheld a decision by the target directors to accept a fully financed $66 all-cash offer in preference to a $70 part-cash, part-securities bid which was subject to uncertain financing. The Court also took into consideration the time value of money, recognizing that it "would require some time to get cash into the shareholders' hands" if the latter offer was accepted.[37]

In re RJR Nabisco, Inc. Shareholders' Litigation, C.A. No. 10389 (Del. Ch. Jan. 31, 1989), focused on whether directors are entitled under Revlon to accept one of two substantially equivalent bids without initiating further bidding. After several initial rounds of bidding, the special committee received a bid from the management group valued at $108.50 to $109 and a bid from KKR valued at $108 to $108.50. The company's investment advisors stated that the two bids were substantially equivalent and fair to the RJR stockholders. Without returning to the bidders, the special committee determined to endorse KKR's proposal. That decision was primarily based on the fact that the KKR proposal provided a 25 percent continuing equity interest to the RJR stockholders, compared with the 15 percent equity interest offered by the management group, and the KKR proposal contemplated the retention of a substantial portion of RJR's businesses, while the management group proposed to retain only the RJR tobacco business.

The Court found in RJR that the failure of the special committee to return to the bidders after the submission of the substantially equivalent bids could not be deemed an indication of bad faith because KKR imposed a strict deadline on its offer and threatened to withdraw from the bidding altogether. In view of the larger equity interest offered by KKR, the different business plans of the two bidders and the more desirable provisions of the KKR debentures, the Court found the special committee's preference for the KKR bid to be a reasonable exercise of business judgment.

The Court in RJR also rejected plaintiff's argument that the special committee could not have informed itself of all material information prior to closing the auction without receiving the highest bids from the two bidders by returning to the management group and KKR after they submitted equivalent bids. In rejecting this argument, the Court emphasized that the duty of directors is only to obtain all information *reasonably* available."[38] In view of the possibility that KKR could have walked away from the transaction because of the time constraint on its bid, the Court concluded that the special committee's decision whether to incur the risk associated with asking for further bids and thereby obtaining additional information is itself a business judgment entitled to the protections of the business judgment rule.

Disparate Treatment of Bidders

Various courts have examined the parameters within which a board must conduct an "auction" for the company. In Revlon, the Delaware Supreme Court held that "measures which end an active auction and foreclose further bidding operate to the shareholders' detriment" and are therefore unlawful.[39] However, the Delaware Supreme Court in Revlon also stated that under certain circumstances, "favoritism" for a preferred suitor in an auction setting "might be justifiable":

> Favoritism for a white knight to the total exclusion of a hostile bidder might be justifiable when the latter's offer adversely affects shareholder interests, but when bidders make relatively similar offers, or dissolution of the company becomes inevitable, the directors cannot fulfill their enhanced Unocal duties by playing favorites with the contending factions. Market forces must be allowed to operate freely to bring the target's shareholders the best price available for their equity.[40]

In Macmillan, the Delaware Supreme Court reiterated this component of Revlon:

> Although we have held that such [lock-up and no-shop] agreements are not *per se* illegal, we recognized [in Revlon] that like measures often foreclose further bidding to the detriment of shareholders, and end active auctions prematurely. *If the grant of an auction-ending provision is appropriate, it must confer a substantial benefit upon the stockholders in order to withstand exacting scrutiny by the courts.*[41]

Notwithstanding the reference to Revlon, the decision in Macmillan confirms that, in analyzing any favored treatment given a bidder, the target directors' actions in structuring and implementing the sales process will be judged under a hybrid formulation of the Unocal test:

> As we held in Revlon, when management of a target company determines that company is for sale, the board's *responsibilities* under the enhanced Unocal standards are significantly altered. Although the board's *responsibilities* under Unocal are far different, the enhanced *duties* of the directors in responding to a potential shift in control, recognized in Unocal, remain unchanged. This principle pervades Revlon, and when directors conclude that an auction is appropriate, the standard by which their ensuing actions will be judged continues to be the enhanced duty imposed by this Court in Unocal.[42]

Under Macmillan, a "two-part threshold test" based on Unocal will result in the application of "enhanced judicial scrutiny" of target directors' actions in the auction setting before the normal presumptions of the business judgment rule will apply. In order to trigger the Macmillan mandate of "enhanced scrutiny," plaintiff must demonstrate and the trial court must find that the target directors "treated one or more of the respective bidders on unequal terms."[43] Upon such a showing, the court must undertake two inquiries:

> In the face of disparate treatment, the trial court must first examine whether the directors properly perceived that shareholder interests were enhanced. In any event the board's action must be reasonable in relation to the advantage sought to be achieved, or conversely, to the threat which a particular bid allegedly poses to stockholder interests.

Assuming the target directors' actions survive the two-prong test, Macmillan dictates that the actions "necessarily are entitled to the protections of the business judgment rule":

> The latitude a board will have in responding to different bids will vary according to the degree of benefit or detriment to the shareholders' general interests that the amount or terms of the bids pose.... Once a finding has been made by a court that the directors have fulfilled their fundamental duties of care and loyalty under the foregoing standards, there is no further judicial inquiry into the matter.[44]

Applying the foregoing standards, the Supreme Court in Macmillan focused on the marginal improvement in the KKR bid which accompanied the lock-up proposal and the assets which KKR sought to acquire under the agreement:

> KKR's "enhanced" bid, being nominal at best, was a *de minimus* justification for the lockup. When one compares what KKR received for the lockup, in contrast to its inconsiderable offer, the invalidity of the agreement becomes patent.
>
> Here, the assets covered by the lock-up agreement were some of Macmillan's most valued properties, its "crown jewels." Even if the lockup is permissible, when it involves "crown jewel" assets careful board scrutiny attends the decision. When the intended effect is to end an active auction, at the very least the independent members of the board must attempt to negotiate alternative bids before granting such a significant concession.[45]

Under Macmillan, directors will be given at least some deference in determining how to structure and conduct the bidding contest:

> We recognize that the conduct of the corporate auction is a complex undertaking both in its design and execution. We do not intend to limit the broad negotiating authority of the directors to achieve the best price available to the stockholders. To properly secure that end may require the board to invoke a panoply of devices, and the giving or receiving of concessions that may benefit one bidder over another. But when that happens, there must be a rational basis for the action such that the interests of the stockholders are manifestly the board's paramount objective.[46]

Indeed, it is clear under Macmillan that directors charged with the duty of conducting an auction do not have to treat all bidders in a like manner or maintain a "level playing field" on which the auction can proceed:

> Directors are not required by Delaware law to conduct an auction according to some standard formula, only that they observe the significant

requirement of fairness for the purpose of enhancing general shareholder interests. *That does not preclude differing treatment of bidders when necessary to advance those interests.* Variables may occur which necessitate such treatment. However the board's primary objective, and essential purpose, must remain the enhancement of the bidding process for the benefit of the stockholders.[47]

In *In re* Holly Farms Shareholders Litigation, Cons. C.A. No. 10350 (Del. Ch. Mar. 22, 1989) ("Holly Farms II") the Court formulated the rule as follows:

> A decision, not tainted by a board under a disability, determining how to best maximize shareholder value during an auction must be given judicial deference if it is rational; i.e., reasonable in relation to the [sic] objective to be achieved. In ascertaining rationality, the Court, of course, must in case of doubt resolve the issue in favor of the Board unless it finds that a majority of the Board were not genuinely independent, adequately informed or did not conduct a good faith thorough review of the transaction.[48]

In Holly Farms I, the Delaware Court of Chancery preliminarily enjoined the effectuation of an asset lock-up, a termination fee, and an expense reimbursement fee entered into by Holly Farms and ConAgra, the target's preferred suitor. The Court found that "an auction aimed at maximizing shareholder value never really took place." The Court concluded that "the sale process itself was so substantially flawed that the Board's actions, considering all the facts and circumstances, were not likely to have maximized the value of the corporation for its shareholders and, therefore, its actions cannot be viewed as being rational."[49]

In *In re* Holly Corp. Shareholders Litigation, Cons. C.A. No. 10350 (Del. Ch. May 18, 1989) ("Holly Farms III"), the Court found Holly Farms' revised auction plan to be unfair to Tyson Foods, in that if Tyson were the high bidder, Tyson's bid would be used to pay any settlement of the lock-up with ConAgra. Thus, shareholders would receive an amount less than the actual bid, yet would receive the full value of the ConAgra bid if ConAgra won. Thus, ConAgra had an unfair advantage. The Court, however, refused to enjoin the auction, as there was no showing of irreparable harm, since the auction itself would not be the equivalent of the merger, which could be enjoined at a later date.

In *In re* Holly Farms Corporation Shareholders Litigation, Cons. C.A. No. 10350 (Del. Ch. June 14, 1989) ("Holly Farms IV"), the Court found that Tyson Foods was not treated equally with ConAgra because it was not given a fair opportunity to submit a bid free of the ConAgra lock-up or to submit a bid contingent upon the lock-up being removed prior to closing. Tyson was only allowed a few hours to prepare a contingent bid after having been told repeatedly that no contingent bid would be acceptable. Moreover, Holly Farms said it would meet with Tyson Foods only if Tyson Foods' bid was better than the best bid of ConAgra, whereas ConAgra would be offered the company immediately if it was the highest bidder. Notwithstanding this unequal treatment, the Court declined to enjoin the merger. Applying Macmillan, the Court found that Holly Farms was faced with the threat that ConAgra's bid would have been withdrawn upon a then-imminent settlement between Tyson Foods and ConAgra, leaving Holly Farms with Tyson Foods' lower bid. Under the circumstances, the Court found that Holly Farms' action in accepting the significantly higher ConAgra offer before it could be withdrawn was reasonable in relation to the threat posed to stockholder interests.

In one of the leading pre-Macmillan decisions on the question—*In re J.P. Stevens*, 542 A.2d 770 (Del. Ch. 1988), appeal refused, 540 A.2d 1088 (Del. 1988)—West Point Pepperell sought a declaratory judgment invalidating provisions of a merger agreement between J.P. Stevens and Odyssey Partners providing for reimbursement of expenses and a "topping fee." The stockholder plaintiffs contended that the special committee acted to protect the interests of J.P. Stevens' management at the expense of the stockholders because Odyssey had indicated that it wanted current management to stay on. The court rejected plaintiffs' contention that the special committee was acting with an inappropriate motivation to favor the interests of J.P. Stevens' management because (i) the challenged provisions of the merger agreement benefited the stockholders, and (ii) the special committee consisted of independent directors operating with due care and receiving outside advice.[50]

West Point advanced the alternative application of Revlon that J.P. Stevens could not take any action tending to impede the achievement of the highest possible price through the auction and that the special committee had a duty to maintain a "level playing field" among the bidders. The Chancellor found that the special committee's only means of getting Odyssey to match the bid of West Point and thereby continue the auction was to approve the topping fee. Accordingly, the Court determined that the special committee acted in furtherance of the board's duty "to seek the best available transaction for the shareholders and to seek no other purpose."[51] The Chancellor specifically recognized the right of target directors to treat bidders differently:

> While it is true, that once agreements of this kind are in place, they do have the effect of tilting the playing field in favor of the holder of such rights, that fact, alone, does not establish that they necessarily are not in the best interests of shareholders. It is the shareholders to whom the board owes a duty of fairness, not to persons seeking to acquire the Company. To continue with the metaphor, *the board may tilt the playing field if, but only if, it is in the shareholders' interest to do so.*[52]

In *In re* Fort Howard Corp. Shareholders' Litigation, the Court addressed the question whether, once a company is for sale, the board must in all events be neutral as between offerors and maintain a level playing field, while not interfering with the free workings of an auction market:

> [A] board need not be passive even in an auction setting. It may never appropriately favor one buyer over another for a selfish or inappropriate reason, such as occurred in Revlon, but it may favor one over another if in good faith and advisedly it believes shareholder interests would be thereby advanced.[53]

In considering the process by which Fort Howard was sold, the Court stated:

> Accordingly, even if the approach adopted could be said to favor the management affiliated group—in the sense that it negotiated its deal without the imposition of time constraints and in a setting in which no other bidders were present—it does not do so in a way that would support the inference that the decision to do so was not made in the good faith pursuit of the interests of the stockholders.[54]

In Freedman v. Restaurant Associates Industries, Inc., the Court recognized that a board may deal selectively with competing bidders, and determined that "steps [may be] taken to defeat a potential suitor" provided such steps are "designed to maximize shareholder returns."[55] The Court, accordingly, declined to compel the corporation to grant a third party a share purchase lock-up option. Referring to the relief sought as "unusual" and "extraordinary," the Court stated that merely because "such a holding would be novel does not preclude it, of course, but the lack of authority is a salient feature of the argument. I need not now, however, express an

opinion as to whether such relief would ever be authorized as an extension of the Revlon teaching."[56]

In Black & Decker Corp. v. American Standard, Inc., the Court
implicitly endorsed the view that a board may treat bidders in an unequal
way, provided that there is some "justification" for such action. The
Court specifically focused on certain proposed amendments to the American Standard retirement plan which were part of a larger defensive recapitalization. The Court recognized that the amendment to the retirement
plan and the adoption of the severance plan gave management a $130
million advantage over any competing bid. Therefore, the Court enjoined
American Standard from taking any action with respect to the two plans
in order to place a competing bidder on an equal footing with management
in the bidding contest. The Court, noting that it was "clear that the
Board's actions places Black & Decker on an unequal footing in its bid
for control," held that "it does not appear that there is any justification for
such continuing unequal treatment." One of the factors that influenced
the Court's decision was the fact that "the value of the competing offers
[were] substantially similar."[57]

Therefore, it appears that, although a target's board may tilt the playing field in order to favor a preferred suitor, it must still allow competing
bidders a fair opportunity to submit the highest bid. Courts in other
jurisdictions have endorsed this approach. For example, in CRTF Corp.
v. Federated Department Stores, Inc., 683 F. Supp. 422 (S.D.N.Y. 1988),
the Court recognized that "the Board may selectively invoke or waive
rights under a previously adopted 'Poison Pill' in order to further the
auction and to raise the bidding."[58] In Edelman v. Fruehauf Corp., 798
F.2d 882 (6th Cir. 1986), the Court found that the Fruehauf board acted in
bad faith in favoring a management-proposed buyout that included a break-
up fee and no-shop provision:

> Fruehauf's Board of Directors unreasonably preferred incumbent man-
> agement in the bidding process—acting without objectivity and requisite
> loyalty to the corporation. Their actions were not taken in a good faith effort
> to negotiate the best deal for the shareholders. They acted as interested
> parties and did not treat the Fruehauf managers and the Edelman group in an
> evenhanded way but rather gave their colleagues on the Board, the inside
> managers, the inside track and accepted their proposal without fostering a
> real bidding process.[59]

The Court issued an injunction that, among other things, required Fruehauf not to take any corporate actions "which are intended to or have the effect of favoring or advantaging any particular bidder over any other bidder."[60]

In Samjens Partners I v. Burlington Industries, Inc., 663 F. Supp. 614 (S.D.N.Y. 1987), plaintiffs claimed that a merger agreement which contained a $50 million break-up fee, between the target board and a friendly bidder, violated the board's duties under Revlon where a hostile bidder (Asher Edelman) was refused the same agreement. The Court cited Revlon in stating "[t]he board is under a further duty, when conducting the auction, to deal fairly with the bidders. It cannot deal selectively to fend off a hostile bidder."[61] However, in rejecting Edelman's effort to invalidate the merger agreement, the Court noted:

> Nor did the Board freeze Edelman out of the auction. The merger agreement the Board signed did not end the auction, it provided a starting point for further bidding. Edelman was free to—and did—raise his bid after it was signed. If the Board was unfair with Edelman, it was only because it forced him to dig deeper into his pockets to the benefit of Burlington shareholders.[62]

Furthermore, the Court recognized that by "[d]enying Samjens a break-up fee [helped] to even the playing field" because Edelman had already made a large "paper" profit from the stock he purchased prior to the auction.[63]

Finally, the Ninth Circuit Court of Appeals in Jewel Cos. v. Pay Less Drug Stores Northwest, Inc., 741 F.2d 1555 (9th Cir. 1984), referred to proposals by commentators suggesting that "even in a negotiated merger transaction the board's role should be limited to the role of auctioneer, i.e., the board should neither express preferences among potential merger parties nor actively negotiate, but should simply solicit bids and pass them on to the shareholders."[64] The Court, however, applying California law, concluded:

> While we express no view on the policy merits of that proposal, we are convinced, after examining California law, that the Corporate Code of California does not adopt the auction model in regulating negotiated acquisitions. To the contrary, California's regulatory scheme for negotiated merger transactions is predicated on the idea that the board of directors of each merging entity will deliberate upon a decision and then negotiate and execute a merger agreement of the type that it, in its business judgment, deems best for the shareholders.

As the Delaware Supreme Court conceded in Macmillan, the Court of Chancery has not "explicitly applied the enhanced Unocal standards" in reviewing board actions in the auction context.[65] This is unsurprising since the Delaware Supreme Court in Revlon apparently agreed with the recognition of the Court of Chancery that the business judgment rule is "the starting point for an analysis of Revlon's conduct" in responding to a hostile acquisition attempt.[66] The Supreme Court spelled out what was implicit in the decision of the Court of Chancery:

> While the business judgment rule may be applicable to the actions of corporate directors responding to takeover threats, the principles upon which it is founded—care, loyalty and independence—must first be satisfied.[67]

In view of the string of decisions by the Court of Chancery following Revlon which apparently applied the business judgment framework of analysis, it is unsurprising that the Delaware Supreme Court in Macmillan cited several of such decisions and stated:

> On the surface, it may appear that the trial court has been applying an ordinary business judgment rule analysis. However, on closer scrutiny, it seems that there has been a *de facto* application of the *enhanced* business judgment rule under Unocal. To the extent that this has caused confusion, we think it is more a matter of semantics than of substance.[68]

In any event, under Macmillan, "[w]hen Revlon duties devolve upon directors, this Court will continue to exact an enhanced judicial scrutiny at the threshold, as in Unocal, before the normal presumptions of the business judgment rule will apply."

The Auction Process and Shareholder Rights Plans

In Revlon, the Supreme Court upheld a rights plan which was found to have been implemented in order to "[protect] the shareholders from a hostile takeover at a price below the company's intrinsic value, while retaining sufficient flexibility to address any proposal deemed to be in the stockholders' best interests."[69] The Court continued by stating:

> To that extent the board acted in good faith and upon reasonable investigation. Under the circumstances it cannot be said that the Rights Plan as employed was unreasonable, considering the threat posed. Indeed, the Plan was a factor in causing Pantry Pride to raise its bids from a low of $42 to an

eventual high of $58. At the time of its adoption of the Rights Plan afforded a measure of protection consistent with the directors' fiduciary duty in facing a takeover threat perceived as detrimental to corporate interests. (Unocal, 493 A.2d at 954-55.) *Far from being a "show stopper," as the plaintiffs had contended in Moran, the measure spurred the bidding to new heights, a proper result of its implementation.*[70]

The Court in CRTF Corp. v. Federated Department Stores, Inc., 683 F. Supp. 422 (S.D.N.Y. 1988) recognized that a target corporation's board of directors may effectively utilize a rights plan in a Revlon-style auction process in order to promote the bidding and ultimately secure the highest price for stockholders. The dispute arose from a bidding contest between Macy's and CRTF for control of Federated. The board of Federated entered into a merger agreement with Macys, pursuant to which Federated agreed to redeem its rights plan with respect to Macy's bid. CRTF, however, alleged that Federated's board had breached its fiduciary duties by its failure to redeem the rights with respect to CRTF's bid. Furthermore, CRTF argued that the target board's fiduciary responsibility requires it to remove all other defensive measures which impede a bid once a Revlon-type auction is underway.[71] However, the Court denied CRTF's application for an order compelling Federated to redeem its rights plan on the grounds that the Federated board was entitled to employ the rights plan to facilitate its role as an auctioneer:

> It provides the directors with a shield to fend off coercive offers, and with a gavel to run an auction. As the facts have shown, it is not a "show stopper." In fact it was clearly a factor in the Board's ability to obtain improvements in the price and financing arrangements offered by CRTF even before the advent of the Macy's offer, as discussed below, and to seek competitive bids from third parties, and to obtain the Macy's bid.[72]

The decisions since Revlon and Federated have focused on whether the board of the target was using the rights plan as a means of facilitating the auction:

(a) BNS Inc. v. Koppers Co., 683 F. Supp. 458 (D. Del. 1988): Beazer, which was making a tender offer for Koppers, alleged that the Koppers board illegally had refused to redeem its rights plan in the face of Beazer's all-cash offer. In denying Beazer's request for relief, Chief Judge Schwartz held that even an all-cash offer can constitute a "threat" to the corporation within the meaning of Unocal, if the target's board finds in good faith that the offer is at an inadequate price. The court found that, at that stage of the bidding, the Koppers board's failure to redeem the rights was a reasonable response to that threat since it was still evaluating how to respond to the BNS offer.

(b) Southdown, Inc. v. Moore McCormack Resources, Inc., 686 F. Supp. 595 (S.D. Tex. 1988): Southdown commenced an all-cash, any-and-all tender offer to acquire shares of Moore McCormack, a Delaware corporation. Moore McCormack was unable to declare that an increased offer by Southdown was inadequate, but responded by announcing a recapitalization proposal—including a cash dividend, debenture, and stub equity—which arguably was superior to the Southdown offer. Viewing the recapitalization proposal as a "scorched earth policy," the court focused on the refusal of the Moore McCormack board to redeem its previously-adopted rights plan (which included a 30 percent flip-in provision). After distinguishing Federated as a case involving a coercive offer and the use of a rights plan to promote an auction, Judge Hughes recognized that Moore McCormack had been unable to solicit any competing bids and that the structure of the Southdown offer posed no threat to the target stockholders. Accordingly, the court enjoined the administration of the rights plan on the ground that "[i]t is time to allow the owners more freedom and less protection." Id. at 604.

(c) Facet Enterprises, Inc. v. The Prospect Group, Inc., C.A. No. 9746 (Del. Ch. Apr. 15, 1988): The Court of Chancery declined to enter a preliminary injunction requiring the board of directors of Facet Enterprises, Inc. to redeem its rights plan in the face of a tender offer by The Prospect Group. Prospect argued that, because its offer was an all-cash offer for 100 percent of the shares, no justification existed for the Facet board to use the rights plan to prevent Facet stockholders from accepting Prospect's offer. The Court refused to order that the rights be redeemed, noting that at oral argument Facet announced that the board had determined to conduct an auction to sell the company. Relying on the rationale of Federated Department Stores that a rights plan may be deployed until the auction is over, Vice Chancellor Jacobs declined to enjoin the Facet rights plan.

(d) Tate & Lyle PLC v. Staley Continental, Inc., C.A. No. 9813, slip op. at 22-23 (Del. Ch. May 9, 1988): The Court determined that the board's refusal to redeem the rights plan was a legitimate method of enhancing the auction process. The Court noted that the rights plan was "obviously serving a useful purpose in allowing the Board to seek a more realistic offer."

(e) Doskocil Co. Inc. v. Griggy, C.A. No. 10095 (Del. Ch. Oct. 7, 1988): The Court allowed the target board to keep a rights plan in place despite the fact that 86 percent of the company's shares had been tendered to a hostile offeror and the board had determined that a lower offer from another bidder was financially adequate. The court reasoned that the rights plan was an effective mechanism by which the company could secure a higher bid from potential offerors who needed more time to evaluate newly received financial information. The court clearly was influenced by an affidavit from a potential offeror stating that it was seriously considering a bid exceeding the price in the pending tender offer and by the statement of the target directors that the process of selling the company probably would be concluded within one week.

(f) Mills Acquisition Co. v. Macmillan Inc., C.A. No. 10168, slip op. at 50 (Del. Ch. Oct. 17, 1988), rev'd on other grounds, 559 A.2d 1261 (Del. 1988): The Court found that no corporate purpose was served by maintaining a rights plan since the auction was over and the two highest bids were on the table. The Vice Chancellor found that both offers were fair and, therefore, "keeping the rights in place [would] only cause the shareholders irreparable harm, since they will be deprived of the opportunity to consider... [a] higher bid."

(g) City Capital Associates v. Interco Inc.: The Court found that the target board's refusal to redeem a rights plan was unreasonable in relation to the minimal threat posed by an all-cash tender offer for all shares which contemplated a back-end merger for the same consideration. The Court found that the target directors did not intend to institute a Revlon-style auction, nor did they intend to negotiate for an increase in the pending offer. In addition, the Court noted that the board had enough time to try to arrange an alternative value-maximizing transaction. Therefore, the Chancellor concluded that "[t]he only function then left for the pill at this end-stage is to preclude the shareholders from exercising a judgment about their own interests..." in deciding whether to accept the proposed tender offer or management's proposed restructuring scheme.[73] Pending Interco's appeal to the Delaware Supreme Court, the Court of Chancery stayed its order requiring the Interco board to redeem the rights. Interco was also required to refrain from taking any further corporate actions relating to its restructuring program and the potential sale of any substantial corporate assets. The order also precluded plaintiffs from purchasing any Interco shares pending the appeal. In the event that the opinion of the Court of Chancery was affirmed, the order allowed the Interco board to determine promptly whether to conduct an auction for the sale of Interco to the highest bidder and, if it determined to do so, allowed the board to keep the rights plan in place for a period of two weeks after such determination "solely for the purpose of enabling the Board to solicit, receive and consider bids for the sale of Interco..." City Capital Associates v. Interco Inc., C.A. No. 10105, slip op. at 3 (Del. Ch. Nov. 3, 1988) (ORDER).

(h) Grand Metropolitan PLC v. The Pillsbury Co., C.A. No. 10323 (Del. Ch. Nov. 7, 1988): The Court held that the target directors' refusal to redeem the poison pill was "consistent with the fiduciary standards established by Delaware law." The Court found that twelve of the fourteen directors were independent, plaintiff had not challenged the board's good faith, and there was no evidence that the board was acting primarily in its own interest. In addition, the board received the advice of two investment bankers that the proposed offer was financially inadequate. The board also requested the investment bankers to explore all financial alternatives including potential restructuring prospects. The Court suggested that an inquiry as to the adequacy of the tender offer may be necessary to determine the nature of the "threat" posed to the target's stockholders.

However, in Grand Metropolitan PLC v. Pillsbury Co., 558 A.2d 1049 (Del. Ch. 1988), the Court ordered the Pillsbury board to redeem the pill. On October 4, 1988, Grand Metropolitan commenced a fully-financed, all-cash tender offer for all the common stock of Pillsbury at $63 per share. The offer was conditioned on redemption of, or other effective invalidation of, Pillsbury's rights plan. Grand Metropolitan informed Pillsbury that it was prepared to negotiate all aspects of the proposal, including price. In response, the Pillsbury board developed a plan which, it maintained, provided a better long-term value for the stockholders, allegedly yielding a present value of $68 to $73 per share. Grand Metropolitan sought a preliminary injunction directing Pillsbury to redeem its stockholder rights plan.

The Court stated that "in the process of validating Rights and Pills, the Supreme Court [in Moran v. Household International] did not give a board of directors unlimited discretion in applying such a plan to tender offers."[74] In addition, the Court recognized:

> Both Moran and Unocal emphasize, strongly, that in the tender offer and poison pill contexts, a board must meet its fiduciary duties to its stockholders. Thus, a board may not "arbitrarily reject the offer" and a "request to redeem the Rights." (Moran at 1354.)[75]

The Court found that there was substantial evidence that the price offered by Grand Metropolitan was fair and adequate. In contrast, the purpose of a rights plan was to create a defense against hostile, coercive acquisition techniques. It also noted that no competitive bid had been made and that Pillsbury's long-term plan, which would allegedly yield a present value of $68–$73, was "ambitious." The Court also stated that a stockholder in Pillsbury could not make a choice between Grand Metropolitan's offer and Pillsbury's long-term plan unless the rights were redeemed. The real threat to shareholder value was said to be the loss to shareholders (approximately $1.5 billion) if the Pillsbury offer was defeated:

> I conclude that the Board's decision to keep the Pill in place was not reasonable in relationship to any threat posed and, therefore, the Board's decision is not protected by the business judgment rule. And since Pillsbury's Rights plan and its Poison Pill serve no purpose under the facts of this case, other than to preclude shareholder acceptance of the Offer, plaintiffs are entitled to appropriate relief.[76]

(i) MAI Basic Four, Inc. v. Prime Computer, Inc., C.A. No. 10428 (Del. Ch. Dec. 20, 1988): MAI sought a preliminary mandatory injunction to set aside the "vast array" of antitakeover defensive devices adopted by Prime. One of Prime's defenses was a "flip-in/flip-out" shareholder rights plan. The Court, however, noted that all Prime's devices could be rescinded by the board without penalty. Relying on Interco, MAI claimed that "the defensive mechanisms enacted by Prime cannot be lawfully maintained absent an active program to pursue alternative transactions to maximize shareholder value."[77] The Court stated that the issue was whether Prime could be forced to redeem the anti-takeover defenses at the present time considering that Prime's board had determined, in good faith, based on the opinions of its financial advisors, that the price offered was inadequate. Prime had also said that it was willing to consider any further offers and that it was studying the available alternatives.[78]

With respect to City Capital v. Interco, the Court held as follows:

> Plaintiff reads more into Interco than is there, however. Interco was predicated on facts which clearly showed that the antitakeover devices had out-lived their purposes. The facts in Interco were quite different than present here. In Interco, the suit came at the end of the long tender offer struggle after the corporation proposed a restructuring in lieu of the pending tender offer and the only purpose for the anti-takeover devices became to

protect the restructuring. And at least one-half of the Board also had economic interests which would be favored by the restructuring. Interco, however, does not hold that anti-takeover devices cannot be used merely to defeat a hostile tender offer which is neither coercive, inadequate, nor a threat to the corporation.[79]

The Court found that MAI had not borne its burden of showing that the directors of Prime had acted unreasonably. Of particular significance to the Court was the short time the tender offer had been pending and the fact that without the antitakeover devices, MAI would not increase its offer. Furthermore, the Court noted that the Prime shareholders could suffer irreparable harm if the takeover defenses were struck down.

(j) Holly Farms I: On October 21, 1988, Tyson Foods commenced a cash tender offer for Holly Farms at $52 per share. The Board of Holly Farms rejected this offer as financially inadequate. Earlier, Holly Farms had been negotiating with a preferred suitor, ConAgra, in connection with a possible business combination. Tyson Foods later increased its offer to $54 cash for all shares. The Holly Farms Board determined that a sale of the Company was in the best interests of the stockholders, and a business combination with ConAgra was agreed upon. ConAgra received an option on Holly Farms' prime operations and agreed to a termination fee of $15 million and expense reimbursement if the deal was not consummated. The Court held that the lock-up agreement was a "show stopper" that effectively precluded an auction. As such, the Board's decision to agree to the lock-up option, as well as the termination fee and reimbursement provisions, were not entitled to the protections of the business judgment rule.

The Court, however, refused to order the board of Holly Farms to redeem its poison pill:

> There is no evidence that the Board is presently using the poison pill for any improper purpose and it may still have a role in maximizing values. At some future time, the poison pill may no longer serve a valid purpose but that time has not yet arrived.[80]

(k) A. Copeland Enterprises, Inc. v. Guste, 706 F. Supp. 1283 (W.D. Tex. 1989): Biscuit Investments, Inc. made a $8 per share all-cash tender offer for the stock of Church's Fried Chicken, Inc., to be followed by a second-step merger. In response thereto, the directors of Church's adopted a poison pill. Applying Texas law, the Court found that, even assuming the directors sought to entrench themselves, the adoption of the pill was proper for three reasons: (1) it bought the directors time to negotiate for alternatives to the tender offer; (2) it gave the directors negotiating power to use in their dealings with the tender offeror and other potential purchasers; and (3) it propped up the value of the target's shares on the market.[81] The Court also found that, as the auction was ongoing, the pill should not be redeemed:

> During the auction, the Court believes the Defendant Directors are not breaching their duty of loyalty, as described above, by keeping the poison pill in place. A poison pill, if properly used, "provides the directors with a shield to fend off coercive offers and with a gavel to run an auction." *After the auction is concluded, however, there will be no reason to keep the pill in place. The negotiating time the Defendant Directors bought with the pill will have expired.* Any increase in market price achieved through the blocking of Biscuit's tender offer with the pill will probably disappear once that offer is withdrawn. Because it would severely and immediately dilute the investment of anyone triggering its provisions, allowing the pill to remain in place past the conclusion of the auction virtually insures that the auction will be unsuccessful and Church's current board will remain in place.[82]

LOCK-UPS AND SPECIAL MERGER PROVISIONS
IN CONTESTED TAKEOVERS

Lock-Ups and Competitive Bidding Contests

The universal view is that lock-ups are not illegal *per se*.[83] Nevertheless, courts reviewing the validity of lock-up devices have recognized that their potential for providing additional benefits to shareholders is accompanied by a danger that they will stifle rather than stimulate bidding for a target corporation's stock.[84] More recently—as courts have come to recognize that "[a]ll auctions must end sometime, and lock-ups by definition must discourage other bidders"—increased attention is focused on whether the auction was conducted fairly and the losing party had an opportunity to submit the highest bid.[85] These concerns were explored in the leading decisions addressing the use of lock-ups in control contests where one party argued that a particular agreement impeded or precluded its ability to present a competitive bid.

In Macmillan, Maxwell challenged the grant by Macmillan to KKR of an option to purchase seven of the company's subsidiaries for $865 million after several rounds of bidding. The Delaware Supreme Court recognized that the lock-up condition of the final KKR bid, along with a no-shop rule and a demand that a definitive merger agreement be executed by 12:00 p.m. the next day, was "effectively designed to end the auction." The final increase in the KKR bid amounted to $.05 per share, while Macmillan added three divisions to the group of optioned assets and increased the exercise price by $90 million. The Delaware Supreme Court contrasted the final lock-up agreement by focusing on Maxwell's prior offer to purchase four of the divisions for $900 million.[86]

After determining that the KKR lock-up agreement "had the effect of prematurely ending the auction before the board had achieved the highest price reasonably available for the company,"[87] the Delaware Supreme Court explained that "[i]f the grant of an auction-ending provision is appropriate, it must confer a substantial benefit upon the stockholders in order to withstand exacting scrutiny by the courts."[88] The criteria for the "enhanced scrutiny" to be applied by the courts in evaluating the propriety of a particular lock-up are contained in a hybrid formulation of the two-step inquiry under Unocal.

Focusing on the increase in the KKR bid which resulted in the grant of the lock-up, the Court recognized:

In this case, a lock-up agreement was not necessary to draw any of the bidders into the contest. Macmillan cannot seriously contend that they received a final bid from KKR that materially enhanced general stockholder interests. By all rational indications it was intended to have a directly opposite effect. As the record clearly shows, on numerous occasions, Maxwell requested opportunities to further negotiate the price and structure of his proposal. When he learned of KKR's higher offer, he increased his bid to $90.25 per share. Further, KKR's "enhanced" bid, being nominal at best, was a *de minimus* justification for the lockup. When one compares what KKR received for the lockup, in contrast to its inconsiderable offer, the invalidity of the agreement becomes patent.

Here, the assets covered by the lockup agreement were some of Macmillan's most valued properties, its "crown jewels." Even if the lockup is permissible, when it involves crown jewel assets, careful board scrutiny attends the decision. *When the intended effect is to end an active auction, at the very least the independent members of the board must attempt to negotiate alternative bids before granting such a significant concession.*[89]

Although the issuance of the injunction in Revlon apparently turned on the unique facts involving the improper motivation of the Revlon directors, the Delaware courts also analyzed the validity of the use of lock-ups in a contested takeover context. The Delaware Supreme Court, in particular, placed heavy emphasis on the fact that the option granted to Forstmann ended what the Court viewed as an "auction." The Court proceeded to discuss the validity of lock-ups granted in a competitive bidding context:

A lock-up is not *per se* illegal under Delaware law. Its use has been approved in an earlier case [Thompson v. Enstar Corp., 509 A.2d 578 (Del. Ch. 1984)]. Such options can entice other bidders to enter a contest for control of the corporation, creating an auction for the company and maximizing shareholder profit. Current economic conditions in the takeover market are such that a "white knight" like Forstmann might only enter the bidding for the target company if it receives some form of compensation to cover the risks and costs involved. However, while those lock-ups which draw bidders into the battle benefit shareholders, similar measures which end an active auction and foreclose further bidding operate to the stockholders' detriment.[90]

The Delaware Supreme Court plainly was unimpressed with Revlon's argument that granting the lock-up was necessary to procure a higher bid:

In reality, the Revlon board ended the auction in return for very little actual improvement in the final bid. The principal benefit went to the directors, who avoided personal liability to a class of creditors to whom the board owed no further duty under the circumstances. Thus, when a board ends an intense bidding contest on an insubstantial basis, and where a significant by-product of that action is to protect the directors against a perceived threat of personal liability for consequences stemming from the adoption of previous defensive measures, the action cannot withstand the enhanced scrutiny which Unocal requires of director conduct.[91]

Thus, the slender increase in the price bid per share attributable to the lock-up apparently contributed to the Court's determination that the Revlon directors acted to promote an impermissible self-interest.

The comments of both the Court of Chancery and the Delaware Supreme Court on the bidding process in Revlon also should be considered in light of the following factors: (1) the white knight was a leveraged buyout specialist which "did not have a long-term 'home and family' relationship in mind" regarding the preservation of Revlon's corporate form; (2) the two bids before the Revlon board were viewed as essentially comparable; and (3) one of the bidders had clearly stated its intention to top every bid by its competitor.[92]

It is not surprising, under these circumstances, that the Revlon opinion states that a board of directors must act as an auctioneer and not allow "considerations other than the maximization of shareholder profit to affect their judgment" when the sale of the corporation becomes inevitable.[93] Nevertheless, the Supreme Court apparently agreed with the recognition of Justice Walsh in the Chancery Court opinion that the business judgment rule is "the starting point for an analysis of Revlon's conduct"—including the decision to grant the lock-up—in responding to a hostile acquisition attempt.[94] The Supreme Court, however, spelled out what was implicit in the decision of the Court of Chancery: "While the business judgment rule may be applicable to the actions of corporate directors responding to takeover threats, the principles upon which it is founded—care, loyalty, and independence—must first be satisfied."[95]

Soon after the Chancery Court decision in Revlon was affirmed by the Delaware Supreme Court, many of the same issues were presented in a case decided in the Second Circuit. In Hanson Trust PLC v. SCM Corp., 623 F. Supp. 848 (S.D.N.Y. 1985), rev'd sub nom., Hanson Trust PLC v. ML SCM Acquisition Inc., 781 F.2d 264 (2d Cir. 1986), SCM sought to counter a hostile bid by Hanson Trust by favoring a competing leveraged buyout proposal advanced by Merrill Lynch.

In response to the Merrill Lynch proposal, Hanson topped the Merrill Lynch bid by raising its initial $60 per share offer to $72. Hanson's $72 offer was conditioned on SCM not entering into any lock-up agreement. Merrill Lynch responded to Hanson's higher bid by offering to increase its bid to $74 per share, but only on the condition that it be granted certain lock-up options. While SCM refused Merrill Lynch's request for stock options amounting to 18 1/2 percent of SCM's stock, Merrill Lynch was granted the right to acquire SCM's pigments and consumer foods businesses at fixed prices upon the acquisition of more than one third of SCM's common stock by a party other than Merrill Lynch. The SCM directors granted the asset options only after concluding that they could not secure the $74 offer by Merrill Lynch without the options. Hanson responded by seeking to enjoin Merrill Lynch and SCM from taking any action in connection with the lock-up options and, shortly thereafter, increasing its bid to $75 on the condition that the lock-up options be either terminated or enjoined.

Reversing the decision of the district court, the Second Circuit placed the burden on the SCM directors to demonstrate the fairness of the lock-up agreement because Hanson made out a *prima facie* case that the SCM directors breached their fiduciary duties by failing to make a reasonable inquiry of the assets' value prior to granting the options. The SCM directors responded, in part, by arguing that the decision to grant the lock-up was valid because it was undertaken for a proper corporate purpose: to induce a higher bid for the company.

The Second Circuit noted initially that the SCM directors had "the difficult task of justifying a lock-up that is suspect for foreclosing bidding, and for thereby impinging upon shareholder decisional rights regarding corporate governance."[96] The court recognized that "[p]rimary purpose analysis is undoubtedly a sound theory of lock-up option justification," but proceeded to test the validity of the directors' motivations by evaluating "whether the lock-up objectively benefits shareholders."[97]

In assessing the objective benefits generated by the lock-up agreement, the court focused on two different classes of SCM stockholders: those interested in disposing of their shares as a result of the bidding process and those who were not inclined to tender. The court concluded that the lock-up consideration did not provide sufficient benefits to the tendering stockholders to justify curtailing the bidding:

> For the benefit of an offer superior to Hanson's $72 cash bid by at best one dollar and change, and which arbitrageurs would value at no more than $.75 to $1.00 higher than Hanson's $72 bid, according to [SCM's investment banker], the [SCM] board approved immediate release of a $6 million "hello again" fee, and approved management's transfer into escrow of the $9 million "break-up" fee payable upon a third party's acquisition of one third of SCM's common stock. The Board additionally optioned 50 percent of SCM's operating income from two prime businesses at conceivably well below fair value, according to the abundant evidence before the district court.[98]

The court also concluded that stockholders desiring not to tender would be coerced into doing so because the mere threat of the exercise of the option raised the unattractive prospect of being a stockholder in a corporation which could be devalued significantly:

> Those who do not tender will either become remaining twenty percent holders with appraisal rights which may be valued less because of the lock-up options, and who will be forced out in the second step of the merger, or, if the requisite two thirds do not tender to Merrill, will be left facing the prospect of the transfer of effectively half the company for inadequate consideration, in addition to the already effected diminution of the corporate treasury resulting from the considerable fees paid by SCM in the course of its defensive tactics. Thus, the SCM-Merrill LBO appears to benefit shareholders, if at all, only so long as it succeeds all the way through the merger stage and the new entity is a financial success. But if the buyout falls short of its ultimate goal, nontendering shareholders may bear all of the potential risks of an aborted effort, including the risk of significant under-valuation.[99]

Finally, after determining that the SCM board knew or should have known that the lock-up option would foreclose competing offers, the court rejected the SCM directors' argument that the asset options were undertaken for the proper corporate purpose of facilitating competition for control of SCM.

In City Capital Associates v. Interco Inc., plaintiff sought injunctive relief which would prohibit a target corporation from shopping what plaintiff alleged to be a crown jewel of the company. Plaintiffs claimed that such a sale would constitute "[defensive action] taken by a board that is interested... [and] ...motivated to entrench itself for selfish reasons."[100] Applying the Unocal standards, the Court held that since the board believed in good faith that plaintiffs' tender offer was inadequate, the board could justifiably attempt to shop a valuable asset if it did so competently, for the best available price, and provided that the negotiated price was fair to the shareholders. The Court also noted that the sale of the asset was not a show stopper since (i) the plaintiffs were free to make an offer for the proposed crown jewel asset, and (ii) plaintiffs were receiving the same financial information regarding the assets as other potential acquirers. Accordingly, the Court found that the proposed sale of the corporate asset was a defensive step that was reasonable in relation to the mild threat posed by a noncoercive cash tender offer.

In Yanow v. Scientific Leasing, Inc., C.A. Nos. 9536 & 9561 (Del. Ch. Feb. 8, 1988), an acquisition agreement was approved between LINC and Scientific Leasing, Inc. ("SLI"). The agreement provided that the SLI directors would be entitled under a window shop clause to provide financial information to a higher bidder in accordance with their fiduciary duties. Furthermore, LINC received an option to purchase 16.6 percent of SLI's shares at the tender offer price and SLI agreed to reimburse LINC's expenses if SLI breached the acquisition agreement or if the LINC offer was not consummated, and a third party acquired 50 percent of SLI's stock.

The Court rejected plaintiff's argument that the foregoing "arrangements constituted the type of provisions condemned as 'lock-up' devices that improperly preclude competing bids in an active auction." The Court held:

> The LINC option is not a "lock up" option that would operate to preclude higher bids. That option, if exercised, would result in LINC owning only 16 percent of SLI and would involve only a minimal cost to a higher bidder ($620,000 for each additional $1 per share offering price). The grant of the option was necessary to induce LINC to make an offer at a premium over market price, and, as such, is the type of arrangement that has met with judicial approval.[101]

In Holly Farms I, the board of Holly Farms, in response to a hostile tender offer by Tyson Foods, entered into a "stock swap" agreement with ConAgra. Holly Farms extended to ConAgra a lock-up option on Holly Farms' prime operations, a termination fee of $15 million, and expense reimbursement if the transaction was not consummated. Tyson Foods attacked these agreements, alleging that it had been unfairly denied the opportunity to bid for Holly Farms and that it had never been informed of the board's decision to sell Holly Farms. Furthermore, Tyson argued that it refrained from submitting a higher bid of approximately $57 cash. The

Court held that even if the board acted in good faith, the sale process itself was so substantially flawed that the actions of the board were not likely to have maximized shareholder value.[102] With respect to the lock-up agreement, the Court held:

> While the granting of a lock-up may be rational where it is reasonably necessary to encourage a prospective bidder to submit an offer, lock-ups "which end an active auction and foreclose further bidding operate to the shareholders' detriment" are extremely suspect.....
>
> Under the circumstances present, the lock-up was nothing but a "show stopper" that effectively precluded the opening act. The Board's granting of the lock-up was, therefore, clearly improper. It is obvious that Tyson Foods cannot bid for Holly Farms as long as the lock-up remains in place and because the lock-up is the product of a fundamentally flawed process and cannot be in the interests of the stockholders, its adoption was not rational and is not protected by the presumption of propriety of the business judgment rule.[103]

One important issue posed by all of the foregoing decisions is how the courts propose to determine the dividing line between lock-ups which impermissibly foreclose competitive bidding and those agreements which are an indispensable element of a negotiated transaction which is beneficial to the stockholders. The answer to this question is suggested by comparing Revlon and Hanson Trust with the earlier decisions involving lock-ups.

In Thompson v. Enstar Corp., 509 A.2d 578, the Delaware Court of Chancery addressed the validity of the decision of the directors during the pendency of a proxy contest for control of the Enstar board to create a voting trust giving Unimar indefeasible voting control over Enstar's "single most valuable asset"—an Indonesian joint venture. Although Enstar had been shopped extensively without success over the previous month by its investment bankers, Unimar emerged as the only firm bidder for the company. Without unconditionally committing to commence a tender offer for Enstar, Unimar demanded and received a lock-up of Enstar's voting rights in the joint venture as a non-negotiable precondition to making a bid for Enstar. Unimar supplied no consideration for the grant of the lock-up other than entering an agreement obligating Unimar to make an offer for Enstar.

The Court found the lock-up "troublesome" because the board had been advised at the time it considered the Unimar bid that another entity might make a higher bid. Nevertheless, the Court rejected plaintiff's argument "that the lock-up provisions were granted for inadequate consideration and were therefore wasteful."[104] The Court's rejection of plaintiff's breach of fiduciary duty claim expressed the inability of the Court to conclude that plaintiff had a reasonable probability of success on the waste claim:

> While reasonable men may differ as to whether the offer was the best which might ever materialize, the plaintiffs have not met their burden of showing that it was unreasonable for the directors to conclude that, in their judgment, the offer of Unimar was the best which could be obtained under the circumstances and that it was possible it might be soon withdrawn, thus leaving the shareholders of Enstar to face the prospect of liquidation for a much lesser price and at some time in the distant future. The adoption of the lock-up provisions was a necessary prerequisite to Unimar making its tender offer and therefore it is probable that it was reasonable for the directors to accede to Unimar's demand under the unusual circumstances present.[105]

The Court found that the Enstar board had acted "reasonably" and did not grant the lock-up prematurely in view of the fact that only one firm bid was on the table, "sufficiently adequate efforts to seek other offers" had been made, and the company demanding the lock-up had firmly threatened to withdraw its offer if it was not accepted immediately.

As Revlon demonstrates, however, the result in Enstar may have been very different if the Enstar board had acted to foreclose the bidding in the face of a firm offer by another suitor. Indeed, the Court noted in a revision to the original opinion that the lock-up might have been invalidated if a firm and viable subsequent offer had been made in a timely manner.[106] Thus, Enstar suggests that a lock-up may be impermissible in a true competitive bidding context and that the normal processes of the marketplace should be allowed to operate without interference to produce the highest price for the stockholders.

In DMG, Inc. v. Ægis Corp., C.A. No. 7619 (Del. Ch. June 29, 1984), the Court of Chancery denied a preliminary injunction sought by DMG (a defeated white knight) to enforce a lock-up option to purchase a majority of the stock of a subsidiary of the target. Minstar had commenced a hostile tender offer for any and all shares of Ægis. As part of its defensive strategy, Ægis entered into an agreement providing for a merger with DMG at a higher price per share. Ægis also granted DMG an option for a period of one year to acquire 51 percent of the stock of Wellcraft Marine, a wholly owned subsidiary of Ægis, if a third party acquired 40 percent or more of Aegis' stock prior to the consummation of merger between DMG and Ægis.

Minstar increased its tender offer price, which was not matched by DMG, and acquired control of Ægis. Thereafter, Minstar replaced the Ægis board with its own nominees and amended the certificate of incorporation of Wellcraft to require a two-thirds vote of all outstanding shares for any action by Wellcraft requiring stockholder approval. DMG brought suit seeking an injunction to prevent the new Ægis board from altering the charter and by-laws of Wellcraft so as to preclude DMG from acquiring control.

The Court noted initially that in exchange for a number of contractual entitlements from Aegis, which included an option to purchase a valuable subsidiary (Wellcraft), DMG neither paid nor promised to pay anything to Ægis. Moreover, the Court recognized that the entitlements which DMG would receive upon acquisition of control over Ægis by a third party were granted by the Ægis directors at a time when such a development was recognized by DMG as a realistic possibility. Under these circumstances, the Court expressed "some doubt" as to whether DMG supplied valid consideration for the options, but did not base its decision to refuse to enforce the Wellcraft option on this ground. Although it recognized the applicability of the business judgment rule to defensive tactics undertaken by the target of a hostile takeover bid, the Court went on to reject the attempt by DMG, in its capacity as a plaintiff, "to claim the benefit of the business judgment rule available by law to the board of directors with which it dealt in an effort to establish its right to preliminary injunctive relief against a corporation now directed by a successor board." The court denied the injunction on the grounds that (a) the business judgment rule could not be utilized in this manner to establish a right to a preliminary injunction against internal corporate action, and (b) DMG failed to establish that the option agreement grants it the unique right to obtain control of Wellcraft.[107]

While the state law considerations were overshadowed by the issues relating to the federal securities laws, in Mobil Corp. v. Marathon Oil Co., the Sixth Circuit left undisturbed the finding by the District Court that Marathon's directors did not breach their fiduciary duty in granting options to U.S. Steel to purchase an extremely valuable oil field and 17 percent of the company's common stock.[108] In Mobil, the target's directors had to decide in less than 24 hours whether to accept a white knight offer containing a sizeable premium over a pending tender offer by another party which the directors deemed inadequate, to allow the white knight offer to expire in order to pursue negotiations with other interested parties who had not submitted firm proposals, or to do nothing at the risk of allowing the inadequate tender offer to succeed. Marathon's directors voted unanimously to accept the white knight's offer.

The District Court in Mobil initially determined that the self-interest of the target directors in the transaction precluded their reliance on the business judgment rule. Nevertheless, the court determined that the directors carried their burden of demonstrating that the options were "fair" and entered into for a proper corporate purpose:

> [D]efendants had a reasonable corporate purpose in granting the options. That purpose was to obtain the best possible deal for Marathon shareholders in the face of an inevitable takeover. The granting of the options must be viewed in the context of the entire negotiated transaction between Marathon and United States Steel. The directors clearly established that the option agreements were required by United States Steel as a part of the transaction; their acceptance by the directors was a necessary step in furtherance of what the directors perceived to be the shareholders' best interests. The record is replete with evidence that the directors thoroughly reviewed the alternatives open to them, diligently investigated the relevant facts, and relied upon the advice of competent professional advisors before accepting the agreements. In sum, the Court concludes from the evidence before it that the defendant directors have borne their burden of showing fairness, corporate purpose, and good faith.[109]

While the Revlon, Hanson Trust, and Enstar decisions expressed concern about stifling competitive bidding, and the courts in DMG and Mobil were not required to focus on the issue, other decisions indicate that the directors' determination to grant a lock-up has a better chance of surviving an injunction proceeding if the agreement does not foreclose the continuation of competitive bidding.

In Buffalo Forge Co. v. Ogden Corp., 555 F. Supp. 892, 906 (W.D.N.Y. 1983), aff'd, 717 F.2d 757 (2d Cir. 1983), cert. denied, 464 U.S. 1018 (1983), the Second Circuit upheld the decision of the directors of Buffalo Forge in the face of a "financially unsatisfactory tender offer" by Ampco to sell treasury shares and grant a stock option to a white knight, Ogden.[110] Ogden specified that the stock sale and lock-up option were indispensable preconditions to its willingness to make a merger proposal. Since the stock sale and option amounted to only 20 percent of the company's voting stock, a bidding war commenced after the target approved the lock-up agreement. Ampco, the initial bidder, ultimately prevailed after increasing its acquisition price from $25 to $37.50 per share. Ampco then sought to rescind the sale and option granted to Ogden and refused to pay for the shares tendered by Ogden.

The District Court in Buffalo Forge reached the following conclusions with respect to sale of treasury shares and the granting of the stock option:

> In this case, the record shows that neither Ogden nor Buffalo Forge intended the sale of the treasury shares and the grant of the option to foreclose additional bidding, either by Ampco or by third parties. And, in fact, the sale of the treasury shares did not foreclose competitive bidding, but rather stimulated it.[111]

The Court of Appeals affirmed the decision of the District Court and concluded that it would not substitute its business judgment for that of the directors. The favorable view of the District Court in Buffalo Forge toward a "leg-up" agreement is consistent with the concern expressed by the state court in Data Probe over the fact that the option granted was sufficiently large that the recipient would gain effective control over the target regardless of the success of its or any other tender offer.[112]

Delaware law (as developed prior to Macmillan) appears to parallel the view set forth in Buffalo Forge that a sale of stock will generally be protected (absent other disabling factors) where the transaction only serves to give one party a leg-up which does not serve as a deterrent to competitive bidding. In Smith v. Pritzker, C.A. No. 6342 (Del. Ch. July 6, 1982), rev'd on other grounds sub nom., Smith v. Van Gorkom, 488 A.2d 858 (Del. 1985), a stockholder of Trans Union Corporation challenged a merger between the company and a third party on the ground that the issuance of 1,000,000 million shares of Trans Union stock (8 percent of the outstanding stock) to an entity controlled by the Pritzker family pursuant to the merger agreement constituted an illegal lock-up. The court rejected this contention after determining that other interested parties would not be precluded from bidding merely because they would have to pay an additional $17 million—in the context of a $690 million transaction—to overcome the leg-up.[113]

Moreover, the decision by the Delaware Court of Chancery in Jacobson v. Idle Wild Foods Inc., C.A. No. 8383 (Del. Ch. Feb. 18, 1986), demonstrates that courts will not presume that directors will wrongfully approve a lock-up and curtail the bidding at a lower price where there is only the suggestion that a higher bid may be presented to the target's board.[114]

It also appears permissible to grant a lock-up after bidding for the target company has ceased.[115]

The Current Status of the Law

Some have argued that an "unrestrained auction" is the best method for the directors to carry out their fiduciary duty to maximize the price obtained for the stockholders.[116] Nevertheless, the judicial review of lock-ups to date suggests that the degree of scrutiny applied to decisions of directors under the business judgment rule depends on the nature of the lock-up (particularly the lock-up and option exercise consideration), as well as the bidding context at the time the directors act to favor one bidder over another.

Notwithstanding the application of the business judgment rule in Enstar, commentary in the decision suggests that the Court's assessment of the validity of the lock-up might have been different, as was also stated clearly in Revlon and Macmillan, if the directors were faced with one buyer willing to continue to make firm and viable bids at higher prices.[117] In Revlon, the Court of Chancery found that the board assumed a higher degree of responsibility in responding to takeover proposals because the adoption of the rights plan gave the board a "plateau of plenary negotiating authority." However, regardless of whether the directors are acting under the cloak of a rights plan, the Delaware Supreme Court decision in Revlon demonstrates that directors have a duty to consider carefully the stockholders' financial interests prior to granting a lock-up to a third party in a competitive bidding contest.[118]

Whenever the board of a target corporation undertakes action without shareholder approval which significantly alters the otherwise free market for corporate control, Macmillan confirms that courts will review those actions with "enhanced scrutiny." Thus, directors should give special consideration to their fiduciary duty to obtain the highest price available for the corporation's assets before granting a lock-up which places an insurmountable obstacle in the path of a party which the directors know is willing and able to continue the bidding. This duty appears to be particularly heavy where the board is responding to proposals, as was the case in Revlon, Hanson Trust, and Macmillan which have three characteristics: (1) the bid is presented to directors who are proceeding on the assumption the corporation will be sold to some third party; (2) the bid offers all stockholders equal treatment and no risk of being either "frozen in" to a disadvantageous minority position or "squeezed out" at a lower back-end price; and (3) the terms of the bids are not materially different. In cases where the board undertakes actions which effectively foreclose the stockholders' ability to receive non-negotiated bids, especially in the presence of a persistent and capable competing bidder, the business judgment rule may not absolve the board from having to demonstrate the reasonableness of its actions.

The cases suggest that courts will consider the following factors in determining the reasonableness of the directors' decision to grant a lockup: (1) the number and nature of offers outstanding on the date of the decision (firm, negotiable, conditional, or simply an expression of interest); (2) the terms of the offer preferred by the directors; (3) whether the offer appears to be the best that could be obtained under the circumstances; (4) the time constraints and other pressures confronting the directors; (5) the relationship between the price of the optioned assets and the incremental price increase in the favored bid; and (6) the value of the consideration to be provided upon the exercise of the lock-up.

While all of the foregoing factors will be considered by a court assessing the validity of a lock-up, the key ingredient—as the courts recognized in Macmillan and J.P. Stevens—should be an examination of the effect of the lock-up on the primary (or intended) beneficiaries of the agreement. Where the lock-up is primarily intended to or effectively serves the interests of shareholders by stimulating an otherwise nonexistent bid or in securing a competing bid (either in terms of quantity or quality of consideration), courts are more likely to uphold the lock-up, as long as the directors act with the proper methodology and are free from disabling conflicts of interest. Compare Macmillan and J.P. Stevens. Where, however, the directors allow considerations other than price to affect their analysis in a context where sale of the company appears inevitable, the courts will scrutinize closely the actions of directors, especially where the lock-up has essentially terminated or materially impeded an active competitive bidding contest.[119]

Lock-Up Consideration and Option Exercise Consideration.

Courts considering the validity of lock-ups have generally examined two separate issues involving questions of contractual consideration. First, was there adequate consideration to the stockholders for the granting of the lock-up ("lock-up consideration")? Second, has the recipient of the lock-up provided adequate consideration for the acquisition of the subject of the lock-up ("option exercise consideration")?[120]

The early decisions involving lock-ups suggested that the courts would not accept uncritically the directors' valuations as to the adequacy of either the lock-up or option exercise considerations. In Hanson Trust, the Second Circuit based its decision squarely on the determination that the grantor failed to demonstrate the fairness of a lock-up following the shifting of the burden of proof. The significance of Hanson Trust becomes manifest when it is compared to the earlier decisions addressing the adequacy of consideration issue.[121]

Even prior to Hanson Trust and Revlon, certain courts in the Second Circuit scrutinized the option exercise valuations where lock-ups were at issue. For example, in Buffalo Forge Co. v. Ogden Corp., 555 F. Supp. 892 (W.D.N.Y.), aff'd, 717 F.2d 757 (2d Cir.), cert. denied, 464 U.S. 1018 (1983), both the District Court and the Second Circuit expressly relied upon the following factors in upholding the issuance of a stock option to a white knight tender offeror: The option price per share substantially exceeded the price of the hostile tender offer; the price was the result of arm's length negotiations; and the price received by the target "exceeded the cost of the stock, its book value and its normal trading price...."[122]

The careful examination of the option exercise consideration question reflected in Buffalo Forge was also evident in Norlin Corp. v. Rooney, Pace Inc., 744 F.2d 255, 259 (2d Cir. 1984). In Norlin, the Second Circuit noted the absence of any cash consideration in transactions giving the directors voting control over 49 percent of the target's stock. The Court of Appeals ultimately enjoined the stock transfers at issue after determining that the directors' actions had no purpose other than perpetuating incumbent management.[123]

The increasing judicial scrutiny of the adequacy of consideration was demonstrated in MacAndrews & Forbes Holdings, Inc. v. Revlon, Inc., 501 A.2d 1239 (Del. Ch. 1985), aff'd sub nom., Revlon, Inc. v. MacAndrews & Forbes Holdings, Inc., 506 A.2d 173 (Del. 1986). In Revlon, the Delaware Supreme Court noted that the white knight, Forstmann Little, conditioned its offer on the receipt of an option to acquire two Revlon subsidiaries at a price "$100–$175 million below the value ascribed to them by [Revlon's investment banker], if another acquirer got 40 percent of Revlon's shares."[124]   The Court ultimately sustained the decision of the Chancery Court to enjoin the lock-up because of the Revlon directors' breach of fiduciary duty, as opposed to the type of waste of assets determination which is inherent in a decision that the option exercise consideration is inadequate. Nevertheless, the low valuation of the optioned assets by the Revlon directors may have contributed to the Court's determination that they acted to promote an impermissible self-interest.[125]

In Hanson Trust PLC v. SCM Acquisition Inc., 623 F. Supp. 848 (S.D.N.Y. 1985), rev'd, 781 F.2d 264 (2d Cir. 1986), the Court of Appeals accepted Hanson's argument that the lock-up prices were below fair value and determined that Hanson established a prima facie case that the SCM board breached its fiduciary duty to exercise due care before granting a lock-up to Merrill Lynch. The court shifted the burden of proof to the SCM directors to demonstrate the fairness of the transaction. The SCM directors unsuccessfully attempted to carry their burden, in part, by demonstrating that the option prices were fairly valued. The court held for several reasons that Hanson presented sufficient evidence to "raise a very serious question that the assets, in terms of what may be the outer parameters of valuation, were significantly undervalued" by the SCM directors. Specifically, the Court criticized the SCM board for (1) not insisting on a price for the optioned assets that would match the percentage of SCM's earnings stream produced by those businesses, and (2) not specifically asking its investment adviser for a fair range of values for the optioned businesses.[126]

In an extremely detailed analysis, the court in Hanson Trust criticized sharply the valuation methodology employed by the board's investment banker, comparing the option prices approved by the directors with valuations prepared by four investment banking firms. The court noted that the evidence suggested that the low end of the range of fair values for one of the two optioned assets was 12 1/2 percent higher and the other 20 percent higher than the option prices agreed to by the SCM directors. Accordingly, the court determined that the board failed to present sufficient evidence to demonstrate the fairness of the lock-up option.

Hanson Trust and Revlon indicate that judicial evaluation of the consideration conferred by the recipient of the lock-up upon the exercise of the option is an increasingly important element in the determination of the validity of the target directors' decision. Courts apparently will not be reluctant to scrutinize the directors' determinations regarding the sufficiency of the consideration to be received when the option is exercised.

Inducement Fees

In order to encourage corporations to enter into merger agreements, various monetary inducements have been devised, including engagement or "hello" fees, which are designed to encourage the bidder to begin or join the auction, termination or "break-up" or "good-bye" fees, in which the bidder is compensated if the target corporation terminates the merger agreement, and "topping" fees, in which a bidder is compensated if its bid is bettered by another bidder. The courts generally have held that although such fees are not invalid per se, they may be struck down if (1) they are the product of disloyal action, (2) they are the product of a grossly negligent process, or (3) they have the effect of precluding any other bids and thereby prematurely terminate the auction.[127]

Some bidders now routinely insist that the target pay a "bust-up fee" in the event the transaction fails to close. One court has recognized that a cancellation fee operates in the manner of a liquidated damages clause and refused to enjoin a transaction containing such an allegedly coercive provision.[128]

The Court of Chancery recognized in Revlon that "a cancellation fee, *per se*, is not unusual in transactions of this magnitude," but proceeded to invalidate the fee in the Revlon-Forstmann merger agreement because it was "linked" to an illegal lock-up agreement between the parties and was "hastily placed in escrow" at the time the lock-up was entered into.[129] The Delaware Supreme Court held that there was no abuse of discretion in enjoining the cancellation fee, pending a determination on the merits.[130]

In Yanow v. Scientific Leasing, Inc., slip op. 12, note 6, break-up and expense reimbursement fees were expressly approved: "[T]he expense reimbursement provision was necessary to induce LINC to bid, since LINC would otherwise have been unwilling to outlay considerable sums for acquisition-related expenses that would be nonrecoverable if a higher bidder succeeded in acquiring SLI. The reimbursement clause, which becomes applicable only if SLI breaches the agreement or if a third party acquires SLI, is also reasonable."

In Edelman, the court found that the board's willingness to pay a break-up fee to the management team, along with other evidence, constituted indicia of unfair dealing under the circumstances, as it demonstrated bias in favor of the management team.[131]

In Macmillan, the KKR-Macmillan merger agreement entitled KKR to a break-up fee of $29.3 million and reimbursement of expenses incurred in good faith up to the time of the termination of the agreement. Those expenses were estimated at $40 million. Plaintiffs attacked the break-up fee and expense reimbursement arrangements, arguing that the amounts were unprecedented and excessive, and designed to deter Maxwell from bidding more to win the company. The Court of Chancery held:

> Break-up fees and related compensation arrangements such as those involved here, are permitted where their adoption is untainted by director interest or other breaches of fiduciary duty. Where such arrangements enhance the bidding by inducing bidders to enter the battle and thereby promote an active auction, they benefit shareholders and are valid. Where such agreements end an active auction and foreclose further bidding, they operate to the shareholders' detriment and will be stricken.[132]

The Court of Chancery found that "the clear effect of the break-up fee and expense reimbursement provisions was to draw KKR into the bidding and to enhance, not end, the auction." The Vice Chancellor also noted that KKR's entry into the bidding contest increased the value offered to the shareholders by approximately $16 and in addition, the fee/expense reimbursement agreement did not deter Maxwell from bidding further. Finally, the Court of Chancery found that the fees had not been shown to be excessive.

The Court of Chancery in J.P. Stevens also recognized that the special committee's agreement to pay Odyssey a break-up fee not to exceed $17 million ($1 per share or 1.6 percent of the bid) was "reasonably conventional and...not invalid per se." In response to West Point's argument that the special committee breached its duty to achieve the best possible deal for the shareholders, the Chancellor agreed that a break-up fee could be invalidated if it was the product of disloyal action or a grossly negligent process. Since the special committee was determined to have acted in good faith and with due care, the Court declined to invalidate the break-up fee.[133]

Other decisions have recognized that termination fees, when reasonable in relation to the bidder's efforts and to the magnitude of the transaction, generally are permissible.[134]

Binding Agreements and Best-Efforts Clauses

The courts have reached different results in determining whether the target directors' fiduciary obligations override a contractual commitment to exercise "best efforts" to secure stockholder approval of a merger agreement when a higher offer arises. One line of cases has upheld the directors' contractual obligations despite the appearance of a more attractive offer. Other decisions have limited the scope of the merger covenant to require the board to consider the subsequent proposal.

In Jewel Cos. v. Pay Less Drug Stores Northwest, Inc., 741 F.2d 1555, 1563–64 (9th Cir. 1984), the leading case upholding the contractual obligations of the target directors, the initial bidder sought to recover damages after the directors of the target ignored a board-approved merger agreement containing a best-efforts clause and entered into a different merger agreement with a third party offering a higher price. The Ninth Circuit, reversing the District Court, determined under California law that the boards of two corporations seeking to merge "may enter into a binding merger agreement governing the conduct of the parties pending submission of the agreement to the shareholders for approval..."

> [T]o permit a board of directors to decide that a proposed merger transaction is in the best interests of its shareholders at a given point in time, and to agree to refrain from entering into competing contracts until the shareholders consider the proposal, does not conflict in any way with the board's fiduciary obligation.[135]

The Court of Appeals recognized the substantial benefits often provided to shareholders by an exclusive board-negotiated agreement. Furthermore, the fact that a transaction may preclude or deter other bids was determined by the Ninth Circuit to be an insufficient justification for allowing the target directors to abandon an agreement which was beneficial to the stockholders at the time the deal was made.[136]

A similar conclusion was expressed in Enstar, where the Court determined that a board decision to accept a particular bid should be measured in terms of the facts known to the directors at the time of their decision.[137]

In Smith v. Van Gorkom, 488 A.2d at 879, the Delaware Supreme Court held that an acknowledgment in a best-efforts clause that the target directors may have a competing fiduciary obligation to the stockholders could not be construed as a "fiduciary duty out" clause. The Court noted that rescinding the merger agreement would raise a "substantial risk" of a breach of contract since the merger agreement provided that the execution of a more attractive agreement was the only basis for withdrawing from the original agreement.

While Jewel recognizes the important role of directors in approving takeover-related agreements, the decision in ConAgra, Inc. v. Cargill, Inc., 382 N.W.2d 576 (Neb. 1986), represents a conflicting view. The board-approved merger agreement between MBPXL and ConAgra contained a best-efforts clause and a fiduciary duty out provision. Just before the MBPXL stockholders were to vote on the ConAgra merger agreement, the MBPXL board cancelled the stockholders meeting, withdrew its recommendation of the ConAgra deal, and urged the stockholders to accept a forthcoming offer from Cargill. After successfully completing an unopposed tender offer for shares of MBPXL, Cargill effected a reverse merger resulting in the operation of MBPXL as a wholly owned subsidiary. The Nebraska Supreme Court applied its interpretation of Delaware law in rejecting the effort of ConAgra, a disappointed suitor, to recover damages from the target, MBPXL, and a subsequent successful bidder, Cargill:

> Once the directors of MBPXL learned of the competing Cargill offer, the "best efforts" clause in the ConAgra proposal could not relieve the MBPXL directors of their duties to act in the shareholders' best interests. They had an obligation at that point to investigate the competing offer, and if, in the exercise of their independent good faith judgment, they found that the Cargill offer was a better offer for the MBPXL shareholders, they were bound to recommend the better offer.[138]

The opinion in ConAgra does not state explicitly whether the decision was based on a contractual interpretation of the merger agreement or broader notions of fiduciary duty. Nevertheless, the majority stated that the target's board "was obligated by its fiduciary duties to the shareholders to investigate the Cargill tender offer" and that "[u]nder the circumstances in this case, the MBPXL board's fiduciary duties have obligated it to withdraw its recommendation of the ConAgra proposal."

In R-G Denver, Ltd. v. First City Holdings of Colorado, Inc., 789 F.2d 1469, 1475 (10th Cir. 1986), the Tenth Circuit, construing Colorado law, affirmed a district court determination that a best-efforts clause "had to be consistent with the fiduciary duty of [First City's] board of directors to exercise independent judgment and inform shareholders of any changed circumstances which would affect the desirability of the contract." In a footnote, the court noted that the Colorado case upon which it relied, Great Western Producers Cooperative v. Great Western United Corporation, 613 P.2d 873 (Colo. 1980), "involved application of Delaware law governing directors' fiduciary duties."[139] In Great Western, the court determined that the best-efforts clause did not require the board to continue to recommend stockholder approval of the transaction when unanticipated events resulted in the board's determination that the deal was not in the best interests of the corporation.[140]

As the dissent recognized in ConAgra, the decision is contrary to the determination of the Ninth Circuit in Jewel that, consistent with its fiduciary duties and pending stockholder approval, a target board may bind itself in limited areas to exert its best efforts to consummate a merger. Thus, to the extent the decision is viewed as persuasive authority by other courts, ConAgra potentially introduces a substantial level of uncertainty regarding the ability of target directors to enter into agreements which foreclose their ability (either directly or indirectly) to consider competing offers.

No-Shop Provisions

As a precondition to entering into a merger agreement, acquirers often insist on the inclusion of a no-shop provision prohibiting the target for soliciting bids from or engaging in negotiations with or supplying confidential information to any other prospective bidder. In Revlon, the Delaware Supreme Court stated that, while no-shop provisions are not illegal per se, they are "impermissible under the Unocal standards when a board's primary duty becomes that of an auctioneer responsible for selling the company to the highest bidder."[141] While this language might seem to suggest that any no-shop provision would be impermissible in the auction context, the Court went on to qualify its ruling:

> Favoritism for a white knight to the total exclusion of a hostile bidder might be justifiable when the latter's offer adversely affects shareholder interests, but when bidders make relatively similar offers, or dissolution of the company becomes inevitable, the directors cannot fulfill their enhanced Unocal duties by playing favorites with the contending factions. Market forces must be allowed to operate freely to bring the target's shareholders the best price available for their equity.[142]

Thus, it appears that no-shop clauses, like lock-ups and inducement fees, are not *per se* illegal, but will only be found to be so when the granting of the no-shop provision prematurely ends the auction process.

In Hastings-Murtagh v. Texas Air Corporation, 649 F. Supp. 479, the court, distinguishing Revlon, refused to strike down a no-shop provision on the ground that, as there were currently no competing offers, it could not be said that the provision precluded an auction.

In Rosenfield v. Becor Western, Inc., No. 87-C-0988 (E.D. Wis. Nov. 5, 1987), the court upheld a no-shop provision in the context of a management LBO after the board had attempted to shop the company, stating that "[t]he directors were justified in deciding to accept what they deemed to be the most favorable offer available, close the bidding process, and permit ... shareholders to decide for themselves whether they want to approve the Merger."[143]

In STV Engineerings, Inc. v. Greiner Engineering, Inc., 861 F.2d 784 (3rd Cir. 1988), the court held that the Greiner board did not breach a no-shop provision when it considered a management buyout. In reversing the decision of the District Court, the Third Circuit stated:

> ...district court's construction would permit a corporation, by agreeing to a standard no-shop clause, to bar its managers from pursuing a management buyout. In addition to limiting the personal freedom of the managers, such a result has the effect of denying stockholders the opportunity to benefit from the potential of a superior bid from a group of people who know the most about the business, and may also have other, sentimental reasons to purchase the company at a premium price.[144]

Thus, the court suggested that, in order for the target board to carry out its Revlon duty to obtain the best price for a corporation, the directors may not be precluded under a no-shop provision in a merger agreement from entertaining other bids.

In Macmillan, the Delaware Supreme Court emphasized its distaste for no-shop clauses in the auction context:

> As for the no-shop clause, Revlon teaches that the use of such a device is even more limited than a lockup agreement. Absent a material advantage to the stockholders from the terms or structure of a bid that is contingent on a no-shop clause, a successful bidder imposing such a condition must be prepared to survive the careful scrutiny which that concession demands.[145]

Although the disposition of the issues raised by the KKR no-shop clause was unnecessary to reaching its decision, the Delaware Supreme Court recognized that KKR gained an "unfair tactical advantage" resulting from the combination of the Evans "tip" and Maxwell's belief that it had submitted the highest offer in light of Wasserstein's communications based on his interpretation of the no-shop clause.[146]

In Rand v. Western Airlines, Inc., C.A. No. 8632 (Del. Ch. Sept. 11, 1989) the Court, citing Macmillan, held that allegations of an improvidently granted no-shop provision, whereby Western could not provide information to other prospective bidders, in conjunction with other allegations were sufficient to withstand a motion to dismiss for failure to state a claim.[147]

Confidentiality Agreements

Confidentiality or "standstill" agreements, whereby corporations agree to make available to bidders confidential financial and other information in exchange for an agreement from the bidder not to use the acquired information to the target's detriment for a set period of time, are commonplace. While such agreements have generally been uncontroversial, they have become relevant in some takeover situations.

In Samjens Partners I, Edelman's refusal to sign a confidentiality agreement was a factor the court considered in denying Edelman's application for a preliminary injunction: "The Board did not deal selectively with Edelman. Instead, he dealt selectively with the Board, according to his own rules."[148] The court also found that the board was justified in not agreeing to inform Edelman of other bids under the circumstances.

In Edelman v. Fruehauf, the court preliminarily enjoined a merger and required the board to conduct a proper auction. As part of the preliminary injunction order, the court explicitly stated that a bidder's request for confidential information was "subject to such bidder agreeing to reasonable provisions to keep such information confidential...."[149]

In *In re* J. P. Stevens & Co., Inc., the court rejected an argument that the standstill agreement constituted a form of favoritism for another bidder, on the ground that all bidders were subject to the same standstill agreement. The court found that there was no evidence of any undisclosed agreement with Odyssey (the successful bidder) which ensured it preferential agreement. Thus, the court held that there was no basis to conclude that the standstill agreement was utilized for an inequitable purpose.[150]

SPECIFIC FIDUCIARY ISSUES IN THE AUCTION/ LOCK-UP CONTEXT

The Necessity of Exercising Due Care in Granting a Lock-Up and Conducting an Auction

In addition to satisfying their duty of loyalty, directors contemplating the issuance of a lock-up or conducting an auction have an obligation to satisfy another critical prong of the business judgment rule: the duty of care.[151]

The critical importance of undertaking an appropriate deliberative process and properly structuring (or at least overseeing) an auction prior to granting a lock-up was illustrated in Macmillan. In that case, the special committee was not formed until a month after management began to develop a restructuring proposal which would transfer effective control over the company to the management group. The special committee did not meet until one week after its formation, and was not informed by management of its prior discussions with the committee's financial advisor during the preceding month. After the Delaware Court of Chancery enjoined the restructuring plan, which had been approved without any negotiation between the special committee and management, the special committee was faced with the responsibility for managing the auction to acquire the company.

The Delaware Supreme Court found that "the board's own lack of oversight in structuring and directing the auction afforded management the opportunity to indulge in the misconduct which occurred."[152] Focusing on the tips given to KKR, the access by one of the bidders to confidential information regarding the bid of another prospective purchaser and the failure of the special committee to negotiate with Maxwell or provide equal access to information, the Court concluded that "this auction was clandestinely and impermissibly skewed in favor of KKR." The Court recognized that "the directors wholly delegated the creation and administration of the auction to an array of [management's] hand-picked investment advisors," and that the bidding process was mismanaged because the "presumably well-intentioned outside directors remove[d] themselves from the design and execution of the auction."[154]

These principles were also illustrated graphically by the Hanson Trust decision, where the Second Circuit determined that the lock-up options granted by SCM to Merrill Lynch should be enjoined as the product of the SCM directors' failure to exercise due care in making their decision. Where the directors' decision is not entitled to the protection of the business judgment rule because of the lack of due care in the process of decision-making, the court may not defer to the directors' valuations. Directors carrying the burden of demonstrating the fairness of a lock-up should expect a searching inquiry into any assertion that the lock-up price of the optioned assets or shares is within the range of fair values.

Applying New York fiduciary duty standards, the court in Hanson Trust stated:

> The law is settled that, particularly where directors make decisions likely to affect shareholder welfare, the duty of due care requires that a director's decision be made on the basis of "reasonable diligence" in gathering and considering material information. In short, a director's decision must be an informed one. Directors may be liable to shareholders for failing reasonably to obtain material information or to make a reasonable inquiry into material matters. Thus, while directors are protected to the extent that their actions evidence their business *judgment*, such protection assumes that courts must not reflexively decline to consider the content of their "judgment" and the extent of the information on which it is based.[154]

The Second Circuit stated that the actions of the board of SCM, which was the subject of a competitive bidding contest between Hanson and Merrill Lynch at the time the option was granted, did not rise to the "level of gross negligence found in Smith v. Van Gorkom...." Nevertheless, the court determined that the SCM directors failed to undertake many of the "prophylactic steps" identified as constituting due care in the Treadway decision:

> By contrast, the SCM directors, in a three-hour late-night meeting, apparently contented themselves with their financial advisor's conclusory opinion that the option prices were "within the range of fair value," although had the directors inquired, they would have learned that Goldman Sachs had not calculated a range of fairness. There was not even a written opinion from Goldman Sachs as to the value of the two optioned businesses. Moreover, the Board never asked what the top value was or why two businesses that generated half of SCM's income were being sold for one third of the total purchase price of the company under the second LBO merger agreement, or what the company would look like if the options were exercised. There was

little or no discussion of how likely it was that the option "trigger" would be pulled, or who would make that decision—Merrill, the Board, or management. Also, as noted in Van Gorkom, the directors can hardly substantiate their claim that Hanson's efforts created an emergency need for a hasty decision, given that Hanson would not acquire shares under the tender offer until [seven days after the decision to grant the lock-up].[155]

The SCM directors also contended that they relied on the advice of their outside legal counsel and investment banker. The Court held that obtaining this advice did not demonstrate compliance with the duty of care since the board was not entitled to rely on its advisers prior to satisfying its "oversight obligations to become reasonably familiar with an opinion, report, or other source of advice...." Similarly, the Court appeared to hold SCM's "working board" to a higher standard of care because of its knowledge of the company and suggested that directors may have an enhanced duty to act with due care in granting a lock-up:

> Given this "working board's" considerable familiarity with SCM, we must question why it did not find the option prices troublesome in light of the considerable evidence . . . that the optioned assets were worth considerably more than their option prices. Indeed, given that the very purpose of an asset option in a takeover contest is to give the optionee a bargain as an incentive to bid and an assured benefit should its bid fail, ...one again might have expected under such circumstances a heightened duty of care.[156]

The court concluded that the corporation's management and the board's outside advisers presented the proposed transactions to the SCM directors "more or less as *faits accompli,* which the Board quite hastily approved."[157]

Thus, Macmillan and Hanson Trust reaffirm that the directors' compliance with the duty of care is a prerequisite to the availability of the business judgment rule, notwithstanding the absence of any suggestion of fraud, bad faith, or self-dealing.[158] Moreover, in view of the apparent difficulty of demonstrating the fairness of a lock-up following a shift in the burden of proof to the defendant directors, a board contemplating the initiation of defensive tactics which may be deemed to preclude competitive bidding should consider undertaking the steps outlined in the Hanson Trust decision, and avoiding the pitfalls which afflicted the special committee in Macmillan. While not a guarantee of success, such steps would tend to enhance the ability of directors to establish the proper discharge of their duty of care.

Director Self-Interest

Several decisions demonstrate that directors contemplating a lock-up agreement should give special consideration to potentially disabling conflicts of interest.

In Macmillan, the Delaware Supreme Court was especially critical of the efforts of the management group to maintain control of the company in the face of hostile bids and the "evident passivity" of the outside directors who apparently were dominated by the financially interested members of management. The special committee was hand picked by the Chairman and Chief Executive Officer, and the special committee's investment and legal advisors were selected by management without any contact with the special committee prior to retention. KKR, working with the management group, ultimately prevailed in an auction process characterized by the Delaware Supreme Court as reflecting "breaches of the duties of loyalty and care by various corporate fiduciaries which tainted the evaluative and deliberative processes of the Macmillan board, thus adversely affecting general stockholder interests."[159] Ultimately, the tips by the management group and the special committee's investment advice to KKR of the Maxwell bid, and the failure of such individuals to disclose the tips to the independent directors of Macmillan, led the Delaware Supreme Court to invalidate the KKR Merger Agreement:

> Under 8 Del.C. § 141(e), when corporate directors rely in good faith upon opinions or reports of officers and other experts "selected with reasonable care," they necessarily do so on the presumption that the information provided is both accurate and complete. Normally, decisions of a board based upon such data will not be disturbed when made in the proper exercise of business judgment. However, when a board is deceived by those who will gain from such misconduct, the protections girding the decision itself vanish. Decisions made on such a basis are voidable at the behest of innocent parties to whom a fiduciary duty was owed and breached, and whose interests were thereby materially and adversely affected.[160]

In Data Probe, Inc. v. CRC Information Systems, Inc., Index No. 92133-1983 (N.Y. Sup. Ct. Dec. 11, 1984), a state trial court in New York addressed the validity of a lock-up option granted by the directors of Datatab to CRC during a contest between CRC and Data Probe for control of Datatab. The option authorized CRC to purchase an amount of Datatab's authorized but unissued voting shares equal to 200 percent of the company's then outstanding voting shares. Following the rejection by the Second Circuit of its effort to invalidate the option as a manipulative practice under Section 14(e) of the Williams Act, Data Probe Acquisition Corp. v. Datatab, Inc., 568 F. Supp. 1538 (S.D.N.Y.), rev'd, 722 F.2d 1 (2d Cir. 1983), cert. denied, 465 U.S. 1052 (1984), Data Probe sought a declaratory judgment in New York state court holding the stock option invalid as a product of a breach of fiduciary duty by the former directors of Datatab.

The state court applied New York fiduciary standards in placing the burden on defendants "to show that the option agreement served the best interests of the corporation and its shareholders" because three of the inside directors of Datatab, all of whom were on month-to-month contracts as officers of the company, "negotiated" with CRC to obtain three-year employment contracts and indemnification warranties in connection with the adoption of the option agreement. When the Datatab directors were informed by counsel that they could become defendants in a lawsuit challenging the options and their employment agreements, the directors insisted upon and received an agreement from the lock-up recipient to provide indemnification.

The court found that the former Datatab directors reached an "extremely cozy" and "sweetheart" relationship with CRC, as well as having "personal interests to protect and further" by insuring that all other tender offers were locked out. In rejecting the application of the business judgment rule, the court found that the Datatab board's "exercise of judgment was deeply influenced by certain tie-in arrangements that were geared to the protection of the directors' jobs, while offering them personal protection from liability, in the event of the very lawsuit they expected by reason of their conduct."

In Revlon, Inc. v. MacAndrews & Forbes Holdings, Inc., 501 A.2d 1239 (Del. Ch. 1985), aff'd, 506 A.2d 173 (Del. 1986), the Delaware Supreme Court expressed concern regarding conflicts of interest when it affirmed the enjoining a lock-up granted by Revlon to Forstmann Little in connection with a leveraged buyout agreement. In response to Pantry Pride's hostile tender offer, the Revlon directors adopted a "back-end" rights plan, caused Revlon to make an exchange offer of senior subordinated notes for ten million shares (approximately 30 percent) of its common stock, and approved a plan to enter into a leveraged buyout agreement with Forstmann at $56 cash per share. Following these developments, Pantry Pride proceeded in several steps to increase its tender offer price to

$56.25 cash per share and advised Revlon that it intended to counter any increased Forstmann bid with a nominal raise in its tender offer. The value of the Revlon notes issued in the exchange offer dropped significantly following announcement of the leveraged buyout agreement because of the latter's impact on certain protective covenants of the notes. The Court of Chancery found, and the Supreme Court agreed, that the Revlon board came to recognize the "importance of doing something for the noteholders" after the threat of litigation by the noteholders became a "source of concern to the outside directors".

Forstmann proceeded to make a revised merger proposal containing several important elements: (1) an increased bid ($57.25 cash per share) to acquire Revlon which exceeded the then pending Pantry Pride offer; (2) a lock-up option which would allow Forstmann to purchase two Revlon subsidiaries at a price arguably far below fair value whenever any person or group acquired 40 percent of Revlon's shares; (3) an offer from Forstmann to exchange a new set of senior notes for all of Revlon's substantially discounted notes issued in the exchange offer; and (4) a demand that Revlon place $25 million in escrow as a cancellation fee in the event it backed out of the transaction to accept another offer. Faced with a no-shopping clause in the revised Forstmann proposal,[161] a one-day deadline to respond and a declaration by Forstmann that its offer was non-negotiable, the Revlon directors approved the revised Forstmann proposal.

Two days later, Pantry Pride obtained a temporary restraining order preventing Revlon from transferring to Forstmann either of the subsidiaries covered by the lock-up option and placing the cancellation fee in escrow. As promised, but only after oral argument on its preliminary injunction motion, Pantry Pride raised its tender offer price again (to $58 per share) and also offered to match Forstmann's proposal to support the value of the exchange offer notes. However, Pantry Pride conditioned this new offer on the lock-up option being withdrawn or invalidated.

The Supreme Court analyzed separately the challenges to the Revlon directors' decisions to adopt the rights plan, conduct the exchange offer, and grant the lock-up options to Forstmann. Applying its decisions in Household and Unocal, the Court found that the Revlon board had not acted improperly in adopting the rights plan or making the exchange offer, and that the Revlon board had not acted to entrench itself. The Court also recognized that the Revlon "board unanimously approved Forstmann's merger proposal because: (1) it was for a higher price than the Pantry Pride bid, (2) it protected the noteholders, and (3) Forstmann's financing was firmly in place."[162]

Nevertheless, the Court found that the Revlon board had acted improperly when, in the face of Pantry Pride's undertaking to top any Forstmann bid, the board agreed to the revised Forstmann merger proposal and granted the lock-up option. The Court of Chancery concluded that the Revlon directors "seemed to want Forstmann...in the picture at all costs" in order "to rid themselves of a vexing and potentially damaging source of litigation" from noteholders.[163] The Supreme Court apparently accepted this determination and proceeded to reject the argument of the Revlon directors that they were entitled to consider the interests of the noteholders in responding to competing offers which would result in the sales of the company:

> The impending waiver of the Notes and covenants had caused the value of the Notes to fall, and the board was aware of the noteholders' ire as well as their subsequent threats of suit. The directors thus made support of the Notes an integral part of the company's dealings with Forstmann, even though their primary responsibility at this stage was to the equity owners.
>
> ***
>
> The Revlon board argued that it acted in good faith in protecting the noteholders because Unocal permits consideration of other corporate constituencies. Although such considerations may be permissible, there are fundamental limitations upon that prerogative. A board may have regard for various constituencies in discharging its responsibilities, provided there are rationally related benefits accruing to the stockholders. (Unocal, 493 A.2d at 955.) However, such concern for non-stockholder interests is inappropriate when an auction among active bidders is in progress, and the object no longer is to protect or maintain the corporate enterprise but to sell it to the highest bidder.[164]

By placing the noteholders' interests above those of the stockholders, and despite the fact that the Forstmann agreement offered a significant financial benefit to the noteholders, the Revlon directors were determined to have acted at the expense of their primary constituency—the stockholders. In affirming the decision below, the Supreme Court ruled that this particular lock-up provision—while not illegal *per se*—could not be sustained in a competitive bidding situation when motivated by director self-interest.

In *In re* Fort Howard, the Court stated that it was irregular for the interested Chief Executive Officer to select the members of the Special Committee:

In so concluding, I note that one's view concerning *bona fides*, will, in settings such as this, almost always rest upon inferences that can be drawn from decisions made or courses of actions pursued by the board (or a Special Committee). Rarely will direct evidence of bad faith—admissions or evidence of conspiracy—be available. Moreover, due regard for the protective nature of the stockholders' class action, requires the court, in these cases, to be suspicious, to exercise such powers as it may possess to look imaginatively beneath the surface of events, which, in most instances, will itself be well-crafted and unobjectionable. Here, there are aspects that supply a suspicious mind with fuel to feed its flame.

It cannot, for example, be the best practice to have the interested CEO in effect handpick the members of the Special Committee as was, I am satisfied, done here.[165]

However, the Court concluded that it drew "no inference of bad faith on behalf of the Special Committee" because the course pursued by the Special Committee "was reasonably calculated to (and did) effectively probe the market for alternative possible transactions."[166]

In Hanson Trust, the Second Circuit noted the argument that independent directors may defer improperly to management and suggested that a board confronted by an insider-led LBO should consider appointing an independent committee of outside directors to negotiate on behalf of the corporation. In addition, the importance of retaining outside, independent advisers by the board of directors is underscored by the Second Circuit's repeated recognition in Hanson Trust that the target board's investment bankers and counsel worked with management to develop a management-led LBO to defeat a hostile takeover bid. Thus, as the Second Circuit stated in Hanson Trust, "[i]n the context of a self-interested management proposing a defensive LBO, the independent directors have an important duty to protect shareholder interests, as it would be unreasonable to expect management, with financial expectancies in an LBO, fully to represent the shareholders."[167]

Thus, Macmillan, Revlon, and other decisions demonstrate that target directors should take special steps to insure that truly independent members of the board participate in the decision to grant a lock-up.[168]

Notes and Citations

1. 559 A.2d at 1285.
2. See Revlon, 506 A.2d at 182; In re Holly Farms Corp. Shareholders Litigation, Cons. C.A. No. 10350, slip op. at 12 (Del. Ch. Dec. 30, 1988) ("Holly Farms I"), "at some point during the late evening or early morning hours of the November 16–17 meeting, the Holly Farms' Board determined that it would sell the corporation. At this point, the Board should have assumed the role of an auctioneer..."; Freedman v. Restaurant Associates Industries, Inc., C.A. No. 9212, slip op. at 16 (Del. Ch. Oct. 16, 1987), the Court recognized an obligation on the part of the board to conduct an auction "once it is clear to the board that the corporation is to be subject to a change in control ...."
3. See Macmillan, 559 A.2d at 1285, Revlon principles apply "whether the 'sale' takes the form of an active auction, a management buyout, or a 'restructuring'...."
4. Id. at 1345 (citations omitted).
5. See Macmillan, 559 A.2d at 1285.
6. Id. at 228.
7. 682 F. Supp. at 781. Compare Bershad v. Curtiss-Wright Corp., 535 A.2d 840 (Del. 1987). In Bershad, the parent corporation decided to cash-out the minority stockholders of a 65 percent owned subsidiary in a merger with the parent. The minority shareholders argued that the parent corporation was under a Revlon-duty to obtain the highest value for the subsidiary. The Court rejected this argument and held that Revlon was not implicated because the subsidiary was not for sale. See also, Kleinhandler v. Borgia, C.A. No. 8334 (Del. Ch., July 7, 1989), Revlon duties are not imposed when a majority shareholder decides to acquire the company in the absence of any showing that the majority shareholder intends to thereafter sell the company to the a third party.
8. 682 F. Supp. at 783–84.
9. 552 A.2d at 1243.
10. See 559 A.2d at 1270, note 13.
11. 551 A.2d at 801–02.
12. 551 A.2d at 802.
13. 551 A.2d at 802–03 (citations omitted; emphasis added).
14. Slip op. at 23–24 (citation omitted).
15. Slip op. at 59–60.
16. Slip op. at 60–63.
17. See Abelow v. Midstates Oil Corp., 189 A.2d at 678–79; Bowling v. Bonneville, Ltd., C.A. No. 1688, slip op. at 7 (Del. Ch. Jan. 14, 1963), the directors' "duty to obtain the best offer...does not require that the assets be placed upon the auction block"; Simkins Industries, Inc. v. Fibreboard Corp., C.A. No. 5369, slip op. at 2 (Del. Ch. July 28, 1977), rejecting plaintiff's contention "that defendant be required by this Court to conduct its proposed sales of its carton producing assets

as if defendant were a governmental agency, namely on the basis of sealed bids or by Court regulated competitive bidding."

18. Edelman v. Fruehauf Corp., 798 F.2d 882, 886–87 (6th Cir. 1986), "once it becomes apparent that a takeover target will be acquired by new owners...it becomes the duty of the target's directors to see that the shareholders obtain the best price possible for their stock"; Thomas v. Kempner, where the Court enjoined a proposed sale of assets and required the corporation to solicit competitive bids; Tate & Lyle PLC v. Staley Continental, Inc., C.A. No. 9813, slip op. at 22–23 (Del. Ch. May 9, 1988), "while the market price is greater than the tender price, the rights plan...[allows] the Board to seek a more realistic offer. To do otherwise could...subject the Board to actions predicated upon their failure to earnestly seek the highest bidder."

19. 559 A.2d at 1288.

20. 559 A.2d at 1288.

21. Slip op. at 14 (emphasis added).

22. Slip op. at 1–2.

23. Slip op. at 3.

24. Slip op. at 32.

25. Slip op. at 32–33.

26. Id. at 802–03 (emphasis added).

27. Slip op. at 10.

28. Id. at 886–87.

29. See Robinson v. Pittsburgh Oil Ref. Corp., 126 A. 46, 49 (Del. Ch. 1924), recognizing that the evaluation of competing bids "involved something more than the simple process of deciding between the flat offers of two sums of money tendered by rival bidders for the same identical thing."

30. See Wilmington Trust Co. v. Coulter, 200 A.2d 441 (Del. 1964); Thomas v. Kempner, C.A. No. 4138 (Del. Ch. Jan. 5, 1977).

31. Smith v. Good Music Station, 129 A.2d 242 (Del. Ch. 1957); Abelow v. Mid States Oil Corp., 189 A.2d 675 (Del. Ch. 1963); Stein v. Orloff, C.A. No. 7276, slip op. at 16–17 (Del. Ch. May 30, 1985).

32. Revlon, 506 A.2d at 182 (emphasis added). The Court in Revlon also stated that the duty of a board in an auction process was "the maximization of the company's value at a sale for the stockholders' benefit." Similarly, in Holly Farms I, the Court referred to "the duty of maximizing the company's value at a sale for the benefit of the stockholders" (slip op. at 10). See also, Freedman v. Restaurant Associates Industries, Inc. (slip op. at 16), the Court referred to "an obligation on the part of a board of directors...to attempt to maximize the amount to be received by shareholders"; City Capital Associates LP v. Interco Inc., 551 A.2d at 803, "the board's duty is to act...so as to encourage the best possible result from the shareholders' point of view"; Mills Acquisition Co. v. Macmillan, Inc., C.A. No. 10168 (Del. Ch. October 18, 1988), p. 4, the Chancery Court referred to the

"Board's bedrock fiduciary duty under Revlon, to achieve, in a sale of the company, the best possible price or transaction for the shareholders"; Paramount Communications Inc. v. Time Incorporated, slip op. at 51, board's duty under Revlon "is to exercise its power in the good faith pursuit of immediate maximization of share value"; TW Services, Inc. v. SWT Acquisition Corp., slip op at 21, the Revlon duty "is the duty to exercise judgment (in good faith and prudently) in an effort to maximize immediate share value"; CRTF Corp. v. Federated Department Stores, Inc., 683 F. Supp. 422, 424 (S.D.N.Y., 1988), "maximize the benefits to the the shareholders once the corporation is the target of competing takeover bids"; Edelman v. Fruehauf Corp., 798 F.2d at 885, the board is obliged to "negotiate the best deal for the shareholders."

33. 559 A.2d at 1282, note 29.
34. Id. at 781.
35. Id. at 781 note 6.
36. Slip op. at 44 note 17.
37. Slip op. at 45. See also In re Fort Howard Corp. Shareholders Litigation, C.A. No. 9991, slip op. at 35 (Del. Ch. Aug. 8, 1988), "even in the auction context, if one deal is all cash and more likely to close and sooner, a disinterested board might prefer it to a deal that may be thought to represent a somewhat higher price, but is not all cash and not capable of closing as quickly"; Cottle v. Storer Communication, Inc., 849 F.2d 570 (11th Cir. 1988), noting that the business judgment rule permits directors to consider not just the aggregate value of competing offers, but also issues such as how much cash is included in each of the respective offers, timing, tax consequences, and financing.
38. Slip op. at 51–52 (emphasis added).
39. 506 A.2d at 183.
40. 506 A.2d at 184.
41. 559 A.2d at 1284 (citations omitted; emphasis added).
42. 559 A.2d at 1287 (citations and footnote omitted; emphasis in original).
43. Id. at 1288.
44. Id.
45. Id. at 1286 (footnote omitted).
46. Id. at 1287.
47. Id. at 1286–87 (footnote omitted; emphasis added).
48. Slip op. at 24 (citations omitted).
49. Slip op. at 13–14.
50. 542 A.2d at 778–79.
51. Id. at 782.
52. Id. (emphasis added).
53. Slip op. at 35.
54. Slip op. at 33. See also Doskocil Cos. v. Griggy, C.A. No. 10095, slip op. at 6 (Del. Ch. Oct. 7, 1988), "when conducting a Revlon auction, the target board may

favor one bidder over another 'if in good faith and advisedly it believes shareholder interests would be thereby advanced."

55. Slip op. at 16.
56. Slip op. at 20.
57. 682 F. Supp. at 786.
58. Id. at 424.
59. Id. at 885.
60. Id. at 890.
61. Id. at 624.
62. Id. at 625–26.
63. Id. at 626.
64. Id. at 1562.
65. Id. at 1287.
66. See MacAndrews & Forbes Holdings, Inc. v. Revlon, Inc., 501 A.2d 1239 (Del. Ch. 1985), aff'd, 506 A.2d 173 (Del. 1986).
67. Revlon, 506 A.2d at 180.
68. 559 A.2d 1288 (footnote omitted).
69. 506 A.2d at 181.
70. Id. (emphasis added).
71. 683 F. Supp. at 439.
72. Cf. Revlon, 506 A.2d at 181, "the Plan was a factor in causing Pantry Pride to raise its bids from a low of $42 to an eventual high of $58."
73. Id. at 798.
74. 558 A.2d at 1054.
75. 558 A.2d at 1055.
76. 558 A.2d at 1060.
77. Slip op. at 4.
78. Slip op. at 5.
79. Slip op. at 8–9.
80. Slip op. at 18. See also In re Holly Farms Corp. Shareholders Litigation, 564 A.2d at 352, refusing to require the redemption of a rights plan as it "is still enhancing legitimate shareholder interests by contributing to a noncoercive vote of the stockholders of Holly Farms and, therefore, should not be redeemed at this time."
81. 706 F. Supp. at 1290.
82. 706 F. Supp. at 1292–93 (emphasis added; citation and footnotes omitted).
83. See, e.g., Cottle v. Storer Communications, Inc., 849 F.2d 570, 575–76 (11th Cir. 1988); Hanson Trust, 781 F.2d 264, 273–74 (2d Cir. 1986); Revlon, 506 A.2d at 183.
84. See, e.g., Mobil Corp. v. Marathon Oil Co., 669 F.2d 366, 374 (6th Cir. 1981), "in our view, it is difficult to conceive of a more effective and manipulative device than the "lock-up" options employed here, options which not only artificially affect, but for all practical purposes completely block, normal healthy market

activity and, in fact, could be construed as expressly designed solely for that purpose."

85. Storer Communications., 849 F.2d at 576.
86. 559 A.2d at 1275–78.
87. Id. at 1264.
88. Id. at 1284.
89. Id. at 1286 (citations and footnote omitted; emphasis added).
90. 506 A.2d at 183. (citations omitted.)
91. 506 A.2d at 184.
92. 501 A.2d at 1248.
93. 506 A.2d at 185.
94. 501 A.2d at 1247. The Supreme Court opinion in Revlon contains a recitation of the Fiduciary standards underlying the availability of the business judgment rule and states that such principles "are the bedrock of [Delaware] law regarding corporate takeover issues" (506 A.2d at 179). This aspect of the Revlon decision is fully consistent with most of the other pre-Macmillan decisions addressing the validity of a board's decision to grant a lock-up. (See, e.g., Hanson Trust, 781 F.2d at 273–74, recognizing the applicability of the business judgment rule to the target board's decision to grant a lock-up; In re Castle & Cooke Derivative Shareholder Litigation, No. C-85-0063, slip op. at 11 (N.D. Cal., June 28, 1985), recognizing that the board's decision to grant an asset option to a merger partner "was a classic exercise of business judgment"; Whittaker Corp. v. Edgar, 535 F. Suppl. 933, 951 (N.D. Ill., 1982), sale of crown jewel falls within the business judgment rule as a "corporate transaction with a third party that the board determines in its business judgment to be in the best interests of shareholders"; DMG, Inc. v. Ægis Corp., C.A. No. 7619, slip op. at 9 (Del. Ch., June 29, 1984), holding that the business judgment rule may be invoked only defensively and might be available to the directors in the event they were sued for granting the lock-up option. Compare, Thompson v. Enstar Corp., 509 A.2d 578, 583 (Del. Ch., 1984), where the Court stated that lock-ups require "careful scrutiny by a court to see if…they are fair to the shareholders" and, thereby, narrowed the broad deference which is afforded traditionally to directors under the business judgment rule.

As a general matter, decisions concerning the sale of the corporation's assets are committed under Delaware law to the business judgment of the board of directors. See Mitchell v. Highland-Western Glass Co., 167 A. 831 (Del. Ch., 1933); Simkins Industries v. Fiberboard Corp., C.A. No. 5369, slip op at 2–3 (Del. Ch., July 28, 1977), denying an injunction sought to promote competitive bidding and holding that the business judgment rule requires deference to the directors' methodology in selling the company "in the absence of a showing of fraud, gross unfairness of price…or unwarranted personal interest in the form of a sharing in the proceeds of such a sale" (citation omitted).

95. 506 A.2d at 180.
96. 781 F.2d at 281 (citation omitted).
97. 781 F.2d at 281.
98. 781 F.2d at 281–82.
99. 781 F.2d at 282 (footnote omitted).
100. 551 A.2d at 800.
101. Slip op. at 11 and 12, note 6 (citations omitted).
102. Slip op. at 13–14.
103. Slip op. at 16–17.
104. 509 A.2d at 584.
105. Id.
106. 509 A.2d at 584, "needless to say, if the subsequent offers had been made sooner a different result might be reached."
107. Slip op. at 9–11.
108. [1981-82 Transfer Binder] Fed. Sec. L. Rep. (CCH) ¶98, 375 (S.D. Ohio Dec. 7, 1981), rev'd on other grounds, 669 F.2d 366 (6th Cir. 1981), cert. denied, 464 U.S. 1018 (1982).
109. Id. at 92, 285.
110. 717 F.2d at 758.
111. 555 F. Supp. at 906.
112. See Data Probe, slip op. at 7–8, the stock option at issue in Data Probe would have allowed the holder to purchase authorized but unissued stock amounting to 200 percent of the grantor's then outstanding shares. Compare, New York Stock Exchange Listed Company Manual §312.00, requiring stockholder approval for the issuance of common stock resulting in the increase of 18-1/2 percent or more of the number of shares outstanding.
113. See also In re KDI Corp. Shareholders Litigation, C.A. No. 10278 (Del. Ch. Nov. 1, 1988), in rejecting plaintiffs' argument that a proposed merger agreement and stock purchase agreement constituted an impermissible lock-up, the Court noted that both agreements, by their terms, did not foreclose a higher bid; Whittaker Corp. v. Edgar, 535 F. Supp. at 949, where the Court, applying Delaware law, found that the sale of an asset "has not created an artificial price ceiling in the tender offer market for Brunswick common shares"; GM Sub Corp. v. Liggit Group, Inc., C.A. No. 6155 (Del. Ch. Apr. 25, 1980), denying application for injunction against sale of assets since the hostile offeror could still mount a tender offer even if the target completed the sale.
114. See also Hastings-Murtagh v. Texas Air Corp., 649 F. Supp. 479, 485 (S.D. Fla. 1986), "an expression of interest in acquiring a corporation that is unsupported by a viable proposal is insufficient to preclude acceptance of lock-up and no-shop provisions, even if they expected another bid to materialize within a few days"; Chas. P. Young & Co. v. Pandick, Inc., C.A. No. 8789, slip op. at 4–5 (Del. Ch. Dec. 29, 1986), Court's Ruling on Plaintiff's Motion for a Temporary Restraining

Order, declining a last-minute effort by a bidder making a conditional, but higher-priced offer to enjoin a management-sponsored acquisition proposal accepted by a committee of outside directors; "Section 141 of the Delaware Corporation Law places the responsibility for evaluating such risks on the board of the company and not on the Court in ordinary circumstances."

115. See Hecco Ventures v. Sea-Land Corp., C.A. No. 8486, slip op. at 14 (Del. Ch. May 19, 1986), "in Revlon and in [Hanson Trust] injunctive relief was required to 'free up' an auction process involving actual bidders that were firmly committed to offer higher prices than the bids that target management was supporting. Here, in contrast, there is no bidder other than CSX, there is no bid other than $28 per share, and there is no showing that an injunction would cause a different bidder or a higher bid to materialize." See also Storer Communications, 849 F.2d at 576, declining to enjoin an asset lock-up granted at the end of the auction process.

116. See Bebchuck, "The Case for Facilitating Competing Tender Offers: A Reply and Extension," *Stanford Law Review, 35,* p. 23 (1984); Note, *Harvard Law Review, 96,* p. 1077.

117. See also Thomas v. Kempner, C.A. No. 4138, slip op. at 12 (Del. Ch. Mar. 22, 1973), enjoining a proposed sale of assets where the directors continued to deal solely with one buyer "after it was readily apparent that at least one other group was not only interested in acquiring the [asset] in issue but was willing to top [the initial bidder's] offer as to cash."

118. See also Hastings-Murtagh v. Texas Air Corp., 649 F. Supp. 479, 484 (S.D. Fla. 1986), lock-up and no-shop provisions "are impermissible only if they are adopted in a situation where there is a live auction with competing bidders. Where lock-up and no-shop provisions are used to encourage a bidder to submit an offer, as distinguished from precluding bidders in an active auction, they have been upheld."

119. See Black & Decker v. American Standard, 682 F. Supp. at 784-786; Hanson Trust, 781 F.2d at 274, in analyzing defensive measures such as lock-ups, the courts must "allow the forces of the free market to determine the outcome to the greatest extent possible within the bounds of the law"; Revlon, 506 A.2d at 184, "market forces must be allowed to operate freely to bring the target's shareholders the best price available for their equity."

120. See EAC Industries v. Frantz Mfg. Co., C.A. No. 8003 (Del. Ch. June 28, 1985), *aff'd,* 501 A.2d 401 (Del. 1985); Thompson v. Enstar Corp., 509 A.2d 578 (Del. Ch. 1984); Repairman's Service Corp. v. National Intergroup, Inc., C.A. No. 7811 (Del. Ch. Mar. 15, 1985).

121. The Revlon decisions reflect the doubts of the Delaware courts as to the adequacy of both the lock-up and option exercise consideration supplied by the recipient of the lock-up. Other decisions based on Delaware law have noted that the challenged transactions contained sufficient option exercise consideration. See

GM Sub Corp. v. Liggett Group, Inc., C.A. No. 6155, slip op at 4 (Del. Ch., April 25, 1980), where the Court noted that the target sold a subsidiary to the highest of nine bidders at a price "very favorable to Liggett"; Whittaker Corp. v. Edgar, 535 F. Supp. at 933–49, where the target sold a subsidiary to a third party at a price exceeding the tender offeror's valuation of the same subsidiary. Compare, Mobil Corp. v. Marathon Oil Co., 669 F.2d at 375–76, where the Sixth Circuit apparently determined that the options granted by Marathon were excessive; DMG v. Ægis Corporation, slip op. at 7, unsuccessful "white knight" granted an option to purchase 51 percent of the stock of a subsidiary was denied relief in attempting to enforce the lock-up, the court expressing "doubt as to whether or not a valid consideration for the...option actually" existed.

122. 717 F.2d at 759.

123. See also Crouse-Hinds Co. v. InterNorth, Inc., 634 F.2d 690 (2d Cir. 1980), where the issuance of target company shares to facilitate a merger occurred at the full merger price. Compare, Mobil Corp. v. Marathon Oil Co., [1981–82 Transfer Binder] Fed. Sec. L. Rep. (CCH) ¶98,375 (S.D. Ohio, Dec. 7, 1981) at 92,274, where the District Court noted that the option to purchase an asset was given to facilitate a substantially higher offer at a price above the valuation provided by the target's investment banker, and the stock option exceeded the market price; and 669 F.2d at 375–76, where the Sixth Circuit in Mobil determined that the stock and asset options granted by the target to a white knight were impermissible because they "significantly discouraged competitive bidding for Marathon stock."

124. 506 A.2d at 178.

125. See also Macmillan, 559 A.2d at 1286, noting critically the grant of an option to acquire seven subsidiaries for $865 million when the disfavored bidder had offered previously to acquire four of the same divisions for $900 million.

126. 781 F.2d at 281. Under the rationale of the Hanson Trust decision, directors bearing the burden of proof may not be able to avoid the issuance of an injunction by demonstrating that the consideration received in exchange for the option represents fair value. See Hanson Trust, 781 F.2d at 278, when the "burden of justification" shifted to the SCM directors, the "inquiry is not whether the asset option prices represented fair value as a factual matter, but whether SCM met its burden of justifying the fairness of the lock-up option."

127. See, e.g., In re J.P. Stevens and Co., Inc. Shareholders Litigation, 542 A.2d at 783; Samjens Partners I, 663 F. Supp. at 624; Cottle v. Storer Communications, Inc., 849 F.2d 570, 578 (11th Cir. 1988); Gray v. Zondervan Corp., 712 F. Supp. 1275, 1282 (W.D. Mich. 1988); Holly Farms I, slip op. at 17.

128. See Beebe v. Pacific Realty Trust, 578 F. Supp. 1128, 1150 (D. Or. 1984), finding a $380,000 cancellation fee to be "reasonable in amount and fully disclosed in the Proxy Statement," and that it did not create an incentive for the stockholders to approve the proposed transaction because it only would have been paid if the

target entered into a better deal. See also *In re* Castle & Cooke Derivative Shareholders Litigation, No. C-85-0663 (N.D. Cal. June 28, 1985), the decision to grant a crown jewel asset option exercisable if the stockholders disapprove a proposed merger is not removed from the business judgment rule simply because the option may tend to induce stockholder approval; Friedman v. Baxter Travenol Laboratories, Inc., C.A. No. 8209 (Del. Ch. Feb. 18, 1986), noting "substantial room to dispute the validity of the assumption" that a liquidated damages clause in a merger agreement would have a coercive impact on the stockholder vote.

129. 501 A.2d at 1252.
130. 506 A.2d at 184. Compare, Hanson Trust, 623 F. Supp. at 858, where the District Court, citing Revlon, stated that the inclusion of a "good-bye" or "break-up" fee and a "hello-again" fee in a white knight agreement is "not unusual in transactions of this type."
131. 798 F.2d at 887.
132. Slip op. at 29–30 (citations omitted).
133. 542 A.2d at 783–84.
134. See Storer Communications, 849 F.2d at 578, cancellation fee amounting to 1 percent of total acquisition price; Samjens, 663 F. Supp. at 625, break-up fee amounting to 2 percent of the target's break-up value did not impede the auction.
135. Id. at 1561–63.
136. Id. at 1563–64.
137. 509 A.2d at 582, "while hindsight might enable me to conclude that if the directors had waited, other offers might materialize, and while I might, in the exercise of my judgment, have decided on May 22nd to postpone the decision, that is not the test. Courts cannot substitute their judgment for the rational judgment of the directors." See also Mobil Corp. v. Marathon Oil Co., [1981–82 Transfer Binder] Fed. Sec. L. Rep. (CCH) at ¶92, 269, note 18; Belden Corp. v. InterNorth, Inc., 413 N.E.2d 98, 102 (Ill. App. 1980), party to a merger agreement with a "best efforts" clause has an "unequivocal right" to have the merger presented and recommended to the target's stockholders.
138. 382 N.W. 2d at 588.
139. Id. at 1475, note 5.
140. 613 P.2d at 878–79, "in short, the 'best efforts' obligation was tempered by the directors' overriding fiduciary duties under [Delaware law]."
141. 506 A.2d at 184.
142. Id. at 184 (footnote omitted).
143. Slip op. at 23.
144. Id. at 789.
145. Id. at 1286.
146. See 559 A.2d at 1283.
147. Slip op. at 7–8.
148. 663 F. Supp. at 625.

149. 798 F.2d at 891.

150. 542 A.2d at 784–85.

151. See Lockwood v. OFB Corp., 305 A.2d 636, 639 (Del. Ch. 1973), directors undertaking to sell assets have a duty to engage in "a reasonably aggressive program which [one] of prudence, discretion and intelligence would have followed in an effort to sell their own property." See also Wilmington Trust Company v. Coulter, 200 A.2d 441, 448 (Del. 1964), "when all is equal, however, it is plain that the Trustee is bound to obtain the best price obtainable."

152. 559 A.2d at 1279.

153. Id. at 1281.

154. 781 F.2d at 274–275 (citations omitted).

155. Id. at 275 (citations omitted). In Hanson Trust, the Second Circuit noted approvingly the following "affirmative directorial steps" undertaken by the directors in Treadway which resulted in a finding of due care: "the directors 'armed' their bankers with financial questions to evaluate; they requested financial sheets; they adjourned deliberations for one week to consider the requisitioned advice; and they conditioned approval of the deal on the securing of a fairness opinion from their bankers." (Hanson Trust, 781 F.2d at 275). Judge Kearse, who wrote the majority opinion for the Second Circuit in Treadway, dissented from the Hanson Trust decision.

156. Id. at 276.

157. Id. at 277. See also Edelman v. Fruehauf Corp., 798 F.2d 882 (6th Cir. 1986), disinterested director approval insufficient to show fairness of transaction where directors merely rubber-stamped management proposal; Norlin Corp. v. Rooney, Pace Inc., 744 F.2d at 265–67.

158. Accord Smith v. Van Gorkom, 488 A.2d 858 (Del. 1985), discussing the directors' duty of care under Delaware law. See also Gimbel v. Signal Cos., 316 A.2d 599, 615 (Del. Ch.), aff'd, 316 A.2d 619 (Del. 1974), enjoining a proposed sale of assets after finding that the "hasty method" employed by the directors to approve the transaction produced "a dollar result which appears perhaps to be shocking."

159. 559 A.2d at 1264–65.

160. Id. at 1283–84 (footnote omitted).

161. See Jewel Cos. v. Pay Less Drug Stores Northwest, Inc., 741 F.2d 1555 (9th Cir., 1984), reversing the District Court and holding that the directors did not breach their fiduciary duties by agreeing, as part of a negotiated merger agreement, to a no-shopping clause.

162. 506 A.2d at 179.

163. 501 A.2d at 1249.

164. 506 A.2d at 182.

165. Slip op. at 30.

166. Id. at 31–32.

167. 781 F.2d at 277.
168. Accord Edelman v. Fruehauf Corp., 798 F.2d 882 (6th Cir. 1986); Packer v. Yampol, C.A. No. 8432 (Del. Ch. Apr. 18, 1986).

CHAPTER 13

A PRIORITY RULE IN
TENDER OFFERS

Yakov Amihud
Moshe Burnovski

INTRODUCTION

The Problem

Consider a bidder making a tender offer to acquire the shares of a target firm. Under the Williams Act, he is required to disclose information about his plans regarding the target firm, and his offer must remain open for 20 business days, during which anybody can enter a competing bid. Making information available to all at no cost is certainly beneficial to society. So is competition between bidders: It enables the most efficient user of the target firm's resources to gain control over them, thus contributing to social welfare.

Yakov Amihud is currently Visiting Professor at New York University, Leonard N. Stern School of Business from the Faculty of Management, Tel Aviv University.

Moshe Burnovski earned his Ph.D. from Tel Aviv University where he is on the Faculty of Management.

The authors thank William Baumol, Lucian Bebchuk, Frank Easterbrook, Daniel Fischel, Ronald Gilson, Deborah Goldstein, Gregg Jarrell, David Leebron, Haim Mendelson, Uriel Procaccia, Roberta Romano, Joseph Williams, participants of the BU Law School faculty seminar, and especially Elizabeth Philipp for valuable comments on parts of this manuscript. The usual disclaimer applies.

This, however, ignores the fact that information is costly to produce. Our initial bidder screened a great number of firms to find potential acquisition candidates, and then carried out detailed research to identify the one most suitable to be an acquisition target. Then he retained the services of investment bankers, accountants, and lawyers to examine the feasibility of the takeover from both a financial and legal standpoint. However, upon making the actual tender offer, he made his privately produced information publicly available. Another bidder may have been waiting just for that. Forgoing the costly process of screening and checking, and focusing on the target firm, he quickly assembled the necessary means and entered a competing offer. In the competition which evolved, our initial bidder lost.

Consequently, potential bidders may be reluctant to engage in the process of searching and bidding for undervalued or inefficiently managed firms. Furthermore, they will prefer to bid not for those firms with the greatest possible improvement in value, but rather for those which are less likely to attract competition from other bidders (e.g., for firms with which the bidders have unique synergies). It is doubtful that these consequences are desirable.

The issue is the free use of the information about the target firm which the initial bidder reveals by his very acquisition attempt. In other areas, however, the rules governing the use of information by the public are altogether different. It is hard to imagine anybody suggesting allowance of free and unrestricted duplication of printed books or of computer software programs, and it is well accepted that patents and designs are protected from unauthorized uses. In general, there are laws which protect intellectual property. Yet, in the case of tender offers, the legal system as well as the public have taken a different course.

The Williams Act has established mandatory disclosure requirement by the bidder of information about the target, as well as a delay period following the making of tender offers. A number of states have enacted takeover laws which require extensive disclosure, effectively delaying the takeover process and extending the period during which a tender offer is to be held open.[1] There is a proposed Senate bill (sponsored by W. Proxmire) which would require that "with respect to a hostile tender offer the time period for completing such a transaction would be extended to 60 business days."[2] This extension is intended to allow time for the target firm's incumbent management "to seek the best deal for target shareholders—by competitive bids."[3]

Supporting this approach, Bebchuk[4] has proposed an "auctioneering rule" which prescribes a mandatory delay period following the initial tender offer. This is designed to facilitate competition among potential acquirers, enabling the firm which can best utilize the target's resources to gain control over them. Bebchuk suggests that this approach would bring about an efficient allocation of resources and greater social welfare. In addition, this proposal is intended to enable the target firm shareholders to extract higher premiums for their shares and will protect them against being pressured to tender at unfavorable prices.

Against this environment, Easterbrook and Fischel[5] argued that takeovers should be facilitated. If the probability of unsuccessful takeover is increased by the auctioneering rule, they contend, the expected gain of the initial bidder[6] will decrease, and there will be lower level of search for undervalued firms.[7] Bebchuk, however, asserted that the efficiency benefits resulting from his rule are "substantial," outweighing its negative effect on search for value-increasing acquisitions.

Our Proposals

In this chapter we propose an altogether different approach to tender offers:

First, we suggest that the issue here is but a special case of how to appropriate information on valuable discoveries and how to treat intellectual property rights. In this context, we point to its resemblance to the case of patents. Thus, we propose to learn about the proper way to regulate takeovers from the way the law has resolved the problem of patent protection.

Second, we propose a "priority rule" which follows the approach of the prevailing laws on intellectual property (e.g., patents and copyright). The rule is designed to protect the right of the initial bidder who, upon being the first to bid for the target firm, reveals his discovery of it as a worthwhile takeover target, and releases information about its worth through his offer price. The priority rule is designed to help the initial bidder to capture the benefits due to his effort in searching and bidding, thus retaining the incentives to carry out these activities. The rule will also enable the initial bidder to elect to carry out an auction for the target, while preserving his rewards.

Third, we propose to allow a new method of tender offers, called "reverse tender offers," which will further protect the initial bidder's information. Rather than offer to buy the target firm's shares at an announced price, and thereby reveal the initial bidder's assessment of the value of the target firm, the bidder may instead invite the target firm's shareholders to submit offers to sell their shares and specify their sale price, buying from each (up to a preannounced quantity) at the price he offered.

Fourth, we suggest that even if our proposed rule is regarded as inferior to the auctioneering rule in protecting the interests of the target firm's shareholders, it is unnecessary to legislate such protection since firms are able to produce "homemade" substitutes for it, if they so wish. Firms can institute charter provisions and by-laws which forestall speedy takeovers and buy time to look for alternative offers. Such measures can also remove from the target's stockholders the "pressure to tender" which was claimed to make the rule necessary. Empirical studies show that the adoption of takeover defensive measures have not increased stockholders' wealth; furthermore, these measures are clearly not adopted by all firms. Hence, the rule can hardly be considered uniformly beneficial. We argue, further, that even if firms could not, on their own, produce adequate homemade substitutes for the auctioneering rule, it would be sufficient to allow this rule to be enacted by the states rather than making it a federal law. Then, firms could elect to be covered by the rule by choosing to incorporate in a state which has passed such a statute. Finally, we consider whether firms could adopt auctioneering-like measures, given the "agency costs" and "collective action" problem in corporate voting, and show that this would be feasible if the rule were indeed valuable to shareholders.

THE APPROPRIATION OF THE DISCOVERY OF TARGET FIRMS

In this section we address the question whether the rewards due to the discovery of a target firm should be appropriated to the initial bidder, or whether subsequent bidders should be given an equal chance at the appropriation (as suggested by the auctioneering rule). This question can be analyzed in the context of the appropriation of intellectual property rights,[8] and, more generally, as a special case in the problem of the production, use, and proprietorship of information. We shall demonstrate the remarkable similarity between the issues in the debate on the appropriation of the rights on the discovery of a target firm and those regarding the patent system,[9] and suggest that principles guiding the latter may be applied to a solution of the problem under study here.

The production of information on undervalued firms and the search for a takeover target may well be like the production of any private good exhibiting technological and reward characteristics[10] which guarantee the attainment of a pareto-efficient solution. However, this optimal solution cannot be attained in this case because of the "ownership externality":[11] The producer of information cannot protect his ownership rights to his output and cannot secure his reward. The very use of information on undervalued target firms by making a public tender offer[12] makes it publicly available; the producer of this information is then unable to force its users to pay him for it. In this case we have ownership externality, leading to "market failure by enforcement."[13] As a result, the producer who bears the full cost of production is not compensated fully for the benefits which have accrued to others without charge. The benefits to the producer being less than they are to society, his willingness to invest resources will be less than the social benefit from his activity. This will result in less than optimal production of information on value-increasing acquisitions.

The value of the information created by takeover and merger proposals can be inferred from the evidence that even when such proposals have fallen through, there has generally been a lasting increase in the target firms' stock prices (net-of-market) compared to the pretakeover price.[14] These price increases can be attributed to the favorable information about the target firms which was produced and revealed by unsuccessful bidders[15] and became public property, available to all. The beneficiaries are the target shareholders who are "free riders" on these value increases; the unsuccessful bidder who has invested resources in producing the information remains uncompensated.

At a first glance it may seem that allowing available information to be used without payment enhances the welfare of both users and society. But this reduces the incentive to produce information and may result in a welfare loss.[16] We then observe market failure in the use of information as a result of nonappropriability, caused by ownership externality. Bator emphasizes that in such cases of market failure, "difficulties reside in institutional arrangements."[17]

Society has developed institutional arrangements to protect the rights of producers of information, lest the level of search, exploration, and innovation be reduced. Laws were enacted which secure the property rights of producers of information, providing them with exclusive rights to use it, at least for a limited time. The more general framework is the protection of intellectual property (such as designs, music, or scientific and technological discoveries) which, once being used, may become public knowledge and be easily exploitable, without necessarily rewarding its originator.

A model solution is the widely prevalent and well-established patent system. The Constitution of the United States provides that Congress shall have power "to promote the progress of science and useful arts, by securing for limited times to authors and inventors the exclusive right to their respective writings and discoveries." These principles were embodied in the U.S. patent system, whose objectives were comprehensively documented in the study of the Senate Subcommittee on Patents, Trademarks, and Copyrights:

> First, it aims to stimulate both invention and the assiduous search for new applications of knowledge, which is the basis of invention. It does this by placing the inventor in a position to secure a reward.
>
> Second, it seeks to create conditions whereby the venture of funds to finance the hazardous introduction into public use of new devices of process will be warranted. This is done by protecting the industrial pioneer for a limited time against the uncontrolled competition of those who have not taken the initial financial risk.
>
> Third, it aims to prevent the creation of an industry permeated by the intense secrecy with regard to its process (...) which can only retard the realization by the public of the benefits of scientific progress. This it does by extending a temporary monopoly to those who (...) will make a full disclosure of their new ideas so that they may be utilized to the full by those skilled in a particular art.[18]

A grant of exclusivity to a patent holder is designed to stimulate search and discovery, but it may also lead to resource misallocation.[19] Given this trade-off, the consensus exhibited by the laws which protect intellectual property (such as the patent laws) is to protect the originator of a discovery. The exclusivity granted by patent laws differ in extent and duration among countries; but all bear witness that, on balance, such exclusivity is considered socially preferable.

We propose that the search and discovery of a target firm and the bidding process which follows have many of the characteristics which are mentioned in the Senate Subcommittee's explanation of the merits of the patent system. (This leads to our proposal of a priority rule in takeovers, discussed in the next section.)

First, the economic value of the discovery of a takeover target is well established:[20] Successful takeovers raise the (average) values of both the target and bidding firms.[21] These takeover-generated value increases can be attributed to gains due to synergy, establishment of more efficient management and better exploitation of financial (and other) advantages.[22] Therefore, as with patents, society has an interest in securing the conditions to perpetuate such activity.

Second, the search for and the discovery of a takeover target requires both skill and financial resources, and the outcome of this activity is uncertain, just as it is with research which may lead to a patent. If those who have not taken the initial financial risk associated with the exploration are allowed to join the process by entering competing bids (as suggested by the auctioneering rule), the venture of the necessary resources may not be warranted. This would lead to the same outcomes as would the abolition of the patent laws: A reduction in search activity and an underproduction of information (in this case, information on undervalued firms). As a result there will be a social welfare loss because of failure of due search and discovery to take place, a loss which is often ignored since it is hardly observable.[23]

As in the case of the patent owner, the initial bidder is a monopolist on information about the target firm at the time the bid is made. But this monopoly dissipates as the period of time during which the bid remains open becomes longer, since then entry by competitors is made more feasible. Competition certainly has its advantages. In patents, allowing the product of the patent to be manufactured competitively may well be socially superior to allowing a monopoly by the patent owner.[24] In takeovers, competition among bidders may prevent the target's assets from ending up in the hands of the initial bidder who may not be their best user.

However, the (temporary) monopoly of the initial bidder need not lead to resource misallocation, and thus its consequences may be less severe than those associated with a monopoly granted to the patent owner. This is because the target firm, having been acquired by the initial bidder, can be resold at a profit to a buyer which is a more efficient user of the target's assets.[25] Optimal resource allocation may then be restored without auctioneering, yet the incentives to search and bid are not diminished since the initial bidder can capture all the benefits of his efforts. The only cost of forgoing auctioneering is the transaction cost associated with the resale of the target, which may be far less than the cost of resource misallocation. It is thus only the saving of transaction costs, rather than the attainment of optimal resource allocation, which constitutes the benefit of the current regime (and of the auctioneering rule).[26]

A temporary monopoly on information of the initial bidder may thus be of less welfare consequence than a temporary monopoly awarded to a patent owner. The latter has the right to produce the product which results from the patent, although this can be socially inefficient when there are better users of the patent. A value-maximizing patent owner would clearly sell the patent right to the best user (incurring some transaction costs), just as would a value-maximizing bidder do with the target firm. However, to maximize his reward from the sale of the patent, the patent owner has an incentive to limit competition among the buyers (because a monopolistic or oligopolistic producer earns more than a competitive one, and part of this rent could be passed on to the seller of the patent). Hence, while in takeovers the resale of the target firm by a value-maximizing initial bidder restores optimal resource allocation, this end cannot be attained under the monopoly of the patent owner. Nevertheless we observe that under the current patent laws, the problem of resource misallocation is considered to be dominated by the need to preserve the incentives to search and discovery.

The equity issues associated with takeovers also resemble those addressed in connection with patents. If there are no competing bidders, the offer of the initial bidder for the target's shares is likely to be lower than under competition. Proponents of the auctioneering rule consider this a form of inequity, which justifies the rule.[27] A similar problem may appear to arise when consumers of the product of the patent (whose owner has a monopoly) pay more than they would if that product were competitively produced. However, there the benchmark for evaluation of the benefit of the patent is not the consumers' welfare under a regime where the patent is available for competitive production, but rather the prepatent situation. If there is an economic gain from the introduction of a patent,[28] reflected by the market value of the patent rights, the monopoly granted to the patent holder is warranted (clearly, if it is limited in extent and duration). Similarly in takeovers, while the price paid to the target's shareholders may not be the highest possible price, it is an improvement compared to the pre-takeover situation, and thus (using the same approach as in patents) it *increases* stockholders' wealth.[29] In addition, the detrimental welfare effect of the monopoly of the patent holder is more severe than that encountered when the initial bidder enjoys a monopolistic position. With patents, the buyers of a monopolistically priced patent's product can do nothing to eliminate the monopolistic profits of the patent owner. In takeovers, however, the consequences of the monopoly on information of the initial bidder are less severe: We show in "The Auctioneering Rule as a State Law," p. 335, that target firms' shareholders can protect themselves against being exploited by the initial bidder by instituting measures against being pressured to tender at unfavorable prices. Again, we observe that despite the persistence of the equity problem in patents, legislatures' reactions suggest that this problem does not justify the removal of the monopoly of the patent owner.

In sum, we argue that the issue of property rights on information in the context of patents and of takeovers can be considered as similar. The patent laws are designed to reserve the incentives for search and discovery by protecting the innovator's share of the ensuing benefits, and this is achieved by granting a monopoly to the patent owner. With tender offers, not only is the information about the target firm produced by the initial bidder unprotected, but the mandatory delay period following a tender offer (under the Williams Act as well as the auctioneering rule) exacerbates the problem. We have demonstrated that the costs associated with the latter are of the same nature, and perhaps even more severe than those resulting from a takeover regime where the initial bidder enjoys an advantage and target firms are not protected by the auctioneering rule. Yet, the legislature implies that these costs are outweighed by the benefits resulting from protection of the benefits to the searcher and producer of information.

Beyond the issue of economic cost-benefit analysis, the exclusivity granted to the patent owner actually corroborates his natural right to the product of his labor and skill. We observe that most developed countries recognized that the fruits of the search which leads to a valuable discovery ought to be protected by granting, in the language of the constitution, an "exclusive right" to the initiator of the discovery.

If the evolution of laws is instructive, it suggests the desirability of establishment of a tender offer system, modeled upon the patent system, which would protect the rights of the initial bidder and preserve the incentive for search and discovery of value-increasing acquisitions. In the next section we propose a takeover rule which contains features similar to those found in patent laws.

A PRIORITY RULE

Description of the Rule

We propose a new rule that we shall call a priority rule, whose purpose is to preserve the incentives to search for value-increasing acquisitions. The rule applies the approach followed by laws which protect intellectual property, such as the patent laws. In addition, it facilitates optimal resource allocation by allowing auctioning.

Under the priority rule, the *initial bidder will have the sole right to bid for the target during a period of time prespecified by law*, hereafter called the "exclusivity period." No other firm will be allowed to make a competing bid during the exclusivity period. After the exclusivity period has expired, everyone will be allowed to bid, as under the current rules. (We later show that despite this exclusivity, the initial bidder cannot make an arbitrarily low bid).

The rule will also enable the initial bidder, after having made his tender offer, to allow others to make offers for the target during the exclusivity period. By the rule, these offers will expire by the end of that period. For the duration of the exclusivity period, while the highest bidder may win this competition, *the initial bidder will be exclusively entitled to the full difference between the value of his offer for the target and of the offer of the winner who eventually ends up taking over the firm;* the target firm's shareholders will receive the price that the initial bidder has offered. This part of the rule is designed to facilitate the transfer of resources to their most efficient user who can offer the best terms, as does the auctioneering rule. But, at the same time, it provides the initial bidder with a reward for the information he has produced regarding the target firm. In fact, this feature of our rule simulates an acquisition of the target by the initial bidder and then auctioning and reselling it to another firm which offers more; however, it saves the transaction costs of completing the initial acquisition and then transferring ownership.

If the initial bidder chooses to invite other offers during the exclusivity period, the rule will allow the initial bidder to offer a premium (a "side payment") over his initial offer price to target firm's stockholders who tender to the bidder of his choice. Those who tender to others will receive only the initial offer price. This is necessary under two circumstances. In the first one, if the initial bidder auctions the target during the exclusivity period, the target's stockholders are indifferent between the bidders since they receive no more than the initial bidder's offer, regardless of whom they tender to. However, the initial bidder prefers that the best bidder wins; he could affect this by offering a premium for target shares tendered to the chosen bidder. To illustrate, suppose the initial offer is P_1 (higher than the preoffer price) and then the initial bidder auctions the target during the exclusivity period, receiving two offers P_2 and P_3, such that $P_3 > P_2 > P_1$. By the priority rule, the target firm's shareholders will receive P_1 and the initial bidder will receive $P_3 - P_1$ on shares tendered to bidder 3 or $P_2 - P_1$ on shares tendered to bidder 2. The initial bidder clearly prefers the shares to be tendered to bidder 3, and thus he will offer a premium of Q for shares sold to 3. This will induce the target's shareholders to tender to bidder 3 to receive $P_1 + Q$ (compared to P_1 if they tender to 2), and the initial bidder's reward will be $P_3 - P_1 - Q$. Clearly,

$$0 \leq Q \leq (P_3 - P_1) - (P_2 - P_1) = P_3 - P_2.$$

That is, the premium is set by the initial bidder to be less than the difference between the best and the next-best offers.

The second situation which calls for a targeted premium is when the initial bidder realizes that the highest offer received in the auction is below the posttakeover value of the target firm to him.[30] Denote that value by V_1 and assume $V_1 > P_3 > P_1$ (using the above notation). In this case, the initial bidder is not interested in bidder 3 winning since then his own reward is $P_3 - P_1$ on shares tendered to 3, whereas his gain on shares tendered to him is $V_1 - P_1 > P_3 - P_1$. Thus, by allowing the initial bidder to offer $P_1 + Q$ for shares tendered to him ($Q < V_1 - P_3$), compared to P_1 if they are tendered to 3, our rule gives preference to the bidder who most values the target's assets, thus facilitating optimal resource allocation.[31]

The initial bidder may, of course, choose to remain the sole bidder and not to auction the firm during the exclusivity period, before the conclusion of the acquisition. Auctioning increases the risk that the target's shareholders, being exposed to a higher offer by some bidder, will be tempted to hold on to their shares until the exclusivity period expires, and then sell directly to the highest bidder and receive the highest price themselves. On the other hand, if he chooses to remain the sole bidder and then sell part or all of the acquired firm after the takeover is completed, he will bear additional transaction costs[32] compared to the cost incurred if the auction of the target occurs during the exclusivity period. Since under our rule, auctioning the target during the exclusivity period (before the conclusion of the acquisition) is at the initial bidder's option, he will make his own calculation and decision whether auctioning is optimal to him. Although it may seem likely that the initial bidder will choose not to allow auctioning during the exclusivity period, the rule is flexible enough to allow auctioning.

It is worth noting that our priority rule could be formulated so as to mandate auctioning of the target during the exclusivity period (rather than leaving the choice with the initial bidder). The social welfare implications of allowing the initial bidder to decide whether to auction is that if he chooses not to auction and he happens not to be the best user of the target's resources, there is a loss equal at most to the transaction costs of reselling the target to a better user.[33] On the other hand, a rule which makes auctioning compulsory could expose the target's shareholders to higher offers than that of the initial bidder and increase their propensity to refrain from tendering during the exclusivity period. This will reduce the probability of success of the initial bidder as well as his expected benefit, with a resultant social cost of a decline in search and discovery of value-increasing acquisitions. It is clearly hard to assess which side of this trade-off is more valuable. Allowing the initial bidder to make the choice, while not necessarily solving the social welfare issue, is consistent with preserving his property rights on the information he has produced.

It could be argued that the initial bidder may refuse to auction the target firm, even when he can gain by selling it to a better user of its assets, if his objective is to expand his firm's size rather than its value.[34] But if this were true, the auctioneering rule too would fail to generate an optimal resource allocation: Then, the winner in the auction will be the firm whose management most values size and expansion (or risk reduction, or any other management-preferred outcomes), possibly outbidding value maximizing firms.[35] Hence, abandoning the assumption of value maximization makes it impossible to determine which rule, our rule or the auctioneering rule, contributes more to optimal resource allocation.

On the Length of the Exclusivity Period

Our priority rule thus follows the well-established pattern of patent laws which award the patent owner a monopoly on his discovery for a limited period of time, after which it becomes public property. The length of this period (which varies among countries) ought to balance the social cost of monopoly with the need to secure incentives for search and discovery.

Similarly, in determining the proper length of the exclusivity period under our priority rule, there is a trade-off to consider. If this period is too short, the target's shareholders will have a greater incentive to refrain from tendering their shares to the initial bidder. After the exclusivity period expires, anyone will be able to bid and the shareholders can expect a higher bid. If the period is too long, it will make it easier for the initial bidder to dictate to the target firm acquisition terms which suit his preferences. Clearly, neither our rule nor the patent laws give unlimited protection to the owner of the initial discovery. In fact, unlimited protection is generally not optimal. Rather, optimal patent life should be designed to maximize social welfare.[36]

The extension of the period for which the tender offer must remain open, under the Williams Act and as suggested by the auctioneering rule, brings about two outcomes:

1. It allows the target firm's shareholders more time to process the information provided by the bidder and to assess the offer.[37]

2. It enables other firms to enter their offers and compete with the initial bidder.[38]

Our criticism of the Williams Act and of the proposed auctioneering rule pertains only to the second outcome, which threatens the initial bidder's incentive to search.[39] The problem is that the two outcomes of extending the offer period are inseparable under the current rules on tender offers. Our priority rule resolves this problem: It is possible to extend the offer period to allow target's shareholders more time to consider the offer while securing the priority right of the initial bidder.

From the target firm's shareholders' viewpoint, if they expect that after the expiration of the exclusivity period they will receive a higher offer than that of initial bidder, they may choose not to tender their shares during that period. Obviously, this decision entails some risk: Against the chance of receiving a higher offer, there is the chance of receiving only lower ones or not receiving any offer at all.[40] Clearly, this risk to the target shareholders increases if the initial bidder chooses not to auction the target during the exclusivity period since, in the absence of explicit offers, there is high uncertainty about obtaining them in the future. But even if auctioning is allowed, under our rule the offers are valid only for the duration of the period, and it is uncertain that they will be extended again later.

To induce the target's shareholders to tender during the exclusivity period, the initial bidder's offer price should at least equal the "certainty equivalent"[41] of the highest anticipated bid. The target firm's shareholders being risk averse, this certainty equivalent is *less* than the highest bid price expected after the exclusivity period. That is, the offer price of the initial bidder, which target shareholders can surely receive, could be less than the expected level of the uncertain highest price they may receive after the exclusivity period. Since the certainty equivalent is a decreasing function of risk (*ceteris paribus*), the greater the uncertainty which the target shareholders have about future offers, the lower the offer price needed in order for the initial bid to succeed. This may induce the initial bidder not to allow auctioning during the exclusivity period.

While the initial bidder may succeed in the takeover even if his offer price is below the expected highest offer after the exclusivity period, his offer cannot be arbitrarily low. It is bounded from below by the certainty equivalent of the highest price attained after the exclusivity period, as assessed by the marginal shareholder whose shares are needed to complete a successful tender offer. After the expiration of that period, the initial bidder can revise his offer upward if faced by higher competing bids, and the situation would be like that we have today.

Under our rule, the target firm's shareholders will possibly receive less than the expected highest offer price. But they will certainly be offered a premium sufficiently high to induce them to sell their shares. Thus, under the priority rule, the wealth of the target firm's shareholders is not reduced but rather increased compared to its pretakeover level. In fact, the premium received by the marginal target's shareholder who tenders during the exclusivity period gives him the *very same* level of welfare (or utility) as could be expected by selling to the highest bidder after the exclusivity period.[42] If the supply function of the target firm's stock is increasing in price,[43] all tendering shareholders will gain,[44] except for the marginal tendering stockholder, for whom the offer price is "just" right.

The value of the target to the bidder may well be greater than his offer price, even after taking into account his search and bidding costs; but any division between the bidder and the target of the takeover-generated added value is arbitrary and can hardly be considered as being more "fair" than another such allocation.[45] Besides, even under unconstrained competition between bidders, the target firm's shareholders cannot expect to receive an offer which equals their firm's value to the highest bidder.[46]

Still, if the target's shareholders feel that the premium which they are awarded by the initial bidder during the exclusivity period is too low, they can refrain from tendering their shares and after the exclusivity period expires they can tender them to a higher bidder. It could be argued that target shareholders may have difficulty doing that if the initial bid is designed to put them under a "pressure to tender." However, as we show in "The Pressure to Tender: A Nonproblem" (page 331 below), there are means available to the target firm to defend its stockholders against being subject to such pressure, enabling them to refrain from tendering their shares.

Concluding Remarks

We outlined a priority rule which follows the ideas reflected in the prevailing patent laws and other laws which protect intellectual property. The rule enables the initial bidder for a target firm to be unchallenged during an exclusivity period (prescribed by law), thus increasing his expected gain from his enterprise. This, we hope, can help to preserve the incentives to search and bid for undervalued firms and keep the search and bidding activity at a level commensurate with the social gains generated by takeovers. Under the priority rule, a larger part of the cost of search and bidding is borne by the target firms' shareholders and it thus may be expected that the profits of the bidders will increase; but given free access to takeover activity, the ensuing competitive equilibrium will guarantee that the expected normal gain to searching and bidding will be zero, as may well be the case under the current rules. However, under the equilibrium generated by our rule, the incidence of search, discovery, and bidding for undervalued firms will be greater than we witness today (or than what would be the case under the auctioneering rule). The gain to the target firms' shareholders thus lies in the higher probability of their firms being sought after for takeover. Then, even if the amount of the takeover premium which they receive is less under our rule, *given* that a bid is made, the *expected* premium may be greater because it is more likely to occur. It follows that the equilibrium under the priority rule may generate a social gain,[47] compared with both the auctioneering rule and today's tender offer laws.

A REVERSE TENDER OFFER

We propose to allow a new type of tender offer, a "reverse tender offer," designed to provide the initial bidder with additional protection of the information he has produced about the value of the target firm. The reverse tender offer will operate as follows:

1. The initial bidder will invite the target firm shareholders to submit offers to sell their shares. Each such offer should specify two numbers: (i) the quantity of shares offered, and (ii) the price at which they are offered. A shareholder can choose to divide his shares into a number of groups and submit a different offer price for each group.

2. The offers will remain sealed until the end of the offer period.

3. The bidder will announce the upper limit on the quantity of shares he is committed to acquire at the offered prices. If desired, the bidder may also specify an upper limit on the price he is willing to pay for the offer. Then, the first limit to be reached—quantity or price—will be the binding constraint which will determine the price and quantity at which the tender offer will be executed.

4. The bidder will select the method of pricing. Under method A, the price paid for each of the executed offers will be the price at which it was offered; under method B, the bidder will pay an equal price for all acquired shares.

5. At the end of the offer period, the bidder will rank the offers he has received by price and construct an offer curve (or supply function) which depicts the sale quantity as an increasing function of the offer price (see Figures 13–1a and 13–1b). That is, the higher the offer price, the greater the aggregate quantity of shares offered to be sold at (and below)

FIGURE 13–1a
Example of Offer Curve—Method A

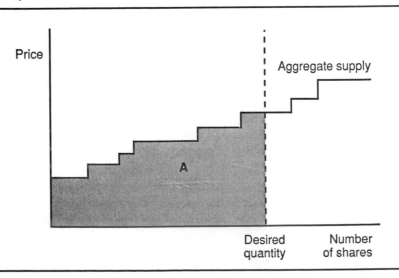

that price. The bidder will then determine the quantity he will acquire, which will be at least the quantity that he has committed himself to acquire. The total amount paid will under method A equal the sum of the product of each offer quantity by that offer price (area A in Figure 13–1a) or, under method B, the product of the whole acquired quantity by the acquisition price (area B in Figure 13–1b).

The advantage of the "reverse tender" is that the bidder does not have to announce a price at which he is willing to acquire the target firm's shares. The bid price usually contains information about the value of the target firm as assessed by the bidder. By announcing the tender offer price, this privately produced information is released and becomes public, enabling its free use by others, including the target firm's shareholders. This may reduce the reward to the initial bidder and reduce the incentives to search and bid for undervalued firms, thus leading to economic inefficiency as discussed in "Appropriation of the Discovery of Target Firms" (page 314, above).

The two methods for paying the target firm's shareholders are both based on methods which are being commonly used in today's markets. For example, Treasury bills are now auctioned weekly by method A, where each offer is executed at the offer price, whereas in the past, Treasury bonds were auctioned by a uniform-price method (method B).[48] Theoretical

FIGURE 13–1b
Example of Offer Curve—Method B

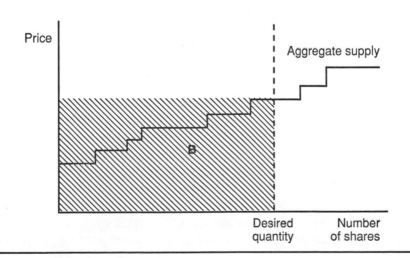

results[49] suggest that the prices that shareholders will demand for their shares depend on which method—A or B—is employed by the bidder. Under method A, knowing that his shares will be bought at the price he offers, a target shareholder may choose to substitute between the probability of his offer being executed and the execution price. Under method B, the individual shareholder is unlikely to affect the (uniform) price at which his shares are bought, hence his offer price will affect only the probability of it being executed. The offer curves will also reflect the policy announced by the bidder with respect to shares which will not be executed or not tendered at all. The offer curves will thus be different under the two methods, and the revenue to the shareholders who tender, and the cost to the bidder, may be different under the two methods.

ON THE AUCTIONEERING RULE

We have proposed enactment of a priority rule, which is designed to increase the probability of success and increase the reward to the initial bidder. On the contrary, the proposal of an auctioneering rule is intended to facilitate the entry of competitors to the bidding process after the initial bid has been made, thus decreasing the expected gain of the initial bidder. This is also the outcome of the Williams Act which prescribes a delay period following the initial offer.

Our criticism of the prevailing legal environment for mergers and acquisitions and of the auctioneering rule has so far rested on our contention that it reduces social welfare. However, it may be argued that mandatory auctioneering is preferable to (potential) target firms' shareholders since, once an offer has been made, auctioneering increases the likelihood that they will obtain a higher offer.[50] Arguing that the priority rule brings about a transfer of wealth from target shareholders to potential bidders, without compensating the target firms' shareholders, the rule could be challenged notwithstanding the greater economic efficiency that it induces.

The question is, then, whether a federally enacted auctioneering rule is necessary to protect the interests of potential target firms' shareholders. In this section, we shall demonstrate that it is not necessary because target shareholders are able to protect themselves, if they so wish, by other means. It is of interest to note here that apparently, the protection of the target shareholders against bidders was not intended by the legislators of the Williams Act, which prescribes a mandatory delay period as advocated by the auctioneering rule. According to the courts, the purpose of the Williams Act was mainly to provide target shareholders with information necessary to make a decision on the proposed bid.[51] The courts interpreted the act as not requiring "judges to oversee takeovers for substantive fairness."[52]

Throughout our analysis, we suggest that it is appropriate to focus on the *ex ante* value of the auctioneering rule. In our opinion, proponents of the rule err in that they focus on the benefits to a target firm's shareholders *given* that a bid for the firm has been made. However, the rule certainly affects the probability of a firm becoming a target firm. While the *conditional* expected gain from auctioneering to the target shareholders could be higher than in the absence of the rule, it may well be that the *unconditional* expected gain is lower. In fact, we shall see in the sequel that many (and perhaps most) firms agree with the latter assessment.

The Availability of Homemade Substitutes

We suggest that the enactment of an auctioneering rule is unnecessary since its objectives can be attained by substitutes which are "homemade" by firms. If target firm's shareholders consider auctioneering valuable, they can devise measures which impede speedy takeovers and buy time to solicit offers from competing bidders or to extract better terms from the initial bidder. In fact, some firms adopt takeover defensive measures whereas other firms elect not to, suggesting that in the view of most shareholders in these firms, obstructing takeovers is *ex ante* undesirable.[53]

There are a number of means by which the firm's shareholders can deter undesired takeover raids and buy time to allow other offerors to enter and compete in the bidding process.[54] To illustrate, consider a recent report about the takeover defensive measures adopted by Time Inc.:

> The main... [measure] was to shift incorporation from New York to Delaware. In a document filed with the Securities and Exchange Commission Time said this would tend "to discourage certain types of transactions which involve an actual or threatened change of control of Time and to encourage any person intending to attempt a takeover of Time to negotiate with its board of directors." Stockholders also approved the division of the board into three classes, with staggered three year terms. Anyone wanting to elect a majority of Time directors, therefore, will have to wait two years. Another major "shark repellant" provides that stockholders with at least 20 percent of Time stock cannot merge it with another company without the

consent of those holding 80 percent of the stock. Any suitor will have to pay Time stockholders either the shares' market value or the highest price that the suitor paid for Time stock in the prior two years, whichever is higher.[55]

A recent popular defense against nonnegotiated takeovers is the "poison pill"[56] which makes the takeover prohibitively expensive for the would-be acquirer, or at least slows down the process. The pill can later be voluntarily "dissolved" by the target, making a takeover feasible. This enables the target to impede an undesired takeover and induce auctioneering. In fact, a number of target firms which had instituted the poison pill ended up being acquired by negotiated bidding.[57]

Such antitakeover measures can provide the target firm time to obtain competing offers, which is the objective sought by the auctioneering rule, or to negotiate better terms with the raider. Yet, "heightened public awareness of takeover activity had lead some shareholders to oppose provisions which are perceived as deterring such activity at their company,"[58] and "companies have a harder time winning shareholders approval for anti-takeover measures."[59] Obviously, shareholders of different companies elect to be governed by different rules with respect to takeovers. While stockholders in some firms seek to impede takeovers, perhaps even to facilitate competition between bidders, stockholders of other firms prefer to facilitate takeovers.[60] Thus, a mandatory delay period, as prescribed by the auctioneering rule, cannot be considered as desirable to *all* firms.

The empirical evidence does not support the hypothesis that takeover defensive measures are valuable (on average) to target firms' shareholders. A number of studies have examined the effect of adopting antitakeover measures on shareholders' wealth by estimating stock price reaction on (and around) the announcement dates.[61] They found that, on average, the adoption of these measures did not increase shareholders' wealth, and in most cases the effect was negative (although usually insignificant). It should be noted that these results may entail an upward-biased estimate of the effect of these measures on stock prices since the board's proposal to adopt antitakeover amendments may signal a greater likelihood of a forthcoming takeover attempt, with its associated gains.[62]

There is, thus, no evidence that investors assign value to the impeding or deflecting of takeovers by antitakeover measures, and there is even evidence that some of these measures are judged by the market to be harmful. This is particularly striking since the studies of the effect of takeover defensive measures were carried out only on firms which have adopted them, indicating that such measures were considered desirable. For firms which chose not to adopt them, these measures would probably produce more negative (or similar) results, if they were imposed; indeed we observe that some firms do not adopt takeover defensive measures.[63] It follows that a mandatory rule which deflects takeovers may well, on balance, be undesirable from the point of view of potential target firms. Stockholders of many such firms apparently prefer the greater probability of takeover to the higher premiums which they may possibly be able to earn when a takeover is impeded and the entry of competing bidders is facilitated.

As for potential acquirers, impediments to takeovers are obviously undesirable. This is corroborated by some indirect evidence[64] showing that firms which were expressly engaged in acquisition plans experienced a decline in stock prices following the 1968–1970 takeover regulations (mainly the Williams Act). Similarly, a number of studies[65] have found that in the postregulation period the gains to bidding firms from takeovers were significantly lower than in the preregulation period.[66]

Summing up, it follows that the auctioneering rule may result in a loss to *both* target and acquiring firms.[67] The available defensive measures not only make the auctioneering rule redundant, but they can also deflect an unwanted raider and nullify our priority rule if it were legislated.

The "Pressure to Tender": A Nonproblem

Our proposed priority rule eliminates competition among bidders during the exclusivity period. Proponents of the auctioneering rule argue that facilitating competition for the target firm among bidders is necessary since "a target's dispersed shareholders are under *pressure to tender*. If they could act in concert, they presumably would agree among themselves to hold out for some limited period and explore the possibility of a competing offer. Since transaction costs make such an agreement impossible, regulation is needed to secure the time that is crucial for competing bids."[68] Further, "as a result of this pressure the target's independence is doomed once a tender offer is made—the target will be acquired by the highest bidder even if many stockholders judge its offer to be less than the target value as an independent entity."[69] The "pressure to tender" exists if "it is expected that, following the expiration of a successful offer, the value of the nontendered shares will be lower than the tender's value."[70] This differential in value between tendered and nontendered shares occurs when the raider makes a two-part offer, under which he pays a higher price for a specified number of tendered shares (which is sufficient to obtain control of the company) than for the remaining shares. This gives rise to a situation known as the "prisoner's dilemma," which pressures stockholders to tender even if the weighted average price paid to them all is lower than what they consider as the fair value of the firm.[71]

Target firms' shareholders may indeed be exposed under the priority rule to pressure to tender their shares to the initial bidder at a price below the value of their firm to him. However, we shall argue that

1. the pressure to tender may be desirable for potential target firms, as well as being socially efficient;

2. shareholders can remove the pressure to tender if they so wish;

3. the evidence suggests that the removal of the pressure to tender is not considered valuable by shareholders.

There is a strong theoretical argument in favor of the pressure to tender:[72] Unless the raider is able to dilute the wealth of the nontendering stockholders (e.g, by a two-part offer or a partial offer), a takeover by a tender offer may not be feasible. Because the raider incurs costs in the takeover process, the offer price must be below the bidder's estimate of the target's posttakeover value, or the bidder expects to incur an overall loss on the transaction. Hence, the target shareholders may refrain from tendering their shares, hoping to take a "free ride" and share in the higher firm value anticipated after the takeover, when they stock value will be at least as high as the offer price. But if all stockholders behave in this way and refrain from tendering, the raider will fail to gain control of the target and the expected increase in its value will not take place. Therefore it may be better to have a mechanism which makes value-increasing take-overs feasible by creating a pressure to tender.

Shareholders then face a trade-off. Enabling the raider to dilute the minority's wealth may reduce the expected gain in a takeover, whereas prohibiting such a dilution will make takeovers altogether infeasible and altogether eliminate gains from a takeover. There is thus an optimal level of dilution of the minority's wealth; that is, it may be in the shareholder's interest to be subjected to a pressure to tender.[73]

But regardless of its merit, the pressure to tender problem can be rendered a non-problem by the stockholders if they so wish. One way to remove the pressure to tender is by guaranteeing that all, or a great majority of, shares receive the same price, without regard to whether they were tendered. This can be attained by instituting a fair price corporate charter provision,[74] or by incorporating in a state whose statutes already include such a provision. The "fair price" provision usually states that any merger or consolidation of the corporation will require an affirmative vote of the holders of a super-majority of the outstanding shares (which may be as high as 95 percent), unless all shareholders of the corporation receive the same value per share as the highest per share price paid by a majority stockholder for any shares acquired in the period prior to the merger proposal, or unless the transaction is approved by a majority of the company's directors, who are usually those unaffiliated with the interested shareholders.[75] The super-majority requirement can be extended to other decisions regarding the firm, such as major sales or acquisitions of assets. It can also be conditioned on the offeror not being engaged in any transaction with the company or not taking any action which might adversely affect the price of the company's stock prior to a freezeout or which might enable the raider to extract some gain from the target company.[76]

The usefulness of the fair price provision as a way to ameliorate the pressure to tender is well known in the business community, and it has been adopted by a large number of firms.[77] The following summarizes its benefits:

> Fair price provisions tend to discourage takeovers in several ways. Firstly, they reduce the pressure on stockholders of the target company to tender at the time of the initial offer by assuring that, if they are subsequently squeezed out, they are likely to receive at least the same price as those who tendered... Secondly, they probably prevent the tender offeror from acquiring a target company at a bargain price by paying a premium for voting control and then squeezing out the remaining stockholders at a lower price. Fair price provisions subject an offeror to a possible loss of control over the ultimate price which it will have to pay.[78]

Raiders can dilute the minority's wealth not only through a straight two-part offer, but also by gaining control of the corporation through a partial offer and then exploiting it, thus diluting the minority's wealth. To defend against this risk, stockholders can institute a mandatory redemption provision of their company's stock at a predetermined price, e.g., the highest price paid by the raider in a specified period for the firm's shares. They can also provide for payment of a dividend of preferred shares that contain features preventing a freezeout in a second-step merger following the takeover, in which case the preferred shares may be convertible into preferred shares of the raider according to a specified formula.[79]

Finally, another defense against a minority squeezeout is available through the legal system. Minority stockholders can challenge the terms of the merger in court and demand an appraisal remedy, which provides them with the right to obtain a "fair value" for their shares from the corporation.[80]

With these protective measures, target shareholders do not have to rush to tender their shares lest they may be squeezed out later. Instead, they can wait for a better offer, knowing that in any case they will get no less than the price paid to the majority of shares that were tendered. There is thus no need for the protection by competitive bids, proposed by the auctioneering rule.

Bebchuk suggested that the pressure to tender may be blocked if stockholders act cooperatively, but such concerted action entails transaction costs which none may wish to bear alone. In recent years, a number of states have enacted statutes which help resolve this problem. For example, Minnesota requires that an acquisition of a specified percentage of the shares of a Minnesota-chartered target corporation be approved by the target's shareholders.[81] Then, if stockholders view the tender offer as unfair, they can *individually* vote against it and block it without the need for costly cooperative action. By choosing to incorporate in a state with such statutes, firms can resolve the pressure to tender problem without a federal auctioneering rule. (We further discuss this issue in the following section.)

The empirical evidence suggests that the removal of the pressure to tender is not valuable to all firms. First, most firms have chosen not to adopt defensive provisions, perhaps because they do not consider them as valuable.[82] Second, studies on the effect of fair-price and super-majority provisions on those firms which have adopted them have produced mixed evidence, mostly negative (although generally insignificant).[83] There is thus no support to the hypothesis that removing the pressure to tender is beneficial.

It is also of interest to note that although two-tier tender offers are viewed as hostile, the great majority of them are in fact negotiated.[84] To the extent that negotiations between the bidder and the target management reflect some agreement between the parties, this evidence may attest that the pressure to tender is not always undesirable.

In conclusion, the pressure to tender does not seem to be a problem which requires governmental regulation under the auctioneering rule or otherwise, nor can opposition to our priority rule be justified on the grounds that the rule permits this pressure. Not only can firms remove the pressure by themselves if they so wish, but both theory and empirical evidence suggest that its removal may well be undesirable. While the auctioneering rule is designed to remove the pressure to tender, our priority rule is substantially neutral with respect to it. Our rule allows it by eliminating competition between bidders during the exclusivity period, but it does not forbid target shareholders to employ protective measures to defend against it. Even if the removal of this pressure is socially inefficient, we do not propose to forbid defensive measures by firms since the property rights of the target shareholders entitle them to decide how they wish to employ their assets.

The Auctioneering Rule as a State Law

Consider a scenario where the priority rule is in effect under federal law while some firms prefer to be protected by the auctioneering rule, and assume that the rule cannot be simulated by homemade defensive measures. These firms would prefer enactment of the auctioneering rule, but the two rules conflict. We however propose that instead of enacting a federal auctioneering rule, it should be left to the states to decide on whether they wish to legislate such a rule,[85] and to the firms to decide whether they wish to be covered by it by incorporating in the states where the rule prevails. If the state auctioneering rule imposes a delay period longer than the exclusivity period under the priority rule, the latter would effectively be nullified.[86] That is, if by state law the tender offer transaction cannot be consummated during a period longer than the exclusivity period, the state law then effectively removes the protection to the initial bidder provided under the priority rule. On the other hand, a priority rule is ineffective unless it is made a federal law. A federal priority rule and state auctioneering rule will enable firms to choose whether they wish to be covered by the one rule or the other.

The demand for a state-legislated auctioneering rule will come from firms which consider it valuable and move to incorporate in a state which has adopted it. The supply of such legislature will come if the auctioneering rule is expected to attract firms, since corporate chartering produces revenues to the states.[87] In this way, market forces of demand (by firms) and supply (by states) will determine the extent to which firms will be protected by the auctioneering rule.[88]

The practice of firms moving to incorporate in states whose laws are more suitable to the firms' interests is quite prevalent. In particular, there are states whose laws contain provisions against surprise attacks by raiders. Examples abound,[89] including the one of Time Inc. cited above. Changes in the state of incorporation in order to deflect raiders may be desirable to some firms[90] whereas other firms may consider state restrictions on takeovers undesirable, as indeed may be the case.[91] Clearly, one state could enact the auctioneering rule and firms which wish such protection would move to incorporate in that state, whereas firms which value more the greater probability of being sought after for a takeover would prefer to incorporate in states whose laws facilitate takeovers.

Competition between states can work if the cost of moving between states is relatively low. Indeed, a change in the place of incorporation by a firm is not very costly since it does not require moving of the actual production and administrative facilities to the state of incorporation. Firms also move for reasons unrelated to competition among jurisdictions, hence the pertinent costs are only the marginal costs of diverting the destination from one jurisdiction to another. Finally, the very pattern of the movement can influence state governments and induce a tendency toward optimal legislation.[92]

Summary

We have demonstrated that target firms' shareholders are able to protect themselves against what they may consider disadvantageous takeovers. The evidence suggests that many do not consider that *ex ante* raising the hurdle for a would-be acquirer is desirable. All this casts doubt on the necessity of a mandatory auctioneering rule. Our priority rule is intended to protect the interests of the initial bidder and, thus, to increase economic efficiency. Since target stockholders are able to protect themselves and nullify to a great extent the advantages given to the initial raider by our rule, the economic benefits of our rule remain.

On the Feasibility of a Homemade Auctioneering Rule

Having suggested that the objectives of the auctioneering rule can be attained by homemade defensive measures, we have to show that their institution is feasible. Here we are confronted by the collective action problem in voting: Even if all shareholders consider this policy beneficial, given the costs of information and coordination, no single small shareholder will expend the resources to bring it to a vote and to marshal support for it because he alone will bear the costs while the gains will be shared by all free-riding shareholders.[93] This implies that (i) the absence of auctioneering-like measures in corporate charters does not mean that they are undesirable to most shareholders; and (ii) there may be a need for government to legislate the auctioneering rule.

The collective action problem in corporate voting can be resolved when the associated costs are borne equally by all shareholders. A natural agent to carry this out is the corporation manager.[94] However, the manager's interests may conflict with those of his principals, and then the costs of monitoring him may make it infeasible to ensure that his actions will serve shareholders' interests.[95]

However, there would be no conflict of interests between shareholders and managers *if* auctioneering were a value-increasing policy. Clearly, a manager whose objective is to maximize the firm's value[96] would initiate and organize a vote on adopting takeover defensive measures, and shareholders would adopt them. But so would a self-serving manager who seeks to entrench in his position (to the detriment of his stockholders) and to reduce the probability of takeover; and again stockholders would adopt the takeover-impeding measures if they were considered to be value-maximizing. In both cases, the interests of managers and shareholders would be aligned, and the collective action problem associated with corporate voting would not be an obstacle.[97]

In sum, the institution of homemade auctioneering rule is feasible and relatively inexpensive.[98] From the fact that most firms did not adopt takeover defensive measures even before the institution of the Williams Act nor do all do so now we can infer that the auctioneering rule (as well as the removal of the pressure to tender) is not uniformly desirable.[99]

It may also be argued that shareholders would object to takeover impeding measures initiated by management lest such measures increase management ability to protect its own interests at their expense. This may be the case with some poison pill or super-majority provisions without an escape clause. But there are measures which provide managers with no more protection than does the auctioneering rule. These are, for example, incorporating in a state which requires substantial disclosure from the raider and imposes a delay period after filing of the tender offer,[100] or instituting a "fair price" provision to remove the pressure to tender. Like the auctioneering rule, such measures serve the incumbent managers by reducing the probability of a takeover, but they do not give management additional protection beyond that intended by the rule.

CONCLUDING REMARKS

In this chapter we have proposed a new approach to the regulation of tender offers with the objective of helping the initial bidder, who has invested in search and bidding, to protect his property rights concerning the information he releases when he bids for the target firm.

We have proposed a priority rule which draws on the established laws protecting intellectual property, such as the patent laws and copyright laws. Under the priority rule, no competitive bid for the target will be allowed during an exclusivity period specified by law. After that, if the takeover does not succeed, anyone will be allowed to bid for the target. The initial bidder will also be able to allow others to bid for the target during the exclusivity period, and he will then be entitled to the difference between his offer price and the offer price of the best bidder. This will facilitate efficient allocation while protecting a reward for the initial bidder. Finally, we suggest allowing the initial bidder to carry out a reverse tender offer procedure pursuant to which the target firm's shareholders will be invited to submit offers to sell their shares at a price they set. This will make it unnecessary for the initial bidder to disclose information, through an announced offer price, about his assessment of the target firm's value.

We expect that our rule will contribute to economic efficiency by helping resolve the ownership externality problem which is prevalent in information, that is, the inability of the producer of information to obtain from its users a reward for his product. Under our rule, the search for, and discovery of, undervalued firms will increase up to a level commensurate with the benefit it generates, making the takeover process more efficient socially.

The priority rule is expected to increase investment in search and bidding for undervalued firms, and thus increase the probability that firms will be sought after for takeovers. But the rule is not designed to protect target firms' shareholders *after* a bid has been made. The priority rule thus contrasts with the current trend in takeover legislation. The Williams Act, the state legislation which followed, and current sentiments among some legislators and academicians are in favor of imposing a mandatory delay period following the tender offer, enabling everyone to enter and compete with the initial bidder. This viewpoint was recently formulated in a proposal by Bebchuk[101] of an auctioneering rule. We, however, suggest that such a rule, as well as the proposed takeover-impeding legislature, are redundant. If shareholders so wish, they can protect themselves against the malaise of speedy takeovers and the pressure to tender by instituting appropriate defensive measures in their company's charter or by choosing to invest in firms with such homemade protection. However, we observe that most firms do not adopt the available protective measures, and those which have done so have not been rewarded with increases in their share prices. We can thus conclude that federal defensive legislation (such as the auctioneering rule) is neither beneficial nor necessary.

On the other hand, our "priority rule" cannot be homemade, but must be legislated and enforced by the government. Still, firms which consider it undesirable can institute takeover defensive measures which make hostile takeovers more difficult and costly. In that way, our rule ameliorates the economic inefficiency caused by the difficulty of protecting the bidder's ownership interests in the information he has produced. At the same time, the availability of homemade takeover defensive measures leaves potential target shareholders with the freedom to choose how to maximize the value of their wealth.

Notes

1. See T. L. Hazen, *The Law of Securities Regulation*, West Publishing 1985, at 386. See also Gregg A. Jarrell and Michael Bradley, "The Economic Effect of Federal and State Regulations of Cash Tender Offers," *Journal of Law and Economics, 23*, 371 (1980).
2. Senator William Proxmire in a senate floor speech on March 20, 1985.
3. Ibid.
4. Lucian A. Bebchuk, "The Case for Facilitating Competing Tender Offers," *Harvard Law Review, 95*, 1028 (1982); Lucian A. Bebchuk, "The Case of Facilitating Competing Tender Offers: A Reply and Extension," *Stanford Law Review, 35*, 23 (1982). Hereafter, "Bebchuk -a" and "Bebchuk-b," respectively.
5. Frank H. Easterbrook and Daniel R. Fischel, "The Proper Role of a Target's Management in Responding to a Tender Offer," *Harvard Law Review, 94*, 23 (1981); Frank H. Easterbrook and Daniel R. Fischel, "Auctions and Sunk Costs in Tender Offers," *Stanford Law Review, 35*, 1 (1982).
6. The "initial bidder" is the entity (e. g., an individual or a firm) who has discovered a firm worthwhile to be a takeover target and is the first to bid for it. This entity has usually invested resources in searching and bidding for the target firm.
7. Unsuccessful bidding imposes a significant cost on the bidder, reflected in the significant decline in its stock price; see evidence in Michael C. Jensen and

Richard D. Ruback, "The Market for Corporate Control," *Journal of Financial Economics, 11*, 183 (1983). Increasing the probability of such a cost, as would the auctioneering rule, will reduce the incentives to search and bid.

8. See, e.g., Mazer v. Stein, 347 U.S. 201, 219 (1954). For a discussion on intellectual property rights in the context of patents, see Ernest B. Lipscomb, *Walker on Patents,* 3rd ed., Rochester, NY: The Lawyer Co-operative Publishing Co., (1984), Vol. 1, 54 ff.

9. For a comprehensive review of economic issues in the debate on the patent system, see F. M. Scherer, *Industrial Market Structure and Economic Performance,* Houghton Mifflin Co., (1980), chapter 16. See also, "Proposals for Improving the Patent System," study of the Subcommittee on Patents, Trademarks and Copyright of the Committee on the Judiciary, United States Senate, (1956); hereafter, "Proposals for Improving the Patent System."

10. These characteristics include increasing marginal cost and decreasing marginal benefit, at least one of them strictly so.

11. See Francis M. Bator, "The Anatomy of Market Failure," *Quarterly Journal of Economics, 351,* 363–65 (1958). See also David K. Whitcomb, *Externalities and Welfare,* Columbia University Press, (1972).

12. There are other possible ways to use the information about an undervalued firm. The producer of the information can acquire control of the target through secret private negotiations with the target firm's management, or he can acquire shares of the target firm and then release his information, thus profiting on the shares he already owns. But these solutions are constrained and thus, as a rule, inferior. To illustrate this point, suppose the rule governing the sale of goods were such that goods displayed for sale could be picked without paying. The producer of goods would thus refrain from displaying them and choose other methods of sale, such as personally dealing with each customer. Even if production and sale were still profitable, there would be a lower level of output, compared with a situation in which free picking of displayed goods is prohibited. In this example, as in the case of information about target firms, the problem arises from the cost of maintaining property rights on output.

13. Bator, *supra* note 11, illustrates this case by an example of apple nectar which is used freely by bee growers. The nectar is an ordinary, private, exhaustible good, but it is impossible to have markets impute to apple blossoms their correct (shadow) value. Hence, since ownership rights of the nectar cannot be enforced, the production of nectar will be suboptimal.

14. Peter Dodd and Richard Ruback, "Tender Offers and Stockholders Returns: An Empirical Analysis," *Journal of Financial Economics, 5,* 351 (1977); Jarrell and Bradley, *supra* note 1; and Frank H. Easterbrook and Gregg A. Jarrell, "Do Targets Gain from Defeating Tender Offers?," *NYU Law Review, 59,* 277 (1984).

15. The increase in value of the target firms should be noted since a rejection of an offer also provides negative information about the entrenchment of the man-

agement, see David P. Baron, "Tender Offers and Managerial Resistance," *Journal of Finance, 38*, 331 (1983). On balance, studies show that the positive information effect dominates. This evidence, however, should be regarded with care since the exact population proportion of target firms to which subsequent offers were made (leading to appreciation in their value) is unknown, and may be different from that covered in these studies. The estimated positive evaluation of the unsuccessful target firms was due primarily to the emergence of a later bid. See Michael Bradley, Anand Desai, and E. Han Kim, "The Rationale behind Interfirm Tender Offers," *Journal of Financial Economics, 11,* 183 (1983). A positive revaluation of stocks of target firms in cases of repurchase or standstill agreements was found by by Wayne Mikkelson and Richard S. Ruback, "Corporate Investments in Common Stock," working paper (1984).

16. See Frank H. Easterbrook, "Insider Trading, Secret Agents, Evidentiary Privileges, and the Production of Information," *Sup. Ct. Rev.*, 313 (1981).

17. Bator, *supra* note 11.

18. *Proposals for Improving the Patent System,* the Senate Subcommittee on Patents, Trademarks, and Copyrights of the Committee of the Judiciary, United States Senate, (1956), at 1.

19. This is well known from microeconomic theory. See Scherer, *supra* note 9.

20. In the language of the court, "the benefits to the economy, the target corporation, and its shareholders from an acquisition are substantial, whether by tender offers or open market operation." Icahn v. Blunt, 612 F. Supp. 1400, 1416 (1985).

21. See a review in Jensen and Ruback, *supra* note 7.

22. The evidence suggests that these value increases cannot generally be attributed to increased market power. See B. Espen Eckbo, "Horizontal Mergers, Collusion, and Stockholders Wealth," *Journal of Financial Economics, 11*, 241 (1983); and Robert Stillman, "Examining Antitrust Policy Against Horizontal Mergers," *Journal of Financial Economics, 11*, 225 (1983). Besides, the legal antitrust system which guards against takeovers is designed to increase market power and subsequently increase the values of the participating firms while having a negative welfare effect. We shall thus continue our analysis assuming that the takeover-generated value increases are socially beneficial.

23. In the fifth section (pp. 271–80), we cite evidence of the detrimental effects of making takeovers more difficult. Many (perhaps most) firms which could protect themselves by a "homemade" auctioneering rule refrain from doing so, perhaps in order not to inhibit potential acquirers from seeking them for takeovers.

24. Permitting free use of the patent is beneficial once the discovery, leading to the patent, has been made. Clearly, while this makes the production and sale more socially beneficial, it will be detrimental to the search process, as discussed above.

25. See Easterbrook and Fischel (1982), *supra* note 5. Indeed, sell-offs of divisions of acquired firms is common as well as profitable. Evidence in Scott C. Linn and

Michael S. Rozeff, "The Corporate Sell-off," *Midland Corp. Finance Journal*, *2*, 17 (Summer 1984), shows that on average, the announcement of a divestiture (or a sell-off) generated a significant increase in the stock price of the selling firm, indicating that the buyer might be paying for the assets more than their value to their current owner.

26. It is worth emphasizing that the resource misallocation problem, which the auctioneering rule intends to ameliorate, is but an outcome of the existence of transaction costs. With negligible transaction costs, the auctioneering rule is unnecessary. Then, the target will eventually be acquired by the best user of its resources.

27. See Bebchuk-b, *supra* note 4.

28. See Scherer, *supra* note 9 at 442–44, on cost-saving patents. Intuitively, the patent product must generally be welfare increasing in order to compete with the prepatent products.

29. We discuss the equity issue in more detail in the third section below.

30. Naturally, the initial bidder's offer is lower than the posttakeover value of the target to him, at least by the amount of his cost.

31. These calculations assume that the initial bidder estimates as certain his ability to conclude the deal during the exclusivity period; otherwise, his strategy may be different.

32. The transaction costs are always borne by the seller since the proceeds of the sale cannot exceed the value of the target to the buyer.

33. The loss is bounded from above by the magnitude of the transaction costs because the initial bidder will refrain from resale if the additional value to be realized is smaller than the related transaction costs. Thus, if a resale occurs, the loss of resources equals the transaction costs, and if a resale does not occur, the loss in forgone improvement is less than the transaction costs.

34. See Bebchuk-b *supra* note 4. He continues his argument, at 44, by stating that "the smaller a director's shareholdings, the greater his inclination to deviate from value maximization in favor of other objectives, such as expansion." Indeed, Yakov Amihud and Baruch Lev, "Risk Reduction as a Managerial Motive for Conglomerate Mergers," *Bell Journal of Economics*, *12*, 605 (1981), found that manager-controlled firms have greater propensity to engage in conglomerate mergers than owner-controlled firms; and Yakov Amihud and Jacob Kamin, "Revenue vs. Profit Maximization: Differences in Behavior by Type of Control and by Market Power," *Southern Economic Journal, 45,* 838 (1979), found that revenue maximization is associated with management control in firms with market power. However, Yakov Amihud, Peter Dodd, and Mark Weinstein, "Conglomerate Mergers, Managerial Motives and Stockholders Wealth," *Journal of Banking and Finance,* (1986), found no significant differences in stock (excess) returns at the merger announcements between the two types of acquiring firms, implying

that the firms are disciplined by the market and the extent of control does not have takeover-related value implications.

35. See also Allan Schwartz, "Imperfect Information and the Tender Offer Auction," University of Southern California Law School, working paper, (June 1985).

36. See W. D. Nordhaus, *Invention, Growth and Welfare,* Cambridge, MA: MIT Press, (1969); F. M. Scherer, "Nordhaus' Theory of Optimal Patent Life: A Geometric Reinterpretation," *American Economic Review, 62,* 422 (1972); M. K. Berkowitz and Y. Kotowitz, "Patent Policy in an Open Economy," *Canadian Journal of Economics, 15,* 1 (1982). These papers analyze the optimal patent life under certainty. M. Rafiquzzaman, "The Optimal Patent Term under Uncertainty," *International Journal of Independent Organisations, 5,* 233 (1987), proved that under uncertainty, the patent term which maximizes social welfare, subject to the inventor's maximization of his welfare, depends on the inventor's attitude towards risk. In particular, in a cost-reducing invention under uncertainty, the optimal patent term is greater under risk aversion (compared to risk neutrality).

37 A related objective of the delay period is to bring about a greater equality in the reward received by the target's shareholders. Bebchuk-b *supra* note 4 argued that a speedy takeover disadvantages those who cannot react to the offer on time, thus receiving less than other shareholders who promptly tender their shares, especially in two-tier or partial offers. However, this equity problem can be resolved by market-based arrangements. Shareholders can protect themselves against being disadvantaged in speedy takeovers by investing only in firms with takeover-impeding measures (such as fair-price or mandatory redemption provisions) as discussed in the fifth section, (pp. 271–80), and by avoiding firms without such measures, in the very same way that they choose between stocks according to risk. If investors indeed care about this problem, then in equilibrium, stocks without protective measures will yield greater returns, adequately compensating their holders for the risk of being disadvantaged in a speedy takeover. Another solution is for unsophisticated investors to have their portfolios managed professionally for a fee. Part of this fee compensates the portfolio manager for being alert and promptly tendering the shares when the opportunity arises. Given the competitive market for portfolio management, such a fee is the exact fair remuneration for the associated effort. In this paper we shall refrain from discussing equity issues and limit ourselves to discussing the efficiency aspects of the problems.

38. It is worth noting that the objective of the Williams Act, as interpreted by the courts, was (1) but not (2); note 51 *infra*.

39. Even the initial bidder may sometimes find it beneficial to allow the target's shareholders more time, so that more shares can be tendered, but this may cost him the entry of competitors and threaten his success.

40. Han, Desai, and Kim, *supra* note 15, found that the stock prices of target firms, where the first offer failed and no subsequent offer was made, declined compared

to the price at the time of the offer. This finding also reflect the outcomes in firms whose management was determined to reject any offer. See also Easterbrook and Jarrell, *supra* note 14.

41   The certainty equivalent of a lottery, or of a risky cash flow, is a sure amount such that a person is indifferent between engaging in the lottery or receiving the sure amount. For a risk neutral person, the certainty (cash) equivalent of a lottery equals its expected cash flow. For a risk averse person, the certainty equivalent of a lottery is *less* than its expected value, the difference being the "risk premium," See, e.g., John Pratt, "Risk Aversion in the Small and in the Large," *Econometrica, 27,* 169 (1965). To illustrate, if the target's shareholders estimate that the expected highest offer price they can get, after the exclusivity period expires, is $P a share, then, being risk averse, they may be as well off if they sell their shares immediately to the initial bidder for a *sure* price (= the certainty equivalent) of less than $P. Since every shareholder has a different level of risk aversion, there will be a positive relationship between individuals' reservation prices and the aggregate quantity tendered. The offer price should be high enough to attract a sufficiently high number of target's shares, but it can still be below $P.

42.   By definition, the utility of the sure amount which is the certainty equivalent of a lottery, equals the expected utility derived from the lottery. That is, a person is as well off when facing the lottery (the future offer price) as when receiving its certainty equivalent (the current initial bidder's offer).

43   The increase in the willingness to sell the stock as the offer price rises may reflect differences between stockholders in their tax basis, and risk aversion and portfolio construction when they are not fully diversified or have different unmarketable assets.

44   The sellers whose reservation prices are lower than the offer price realize a "seller's surplus," equal to the difference between the offer price and the reservation price.

45.   We have here a super-additive game (i.e., a game whose value when the players cooperate is higher than the sum of its values to the players when they do not cooperate), whose "core" consists of undominated allocations of the added value created by the merger, all being equally "fair." The allocation of the *entire* merger benefits to the raider or to the target are also in the core. See, e.g., Jan Mossin, "Merger Agreements: Some Game Theoretic Considerations," *Journal of Business, 41,* 460 (1968).

46.   This is a well-known outcome of an English auction, where the price is raised until the penultimate bidder drops out of the competition (when the price just exceeds his reservation price). The remaining (highest) bidder can then acquire the target at the last price which is just above its value to the second bidder but still below his own.

47.   This would generally be the case when externalities are internalized.

48.   See in Yakov Amihud (ed.), *Bidding and Auctioning for Procurement and Al-*

location, NYU Press, 1976. See a comparative analysis of auctioning methods in Milton Harris and Artur Raviv, "Allocation Mechanisms and the Design of Auctions," *Econometrica, 49,* 1477 (1981).

49   Harris and Raviv, ibid., analyzed demand functions and we make here an analogy to supply functions.

50.   Note, however, that the expected gain to target shareholders, unconditional on whether an offer has been made, may be lower under the current tender offer regime. See discussion *infra.*

51.   "The Purpose of the Williams Act is to ensure that public shareholders who are confronted by a cash tender offer for their stock will not be required to respond without adequate information." Rondeau v. Mosinee Paper Corp., 422 U.S. 49, 58.

52.   Schreiber v. Burlington Northern Inc., 86 L. Ed. 2d. 1, 7.

53   Evidence on the fact that opposing takeovers is inconsistent with stockholders' interests may be inferred from Ralph A. Walkins and Michael S. Long, "Agency Theory, Managerial Welfare, and Takeover Bid Resilience," *Rand Journal of Economics,* 54 (1984). They found that tender offers are more likely to be contested by managers with low ownership positions in their corporations, whereas uncontested offers are associated with significantly higher ownership positions in the corporation by the officers. This implies that facilitating takeovers is more consistent with maximization of shareholders' wealth, while obstructing them may be associated with managerial interests. This is corroborated by (weak) evidence that managers who contested offers were overpaid compared to managers in uncontested offers. They also found that the opposition to takeovers is not a function of the bid premium.

54   For a comprehensive discussion of charter and bylaw techniques to deflect takeovers, see Stephen A. Hochman and Oscar D. Fogler, "Deflecting Takeovers: Charter and By-Law Techniques", *Business Lawyer, 34,* 537 (1979); Arthur Fleicher, *Tender Offers: Defences, Responses, and Planning,* chapter VI (1985); Ronald J. Gilson, "A Structural Approach to Corporations: The Case Against Defensive Tactics in Tender Offers," *Stanford Law Review, 33,* 819 (1981); and Ronald J. Gilson, "Seeking Competitive Bids Versus Pure Passivity Rule," *Stanford Law Review, 35,* 51 (1982). This information also appears in practitioners' publications, see, e.g., James E. Moon, "Tender Offers: How to Win," *Financial Executive,* 28 (1983).

55.   R. J. Cole, *New York Times,* (October 3, 1984).

56.   The "poison pill" arrangement gives stockholders the right to buy additional securities of the firm at a special price (or obtain other benefits) when a hostile bidder tries to take over the firm, and it can be instituted by management without the need for stockholders' approval.

57.   Gregg A. Jarrell and John Pound, "The Economics of Poison Pills", SEC Working Paper, (March 1986). The legality of the poison pill in precluding

hostile takeover altogether was recently challenged and it was enjoined. See Dynamics Corp. of America v. CTS Corp., 794 F.2d. 259 (7th Cir. 1986).

58. Michael A. Schwartz and Sharon L. Tillman, "Recent Proxy Contest Development", mimeograph, Wachtel, Lipton, Rosen and Katz, New York, (1984).

59. *Wall Street Journal*, (European ed.), May 30, 1986.

60. The most ardent opposition to antitakeover measures comes nowadays from sophisticated institutional investors: "big investors don't want to discourage lucrative acquisitions by putting another wall around the company," Id. See also discussion below in "Pressure to Tender: A Nonproblem," p. 331.

61. Harry DeAngelo and Edward Rice, "Antitakeover Charter Amendments and Stockholders' Wealth, *Journal of Financial Economics, 11,* 329 (1983), found no evidence that antitakeover amendments—super majority, staggered board, fair price, and lock-ups—affect stock prices; they found a minor but insignificant negative price reaction. Scott C. Linn and John Y. McConnell, "An Empirical Investigation of the Impact of Antitakeover Amendments on Common Stock Prices" *Journal of Financial Economics, 11,* 361 (1983), presented findings which, while not unambiguous, show some favorable reaction of stock prices to these amendments. Gregg A. Jarrell, Annette Poulsen, and Lynne Davidson, "Shark Repellants and Stock Prices: The Effect of Antitakeover Amendments since 1980," The SEC working paper, (April 1985), found a statistically significant negative stock price reaction in firms proposing "super majority" rules and having relatively high insiders' holdings and low institutional holdings, whereas the price reaction to other antitakeover amendments was negative but statistically insignificant. Finally, Jarrell and Pound, *supra* note 57, found that the adoption of poison pill plans led to a significant decline in stock prices; but note that unlike the other antitakeover measures, the latter does not require stockholder approval.

62. While the absence of a positive effect on prices of antitakeover measures can be viewed as an indication that stockholders do not welcome attempts to deflect takeovers, it could also be argued that the evidence of mostly insignificant price reaction reflects a perception that the antitakeover measures are ineffective. Then, the question is why managements go through the effort and cost to institute them. For a practitioner's view on the value of theses measures in impeding takeovers, see *Investment Dealers Digest,* 49 (February 1, 1983).

63. It could be argued that takeover defensive measures cannot perfectly simulate the auctioneering rule, since the latter mandates a delay period in tender offers whereas the former merely makes tender offers more difficult. However, it is well known that these measures go a long way to impede undesirable takeovers and to buy the target firm time to obtain competing offers, as intended by the auctioneering rule. Thus, if *all* firms considered that rule to be valuable, they would have *all* established these measures. From the absence of a unanimous

adoption of takeover defensive measures, we can learn that impeding takeovers is not always considered desirable.

64. Katherin Schipper and Rex Thompson, "Evidence on the Capitalized Value of Merger Activity for Acquiring Firms," *Journal of Financial Economics, 11*, 85 (1983).

65. Jarrell and Bradley, *supra* note 1; Paul Asquith, Robert F. Bruner, and David W. Mullins, "The Gains to Bidding Firms from Mergers", *Journal of Financial Economics, 11*, 121 (1983); Michael Bradley, Anand Desai, and E. Han Kim, "Determinants of the Wealth Effects of Corporate Acquisition: Theory and Evidence," University of Michigan working paper (1983).

66. Jensen and Ruback, *supra* note 7, point out that the excess returns in the post-regulation period may even be overestimated since then low-profit mergers were avoided.

67. Evidence on this loss can be inferred from Bradley, Desai, and Kim, *supra* note 66. They found that the gains to target firms in the post-regulation period were higher, and those of the bidding firms were lower, than in the pre-regulation period; but when put together, relative wealth changes were not distinguishably different before and after the antitakeover regulation period. Given the negative effect that these regulations must have had on the level of search for undervalued targets, the evidence implies that their social welfare effect was negative. The same may apply to the auctioneering rule.

68. Bebchuk-b, *supra* note 4 at 5, our italics.

69. Id., at 35.

70. Id., at 23.

71. On the prisoner's dilemma, see R. Duncan Luce and Howard Raiffa, *Games and Decisions,* New York: John Wiley and Sons, Inc., (1957). For the application of the prisoner's dilemma approach to two-part tender offers, see Gilson, *supra* note 54 (1981) at 859-862; Jensen and Ruback, *supra* note 7; Michael Bradley, and E. Han Kim, "The Tender Offer as a Takeover Device: Its Evolution, The Free Rider Problem, and the Prisoner's Dilemma," University of Michigan Graduate School of Business Administration working paper, (April 1985).

72. Sanford Grossman and Oliver D. Hart, "Takeovers Bids, the Free-Rider Problem, and the Theory of the Corporation," *Bell Journal of Economics, 11,* 42 (1980).

73. Recent papers demonstrate how the free-rider problem may be resolved in some cases without dilution of the non-tendering stockholders' wealth. See Jean-François Dreyfus, "Takeover Bids and Personal Income Taxes" NYU-GBA working paper, (1985); Robert W. Vishny and Andrei Shleifer, "Large Shareholders and Corporate Control," *Journal of Political Economy,* 461 (1986); Ishak Diwan, "Greenmail, Managerial Entrenchment and the Free-Rider Problem," NYU-GBA working paper, (June 1985).

Sanford Grossman and Oliver Hart, "Allocational Role of Takeover Bids in Situations of Asymmetric Information," *Journal of Finance, 36,* 253 (1981), show that the socially optimal level of dilution of the minority's wealth is even greater than that optimal for shareholders. See also, Frank H. Easterbrook and Daniel R. Fischel, "Corporate Control Transactions," *Yale Law Journal, 91*, 698 (1982), who argue that unless minority freezeouts were allowed there would be intolerable holdout problems and efficient corporate transactions would be frustrated. However, they point out that the courts sometimes decide against the dilution of the minority's wealth.

74.   For example, General Foods corporation, which adopted a fair-price charter amendment to ameliorate this very same problem, asserted in its proxy statement: "Two tier pricing tends to pressure stockholders into making hasty decisions and can be unfair to stockholders whose shares are not purchased in the first stage of the acquisition." N. S. Poser, *Investment Dealers Digest*, 15 (July 24, 1984).

75.   The fair-price provision was preceded by the "super-majority" provision. Unlike the former, the latter lacks an automatic escape clause which nullifies the super majority requirement when certain conditions are satisfied. Thus the super-majority provision gives large stockholders or entrenched self-serving managements a blocking power concerning some policies to the disadvantage of other stockholders. This may explain the significant negative effect of the adoption of super-majority provisions on stock prices in firms with relatively high insiders' holdings; see Jarrell, Poulsen, and Davidson *supra* note 61. In fact, the super-majority provision lost favor in recent years, being increasingly replaced by fair-price provisions. The Investor Responsibility Research Center reported (February 1985) that while fair-price provisions were a relative novelty in 1983, they all but replaced the super-majority proposals in 1984, becoming the most prevalent form of antitakeover measure. Institutional investors who have ardently opposed super-majority proposals have become increasingly receptive to the fair-price proposals. *The Wall Street Journal* (May 30, 1986) reports that institutional investors are leading the fight against super-majority requirements. Jarrell, Poulsen, and Davidson, ibid., found that firms proposing super-majority measures had low institutional holdings, whereas fair-price measures were more prevalent in firms with high institutional holdings.

76.   Hochman and Fogler, *supra* note 54 at 554.

77.   See, e.g., the interview with James Dwyer, Senior Vice President of investment banking at Donaldson, Lufkin and Jenrette: "Another defense mechanism...is the fair price charter, meant to prevent big-premium offers for a portion of the stock. Such front-end loaded offers are combatted these days...with super majority amendments. Some of the best merger lawyers are urging their clients to use them. With such a clause, unless the bidder pays a high price to everyone, they will need an 80 percent vote to get approval for the second stage of the merger" (*Investment Dealers Digest,* February 1, 1983, p. 10). Fair price and super-majority provisions have been adopted by over 200 corporations in 1983, over 400 in 1984 and over 500 (expected) in 1985. These firms comprise about 11

percent of all publicly owned companies. See John Shad, discussion on the Securities and Exchange Commission Economic Forum on Tender Offers, February 20, 1985.

78. Hochman and Fogler, *supra* note at 554.

79. See, for example, the cases of Rubbermaid Corporation (3-24-1978), and Bell and Howell whose issuance of convertible preferred was upheld; National Education Corp. v. Bell and Howell Co., C.A. 7278, Del. Ch., (August 25, 1983).

   The raider may find such a policy costly even in the absence of the mandatory redemption provisions since, lacking a super majority, he may have problems in passing a variety of resolutions. This constraint may force the raider to forgo decisions which require the minority's approval and impose a cost, serving as a disincentive to take over the firm without paying an equal price to all.

80. See Victor Brudney and Marvin A. Chirelstein, "A Restatement of Corporate Freezeouts," *Yale Law Journal, 87,* (1978); and Daniel R. Fischel, "The Appraisal Remedy in Corporate Law", *Am. Bar Found. Res. Journal,* 875 (1983). Such protection is particularly available in states whose statutes provide appraisal rights in mergers.

81. See the 1984 amendment to the state of Minnesota Corporate and Blue-Sky statutes. Furthermore, shares acquired in violation of the law from a Minnesota resident are denied voting rights for a period of one year after acquisition. Then, even if the raider acquires a majority of the voting stock in a two-part offer, it may still be unable to control the target company. See Leigh B. Trevor and John W. Edwards, "State Regulation of Corporate Takeovers: Developments Since Edgar vs. Mite Corp.," *Journal of Buyouts and Acquisitions, 3, 3* (April/May 1984). See also Shad, *supra* note 77.

82. The fact that a fair-price amendment is not even brought to a vote in most corporations does not reflect an ignorance of its benefits which, as shown above, are well known. It may rather reflect shareholders' preferences (explicit or implicit). For example, the management of Household International wanted to forestall a prospective takeover, but received information from proxy solicitation firms that a fair price amendment would not pass; hence it devised a poison pill. See Michael Jensen in the SEC Economic Forum on Tender Offers, February 1985, p. 82.

83. Linn and McConnell, *supra* note 61, found that pre-1980 amendments with a super-majority requirement for mergers (with a lock-in amendments requiring a super-majority to amend this provision) produced a weak positive reaction in stock prices, while the study by Jarrell, Poulsen, and Davidson, *supra* note 61, of a post-1980 sample showed that the adoption of super-majority amendments significantly decreased stock prices in firms with large insider and low institutional stock holdings, while the adoption of fair-price provisions had an insignificant negative effect on stock prices. Some of the super-majority cases which were included in these studies might be devised to protect managers' interests, in

particular when these provisions did not include escape clauses which nullify them when fair price requirements, or the target board's requirements (preferably those of the outside directors) are satisfied. This might have caused a negative price reaction. On the other hand, if the proposal of an antitakeover amendment signals a forthcoming takeover, the results would be upward biased. The difference in the results for the two periods may be due to the change in the public's evaluation of the strict super-majority provisions (perhaps through learning) which recently became less desirable; see the IRRC report, *supra* note 75. Such differences may also be due to changes in the features of the super-majority provisions through the years.

84. Robert Comment, Gregg A. Jarrell, Hugh Hayworth, and Annette Poulsen, "The Economics of Any-or-All, Partial and Two-Tier Tender Offers," SEC working paper, (April 1985), found that in their sample of takeovers during 1981–1984, 92.1 percent of the ultimate two-tier tender offers were negotiated, compared to 83.6 percent of any-or-all offers and 38.9 percent of partial offers. The two-tier offers were applied in the largest takeovers on average, attesting to their importance. Finally, the premiums paid in two-tier offers averaged 54.5 percent compared to 59.6 percent in any-or-all offers (no test of significance is provided). Further study is necessary to establish the effect of the type of offer on the premium paid, controlling for size and other factors.

85. In fact, the Illinois Business Takeover Act (September 8, 1977) intended, like the auctioneering rule, to provide target companies with additional time to combat tender offers. The Supreme Court declared this unconstitutional under the Commerce Clause of the U.S. Constitution, and also because it imposed a burden on interstate commerce and frustrated the objectives of the Williams Act; see Edgar v. Mite, 102 S. Ct. 2629 (1982). For a comprehensive discussion, see Gregg A. Jarrell, "State Anti-Takeover Laws and the Efficient Allocation of Corporate Control: An Economic Analysis of Edgar v. Mite Corp.," 2 Sup. Ct. Econ. Rev., (1983). Still, a number of states have tender offer statutes including extensive disclosure requirements which effectively delay the execution of takeovers; see Hazen *supra* note 1, Jarrell and Bradley, *supra* note 1; and Trevor and Edwards, *supra* note 81. While the validity of such state laws is questionable, our proposals do not pertain to restrictions in current legislation.

86. This implies that the priority rule is dispositive. We shall not address here the issue of the conflict between federal and state laws.

87. On the revenues generated to the states by corporate chartering, see Peter Dodd and Richard Leftwich, "The Market for Corporate Charters: 'Unhealthy Competition' versus Federal Regulation," *Journal of Business, 53,* 260 (1980), and the references therein; and Roberta Romano, "Law as a Product: Some Pieces of the Incorporation Puzzle," *Journal of Law, Economics and Organizations, 1,* 225 (1985).

88. On the theory of demand for and supply of regulations within states, see George

J. Stigler, "The Theory of Economic Regulation," *Bell Journal of Economics, 2,* 3 (1971). For a discussion of the effect on state legislation of competition between states, see Frank H. Easterbrook, "Antitrust and the Economics of Federalism," *Journal of Law and Economics, 26,* 23 (1983). Firms have incentives to locate in states where they can adopt welfare increasing voting procedures, see Frank H. Easterbrook and Daniel R. Fischel, "Voting in Corporate Law," *Journal of Law and Economics, 26,* 395 (1983). Romano, ibid., proposes a transactions explanation of reincorporation: Firms shift their state of domicile at the same time they undertake, or anticipate engaging in, discrete transactions involving changes in firm operation and/or organization; in some cases, reincorporation benefits stockholders.

89. The following quotation may illustrate the effectiveness of such provisions: "Offerors were reluctant to keep a tender offer, involving large sums, in suspense while the Ohio or the Virginia Division of Securities pondered its fairness", Hochman and Fogler, *supra* note 54 at 577. See also Hochman and Fogler, *supra* note 54, on the antitakeover features of the Delaware law. The state of Minnesota has consistently expanded its takeover-constraining legislation, see *supra* note 81. Poser describes the flight to Delaware of Gulf Oil, since Delaware laws were perceived by Gulf as more suitable to forestall a threatened takeover by Mesa Petroleum. Under the reorganization, Gulf's shareholders would become shareholders of a Delaware holding company which would hold all the shares of the Pennsylvania-based operating company. For details on the advantages of incorporating in Delaware rather than in Pennsylvania, see Norman S. Poser, "Flight to Delaware as a Takeover Defense," *Investment Dealers Digest,* 12 (1983).

90. Changes in the state of incorporation were associated with increases in stock prices of firms which chose to do that (although these changes were not necessarily motivated by takeover laws); see Dodd and Leftwich, *supra* note 90. Note that such changes may signal an impending takeover, hence the price increases.

91. State laws which restrict corporate acquisitions had a significant adverse effect on managerial efficiency in the case of banks; see Christopher James, "An Analysis of the Effect of State Acquisition Laws on Managerial Efficiency: The Case of the Bank Holding Company Acquisitions," *Journal of Law and Economics, 27,* 211 (1984). Romano, *supra* note 90, found that reincorporation motivated by antitakeover defense had no significant effect on firms' stock prices.

92. It may be argued that even if a firm prefers the auctioneering rule, it may refrain from incorporating in the state which enacted it if some other rules in that state are undesirable. However, state rules concerning corporate charters are not necessarily mandatory; in many cases, such rules are or can be made permissive and include default provisions which can be exercised by the firm. For example, a corporation in Maryland can choose not to be governed by this state's fair price

statute by properly approving a charter amendment to that effect. Hence the legislation of the auctioneering rule by a number of states will offer a variety of combinations of corporate laws, and the response of firms will give legislators an indication on the desirability of the rule. Dennis W. Carlton and Daniel R. Fischel, "The Regulation of Insider Trading," *Stanford Law Review, 35*, 857 (1983), suggested legislation at the state level as a possible substitute for federal regulation of insider trading.

93. See Frank H. Easterbrook and Daniel R. Fischel, "Voting in Corporate Law," *Journal of Law and Economics, 26*, 395 (1983).

94. Indeed, shareholders delegate extensively to managers and almost always endorse their decisions; Easterbrook and Fischel, ibid.

95. See Michael C. Jensen and William H. Meckling, "Theory of the Firm: Managerial Behavior, Agency Costs and Ownership Structure," *Journal of Financial Economics, 4*, 305 (1976). The manager's actions could, however, be aligned with shareholders' interests by proper managerial employment contracts [Clifford W. Smith and Ross L. Watts, "The Structure of Managerial Compensation Contracts and the Control of Management," University of Rochester working paper, (1983)], or by the monitoring of the market for managers [Eugene F. Fama, "Agency Problems and the Theory of the Firm," *Journal of Political Economics, 88*, 288 (1980)]. Carlton and Fischel *supra* note 92 at 863, suggested that in the long run, the evolutionary process will bring about the optimal set of contracts since firms with the "wrong" charters will be at a competitive disadvantage.

96. This goal can be attained by a properly designed managerial compensation scheme and by proper monitoring of the manager.

97. It could be argued that the absence of takeover-impeding measures would not necessarily reflect shareholders' preferences if we assume that facilitating takeovers were in the management interests while conflicting with those of stockholders; but this is unreasonable. Antitakeover measures are known to be often desirable by target firms' incumbent managements who seek to protect their interests at the shareholders' expense. For an in-depth analysis of the conflict of interest between management and shareholders in tender offers see Gilson, *supra* note 54.

98. A vote on auctioneering-type measures can be taken in annual meetings of shareholders which convene in any event, or it can be added to the list of issues stockholders are asked to vote on by proxy.

99 While we derive conclusions from the absence of antitakeover measures, we can hardly infer from their presence that they necessarily benefit shareholders: Managers who prefer such measures may sometimes succeed in inducing uninformed shareholders to adopt them, and shareholders may sometimes err Also, differences in ownership structure (diffused versus concentrated ownership) and in the cost of monitoring (e.g., it is more costly to monitor a firm with "noisy" information) may also account for the ability of managers to institute

antitakeover measures even when they are against shareholders' interests. This may account for the negative returns we observe in some firms when these measures have been adopted, perhaps reflecting the response of informed investors. Yet learning is not inconsistent with stockholders' rationality, and we observe (see pp. 329–31) that in time, firms tend to abandon value-decreasing measures. But once instituted, removing these measures may not be feasible because of managerial opposition and the collective action problem in voting. Still, there may be cases where antitakeover measures coincide with shareholders' objectives: Some firms may use these measures to signal inside information to potential raiders, even though it is costly. Or, in Bebchuk's view, some shareholders may prefer to reduce the probability of takeover for a higher premium once a takeover takes place.

100. A long delay period may be considered invalid under present laws; see notes 57 and 85 *supra*.
101. Bebchuk-b, *supra* note 4.

CHAPTER 14

TAKEOVER DEFENSE V. CORPORATE AUCTIONS: LAW AND PRACTICE AFTER MACMILLAN

Theodore N. Mirvis

INTRODUCTION

In considering corporate auction law and practice and its relationship to the legal rules applicable to takeover defense, I would divide the presentation into three parts:

1. Under what circumstances does the law impose on a board of directors the special legal rules pertaining to what we loosely call corporate auctions, that is, the so-called Revlon duty to seek the highest price for the stockholders;[1]

2. What is the substantive content of these special legal rules, considering in particular the Delaware Supreme Court's recent opinion in Macmillan;[2] and

3. How are these rules likely to be refined as the legal constructs meet reality in the cases ahead.

Theodore N. Mirvis is a partner in the law firm of Wachtell, Lipton, Rosen & Katz. Mr. Mirvis received his J.D. degree from Harvard Law School in 1976.

REVLON LAND

The issue of when a board will find itself in Revlon land is, analytically, the flip-side of the "just say no" coin.

When and if we permit a target's board of directors to "just say no"—to reject a merger proposal or a tender offer and simply stand behind its poison pill rights plan without embarking on any short-term value creation in competition with the takeover bid—we are recognizing that there is no reason for the law of fiduciary duty to force the directors to depart from their traditional role of managing the business and affairs of the company. That traditional role, of course, is subject to the duties of loyalty and care, which are generally thought to be consistent with the promotion of *long-term* stockholder and corporate values, with minimal legal interference.

The opposite end of the spectrum is Revlon's imposition of a confining duty to seek to maximize immediate stockholder value—a legal duty that Chancellor Allen in the TW Services case[3] recently described as a "radically altered state."

The easy case, of course, is when the board itself puts the company up for sale (as in Revlon itself and in such cases as RJR Nabisco,[4] J.P. Stevens,[5] and Macmillan).

The middle case, or series of cases, is when the board reacts to a takeover bid by proposing itself to radically change the company through a restructuring—which may involve a change of effective or negative control (as in American Standard[6] and Macmillan I[7]), or may by itself be neutral as to control (as in Interco[8] and Pillsbury[9]). Macmillan does seem to decide that if the restructuring has control impacts, then the board can no longer claim to be basing its conduct on the long term but rather will be subjected to the Revlon requirement of immediate value maximization.

And then there is "just say no." Seen from the Revlon vantage point, the "just say no" issue is whether a board can be Revlon'ed against its will: whether the receipt of a takeover bid justifies removing the board's long-term management power, and forcing it to go out and seek the highest immediate sale price.

This way of looking at "just say no" is suggested both by the TW Services case and by Macmillan itself.

In TW Services, the Court of Chancery had before it a hostile all-shares, all-cash premium tender offer; 88 percent of the shares had been tendered; the target board had refused to negotiate; and the hostile bidder was asking the court to knock out the pill. For all the world, it looked like a knock-out case after the one-two punch of Interco and Pillsbury.

But, unlike Interco and Pillsbury, the tender offer was conditioned on board approval—it was a "first say yes" condition. And the court held that this condition changed everything since under the Delaware statute—as is universally the case—board approval is an absolute prerequisite to stockholder consideration of a merger. There can never be a merger unless the board first says yes. Whether or not to say yes, the court held, was to be judged by the plain vanilla business judgment rule requirements of loyalty and care—unlike whether or not to say no to a pill redemption request, which is judged under the additional Unocal test of objective proportionality between the board's position and the threat to the corporation represented by the takeover bid.[10]

While the TW opinion recognized the "anomaly" in such disparate treatment of merger decisions versus pill decisions, the opinion also distinguishes the recap/pill cases (Interco and Pillsbury) from the "just say no" case by making the point that the Revlon short-term duty operates much differently when a board itself radically changes the company in a manner functionally equivalent to a sale. The Chancellor contrasted the case of simple resistance:

> But what of a situation in which the board resists a sale? May a board find itself thrust involuntarily into a Revlon mode in which it is required to take only steps designed to maximize current share value and in which it must desist from steps that would impede that goal, even if they might otherwise appear sustainable as an arguable step in the promotion of "long term" corporate or share values? Revlon did not address that subject but implied that a board might find itself in such a position when it said that the duty it speaks of arose "when the break-up of the company is inevitable."

In Macmillan, the Delaware Supreme Court succinctly raised the "just say no" issue in similar terms. The Court noted that the initial inquiry under Revlon is whether the company is "for sale," and further: "Clearly not every offer or transaction affecting the corporate structure invokes the Revlon duties." While the Court was not called upon to delineate which offers, if any, do and which do not invoke the Revlon duties, there is great significance in how the issue is framed. It is one thing to consider the question to be governed by concepts of stockholder choice and corporate democracy; it is another to speak of compelling the board to the single-minded duty to maximize immediate value.

The question that "just say no" raises is thus a Revlon/Macmillan

question—is the fact of a premium all-cash, all-shares tender offer sufficient to trigger the Revlon duty and usurp the directors' usual management powers. Or, in a formulation suggested by TW Services, should a
board be any more forbidden to "just say no" to a tender offer than it
should be forced to "first say yes" to a merger.

AUCTION LAW

As to the content of the Revlon duty when it does attach, we now have the
Macmillan opinion.

I would take as my thesis that Macmillan will prove to have created a
doctrinal structure that is appropriately deferential to the complexity of
the corporate auction process. Just as Unocal—a case that upheld very
strong defensive action (a self-tender that excluded the bidder)—is now
seen as a powerful limit on takeover defense via the objective proportionality test, so too Macmillan—a case that threw out a result it found to be
the product of a tainted process—has endorsed broadly the concepts necessary to preserve the exercise of business judgment in the design and
effectuation of corporate auctions.

In short, I would suggest that both Unocal and Macmillan will prove
to be examples of hard cases making good law.

The key point here, to my mind, is that Macmillan recognizes the
conflict between, on the one hand, the goal of stockholder value maximization
and, on the other hand, the rhetoric of procedural "fairness" or "even-
handedness" or "neutrality" in the conduct of the sale process.

Before Macmillan, there was fear that the courts would compel absolute
equal treatment of bidders, and take the auction analogy literally to displace
all business judgment; there was fear that courts would create legal rules
that would not take into account the fact that a fair and neutral auction in
many cases will not get the best price.

Macmillan should quiet that fear. Macmillan defines the required fairness as "fairness in the interest of promoting the highest values reasonably
attainable for the stockholders' benefit." It is "fairness in the sense that
stockholder interests are enhanced." Macmillan thus recognizes that the route
to the highest price will often not be the route that is most "fair" to all
bidders—it is fairness to the stockholders, not bidders, that ought to count.

Indeed, uneven, discriminatory treatment of bidders is often unavoid-
able and essential to promote the highest price, whether

- in access to confidential information, where a board tries to lay down equal ground rules that impact unequal bidders differently;
- in access to management presentations, where this valuable and short-supply asset must be expended in a discriminatory way;
- in inducements to bid, where competing bidders often are absolutely unwilling to play without assurance of compensation for their time and prestige should they lose, especially against the original bidder who has a tremendous research head start and usually, via a toehold stake in the target, a built-in bidding advantage and break-up fee.

Macmillan makes clear that discrimination between bidders to enhance shareholder interests is valid; that discrimination will be struck down only if there is no "rational basis for the action" in terms of stockholder interests; that there is no standard formula to run an auction; and that, in a grafting of the Unocal defense test, if there is unequal treatment (that is, any departure from the Sotheby/Christie's model of "here is a painting, what am I bid"), there must be:

1. a perception by the directors that shareholder interests are being enhanced, and

2. a reasonable relationship between the discrimination and the stockholder advantage sought to be achieved.

Macmillan thus recognizes that the running of corporate auctions, like takeover defense, is an art not a science, but need not simplistically resemble an art auction. And Macmillan promises that the board will be given the power to set the auction rules, to be an effective not a passive auctioneer—subject only to ensuring that the rules and practices are designed to promote the maximum bid.

APPLYING MACMILLAN

The challenge for the courts now will be in applying Macmillan, in fleshing out the common law, just as the challenge after Unocal was, and continues to be, the ever more subtle application of the proportionality test.

To posit a few possible issues and variants:

1. *The typical lock-up case:* Assume that the hostile bidder begins at $80; a competing bidder (the white knight) bids $82; the bidding continues in similar increments until there is an announced final round with the original hostile bidder at $90. The competing bidder then says: "I'll bid

$91 subject to an asset lock-up; without it, I will walk and publicly announce that I'm walking."

Of course, there are no legal constraints on what bidders may demand. Bidders are not subject to any fiduciary duties. A bidder can demand that the directors paint their faces blue as a condition to its bid. The board must assess if the competing bidder really will walk, and, if so, what will the hostile bidder do. It is one thing to guess whether refusal of a bidder's unreasonable demand (blue paint) will result in the bidder's taking a walk; it is quite another matter when the demand (a lock-up) makes economic sense from the viewpoint of a bidder who views his franchise as being on the line.

If the board believes the competing bidder will walk, the risk is that the hostile bidder is no longer at $90, but back to $80, or perhaps $85. Under the Macmillan test, what the lock-up gets is not $1 for shareholders, but $11 or $6—that is, there is a *substantial* benefit.

Note that hostile bidders, like Perelman in Revlon and Maxwell in Macmillan, often claim they will beat any other bid by some small amount (25¢ in Revlon). But without a lock-up, there is no other bid. Can it be that to *fulfill* its Revlon fiduciary duty—to get the last 25¢ from bidder X—a board must *breach* its fiduciary duty by giving a lock-up to bidder Y? And query whether a board may properly say at the outset that it will not consider this kind of stalking horse bid—as the RJR Nabisco special committee apparently did when its guidelines specified that it would give no consideration to a bid whose price varied depending on the price of another party's bid (Rule G of the RJR Rules and Procedures.)

2. *The disclosed lock-up case:* One possible result of Macmillan may be for the target to lay out in advance to all bidders what impediments it is willing to give to the high bidder, assuming it is using the technique of competing bids with a deadline. In that case, query if the lock-up is disparate treatment at all, since it was available to everyone.

While the hostile bidder who knows he can go 25¢ higher than anyone else will cry foul, why shouldn't a board be permitted to say in advance that there will be a deadline for best bids, and that it will enforce that deadline with a lock-up to the best bidder? It is certainly reasonable for an auctioneer to use the technique of one-round sealed bids. Without an effective auction-ending lock-up, the board/auctioneer has no way to enforce a best-bids deadline. The result is a second look for the low bidder, who now knows how little he can bid and still top. If an auctioneer has the responsibility to seek the highest bid, he must also have the power to cajole, threaten, and force the bidders to do things they don't want to do, but which are designed to make them pay more than they want to.

3. *Just say no:* Finally, to return to "just say no": If we continue the auction analogy, just saying no to a bid on grounds of price inadequacy is in effect setting a reserve price, and implementing a defensive restructuring with a blended price above the bid price is in effect using a house bidder to enforce the reserve price.

If we are serious about not interfering with a board's ability to run an effective auction, then shouldn't the right and practical ability to set a reserve price also be protected?

CONCLUSION

The lawyers, of course, will look to the courts for the answers—or, rather, the courts will give them to us whether we want them or not. But we both look to the financial theorists to buttress the point that there is no one way to sell a company, and that impediments and inducements are a necessary part of the effort to maximize price.

Notes

1. Revlon, Inc. v. MacAndrews & Forbes Holdings, Inc., Del. Supr., 506 A.2d 173 (1986).
2. Mills Acquisition Co. v. Macmillan, Inc., Del. Supr., No. 4156, 1988 (May 3, 1989) (written decision).
3. TW Services, Inc. v. SWT Acquisition Corp., Del. Ch., C.A. No. 10427, Allen, C. (March 2, 1989).
4. *In re* RJR Nabisco, Inc. Shareholders Litigation, Del. Ch., C.A. No. 10389 (Consolidated), Allen, C. (Jan. 31, 1989).
5. *In re* J. P. Stevens & Co., Inc. Shareholders Litigation, Del. Ch., 542 A.2d 770 (1988).
6. Black & Decker Corp. v. American Standard Inc., D. Del., 682 F. Supp. 772 (1988).
7. Robert M. Bass Group, Inc. v. Evans, Del. Ch., 552 A.2d 1227 (1988).
8. City Capital Associates Ltd. Partnership v. Interco Inc., Del. Ch., 551 A.2d 787 (1988).
9. Grand Metropolitan Public Ltd. Co. v. Pillsbury Co., Del. Ch., C.A. Nos. 10319, 10323 (Consolidated), Duffy, J. (Dec. 16, 1988).
10. Unocal Corp. v. Mesa Petroleum Co., Del. Supr., 493 A.2d 946 (1985).

CHAPTER 15

AUCTION DUTIES AND OTHER PRACTICES: COMMENTS ON CHAPTERS 11–14

William Rifkin
Andrew G. T. Moore II
Lowell E. Sachnoff

WILLIAM RIFKIN

I will take a business rather than a legal perspective in discussing the issue of whether companies should be auctioned off at all rather than sold on a negotiated basis. The issue whether or not to auction a company once the decision to sell has been made is relevant not only to the sale of public companies but the sale of the subsidiaries as well. Yet, in the case of a subsidiary, because the seller is a company rather than public shareholders, these types of transactions have avoided judicial scrutiny. However, these transactions were often quite significant and could have a great impact on shareholder value.

William D. Rifkin (A.B. degree Stanford and M.B.A. Harvard) is a Managing Director of Salomon Brothers Inc. and Co-Head of the Merger and Acquisition (M&A) Group.

The Honorable Andrew G. T. Moore II has been Justice of the Delaware Supreme Court since 1982. His J.D. degree was from Tulane University. As a member of the Delaware Supreme Court, Justice Moore has authored many corporate opinions of national interest, including the following cases: *Macmillan, Newmont Mining, Revlon, Inc.,* and *Unocal.*

Lowell E. Sachnoff is a senior partner in the firm of Sachnoff & Weaver, Ltd. He is a graduate of Harvard Law School.

There is no question that auctions have helped to propel prices to higher levels. Take the RJR-Nabisco deal for instance. The initial bid by management was $70, the management group ultimately raised its bid to $112. In the Holly Farms deal, the original offer was on the order of $50, but soon after an offer was made at $73.50. Arguably, however, the poison pill has had more to do with raising bidding prices than the auction itself. Nevertheless, auctions have contributed to this increase in values.

In my view, it is very important that the courts continue to avoid prescribing precise rules as to how the auctions should be conducted. In this respect I think the Macmillan decision was exceptionally thoughtful; colorful language notwithstanding, I think it was quite restrained.

It is necessary to establish clear objectives for auctions such as the maximization of shareholders' value within a reasonable time frame. But it is also necessary to avoid creating cosmetic auction procedures which could lead to suboptimal results. It is important to allow experienced brokers the discretion to exercise their judgment in the sale process. The key is that an auction be *effective* rather than what the layman might consider to be *fair*. There is a lot of talk in our business about creating a level playing field. On a level playing field, the San Francisco 49'ers would crush Colombia every time. And sometimes a tilted playing field might propel certain participants to even higher bids.

Next, consider the question whether or not an auction should be held, when it is at the discretion of the seller; consider, for example the case when no public disclosure has been made or the business being sold is private. The first issue that we have to face is the risk that as a matter of policy certain highly qualified bidders may simply refuse to participate in a wide open auction process. As a broker or a seller of business, we have to weigh the trade-off between the quantity or number of bidders and the quality of the sale process. It has been my experience that bidders will discount the price they are prepared to offer for uncertainty. The more comfort they have with the property they are bidding on, the more likely they are to bid their maximum price. And from a practical standpoint a company can only entertain so many bidders and allow them to conduct only a limited amount of diligence. The RJR deal makes it very clear that you only need two bidders to have an effective auction. You do not need multiple bidders.

When selling private companies, it is not unusual for an investment banker to approach well over 100 bidders initially. If that is an open auction, I question whether it necessarily will result in the highest price. Further, consider the likelihood that you will discourage bidders from participating just because they perceive their probability of success to be quite low. If the bidder feels he has a legitimate chance of winning because only a few parties have been invited to bid, he is more likely to participate. And most people once they get involved in bids hate to lose; quite often they end up bidding more than they ever had imagined. Finally, in many cases it is not important even to have a second bidder because of the strength of the poison pill. The seller always has the ability simply to refuse to redeem the pill at least over some period of time. This has been quite effective in getting bidders to raise their price. The Kraft sale, I think, was ample evidence of this. Sometimes from the business standpoint, confidentiality can be quite critical. A premature leak of a deal could kill it and create irreparable harm to the target. This is particularly true with respect to professional service businesses. An example might be Drexel's recent sale of its brokerage business . Once it announced that it was going to sell the business, a number of key salesmen simply left the firm. They were quite mobile. Had this deal been announced as *fait accompli*—had these brokers known where their future home was going to be—it is quite conceivable that fewer of them would have left. What do auction rules mean in such cases?

After RJR, I think most bidders presume there will be multiple rounds of bidding, and as a result, I think, they are more and more likely to hold back increasingly large amounts of money. How will the seller ever know that they have squeezed the last dollar out of the bidder? How will the bidder know that this round is going to be the last round? Eventually the bidders will figure out how this system works. Quite possibly nothing will be gained by subjecting bidders to more than one round.

Finally, I would like to touch upon lock-ups more from a human behavior standpoint than a legal standpoint. In my experience the last price raise by a buyer is typically a very emotional and politically difficult decision. Bidders often hire a financial adviser who told them what would be a reasonable price for the property. But more often than not the final price that is offered is well above the maximum value that the bidder had initially envisioned bidding. A lock-up is important as much as anything else as a face-saving measure to the bidder. If the bidder is topped, some sort of a lock-up such as a breakup fee or optional shares is a consolation price; they lost but they go back to their board of directors and say that we gained something from the process. If, on the other hand, they win the bid, having paid a very large price, it will be many years before it can be determined whether the price was a reasonable one or not.

JUDGE ANDREW G. T. MOORE II

I think I agree with most of what the legal members of the panel have been saying. As for the other very interesting comments I was once accused of speaking about Alice in Wonderland but I won't; I will restrain myself on that today. I want to consider the history of the role of directors as we have seen it evolve. And I am going to speak of pre-Van Gorkom. That means pre-the announcement of the decision—the so-called Trans Union decision—which I always referred to as Smith versus Van Gorkom or Van Gorkom and post-Van Gorkom.

It was very interesting to hear Mr. Evans this morning. He expressed what I would consider the pre-Van Gorkom philosophy of the role of directors. The problem presented in Van Gorkom was precisely that which results when directors who fail to recognize that their role is one based upon very serious, very demanding fiduciary requirements. The director who believes that the role is to come to a meeting once a month, never challenge the CEO because that would be considered bad form, and not criticize one's fellows and ask the hard questions, those are the types of directors who end up with the problems that the Trans Union directors faced. If independent directors are to achieve the role that, at least our Court believes is required of them, then one is going to expect those directors to be prepared to make the hard choices and to be prepared to spend the time, at least in the big takeover cases where we have seen maximization of shareholder value. In the Federated case, for example, and in the RJR case and in many others, directors found themselves virtual prisoners, locked in almost continuously dealing with the problems that each day's events required them to address.

I heard the reference this morning again from Mr. Evans to the effect that it is now necessary to build a record. Well, if the purpose is solely to build a record and not to have utilized your role in a substantive manner, then I find that to be consistent with *pre*-Van Gorkom philosophy. If anyone thinks that Van Gorkom is directed to setting or establishing a method by which lawyers and investment bankers can simply build a record, they are making a very serious mistake because it overlooks the very substantive requirements that those decisions impose upon the directors. It would be the greatest mistake for a director to think that the decision in Smith v. Van Gorkom is a relief act for lawyers and investment bankers, although I have heard it described that way.

Now let us turn for the moment to the question of an auction. It was the law before Macmillan that you do not have to auction a company at the mere drop of a hat or upon a receipt of any bid or bear hug or whatever overture might come your way. The Delaware Courts have said that and I don't think there is anything unique in that principle. The failure of a board to accept an offer, if it is based upon all the factors that enter into a business judgement, is as much a business decision as any other.

There are two footnotes in the Macmillan opinion that I would recommend to any serious reader. One is footnote 29 which appears on page 48 of the opinion; there we were talking about receipt of bids where we say the proper objective of Macmillan's fiduciary was to obtain the highest price reasonably available for the company provided it was offered by a reputable and responsible bidder. And then we said, "In accessing the bid and the bidder's responsibility, a board may consider among various proper factors the adequacy and terms of the offer, its fairness and feasibility, the proposed or actual financing for the offer and the consequences of that' financing; questions of illegality, the impact on both the bid and the potential acquisition on other constituencies provided that it bears some reasonable relationship to general shareholder interests; the risk of nonconsummation, the basic stockholder interests at stake, the bidders identity, prior background, and other business venture experiences, and the bidder's business plans for the corporation and their effects on stockholder interests," citing Unocal, Newmont and Revlon.

And then we talked about the power of a Board to refuse to entertain a bid. In footnote 35 we said this Court has been required to determine on other occasions since our decision on Revlon whether a company is for sale. Clearly not every offer or transaction affecting the corporate structure invokes the Revlon duties. A refusal to entertain offers may conform with a valid exercise of business judgement. And then there is a much more extended discussion about what that might mean. What we see here, having evolved from Smith v. Van Gorkom is a greater sense of duty placed upon the outside independent directors. Without their participation, the business judgment rule under the present decisions is simply unavailable.

It certainly behooves management not only to insulate itself from the process (which was not done in Macmillan) but to remove itself from the process where the management is not disinterested and to place upon the independent outside directors the true responsibilities. That means when you talk about independent outside directors, as another footnote of Macmillan would seem to indicate, it does not mean bringing in dad's old college classmate to head up the committee and the committee actually not doing much work. It means imposing upon the committee all of the obligations that one understands to be the fiduciary duties of directors. So what you have heard today from the other practicing members of the bar I think is very consistent with what our decisions have been saying in the takeover field both from the standpoint of maximizing shareholder value in the face of an auction and also perhaps maximizing shareholder value under circumstances where it does not appear that this is the moment to sell the company.

LOWELL E. SACHNOFF

In the old days Harold Geneen, a famous corporate tycoon, used to describe the role of the outside directors the way he liked to see them—as mushrooms. That is, they were to be kept in the dark, they were to be plied with liquid refreshments, and they were to be fed plenteous quantities of horse manure. It is a funny story but not really. And anybody who thinks that Justice Moore is not really serious when he said that in large part the responsibility for corporate governance in these control contests rests with outside directors, ought to take a look at yet another footnote that he put in the Macmillan case. Namely, footnote 32. Footnote 32 is something we lawyers call *dictum*. That is, he did not have to put this in the case because it was not necessary for a decision. But he said the question of the independent director's personal liability—the directors who are getting their $25,000 a year in this $3 billion takeover—is not the issue in the challenged decisions reached under circumstances borne of the board's lack of oversight. Now, Justice Moore could have stopped there. But he did not. Rather he said, that we entertain no doubt of this board's virtual abandonment of its oversight functions in the face of Evans's and Raleigh's patent self-interests breached its fundamental duties of loyalty and care in the conduct of an auction.

Now somewhere there is a tension between the notion of independent directors who all have other jobs (whether they run companies or they used to run companies or they are professors or retired lawyers or accountants) and the notion that in a very realistic sense they sit at the very bottom of an inverted pyramid in our country's economy. In one sense the future of free enterprise as we know it rests on the ability of independent directors to discharge their duties in faithful way. If they don't, we are going to get government regulation or federal chartering of corporations. Everybody who is an independent director or who is going to be one ought to read this footnote very carefully because the law of Delaware as articulated in the Revlon and Unocal and now in Macmillan imposes immense responsibilities on independent directors. Since most public companies have boards that are dominated by independent directors, they cannot be mushrooms anymore. They have to take an active role in these decisions of real consequence.

Now, who are these independent directors? They are the ones who serve on the special committees, and who can't blindly rely on expert opinions; they have to go behind the opinions of lawyers, bankers, and other expert witnesses. Maybe they have to get second opinions too on some of these things. The independent investors research group has done a study of the Fortune 500 companies and almost 70 percent of the outside directors of these companies are made up of men who are either current CEOs, former CEOs who are retired, or people in management who are on the CEO career path. There is a great potential here for structural bias, a kind of old-boy clubbing that Justice Moore alluded to in a metaphorical way in his opinion in Macmillan. So I take issue with Mr. Evans's conclusion that "they should be supportive and they should be quietly counseling management." I think that if that is customary behavior of directors of public companies, it is an abdication of their responsibility to monitor in an effective way the performance of the management.

I do not think everybody has to go to the extreme of Ross Perot and get on the public soap box and lambaste the company that he is director of. Somewhere between Mr. Evans's view on the responsibility of the outside directors and the Perot type is the golden mean. Otherwise these directors who are exposed to the immense responsibility simply will not be able to discharge it.

Now, my second point, that relates to auctions, has to do with the very next footnote which is footnote 33. Footnote 33 has to do not so much with the outside directors who got a profound shock in footnote 32, but this is another piece of dictum in the case in which Justice Moore is talking about the investment bankers. He said although the investment banker was not a Macmillan officer or director it is bedrock law that the conduct of the one who knowingly joins with a fiduciary including corporate officials in breaching the fiduciary obligation is equally culpable. Clearly investment bankers are major players in these struggles for corporate control with the bidders and the targets, but there are a host of other experts who play roles, who would fit squarely into this category: lawyers, accountants, engineers, appraisers, proxy solicitors. Like when rhinoceroses fight, they always have little birds that sit on their backs waiting to peck off things to eat; birds who pick up the golden crumbs in all of these transactions. If these people are in league with faithless fiduciaries who are breaching their duties, and if they give them substantial assistance, they are liable for large amounts of money in potential later lawsuits.

Next, I want to comment on a very serious point that I heard Professor Grossman make about his concern that since all marginal discussions are business decisions, are they all subject to judicial evaluation? The decisions whether you make widgets or gadgets are business decisions for sure but those are decisions about institutional competence in which courts don't have any expertise. Some judges may have the ability but they do not have the staff, the inclination, and the time necessary to say that if you decide to go into widgets rather than the gadgets and lose a lot money, that you or the managers and directors should be liable. I do think that there is a distinction in the context of *contests* for corporate control of auctions because there the issue is whether a bidder can make a direct contact with an owner or the shareholder and say I would like to buy your stock at *x* dollars, and get a direct answer. The great strength of the Unocal opinion is that when management is involved in potential conflicts of interest—for example, its own self-interest in seeking to maintain its jobs and its perks—that is something that the courts have very special competence to handle. That is quite unlike questions as to whether to make widgets or gadgets. It links in to hundreds of years of equitable jurisdiction in the law of trusts and other fiduciary relationships where courts can look at situations and say here is one where managers as fiduciaries are acting in their own self-interest rather than putting their interests aside at the door in favor of the beneficiaries of their fiduciary relationship, in this case the stockholders. I think that there is an important conceptual difference in business decisions that relate to real output/input decisions in a corporation as opposed to what happens in contests for corporate control of a corporation.

The last point I wanted to make about Macmillan refers to a footnote, too. Sometimes absolutely the best things come in footnotes. Many times expert opinions are like real estate appraisals which are made as instructed. Take the typical clash between high-priced experts: one who says the value is *X and* the other says it is *Y*. And then, three days or two weeks later they all change their calculations for reasons that sometimes are not explicable. Justice Moore in footnote 40 on page 62 of the Macmillan decision quoted an earlier decision by Chancellor Allen, in the Fort Howard decision where he said "due regard for the protective nature of stockholders in class action requires in these cases to be suspicious, to exercise such powers as it may possess to look imaginatively beneath the surface of events which in most instances will be well crafted and unobjectionable." I suggest that courts maintain healthy skepticism, perhaps even a touch of cynicism, about some of the expert opinions that they are confronted with these cases.

As long as courts look beneath the surface of events to the realities of what is going on coupled with better ways to pick independent outside directors, this will comprise a two-prong force capable of protecting shareholder interests throughout this string of corporate takeover fights that we face.

PART 4

VALUE ADDITIVITY BY CORPORATE RESTRUCTURING

CHAPTER 16

THE ECONOMICS OF CORPORATE RESTRUCTURING: AN OVERVIEW

James L. Bicksler
Andrew H. Chen

INTRODUCTION

The primary purpose of this paper is to provide an economic overview of the major issues relating to corporate restructurings. In the 1980s, restructuring has become a major activity in the U.S. corporate world. Further, some frequently used methods of corporate restructuring have been controversial and have attracted a great deal of attention among corporate executives, investment bankers, institutional and individual investors, regulators, and financial economists. Indeed, there is a continuing debate on whether or not corporate restructurings are productive and beneficial for the U.S. economy and what constitutes the specific sources of value for corporate restructurings. A corporate restructuring involves, for example, an alteration of a firm's business goals and strategies through a change in the composi-

James L. Bicksler, who holds a Ph.D. in finance from the Stern School of Business, NYU, is a Professor of Finance at Rutgers University Graduate School of Management. He has published in professional journals and has edited books in corporate finance, capital markets, and portfolio analysis.

Andrew H. Chen is Distinguished Professor of Finance, Edwin L. Cox School of Business, Southern Methodist University. Professor Chen holds a Ph.D. degree from the University of California, Berkeley.

tion of its assets and/or the composition of its liabilities as well as its organizational form—ownership structure. In a broad sense, corporate restructurings encompass virtually all of the corporate activities, including the less routine decisions such as relocating corporate headquarters and hiring or firing the corporate CEOs, and the possibly more frequent decisions such as temporarily closing down certain operation units, the sale or disposition of assets or business units, and corporate mergers and acquisitions. Also, corporate restructuring has emerged as a potent defensive mechanism in the environment of hostile corporate takeover activities. However, our analysis in this paper will focus primarily, though not exclusively, on corporate restructurings undertaken outside of a corporate control contest. In other words, we shall examine corporate restructuring as a corporate strategy that enhances the shareholder value, rather than as a defensive technique pertinent to the threat of hostile takeovers. However, it should be noted that the enhancement in a firm's public stock market value will reduce the threat of actual and potential hostile takeovers.[1] Therefore, many of the considerations relevant to a corporate restructuring within a nontakeover context are also relevant to corporate antitakeover strategy and tactics. If a corporation periodically reformulates and implements its re-structuring plans to enhance its shareholder value, it can also have the side effect of fending off actual or potential hostile takeovers.

By corporate restructuring is meant firm decisions about its choices of real and financial assets, capital structure mix, organizational form, and executive compensation policies that enhance the market value of the firm's shares. Although the major methods employed in corporate restructuring plans often involve several complex and interrelated decisions and transactions, it is useful to classify the methods of corporate restructurings into two major categories: (1) *assets restructurings* that include the transactions that change the ownership and the composition of the firm's assets for saving taxes and for better utilization of the resources, such as sales or dispositions of assets and business units, corporate split-ups and spin-offs; and (2) *financial restructurings* or recapitalizations that include transactions that significantly change the composition of equity ownership as well as the leverage of the firm, such as share repurchases through self-tenders, exchange offers, and the creation of leveraged ESOPs. Our economic perspective with regard to corporate restructurings is that of the normative goal of maximizing present shareholder wealth.

The reasons why corporate restructuring is an important and timely topic in today's global economy include its impact on the markets for products, labor, financial services, and corporate control. More specifically, it has major implications for corporate efficiency and productivity, which in turn influence our global competitiveness. Corporate restructuring is presently a high dollar volume activity in which a large portion of corporate America participates.

The paper is organized as follows. The following section sets forth the foundations of corporate share valuation. The third section details the possible sources of shareholder wealth creation from restructurings. The fourth section describes major types of corporate restructurings widely employed by large U.S. corporations in the recent past. An optimal corporate restructuring strategy is developed in the fifth section. The final section summarizes our major conclusions.

FOUNDATIONS OF CORPORATE SHARE VALUATION

Maximizing the present market value of shares of a corporation is the goal of both corporate strategy in general and corporate restructuring in particular. Therefore, in the analysis of economic issues in corporate restructuring and recapitalization, it is helpful to start with brief discussions of share valuation. In general economic terms, the market value of any financial asset is equal to the present value of the stream of expected future cash flows accruing to the owner of the asset. The uncertainty and the timing of the future cash flows accruing to the owner of the asset are the key determinants of the market value of the asset.

Two conceptually equivalent approaches to the asset valuation have been commonly used in the literature: (1) the *risk-adjusted-discount-rate* (RADR) approach, which states that the market value of a financial asset is equal to the present value of the stream of expected future cash flows discounted at an appropriate discount rate or the cost of capital which reflects the risks of the cash flows, and (2) the *certainty-equivalent* (CEQ) approach, which states that the market value of a financial asset is equal to the present value of the stream of certainty-equivalents of future cash flows discounted at a risk-free rate of interest. In the RADR approach, the risks or uncertainties of a financial asset's future cash flows are reflected in the appropriate discount rate or the cost of capital for the asset. A financial asset's cost of capital should consist of a risk-free rate of interest, a premium for the business risk as well as a premium for financing risk of the asset. A financial asset which has a higher risk in its future cash flows will require a higher appropriate discount rate in valuation and hence will result in a lower market value. On the other hand, in the CEQ approach, the risks or uncertainties of the asset's future cash flows are reflected in the certain-equivalents of the cash flows, obtained by subtracting the risk premiums from the expected cash flows. A financial asset which has a higher degree of uncertainty in its cash flows means a lower amount of certain-equivalent and thus a lower market value. The standard representations of these two valuation approaches are as follows:

1. *The RADR Approach:*

$$V_0 = \sum_{t=1}^{n} \frac{\overline{C}_t}{(1 + k)^t} \qquad (16.1)$$

where
V_0 = the market value of the financial asset;
C_t = the expected net cash flows in period t ;
k = the appropriate or risk-adjusted discount rate.

2. *The CEQ Approach:*

$$V_0 = \sum_{t=1}^{n} \frac{C_t^*}{(1 + r)^t} \qquad (16.2)$$

where
C_t^* = the certainty-equivalent of cash flows in period t ;
r = the risk-free rate of interest.

The common shares of a corporation represent the residual claims of the firm. Therefore, the net cash flows available to the shareholders are defined as the total cash inflows generated by the firm from sales minus the cash costs of productions that include the cost of raw materials, the cost of labor, and the cost of debt. In the presence of corporate income taxes, the tax deductions and the tax payments should be included in the calculation of net aftertax cash flows in the valuation of shares. Thus, corporate strategies are differentiated by their impact on the magnitudes and uncertainties of expected future residual cash flows accruing to the shareholders. Indeed, conceptually corporate strategies are simply different vectors of corporate decision options affecting and significantly altering the magnitude and the timing of both the firm's cash inflows and cash expenditures and hence the market value of its shares. A corollary proposition is that the expected future net cash flows are determined by the vector of corporate decisions with regard, for example, to the choice of the assets, the expenditures, and the capital structure. At any future point in time, the firm has a number of alternative strategies which impact differently upon the future cash flows and hence have varying valuation consequences. This means that an understanding of the determinants of the expected future net cash flows to shareholders is essential in formulating

FIGURE 16–1
Relations among Firm's Decisions and Product and Financial Markets

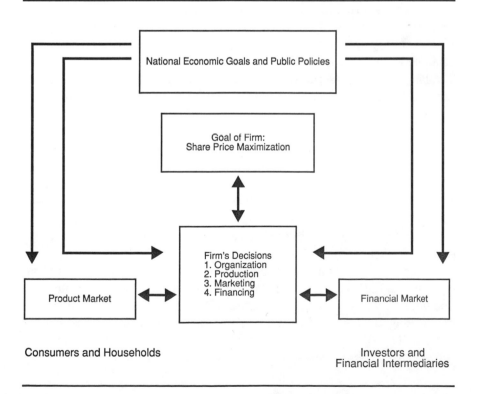

value maximizing corporate strategies. Figure 16–1 shows the relationships among various firm decisions and their linkage with both the product and financial markets. It is the interplay of corporate decisions within markets overtime that determines the net future cash flows and the market value of common shares of the firm.

POSSIBLE SOURCES OF VALUE CREATION

In the following we shall discuss some factors from which corporate restructurings can generate value for the shareholders of the firm.

Tax Benefits

Evidence from several recent studies has shown that obtaining tax benefits is one of the most important factors that encourage corporations to restructure themselves for the purpose of enhancing shareholder value.[2] Tax benefits in corporate restructurings and recapitalizations may come from several sources. First, a sale of assets with substantially high fair market value in a restructuring transaction may step up the tax basis of the assets and generate value for shareholders by increasing the depreciation deductions. Similarly, a sale of assets with their fair market value below the tax basis can also increase shareholder value by allowing the firm to cash in immediately the tax deduction from the "unrealized" loss.

Second, an increase in interest deductions generated by larger amount of debt typically used in LBOs, leveraged MBOs, leveraged asset acquisitions, and in the leveraged recapitalizations such as leveraged share repurchases certainly will create shareholder value. Besides the beneficial tax effect, high leverage will increase wealth for shareholders by the "debt control hypothesis" of Jensen [1986] wherein agency costs will be reduced by the improved monitoring processes for management actions and the improved managerial incentives.[3]

Third, a substantial amount of tax benefits can be obtained from using leveraged ESOP financing in recapitalizations and management buyouts. The unusual tax benefits in leveraged ESOPs come from two sources: (1) In a leveraged ESOP, the portion of the company contribution that is used to repay the principal amount of the ESOP debt is tax deductible up to 25 percent of the eligible payroll. In addition, the portion of the company contribution that is used to pay interest is deductible without limitation. Thus, the principal of ESOP debt is repaid in pretax dollars. Furthermore, this unusual tax shield may be augmented by making stock rather than cash contributions from the employer corporation, which creates a new opportunity for tax-deductible equity financing. (2) As allowed in the Tax Acts of 1984 and 1986, there is a 50 percent income exclusion for tax purposes for financial institutions (banks as well as mutual funds) receiving interest on loans to ESOPs—the savings from which are often shared with the borrowing employer corporation.[4]

In a recent study on management buyouts, Kaplan [1987] has observed that ESOPs were used in only 5 of the 76 buyouts examined in his study and has indicated that some cost factors associated with leveraged ESOP financing might preclude them from being widely employed in the MBOs. It should be noted, however, that the sample in his study consists of the large MBOs completed between 1980 and 1986. Since the major tax benefits of leveraged ESOP financing were introduced in the 1984 and the 1986 Tax Acts, a new study basing upon more recent sample data might produce different results. The nontax advantages and disadvantages of ESOP financing within the corporate control context were discussed in detail by Chen and Kensinger [1988]. Sholes and Wolfson [1989b], however, have argued that the main motivation for the growth of ESOPs is their antitakeover characteristics rather than their tax or incentive advantages.

Deconglomeration

The business and financial environment of the late 1980s is quite different from that in the 1960s. Rapid technological change, worldwide competition for major products, and the fluctuating global financial market conditions are important characteristics of the business environment in the 1980s that were not present in the 1960s. Under the relatively stable economic conditions as well as the presence of strong antitrust laws in the late 1960s, acquiring some unrelated and undervalued businesses was alleged to be the best way to spend the internally accumulated cash for many corporations. Further, conglomerate mergers were alleged to have an important diversification rationale which resulted in the creation of shareholder value. This argument justifying conglomerates needs to be examined. Conglomerate firms are companies whose different components involve business activities in unrelated product lines whereby there are no economies of scale or scope or economies of vertical integration. The economic justification for conglomerate mergers in a market valuation context has never been clear. However, a commonly suggested economic rationale for conglomerate mergers, for example, such as the merger of Mobil Oil and Montgomery Ward, has been the reduction of corporate risk due to the independence on low covariance of their respective future cash flows. This diversification is redundant given the extensive portfolio diversification opportunities available to shareholders in the financial markets. Alternatively stated, the diversification rationale for corporate conglomerization wherein the firm functions as a mere investment trust is fallacious given the presence of more extensive and less costly portfolio diversification opportunities for investors. In any case, in the competitive environment of the 1980s, a firm with a simplified focused business activity can concentrate its efforts in areas of expertise.[5] Furthermore, the breaking up of different businesses within a firm into separate entities may permit a better compensation structure that will tie the manager and employee incentives closer to their specific operations and increase the firm's efficiency and productivity. Therefore, the "conglomerate theory" of value creation of the '60s has been replaced by the "deconglomerate theory" of value creation of the '80s. Martin Davis [1987], based upon his personal experience at Gulf & Western, has pointed out that "pruning" and "focus" on business operations should be the key considerations in the corporate strategic planning processes for the purpose of enhancing shareholder value in today's dynamic business environment.

Today, U.S. corporations face both more global competition in the product markets as well as more competition in the market for corporate control.[6] Corporate restructuring addresses both of these issues. The incentive and efficiency gains from improved management as a result o corporate restructuring should create and increase the shareholder value A larger equity position held by managers through leveraged MBOs leveraged recapitalizations, and leveraged ESOPs could strengthen th managerial incentives and could align their economic self-interests wit those of the shareholders. Furthermore, a better debt control of manageri decisions resulting from the increase in the firm's leverage should improv management efficiency and productivity. Indeed, as can be seen fro Table 16–1, there has been a positive correlation between the intensity restructuring and the improvement in productivity in selected industrie This leads to improved corporate performance in the product markets.

TABLE 16–1
Productivity Trends and Restructuring in Selected Industries

Industry	Restructuring Intensity Measure (RIM) 1980 to 1985	Average Annual Productivity Change		
		1973 to 1980	1980 to 1985	Change in Trend
Metal Mining	16.4			
Iron Ore		1.4%	8.1%	6.7%
Copper		1.1	9.9	8.7
Coal Mining	2.5	−1.6	6.5	8.1
Total Manufacturing	1.6	1.2	3.7	2.5
Lumber & Wood Products	2.2			
Sawmills & Planing Mills		0.6	5.4	4.9
Stone, Clay, and Glass	0.9			
Hydraulic Cement		−1.9	8.7	10.6
Primary Metals	1.5			
Steel		−0.5	6.1	6.6
Gray Iron Foundries		−0.6	3.8	4.3
Primary Copper, Lead, and Zinc		1.3	13.0	11.7
Primary Aluminum		0.1	3.7	3.6
Copper Rolling & Drawing		0.1	6.5	6.4
Fabricated Metals	1.4			
Automotive Stampings		1.0	4.6*	3.6
Machinery, Except Electrical	1.0			
Refrigeration and Heating Equipment		−1.3	2.1*	3.4
Electric and Electronic Equipment	1.6			
Radio and TV Sets		4.2	14.4*	10.2
Transportation Equipment	1.6			
Motor Vehicles and Parts		0.8	6.2	5.3
Textile Mill Products	1.2			
Nonwool Yarn Mills		2.3	5.3	3.0
Rubber & Misc. Plastic Products	0.8			
Tires and Inner Tubes		1.1	7.3	6.3
Railroad Transportation	3.1	1.5	8.6	7.1

*Productivity statistics are available through 1984.

Source: *Worldwide Economic Outlook 1987,* Morgan Stanley & Co.

Real Options

Specific corporate capital budgeting decisions such as manufacturing capacity decisions involve a number of real options such as the firm's ability to change the scale of its plant, to change the investment timing of adding the plant, to abandon the plant, to shut down or to partially shut down the plant, to sell and lease back the plant, and to have a number of alternative ownership decisions with regard to the plant. Furthermore, a firm has many other types of real options. These options are formally similar to the American put and call options. Thus, the Black-Scholes option pricing techniques have been applied in the analysis of a firm's real options.[7] These corporate real options represent value additivity possibilities for the firm in creating shareholder value and are a major component of corporate strategies. Indeed, an asset with a greater degree of flexibility possesses a real option with a higher "call option" value to its owner. Therefore, separating the ownership of certain assets through the sale of assets provides the owner the flexibility to exercise the options separately and hence increase the real option value of the assets. Indeed, from option pricing theory, we know that the sum of the call options of the assets has a greater value than that of a call option on the portfolio of the assets. The option dimension of corporate strategy and restructuring is at the core of maximizing shareholder wealth.

Transfer From Other Stakeholders

Corporate restructuring could also result in transferring wealth from other stakeholders to the shareholders. As we have argued above, corporate restructurings may result in more efficient allocation of resources and thus are positive-sum games which are of beneficial for the economy. In this case, the increase in the shareholder value would not necessarily come from the wealth transfer from other stakeholders, such as bondholders and labor. If, however, a corporate restructuring were a zero-sum game, then any gain in the shareholder value must come from wealth transfer from some passive participants of the game. For instance, the tax benefits received by a firm through corporate restructuring represent the losses to the U.S. Treasury and ultimately to the taxpayers. In a recent study on the impact of major divestiture of AT&T, Chen and Merville [1986] have presented empirical evidence showing that the equity holders of AT&T have gained abnormal returns, while the bondholders of AT&T have not incurred any abnormal losses during the extended split-up period. Thus the gains received by the shareholders of AT&T from the company's divestiture could come from the elimination of certain deadweight losses from the drop of the government's 1974 antitrust charges or from the possible wealth transfer from the utilities consumers.

CORPORATE RESTRUCTURINGS

Assets Restructurings

Sales of Assets or Business Units
Many corporations restructure themselves by selling assets or business units for tax as well as nontax reasons. Separating the ownership of assets could increase the sum of the values of the assets' real options. It has been noted that one of the most effective ways to discourage a bidder is to sell off those assets which are most attractive to the bidder. This tactic, sometimes called a scourged earth or crown jewel defense, would be most effective if the bidder values some aspect of the target's assets more highly than does financial market or the target itself. In other words, there is a misvaluation with regard to appropriate market prices. This financial market misvaluation could be due to asymmetric information or to a difference in the relative values of the assets to buyers and sellers due to the assets' different synergies.

Corporate Split-Ups and Spin-Offs
Corporate split-ups and spinoffs can also generate tax benefits and increase corporate efficiency and productivity to enhance the shareholder value. They also have been used as a response to actual and potential takeover threat. By placing the firm's "crown jewel" divisions or assets in a new separate corporation and selling off some of the shares of the new corporate entity in an initial public offering, a firm may focus the financial market's attention on its assets and enhance the shareholder value. The shares of the new corporation are or could be distributed to "friendly" shareholders in the event of a takeover of the parent company. The purposes and effects of corporate split-ups and spin-offs in the context of corporate control can be illustrated by analyzing a few recent restructurings.

    Diamond Shamrock Corporation. In response to a partial cash tender offer (for about 18 percent of the outstanding common shares) by Mesa in

January 1987, Diamond Shamrock's Board of Directors adopted a major restructuring plan which contained the following key points: (1) The company spun off its two core businesses and formed a new entity, Diamond Shamrock R&M, and distributed R&M stock to its shareholders; (2) the company made a cash tender offer of $17 per share (Mesa's offer was $15 per share) for up to 20 million shares; (3) the company sold $300 million or 3 million shares of Diamond Shamrock's newly created Cumulative Convertible Preferred Stock to Prudential for the equity capital for the restructuring plan.

In reaction to Diamond Shamrock's restructuring, Mesa amended its offer to an all cash bid at $15 per share for all the outstanding shares. The amended offer was dropped two weeks later after being rejected by Diamond Shamrock.

Carter-Hawley Hale Stores, Inc. On December 1, 1986, The Limited, Inc. and The Edward J. DeBartolo Corporation proposed to acquire all outstanding common stock of Carter-Hawley at a price of $55 per share in cash and all outstanding shares of convertible preferred stock at a price of $672.51 per share in cash. Carter-Hawley's Board of Directors rejected the Limited-DeBartolo's offer and adopted a restructuring plan, spun off its specialty store chains into a new "Specialty Company," and distributed the stock of the new company to the firm's current shareholders. As a result of the restructuring plan, the management and benefit plan ownership was increased to 44 percent of the Common Stock of Carter-Hawley, and the ownership holdings of the General Cinema management and benefit plan were 67 percent of the equity and 59 percent of the voting power of Specialty Company.

It should be pointed out that if the requirements of Section 355 of the Income Revenue Code are met, a split-up or spin-off may be accomplished free of tax to the corporation and its shareholders. One of the requirements under Section 355 is that the spin-off not be a device for the distribution of earnings and profits of the distributed or the distributing company.

Financial Restructuring

Self-Tender Offers/Open-Market Purchase
Financial restructuring or recapitalization has routinely resulted in a firm increasing its financial leverage. The repurchase of a company's

shares through a self-tender offer program or a stock repurchase program in an open market will reduce the shareholders' equity position in the company and result in the constructive effects of leverage that we have noted earlier. Share repurchase has become an integral part of a firm's defensive restructuring as well. The benefits of share repurchases as an antitakeover defense tactic include the following: (1) The repurchase may divert shares from the bidder's offer; (2) the repurchase may increase the share's public stock market price, which will force the potential acquirer to offer a higher price in order to gain the control of the firm; (3) it will deplete the firm's cash or other liquid assets; (4) it will reduce the outstanding number of the firm's shares and hence increase the equity ownership of management and benefit plans; and (5) the repurchased shares may be resold to a "friendly" group or an employee benefit plan.

Targeted Repurchase or Greenmail

In order to fend off the threat of hostile takeover, a company might engage in targeted repurchase of shares. Unlike the open-market repurchases where the shares are purchased from the company's shareholders generally, a targeted repurchase involves the purchase by the company of its shares at a premium from a bidder without offering a similar value to the other shareholders. It should be noted that a targeted repurchase of shares at a premium for management entrenchment are not only discriminatory but is likely to be economically disadvantageous to the firm's present shareholders.

Public LBOs

A leveraged recapitalization (or public LBO) usually involves the exchange of the "public" shareholders' stock for a smaller equity position in a newly recapitalized corporation, plus a payment of cash, debt securities, preferred stock, or a combination thereof. The public LBOs are different from the pure leveraged buyout transaction that eliminates the public shareholders' ownership interest in the firm. In a typical public LBO, management and ESOPs receive only the common stock of the newly recapitalized corporation instead of cash or any debt securities. Thus, the public shareholders have reduced their equity ownership position in the corporation, while management has increased both its equity ownership and control of the corporation, resulting in a clear increase in both incentives and productivity in the new corporation.

LBO or "Going Private"

A leveraged buyout (LBO) or "going private" transaction may or may not involve the management of the corporation. However, all of the public shareholders of the firm are cashed out as a result of an LBO. In the case that the management of the corporation is part of the LBO group, especially in management buyout, the control of the corporation is consolidated in the management and the positive effects of insider ownership should produce some economic gains.[8] Since the LBO group typically includes key corporate officers, directors, and major shareholders of the company, the directors' fiduciary duties and the business judgment rule should be strictly applied in the LBO transactions to ensure that the present shareholders are not in the disadvantage. In other words, the board of directors should be particularly sensitive to the fairness of the transaction to the shareholders and the corporation.

Leveraged ESOPs

Since the passage of the Tax Reform Acts of 1984 and 1986, leveraged ESOPs have become one of the most used methods in corporate restructuring. It is also one of the most potent takeover defenses and is presently in vogue as a method to reduce competition in the market for corporate control.[9] We have already discussed the unusual tax benefits associated with the leveraged ESOPs in financial restructuring.

Here we describe how the structure of leveraged ESOP can be used to increase the value of large companies in mature, slow-growth industries. As discussed in Chen and Kensinger [1988] and summarized in Figure 16–2, a leveraged ESOP can transfer the internal cash flows and control to the marketplace. On the one hand, when the shareholders sell the stock to an ESOP, they redeploy the funds into higher valued uses in the capital market. And as the corporation is forced to repay the debt created by the leveraged ESOPs, the debt service payments are forced out of the employer corporation by the ESOP financing. When a mature and slow-growth corporation throws off large sums of cash and has few attractive internally generated growth opportunities, stockholders may fear that managers will squander free cash flows on ill-advised attempts to expand the firm into areas in which it lacks experience, expertise, and competitive advantage. Therefore, shareholders will value any arrangement which commits management to pay out the free cash flows to investors. With a higher degree of debt in the capital structure, the cash flows become committed to the retirement of interest and principal of debt. Therefore, new projects would

FIGURE 16–2
How ESOP Financing Works

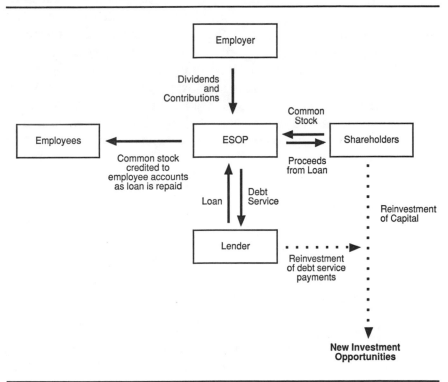

have to compete for external funding, rather than be sustained by the employer's cash flows. Driving the cash flows to the highest value uses enhances economic efficiency.

OPTIMAL CORPORATE RESTRUCTURING STRATEGIES

We briefly described the optimal dynamic corporate restructuring strategies based upon the generalized capital asset pricing model, which is related to the CEQ approach discussed in the second section (p. 376). A formal discussion of this type of strategy is presented in the Appendix to this chapter (p. 393). Optimal corporate restructuring strategies in a dynamic setting involves portfolio revisions through which the managers restructure the portfolio of strategic business units (SBU) of the corporation periodically to maximize the shareholder value. Dynamic corporate restructuring includes: (1) restructuring of the portfolio of SBUs; (2) based on shareholder-value-maximization; and (3) incorporation of the relevant dynamic factors. With a properly constructed valuation model, the contribution of each SBU's cash flows to that of the aggregate cash flows of the market as well as its contribution to hedging against the exogenous state variables such as inflation risk and competition risk from both domestic and foreign rivals can be identified and evaluated. A comparison of the public market price and the private valuation should provide a sound criterion for corporate restructuring decisions.

CONCLUSIONS

We have provided an economic overview of major issues relating to corporate restructurings. We have suggested some possible sources of shareholder value creation from corporate restructurings. Both tax as well as nontax economic factors are important impetuses for the recent surge in corporate restructurings. In addition, defensive restructuring constitutes an important antitakeover tactic and has likewise resulted in numerous restructurings. Different strategies and methods of corporate restructuring result in varying economic impacts on macroeconomic variables, stakeholders, shareholders, incumbent management, and different sectors of the economy. An important public issue is how to devise policies that will maximize the constructive aspects of corporate restructuring in terms of improving economic efficiency and competitiveness and that, at the same time, will minimize the possible economic ill effects from such activities.

Notes

1. The converse is, however, not true, that is, successful defensive restructuring can reduce competition in the market for corporate control and entrench management. This will result, *ceteris paribus,* in the share price not being maximized.
2. See, for example, the most recent study of Scholes and Wolfson [1989], wherein they have presented evidence that the changes in tax laws passed in the 1980s had a first order effect on observed merger and acquisition activity in the U.S.
3. This constructive effect of leverage has been advanced by Michael Jensen in his

article, "Agency Costs of Free Cash Flow, Corporate Finance and Takeovers," *American Economic Review* (May 1986).

4. The tax benefits associated with leveraged ESOPs have been discussed by Chen and Kensinger in "Innovations in Corporate Financing: Tax-Deductible Equity," Financial Management (Winter 1985).

   An analysis of the myriad economic-financial dimensions, such as employee nonoptimal portfolio diversification, fiduciary responsibilities of the plan's trustees, the specifics of how the stock is voted, ownership of the shares after the employees leave the firm, possible NYSE delistings and their impact upon whether shareholders, employees and/or executives management gain or lose from ESOPs is not addressed. However, the viewpoint that ESOPs established in corporate contests are optimal for shareholders and employees is viewed with skepticism.

5. This is equivalent to the "stick to the knitting" principle advocated in the popular book by Peters and Waterman in *In Search of Excellence: Lessons from America's Best-Run Companies.*

6. See Scholes and Wolfson [1989] for the evidence showing that the Tax Reform Act of 1986 has stimulated foreign demand for U.S. business.

7. See, for example, McDonald and Siegel's [1985, 1986] analyses on a firm's shutdown and waiting to invest options; Myers and Majd's [1983] study of project abandonment option; and Majd and Pindyck's analysis of the time-to-build option. Recently, Kulatilaka and Marks [1988] have derived a general formulation of corporate real options.

8. Although numerous studies have produced evidence showing positive economic gains from LBOs, some critics continue to raise questions about the methodologies and the measures of such gains. In a most recent study, Hite and Vetsuypens [1989] have presented evidence showing some economic gains from management buyouts of divisions.

9. ESOPs have been the subject of the featured main story of "The Rush to ESOPs' Employee Ownership: Is It Good for You or Your Company?" *Business Week,* May 15, 1989.

References

Auerbach, A. J., and Reishus, D. (1988). "The Impact of Taxation on Mergers and Acquisitions," in (A. J. Auerbach, ed.), *Mergers and Acquisitions,* University of Chicago Press.

Block, D., Landau, E., and Toes, S. (1987). "Restructuring the Corporation—As a Response to a Hostile Takeover Bid."

Chen, A., and Kensinger, J. (winter 1985). "Innovations in Corporate Financing: Tax-Deductible Equity," *Financial Management* .

Chen, A., and Kensinger, J. (spring 1988). "Beyond the Tax Benefits of ESOPs," *Journal of Applied Corporate Finance*.

Chen, A., and Merville, L. (December 1986). "An Analysis of Divestiture Effects Resulting from Deregulation," *Journal of Finance*.

Davis, M. (1987). "Strategic Formulation: Pruning and Focus," in (R. Kuhn, ed.), *Handbook for Creative and Innovative Managers*.

Fama, E., and Jensen, M. (June 1983). "Separation of Ownership and Control," *Journal of Law and Economics*.

Fama, E., and Jensen, M. (June 1983). "Agency Problems and Residual Claims," *Journal of Law and Economics*.

Fama, E., and Jensen, M. (June 1985). "Organizational Forms and Investment Decisions," *Journal of Financial Economics*.

Hite, G., and Vetsuypens, M. (1989). "Management Buyouts of Divisions and Shareholder Wealth," *Journal of Finance*.

Jensen, M. (May 1986). "Agency Costs of Free Cash Flow, Corporate Finance and Takeovers," *American Economic Review*.

Kaplan, S. (November 1987). "Management Buyouts: Evidence on Taxes as a Source of Value." Harvard University working paper.

Kulatilaka, N., and Marks, S. G. (1988). "The Strategic Value of Flexibility," *American Economic Review*.

Majd, S., and Pindyck, R. (1987). "Time to Build, Option Value, and Investment Decisions," *Journal of Financial Economics*.

McDonald, R., and Siegel, D. (1985). "Investment and the Valuation of Firms When There Is an Option to Shut Down," *International Economic Review*.

McDonald, R., and Siegel, D. (1986). "The Value of Waiting to Invest," *Quarterly Journal of Economics*.

Myers, S., and Majd, S. (1983). "Calculating the Abandonment Value of a Project Using Option Pricing Theory," Cambridge, MA: MIT, Sloan School working paper.

Peters, T., and Waterman, R. (1982). *In Search of Excellence: Lessons from America's Best-Run Companies*. New York: Harper & Row.

Ragazzi, G. (1981). "On the Relation between Ownership Dispersion and the Firm's Market Value," *Journal of Banking and Finance*.

Scholes, M., and Wolfson, M. (1989a). "The Effects of Changes in Tax Laws on Corporate Reorganization Activity," Stanford University working paper.

Scholes, M., and Wolfson, M. (1989b). "Employee Stock Ownership Plans and Corporate Restructuring: Myths and Realities," this volume, Chapter 15.

Williamson, O. (June 1988). "Corporate Finance and Corporate Governance," *Journal of Finance*.

APPENDIX TO CHAPTER 16

OPTIMAL CORPORATE RESTRUCTURING UNDER UNCERTAINTY

Introduction

An optimal corporate restructuring in a dynamic setting involves mainly portfolio revisions through which the managers of a company restructure the portfolio of strategic business units (SBU) periodically to maximize the market value of the firm. The changing business conditions, both endogenous and exogenous make it necessary for managers to conduct periodical portfolio revisions in corporate strategic planning. The central problem in the optimal dynamic corporate strategies includes the following three key issues: (1) It involves the restructure of portfolio of SBUs, adding new businesses or deleting the existing ones, or merely shifting the relative weights among the existing businesses; (2) the evaluation and selection of optimal corporate strategies should follow the value-based criterion; and (3) the corporate strategic planning is dynamic in nature, so the relevant dynamic factors should be incorporated into the valuation models and the decision processes.

The purpose of this appendix is to develop a simple conceptual framework for optimal corporate restructurings that is complete in incorporating the above three key elements in strategic planning and is feasible for practical implementation. In the second section (p. 393), the generalized capital asset pricing model and its special features that are most suitable for corporate restructuring decisions are discussed. In the third section (p. 395), the application of the generalized capital asset pricing model to evaluate a firm's SBUs and the decision rules for acquiring or divesting a business consistent with value-based approach are discussed.

The Generalized Capital Asset Pricing Model

Allowing investors to consider the possible shifts in the future investment opportunities in their optimal investment-consumption decisions, Merton (1974, 1976) has extended the static Markowitz portfolio selection model to a dynamic optimal portfolio decision model and developed a generalized capital asset pricing model (GCAPM). The main result in Merton's developments is that in the equilibrium risk-return relation for each asset, the *relevant* or *systemic* risk of an asset includes not only its *market-volatility risk* but also its *state-variable risk*. The market-volatility risk of an asset is measured by the covariance between the asset return and the return on the market portfolio, while the state-variable risk of an asset is measured by the covariance between the asset return and the unfavorable shifts in future investment opportunities. The unfavorable shifts in the future investment opportunities faced by the investors are generally caused by changes in the state variables such as inflation, the market interest rates, the production technologies, and the foreign competitions, etc. Therefore, in contrast to a single beta in the traditional Sharpe-Lintner-Mossin capital asset pricing model (CAPM), there are multiple betas in the equilibrium risk-return relationship in the GCAPM.

As will become clearer later in this Appendix, the GCAPM that captures the characteristics of a firm's SBUs through its state-variable risks is a better valuation model than the CAPM in corporate restructuring decisions. In the GCAPM, the relevant risk of any asset in equilibrium consists of both the market-volatility risk and the state-variable risk. Formally, the GCAPM can be expressed in terms of cash flows as follows:

$$V_j = \frac{1}{\gamma} \{ \bar{D} - [\gamma_1 \, \text{COV}(\tilde{D}_j, \tilde{D}_m) - \gamma_2 \, \text{COV}(\tilde{D}_j, \tilde{\theta})] \} \qquad (A16.1)$$

where

V_j = the equilibrium value of firm or asset j;

γ = one plus the risk-free rate of interest;

$\tilde{D}_j$ = the uncertain future cash profit of firm or asset j, a random variable with expected value $\bar{D}_j$ and variance σ_j^2;

$\tilde{D}_m$ = the aggregate uncertain future cash profit of all firms or assets in the market, including that of the jth firm or asset;

$\tilde{\theta}$ = the uncertain changes in the state variable (or state variables if it denotes a vector);

γ_1 = the equilibrium market price of volatility risk;

γ_2 = the equilibrium market price of state-variable risk; and,

COV = the covariance operator.

Equation (A16.1) states that the equilibrium value of firm or asset j is equal to the present value of the certainty-equivalent (CEQ) of its future cash profits, discounted at the risk-free interest rate. The CEQ of an uncertain end-of-period cash profit is equal to its expected value minus the appropriate risk premium of the cash profit, which consists of the market-volatility risk ($\text{COV}(\tilde{D}_j, \tilde{D}_m)$) and the state-variable risk ($\text{COV}(\tilde{D}_j, \tilde{\theta})$), weighted by their respective factors, γ_1 and γ_2. The traditional capital asset pricing model (CAPM) which does not include the uncertain changes in the state variable is a special case of the GCAPM. Therefore, the traditional CAPM *overstates* the firm's or asset's systematic risk if its cash profits are positively correlated with the uncertain changes in the state variable, and it *understates* the firm's or asset's systematic risk if its cash profits are negatively correlated with the uncertain changes in the state variable.

The Value-Based Criterion in Corporate Restructuring

A successful and complete corporate restructuring requires an appropriate evaluation of SBUs and the value-based evaluation criterion for decisions. The GCAPM described in the previous section provides a proper way to evaluate a firm's SBUs under uncertainty. Suppose that firm j owns a portfolio of m strategic business units (SBU) with future cash flows denoted by $\tilde{D}_{jk}$, for $k = 1, 2, ...m$. The total cash profit of firm j is a sum of the cash profits of all the SBUs managed by the company, that is $\tilde{D}_j = \sum_{k=1}^{m} \tilde{D}_{jk}$. Utilizing the GCAPM as shown in Equation (A16.1), the equilibrium value of the kth SBU of firm j can be expressed as follows:

$$V_{jk} = \frac{1}{\gamma} \{\bar{D}_j - [\gamma_1 \, COV(\tilde{D}_{jk}, \tilde{D}_m) - \gamma_2 \, COV(\tilde{D}_{jk}, \tilde{\theta})]\} \qquad (A16.2)$$

Similar to the equilibrium value of a firm, the equilibrium value of a SBU is equal to the present value of the CEQ of its cash profits discounted at the risk-free rate of interest. In the determination of CEQ of the cash profits of a SBU, the relevant risk premium consists of both the market-volatility risk and the state-variable risk. To gain more insights in the value-based criterion for evaluating the SBUs within a company, we shall analyze these two components of systematic risk separately in detail in the following.

(A) The Market-Volatility Risk of SBU

As shown in Equation (A16.2), the market-volatility risk of the kth SBU in firm j is as follows:

$$
\begin{aligned}
COV(\tilde{D}_{jk}, \tilde{D}_m) \\
= COV(\tilde{D}_{jk}, \tilde{D}_j + \tilde{D}_w) \\
= COV(\tilde{D}_{jk}, \tilde{D}_{jk} + \sum_{\substack{i=1 \\ i \neq k}}^{m} \tilde{D}_{ji} + \tilde{D}_w) \\
= VAR(\tilde{D}_{jk}) + \sum_{\substack{i=1 \\ i \neq k}}^{m} COV(\tilde{D}_{jk}, \tilde{D}_{ji}) + COV(\tilde{D}_{jk}, \tilde{D}_w)
\end{aligned}
$$

where

$\tilde{D}_w$ = the aggregate uncertain future cash profits of all other firms (i.e., all firms, except firm j, in the market).

Therefore, in the value-based pricing model for each SBU, the market-volatility risk consists of the following three key components:

(i)   the variance of the cash profits of the kth SBU in firm j (i.e., Var $(\tilde{D}_{jk})$), to be called the kth SBU's *internal-internal risk;*

(ii)   the covariance between the kth SBU's cash profits and that of all other SBUs in firm j (i.e., $\sum\limits_{\substack{i=1 \\ i \neq k}}^{m} \text{COV}(\tilde{D}_{jk}, \tilde{D}_{ji})$),to be called the kth SBU's *internal-external risk.*

(iii)   the covariance between the kth SBU's cash profits and aggregate cash profits of all other firms (i.e., $\text{COV}(\tilde{D}_{jk}, \tilde{D}_w)$), to be called the kth SBU's *external-external risk.*

The multiples determining factors that affect the market-volatility risk of a SBU clearly indicate that evaluation of any SBU cannot and should not be carried out in isolation without examining its relations to other SBUs in the firm and to other firms in the market. In other words, the value-based criterion for evaluating a SBU calls for an integrated approach. Without such a complete evaluation approach, the decisions in corporate strategic planning will be biased and non-optimal.

(B)   The State-Variable Risk of SBU

As indicated in Equation (A16.2), the state-variable risk of the kth SBU in firm j is measured by the covariance of its cash profits with the *unfavorable certain changes in the state variable,* (i.e., $\text{COV}(\tilde{D}_{jk}, \tilde{\theta})$). A positive covariance between the cash profits of the kth SBU and the unfavorable uncertain changes in the state variable indicates that the cash profits of the SBU tend to be higher in the event that an unfavorable state occurs. For example, if the uncertain rate of inflation in the economy is the unfavorable state variable of the major concern in corporate strategic planning decisions, a SBU with $\text{COV}(\tilde{D}_{jk}, \tilde{\theta}) > 0$ tends to have a larger cash profit during the period of higher rate of inflation, and hence, it will be valued higher by the investors and the corporate financial managers. Such a business unit will be termed an *inflation-hedging* SBU and it will command a greater value in the marketplace. Likewise, a SBU with $\text{COV}(\tilde{D}_{jk}, \tilde{\theta}) < 0$ tends to have a smaller cash profit during the period of higher rate of inflation, and hence, it will be valued lower because it is an *inflation-adversed* SBU. The sign and the magnitude of $\text{COV}(\tilde{D}_{jk}, \tilde{\theta})$ indicate the state-variable risk of the kth SBU. Since the state-variable risk of firm j is simply the sum of the state-variable risks of all SBUs within the company $(\text{COV}(\tilde{D}_j, \tilde{\theta}) = \sum_{k=1}^{m} \text{COV}(\tilde{D}_{jk}, \tilde{\theta}))$, by changing the relative sizes of SBUs in the firm and by changing $\text{COV}(\tilde{D}_{jk}, \tilde{\theta})$ of all SBUs under the control through the advertisement and R&D expenditures, a company can adjust its state-variable risk in strategic planning.

(C) The Value-Based Criterion in Acquiring or Divesting an SBU

The GCAPM for evaluating SBUs provides a useful tool in corporate restructuring—it is a value-based approach and it explicitly incorporates the *characteristics of strategic businesses.* As we have already pointed out, the equilibrium *value of a SBU is determined by both its market-volatility risk and its state-variable risk.* Furthermore, the stochastic relationship of the SBU's cash profits and that of other SBUs within the firm as well as that of other firms in the market have to be considered in the process of evaluating a SBU. *In other words, the value-based approach to the evaluation of a SBU requires a comprehensive and integrated view of the unit.* Any SBU cannot be evaluated independently.

It can be easily seen that the risk-adjusted net present value (*RANPV*) rule can be *employed in the acquisition or the divestiture of a SBU in the corporate restructuring decisions.* The rule calls for acquiring a new SBU if its *RANPV* is greater than zero. The *RANPV* of acquiring a new SBU is defined as follows:

$$RANPV_k = V_k - B_k$$

$$= -\frac{1}{\gamma} \{\bar{D}_k - [\gamma_1 \; \text{COV}(\tilde{D}_k, \tilde{D}_m) - \gamma_2 \, \text{COV}(\tilde{D}_k, \tilde{\theta})]\} - B_k, \quad (A16.3)$$

where B_k = the asking price for the kth new strategic business unit.

If the $RANPV_k$, as shown in Equation (A16.4), is greater than zero, then the kth new SBU is worth being acquired because the acquisition of the SBU will increase the value of the firm. On the other hand, acquiring a SBU with a negative *RANPV* will reduce the value of the firm, which will not be in the best interest of the firm's shareholders.

Similarly, we can easily devise a simple rule for divesting a SBU under the control of the firm. If the $RANPV_k$ as shown below is positive, then the kth SBU currently under control should be divested:

$$RANPV_k = S_k - V_k$$

$$= S_k - \frac{1}{\gamma} \{\bar{D}_k - [\gamma_1 \; \text{COV}(\tilde{D}_k, \tilde{D}_m) - \gamma_2 \, \text{COV}(\tilde{D}_k, \tilde{\theta})]\}, \quad (A16.4)$$

where S_k = the external bid price for the firm's kth strategic business unit.

Following the positive *RANPV* decision rules in Equations (A16.3) or (A16.4), the acquisition or the divestiture of a SBU will increase the value of the firm. Therefore, the managers following the value-maximization rule should acquire a SBU if the expression in Equation (A16.4) is greater than zero, and should sell a SBU if the expression in Equation (A16.5) is greater than zero. Note that these decision rules are perfectly consistent with the value-based criterion in corporate restructuring decisions.

CHAPTER 17

THE BUSINESS JUDGMENT RULE IN CORPORATE RESTRUCTURING AND RECAPITALIZATION TRANSACTIONS

Dennis J. Block
Stephen A. Radin
Isaac M. Jaroslawicz

Restructuring and recapitalization plans encompass a wide variety of corporate strategies designed to enhance shareholder values, typically by reducing the differential between market value and intrinsic value. The corporation accordingly becomes a less attractive acquisition target, which increases the likelihood that the corporation will be able to remain an independent entity.

The terms *restructuring* and *recapitalization* are difficult to define with any precision, but it can generally be said that the term *restructuring* refers to the sale or other disposition or reconfiguration of assets pursuant to which a company focuses on its core business, and that the term *recapitalization* refers to the company's altering of its shareholder population through the purchase or sale of stock either by the company itself or by a friendly third party. Many transactions, such as extraordinary dividends

Dennis J. Block, Stephen A. Radin, and Isaac M. Jaroslawicz, of Weil, Gotshal and Manges, are corporate counselors and litigators who specialize in mergers and acquisitions and corporate and securities litigation.

consisting of cash, securities, or a combination of both, include elements of both restructuring and recapitalization.

This outline examines the legal standards governing directorial conduct generally and in the context of corporate takeovers, with emphasis on restructuring and recapitalization transactions including the sale or other disposition of corporate stock or assets, the repurchase of corporate stock either on the open market or pursuant to a self-tender offer or exchange offer, the declaration of an extraordinary dividend, and the creation of a class of super-voting stock.

I.   The Business Judgment Rule

A. Introduction
  1. Corporate directors owe fiduciary duties to the corporation they serve and its shareholders. These fiduciary duties include the duty of care and the duty of loyalty. In simplest terms, the duty of care requires that directors exercise the care that an ordinarily prudent person would exercise under similar circumstances, and the duty of loyalty prohibits faithlessness and self-dealing. See, e.g., Norlin Corp. v. Rooney, Pace Inc., 744 F.2d 255, 264 (2d Cir. 1984).
  2. The business judgment rule is a specific application of the directorial standard of conduct to the situation where, after reasonable investigation, disinterested directors adopt a course of action which, in good faith, they honestly and reasonably believe will benefit the corporation. Should the directors be sued because of their decision, the court—at least in theory—will not second-guess the merits of the decision, but rather will examine the decision only to the extent necessary to verify the presence of the rule's five elements—a business decision, disinterestedness, due care, good faith, and no abuse of discretion. These elements of the rule are discussed in § I D infra.
  The business judgment rule is thus a tool of judicial review rather than a standard of conduct.
  3. The rule applies both in actions seeking to impose liability for damages upon directors for their decisions and in actions seeking injunctive relief against particular board actions.
      a. One commentator has articulated a distinction between the business judgment *rule* and the business judgment *doctrine.* See Hinsey, Business Judgment and the American Law Institute's Corporate Governance Project: The Rule, the Doctrine, and the Reality, 52 Geo. Wash. L. Rev. 609, 611–

13 (1984) (the business judgment rule "shields individual directors from personal liability for damages stemming from decisions"; the business judgment doctrine, by contrast, "protects the decision itself").

   b. Both courts and commentators, however, have generally referred to both the rule and the doctrine as one. See id. at 611; Revlon, Inc. v. MacAndrews and Forbes Holdings, 506 A.2d 173, 180 n.10 (Del. 1986) (noting the "practice of referring only to the business judgment rule, although in transactional justification matters such reference may be understood to embrace the concept of the doctrine").

B. Rationale

   1. By recognizing human fallibility, the rule encourages competent individuals to serve as directors. See, e.g., Briggs v. Spaulding, 141 U.S. 132, 149 (1891); Dynamics Corp. of Am. v. CTS Corp. ("CTS I"), 794 F.2d 250, 256 (7th Cir. 1986), rev'd on other grounds, 481 U.S. 69 (1987); Godbold v. Branch Bank, 11 Ala. 191, 199 (1847); Percy v. Millandon, 8 Mart. (n.s.) 68, 78 (La. 1829).

   2. The rule recognizes that business decisions frequently entail risk, and thus provides directors the broad discretion they need to formulate dynamic and effective corporate policy without fear of judicial second-guessing. See, e.g., CTS, 794 F.2d at 256; Cramer v. General Tel. and Elecs. Corp., 582 F.2d 259, 274 (3d Cir. 1978), cert. denied, 439 U.S. 1129 (1979); Levin v. Mississippi River Corp., 59 F.R.D. 353, 364 (S.D.N.Y.), aff'd mem., 486 F.2d 1398 (2d Cir.), cert. denied, 414 U.S. 1112 (1973).

   3. The rule keeps courts from becoming enmeshed in complex corporate decision-making, a task which they are ill-equipped to handle. As the Second Circuit observed in Joy v. North, 692 F.2d 880 (2d Cir. 1982), cert. denied, 460 U.S. 1051 (1983):

> [A]fter-the-fact litigation is a most imperfect device to evaluate corporate business decisions. The circumstances surrounding a corporate decision are not easily reconstructed in a courtroom years later, since business imperatives often call for quick decisions, inevitably based on less than perfect information. The entrepreneur's function is to encounter risks and to confront uncertainty, and a reasoned decision at the time made may seem a wild hunch viewed years later against a background of perfect knowledge.

692 F.2d at 886. In the words of the courts in Solash v. Corp., [1987–88 Transfer Binder] Fed. Sec. L. Rep. (CCH) ¶ 93,608, at 97,727 (Del. Ch. Jan. 19, 1988), and In re J.P. Stevens and Co. Shareholders Litigation, 542 A.2d 770, 780 (Del. Ch. 1988):

Because businessmen and women are correctly perceived as possessing skills, information and judgment not possessed by reviewing courts
and because there is great social utility in encouraging the allocation of
assets and the evaluation and assumption of economic risk by those with
such skill and information, courts have long been reluctant to second-
guess such decisions when they appear to have been made in good faith.
See Frances T. v. Village Green Owners Ass'n, 42 Cal. 3d 490, 507 n.14,
229 Cal. Rptr. 456, 465 n.14, 723 P.2d 573, 582 n.14 (1986) ("directors
should be given wide latitude in their handling of corporate affairs because
the hindsight of the judicial process is an imperfect device for evaluating
business decisions"); Kamin v. American Express Co., 86 Misc. 2d 809,
812–13, 383 N.Y.S.2d 807, 810–11 (Sup. Ct.) ("[t]he directors' room
rather than the courtroom is the appropriate forum for thrashing out purely
business questions"), aff'd mem., 54 A.D.2d 654, 387 N.Y.S.2d 993 (App.
Div. 1976).

C. The Rule's Presumption

The courts have frequently described the business judgment rule as a
presumption of regularity. The Delaware Supreme Court has during the last
five years repeatedly reaffirmed the long-standing presumption in that
jurisdiction. See Aronson v. Lewis, 473 A.2d 805, 812 (Del. 1984) (the
business judgment rule "is a presumption that in making a business decision
the directors of a corporation acted on an informed basis, in good faith, and
in the honest belief that the action taken was in the best interests of the
company"), quoted in Smith v. Van Gorkom, 488 A.2d 858, 872 (Del. 1985),
Unocal Corp. v. Mesa Petroleum Co., 493 A.2d 946, 954 (Del. 1985), Moran
v. Household Int'l, Inc., 500 A.2d 1346, 1356 (Del. 1985), Revlon, Inc. v.
MacAndrews and Forbes Holdings, 506 A.2d 173, 180 (Del. 1986), Polk v.
Good, 507 A.2d 531, 536 (Del. 1986), and Ivanhoe Partners v. Newmont
Mining Corp., 535 A.2d 1334, 1341 (Del. 1987). See also Grobow v. Perot,
539 A.2d 180, 187 (Del. 1988) ("the business judgment rule is...a presumption that directors making a business decision, not involving self-interest, act
on an informed basis, in good faith and in the honest belief that their actions
are in the corporation's best interest").

D. The Elements of the Rule

The business judgment rule shields corporate decision-makers and their
decisions from judicial second-guessing where the five elements of the rule—
a business decision, disinterestedness, due care, good faith, and no abuse of
discretion—are present. It is presumed that each of these requirements have
been satisfied, and the party challenging the board's decision has the burden

of rebutting the rule's presumption. See generally 1 R. Balotti and J. Finkelstein, The Delaware Law of Corporations and Business Organizations §§ 4.6A and 4.6D, at 73–74 and 87–88 (1988); 3A W. Fletcher, Cyclopedia of the Law of Private Corporations § 1040, at 58 (1986); Arsht, The Business Judgment Rule Revisited, 8 Hofstra L. Rev. 93, 114–30 (1979).

Where the party challenging the board's decision overcomes this burden, the business judgment rule will have no applicability, and the transaction at issue will be scrutinized by the court to determine whether it is entirely or intrinsically fair. See, e.g., Van Gorkom, 488 A.2d at 893; Shamrock Holdings v. Polaroid Corp., [1988–1989 Transfer Binder] Fed. Sec. L. Rep. (CCH) ¶ 94,176, at 91,620 (Del. Ch. Jan. 6, 1989).

1. A Business Decision

    a. Only director action is covered by the rule. "Technically speaking, [the rule] has no role where directors have either abdicated their functions, or absent a conscious decision, failed to act." Aronson v. Lewis, 473 A.2d 805, 813 (Del. 1984). See also Hanson Trust PLC v. ML SCM Acquisition Inc., 781 F.2d 264, 275 (2d Cir. 1986).

    b. Inaction, while judged under the duty of care, is not protected by the business judgment rule unless it is the result of "a conscious decision to refrain from acting." Aronson, 473 A.2d at 813. Thus in Kaplan v. Centex Corp., 284 A.2d 119 (Del. Ch. 1971), for example, the court found that although the evidence revealed some references by the directors to the challenged transactions, "none of these, singly or cumulatively, show that director judgment was brought to bear with specificity on the transactions." Id. at 124. See also Rabkin v. Philip A. Hunt Chem. Corp., 547 A.2d 963, 972 (Del. Ch. 1986) ("[t]he business judgment rule may apply to a deliberate decision not to act, but it has no bearing on a claim that directors' inaction was the result of ignorance"), motion for reargument denied, No. 7547 (Del. Ch. Dec. 17, 1987).

2. Disinterestedness

    a. Only disinterested director conduct is protected by the business judgment rule. Aronson, 473 A.2d at 812.

    b. To establish that directors were interested in a challenged transaction, a plaintiff "must plead particularized facts demonstrating either a financial interest or entrenchment." Grobow v. Perot, 539 A.2d 180, 188 (Del. 1988). See also Pogostin v. Rice, 480 A.2d 619, 624 (Del. 1984) ("[d]irectorial interest exists whenever divided loyalties are present, or a director either has received, or is entitled to receive, a personal financial benefit from the challenged transaction which is not equally shared by the stockholders"); Aronson, 473 A.2d at 812 (defining interested directors as directors who either "appear on both sides of a transaction [or] expect to derive any personal financial benefit from it in the sense of self-dealing, as opposed to a benefit which devolves upon the corporation or all stockholders generally").

    c. This interestedness must afflict a majority of the corporation's directors. See Pogostin, 480 A.2d at 626; Aronson, 473 A.2d at 815 and n.8.

    d. The receipt of director's fees does not establish interestedness. See, e.g., In re E.F. Hutton Banking Practices Litig., 634 F. Supp. 265, 271 (S.D.N.Y. 1986); Grobow, 539 A.2d at 188.

    e. The ownership of stock by directors, even where different groups of stockholders have different interests in a challenged transaction, does not by itself create divided loyalties sufficient to trigger directorial interestedness and a shifting of the burden of proof.

        (1) Thus in Unocal Corp. v. Mesa Petroleum Co., 493 A.2d 946 (Del. 1985), for example, the Delaware Supreme Court stated that the mere fact that board members are also large stockholders who stand to gain from a transaction along with only some of the corporation's remaining stockholders "does not create a disqualifying 'personal pecuniary interest' to defeat the operation of the business judgment rule." Id. at 958, citing Cheff v. Mathes, 199 A.2d 548, 554 (Del. 1964).

        (2) Similarly, in Freedman v. Restaurant Associates Industries, [1987–1988 Transfer Binder] Fed. Sec. L. Rep. (CCH) ¶ 93,502 (Del. Ch. Oct. 16, 1987), the Delaware Chancery Court stated its "impression" that conflicts among shareholder constituencies involving an issue such as the apportionment of merger consideration between differing classes of stock does not deprive directors of the "presumptions ordinarily accorded to their good faith decisions and require them to establish the intrinsic fairness of the apportionment." Id. at 97,221.

3. Due Care

    a. Due care in this context mandates that directors make a reasonable effort to ascertain and consider all relevant information. Accordingly, the business judgment rule only protects "informed" decisions. See, e.g., Hanson Trust PLC v. ML SCM Acquisition Inc., 781 F.2d 264, 274–75 (2d Cir. 1986); Smith v. Van Gorkom, 488 A.2d 858, 872 (Del. 1985).

(1) As the Second Circuit has put it, "directors are protected to the extent that their actions evidence their business judgment," but such protection "assumes that courts must not reflexively decline to consider the content of their 'judgment' and the extent of the information on which it is based." Hanson, 781 F.2d at 275 (emphasis in original), quoted in Edelman v. Fruehauf Corp., 798 F.2d 882, 886 (6th Cir. 1986).

(2) In Delaware, at least, the standard for determining whether a business judgment is an informed one is "gross negligence." See, e.g., Van Gorkom, 488 A.2d at 872–73; Aronson, 473 A.2d at 812; Rabkin v. Philip A. Hunt Chem. Corp., 547 A.2d 963, 970 (Del. Ch. Dec. 4, 1986); Repairman's Serv. Corp. v. National Intergroup, Inc., 10 Del. J. Corp. L. 902, 909 (Del. Ch. Mar. 15, 1985); Reading Co. v. Trailer Train Co., 9 Del. J. Corp. L. 223, 229 (Del. Ch. 1984). Cf. Rabkin v. Philip A. Hunt Chem. Corp., No. 7547, slip op. at 7–8 (Del. Ch. Dec. 17, 1987) ("ordinary negligence is the appropriate standard of liability" in cases involving allegations that directors have "abdicate[d] their managerial responsibilities").

b. Two well-publicized 1985 and 1986 decisions involving conduct by the boards of Trans Union Corporation and SCM Corporation have focused considerable attention upon this aspect of the directorial duty of care.

(1) Van Gorkom

(a) Smith v. Van Gorkom, 488 A.2d 858 (Del. 1985), involved the Trans Union board's decision to approve and recommend to shareholders a $55 per share cash-out merger proposal pursuant to which Trans Union would be merged into a company controlled by Jay Pritzker. Trans Union's Chairman and Chief Executive Officer, Jerome Van Gorkom, suggested the transaction to Pritzker without consulting the corporation's board, and, following several meetings between these two men, Pritzker agreed. Van Gorkom called a special board meeting for the following day (a Saturday) without advising the directors of the meeting's purpose. The meeting began with a 20-minute presentation by Van Gorkom which outlined the terms of the proposed merger but never mentioned that he (not Pritzker) was the one who had suggested the merger price. Because the proposed agreement permitted Trans Union to receive (but not actively solicit) competing offers for 90 days,

Van Gorkom stated that the free market would judge whether $55 was a fair price. The corporation's chief financial officer—who opposed the merger but whose recommendation was neither requested nor given at the meeting—advised the board that he had not learned about the merger proposal until that morning, and that rough calculations he had earlier prepared in connection with consideration of a possible leveraged buy-out transaction "did not indicate either a fair price for the stock or a valuation of the Company." The financial officer stated that although he "did not see his role as directly addressing the fairness issue," his opinion was that "$55 was 'in the range of a fair price,' but 'at the beginning of the range.'" No investment banker was present at the meeting. The directors approved the proposed merger agreement after two hours, and the document was executed by Van Gorkom at a social event that evening, before either he or any other director had read it. Trans Union then announced its "definitive" merger agreement, omitting any reference to the corporation's limited right to receive higher offers. 488 A.2d at 864–69.

(b) The court concluded that the directors had not exercised due care:

The directors (1) did not adequately inform themselves as to [their board chairman's] role in forcing the "sale" of the Company and in establishing the per share purchase price; (2) were uninformed as to the intrinsic value of the Company; and (3) given these circumstances, at a minimum, were grossly negligent in approving the "sale" of the Company upon two hours' consideration, without prior notice, and without the exigency of a crisis or emergency. Id. at 874.

(c) See also Victor, "Rhetoric is Hot When the Topic is Takeovers," *Legal Times,* Dec. 23, 1985, at 2 (quoting Delaware Supreme Court Judge Andrew G.T. Moore, who joined the majority opinion, for the proposition that Van Gorkom "doesn't stand for new law. The court was just applying old law to egregious facts.").

(2) Hanson

(a) Hanson Trust PLC v. ML SCM Acquisition Inc., 781 F.2d 264 (2d Cir. 1986), involved a lock-up option granted by SCM Corporation to Merrill Lynch, one of two competing bidders for SCM. The lock-up option granted Merrill the irrevocable right to purchase two of SCM's most attractive businesses at "significantly undervalued" prices (the lowest values adduced at a preliminary injunction hearing revealed that the $430 million option price was at least $80 million below fair value, and there was evidence that the option price could have been as much as $230 million below fair value) in the event a third party acquired one third of SCM's shares. 781 F.2d at 266–67 and 279–81.

(b) The court concluded that the SCM directors' grant of the option, while "not ris[ing] to that level of gross negligence found in Smith v. Van Gorkom," still constituted a breach of their duty of care. Id. at 275. The court summarized the critical board meeting as follows:

> [T]he SCM directors, in a three-hour late-night meeting, apparently contented themselves with their financial advisor's conclusory opinion that the option prices were "within the range of fair value," although had the directors inquired, they would have learned that Goldman Sachs [SCM's investment banker] had not calculated a range of fairness. There was not even a written opinion from Goldman Sachs as to the value of the two optioned businesses.... Moreover, the Board never asked what the top value was or why two businesses that generated half of SCM's income were being sold for one third of the total purchase price of the company under the second LBO merger agreement, or what the company would look like if the options were exercised.... There was little or no discussion of how likely it was that the option "trigger" would be pulled, or who would make that decision— Merrill, the board, or management. Id.

(c) The court emphasized that the SCM directors had "manifestly declined to use 'time available for obtaining information' that might be critical, given 'the importance of the business judgment to be made.'" Id., quoting *Principles of Corporate Governance: Analysis and Recommendations* § 4.01 Comment at 66 (Tentative Draft No. 4 Apr. 12, 1985).

(d) The Hanson decision is discussed in more detail in § IV B 2 b infra.

(3) For a discussion of a series of more recent cases following or distinguishing Van Gorkom and Hanson, see Radin, The Director's Duty of Care Three Years After Smith v. Van Gorkom, 39 Hastings L.J. 707 (1988).

(4) Good Faith

    (a) A director may also lose the protection of the business judgment rule if he acts without a good faith belief that his business judgment is in the best interest of the corporation.

    (b) Good faith involves all aspects of honesty and integrity, and presupposes no personal financial interest or self-dealing. Put another way, directorial action must be genuinely motivated by an honest desire to benefit the corporation's shareholders, and not by some other purpose, such as personal gain.
See generally R. Balotti and J. Finkelstein, The Delaware Law of Corporations and Business Organizations § 4.6D, at 94.1–94.2 (1988); Arsht, The Business Judgment Rule Revisited, 8 Hofstra L. Rev. 93, 127 (1979).

5. No Abuse of Discretion

  a. Even where the above four elements are present, the directors' decision will be respected by the courts only absent an abuse of discretion. See, e.g., Aronson v. Lewis, 473 A.2d 805, 814 (Del. 1984). This concept, of course, "presupposes discretion, a term which reaffirms the broad latitude granted to the directors." Veasey and Seitz, The Business Judgment Rule in the Revised Model Act, the Trans Union Case, and the ALI Project—A Strange Porridge, 63 Tex. L. Rev. 1483, 1487 (1985).

  b. Accordingly, several courts and commentators have stated that the business judgment rule does not extend so far as to oust the courts completely from any role in scrutinizing the merits of a board's decision. Rather, judges may—and in fact often do—examine the merits of the decision not in order to substitute their views for those of the corporation's directors, but merely to determine whether the directors' actions constitute gross overreaching or an abuse of discretion. See Cramer v. General Tel. and Elecs. Corp., 582 F.2d 259, 275 (3d Cir. 1978), cert. denied, 439 U.S. 1129 (1979) ("where the shareholder contends that the directors' judgment is so unwise or unreasonable as to fall outside the permissible bounds of the directors' sound discretion, a court should, we think, be able to conduct its own analysis of the reasonableness of that business judgment"); In re J.P.

Stevens and Co. Shareholders Litig., 542 A.2d 770, 780–81 and n.5 (Del. Ch. 1988) ("[a] court may... review the substance of a business decision by an apparently well-motivated board for the limited purpose of assessing whether that decision is so far beyond the bounds of reasonable judgment that it seems essentially inexplicable on any ground other than bad faith") (emphasis in original); AC Acquisitions Corp. v. Anderson, Clayton and Co., 519 A.2d 103, 111 n.9 (Del. Ch. 1986):

> I recognize that some cases acknowledge a possibility—perhaps more theoretical than real—that a decision by disinterested directors following a deliberative process may still be the basis for liability if such decision cannot be "attributed to any rational business purpose,"...or is "egregious."

See also Arsht, The Business Judgment Rule Revisited, 8 Hofstra L. Rev. 93, 122 (1979):

> This particular limitation to the business judgment rule is, perhaps, not a limitation at all, but simply an application of the fundamental principle behind the rule. An honest error in judgment is allowed. But a judgment that cannot be sustained on some rational basis falls outside the protection of the business judgment rule; the transaction's results may often belie the honest, good faith exercise of judgment.

c. In In re RJR Nabisco, Inc. Shareholders Litigation, [1988–1989 Transfer Binder] Fed. Sec. L. Rep. (CCH) ¶ 94,194 (Del. Ch. Jan. 31, 1989), the Delaware Court of Chancery focused specifically upon the question whether there remains room for a judicial judgment concerning the merits of (i) a business decision (ii) by disinterested directors (iii) acting with due care and (iv) acting in good faith, and concluded that the answer was "no." The court explained:

> [S]uch limited substantive review as the rule contemplates (i.e., is the judgment under review "egregious" or "irrational" or "so beyond reason," etc.) really is a way of inferring bad faith. I am driven to this view because I can understand no legitimate basis whatsoever to impose damages (or enter an injunction) if truly disinterested directors have in fact acted in good faith and with due care on a question that falls within the directors' power to manage the business and affairs of the corporation. To recognize in courts a residual power to review the substance of business decisions for "fairness" or "reason-

ableness" or "rationality" where those decisions are made by truly disinterested directors in good faith and with appropriate care is to make of courts super-directors. It might be correctly said that whether one infers bad faith from an egregious or irrational decision (thus depriving it of business judgment rule protection) or directly strips the decision of that protection upon such a finding is of little practical importance. I am not sure that this is the case, but in any event in the law, to an extent present in few other human institutions, there may be in the long run as much importance ascribed to the reasoning said to justify action, as there is in the actions themselves. Id. at 91,710 n.13 (citations omitted).

d.   The most common example of an abuse of discretion mentioned by courts and commentators which recognize the "no abuse of discretion" element of the rule is the waste of corporate assets, a cause of action separate and apart from a breach of fiduciary duty. See Hanson, 781 F.2d at 279 n.9. Thus, for example, in Gimbel v. Signal Cos., 316 A.2d 599 (Del. Ch.), aff'd, 316 A.2d 619 (Del. 1974), the court was faced with a board decision to sell a corporate subsidiary for $280 million less than its alleged value. While the plaintiff could not make a sufficient showing of imprudence in deliberation by the board (id. at 615), the court held that "[t]here are limits on the business judgment rule which fall short of intentional or inferred fraudulent misconduct and which are based simply on gross inadequacy of price" (id. at 610):

> [T]he ultimate question is not one of method but one of value. The method does not appear so bad on its face as to alter the normal legal principles which control. But hasty method which produces a dollar result which appears perhaps to be shocking is significant. Id. at 615. Accordingly, the court enjoined the transaction in order to facilitate "an immediate fuller investigation into this matter of fair value." Id. at 617.

II.   The Business Judgment Rule's Application in Transactions Involving Corporate Control

A. Should the Business Judgment Rule Apply at All?

1. Most courts, both in Delaware and elsewhere, seem to agree that the business judgment rule generally should apply in one form or another in

cases challenging actions taken by corporate directors to defend against hostile takeover attempts.

   a. Examples of Delaware Cases: Ivanhoe Partners v. Newmont Mining Corp., 535 A.2d 1334, 1341 (Del. 1987); Revlon, Inc. v. MacAndrews and Forbes Holdings, 506 A.2d 173, 179–82 (Del. 1986); Moran v. Household Int'l, Inc., 500 A.2d 1346, 1350 (Del. 1985); Unocal Corp. v. Mesa Petroleum Co., 493 A.2d 946, 954 (Del. 1985); Pogostin v. Rice, 480 A.2d 619, 627 (Del. 1984).

   b. Examples of Non-Delaware Cases: Terrydale Liquidating Trust v. Barness, 846 F.2d 845, 847–48 (2d Cir. 1988), aff'g 642 F. Supp. 917, 919–23 (S.D.N.Y. 1986); Radol v. Thomas, 772 F.2d 244, 257–58 (6th Cir. 1985), cert. denied, 475 U.S. 1086 (1986); Jewel Cos. v. Pay Less Drug Stores Northwest, 741 F.2d 1555, 1560–61 (9th Cir. 1984); Panter v. Marshall Field and Co., 646 F.2d 271, 295 (7th Cir.), cert. denied, 454 U.S. 1092 (1981); Crouse-Hinds Co. v. InterNorth, Inc., 634 F.2d 690, 702-03 (2d Cir. 1980); Johnson v. Trueblood, 629 F.2d 287, 293 (3d Cir. 1980), cert. denied, 450 U.S. 999 (1981).

2. Several courts have gone one step further, stating that directors may be obligated to oppose takeover attempts which they consider detrimental to the corporation. See, e.g., Treco, Inc. v. Land of Lincoln Sav. and Loan, 749 F.2d 374, 378 (7th Cir. 1984); Heit v. Baird, 567 F.2d 1157, 1161 (1st Cir. 1977); Gelco Corp. v. Coniston Partners, 652 F. Supp. 829, 849 (D. Minn. 1986), aff'd on other grounds, 811 F.2d 414 (8th Cir. 1987); Turner Broadcasting Sys. v. CBS, Inc., 627 F. Supp. 901, 908 (N.D. Ga. 1985); Unocal Corp. v. Mesa Petroleum Co., 493 A.2d 946, 955 (Del. 1985).

3. This view, however, is not unanimous.

   a. Two dissenting opinions in Third and Seventh Circuit decisions have contended that directors should not be entitled to utilize the business judgment rule as a shield protecting defensive tactics against hostile takeover efforts. See Panter v. Marshall Field and Co., 646 F.2d 271, 299 (7th Cir. 1981), cert. denied, 454 U.S. 1092 (1981) (Cudahy, J., dissenting); Johnson v. Trueblood, 629 F.2d at 301 (Rosenn, J., concurring and dissenting). As Judge Cudahy put it in Panter:

> I emphatically disagree that the business judgment rule should clothe directors, battling blindly to fend off a threat to their control, with an almost irrebuttable presumption of sound business judgment, prevailing over everything but the elusive hobgoblins of fraud, bad faith or abuse of discretion. 646 F.2d at 299.

   b. Similarly, in Minstar Acquiring Corp. v. AMF Inc., 621 F. Supp. 1252

(S.D.N.Y. 1985), a judge in the Southern District of New York found application of the business judgment rule in the context of a board's decision to defend against a corporate takeover both "questionable" and "troublesome":

> The business judgment rule is a rule of judicial restraint which holds that courts will not inquire into the business judgment of directors who are acting without self-interest and in good faith. As an initial matter we question whether it is appropriate to apply the rule in the context of defensive tactics. The rule was developed to protect directors' judgments on questions of corporate governance. Questions like 'should we buy a new truck today?' or 'should we give Joe a raise?' are simplistically, types of business judgments which the rule was developed to protect. Courts have no place substituting their judgments for that of the directors.
>
> Defensive tactics, however, raise a wholly different set of considerations. The problem is that defensive tactics often, by their very nature, act as a restraint on business purposes. Therefore, the application of the business judgment rule in this context seems, to us, questionable, however, the weight of authority dictates that the rule be applied.
>
> ***
>
> The right of a shareholder to sell his stock is a private transaction between a willing seller and a willing purchaser and in no way implicates the business judgment rule. Therefore, a board of directors' assertion of a unilateral right, under the business judgment rule, to act as a surrogate for the shareholder's independent right of alienation of his stock is troublesome. Id. at 1259–60 and 1260 n.6. The court did not decide this issue, however, because under the facts before it a "strong inference" could be found that the board acted "only to entrench itself," thus enabling the court—even under traditional business judgment rule standards—to shift the burden of proof to the directors to show that the transaction was fair and reasonable. Id. at 1261.

4. In the authors' view, the cases decided to date demonstrate a judicial willingness to uphold reasonable defensive measures which are part of a viable business strategy and which are likely to facilitate a favorable result for shareholders. Courts are unwilling to uphold defensive strategies which do not further such a result and/or alter the basic decision-making structure between directors and shareholders.

B. The Delaware Approach

A series of Delaware Supreme Court cases decided between mid–1985 and today—Unocal Corp. v. Mesa Petroleum Co., 493 A.2d 946 (Del. 1985); Moran v. Household International, Inc., 500 A.2d 1346 (Del. 1985); Revlon, Inc. v. MacAndrews and Forbes Holdings, 506 A.2d 173 (Del. 1986); Polk v. Good, 507 A.2d 531 (Del. 1986); Ivanhoe Partners v. Newmont Mining Corp., 535 A.2d 1334 (Del. 1987); and Mills Acquisition Co. v. Macmillan, Inc. ("Macmillan II"), No. 415 (Del. May 3, 1989)—set forth the view in that jurisdiction concerning the business judgment rule's applicability to defensive measures adopted by Delaware corporations, either as a reaction to a particular threat or simply as a means of warding off possible future advances.

1. The Delaware Supreme Court has emphasized in these cases that a board addressing a pending takeover bid "has an obligation to determine whether the offer is in the best interests of the corporation and its shareholders." Unocal, 493 A.2d at 954; Household, 500 A.2d at 1350. The board's duty in this respect "is no different from any other responsibility" shouldered by the board, and the board's decisions on this subject "should be no less entitled to the respect they otherwise would be accorded in the realm of business judgment." Unocal, 493 A.2d at 954; Household, 500 A.2d at 1350. See also Revlon, 506 A.2d at 179–80; Newmont, 535 A.2d at 1341.

   a. The Household court noted that "in reviewing a pre-planned defensive mechanism it seems even more appropriate to apply the business judgment rule," since "pre-planning for the contingency of a hostile takeover might reduce the risk that, under the pressure of a takeover bid, management will fail to exercise reasonable judgment." Household, 500 A.2d at 1350. See also, e.g., CRTF Corp. v. Federated Dep't Stores, 683 F. Supp. 422, 437 (S.D.N.Y. 1988); Buckhorn, Inc., v. Ropak Corp., 656 F. Supp. 209, 233 (S.D. Ohio), aff'd mem., 815 F.2d 76 (6th Cir. 1987) (both applying Delaware law).

   b. By contrast, corporate action that inequitably seeks to defeat a takeover by means of a retrospective defensive measure (rather than a prospective or reactive step) does not fall within the ambit of the business judgment rule. See Frantz Mfg. Co. v. EAC Indus., 501 A.2d 401, 408 (Del. 1985).

2. Nevertheless, the Delaware Supreme Court has imposed an "enhanced" duty on the board in a takeover situation because of the "omnipresent specter that a board may be acting primarily in its own interests, rather than those of the corporation and its shareholders." Unocal, 493 A.2d at 954;

Revlon, 506 A.2d at 180; Newmont, 535 A.2d at 1341; Macmillan II, slip op. at 61. This "enhanced" duty dictates "judicial examination at the threshold before the protections of the business judgment rule may be conferred." Unocal, 493 A.2d at 954; Newmont, 535 A.2d at 1341.

3. Accordingly, unlike traditional business judgment rule cases where the burden of proof is on the party challenging the transaction, the initial burden in a takeover situation lies with the directors, who must show

   a. First, that they had "reasonable grounds for believing that a danger to corporate policy and effectiveness existed," and

   b. Second, that the defensive measure decided upon was "reasonable in relation to the threat posed."

   Unocal, 493 A.2d at 955; Household, 500 A.2d at 1356; Revlon, 506 A.2d at 180; Polk, 507 A.2d at 537; Newmont, 535 A.2d at 1341.

   A board undertaking this analysis must analyze "the nature of the takeover bid and its effect on the corporate enterprise." Unocal, 493 A.2d at 955; Newmont, 535 A.2d at 1341–42. This involves consideration of among various proper factors, the adequacy and terms of the offer; the proposed or actual financing for the offer, and the consequences of that financing; questions of illegality; the impact of both the bid and the potential acquisition on other constituencies, provided that it bears some reasonable relationship to general shareholder interests; the risk of nonconsummation; the basic stockholder interests at stake; the bidder's identity, prior background, and other business venture experiences; and the bidder's business plans for the corporation and their effects on stockholder interests. Macmillan II, slip op. at 48 n.29.

4. This two-pronged burden has come to be known as the Unocal test or standard, and may be satisfied "by showing good faith and reasonable investigation." Unocal, 493 A.2d at 955; Household, 500 A.2d at 1356; Revlon, 506 A.2d at 180; Newmont, 535 A.2d at 1341.

5. Once the board satisfies its initial Unocal burden, the burden of proof shifts back to the plaintiff, who has the burden of persuasion, to demonstrate by a preponderance of the evidence a breach of the directors' fiduciary duties. Unocal, 493 A.2d at 958; Household, 500 A.2d at 1356.

6. The Delaware Court of Chancery's 1988 opinion in City Capital Associates v. Interco Inc., 551 A.2d 787 (Del. Ch. 1988), emphasizes that the Unocal test poses the danger that "courts—in exercising some element of substantive judgment—will too readily seek to assert the primacy of their own view on a question upon which reasonable, completely disinterested minds might differ." Id. at 796. "Inartfully applied," the Interco court thus

observed, the test "could permit an unraveling of the well-made fabric of the business judgment rule." Id. The Delaware courts therefore apply this form of judicial review cautiously, according to the Interco court, "with a clear appreciation for the risks and special responsibility this approach entails." Id. at 796–97. See also Veasey, The New Incarnation of the Business Judgment Rule in Takeover Defenses, 11 Del. J. Corp. L. 503, 512 (1986):

> Recent cases purport to apply the business judgment rule and merely shift the burden of going forward with the evidence in some respects. There is a danger, however, that this approach could lead to random, ad hoc decisions. Courts tend to be result-oriented. If a particular defensive tactic does not pass the "smell test," i.e., it looks like an effort to entrench the incumbents and that there is a reasonable likelihood that stockholders are not getting the best price obtainable, the court may employ the new standards of judicial review to justify an injunction.

7. To date, the Delaware courts have found that threats sufficient to satisfy the first prong of the Unocal standard include (but are not limited to):

a. Coercive "front-end loaded" cash offers for less than all shares, pursuant to which "back-end" shareholders may be "squeezed out" with junk bonds or other securities worth less than the cash paid to shareholders who tender their shares into the front end of the offer. See, e.g., Newmont, 535 A.2d at 1342; Unocal, 493 A.2d at 956 and n.12; Household, 500 A.2d at 1357.

b. Noncoercive cash offers for all shares which are inadequate because (in the board's judgment) the price offered does not reflect the stock's true value and/or does not provide shareholders the highest price possible for their shares. See, e.g., Shamrock Holdings v. Polaroid Corp. ("Polaroid II"), [Current] Fed. Sec. L. Rep. (CCH) ¶ 94,340, at 92,223 (Del. Ch. Mar. 17, 1989); Grand Metro. PLC v. Pillsbury Co., [1988–1989 Transfer Binder] Fed. Sec. L. Rep. (CCH) ¶ 94,104, at 91,193 and n.8 (Del. Ch. Dec. 16, 1988); Interco, 551 A.2d at 797–98; Robert M. Bass Group v. Evans ("Macmillan I"), 552 A.2d 1227, 1239–41 (Del. Ch. 1988).

(1) Absent unusual circumstances, several courts have suggested this threat remains a threat only until "there has been sufficient time for any alternative to be developed and presented and for the target corporation to inform its stockholders of the benefits of retaining their equity position." Polaroid II, [Current] Fed. Sec. L. Rep. (CCH) at 92,223. See also Interco, 551 A.2d at 798.

(2) Such unusual circumstances permitting a board to view a noncoercive but (according to the board) inadequate offer as a continuing threat were found in Polaroid II. Polaroid had obtained a judgment in its favor in a patent infringement litigation against Kodak, and was seeking $5.7 billion, or $44.14 per share, in damages. The court emphasized that "Polaroid's stockholders really have very little way of assessing the present worth of this extremely valuable asset," and that Polaroid's board accordingly had "a valid basis for concern that the Polaroid stockholders will be unable to reach an accurate judgment as to the intrinsic value of their stock." Id. at 92,223–24.

(3) At least one court, however, has suggested that a board may have the authority to "just say no" to any sale of the company or the pursuit of any alternative maximization of current value or other extraordinary transaction, and instead simply "continue managing the enterprise in a long-term mode." TW Servs. Shareholders Litig., [Current] Fed. Sec. L. Rep. (CCH) ¶ 94,334, at 92,178 and 92,181 (Del. Ch. Mar. 2, 1989).

c. Noncoercive and adequate cash offers for all shares which do not provide shareholders an option of remaining shareholders in the corporation as the board believes it should be restructured. See AC Acquisitions Corp. v. Anderson, Clayton and Co., 519 A.2d 103, 112 (Del. Ch. 1986).

8. The cases decided to date also demonstrate that the circumstances surrounding the particular threat involved in a particular case determine the reasonableness of the defensive measure taken by a board in response to the threat, with mild threats to the corporate entity requiring more carefully tailored board responses than more severe threats. See, e.g., Interco, 551 A.2d at 798–800; Macmillan I, 552 A.2d at 1241–46; Anderson Clayton, 519 A.2d at 112–15. As the Unocal court put it, a "corporation does not have unbridled discretion to defeat any perceived threat by any Draconian means available." Unocal, 493 A.2d at 955.

9. An open question is whether the courts may undertake a Unocal analysis in cases in which the target corporation's board of directors has not itself done so. The Delaware Court of Chancery declined to answer this question in Shamrock Holdings v. Polaroid Corp. ("Polaroid I"), [1988–1989 Transfer Binder] Fed. Sec. L. Rep. (CCH) ¶ 94,176, at 91,619–20 (Del. Ch. Jan. 6, 1989), but noted that it had applied a Unocal analysis in Henley Group v. Santa Fe Southern Pacific Corp., No. 9569 (Del. Ch. Mar. 11,

1988), notwithstanding the contention of the Santa Fe directors that Unocal had no applicability in that case because the board's conduct was not defensive in nature. Id., slip op. at 37.

 The Polaroid I court also declined to decide whether board approval of a challenged transaction should be judged pursuant to the ordinary business judgment rule standard or the Unocal standard in cases in which management directors who propose a transaction are found to have acted in a defensive mode but the corporation's outside directors— who constitute a majority of the board—contend that their conduct was not defensive. [1988–1989 Transfer Binder] Fed. Sec. L. Rep. (CCH) at 91,619–20.

10. Federal courts construing Indiana, Minnesota and Wisconsin law have utilized Delaware's two-pronged Unocal test to evaluate the propriety of various defensive measures, and it can be expected that additional courts will do the same as cases arise in other jurisdictions. See Dynamics Corp. of Am. v. CTS Corp. (CTS II), 805 F.2d 705, 708 (7th Cir. 1986) (Indiana law); Amanda Acquisition Corp. v. Universal Foods Corp., No. 88-C–1296(JPS), slip op. at 50–53 (E.D. Wis. Mar. 18, 1989) (Wisconsin law); Gelco Corp. v. Coniston Partners, 652 F. Supp. 829, 845 (D. Minn. 1986), aff'd on other grounds, 811 F.2d 414 (8th Cir. 1987) (Minnesota law).

11. Different and more stringent rules apply when the sale or break-up of the corporation becomes inevitable and an "auction" is required. The specific circumstances under which such an auction must be conducted and the rules which govern auctions when they are required are beyond the scope of this outline. See Chapter 11, this volume, and generally, e.g., Mills Acquisition Co. v. Macmillan, Inc. ("Macmillan II"), No. 415, slip op. at 40–65 (Del. May 3, 1989); Ivanhoe Partners v. Newmont Mining Corp., 535 A.2d 1234, 1345 (Del. 1987); Bershad v. Curtiss-Wright Corp., 535 A.2d 840, 845 (Del. 1987); Revlon, Inc. v. MacAndrews and Forbes Holdings, 506 A.2d 173, 182–84 (Del. 1986); TW Servs. Shareholders Litig., [Current] Fed. Sec. L. Rep. (CCH) ¶ 94,334, at 92,178–80 (Del. Ch. Mar. 2, 1989); In re RJR Nabisco, Inc. Shareholders Litig., [1988–1989 Transfer Binder] Fed. Sec. L. Rep. (CCH) ¶ 94,194, at 91,714–15 (Del. Ch. Jan. 31, 1989); In re Holly Farms Corp. Shareholders Litig., [1988–1989 Transfer Binder] Fed. Sec. L. Rep. (CCH) ¶ 94,181, at 91,643–45 (Del. Ch. Dec. 30, 1988); City Capital Assocs. v. Interco Inc., 551 A.2d 787, 801-03 (Del. Ch. 1988); In re J.P. Stevens and Co. Shareholders Litig., 542 A.2d 770, 781–84 (Del. Ch. 1988); Yanow v. Scientific Leasing, [1987–1988 Transfer Binder] Fed. Sec. L. Rep. (CCH) ¶ 93,660, at 98,034 (Del. Ch. Feb. 5, 1988).

12. Finally, it is well-settled under Delaware law (and the law of virtually every other jurisdiction) that neither the traditional business judgment rule nor the Unocal variation of the rule has any applicability where directors act "solely or primarily out of a desire to perpetuate themselves in office" or in some other inequitable manner. See, e.g., Macmillan II, slip op. at 41; Newmont, 535 A.2d at 1341; Unocal, 493 A.2d at 955; Schell v. Chris-Craft Indus., 285 A.2d 437, 439 (Del. 1971); Condec Corp. v. Lunkenheimer Co., 230 A.2d 769, 775–76 (Del. Ch. 1967).

III. Stock Sales to "Friendly" Investors

A. White Squire Transactions

1. One means by which a corporation may restructure or recapitalize itself is by placing a block of stock in the hands of a friendly "white squire"—i.e., a third party that is interested in making an investment but not acquiring complete control over the target. Such white squire arrangements are typically judged pursuant to business judgment rule standards, although it should be noted that stock exchange rules provide that listed companies are subject to delisting for issuances of stock in excess of specified percentages of outstanding shares. See New York Stock Exchange Listed Company Manual § 312.00 (18.5 percent); AMEX Company Guide §§ 712–13 (20 percent).

2. In Carter Hawley Hale Stores v. The Limited, Inc., No. 84–2200-AWT (C.D. Cal. Apr. 17, 1984), for instance, Carter Hawley Hale ("CHH") responded to a takeover attempt by The Limited by selling convertible preferred stock possessing votes equivalent to 22 percent of CHH's outstanding voting shares to General Cinema, with General Cinema agreeing to vote its shares pursuant to the recommendation of CHH's board. The court refused to enjoin the stock sale:

> [U]nder the facts as presented to me now this was a prudent exercise of business judgment made by independent directors and not insiders, although the insiders, I think, confirmed the actions of the outside directors.
>
> [I]t not for me to say…whether I think it is wise or not; it is whether it is within the ambit of reasonable judgment by prudent businessmen, and [it] appears to me on the evidence today that it is.
>
> [I] can't say it is any worse than the offer of The Limited. I think once the board determines that it believes the unfriendly offer is not adequate for its shareholders, then I think it has the obligation

> to take such actions as it feels is necessary to protect the rights of
> the shareholders. And if that is a reasonable course of action
> chosen, I think it should be upheld. Id., Tr. op. at 78–79.

3. Similarly, in News International PLC v. Warner Communications, No.
7420 (Del. Ch. Jan. 12, 1984), Warner responded to a threatened takeover
by Rupert Murdoch's News International by selling a 19 percent equity
interest in Warner to a Chris-Craft subsidiary in exchange for a 42.5
percent interest in the subsidiary. Id., slip op. at 1. Despite the fact that
Warner had an 80 percent supermajority voting requirement for certain
shareholder actions, including the removal of directors, the court refused
to enjoin the transaction. The court rejected News International's argument that "by issuing what in practical effect is a 20 percent interest to the
subsidiary of Chris-Craft, Warner's management is depriving plaintiff for
all time of the opportunity, either through the acquisition of stock or
through proxies obtained from other Warner shareholders, to exercise the
required 80 percent vote":

> [I]n theory, there is nothing to prevent Chris-Craft, should it so desire,
> from voting its shares with those of the plaintiff in an effort to produce
> the 80 percent vote necessary to take action against the wishes of
> Warner's present management. It could accomplish the same thing in
> league with 60 percent of Warner's present shareholders other than the
> plaintiff. Thus, it does not appear that the proposed transaction itself
> will necessarily deprive plaintiff and the shareholders of Warner other
> than management from the opportunity of ever taking action against
> management. Id. at 3–4.

4. The same result was reached in Shamrock Holdings v. Polaroid Corp.
("Polaroid II"), [Current] Fed. Sec. L. Rep. (CCH) ¶ 94,340 (Del. Ch. Mar.
17, 1989).

a. This case involved Polaroid's sale to Corporate Partners of $300
   million worth of voting preferred stock during the pendency of an
   unwanted all-cash tender offer by Shamrock.

   (1) The court identified Corporate Partners as a partnership "organized
       to make friendly investments" whose participation resulted in "an
       infusion of capital" and "a block of voting securities in the hands
       of one sophisticated entity which will support management and the
       board of directors" and thus provide "insulation from...hostile
       acquirors." Id. at 92,216–17.

   (2) The terms of the preferred stock granted Corporate Partners the
       right to "put" its preferred stock to Polaroid at a 7 percent rate of

return in the event of a change of control within 6 months, and at a 28–30 percent rate of return in the event of a change of control within 6 to 24 months. Id. at 92,219.

(3) There was no agreement concerning how Corporate Partners would vote its stock so long as Corporate Partners' total voting power remained below 20 percent, but if Corporate Partners' voting power rose above 20 percent then all votes held by Corporate Partners in excess of 19.9 percent would be cast—at Corporate Partners' option—either in proportion to the votes of all other shareholders or as directed by Polaroid's board. Id.

(4) Corporate Partners' ability to transfer its shares was restricted, but Corporate Partners was not barred from tendering its shares into Shamrock's offer or any other cash tender offer for all Polaroid shares. Id.

b. The court declined to issue a preliminary injunction against the sale of this stock to Corporate Partners due to "credible evidence" in "a very limited record" that:

(1) Polaroid and Corporate Partners had engaged in "fairly extensive arm's-length negotiations" during which Polaroid was able to reduce the number of votes the preferred stock would carry,

(2) The terms upon which the preferred stock was issued were commercially reasonable, and

(3) The preferred stock allowed Polaroid "significantly more flexibility" than it would have had if the $300 million invested in Polaroid by Corporate Partners had been obtained through corporate borrowing. Id. at 92,224–25.

The court acknowledged that there was also evidence that the terms of the preferred stock were not commercially reasonable and that "[i]t seem[ed] a bit too convenient" that Corporate Partners— the only entity Polaroid claimed it could find which was willing to invest on terms acceptable to Polaroid—was an entity that promoted itself as a "friendly" investor providing "insulation from...hostile acquirors," but concluded that there was an insufficient basis upon which it could find the transaction to have been improperly motivated or unreasonably disproportionate to the threat posed by Shamrock's tender offer. Id. at 92,224–25.

5. The court in Ivanhoe Partners v. Newmont Mining Corp., 535 A.2d 1334 (Del. 1987), upheld Newmont Mining's declaration of a large dividend during the pendency of an unwanted two-tier offer by Ivanhoe Partners, a

T. Boone Pickens-controlled entity. The dividend was intended to finance a "street sweep" by Consolidated Gold Fields, a white squire already holding 26 percent of the corporation's stock.

   a. A standstill agreement negotiated prior to this transaction allowed Gold Fields to increase its position to 49.9 percent, and Gold Fields in fact raised its holdings to 49.7 percent. The agreement also limited Gold Fields to 40 percent of the seats on Newmont's board, required Gold Fields to support the board's slate of nominees for the directorships, and prohibited the transfer of Gold Fields' interest to any third party which would not agree to be bound by these terms. See id. at 1338–40.

   b. The court concluded that Newmont's actions were reasonable in relation to the threats posed by

     (1) Ivanhoe's financially inadequate and coercive tender offer, and

     (2) The possibility that Gold Fields—a large shareholder which had made clear its intent to act in accordance with its own best interests—might itself try to take control of the corporation at an unfair price. See id. at 1342. The court stated:

> The comprehensive defensive scheme consisting of the dividend, standstill agreement, and street sweep accomplished the two essential objectives of thwarting the inadequate coercive Ivanhoe offer, and of insuring the continued interest of the public shareholders in the independent control and prosperity of Newmont. Under the circumstances, the board's actions taken by a majority of independent directors, are entitled to the protection of the business judgment rule. Id. at 1345.

6. Manbourne, Inc. v. Conrad, 796 F.2d 884 (7th Cir. 1986), provides an example of a stock issuance which has been enjoined. This case involved the issuance of stock-to-option holders shortly after an unwanted acquiror had obtained control of 50.23 percent of the corporation's stock, and after the corporation's directors had "arranged for the option holders to exercise their options for the purposes of placing majority control in friendly hands, and maintaining themselves in office." Id. at 886 and 890. The court emphasized that the case did not involve "unaffiliated individuals independently exercising their options to purchase stock in a corporation that is the subject of a takeover bid, and we do not decide whether the exercise of stock options could ever be enjoined in such a case." Id.

7. Similarly, in Phillips v. Insituform of North America, 13 Del. J. Corp. L. 774 (Del. Ch. 1987), the court enjoined the sale of 51,000 shares to the chairman and chief executive officer of the company (only 10 percent of

the stock was paid for in cash) in order to reduce the percentage of that class of stock held by a court-appointed receiver to 49 percent, and thus eliminate the possibility of immediate shareholder action. The court emphasized that "no justification has been shown that would arguably make the extraordinary step of issuance of stock for the admitted purpose of impeding the exercise of stockholder rights reasonable in light of the corporate benefit, if any, sought to be obtained." Id. at 788–89.

B. Employee Stock Ownership Plans ("ESOPs")

  1. Introduction

    a. Employee Stock Ownership Plans ("ESOPs"), historically created to provide retirement benefits for corporate employees and substantial tax savings for corporations, have increasingly been utilized by corporate directors as a defensive measure. See ESOPs: Are They Good for You? Business Week, May 15, 1989, at 116; Stuffing Nest Eggs with ESOPs, Bus. Week, Apr. 24, 1989; Hilder and Smith, ESOP Defenses are Likely to Increase, Wall St. J., Apr. 6, 1989, at A2; Suddenly, Blue Chips are Red-Hot for ESOPs, Bus. Week, Mar. 20, 1989, at 144; A New Way to Keep Raiders at Bay, Bus. Week, Jan. 23, 1989, at 39.

    b. Stock held by an ESOP is typically assumed to be in friendly hands because unsolicited takeover efforts almost inevitably raise concerns about job security, and individual employees holding ESOP shares worth a small fraction of their individual salaries, it is generally believed, will forgo higher returns on their ESOP investment in favor of job security. Shamrock Holdings v. Polaroid Corp. ("Polaroid I"), [1988–1989 Transfer Binder] Fed. Sec. L. Rep. (CCH) ¶ 94,176, at 91,621 (Del. Ch. Jan. 6, 1989). To the extent that this assumption is true, ESOPs provide a block of voting stock which will generally act in accordance with management's recommendations.

    c. ESOP blocks are particularly significant in light of § 203 of the Delaware General Corporation Law. This statute, enacted in 1988, provides that a prospective acquiror may not engage in a business combination with the target corporation for three years after becoming a 15 percent shareholder unless, among other things, the acquiror obtains at least 85 percent of the target company's voting stock in the same transaction that causes it to become a 15 percent stockholder. Del. Gen. Corp. Law § 203(a)(2).

    d. Even apart from § 203, substantial ESOP blocks may effectively bar the consummation of a hostile bid by making it impossible for a bidder to acquire enough shares to ensure completion of a second-step or back-end merger. See generally Nassau, Schwartz and Sobel, ESOPs After Polaroid—Opportunities and Pitfalls, I Mergers and Acquisitions L. Rep. 1191 (1989).

e. Numerous courts have held that ESOPs, like other employee benefit plans, may serve legitimate corporate purposes, including supplementing employee compensation and retirement benefits, improving employee morale and loyalty, and raising capital. See, e.g., Norlin Corp. v. Rooney, Pace Inc., 744 F.2d 255, 266 (2d Cir. 1984); Polaroid I, [1988–1989 Transfer Binder] Fed. Sec. L. Rep. (CCH) at 91,620–21 and n.16.

As discussed below, however, difficult questions arise in the context of ESOPs adopted during or immediately before contests for corporate control.

2. Cases Invalidating ESOPs

a. Several courts have refused to accord business judgment rule protection to ESOPs adopted in the midst of a takeover battle, on the ground that such "precipitous timing" gives rise to a strong inference of entrenchment-based conduct.

b. In Norlin Corp. v. Rooney, Pace Inc., 744 F.2d 255 (2d Cir. 1984), for example, the Second Circuit Court of Appeals struck down an ESOP created five days following a district court's refusal to enjoin further stock purchases by an unwanted bidder.

(1) The court emphasized that the ESOP was created at a time when the corporation's officers were "clearly casting about for strategies to deter a challenge to control," that members of the target corporation's board had been appointed trustees of the ESOP, that the board retained voting control of the ESOP shares, that no real consideration was received from the ESOP in exchange for the transferred shares, and that no rationale for the transfers was offered to shareholders other than the board's determination to oppose an unwanted takeover at all costs. Id. at 265–66.

(2) The court also noted the directors' awareness that, absent shareholder approval, the combination of the ESOP creation and other stock issuances violated New York Stock Exchange rules, and could result in delisting. Id. at 259–60.

(3) The court accordingly found that "the ESOP was created solely as a tool of management self-perpetuation," id. at 266, and was therefore invalid. Id. at 267.

c. Similar results have been reached by the Ninth Circuit in Klaus v. Hi-

Shear Corp., 528 F.2d 225, 233 (9th Cir. 1975), by district courts construing Delaware law in Buckhorn, Inc. v. Ropak Corp., 656 F. Supp. 209, 232 (S.D. Ohio), aff'd mem., 815 F.2d 76 (6th Cir. 1987), and Podesta v. Calumet Industries, [1978 Transfer Binder] Fed. Sec. L. Rep. (CCH) ¶ 96,433, at 93,550–54 and 93,556–57 (N.D. Ill. May 9, 1978), and by the Delaware Supreme Court in Frantz Manufacturing Co. v. EAC Industries, 501 A.2d 401, 407-08 (Del. 1985).

3. Cases Upholding ESOPs on Business Judgment Rule Grounds

   a. ESOPs have been upheld on business judgment rule grounds notwithstanding the close proximity of the decision to adopt the ESOP and the contest for corporate control in cases involving Chicago Pneumatic Tool, Anderson Clayton and Harcourt Brace Jovanovich.

   b. Chicago Pneumatic Tool

      (1) Danaher Corp. v. Chicago Pneumatic Tool Co., 633 F. Supp. 1066 (S.D.N.Y. 1986), involved an ESOP which was funded within days of the start of a stock accumulation program by a hostile acquiror, and which named the corporation's Chief Executive Officer as trustee. See 633 F. Supp. at 1068–70.

      (2) The court upheld the ESOP on the grounds that "the establishment and funding of the ESOP had been a subject of attention and repeated discussion by the Board throughout the twelve previous months," that the funding had been authorized four months before the hostile bidder's stock acquisitions had begun, and that "[t]here is every indication that [the funding] was undertaken because the Board and management of CP believed it would be a good thing for their corporation." Id. at 1071.

   c. Anderson Clayton

      (1) In In re Anderson, Clayton Shareholders Litigation, 519 A.2d 680 (Del. Ch. 1986), the court refused to enjoin an ESOP that was part of a restructuring plan (discussed in § V B 2 b infra) recommended by a board in order to (i) permit a cash distribution which was part of the restructuring to be on a capital gains basis, and (ii) provide "an attractive technique (from a tax point of view)" for compensating corporate officers and employees. 519 A.2d at 688.

      (2) The court emphasized that the ESOP trustee was an independent bank with no significant relationship with the corporation, that voting of the ESOP shares was to be directed by the trust beneficiaries, and that management directors would, following the completion of the restructuring, control the votes of

only 1.3 percent of the corporation's total outstanding stock. Id. at 689.

d. Harcourt Brace Jovanovich

   (1) The court in British Printing and Communication Corp. plc v. Harcourt Brace Jovanovich, Inc., 664 F. Supp. 1519 (S.D.N.Y. 1987) denied preliminary injunctive relief against a restructuring plan (discussed in § VI B 2 infra), which was adopted in response to an unwanted bid, and which included a sale and contribution by the target corporation of a substantial amount of stock to an ESOP. See 664 F. Supp. at 1521 and 1525–26.

   (2) The court based the ESOP aspect of its decision upon its finding that a pre-existing ESOP had been created for a valid purpose long before the appearance of the unwanted bidder, and that the ESOP was "intended to serve as an incentive for increased employee productivity, an essential element of the plan's success." 664 F. Supp. at 1531. This was particularly important, the court emphasized, because the cost of the restructuring would require the company "to restrict its spending in the near future, thus impinging on its ability to offer other financial incentives to its employees." Id. at 1526.

   (3) The Harcourt Brace court also emphasized that the "possibility of an entrenchment motive…is belied by the fact that neither management as a whole nor the ESOP trustees control how the stock held by the ESOP is voted." Id. at 1531.

      (a) Rather, the ESOP plan contained a "pass-through" provision pursuant to which all shares allocated to individual employee participants' accounts would be voted by the participants themselves. Unallocated shares would be voted for and against proposals to shareholders in the same proportion as the allocated shares are voted. Id. at 1526 and 1528.

      (b) The court emphasized that decisions regarding whether to tender to a potential acquiror "would be decided by the trustees under the constraints of their legal obligation to act in the best interests of the ESOP beneficiaries." Id. at 1531. See also id. at 1529, citing 29 U.S.C. § 1104, and Donovan v. Bierwirth, 680 F.2d 263 (2d Cir.), cert. denied, 459 U.S. 1069 (1982) (discussed in § III B 5 c infra).

      (c) The court was not troubled by the fact that the ESOP trustees were members of management because the trustees had obtained advice from independent legal and financial advisers. See 664 F. Supp. at 1526.

4. Polaroid and the Entire Fairness Standard

  a. The ESOP decision which has received the most attention to date is the Delaware Court of Chancery's 1989 decision in Shamrock Holdings v. Polaroid Corp. ("Polaroid I"), [1988–1989 Transfer Binder] Fed. Sec. L. Rep. (CCH) ¶ 94,176 (Del. Ch. Jan. 6, 1989).

  b. Polaroid I involved the adoption of a $300 million ESOP holding 14 percent of Polaroid's stock less than one month after the corporation learned that a potentially hostile bidder—Shamrock Holdings—had acquired just under 5 percent of Polaroid's stock. See id. at 91,614–15 and 91,617–18.

  c. The ESOP plan was intended to be "shareholder neutral" (id. at 91,617 and 91,620)—i.e., the ESOP "would be funded by an exchange of employee benefits and the ESOP shares would be purchased in the open market with the result that the ESOP would not impose any additional cost on the company or have any dilutive effect on the stockholders." Id. at 91,613. The $300 million in exchanged employee benefits included a five percent pay cut for all employees, § 401(k) matching funds, a delay in pay scale increases, and profit sharing retirement plan contributions. Id. at 91,616.

  d. The 14 percent ESOP was approved at a special meeting of Polaroid's board held the day before Polaroid's management had been scheduled to meet with Shamrock at Shamrock's request for a "friendly meeting." Id. at 91,615, 91,616–17 and nn. 6–7.

    (1) Shamrock had first requested this meeting on June 16, 1988. Polaroid agreed on June 24 to schedule a meeting for July 13, but only if Shamrock agreed not to buy any additional Polaroid stock prior to the meeting or for a reasonable amount of time after the meeting. Shamrock agreed to these conditions. Id. at 91,615.

    (2) The board meeting was called on less than a week's notice, resulting in three outside directors being unable to attend and a fourth director having to leave before any votes were taken. Id. at 91,617.

    (3) No written materials were provided to the directors prior to the meeting. Id. The ESOP was discussed for about two hours, with attention given to shareholder neutrality, how the $300 million needed to fund the ESOP would be obtained from employees, whether employees would make shareholder decisions (involving

tendering and voting) from a long-term rather than a short-term perspective, the likelihood of morale problems when employees were told that a five percent pay cut would be required to fund the ESOP, and the prospect that the ESOP would provide employees greater incentive to make the company profitable. Id.

(4) The directors did not question the ESOP size chosen by management, id., and there was no discussion of alternative funding sources or the known opposition of certain employee groups to the proposed pay cuts. Id. at 91,617–18 and 91,619 n.12.

(5) There was also no discussion of the effect of a 14 percent ESOP in light of § 203 of the Delaware General Corporation Law, which, as discussed earlier (see § III B 1 b supra), precludes business combinations between a corporation and a shareholder which acquires more than 15 percent but less than 85 percent of the corporation's outstanding stock without prior board approval for three years following the acquisition. See Del. Gen. Corp. Law § 203(a).

e. Following a full trial on the merits, the Delaware Court of Chancery upheld the ESOP's creation on the ground that the transaction satisfied the entire fairness test applied where the business judgment rule does not shield a transaction from judicial scrutiny. Id. at 91,620. See § I D supra.

The court emphasized that this conclusion made it unnecessary to decide whether Shamrock was correct in contending that the business judgment rule was inapplicable due to Polaroid's directors' alleged (1) failure to inform themselves, see id. at 91,619, and (2) failure to consider whether their conduct conformed to the standards (reasonable grounds for believing that a danger to corporate policy and effectiveness existed and a reasonable response in relation to the threat posed) as mandated, according to Shamrock, by Unocal Corp. v. Mesa Petroleum Co., 493 A.2d 946 (Del. 1985). See Shamrock, [1988–1989 Transfer Binder] Fed. Sec. L. Rep. (CCH) at 91,618–20.

f. The court outlined and applied several factors relevant to the fairness of an ESOP.

(1) First and foremost, the court emphasized, is whether the ESOP is funded by employees or by the corporation and its shareholders. Polaroid I, [1988–1989 Transfer Binder] Fed. Sec. L. Rep. (CCH) at 91,620.

(a) Here, the court concluded, the ESOP was funded by employees and was thus "shareholder neutral " Id

    (b) Since ESOPs generally promote morale and productivity, the court added, the plan was if anything "shareholder positive." Id.

(2) Second, the court considered the impact of the ESOP upon the corporation's business operations—i.e., whether the ESOP would enhance or impair productivity.

    (a) The court observed that ESOPs generally promote employee morale and productivity, but recognized that this ESOP differed from many ESOPs by being funded with a mandatory 5 percent pay cut.

    (b) The court concluded, however, that there was no evidence that the ESOP contained a "hidden cost" to be reflected in an employee cutback on productivity as an expression of displeasure with the pay cut. Id. at 91,620–21.

(3) Third, the court considered the antitakeover effect of the ESOP.

    (a) The court acknowledged the general belief that ESOP stockholders will be friendly to management. Id. at 91,621.

    (b) The court also acknowledged the significance of the size of Polaroid's ESOP in light of § 203 of the Delaware General Corporation Law, which, as noted above, provides that a bidder which acquires more than 15 percent but less than 85 percent of the company's shares without board approval may not engage in a business combination with the company for 3 years. Id.

    (c) The court also observed, however, that the Delaware statute provides that shares held by employee stock plans that do not provide for confidential tendering by employees are not included in the total number of outstanding shares in the 85 percent calculation, and that Polaroid's plan did provide for confidential tendering by employees. Id. at 91,622.

        [The court noted in a subsequent opinion that the ESOP plan document did not in fact require confidential voting. The court declined to modify its Polaroid I decision on this basis, however, because Polaroid's directors and ESOP trustee had treated the ESOP as if it required confidential voting even before being challenged on this point, and that the document had since been amended to require confidential voting. Shamrock Holdings v. Polaroid Corp., [Current] Fed. Sec. L. Rep. (CCH) ¶ 94,340, at 92,225 (Del. Ch. Mar. 17, 1989) ("Polaroid II").]

(d) The court viewed the statutory provision regarding confidential tendering as a "policy statement" suggesting that ESOPs with confidential tendering are "not suspect—they will not necessarily interfere with an acquiror's ability to obtain 85 percent of the voting stock of a target corporation." Polaroid I, [1988–1989 Transfer Binder] Fed. Sec. L. Rep. (CCH) at 91,622.

(e) The court emphasized, however, that the statutory provision regarding confidential tendering should not be read as "automatically blessing any ESOP with confidential tendering." Id. The court recognized that the existence of the 14 percent ESOP "may mean that a potential acquiror will have to gain the employees' confidence and support in order to be successful in its takeover effort," but concluded that there had been "no showing that such support is or would be impossible to obtain." Id.

(4) Finally, the court considered the dilutive effect of the ESOP.

(a) The court observed that the ESOP shares were issued by the company instead of being purchased by the ESOP in the market, and thus (at least temporarily) diluted the holdings of public shareholders. Id.

(b) The court explained that the $300 million paid by the ESOP for 10 million shares was available to the corporation for open market repurchases, and that whether the ESOP would ultimately have a dilutive effect depended upon the corporation's ability to make open market purchases at the same $30 per share price that was paid by the ESOP and/or the ESOP's generating additional revenues for the company by increasing productivity. Id.

(c) The court recognized that a 5 percent reduction in earnings per share was a possibility, but concluded that "[o]n balance…a minimal reduction in earnings per share is fair where, as here, it is necessary to promptly implement a large ESOP that is intended to increase corporate earnings." Id.

(d) The result would be different, the court noted, "[i]f the ESOP's only purpose were to help thwart hostile takeovers." Id.

(5) The Polaroid I court concluded by emphasizing that it was "unaware of any case where an entire fairness analysis was applied

to an ESOP," but that a "strong indicia of fairness is established" in the ESOP context where the ESOP is "fully funded by the employees and where they control the disposition and voting of the ESOP stock." Id. at 91,623.

   (a) The court acknowledged that Polaroid's directors "rushed to put this ESOP in place...motivated, at least in part, by a desire to add one more obstacle to Shamrock's potential acquisition bid." Id.

   (b) The court determined, however, that this defensive device "is designed to and appears likely to add value to the company and all of its stockholders," and "does not prevent the stock-holders from receiving or considering alternatives." Id.

5. ERISA Considerations

   a. The Employee Retirement Income Security Act of 1974 (ERISA), 29 U.S.C. § 1001 et seq., mandates that employee benefit plan fiduciaries must act "solely in the interest of the participants and beneficiaries" of the plan, and "for the exclusive purpose" of providing benefits to these beneficiaries. Id. § 1104(a). Trustees of employee benefit plans not falling within the scope of ERISA have a similar common law duty. See, e.g., Restatement (Second) of Trusts § 170 (1957).

   b. These obligations place ERISA trustees in a difficult position when a tender offer, opposed by the corporation's board of directors as contrary to the corporation's best interests, provides the trustees with an opportunity to sell the plan's shares of the corporation's stock at a substantial premium over the stock's prevailing market price. See generally Note, Dual Standards for the Use of Employee Benefit Plans in Corporate Takeovers: ERISA and the Business Judgment Rule, 59 St. John's L. Rev. 751 (1985); Note, Fiduciary Duties of Pension Fund Managers in Corporate Take-Overs, 11 N. Ky. L. Rev. 553 (1984); Note, The Duties of Employee Benefit Plan Trustees Under ERISA in Hostile Tender Offers, 82 Colum. L. Rev. 1692 (1982).

   c. These conflicting interests provided the basis for the Second Circuit's decision in Donovan v. Bierwirth, 680 F.2d 263 (2d Cir.), cert. denied, 459 U.S. 1069 (1982).

      (1) Here, the Second Circuit found that the Secretary of Labor had demonstrated a "likelihood of success" supporting the issuance of preliminary injunctive relief on his claim that the purchase by pension fund trustees of over 1 million shares of the corporation's stock (at a total cost of over $44 million) during the course of a hostile battle for corporate control

constituted a breach of the "high standard of duty" imposed by ERISA. Id. at 272.

(2) The Second Circuit emphasized that the fund trustees were also officers of the target corporation who in that capacity were devoting a substantial portion (if not most) of their time to efforts opposing the unwanted offer:

> We accept that [the trustee-directors] were honestly convinced that acquisition of [the corporation] by the debt-ridden [offeror] would mean a less bright future for [the corporation] and also that an [offeror] acquisition posed some special dangers to the participants of the Plan. However, they should have realized that, since their judgment on this score could scarcely be unbiased, at the least they were bound to take every feasible precaution to see that they had carefully considered the other side, to free themselves, if indeed this was humanly possible, from any taint of the quick negative reaction characteristic of targets of hostile tender offers displayed at the [board meeting at which the offer was rejected] and particularly to consider the huge risks attendant on purchasing additional [corporation] shares at a price substantially elevated by the tender offer. We need not decide whether even this would have sufficed; perhaps...resignation was the only proper course. Id. at 276.

(3) Additional evidence was offered at a subsequent trial, the Second Circuit noted in a later proceeding, which "tended to show that at the time the Trustees purchased the stock, they expected its price to drop because they expected to successfully frustrate the tender offer." Donovan v. Bierwirth, 754 F.2d 1049, 1052 n.2 (2d Cir. 1985).

d. Directors who select and retain ERISA fiduciaries themselves have a fiduciary duty under the statute, even where the trustees selected are not directors or officers of the corporation.

Thus, in Leigh v. Engle, 727 F.2d 113 (7th Cir. 1984), the Seventh Circuit held that directors may be held liable for the fiduciary duty violations of ERISA trustees if the directors fail to act "reasonably and prudently in light of their knowledge of the [trustees'] conflicting interests and the trust's investments." Id. at 136; see also id. at 133–36.

(1) The court in Leigh found that "[n]othing in the record" demonstrated that the corporation's board or its chairman "took steps either to insure that

[the trustees] were fulfilling their fiduciary obligations or to remedy any violations which might have already occurred," id. at 136, and noted the evidence suggested that the selection of the ESOP trustees assured the chairman of the corporation "substantial de facto control over plan investment decisions." Id. at 134 n.33.

(2) On remand, the trial court determined that the corporation and its chairman "did not take reasonable action to ensure that [the trustees] were fulfilling their fiduciary obligations." See Leigh v. Engle, 669 F. Supp. 1390, 1395 (N.D. Ill. 1987), aff'd, 858 F.2d 361 (7th Cir. 1988). To the contrary, the trial court found, the corporation and its chairman "knew of, but chose to ignore" improper investment decisions. Id. The corporation and its chairman were thus found liable for breaching their fiduciary duties to the trust. Id. This finding was upheld by the Seventh Circuit on appeal. See Leigh v. Engle, 858 F.2d 361, 364–65 (7th Cir. 1988).

e. Many Employee Stock Ownership Plans today shift the decision whether to tender shares in the event of a tender offer from the ESOP trustee to the individual participants.

(1) The court in Moran v. Household International, Inc., 490 A.2d 1059 (Del. Ch.), aff'd on other grounds, 500 A.2d 1346 (Del. 1985), held that a board's adoption of such a provision did not constitute a breach of the directors' fiduciary duty to the corporation's shareholders because there had been no showing that "the primary purpose of the resolution was to retain control." Id. at 1082. The court left open the effect of the change upon the fiduciary duty owed by the ESOP trustee to the ESOP participants. See id. at 1081.

(2) The United States Department of Labor has concluded that an ESOP plan may grant participants the authority to direct the plan trustee whether to tender or how to vote shares allocated to the participants' individual accounts, and that the trustee may follow directions given pursuant to such a plan provision, so long as the directions are "not...contrary to the provisions of ERISA" and no "violation of ERISA would occur if participants' directions were followed." Unpublished Letter from U.S. Department of Labor to Unnamed Corporation at 3 and n.2 (Feb. 23, 1989).

(3) The Labor Department has emphasized that the trustee always remains "responsible for assuring that the participants receive necessary and accurate information in order to allow them to be fully informed as they consider how to vote or whether to tender."

Id. at n.2. The trustee is also required to ignore participant instructions if the participants are subjected to undue pressure in making their decisions. Id. See also Letter from U.S. Department of Labor to John Welch re Profit Sharing Retirement Income Plan for the Employees of Carter Hawley Hale Stores, Inc. (CCH), printed in Pens. Rep. (BNA) Vol. 11, No. 19, at 633 (Apr. 30, 1984).

(4) The Labor Department has also taken the position that an ESOP trustee must vote unallocated or unvoted ESOP shares in accordance with the trustee's own judgment. Unpublished Letter from U.S. Department of Labor to Unnamed Corporation at 3 (Feb. 23, 1989). The trustee may not, according to the Labor Department, "blindly follow" a trust provision directing the trustee to vote unallocated or unvoted shares in the same proportion as allocated shares are voted by employees. Id.; Ingrassia, Polaroid ESOP Has Independent Role in Shamrock Bid, Labor Agency Advises, Wall St. J., Mar. 10, 1989, at A4 (quoting Alan D. Lebowitz of the Labor Department).

(a) This raises an important question under Delaware General Corporation Law § 203, which precludes business combinations between a corporation and a shareholder which acquires more than 15 percent but less than 85 percent of the corporation's outstanding stock without prior board approval for three years following the acquisition. Del. Gen. Corp. Law § 203(a). As noted above (see § III B 4 f 3 supra), this 85 percent figure excludes shares held by "employee stock plans in which employee participants do not have the right to determine confidentially whether shares held subject to the plan will be tendered in a tender or exchange offer." Del. Gen. Corp. Law § 203(a). Thus, if 20 percent of a corporation's stock is owned by a stock plan in which participants do not have the right to determine confidentially whether shares will be tendered, then the acquiror must acquire 85 percent of 80 percent (i.e., a total of 68 percent) of the corporation's total shares.

(b) If the Labor Department's view is correct and unallocated shares must be voted by the trustee independently of whatever employees do with allocated shares, then the existence of unallocated shares in an ESOP will lower the percentage an acquiror must obtain in order to avoid triggering § 203.

C. Leg-Up and Lock-Up Stock Options

1. Where a board has determined to sell the corporation, a leg-up or lock-up stock option may provide a favored bidder with an opportunity to purchase

a block of stock, typically exercisable if some other third party acquires a specified percentage of the target corporation's stock.

   a. A leg-up stock option typically assures the favored bidder 10 or 20 percent of the corporation's stock, thus providing that bidder a "leg up" over other bidders and ensuring that bidder a financial benefit should it fail to acquire control.

   b. A lock-up stock option, by contrast, virtually ensures that the recipient of the option will take control of the corporation by granting the option recipient the right to acquire a majority of the target corporation's stock.

2. Cases Upholding Leg-Up Options

   a. Buffalo Forge

     (1) Following Ampco-Pittsburgh's initial and, as the court found in Buffalo Forge Co. v. Ogden Corp., 717 F.2d 757 (2d Cir.), aff'g 555 F. Supp. 892 (W.D.N.Y.), cert. denied, 464 U.S. 1018 (1983), "financially unsatisfactory" offer of $25 per share, Buffalo Forge entered into a merger agreement at $32.75 per share with a white knight, Ogden. As a condition of the merger, Buffalo Forge agreed

        (a) To sell Ogden 425,000 shares of treasury stock at $32.75 per share, and

        (b) To grant Ogden an option to purchase an additional 143,000 shares on similar terms.

           A bidding war between Ampco and Ogden ensued, with Ampco ultimately acquiring Buffalo Forge at $37.50 per share. 717 F.2d at 758–59; 555 F. Supp. at 895.

     (2) The trial court found that "neither Ogden nor Buffalo Forge intended the sale of the treasury shares and the grant of the option to foreclose additional bidding, either by Ampco or by third parties," and that "the sale of the treasury shares did not foreclose competitive bidding but rather stimulated it." 555 F. Supp. at 906. The court emphasized that the price received by Buffalo Forge for its treasury stock from Ogden "exceeded the cost of the stock, its book value and its normal trading price." 717 F.2d at 759, quoting 555 F. Supp. at 904-05.

     (3) The Second Circuit concluded that under these circumstances it would be a mistake for a court "to substitute its judgment for the business judgment of the directors, the exercise of which brought about" a 50 percent increase in Ampco's offer, from $25 a share to $37.50 a share. 717 F.2d at 759.

b. Texas Air
   (1) In Hastings-Murtagh v. Texas Air Corp., 649 F. Supp. 479 (S.D. Fla. 1986), the court upheld a merger agreement which included an option granted by Eastern Air Lines to Texas Air to purchase 10.9 million recently issued shares, or approximately 15 percent of the 72 million Eastern shares which would be outstanding following the exercise of the option. 649 F. Supp. at 481.
   (2) The court emphasized that
      (a) The option had been insisted upon by Texas Air,
      (b) No competing proposals were on the table at the time the option was granted,
      (c) In return for the option Eastern's board had secured more favorable terms (these terms included a "lock-in" provision requiring performance of the merger agreement even if Eastern, which had suffered serious financial and labor difficulties in preceding months, filed for bankruptcy or developed further labor problems before the transaction was completed),
      (d) Four independent banking firms had stated that the Texas Air offer represented fair value to Eastern's shareholders.
   (3) The court rejected the plaintiff's suggestion that Eastern's board was obligated "to jeopardize one bid" and "wait for an indefinite time to permit [a potential alternative union bidder] to construct a proposal and arrange financing for a bid." Id. at 484–85.
c. Similar principles were applied by the courts in Yanow v. Scientific Leasing, [1987–1988 Transfer Binder] Fed. Sec. L. Rep. (CCH) ¶ 93,660 (Del. Ch. Feb. 5, 1988); and Hecco Ventures v. Sea-Land Corp., 12 Del. J. Corp. L. 282 (Del. Ch. 1986), in refusing to interfere with grants of options to purchase approximately 12 percent and 22 percent, respectively, of the stock of the corporations involved in these two cases. Scientific Leasing, [1987–1988 Transfer Binder] Fed. Sec. L. Rep. (CCH) at 98,032 and 98,033 n.6; Sea-Land, 12 Del. J. Corp. L. at 286. As the Scientific Leasing court noted, stock options which do not "improperly preclude competing bids in an active auction" and are "necessary to induce...an offer at a premium over market price" are not unlawful. [1987–1988 Transfer Binder] Fed. Sec. L. Rep. at 98,033 and n.6, citing Sea-Land, 12 Del. J. Corp. L. at 289–90.
d. See also Keyser v. Commonwealth Nat'l Fin. Corp., 644 F. Supp. 1130, 1145–49 (M.D. Pa. 1986) (refusing to enjoin grant of warrants to purchase 24.9 percent of corporation's stock), subsequent proceedings, 675 F. Supp.

238, 254–66 (M.D. Pa. 1987) (denying directors' motion for summary judgment due to existence of fact issues).

3. Case Not Upholding Lock-Up Options—Data Probe, Inc. v. CRC Information Sys., N.Y.L.J., Dec. 28, 1984, at 7 (N.Y. Sup. Ct. 1984).

   a. The bidding for Datatab opened when CRC offered to purchase all outstanding Datatab shares at $1.00 per share, and agreed to grant Datatab's principal officers three-year employment contracts at increased salaries. A second bidder, Data Probe, then made a cash tender offer at $1.25 per share. CRC then raised its bid to $1.40, and in return received an option to purchase voting shares of Datatab amounting to 200 percent of Datatab's previously outstanding shares. This option "in effect guaranteed CRC the power to accomplish the proposed merger even if disapproved by Datatab's...shareholders." Data Probe Acquisition Corp. v. Datatab, Inc., 568 F. Supp. 1538, 1541–42 (S.D.N.Y.), rev'd, 722 F.2d 1 (2d Cir. 1983), cert. denied, 465 U.S. 1052 (1984). Data Probe subsequently increased its bid to $1.55 per share, conditioned upon the invalidation of the option to CRC. Id. at 1543.

   b. The New York state court concluded that the Datatab directors' "exercise of judgment was deeply influenced by concerns other than the corporation's best interests":

      It is difficult to escape the view that the former directors of Datatab had established an extremely cozy relationship with CRC.... It appears that the former directors were anxious to lock out any other tender offer, no matter how low CRC's [bid] might be.

      N.Y.L.J., Dec. 28, 1984, at 7. Accordingly, the court concluded, "retreat behind the business judgment rule has been barred." Id. at 11.

IV. Asset Redeployment Transactions

A. Asset Sales

   1. A corporation may restructure itself by selling a key asset or division— often the corporation's "crown jewel"—believed to be particularly desirable to a potential acquiror. Such transactions have typically been upheld by the courts on business judgment rule grounds.

   2. For example, in Whittaker Corp. v. Edgar, 535 F. Supp. 933 (N.D. Ill. 1982), aff'd mem., Nos. 82–1305 and 82–1307 (7th Cir. Mar. 5, 1982), the court held that the proposed sale of the target company's lucrative medical division following an unwanted tender offer was within the bounds of a valid business judgment.

a. The court explained:
> When confronted with a threatened change in control, a board of directors of a target company may engage in a corporate transaction with a third party that the board determines in its business judgment to be in the best interests of shareholders.... In so doing, the board of directors may enter into various arrangements with the third party to promote consummation of the transaction even though to do so might cause the hostile tender offeror to withdraw. Id. at 951.

b. Significantly, there was no challenge in Whittaker to the consideration paid for the medical division (indeed, the purchaser was to pay $450 million for an asset the unwanted tender offeror had valued at only $350 million). Id. at 938 and 942.

3. In City Capital Associates v. Interco Inc., 551 A.2d 787 (Del. Ch. 1988), the court refused to enjoin the sale of Interco's "crown jewel" Ethan Allen furniture division during the pendency of an unwanted tender offer.

a. The court labeled the issue "rather easy":
> Of course, a board acts reasonably in relation to an offer, albeit a noncoercive offer, it believes to be inadequate when it seeks to realize the full market value of an important asset. Moreover, here the board puts forth sensible reasons why Ethan Allen should be sold under its new business plan.... Finally, as a defensive measure, the sale of Ethan Allen is not a "show stopper" insofar as this offer is concerned. This is not a crown jewel sale to a favored bidder, it is a public sale. On my assumption that the price will be a fair price, the corporation will come out no worse from a financial point of view. Moreover, the [unwanted tender offeror is] being supplied the same information as others concerning Ethan Allen and they may bid for it. I do understand that this step complicates [its] life and indeed might imperil [its] ability to complete its transaction. [The unwanted tender offeror], however, has no right to demand that its chosen target remain in status quo while its offer is formulated, gradually increased and, perhaps, accepted. I therefore conclude that the proposed sale of Ethan Allen Company is a defensive step that is reasonable in relation to the mild threat posed by th[e] noncoercive...cash offer. Id. at 801.

b. The court reached this conclusion notwithstanding its holding in another part of its decision that Interco could not utilize its poison pill rights plan to protect a restructuring including the sale of Ethan Allen.

551 A.2d at 797–800 (discussed in § VII A infra). Cf. Grand Metro. PLC v. Pillsbury Co., [1988–1989 Transfer Binder] Fed. Sec. L. Rep. (CCH) ¶ 94,104, at 91,196–97 (Del. Ch. Dec. 16, 1988) (holding that Pillsbury could not utilize its poison pill rights plan to protect a restructuring which included the spin-off of its Burger King subsidiary (discussed in § VII B infra), but enjoining the spin-off until the conclusion of pending litigation due to "the uncertainties which now shroud corporate affairs").

4. In GM Sub Corp. v. Liggett Group, No. 6155 (Del. Ch. Apr. 25, 1980), the court denied a request for a temporary restraining order enjoining the sale of a subsidiary, which was allegedly the target corporation's prize asset, in response to a hostile tender offer.

   a. The court noted that the target corporation had engaged an investment banking firm, that the investment banking firm had solicited nine bids over a three-week period, and that the highest of these bids, which the target accepted, was 22 times the earnings of the subsidiary. Accordingly, the court concluded, the price "is said to be very favorable to [the corporation] and will enhance its overall position. Opposed to this, there is nothing offered by [plaintiff] to show that the price is in any way inadequate." Id., slip op. at 4.

   b. The court acknowledged that "it seems realistic to assume that it was contemplated by [the target corporation] that the practical effect of the sale of its sought-after asset might be to cause [the unwanted bidder] to lose interest in its tender offer." Id. at 3. Nevertheless, the court determined, the corporation's sale of its prize asset "does not provide any guarantee that control…will not change." Id. Indeed, the court explained, if the tender offer is resumed and ultimately is successful, the unwanted bidder will be in control of the corporation, with the only difference being that one asset—a particular subsidiary—will have been exchanged for another asset—cash. Id. at 4.

5. The Second Circuit in Terrydale Liquidating Trust v. Barness, 846 F.2d 845 (2d Cir. 1988), aff'g 642 F. Supp. 917 (S.D.N.Y. 1986), and 611 F. Supp. 1006 (S.D.N.Y. 1984), held that the trustees of a real estate investment trust did not breach their fiduciary duties during the pendency of an unwanted tender offer by selling four office buildings representing approximately 80 percent of the trust's assets and distributing the proceeds of the sale, and then liquidating all remaining trust assets. 846 F.2d at 846.

   a. Construing Missouri law, the court emphasized that the trustees had first sought to obtain an offer to acquire all of the trust's outstanding shares, since, in the district court's words, a takeover by the unwanted bidder could have "wreak[ed] havoc" and left minority shareholders in a "very disfavorable position." Id. and 642 F. Supp. at 923.

b. The court also emphasized that the trustees had solicited bids from numerous corporate and real estate investors, and that the offer to purchase the four properties which constituted 80 percent of the trust's assets was the best offer available. 846 F.2d at 846 and 847.

c. The court thus concluded that the trustees had fulfilled their "duty... under the circumstances of this case... to maximize the value for all shareholders." Id. at 847.

6. Joseph E. Seagram and Sons, Inc. v. Abrams, 510 F. Supp. 860 (S.D.N.Y. 1981), demonstrates that asset redeployment tactics will not automatically be upheld no matter what the circumstances.

a. The Seagram court issued a temporary restraining order enjoining a target board's alleged plan "to sell off its assets and, failing this, to destroy the charter of the company" in order to defeat a hostile tender offer. Id. at 861.

b. The court made clear its perception that incumbent management had determined "to keep control of the company entrenched within the present board of directors regardless of the company's real best interests or else to dismember it piece by piece, even to the point of liquidation of the enterprise." Id. at 862. In the court's words:

> There must be some radical defect or gap in existing securities and corporation law and regulation which would allow an assumption of power by caretakers of a corporation to deal with its assets and its life in retaliation for a hostile tender not otherwise intended or defensible as good corporate business. Surely they were not elected and permitted to serve as directors on any such platform. It is inconceivable that an alleged flourishing enterprise has authorized its board to subject the assets and charter of the company to a scorched earth policy to be accomplished in the name of an exercise of business judgment but in fact, it is alleged, merely to thwart a change in the existing stock ownership which may end the tenure of the present directors and key officers of the company. Id. at 861.

B. Asset Lock-Up Options

1. Where a board has determined to sell the corporation, an asset lock-up option may provide a favored bidder an option to purchase a key corporate division or other asset in the event another bidder acquires a specified percentage of the target corporation's stock. The effect is to ensure that the

favored bidder will receive the optioned asset no matter who ends up with the rest of the corporate entity.

2. Asset lock-up options granted during the course of bidding contests for Revlon, SCM, Macmillan and Holly Farms have been enjoined by the courts.

a. Revlon

(1) The facts underlying the lock-up aspect of the court's decision in Revlon, Inc. v. MacAndrews and Forbes Holdings, 506 A.2d 173 (Del. 1986), aff'g 501 A.2d 1239 (Del. Ch. 1985), began with a $53 cash tender offer by Pantry Pride for any and all Revlon shares. In response, Revlon's board approved a plan to enter into a leveraged buyout agreement with Forstmann Little in which each Revlon shareholder would receive $56 cash per share. 506 A.2d at 177–78; 501 A.2d at 1245.

Pantry Pride then raised its offer to $56.25 in cash per share, and stated its intention to "top any Forstmann offer by a slightly higher one." 506 A.2d at 178.

Forstmann responded by raising its bid by $1 to $57.25 per share (this time in cash and debt securities). In return for this $1 in increased value for Revlon shareholders, Forstmann demanded and received an option to purchase two divisions of Revlon for $525 million in the event another person acquired 40 percent of Revlon's shares. 506 A.2d at 178–79; 501 A.2d at 1245. This $525 million option figure, according to Revlon's own investment banker, was at least $100–175 million below the actual value of the two divisions. 506 A.2d at 178.

(2) The Delaware Chancery Court asked "[w]hat motivated the Revlon directors to end the auction with so little objective improvement?" The court concluded that Revlon's board "seemed to want Forstmann Little in the picture at all costs," perhaps—the court surmised— because Forstmann had agreed to take steps to protect the rights of certain Revlon noteholders who had threatened litigation against the Revlon board because the sale of the company would involve the waiver of covenants in the notes which protected the value of those notes. 501 A.2d at 1250–51.

(3) The Delaware Supreme Court agreed with the Chancery Court's criticism of the Revlon board's "emphasis on shoring up the sagging market value of the Notes in the face of threatened litigation by their holders" at a time when, having recognized that a sale of the corporation was inevitable, the directors' role was to

secure the best price for the stockholders in a sale of the company. 506 A.2d at 182. The Supreme Court therefore agreed with the Chancery Court's determination that the granting of the asset lock-up option constituted a breach of fiduciary duty:

> While Forstmann's $57.25 offer was objectively higher than Pantry Pride's $56.25 bid, the margin of superiority is less when the Forstmann price is adjusted for the time value of money. In reality, the Revlon board ended the auction in return for very little actual improvement in the final bid. The principal benefit went to the directors, who avoided personal liability to a class of creditors to whom the board owed no further duty under the circumstances. Thus, when a board ends an intense bidding contest on an insubstantial basis, and where a significant by-product of that action is to protect the directors against a perceived threat of personal liability for consequences stemming from the adoption of previous defensive measures, the action cannot withstand the enhanced scrutiny which Unocal requires of director conduct. Id. at 184.

(4) The Supreme Court emphasized, however, that asset lock-up options are not *per se* illegal:

> Such options can entice other bidders to enter a contest for control of the corporation, creating an auction for the company and maximizing shareholder profit. Current economic conditions in the takeover market are such that a white knight... might only enter the bidding for the target company if it receives some form of compensation to cover the risks and costs involved.... However, while those lock-ups which draw bidders into the battle benefit shareholders, similar measures which end an active auction and foreclose further bidding operate to the shareholders' detriment. Id. at 183.

b. Hanson

(1) In Hanson Trust PLC v. ML SCM Acquisition Inc., 781 F.2d 264 (2d Cir. 1986), rev'g 623 F. Supp. 848 (S.D.N.Y. 1985), the Second Circuit enjoined the exercise of a lock-up option granted to a favored bidder under circumstances similar to those involved in Revlon.

(a) The bidding opened with Hanson making a $60 per share all-cash tender offer, which was followed by a leveraged buyout offer by SCM's management and Merrill Lynch at $70 per share (85 percent cash, 15 percent debt securities).

(b) Hanson answered with a $72 all-cash bid, and the SCM management–Merrill group raised its bid to $74 per share (this time 80 percent cash, 20 percent debt securities).

(c) In return for this $74 bid, SCM's board granted Merrill a lock-up option, providing Merrill the right to buy two of SCM's most attractive businesses for $350 million and $80 million, respectively, if any party other than Merrill acquired more than one-third of SCM's outstanding shares. Id. at 266–67.

(2) The Second Circuit held that the SCM board's approval of the lock-up option was not protected by the business judgment rule because the board had failed to make an informed decision.

(a) The court emphasized that SCM's directors had failed to ask any of the questions which would have led them to the conclusion that the $350 million and $80 million option prices represented "serious undervaluation" and possibly even a "*prima facie* case of waste" of corporate assets. 781 F.2d at 279 and n.9.

(b) "Indeed," the court suggested, "given that the very purpose of an asset option in a takeover context is to give the optionee a bargain as an incentive to bid and an assured benefit should its bid fail," a heightened duty of care might have been appropriate: The price may be low enough to entice a reluctant potential bidder, but no lower than "reasonable pessimism will allow…." To ascertain that [the] proposal has not crossed this critical line, the Board certainly should have subjected the proposal to some substantial analysis. Id. at 276.

This is particularly so, the court added, where the proposal comes from a self-interested management which has a 15 percent equity interest in the transaction. Id. at 277.

(3) As in Revlon, the Hanson court emphasized that "some lock-up options may be beneficial to the shareholders, such as those that induce a bidder to compete for control of a corporation, while others may be harmful, such as those that effectively preclude bidders from competing with the optionee bidder." Id. at 274.

Here, the court emphasized, SCM's grant of the lock-up option "foreclose[d] rather than facilitate[d] competitive bidding" for SCM since the sale of major corporate assets at discounted prices—as would happen if the option were triggered by Hanson's acquisition of the company—would leave Hanson holding a company worth substantially less than its present value. Id. at 282–83.

(4) Thus the court returned to "the question the [Delaware Chancery Court] in Revlon wisely raised: 'What motivated the directors to end the auction with so little objective improvement?'"

    (a) In Revlon, according to the Hanson court, the "inescapable conclusion" was that the board, in breach of its duty of loyalty, "seemed to want the LBO partner 'in the picture at all costs.'"

    (b) In Hanson, the court concluded, the SCM board, in breach of its duty of care, "achieved the same questionable result." Id. at 283.

(5) The duty of care aspect of the Hanson decision is discussed in more detail in § I D 3 b 2 supra.

c. Macmillan

    (1) The Delaware Supreme Court in Mills Acquisition Co. v. Macmillan, Inc. ("Macmillan II"), No. 415 (Del. May 3, 1989), preliminarily enjoined an asset option granted to a bidder group which included management and KKR on the ground that this bidding group was given an unfair advantage over a competing bidder (Robert Maxwell) during the course of an auction for Macmillan.

    (2) The auction process which preceded the grant of this asset option, according to the court, was "clandestinely and impermissibly skewed" in favor of the KKR group. Id., slip op. at 46. In particular, the court noted:

        (a) Macmillan's directors "wholly delegated the creation and administration of the auction to an array of [management's] handpicked investment advisors." Id. at 45. The court stated that the investment advisor to Macmillan's independent directors would have been "a far more appropriate candidate to conduct this process on behalf of the board." Id.

        (b) KKR "repeatedly received significant material advantages to the exclusion and detriment of Maxwell to stymie, rather than enhance, the bidding process." Id. at 46. These advantages included (1) a telephone tip by Macmillan's chief executive officer to KKR concerning one of Maxwell's bids and the board's then current view of the two competing bids and (2) differing scripts read to the competing bidders by the investment advisor conducting the auction. See id. at 31–39 and 49–52.

        (c) The court noted that Macmillan's outside directors were

unaware that the auction was not run on an evenhanded basis, but concluded that the decisions made by these directors in connection with the auction were not protected by the business judgment rule because (1) the directors' "own lack of oversight in structuring and directing the auction afforded management the opportunity to indulge in the misconduct which occurred" (id. at 41; see also id. at 42 and 45–46), and (2) "when a board is deceived by those who will gain from such misconduct, the protections girding the decision itself vanish." Id. at 52.

    d. Holly Farms

        (1) The Delaware Court of Chancery invalidated an asset lock-up option granted to a favored bidder in In re Holly Farms Corp. Shareholders Litigation, [1988–1989 Transfer Binder] Fed. Sec. L. Rep. (CCH) ¶ 94,181 (Del. Ch. Dec. 30, 1988), subsequent proceedings, id. ¶ 94,349 (Del. Ch. Mar. 22, 1989), and No. 10350 (Del. Ch. May 18, 1989), on the ground that the board had failed to conduct an auction under circumstances where the court found that the corporation was for sale.

        (2) The court observed that the board negotiated with one bidder throughout the course of a marathon board meeting but made no serious effort to encourage a second bidder to put its best offer on the table. The court emphasized that the second bidder was never told that the corporation was for sale, even in the face of direct questioning on this subject. The court also noted that it was undisputed that the second bidder was ready and willing to make a bid that was higher than that which was accepted, but refrained from doing so because it was never told that the corporation was to be sold. Id. at 91,644.

3. Notwithstanding the Revlon, Hanson, Macmillan II and Holly Farms decisions, the Eleventh Circuit's 1988 decision in Cottle v. Storer Communication, 849 F.2d 570 (11th Cir. 1988), illustrates that asset lock-up options may still be utilized under at least certain circumstances.

    a. The Storer court stated that "as a general rule, courts have held that lock-ups that draw new contestants into the bidding war are permissible, while lock-ups that tend to preclude new bidders or exclude hostile ones are not." Id. at 575–76. The court continued, however, by noting that "this formulation...is not particularly helpful in determining the validity of any particular option" since "[a]ll auctions must end sometime, and lock-ups by definition must discourage other bidders."

Id. at 576. Accordingly, the court concluded, "[t]he question…is not whether the asset lock-up granted…effectively ended the bidding process," but instead "whether [the corporation] conducted a fair auction, and whether [the winning bidder] made the best offer." Id.

b. Applying this standard, the court emphasized that

(1) Four of Storer's seven outside directors had been elected on the platform that they would "obtain the best price possible for the shareholders, rather than…defend 'the corporate bastion,'"

(2) Storer had searched for four months for potential bidders,

(3) Only two bidders had indicated any interest,

(4) Storer's board had rejected the winning bidder's first offer as inadequate,

(5) Storer had negotiated extensively and deliberately with both bidders,

(6) The asset option was not granted until after both bidders had made full presentations concerning their most recently revised offers, and

(7) The two bids were about to expire at the time the auction was ended. Id. at 576.

c. The court placed particular emphasis upon two important distinctions between this case and the Revlon and Hanson cases:

(1) First, Storer had used the asset option to secure a substantial improvement in the winning bidder's offer—from $75 in cash to $91 in cash, which was at least $2.25 (and, under certain circumstances, $7.50) higher than the competing bidder's offer. Id. at 576–77.

(2) Second, it was undisputed that the prices set in the asset option were reasonable and within the range of fair value. Id. at 577.

d. See also Thompson v. Enstar Corp., 509 A.2d 578, 583 (Del. Ch. 1984) (upholding an asset lock-up option granted under circumstances where the directors had "only one bona fide offer" in hand after "sufficiently adequate efforts to seek other offers," that offer was conditioned upon approval of the lock-up option, and rejection of the offer may have left shareholders facing liquidation at a much lower price).

V. Nontargeted Repurchases, Self-Tender Offers, and Exchange Offers

A. Introduction

1. A corporation may also restructure or recapitalize itself by repurchasing some percentage of its own shares for a price in excess of the prevailing

market price. These repurchases may be by means of open market repurchases, a self-tender offer, or an exchange offer.

    a. Open market repurchases, also known as "nontargeted repurchases," differ from "targeted repurchases"—or "greenmail"—in that shares are purchased from the corporation's shareholders generally rather than from just one unwanted shareholder or group of shareholders.

    b. Self-tender offers are offers by the corporation for the corporation's own shares for an all-cash package.

    c. Exchange offers are offers by the corporation for the corporation's own shares for either (i) an all-paper package or (ii) a cash plus paper package.

2. Potential benefits of nontargeted repurchases, self-tender offers, and exchange offers include the following:

    a. Divert shares from both hostile bidders and arbitrageurs looking to accumulate blocks of shares.

    b. Make the corporation less attractive to a potential acquiror by depleting the corporation's cash or other liquid assets, or burdening it with debt.

    c. Covenants in debt securities distributed to shareholders in exchange offers may bar major dispositions of corporate assets, and thus preclude bids by offerors hoping to finance an acquisition of the corporation by selling corporate assets.

    d. Increase the proportionate size of a substantial block of the corporation's stock held by a person or group friendly to management.

    e. Shares acquired by the corporation may be resold to a white squire or to an employee benefit plan.

        See generally, R. Balotti and J. Finkelstein, The Delaware Law of Corporations and Business Organizations §§ 6.27 and 6.28, at 312–14 (1988); Brown, Recapitalization Used to Avoid Takeovers, N.Y.L.J., Mar. 16, 1987, at 29; Lederman and Goroff, Recapitalization Transactions, 19 Rev. Sec. and Comm. Reg. 241 (1986); Cowan, The Allure of Stock Buybacks, N.Y. Times, Mar. 5, 1987, at D1; Vartan, Corporations' Stock Buyback, N.Y. Times, Aug. 5, 1987, at D8.

3. The practitioner should be aware that many state corporation statutes do not permit a corporation to vote repurchased shares. See, e.g., Del. Gen. Corp. Law § 160(c). Accordingly, where an offeror is already a substantial shareholder, a nontargeted repurchase program may serve only to increase the percentage of shares held by the offeror, and in turn decrease the amount of money required for the offeror to make a successful bid.

4. The practitioner should also be aware of state statutes which impose

limitations on stock repurchases designed to protect the corporation's capital. See generally 1 E. Folk, R. Ward and E. Welch, Folk on the Delaware General Corporation Law §§ 160.1–.10 (2d ed. 1988); Goldfus and Hamermesh, Repurchases of Shares—State of State Law, printed in 3 Securities Law Techniques § 69 (A. Sommer ed. 1988).

B. The Case Law

Decisions to commence open market repurchase programs or self-tender or exchange offers have generally been tested by the courts on business judgment rule grounds.

1. Unocal

    a. The Delaware Supreme Court's landmark decision in Unocal Corp. v. Mesa Petroleum Co., 493 A.2d 946 (Del. 1985), involved a "two-tier" "front end loaded" tender offer for Unocal's stock by Mesa Petroleum (i.e., T. Boone Pickens), the owner of 13 percent of Unocal's stock. Specifically, Mesa offered

        (1) $54 per share for 37 percent of the stock (which would give Mesa a total of just over 50 percent), and

        (2) Highly subordinated "junk bond" securities purportedly worth $54 for Unocal's remaining shares. Id. at 949–50.

    b. Unocal's board rejected Mesa's tender offer as coercive and grossly inadequate, and approved an exchange offer providing that if Mesa acquired 50 percent of Unocal's stock, then Unocal would offer the holders of the remaining 49 percent of Unocal's shares (i.e., all shares not held by Mesa) an exchange of their shares for debt securities having an aggregate value of $72 per share. The condition requiring that Mesa purchase 50 percent of Unocal's stock was waived a few days later. Id. at 950–51.

    c. The Delaware Supreme Court first set forth what has now been labeled the Unocal test, pursuant to which all defensive tactics are tested in Delaware courts. See § II B supra.

    d. Applying this standard, the court found that the selective exchange offer was "reasonably related" to the "destructive threat Mesa's tender offer was perceived to pose." 493 A.2d at 956 and 958.

        (1) The Threat

            (a) The Unocal directors concluded that "the value of Unocal was substantially above the $54 per share offered in cash at the front end" by Mesa. Id. at 956.

            (b) The Unocal directors also concluded that "the subordinated securities to be exchanged in Mesa's announced squeeze out of the remaining shareholders in the 'back-end' merger were 'junk bonds' worth far less than \$54." Id.

(c) The court emphasized that it is "now well recognized that such offers are a classic coercive measure designed to stampede shareholders into tendering at the first tier, even if the price is inadequate, out of fear of what they will receive at the back end of the transaction." Id.

(d) The court also emphasized that "[w]holly beyond the coercive aspect of an inadequate two-tier tender offer, the threat was posed by a corporate raider with a national reputation as a "greenmailer." Id.

(2) The Response

(a) The court observed that "[i]n adopting the selective exchange offer, the board stated that its objective was either to defeat the inadequate Mesa offer or, should the offer still succeed, provide the 49 percent of its stockholders, who would otherwise be forced to accept 'junk bonds,' with \$72 worth of senior debt." Id.

(b) The court found both of these purposes to be valid purposes, and concluded that Unocal's efforts to accomplish these purposes "would have been thwarted by Mesa's participation in the exchange offer." Id.

[1] "First, if Mesa could tender its shares, Unocal would effectively be subsidizing the former's continuing effort to buy Unocal stock at \$54 per share." Id.

[2] "Second, Mesa could not, by definition, fit within the class of shareholders being protected from its own coercive and inadequate tender offer." Id.

(3) Additional Significant Passages by Court

(a) "[T]he principle of selective stock repurchases by a Delaware corporation is neither unknown nor unauthorized.... The only difference is that heretofore the approved transaction was the payment of 'greenmail' to a raider or dissident posing a threat to the corporate enterprise. All other stockholders were denied such favored treatment, and given Mesa's past history of greenmail, its claims here are rather ironic." Id. at 957.

(b) "Nothing precludes Mesa, as a stockholder, from acting in its own self-interest.... However, Mesa, while pursuing its own interests, has acted in a manner which a board consisting of a majority of independent directors has reasonably determined to be contrary to the best interests of Unocal and its other shareholders. In this situation, there is no support in Delaware law for the proposition that, when responding to a perceived harm, a corporation must guarantee a benefit to a stockholder who is deliberately provoking the danger being addressed. There is no obligation of self-sacrifice by a corporation and its shareholders in the face of such a challenge." Id. at 958.

e. The All-Holders Rule

   (1) The Securities and Exchange Commission responded to the Unocal decision by amending Rule 13e–4(f) and adopting Rule 14d–10 (the "all-holders rule"), which requires equal treatment for all shareholders of the same class of stock. See 17 C.F.R. §§ 240.13e–4(f) and 240.14d–10; Securities Act Release No. 33–6653 and Exchange Act Release 34–23421 (July 11, 1986), printed in [1986–1987 Transfer Binder] Fed. Sec. L. Rep. (CCH) ¶ 84,016.

   (2) The Third Circuit held in Polaroid Corp. v. Disney, 862 F.2d 987 (3d Cir. 1988), that Rule 14d–10 is properly within the scope of the Exchange Act's enabling provision and that a private right of action exists pursuant to which target corporation shareholders have standing to assert violations of the Rule, but that target corporations themselves do not have such standing. Id. at 991–1003.

2. Anderson Clayton, Gelco and Burlington

   a. Three post-Unocal decisions involving Anderson Clayton, Gelco and Burlington Industries consider restructurings including self-tender or exchange offers having at least some coercive effect upon shareholders, and which, if completed, would result in a substantial block of stock being shifted from public to more friendly management or employee hands.

   b. Anderson Clayton

   (1) The Delaware Court of Chancery's 1986 decision in AC Acquisitions Corp. v. Anderson, Clayton and Co., 519 A.2d 103 (Del. Ch. 1986), involved what the court described as a "front-end loaded" $60 per share self-tender offer for 65.5 percent of the corporation's stock, to be accompanied by the sale of stock to a newly formed employee stock ownership plan in an amount equal to 25 percent of the corporation's outstanding stock following the sale. Anderson Clayton's self-tender offer was made in response

to a concededly fair $56 per share all-cash offer to all shareholders. Id. at 104-05 and 112.

(2) The economic effect of Anderson Clayton's self-tender offer, according to the court, was to create a situation in which "no rational shareholder could afford not to tender into the Company's self-tender offer," since the value of Anderson Clayton stock would be materially less than $60 per share (estimates presented to the court ranged from $22 to $52 per share) following consummation of the self-tender. Therefore, the court explained, a shareholder "who elects not to tender into the self-tender is very likely…to experience a substantial loss in market value of his holdings." "[T]he only way…that a shareholder can protect himself from such an immediate financial loss…," the court continued, "is to tender into the self-tender so that he receives his pro rata share of the cash distribution that will, in part cause the expected fall in the market price of the Company's stock." Id. at 113–14.

(3) The court enjoined the self-tender on the ground that the board's decision to commence the offer satisfied the first leg but not the second leg of the Unocal test.

   (a) With respect to the first leg, the court observed that the "threat" posed by the outside bidders' $56 all cash offer rested "on the assumption that a majority of the Company's shareholders might prefer an alternative…offer," and "[t]he creation of such an alternative" thus "serve[d] a valid corporate purpose. Id. at 113 and 112. The court accepted the corporation's characterization of its self-tender offer "as the creation of an option to shareholders to permit them to have the benefits of a large, tax-advantaged cash distribution together with a continuing participation in a newly structured, highly leveraged Anderson Clayton":

   The board recognizes that the [$56] offer—being for all shares and offering cash consideration that the board's expert advisor could not call unfair—is one that a rational shareholder might prefer. However, the board asserts—and it seems to me to be unquestionably correct in this—that a rational shareholder might prefer the company transaction. One's choice, if given an opportunity to effectively choose, might be dictated by any number of factors most of which (such as liquidity preference, degree of aversion to risk, alternative investment opportunities and even desire or disinterest in seeing the continuation of a distinctive Anderson Clayton identity) are distinctive functions of each individual decision-maker. Id. at 112.

(b) With respect to the second leg of the Unocal test, however, the court concluded that the self-tender offer was not "reasonable in the light of the 'threat' posed." Id. at 113–14. The court emphasized that "an Anderson Clayton stockholder, acting with economic rationality, has no effective choice as between the contending offers as presently constituted," since "[e]ven if a shareholder would prefer to sell all of his or her holdings at $56 per share...he or she may not risk tendering into that proposal and thereby risk being frozen out of the front end of the company transaction, should the [$56] offer not close." Id. at 114.

(4) The court thus enjoined the transaction on the ground that the "coercive" and "obvious entrenchment effect" of the self-tender offer transaction constituted "a breach of a duty of loyalty, albeit a possibly unintended one." Id. at 113 and 114 (emphasis in original).

(5) The court noted its view that an alternative transaction such as the corporation's self-tender offer in Anderson Clayton would be "manifestly reasonable" were it timed in a manner which would provide shareholders with a real choice between alternatives. For example, the court suggested, a self-tender offer allowing shareholders to continue to own part of the corporation, but which would be available only following a decision by a majority of shareholders not to tender into a competing all-cash tender offer, might well be permissible. Id.

c. Gelco

(1) Gelco Corp. v. Coniston Partners, 652 F. Supp. 829 (D. Minn. 1986), aff'd on other grounds, 811 F.2d 414 (8th Cir. 1987), involved the adoption by Gelco Corporation, as part of an ongoing business plan to streamline company operations, of a restructuring program which included the sale of four of the corporation's business units and a self-tender offer to purchase up to three million outstanding shares through a "dutch auction" at prices of $17 to $20 per share. The self-tender offer was to be financed by the sale of newly issued voting preferred stock to Merrill Lynch. Id. at 834–35.

(2) The day before the self-tender was due to expire, Coniston Partners purchased 17.6 percent of Gelco's outstanding shares and proposed a merger pursuant to which all Gelco shareholders would receive $22.50 per share. Coniston's proposal was conditioned upon the termination of Gelco's pending self-tender offer and rescission of the sale of preferred stock to Merrill Lynch. Id.

(3) Gelco rejected Coniston's offer as financially inadequate, but since its stock was by this point trading at $23 per share, cancelled the $17 to $20 self-tender offer. Instead, Gelco announced an exchange offer in which Gelco would purchase up to 6 million of its shares, with each shareholder receiving $10 in cash plus a fraction of a share of preferred stock having a liquidation preference of between $16 and $20 (the precise number would be determined, as in Gelco's original self-tender offer, by a dutch auction procedure). Id. at 836. According to Gelco, the exchange offer was "designed to give stockholders a choice between liquidating their holdings now and still holding a stake in future growth or maintaining their current investment position, or a mix of both." Id. at 837.

(4) Gelco's offering materials acknowledged that the transaction "may adversely affect the market price of the shares that remain outstanding," and the court found "that the structure of the offer encourages all shareholders to tender, and to tender at the low end of the liquidation preference—for if shareholders do not tender all of their shares, they will be left holding common stock that may decrease in value." The completion of Gelco's exchange offer (which would reduce the number of shares held by the public, since management would not tender its shares), combined with Merrill Lynch's acquisition of voting preferred stock in return for providing financing for the transaction, would place control of over 53 percent of Gelco's voting stock in the hands of Gelco directors and management and Merrill Lynch. Id.

(5) Coniston responded to Gelco's exchange offer by commencing an offer to purchase all of Gelco's outstanding shares for $26 in cash, conditioned upon either Gelco's withdrawal or judicial invalidation of the exchange offer. Id.

(6) Applying Minnesota law, the court recognized that the exchange offer had a coercive effect similar to that in Anderson Clayton since shareholders "may feel obligated to tender to Gelco's offer for fear their shares will decrease in value if not tendered," but concluded

that the similarities between the Gelco offer and the Anderson Clayton offer ended there. Id. at 846.

    (a) First, the court explained, Gelco's investment banker had concluded that Coniston's $26 offer was inadequate, while Anderson Clayton's investment banker had not found that the competing offer in that case had been inadequate. Id.

    (b) Second, Gelco's board, unlike Anderson Clayton's board, had made a good faith determination that the restructuring program promised greater long-term value for shareholders than a sale of the company. Id. The court noted that Gelco's investment advisor had estimated the break-up value of the company first at $29.85 to $37.86 per share, and later at $31.57 to $39.03 per share. The court cautioned, however, that "to the extent the Board rejected a potential acquiror's all-cash offer closer to these ranges, the judgment of the Board becomes suspect." Id.

    (c) Third, Gelco's exchange offer had been part of a restructuring plan adopted a full month prior to Coniston's initial $22.50 per share merger proposal, while Anderson Clayton's self-tender offer, according to the Gelco court, had had no underlying business purpose other than to react to a hostile offer. Id.

(7) The court acknowledged that the estimated $21 to $24 blended value of Gelco's exchange offer (with blended value representing an average of the price to be paid to shareholders in the exchange offer and the expected trading price of the remaining common shares at the time the offer was completed) was lower than Coniston's $26 offer, but concluded that this fact did not prove that Coniston's bid was adequate. Id. at 837 and n.6 and 846.

(8) The court also rejected Coniston's contention that the combination of Gelco's exchange offer and Merrill Lynch's acquisition of voting preferred stock, which would place control of over 53 percent of Gelco's voting stock in the hands of Gelco directors and management and Merrill Lynch, constituted an irreparable shift of control. Id. at 837 and 846–47. The court explained that "the preferred stock held by Merrill Lynch can be redeemed at any time, and in all likelihood will be redeemed in the relatively near future. In the meantime, Merrill Lynch is not bound to vote a particular way." Id. at 847.

(9) The Eighth Circuit affirmed the district court's denial of preliminary injunctive relief in Coniston Partners v. Gelco Corp., 811 F.2d

414 (8th Cir. 1987), but only on the ground that Coniston had failed
to demonstrate irreparable injury. The appellate court based its
decision on the district court's finding that Coniston intended to
liquidate Gelco, and that any injury to Coniston could therefore be
remedied in a suit for money damages seeking the lost liquidation
value. Id. at 418–20.

d. Burlington

(1) Samjens Partners I v. Burlington Industries, 663 F. Supp. 614
(S.D.N.Y. 1987), involved a self-tender offer by Burlington Industries for 25 percent of its common stock at a price of $80 per
share. The self-tender offer was commenced in response to
Samjens' tender offer at $67 per share—a price determined by
Burlington's board to be inadequate—for all of Burlington's
outstanding stock, conditioned upon the tendering of at least 80
percent of the stock. Id. at 618 and 622. The self-tender offer, in
Burlington's words, was intended:

> to preserve the flexibility of the Company while...alternatives
> are being explored, to avoid any significant time delay in
> shareholders realizing the benefit of any...restructuring and
> to give shareholders desiring to receive cash for a portion of
> their shares an alternative to the inadequate...[t]ender [o]ffer,
> while permitting them to retain at the present time a continuing
> interest in the Company. Id. at 619.

(2) One week later, Burlington entered into a friendly merger agreement with a Morgan Stanley subsidiary, pursuant to which Morgan
commenced a tender offer at $76 (later raised to $78) per share for
all shares. Burlington then extended its self-tender offer so that it
would expire the same day that Morgan's offer would expire,
recommended that shareholders tender into Morgan's offer, and
announced that the self-tender offer would be terminated if Morgan's
offer were successful. Id. at 621 and 626.

(3) While the court found that there was no agreement between
Burlington management and Morgan regarding management's
equity participation following the proposed merger, the Burlington
board's recommendation of the Morgan offer disclosed that Morgan
representatives had indicated their willingness to allow Burlington
management to obtain an equity position in the new corporation.
Id. at 622.

(4) Applying Delaware law, the court rejected the unwanted tender

offeror's contention that the self-tender offer—which, if successful, would have defeated the tender offer since the tender offer was conditioned upon receipt of at least 80 percent of all outstanding Burlington shares—constituted a breach of fiduciary duty:

> When the Burlington Board first issued the self-tender offer, it was in response to a threat to Burlington shareholders: an inadequate tender offer. The self-tender was designed so that if the maximum number of shares were tendered, the inadequate tender offer would be defeated. The self-tender was thus enacted for a legitimate purpose. It also was reasonable in light of the threat. It was designed to allow the Board time to consider alternatives that would maximize shareholder value. There is also no evidence that the original tender offer was structured such that no rational shareholder could turn it down. There is no evidence that the price of Burlington shares would have drop[p]ed drastically after the self-tender such that a shareholder would have to tender into it to preserve any value. Furthermore, the self-tender was to expire...eight days after the [original tender] offer expired. This allowed shareholders more time to consider their options. Id. at 626. The court also emphasized that the board's ultimate decision to back the Morgan offer instead of the self-tender offer took the self-tender "out of the picture." Id.

(5) See also Rosen v. Burlington Indus., N.Y.L.J., June 3, 1988, at 22 (N.Y. Sup. Ct. 1988) (dismissing state court action alleging that Burlington's directors breached their fiduciary duties in entering into transaction with Morgan).

3. Revlon, CBS, and Union Carbide
   a. Three post-Unocal decisions involving Revlon, CBS, and Union Carbide consider restructurings including debt securities containing covenants restricting the sale of corporate assets or the incurrence of corporate debt beyond specified limits. Such covenants typically preclude the use of the corporation's assets to finance a takeover of the corporation.
   b. Revlon
      (1) The exchange offer aspect in the Delaware Supreme Court's decision of Revlon, Inc. v. MacAndrews and Forbes Holdings, 506 A.2d 173 (Del. 1986), centered around Pantry Pride's initial $47.50 cash tender offer for any and all Revlon shares. Revlon's

board recommended rejection of this offer on the ground that $47.50 was a grossly inadequate price, and commenced an exchange offer for approximately 25 percent of the corporation's outstanding shares. The exchange offer provided each shareholder:

(a) One note ($47.50 principal at 11.75 percent interest) which would trade at face value, and

(b) One-tenth of a share of convertible exchangeable stock valued at $100 per share.

The notes contained covenants which limited Revlon's ability to incur additional debt, sell assets or pay dividends unless approved by the independent, nonmanagement directors on Revlon's board. Id. at 177.

(2) The court applied the Unocal standard to uphold the board's decision to commence this exchange offer, emphasizing that

(a) The board had reasonable grounds to believe that a harmful threat (i.e., an inadequate takeover bid) to the corporation existed, and

(b) The exchange offer was a reasonable response to the threat. Id. at 181.

c. CBS

(1) The court in Turner Broadcasting System v. CBS, Inc., 627 F. Supp. 901 (N.D. Ga. 1985), refused to enjoin an exchange offer in which CBS offered to acquire 21 percent of its outstanding stock for $150 per share, with $40 of the consideration to be in cash, and $110 to be in debt securities. This offer was made in response to the Turner Broadcasting System's exchange offer for all outstanding shares of CBS stock, with all of the consideration to be in debt securities. Id. at 902 and 903-04.

(2) Turner intended to finance the debt incurred in purchasing CBS by selling all CBS assets not related to CBS's national television broadcast and network businesses, and the notes offered by CBS to their shareholders in the corporation's exchange offer accordingly contained covenants (i) limiting the debt CBS could incur and (ii) prohibiting the sale or transfer of CBS assets unless authorized by a majority of the corporation's independent directors. Id. at 903-04. The term *independent director* was defined as "a director who is not and has never been an employee of the company and who was either a member of the board on July 31, 1985, or who subsequently becomes a director of the company and whose

election [is] approved by a majority of the independent directors then on the board." Id. at 904.

(3) Applying New York law, the court found that "the CBS directors could reasonably conclude that the Turner offer, with its high risk securities and questionable financial viability, was not in the best interests of the CBS shareholders." Id. at 909.

(4) CBS's stock repurchase plan, the court also found, resulted from the CBS directors' exercise of "their best business judgment," and "was not designed, in and of itself, to defeat the Turner tender offer to the detriment of the CBS shareholders." Id.

(5) The court concluded that even if it were to assume that the stock repurchase plan was "intended to affect control" of the corporation, Turner had still failed to carry its burden of "showing that the transactions were unfair or unreasonable" because the directors had made "a sufficient showing of fairness by demonstrating through the evidence presented that the transactions entered into were for a proper corporate purpose." Id. at 910.

(6) The court added that even if it were to apply the Delaware courts' requirement that directors bear the burden of justifying share repurchases as primarily in the corporate interest, the CBS repurchase plan would still withstand judicial scrutiny. Id. at 910–11.

d. Union Carbide

(1) Like the CBS exchange offer, the Union Carbide exchange offer for 35 percent of its shares, examined in GAF Corp. v. Union Carbide Corp., 624 F. Supp. 1016 (S.D.N.Y. 1985), was a response to an offer to be financed, in large part, by utilizing Carbide's own assets and borrowing capacity. The Carbide offer accordingly offered shareholders "high interest corporate debentures and notes containing covenants to protect their credit value which restrict...the sale, in any year, of more than 25 percent of the Company's net assets and, in certain circumstances, not more than 5 percent thereof." Id. at 1017.

(2) Upholding the exchange offer and the restrictive covenants under New York law, the court observed that Union Carbide had satisfied the "burden of going forward with proof of reasonableness and fairness that satisfies invocation of the Business Judgment Rule." Id. at 1022. The court elaborated:

The transactions complained of were grounded on sound reason, made with a good-faith intent to serve the shareholders' best interests and, in the case of the debt securities under the Exchange Offer, to provide conscionable security for and protection of their credit value. Independent outsiders, comprising a majority of the Board, legally and factually disinterested in the benefits of their decisions approved the actions taken. The board did not act, as charged by plaintiff, to keep control of the Company entrenched within the present Board of Directors regardless of Carbide's real best interests. The Carbide offer was not intended to and does not discriminate against bidders for control. It was an alternative available for the stockholders' consideration. It is a measured and responsible action taken with a purpose to protect the best interests of Carbide and its shareholders, and those who acquired the debt securities to be issued. Id. at 1018.

4. Polaroid

    a. In Shamrock Holdings v. Polaroid Corp. ("Polaroid II"), [Current] Fed. Sec. L. Rep. (CCH) ¶ 94,340 (Del. Ch. Mar. 17, 1989), the Delaware Court of Chancery refused to enjoin a series of transactions adopted by Polaroid's board during the pendency of an unwanted $45 per share cash tender offer for all outstanding Polaroid shares by Shamrock Holdings. Id. at 92,217.

    (1) These transactions included a $1.1 billion stock repurchase plan, consisting of (i) $800 million self-tender offer for up to 16 million shares of common stock at $50 per share and (ii) a subsequent repurchase of an additional $325 million worth of shares in the open market or in privately negotiated transactions. Id. at 92,219 and 92,220.

    (2) These stock purchases came shortly after the board's (i) creation of an Employee Stock Ownership Plan which owned 14 percent of Polaroid's shares (id. at 92,217), and (ii) sale of $300 million worth of preferred stock to Corporate Partners, a partnership "organized to make friendly investments" which result in "an infusion of capital" and "a block of voting securities in the hands of one sophisticated entity which will support management and the board of directors" and thus provide "insulation from...hostile acquirors." Id. at 92,216–17 and 92,219. These two aspects of the Polaroid defense are discussed in §§ III A 4 and III B 4 supra.

    (3) Together, these transactions would place approximately 33 percent of Polaroid's stock in the apparently friendly hands of

the ESOP and Corporate Partners. Id. at 92,222 and 92,223.
b. The court began by noting its view that an inadequate, noncoercive offer may constitute a threat for some reasonable period of time after it is announced, but that once "there has been sufficient time for any alternative to be developed and presented and for the target corporation to inform its stockholders of the benefits of retaining their equity position, the 'threat' to the stockholders of an inadequate, noncoercive offer seems, in most circumstances, to be without substance." Id. at 92,223.

Here, however, the court determined that the Polaroid directors' decision to view a noncoercive but inadequate tender offer as a threat was justified by "unusual circumstances" present in the case. These "unusual circumstances" involved a damage award of a still to be determined amount of up to $5.7 billion, or $44.14 per share, in a patent infringement litigation against Kodak in which Polaroid had already obtained a judgment in its favor. Id. The court explained:

> In the foreseeable future, the amount of the damage award will be quantified if not paid. Until that time, it seems appropriate to consider a noncoercive but inadequate tender offer to be a threat. Although the stock market has "valued" the Kodak judgment and analysts have made estimates, Polaroid's stockholders really have very little way of assessing the present worth of this extremely valuable asset. Under these circumstances, there is a real possibility that the Polaroid stockholders will undervalue the Kodak judgment and it does not appear that the mere dissemination of information will cure this problem. Thus, I am satisfied that the Polaroid directors were entitled to treat the Shamrock tender offer as a threat. There is evidence that the offered price is inadequate (and the board so found) and there is a valid basis for concern that the Polaroid stockholders will be unable to reach an accurate judgment as to intrinsic value of their stock in light of the current status of the Kodak litigation. Id. at 92,224.

c. Having acknowledged this threat, the court found that the self-tender offer and buyback plan constituted a reasonable response which offered "some immediate value to those shareholders interested in cash while increasing the equity interest held by the remaining stockholders." Id. "Ignoring Corporate Partners and the ESOP," the court also observed, "the likely shift in the stockholder profile in favor of Polaroid appears to be minimal." Id.

d. The court recognized that the combination of the repurchase plan, Polaroid's already adopted ESOP, and Polaroid's stock issuance to Corporate Partners was "likely to increase the combined voting power of the ESOP and Corporate Partners above 30 percent," and that the planned post-tender buyback would likely be used to reduce the holdings of those Polaroid stockholders identified by management as short-term investors. Id. The court also recognized that the result of all this was the placement of "significantly more voting power...in the hands of groups that oppose Shamrock." Id.

As discussed elsewhere in this outline, however, the court upheld the stock issuance and ESOP components of the transaction (see §§ III A 4 and III B 4 supra), and concluded that the series of transactions as a whole was neither unreasonably disproportionate to the Shamrock threat nor improperly motivated. [Current] Fed. Sec. L. Rep. (CCH) at 92,225.

VI. Extraordinary Dividends

A. Introduction
   1. Another means by which a corporation may recapitalize itself is by declaring a dividend pursuant to which all shareholders:
      a. Receive cash and/or preferred stock or debentures (or other paper), and
      b. Retain their common stock, shares of which are then referred to as "stub" or "rump" shares.
   2. An important practical difference between a board decision to commence a self-tender or exchange offer and a board decision to declare a dividend is that:
      a. A self-tender or an exchange offer requires some shareholder action to succeed as a defensive strategy (i.e., the required percentage of the corporation's shareholders must tender their shares), while
      b. A dividend can be accomplished quickly and without any affirmative shareholder action.
B. The Case Law
   Dividend recapitalizations have been reviewed by the courts pursuant to the same standards utilized in other restructuring and recapitalization cases.
   1. Newmont Mining
      a. Ivanhoe Partners v. Newmont Mining Corp., 535 A.2d 1334 (Del. 1987), aff'g 533 A.2d 585 (Del. Ch.), involved the situation where Newmont Mining, a large gold producer, declared a $33 per share

dividend in response to perceived threats to the corporate entity posed by the combination of

(1) An inadequate and coercive partial tender offer by a 10 percent shareholder, Ivanhoe Partners (an entity controlled by T. Boone Pickens), and

(2) The presence in the corporation's shareholder body of a potentially unfriendly 26 percent shareholder, Gold Fields.
535 A.2d at 1336–40 and 1342.

b. The dividend, which represented the liquidation value of Newmont's nongold assets, was declared in accordance with an agreement between Newmont and Gold Fields pursuant to which Gold Fields would utilize its share of the dividend to "sweep the street" to increase its Newmont holdings to 49.7 percent, and then conduct itself in accordance with a pre-arranged standstill agreement. Id. at 1340.

c. Upholding the dividend against a challenge by Ivanhoe, the Delaware Supreme Court stated the following:

> [T]he $33 dividend...served two significant purposes in defending against Ivanhoe's inadequate and coercive tender offer. First, the dividend distributed the heretofore undervalued nongold assets to all of Newmont's shareholders. In doing so Newmont effectively eliminated the means by which Ivanhoe might have acquired Newmont's gold assets at a substantial discount to the detriment of the other stockholders. Second, the dividend provided the financial impetus needed to persuade Gold Fields to engage in the street sweep. Although Gold Fields had the requisite financing to implement such action independently of the dividend, its board was reluctant to invest the $1.6 billion dollars needed to obtain a majority interest in Newmont. Id. at 1343.

2. Harcourt Brace Jovanovich

a. A federal court applying New York law in British Printing and Communi-cation Corp. plc v. Harcourt Brace Jovanovich, Inc., 664 F. Supp. 1519 (S.D.N.Y. 1987), upheld a recapitalization adopted by Harcourt Brace Jovanovich ("HBJ") in response to a $44 per share merger proposal by British Printing and Communication Corp. ("BPCC").

(1) This recapitalization plan included a special dividend of $40 in cash plus a share of preferred stock to be valued at approximately $10. HBJ shareholders would also retain their existing "stub" shares,

which would be worth $5 to $7 per share and would allow shareholders to participate in the corporation's future economic growth. Id. at 1525.

(2) The recapitalization also included ownership of HBJ securities by an investment banking advisor providing bridge financing for the transaction and by an employee stock ownership plan.

The sum total of all this, according to BPCC, was to place substantial voting power in friendly hands. Id. at 1525–26 and 1531.

b. The court rejected BPCC's contention that HBJ's shareholders received less than what otherwise might be available because the board had acted to entrench incumbent management, stating that this contention was not supported by evidence. Id. at 1531.

c. The court also held that the payment of the special dividend posed no threat of irreparable injury to HBJ's shareholders since the "debt incurred in order to provide that dividend will be offset by the payment of the dividend (plus cost reductions implemented because of the recapitalization)." Id. at 1529. The net result, the court therefore concluded, was neither an increase nor a decrease in the value of HBJ to its shareholders, but simply "to allow them to realize that value, in part immediately, more fully than they might otherwise." Id.

d. Another important aspect of the HBJ recapitalization was the temporary financing of the plan by a bridge loan provided by HBJ's financial advisor, First Boston Corporation, until high-risk, high-yield subordinated "junk bond" securities could be sold. Id. at 1526.

(1) As a condition for providing this bridge financing, First Boston insisted upon "some voice in the running of the company." Id.

(a) First Boston was accordingly allowed to purchase 40,000 shares of a new issue of redeemable preferred stock at a price exceeding $80 million. These shares carried a total of 8,160,000 votes, representing a cost of approximately $10 per vote, the estimated price per share at which HBJ common stock was expected to trade following the distribution of the special dividend. Id.

(b) In addition, in order "to ensure that [First Boston] would not be faced with a lengthy commitment to new management which might not be as reliable in running HBJ as First Boston believed HBJ's present management to be," the loan agreement provided that First Boston could call in its loan in the event of a change in control. Id. at 1527.

(2) The court rejected Maxwell's contention that this aspect of the transaction was "designed solely to place votes in friendly hands in order to entrench management":

> The record reveals...that it was First Boston that insisted on the right to purchase the stock as a condition of providing the bridge financing, as a way of ensuring that it had a voice in HBJ's management (so as to protect its loan to HBJ) and as an investment. [Maxwell] adduced no evidence of a secret or open agreement between First Boston and any other entity concerning how it would vote or dispose of its shares. In addition, First Boston paid a price for that stock equivalent to the market price for the comparable common stock being traded on the market ex dividend. Id. at 1531

> The court also rejected Maxwell's contention that the change of control provisions in the HBJ–First Boston loan agreements would have the effect of precluding a takeover of the company:

> > The would-be acquirer need only obtain sufficient financing of its own with which to replace the loans in order to render those provisions nugatory. Even absent such alternative financing, the acquirer would quite possibly be able to assure [the lenders] that it is capable of running HBJ as efficiently as does present management and there-by dissuade them from calling in the loans. Id. at 1529.

3. Santa Fe
    a. Henley Group v. Santa Fe Southern Pacific Corp., No. 9569 (Del. Ch. Mar. 11, 1988), involved a Santa Fe restructuring plan adopted at the time the corporation was required by an Interstate Commerce Commission Order to divest itself of substantial assets. Id., slip op. at 3 and 16.
        (1) The plan involved the distribution to shareholders of a $30 per share dividend consisting of $25 per share in cash and a $5 payment-in-kind ("PIK") debenture, which made "a portion of Santa Fe's existing value liquid, and [allowed] the common shareholders to realize some of that liquidity, by transforming $5 of Santa Fe's equity into debt that can be publicly traded and sold on the open market for cash. Alternatively, a shareholder may...hold the debenture until maturity and collect interest" at 16

percent per year for 15 years, with the interest during the first 6 years to be paid in additional debentures rather than cash. Id. at 16–17, 32 and 40.

(2) The debentures were nonredeemable for two years, and contained restrictions—referred to by the court as "PIK restrictions"—significantly limiting the corporation's "ability to pay dividends, to borrow, and to enter into certain types of fundamental transactions, including mergers and further restructurings that involve spin-offs or other extraordinary distributions to shareholder." Id. at 33.

b. The court began its analysis by rejecting Santa Fe's claim that the PIK debenture restrictions were not adopted as an antitakeover measure, and accordingly held that the two-pronged Unocal test provided the applicable standard for judicial review. Id. at 35–36.

(1) The court supported this conclusion by emphasizing the "indisputable (though limited) antitakeover effect" created by "the stringent PIK restrictions," which "would preclude a leveraged acquisition of Santa Fe, or a restructuring that involves a spin-off or a recapitalization for as long as the debentures remain outstanding (at least the two year nonredemption period)." Id. at 35.

(2) The court also noted that Santa Fe's board adopted the restructuring plan, including the PIK debentures, on "the very day it also adopted a package of antitakeover measures," and that the debenture component of the dividend could have been financed on more conventional terms. Id. at 35–36.

c. Applying the first prong of the Unocal test, the court held that the corporation's directors reasonably perceived two substantial shareholders as threats to corporate policy and effectiveness at a time when the board was "justifiabl[y] concern[ed] that Santa Fe might be vulnerable to a takeover that would deprive shareholders from receiving full value for their equity." Id. at 37–38.

d. Applying the second prong, the court upheld the reasonableness of the debentures—and in particular the PIK restrictions—as a response to this threat:

First, the restrictive (antitakeover) features of the PIK debenture are limited in scope and time. Although the PIK restrictions do preclude highly leveraged acquisitions, they do not deter acquisitions that are not dependent upon substantial additional leveraging of Santa Fe's assets. Nor do they preclude a proxy contest for control of the Board. Moreover, the restrictions can be eliminated after the first two years (in 1990) by redeeming the debentures.

Second, the debentures, by preventing highly leveraged take-overs of Santa Fe for a minimum of two years, protect the restructuring by enabling the asset sales to take place without disruption. The debentures' PIK restrictions, plus...their six year deferral of cash interest payments, will enable Santa Fe to generate the cash flow required to pay down its indebtedness, including interest on the PIK, and otherwise allow Santa Fe to implement the restructuring.

Third, according to [an investment advisor's affidavit], the restrictions are standard high yield debenture provisions that will preserve the debenture's trading value by preventing an acquirer from (i) leveraging the company's assets so as to render it unable to meet its debt obligations under the PIK, or (ii) subordinating the PIKs under significant additional senior debt that would jeopardize the company's ability to meet its payment obligations to PIK holders. The restrictions are not unusual for financial instruments of this type. According to [the affidavit], comparable debt securities have interest deferral periods ranging from five to seven years, and nonredemption periods ranging from one to five years. Moreover, dividend restrictions are standard features of virtually all debt securities and the dividend restrictions in the [Santa Fe] debentures are less stringent than those contained in Santa Fe's bank credit agreement for financing the cash portion of the dividend. [The affadivit] testimony in these respects is uncontroverted. Id. at 41–42.

4. Macmillan

   a. The litigation in Robert M. Bass Group v. Evans, 552 A.2d 1227 (Del. Ch. 1988) ("Macmillan I"), involved a proposed restructuring of Macmillan, Inc. into two separate entities, one consisting of Macmillan's publishing business ("Publishing") and the other consisting of Macmillan's information business ("Information"). Id. at 1231.

      (1) The court noted Macmillan's assertion that "a two-company structure would allow shareholders to receive a greater dividend than in a single company transaction, and would lead to a higher stock value for each of the separate entities." Id. at 1231.

      (2) The court also noted plaintiffs' contention that "the two-company recapitalization would make a hostile takeover more difficult,

since management could own a greater percentage of one of the two separate entities than would be the case in a single company recapitalization." Id.

The restructuring had been under consideration for a full year, but was adopted two weeks after a group including Robert M. Bass offered to acquire all of Macmillan's common stock for $64 per share in cash. Id. at 1236.

b. The plan was implemented by the declaration of a dividend providing that Macmillan's public shareholders would
   (1) Receive $52.35 in cash and a $4.50 debenture,
   (2) Retain their shares of Macmillan, which would be called Publishing (valued at $5.10), and
   (3) Receive one half of a share of a new Information entity to be spun off from Macmillan (valued at $2.20).
      The entire package was valued at $64.15 per share.
      The plan also provided that a four-member management team would forgo the cash and debenture components of the dividend, and exchange most of their Macmillan stock and options—which represented 4.5 percent of Macmillan's equity—for Information stock representing 39.2 percent of Information's equity. Id. at 1236–37.

c. The Bass Group responded by proposing, in the alternative,
   (1) An increase of its $64 cash offer for all Macmillan shares to $73, or
   (2) A restructuring modeled after the already approved company plan, but providing that the cash component of the dividend would be $58 rather than $52.35 per share, that Macmillan's management would receive the same dividend as Macmillan's public shareholders, and that the Bass Group would pay cash for the 39.2 percent interest in Information that would, under the Macmillan plan, go to Macmillan management.
      Both of these proposed alternatives were rejected by Macmillan. Id. at 1238.

d. Granting the Bass Group's motion for a preliminary injunction, the Delaware Court of Chancery noted first that the Macmillan board's approval of the dual-company restructuring program was governed by the two-pronged Unocal standard since "the restructuring was intended as a response to the Bass offer." Id. at 1239 and n.31.

e. With regard to the first prong of the Unocal test, the court concluded that "if the Bass offers posed a cognizable, reasonably perceived threat, it was only in the minimal sense that the Bass Group's current proposal of $73 per share, although fair, is less than the highest price that the defendants' financial advisors believe might be obtained if the entire company were put up for sale." Id. at 1241 (footnote omitted).

The court reached this determination by rejecting three contentions by Macmillan.

(1) First, the court rejected Macmillan's claim that the announcement of the Bass proposal itself constituted a threat since it put the company "into play" by causing significant open market trading. That fact alone, according to the court, does not demonstrate actionable harm since, rather than being coerced, Macmillan's shareholders "[p]resumably...wished to take immediate advantage of the market price increase resulting from disclosure of the Bass proposal. Id. at 1240.

(2) Second, the court rejected Macmillan's contention that the Bass Group posed a threat to the corporation due to the Group's reputation as "greenmailers" whose *modus operandi,* as evidenced by previous acquisitions, was detrimental to public shareholder interests." Id. at 1240.

   (a) The court cited the absence of support in the record for this claimed perception, and noted its belief that Macmillan had not expressed a genuine willingness to listen to the Bass Group's response to concerns regarding past "predatory acquisition practices." Id.

   (b) The court added that the board's "education on [this] subject was provided by management," was "less than accurate" and "served more to propagandize the Board than to enlighten it." Id. at 1232.

(3) Third, the court rejected Macmillan's contention that the $64 Bass offer constituted a threat because it was substantially below the range of values Macmillan's financial advisors considered fair.

   (a) The court described the $64 offer as "only an opening bid, by its own terms subject to negotiation," and concluded that management "chose to close their eyes and to treat the offer as firm and unalterable," with Macmillan's board and a special committee of outside directors "follow[ing] in lockstep" rather than taking "reasonable measures to uncover the facts." Id. at 1240–41.

(b) The court also emphasized the Bass Group's subsequent proposal of two alternative transactions, both of which neither of Macmillan's financial advisors had labeled unfair. Id. at 1241.

(4) Finally, the court stated, "the antitakeover devices already at [Macmillan's] disposal," including a poison pill rights plan "which would effectively deter the Bass Group (or anyone else) from acquiring over 15 percent of Macmillan's stock," left the board in a position in which "[e]ven if, *arguendo*, the Bass offers were hostile, coercive and/or unfair, the Board scarcely needed to fear any threat to corporate policy and effectiveness." Id. at 1241.

f. With regard to the second prong of the Unocal test, the court concluded that the Macmillan restructuring was not reasonable in relation to the threat posed. The court emphasized that "given the nature of the threat"—i.e., that the Bass proposal was not the highest price that might be obtainable—"a reasonable response would, at a minimum, offer stockholders higher value than the Bass Group offer or, at the very least, offer stockholders a choice between equivalent values in different forms." Id. at 1242. The company restructuring plan, according to the court, did not satisfy this standard because it offered "inferior value to the shareholders" and "force[d] them to accept it" since the restructuring took the form of a dividend not requiring shareholder approval. Id.

(1) The court noted Macmillan's contention that the restructuring was reasonable because it

   (a) Allowed shareholders "to realize immediate value while retaining their equity interest, with the prospect of receiving long term value,"

   (b) Created a structure "designed to result in a higher market value for each separate component," and

   (c) Encouraged management "to efficiently manage the companies by 'tying up' a large portion of management's net worth in the equity of these companies, thereby inducing them to increase their stock value." Id. at 1243.

(2) The court concluded, however, that:

these rationales, even if accepted, do not justify forcing shareholders to accept an economically inferior transaction while, at the same time, precluding them from considering an economically superior one. The directors certainly were free to propose the restructuring to their shareholders. However, as fiduciaries they were not free to "cram down" that transaction in order to "protect" their shareholders from a noncoercive, economically superior one. Under Unocal the directors were obligated to give the shareholders a choice. The restructuring, because it deprives them of that choice, is manifestly unreasonable. Id. at 1243–44 (footnote omitted).

(3) The court also rejected Macmillan's contention that the difference in consideration to be received by Macmillan's public shareholders in the company restructuring and the Bass Group's alternative restructuring proposal was justified by the fact that the latter but not the former constituted a sale of control mandating a control premium. In the court's words:

> There is no evidence that any member of the Board or the Special Committee questioned how a sale of 39 percent of Information would constitute a sale of the company if sold to the Bass Group, yet would not be if that same 39 percent interest is sold to the management group. The defendants have failed to explain that reasoning, and its logic continues to elude the court. Id. at 1242.

> The court explained that the Macmillan financial advisors' $64.15 valuation of the management restructuring included the value of the equity that shareholders would retain, and thus presumably took into account whatever control premium might be realized in the future. The court also emphasized its view that the management restructuring constituted the sale of effective control even though the 39 percent interest in Information to be owned by management was not an absolute majority interest. The court supported this statement by citing internally generated Macmillan documents reporting that the management group would have effective control over Information even with a block of less than 50 percent of Information's stock. The effect of this, the court concluded, was to "make Information 'takeover proof,' because it will tend to entrench the management group and virtually eliminate the public shareholders' opportunity to realize a 'takeover premium' for their shares without obtaining management's consent." Id. at 1244.

5. Moore McCormack
   a. Southdown, Inc. v. Moore McCormack Resources, 686 F. Supp. 595 (S.D. Tex. 1988), involved a $31 cash per share offer by Southdown

for all outstanding shares of Moore McCormack stock (the stock was trading at $24 per share at the time, and had historically traded in the $20 price range). The offer was subsequently increased first to $35 cash per share, then to $35 cash plus a $5 bond per share, and finally to $40 per share. Id. at 598.

b. Moore McCormack's board determined to pursue what the court described as a "scorched earth" restructuring strategy, intended "to change the financial structure of the company in order to make it unattractive to a buyer" without regard to the corporation's operating or financing needs. Id. at 599. Pursuant to this plan, each shareholder would receive

    (1) A $24.60 cash dividend, $15.50 of which was payable immediately and $9.10 of which would be paid in a later installment, conditioned upon the corporation's receipt of an appraisal revaluing the company's assets significantly upward and

    (2) A $6.62 15-year subordinated debenture. Shareholders would also continue to hold their "stub" or "rump" common shares, which would then carry a value of between $1 and $3 per share.

c. Moore McCormack conceded that the recapitalization plan's total value was less than the $40 per share offered by Southdown, but contended that the plan was superior to Southdown's offer since it "created" more value for shareholders. Id. at 599–600.

d. The court rejected this contention, concluding instead that "ample financial data indicate[d] that Moore McCormack's conclusory statement about the inadequacy of Southdown's offer is, at best, a market-manipulative falsehood to perpetuate…management's incumbency." Id. at 603.

    (1) The court emphasized that the highest price at which the stock had traded during the two years prior to Southdown's initial offer was $28.75 per share, and that Southdown's $40 offer reflected a 68 percent premium over Moore McCormack's preoffer trading price. Id.

    (2) The court also emphasized that the $40 offer fell "well within Moore McCormack's own valuation" of the company, and that Moore McCormack lacked sufficient collateral or value to obtain more than $35 per share in a liquidation. Id.

e. The court accordingly concluded that Southdown had demonstrated a likelihood of success on its claim that the recapitalization plan was not protected by the business judgment rule, and thus enjoined the transaction. Id. at 604 and 596.

VII. Use of Poison Pill Shareholder Rights Plans to Protect Restructuring Transactions

Much attention has been devoted in recent months to the use of poison pill shareholder rights plans to protect restructuring or recapitalization transactions against noncoercive all-cash tender offers deemed inadequate by the target corporation's board. The redemption of poison pill rights under such circumstances has been ordered in transactions involving Interco and Pillsbury.

A. Interco
   1. In City Capital Associates v. Interco Inc., 551 A. 2d 787 (Del. Ch. 1988), the Delaware Court of Chancery addressed a takeover battle in its "end-stage," meaning that negotiating leverage provided by the target's poison pill could "not be further utilized by the board to increase the options available to shareholders or to improve the terms of those options." Id. at 790.
   2. Two options were on the table at that point:
      a. First, a noncoercive $74 all-cash offer for all shares by the Rales brothers. Id. at 794.
      b. Second, a $76 Board approved restructuring, consisting of:
         (1) The sale by Interco of assets (including Interco's Ethan Allen "crown jewel") generating approximately 50 percent of Interco's gross sales,
         (2) The borrowing of approximately $2 billion,
         (3) The declaring of a part-cash and part-securities dividend having a claimed aggregate value of $66 per share, and
         (4) The retention by shareholders of an equity interest or stub estimated to trade at a price of at least $10 per share. Id. at 793.
            The court emphasized that the board believed in good faith that the restructuring transaction was worth at least $76 per share, but that in the court's view this was an inherently debatable proposition due to the nature of the involved securities. Id. at 795.
   3. Under these circumstances, the court concluded that the board's refusal to redeem its poison pill rights in order to protect the restructuring transaction constituted a defensive step that was not reasonable in relationship to any threat to the corporation or its shareholders.
      a. According to the Interco decision, a board determination that an offer is inadequate by itself justifies leaving a poison pill in place even in the setting of a noncoercive offer for a period of time during which the

board exercises its good faith business judgment to take appropriate steps to advance shareholder interests. Id. at 798.

    b. Once that period has ended, however, the role of the poison pill in the context of a noncoercive offer is completely fulfilled, and shareholders should be allowed to exercise their own judgment about their own interests. Id.

    c. Put simply, the Interco court concluded, it is "inarguable" that a shareholder could prefer a $74 cash payment now to the potentially $76 but in fact "complex and uncertain future consideration" offered through the board-approved restructuring. Id. at 799.

B. Pillsbury

    1. A second Delaware Court of Chancery decision, Grand Metropolitan PLC v. Pillsbury Co., [1988–1989 Transfer Binder] Fed. Sec. L. Rep. (CCH) ¶ 94,104 (Del. Ch. Dec. 16, 1988), involved a $63 per share all-cash offer by Grand Metropolitan for all outstanding shares of Pillsbury, conditioned upon Pillsbury's redemption of its poison pill. The $63 per share price, according to the court's calculation, represented a 60 percent premium over the pre-offer Pillsbury market price. Id. at 91,190.

        According to the court, the only possible danger posed by Grand Met's offer to Pillsbury related solely to the price Pillsbury shareholders would receive for their stock. Id. at 91,193.

    2. Pillsbury's board responded to Grand Met's offer with a restructuring plan which Pillsbury said would provide $68 in long-term value for shareholders by spinning off and selling various Pillsbury businesses over a 2 1/2- to 5-year period. Id. at 91,193–94.

    3. The court found no reason to question the good faith of Pillsbury's directors in believing that their restructuring plan would better serve shareholder interests than Grand Met's all-cash offer. Nevertheless, the court held that Pillsbury's use of the pill to preclude shareholders—87 percent of whom had tendered their shares—from concluding that "$63 in present cash is preferable to the possibility of $68 if all of the 'ifs' in Pillsbury's plan disappear and its hopes for the future become realized" was far out of proportion to the at most minimal threat facing Pillsbury's shareholders. Id. at 91,194. The court added that, in its view, the real threat to shareholder value was not the difference between $63 and $68 (Pillsbury's value if shareholders are "patient and endure for a long time, perhaps until 1992 or 1993"), but rather the difference between $63 and the high 30s, where the court believed the stock would likely fall if Grand Met's offer were withdrawn. Id.

4. The court therefore ordered the poison pill redeemed, thus permitting Pillsbury's shareholders to make their own determination about their own best interests. Id. at 91,197.

C. The evolving law surrounding the redemption of poison pill shareholder rights outside of the specific context of restructuring transactions is beyond the scope of this outline. See generally Amanda Acquisition Corp. v. Universal Foods Corp., No. 88-C–1296 (JPS), slip op. at 50–69 (E.D. Wis. Mar. 18, 1989) (Wisconsin law); Desert Partners v. USG Corp., 686 F. Supp. 1289, 1298–301 (N.D. Ill. 1988) (Delaware law); CRTF Corp. v. Federated Dep't Stores, 683 F. Supp. 422, 439–42 (S.D.N.Y. 1988) (Delaware law); Southdown, Inc. v. Moore McCormack Resources, 686 F. Supp. 595, 600-04 (S.D. Tex. 1988) (Delaware law); BNS Inc. v. Koppers Co., 683 F. Supp. 458, 474–76 (D. Del. 1988) (Delaware law); Gelco Corp. v. Coniston Partners, 652 F. Supp. 829, 849–50 (D. Minn. 1986), aff'd on other grounds, 811 F.2d 414 (8th Cir. 1987) (Minnesota law); Moran v. Household Int'l, Inc., 500 A.2d 1346, 1354, 1357 (Del. 1985), aff'g, 490 A.2d 1059 (Del. Ch.) (Delaware law); TW Servs. v. SWT Acquisition Corp., [Current] Fed. Sec. L. Rep. (CCH) ¶ 94,334, at 92,178–82 (Del. Ch. Mar. 2 1989) (Delaware law); In re Holly Farms Corp. Shareholders Litig., [1988–1989 Transfer Binder] Fed. Sec. L. Rep. (CCH) ¶ 94,181, at 91,645 (Del. Ch. Dec. 30, 1988) (Delaware law); MAI Basic Four, Inc. v. Prime Computer Inc., [1988–1989 Transfer Binder] Fed. Sec. L. Rep. (CCH) ¶ 94,179, at 91,633–35 (Del. Ch. Dec. 20, 1988) (Delaware law); Grand Metro. PLC v. Pillsbury Co., [1988–1989 Transfer Binder] Fed. Sec. L. Rep. (CCH) ¶ 94,104, at 91,141–94 (Del. Ch. Dec. 16 1988) (Delaware law); Grand Metro. PLC v. Pillsbury Co., No. 10319 (Del. Ch. Nov. 7, 1988); Mills Acquisition Co. v. Macmillan, Inc., [1988–1989 Transfer Binder] Fed. Sec. L. Rep. (CCH) ¶ 94,071 at 91,024-25 (Del. Ch. Oct. 17, 1988), rev'd on other grounds, [1988–1989 Transfer Binder] Fed. Sec. L. Rep. (CCH) ¶ 94,072 (Del. oral opinion Nov. 2, 1988, written opinion forthcoming) (Delaware law); Doskocil Cos. v. Griggy, No. 10095, slip op. at 5–11 (Del. Ch. Oct. 7, 1988) (Delaware law); Nomad Acquisition Corp. v. Damon Corp., [1988–1989 Transfer Binder] Fed. Sec. L. Rep. (CCH) ¶ 94,040, at 90,871–72 (Del. Ch. Sept. 16, 1988) (Delaware law); Tate and Lyle PLC v. Staley Continental, Inc., [1987–1988 Transfer Binder] Fed. Sec. L. Rep. (CCH) ¶ 93,764, at 98,587 (Del. Ch. May 9, 1988); Facet Enters. v. Prospect Group, No. 9746, slip op. at 15–19 (Del Ch. Apr. 15, 1988) (Delaware law).

VIII. Super-Voting Common Stock

A. Introduction
  1. A final restructuring or recapitalization strategy is the issuance of "super-voting," "disparate-class" or "dual-class" common stock to existing common shareholders either as a dividend or as part of an exchange offer. This super-voting common stock:
     a. Must be authorized in the corporation's charter and thus requires shareholder approval,
     b. Typically has disproportionately high voting rights but lower dividend and liquidation rights than the corporation's ordinary common stock, and
     c. Generally is subject to substantial transfer restrictions, but may be converted into common stock at any time.
        See generally 1 R. Balotti and J. Finkelstein, The Delaware Law of Corporations and Business Organizations § 6.03B, at 324.21-.22 (1988); 2 R. Winter, M. Stumpf and G. Hawkins, Shark Repellents and Golden Parachutes: A Handbook for the Practitioner § 9.11, at 270.2–4 (1988); Wander and LaCoque, Boardroom Jitters: Corporate Control Transactions and Today's Business Judgment Rule, 42 Bus. Law. 29, 49–50 (1986).
  2. The antitakeover effect "stems from the fact that shareholders other than insiders…have less desire to retain the nontransferable super-voting stock and, therefore, over time will convert their shares of super-voting stock into common stock. As conversions by shareholders other than insiders occur, the percentage of the total voting power held by the insiders will increase." Lipton and Brownstein, Takeover Responses and Directors' Responsibilities—An Update, 40 Bus. Law. 1403, 1415 (1985).
  3. Accordingly, as a defensive strategy, dual-class common stock plans are "designed for and are most effective" where one or more blocks of stock are in the hands of holders "willing to forgo dividends and/or retain nontransferable shares." R. Balotti and J. Finkelstein § 6.30B, at 324.22. See also Note, Dual-Class Recapitalization, and Shareholder Voting Rights, 87 Colum. L. Rev. 106, 112–13 (1987); Sandler, Dual Stock Categories Spur Powerful Debate Over Stability vs. Gain, Wall St. J., May 17, 1988, at 1; Sontag, Dual-Class Stock Plans Face Possible SEC Ban, Nat'l L. J., June 27, 1988, at 1.
  4. There are, of course, numerous business uses for multiple classes of

common stock carrying differing voting rights that have nothing to do with maintaining corporate control. The financing of both day-to-day corporate activities and extraordinary corporate acquisitions and the providing of entrepreneurial incentives to the management of discrete units of a corporation are examples of such business uses. See Fischel, Organized Exchanges and the Regulation of Dual Class Common Stock, 54 U. Chi. L. Rev. 119, 140 (1987); Johnson, Classes of Common Stock Achieve Key Goals, Legal Times, Mar. 17, 1986, at 15; Exchange Act Release No. 34–25891, 53 Fed. Reg. 26376, 26381 and 26383–84 and n.89 (July 12, 1988); Exchange Act Release No. 34–24623, 52 Fed. Reg. 23665, 23671 (June 24, 1987).

5. Although there are no cases on the subject, the creation of multiple classes of stock with differing voting rights for one or more of these purposes presumably would be protected by the business judgment rule. See Johnson, Legal Times, Mar. 17, 1986, at 15.

B. Statutory Authority

1. Section 212(a) of the Delaware General Corporation Law provides that each stockholder of a corporation is entitled to one vote for each share held "[u]nless otherwise provided in the certificate of incorporation." Del. Gen. Corp. Law § 212(a).

2. The Delaware Supreme Court in Providence and Worcester Co. v. Baker, 378 A.2d 121 (Del. 1977), thus upheld a certificate provision granting shareholders one vote for each of the first 50 shares held, and one vote for every 20 shares held beyond the first 50 shares. Id. at 121 n.2 and 122–24.

3. Several Delaware courts, following the Providence and Worcester decision, have reaffirmed the statutory authority of Delaware corporations to issue dual class voting stock. See, e.g., Williams v. Geier, [1987 Transfer Binder] Fed. Sec. L. Rep. (CCH) ¶ 93,283, at 96,407-08 (Del. Ch. May 20, 1987); Lacos Land Co. v. Arden Group, Inc., 517 A.2d 271, 275 (Del. Ch. 1986). See also Weiss v. Rockwell Int'l Corp., No. 8811, Tr. op. at 9 (Del. Ch. Feb. 6, 1987) (noting that plaintiff did not contest corporation's statutory authority to adopt dual class voting stock); Packer v. Yampol, 12 Del. J. Corp. L. 332, 351 (Del. Ch. 1986) (same).

4. Federal courts construing the laws of Iowa and Pennsylvania similarly have found statutory bases for shareholder-approved disparate-class reclassification charter provisions. See Baron v. Strawbridge and Clothier, 646 F. Supp. 690, 698 (E.D. Pa. 1986); Kersten v. Pioneer Hi-Bred Int'l, Inc., 626 F. Supp. 647, 649 (N.D. Iowa 1985).

5. By contrast, however, federal courts construing Colorado, Delaware, Georgia, New Jersey, and Wisconsin law and a state court in New York have (explicitly or implicitly) refused to follow Providence and Worcester in cases involving flip-in and disproportionate voting poison pill provisions put into place without shareholder approval. See West Point-Pepperell, Inc. v. Farley Inc., No. 3:88-CV57-GET, slip op. at 16–17 (N.D. Ga. Nov. 14, 1988) (Georgia law); Amalgamated Sugar Co. v. NL Indus., 644 F. Supp. 1229, 1234–37 (S.D.N.Y. 1986) (New Jersey law); R.D. Smith and Co. v. Preway Inc., 644 F. Supp. 868, 873–75 (W.D. Wis. 1986) (Wisconsin law); Spinner Corp. v. Princeville Dev. Corp., No. 86-0701, slip op. at 5–7 (D. Haw. Oct. 31, 1986), vacated, [1987 Transfer Binder] Fed. Sec. L. Rep. (CCH) ¶ 93,157 (D. Haw. Jan. 30, 1987) (Colorado law); Minstar Acquiring Corp. v. AMF Inc., 621 F. Supp. 1252, 1259 (S.D.N.Y. 1985) (New Jersey law); Unilever Acquisition Corp. v. Richardson-Vicks, Inc., 618 F. Supp. 407, 409–10 (S.D.N.Y. 1985) (Delaware law); Asarco Inc. v. MHR Holmes A Court, 611 F. Supp. 468, 478 (D.N.J. 1985) (New Jersey law); Bank of New York Co. v. Irving Bank Corp., N.Y.L.J., July 8, 1988, at 22 (N.Y. Sup. Ct. 1988), subsequent proceedings, No. 10217/88 (N.Y. Sup. Ct. July 21, 1988), aff'd mem., No. 34386 (N.Y. App. Div. Oct. 4, 1988). But cf. City Fed. Sav. and Loan Ass'n v. Mann, No. 84–4010, Tr. op. at 62–63 (D.N.J. Aug. 2, 1985) (denying preliminary injunctive relief in case involving Delaware law on the ground that "each side has tenable arguments"), aff'd mem., 782 F.2d 1027 (3d Cir. 1986).

Legislation enacted in the mid-to-late 1980s in Georgia, Ohio, Pennsylvania, and Wisconsin specifically permits the creation and issuance of poison pill provisions which include discriminatory conditions, unless otherwise provided in the corporation's charter. See Ga. Bus. Corp. Code § 14–2–624 (effective July 1, 1989); Ohio Gen. Corp. Law §§ 1701–16(A) and (B)(1)(f); Pa. Bus. Corp. Law § 611(D); Wis. Bus. Corp. Law § 180.155.

The Georgia and Wisconsin legislation judicially overruled the West Point-Pepperell and Preway decisions. See Amanda Acquisition Corp. v. Universal Foods Corp., No. 88-C–1296 (JPS), slip op. at 51 (E.D. Wis. Mar. 18, 1989) (Wisconsin law). New York adopted similar legislation in December 1988 on a temporary basis to overrule the Irving Bank decision, but that legislation expired on April 1, 1989 without further action by the legislature. See N.Y. Bus. Corp. Law § 505(a); Bid to Extend Shareholder Plans Fails, N.Y.L.J., Mar. 31, 1989, at 1. A new statute was enacted in

New York in early May, but that legislation expires on June 30. See Cole, The Trade-Off for a 'Poison Pill', N.Y. Times, May 11, 1989, at D2.

The application of these decisions and statutes in the context of super-voting stock as opposed to poison pill provisions is uncertain.

C. SEC Rule 19c–4

1. In July 1988, following four years of discussion and debate, the Securities and Exchange Commission adopted Rule 19c–4. Exchange Act Release No. 34–25891, 53 Fed. Reg. 26376 (July 12, 1988). This Rule—as of its July 7, 1988 effective date—prohibits the listing or continued listing on any national exchange or by the NASD if "the issuer of such security issues any class of security, or takes other corporate action, with the effect of nullifying, restricting, or disparately reducing the per share voting rights of holders of an outstanding class or classes of common stock." Rule 19c–4(a)and(b), printed in Exchange Act Release No. 34–25891, 53 Fed. Reg. at 26394 (codified at 17 C.F.R. § 240.19c–4).

2. The Rule includes nonexclusive lists of corporate actions presumed to be prohibited or permitted:

    [T]he following shall be presumed to have the effect of nullifying, restricting, or disparately reducing the per share voting rights of an outstanding class or classes of common stock:

    (1) Corporate action to impose any restriction on the voting power of shares of the common stock of the issuer held by a beneficial or record holder based on the number of shares held by such beneficial or record holder;

    (2) Corporate action to impose any restriction on the voting power of shares of the common stock of the issuer held by a beneficial or record holder based on the length of time such shares have been held by such beneficial or record holder;

    (3) Any issuance of securities through an exchange offer by the issuer for shares of an outstanding class of the common stock of the issuer, in which the securities issued have voting rights greater than or less than the per share voting rights of any outstanding class of the common stock of the issuer;

    (4) Any issuance of securities pursuant to a stock dividend, or any other type of distribution of stock, in which the securities issued have voting rights greater than the per share voting rights of any outstanding class of the common stock of the issuer.

                        ***

    [T]he following, standing alone, shall be presumed not to have the effect of nullifying, restricting, or disparately reducing the per share voting rights of holders of an outstanding class or classes of common stock:

(1) The issuance of securities pursuant to an initial registered public offering;

(2) The issuance of any class of securities, through a registered public offering, with voting rights not greater than the per share voting rights of any outstanding class of the common stock of the issuer;

(3) The issuance of any class of securities to effect a bona fide merger or acquisition, with voting rights not greater than the per share voting rights of any outstanding class of the common stock of the issuer;

(4) Corporate action taken pursuant to state law requiring a state's domestic corporation to condition the voting rights of a beneficial or record holder of a specified threshold percentage of the corporation's voting stock on the approval of the corporation's independent shareholders.

Rule 19c–4(c) and (d), printed in Exchange Act Release No. 34–25891, 53 Fed. Reg. at 26394 (codified at 17 C.F.R. § 240.19c–4).

3. In support of its decision to promulgate Rule 19c–4, the Commission emphasized that while it "does not believe that the issuance of less than full voting rights stock is *per se* inappropriate," "[s]hareholders who purchase voting rights stock in a company do so with the understanding that the shares will be accompanied by the voting rights attendant to the stock at the time of the purchase." The diminution or limitation of these rights, according to the Commission, "is inconsistent with the investor protection and fair corporate suffrage policies" embodied in the Exchange Act. Exchange Act Release No. 34–25891, 53 Fed. Reg. at 26381. The Commission emphasized its view that "the shareholder voting process is not fully effective in preventing the adoption of disparate voting rights plans that disenfranchise shareholders, and noted the rights of minority shareholders, who may be "permanently disenfranchised" by a dual-class proposal against which they voted. Id. In short, the Commission concluded, "it is preferable for a company's insiders wishing to gain voting control to do so through a repurchase of shares in which such repurchase is subject to market discipline and judicial review regarding state corporate fiduciary requirements. Id.

4. The Commission determined to "grandfather" all issuers who issued disparate voting stock prior to the Rule's July 7, 1988 effective date, and to allow companies that filed proxy materials with respect to disparate

voting stock between January 1, 1987, and the Rule's effective date, but had not yet issued the disparate class or classes of stock, to issue the stock within 90 days of the publication of the Rule 19c-4 in the Federal Register. Id. at 26386.

The Commission noted that as of June 1, 1988, 55 NYSE listed companies had adopted and implemented disparate voting rights plans, and an additional five NYSE listed companies had adopted but not yet implemented such plans. As of this same date, the AMEX and NASDAQ listed 117 and 182 companies, respectively, with disparate voting rights plans. Id. at 26376 and n.12.

5. See also AMEX and NASD Statement on and Selected Interpretations of Rule 19c-4, with Lists of Letters Issued to Date, printed in 21 Sec. Reg. and L. Rep. (BNA) 574–79 (Apr. 14, 1989).

D. Cases Upholding Super-Voting Stock
1. Once it is determined that the issuance of super-voting stock does not violate the governing state corporation law and, for listing purposes, Rule 19c-4, the next level of inquiry is whether the board of directors' adoption of a reclassification plan or its implementation is a valid exercise of business judgment.

    To date, preliminary injunctive relief has been denied in several cases challenging board decisions to adopt such plans subject to shareholder approval. No court has yet addressed the business judgment rule's applicability to a dual-class plan on the merits in the context of a trial or on a motion to dismiss or for summary judgment.

2. Strawbridge and Clothier
    a. Baron v. Strawbridge and Clothier, 646 F. Supp. 690 (E.D. Pa. 1986), involved a proposed reclassification plan which would double the number of the corporation's common shares, and then reclassify these shares into Series A and Series B shares. The Series A shares would have one vote per share, be freely transferable, and be entitled to dividends at least 10 percent higher than the Series B shares. The Series B shares would receive 10 votes per share, be transferable only to certain limited persons, and be freely convertible to Series A shares.
    b. The plan was proposed in response to a two-tier tender offer opposed by the corporation's board of directors, all but one of whom were current or former senior officers or their relatives. Pursuant to this tender offer, two thirds of the company's stock would be purchased for $60 per share, with the remaining one third of the company's share-

holders to receive cash and/or debt securities in a back-end merger with as yet unspecified terms.

c. The corporation's proxy materials explicitly stated that the purpose of the reclassification was to "further strengthen our defenses against hostile takeover threats from outside sources," id. at 693, and that "[s]hould the plan be approved by the shareholders, it will be possible for the controlling shareholders to control a majority of the voting power while holding as little as 9.1 percent of the outstanding voting stock of the company." Id. at 698.

d. Denying a motion for preliminary injunctive relief by the unwanted offeror, the court emphasized that the reclassification plan served legitimate corporate purposes, including protection of shareholders from an offer considered "financially inadequate" and protection of the company's employees, customers, and community from "detrimental" effects of the offer. Id. The court also emphasized the absence of any evidence indicating that the value of the corporation's stock would be harmed by implementation of the plan. Id. The court added that noncontrolling shareholders would have the option at any time of converting their Series B stock into Series A stock, thus giving each individual shareholder the option of holding shares in whichever class he considered more valuable. Id. The court noted that

> [i]f the plan had been structured so as to preclude the noncontrolling shareholders from electing a particular series of stock, the court may have found the plan to be a violation of the directors' trust obligation.... However, that is not this case; since each shareholder has the same choice, it cannot be said that the plan discriminates against any group. Id.

3. Rockwell

a. Weiss v. Rockwell International Corp., No. 8811 (Del. Ch. Feb. 6, 1987), involved the issuance of a new class of Class A common stock carrying 10 votes per share as a stock dividend to existing holders of common stock on a share-for-share basis. Once put in place, the new Class A stock would be subject to restrictions on transfer to anyone outside a narrow class of disqualified persons, and transfer to anyone else would cause the Class A stock to convert automatically into ordinary common stock. The court stated that "[t]he admitted purpose, or at least one admitted purpose of the proposal, is to deter hostile takeover proposals without prior negotiation with the board." Id., slip op. at 2.

b. Refusing to grant a preliminary injunction, the court emphasized that the directors were "only recommending" the proposal and that it was the shareholders "who will be the ones to adopt it." Id. at 10. Under Delaware law, the court stated, a proposal approved "by an informed shareholder vote will be upheld unless it is shown to be wasteful"— something that had not been alleged, much less proven. Id.

c. Additionally, the court stated, "[e]ven if viewed as a unilateral action by the directors alone, which this transaction would not be, the proposal is valid...under the business judgment rule." Id. The court explained that the corporation's board included a majority of independent outside directors who had no financial stake in recommending the proposal. The directors acted "on the advice of independent investment bankers and lawyers," and did so, in the court's words, "in a deliberate fashion worthy of directors of a major public corporation." Id. at 11.

4. Carter-Wallace

a. The court in Hahn v. Carter-Wallace, Inc., No. 9097 (Del. Ch. Oct. 9, 1987), likewise denied preliminary injunctive relief against a stock reclassification plan pursuant to which the corporation planned to issue new super-voting stock on a share-for-share basis. Under the plan, most transfers of this new class of stock outside of a controlling family group would trigger an automatic conversion of the stock into ordinary common stock. The court stated that "[i]t is not really denied that the purpose of the reclassification is to concentrate voting control...for the foreseeable future" in members of the controlling family group, who are "viewed by the corporation as being 'long-term investors,'" and noted that the plan had been approved by a special independent committee, the corporation's directors, and 80 percent of the corporation's minority stockholders. Id., slip op. at 1–2.

b. The court held that the affirmative vote of a majority of the minority placed the burden of proof on the plaintiff, id. at 4, and rejected the plaintiff's claim that the reclassification was implemented for the primary purpose of perpetuating the family's voting control:

> It appears from the present record...that there are other reasons for the restructuring, i.e., to insure that the corporation will continue to be managed in accordance with its traditional business philosophy which emphasizes long-term growth rather than short-term profit performance.
>
> While reasonable men may disagree as to whether long-term growth objectives should prevail over short-term profit con-

siderations, the decision to pursue a long range objective is a business decision subject to a presumption of propriety under the business judgment rule. Id. at 5.

E. Cases Not Upholding Super-Voting Stock

1. A preliminary injunction against a recapitalization plan involving super-voting stock was granted in Packer v. Yampol, 12 Del. J. Corp. L. 332 (Del. Ch. 1986).

   a. This litigation involved the issuance by Graphic Scanning Corporation of Class A and Class B super-voting preferred stock in the midst of a proxy contest.

      (1) The Class A super-voting stock carried 120 votes per share, and was issued to Barry Yampol, Graphic's Chairman and Chief Executive Officer, in exchange for Yampol's advancing funds needed by the company to meet a $5.25 million interest payment on outstanding debentures. Id. at 343 and 346.

      (2) The Class B super-voting stock carried 114 votes per share, and was issued to Battery, N.V. and Monar Company, N.V., two corporations specifically formed by an investor friendly to Yampol, in return for an equity investment of $10 million. The terms of the Class B super-voting stock granted its holders an effective veto power over certain mergers, asset sales, and other significant corporate transactions in the event that either Graphic's directors were replaced in a proxy contest or Yampol's ownership of Series A shares was reduced by 20 percent or more. Id. at 345–47.

      (3) Together, the court emphasized, the Series A and Series B preferred stock represented almost 33 percent of the corporation's total voting power. Combined with Yampol's previous common stock holdings, the effect of the stock issuance was to place 44 percent of the corporation's voting power in the hands of Yampol, Battery, and Monar. Id. at 347.

      (4) The court also emphasized that the Series A and Series B stock was obtained by Yampol, Monar, and Battery at an average cost per vote of $.86. Since Graphic common stock was trading at the time at $8.75 per share, the court observed, a common stock purchaser would have had to invest approximately $155 million to obtain voting power equivalent to that obtained by Yampol, Battery, and Monar for approximately $15 million. Id. at 336–37 and 347.

   b. The court preliminarily enjoined the transaction, finding that the Graphic board's primary purpose was to obtain an unfair or improper advantage in a proxy contest in order to maintain control. Id. at 356.

(1) The court rejected the Graphic directors' contention that their sole objective was to "raise capital and save Graphic from an impending cash crisis under circumstances where the only available means was to issue super-voting preferred stock and the only available sources of cash" were Yampol, Battery, and Monar. The court explained that the directors "knew full well" that the consequences of their actions would be "to inflict a severe, if not fatal, wound" upon an on-going proxy solicitation. Id. at 356. See also id. at 356–60.

(2) The court also noted that the transaction was not protected by the business judgment rule because Graphic's directors were interested in the transaction. Yampol, the court explained, was clearly interested in a transaction conferring voting power upon him, and Graphic's other directors, according to the court, were interested due to their "professional, financial and personal relationships" with Yampol. Id. at 354.

2. Preliminary injunctive relief against a super-voting stock recapitalization plan was also granted in Lacos Land Co. v. Arden Group, Inc., 517 A.2d 271 (Del. Ch. 1986).

a. This case involved a dual-class voting stock plan "deliberately fashioned to be attractive" to Bernard Briskin, the corporation's chief executive officer and principal shareholder (Briskin owned or controlled 16.9 percent of the corporation's stock, and held exercisable stock options for an additional 5.2 percent). Pursuant to the plan, shares of a new Class B common stock would be issued on a one-for-one basis to any common shareholders electing to exchange their stock. Holders of this new Class B stock were to have ten votes per share and the right to elect 75 percent of the corporation's board of directors, but could transfer their stock only to a restricted group of persons. Id. at 272 and 273–74.

Arden's proxy solicitation materials openly stated Briskin's position that he would not support future corporate transactions which might make the company vulnerable to hostile takeover or "greenmail" attempt but which could nevertheless be determined by the board to be in the best interests of all shareholders unless affirmative steps—i.e., adoption of the super-voting stock—were taken to secure his voting position. Id. at 276–77.

b. Enjoining the issuance of the Class B stock, the court emphasized that as a corporate fiduciary Briskin could not take such a position even if he was "benevolently motivated" to put into place "the most powerful of antitakeover devices so that he could be assured the opportunity to reject (for all the shareholders) any offer that he—who presumably knows more about the Company than anyone else—regards as less than optimum achievable value." Id. at 278. The court explained:

> Shareholders who respect Mr. Briskin's ability and performance— and who are legally entitled to his undivided loyalty—were inappropriately placed in a position in which they were told that if they refused to vote affirmatively, Mr. Briskin would not support future possible transactions that might be beneficial to the corporation. A vote of shareholders under such circumstances cannot, in the face of a timely challenge by one of the corporation's shareholders, be said, in my opinion, to satisfy the mandate of Section 242(b) of our corporation law requiring shareholder consent to charter amendments. Id. at 278–79.

c. The court also held that certain statements in Arden's proxy solicitation materials were misleading, and thus provided an alternative ground for preliminary injunctive relief. See id. at 279–81.

CHAPTER 18

EMPLOYEE STOCK OWNERSHIP PLANS AND CORPORATE RESTRUCTURING: MYTHS AND REALITIES

Myron S. Scholes
Mark A. Wolfson

During the first six months of 1989, U.S. corporations acquired over $19 billion of their own stock to establish employee stock ownership plans (ESOPs). This compares to only $5.6 billion for all of 1988 and less than $1.5 billion per year from the passage of the Employee Retirement Security Act in 1974 through 1987.[1] Special tax advantages appear to be available to companies using ESOPs. For example, such firms can sometimes deduct dividends paid on ESOP shares as well as benefit from a tax-subsidized borrowing rate on loans used to buy ESOP shares. There are also important nontax considerations such as the claimed incentive advantages of employees owning company stock and the use of ESOPs to defend against hostile tender offers by placing shares in the hands of

---

Mark A. Wolfson is Joseph McDonald Professor at Stanford University. He has a Ph.D. degree from the University of Texas.

Myron Scholes is currently a Senior Advisor at Salomon Brothers, Inc., on leave from Stanford University Graduate School of Business. Scholes, best known for his seminal work in options analysis with Fisher Black, has published numerous important journal articles. He is President-elect of the American Finance Association.

The authors have benefited from conversations with Alan Auerbach, Jeremy Bulow, and John Shoven.

relatively friendly employees. Our analysis brings into question the notion that ESOPs provide unique tax and incentive advantages. Depending on the benchmark against which they are compared ESOPs can often be beaten along both dimensions.

Our analysis suggests that, particularly for large firms, where the greatest growth in ESOPs has occurred, the case is very weak for taxes being the primary motivation to establish an ESOP. Yet Congress appears to believe that tax benefits explain the growth in popularity of ESOPs over the last few years. In July, 1989, proposed legislation in H.R. 2572 would result in the elimination of both the dividend deduction and the interest subsidy for plans established after July 10, 1989. The case is also weak for employee incentives being the driving force behind the establishment of ESOPs. We conclude that the main motivation for the growth of ESOPs is their antitakeover characteristics.

The paper proceeds as follows. We begin with an overview of tax and nontax motivations for adopting ESOPs. This is followed by a closer look at the operational characteristics of ESOPs. Our discussion here includes an evaluation of the risk-sharing and incentive features of these plans. We turn next to a closer look at some of their alleged tax advantages. Finally, we present some evidence on the growing importance of ESOPs in the U.S. and conclude with some brief summary remarks.

OVERVIEW OF TAX AND NONTAX MOTIVATIONS
FOR ADOPTING ESOPS

The ESOP is a special type of defined-contribution plan (like an individual retirement account, a Keogh account, or a Code Sec. 401(k) pension plan). The corporation makes tax deductible annual contributions to the ESOP, and the contributions are generally used to buy company stock or to pay down a loan that that was used to acquire company stock when the program was initiated. Employees are allocated company shares each year tax-free and any investment income accumulates tax-free within the ESOP. Employees pay tax when they receive dividend distributions on ESOP shares during their working lives or other distributions from the ESOP during retirement or when they otherwise leave the firm.

Unlike most other defined-contribution plans, the ESOP is required to invest primarily in the stock of the company establishing the plan, and this is commonly taken to mean that the ESOP must hold at least 50 percent of its assets in the stock of the sponsoring company. Unlike any other defined-contribution plan, the ESOP can borrow to buy company stock, to prefund the required number of shares that the firm expects to credit to its employees over the life of the plan. Such plans are called "leveraged ESOPs." As the firm contributes to the ESOP, shares are credited to employees' accounts. Moreover, qualified lenders can exclude 50 percent of the interest that they receive on the ESOP loan and the corporation can deduct any dividends that are used to pay down the ESOP loan or are paid directly to employees on their ESOP shares. As we will see, these tax benefits must be balanced against both tax and nontax costs of establishing an ESOP.

ESOPs have become popular in recent years because (1) there are several important tax benefits that are available through an ESOP that are not available through other tax-qualified and nonqualified compensation programs, (2) they can be used to restructure employee work incentives and retirement benefits, and (3) they can be used in corporate finance strategies as substitutes for, or in conjunction with, recapitalizations (changes in corporate capital structures) and leveraged buyouts. For example, ESOPs have been used to sell company divisions to employees. In addition, the deductibility of net operating losses (both existing and so-called "built-in losses") against future taxable income are not restricted if a corporate control change occurs through ownership interests acquired by an ESOP. The 1986 Act restricted the deductibility of such losses upon certain control changes when ownership interests are sold to parties other than ESOPs. Moreover, ESOPs have been used to secure tax deductions on the payment of dividends, to achieve a subsidized borrowing rate on ESOP loans, and to defer the capital gains tax incurred by owners of private companies on the sale of their shares to the ESOP. ESOPs have also been used to allocate interest payments domestically to free up foreign tax credit limitations. The 1986 Act made foreign tax credit limitations a significantly greater concern than it had been previously. The U.S. restricts foreign tax credits to an amount equal to foreign taxable income divided by worldwide taxable income, multiplied by U.S. tax on worldwide taxable income. One way to mitigate this problem is to make foreign-source income, as a fraction of worldwide income, as large as possible. Under Code Sec. 861, interest generated on domestic debt must typically be allocated partially to foreign activities, thereby reducing foreign-source income. It appears possible to allocate 100 percent of the interest on certain ESOP debt to domestic income, thereby increasing the allowable foreign tax credits.

There are other nontax reasons why ESOPs have become popular. An important one is that they have been used effectively to thwart hostile takeover attempts, particularly in the state of Delaware.[2] In early 1989, Polaroid won an important decision in the Delaware Chancery Court, which upheld Polaroid's issuance of 14 percent of its stock to an ESOP prior to the initiation of a hostile tender offer by Shamrock Holdings. The ESOP helped Polaroid's management defeat Shamrock's bid for its stock because employees voted their Polaroid shares with management. Delaware law requires that a firm wait three years after it acquires a 15 percent interest in a target before it can merge with the target unless it can secure an 85 percent vote of the target's shareholders.[3] The waiting period can impose substantial costs on the acquiring firm if it had plans to use the assets of the target as collateral for interim or longer-term loans to finance a leveraged buyout. Firm management might establish an ESOP because they believe that employee-shareholders are more likely to vote with them than are outside shareholders. As a result, Polaroid's use of an ESOP as a successful takeover defense stimulated considerable interest in ESOPs.

It is interesting to note that the New York Stock Exchange requires shareholder approval for adoption of an ESOP only when ESOPs acquire more than 18.5 percent of employer stock.[4] In addition, while employees must be granted voting rights in public-company ESOPs, acting on a tender offer is not a voting rights issue, so an ESOP provides a particularly strong tender offer defense. With respect to the Delaware 85 percent rule, however, stock held by an ESOP is counted as outstanding shares only if the participants have the right to tender their shares confidentially.

ESOPs are also being used to replace existing defined-benefit pension programs, to replace other types of defined-contribution programs, and to replace postretirement health care programs. In the case of postretirement health care programs, some corporations are substituting an ESOP for their previous promise to fund the postretirement health care costs of their employees.[5] Most postretirement health care programs are unfunded and are open-ended as to medical costs. In other words, the corporation makes an unsecured promise to provide health care for employees after they retire, whatever the costs might be. As an alternative, some companies contribute their stock to an ESOP and employees fund their own postretirement health care costs from their accumulation in the ESOP. By establishing an ESOP, the corporation transfers both the uncertainty of future health costs and the selection of the level of health care to employees.[6] But the advance funding of postretirement benefits through an ESOP (or any other pension fund) reduces the risk that the employer will default on the promise to provide the future benefits.

As pointed out by Freiman (1989), however, advance funding of retiree medical benefits through an ESOP is not necessarily tax advantageous. While the employer secures an immediate tax deduction for the contribution into the pension trust, employees eventually pay tax on withdrawals from the fund. By contrast, pay-as-you-go retiree medical benefit plans allow employees to receive tax-free benefits in retirement, but at the expense of a deferred tax deduction for the employer and the loss of tax-free compounding for advance funding. Section 401(h) plans allow the firm to have the benefits both ways: immediate deduction for advance funding and tax-free compounding of investment returns, along with tax-free benefits to retirees. But it is not yet clear whether these benefits are available to defined-contribution pension plans, and no more than 25 percent of a pension plan's contributions can be invested in a tax-exempt account to be used to provide for tax-free health care benefits.

That advance funding of retiree medical benefits through an ESOP may be dominated along the tax dimension by other funding alternatives is interesting because it increases the likelihood that nontax factors, such as an enhanced takeover defense, have a first order effect on the decision to fund such benefits through an ESOP. Since tax considerations are reasonably complicated in the pension area, in general, and in the ESOP area, in particular, it is important that both independent members of corporate boards, as well as the courts, understand whether there really exist tax benefits for proposed retirement benefit plans, because the adoption of such plans may serve the interests of incumbent management, but not shareholders, along nontax dimensions.

There are many substitute vehicles through which the corporation can achieve the many nontax and tax benefits of ESOPs listed above. However, there are some special tax benefits available to an ESOP that are not available elsewhere. For example, an ESOP can borrow to finance its purchase of company stock at a tax-subsidized rate and deduct the interest on the loan. No other pension plan can do this. Moreover, a corporation can take a deduction for dividends it pays on the stock held in the ESOP if the dividends are paid directly to the employees in cash or if the dividends are used to pay down part of an ESOP loan. The ability to deduct from corporate taxable income both dividends on ESOP shares and the interest payments on the ESOP loan enables part of corporate income to avoid an entity-level tax, as in S corporations, partnerships, and proprietorships. This has become particularly important with the passage of the 1981 and 1986 Tax Act.

The tax laws in the U.S. have always treated debt (and other claims that give rise to tax deductible payments to the corporation such as obligations to employees, lessors, and suppliers) differently from corporate equities. Whereas interest paid on debt is tax-deductible to corporate borrowers, dividends paid on common and preferred stock are not. In addition, whereas gains and losses on the repurchase of corporate bonds are taxable events to corporate issuers, the same is not true of share repurchases. On the investor side, interest from bonds is taxable as ordinary income whether paid out currently or not, while dividends and changes in the value of stocks are taxable only when realized. Moreover, dividends receive tax-favored treatment to corporate shareholders, and capital gains, besides being granted favorable tax-deferral treatment, have also been taxed at rates well below that of ordinary income to many shareholders.

Since the returns to corporate stock are tax-favored relative to bonds, investors are willing to accept lower pretax equity returns, on a risk-adjusted basis, to invest in them. This is similar to what we observe in the market for tax-exempt bonds, where the pretax yields are substantially below those of fully taxable bonds. The same can readily be observed in the market for adjustable-rate preferred stocks, held almost exclusively by corporations for whom the dividend income is largely tax exempt. This reduction in rates exacts an implicit tax from investors. Symmetrically, the rate reduction represents an implicit tax subsidy to issuers of corporate stocks that compensates, at least partially, for the nondeductibility of dividends.[7]

Note that holding everything else constant, increasing the tax rate to investors on income from share ownership reduces the pretax wedge between shares and bonds (and therefore reduces the implicit tax subsidy to issuing shares). This makes stock more expensive for corporations to issue relative to bonds. Similarly, increasing corporate tax rates relative to personal tax rates favors corporate debt financing to the extent that such financing moves taxable income from the corporate sector to the noncorporate sector.

Prior to 1981, top marginal tax rates in the corporate sector were well below top marginal personal tax rates. Top personal rates were 70 percent from 1965 to 1981 whereas top corporate rates were in the 50 percent range. In the two decades preceding 1965, top personal rates were in the

90 percent range. During this period of time, top long-term capital gains rates to individuals ranged from 25 percent to 35 percent. Such a configuration of tax rates should have caused common stocks to bear substantial implicit taxes, and corporate debt financing might not have been the least bit tax-favored for many corporations during this period.

With the passage of the Economic Recovery Tax Act in 1981, personal tax rates were reduced dramatically while corporate rates were not. But at the same time, capital gains rates were also slashed. Moreover, with interest rates at record levels, the tax advantage of capital gains deferral was particularly high at this time. With top personal tax rates set at a level just above top corporate tax rates, the 1981 Tax Act began to move incentives in the direction of increased corporate borrowing, although this effect was mitigated by the reduction in capital gains tax rates and high interest rates. By 1984, interest rates had subsided dramatically, reducing the tax-sheltered nature of common stocks to some extent, and this further promoted debt financing over equity financing by corporations.

As always, important nontax factors were also bearing on the corporate financing decisions during the early 1980s. In particular, mature corporations were discovering that it was efficient, from a corporate control standpoint, to restructure by buying back equity with the proceeds of debt issues, thereby committing to distribute "free cash flows" to investors through bond interest and principal repayments.[8] Moreover, increased reliance on strip financing (where institutional investors acquire combinations of junior debt along with equity and/or senior debt, to reduce conflicts of interest among classes of investors) and the rise of active bondholders enabled more debt to be issued without the prospect of incurring excessive deadweight restructuring and bankruptcy costs in the event of default on corporate commitments to creditors.[9] But it does not seem appropriate to view these developments as being completely independent of the evolution of the tax law. The tax law may well have provided important incentives for the proliferation of these institutional arrangements.

Corporate restructuring took a decided turn in 1984. Net new borrowing by corporations exploded to nearly $160 billion a year during 1984–1986 from $66 billion per year during 1978–1983. At the same time there was a quantum leap in the magnitude of both share repurchases ($37 billion per year 1984–1986 versus $5 billion per year 1978–1983) and other equity retirements via corporate acquisitions ($75 billion per year 1984–1986, versus $15 billion per year 1980–1983).[10]

The 1986 Tax Reform Act had an even more dramatic impact on

favoring corporate debt financing. Personal rates were reduced to a level well below that on corporations (28 percent for wealthy individuals versus 34 percent for corporations by 1988) and capital gains tax rates were increased dramatically. This, in conjunction with relatively low interest rates, substantially reduces the implicit tax on shares, thereby making equity financing a particularly expensive way to finance corporate investment.

That debt financing has become more tax-favored with the 1981 and 1986 Tax Acts is closely related to noncorporate forms of organization becoming more tax-favored relative to the corporate form. If all corporate earnings before interest and taxes could be distributed to investors as interest (or interest substitutes), the corporation would essentially be converted to a partnership for tax purposes. There would be no entity-level tax imposed on the corporation,[11] and all owners would pay tax at the personal level on interest income.[12]

There are many ways in which the firm can "lever up." One method that has received considerable attention is leveraged buyouts or LBOs. Others include (1) debt-for-equity swaps, (2) dividend-for-debt exchanges, (3) cash redemption of stock financed with debt, (4) deferred compensation plans, (5) partnership arrangements involving deferred payments, and (6) leveraged ESOPs. All of these alternatives are limited in their ability to eliminate the corporate-level tax. Although a 100 percent-employee-owned ESOP firm can pay out all of its before-tax income in the form of compensation payments to employees, or dividend payments on ESOP stock or interest payments on ESOP loans, we will see that there are enough tax rule restrictions, natural market frictions, or other nontax costs to prevent the elimination of the entity-level tax.

A CLOSER LOOK AT THE OPERATIONAL CHARACTERISTICS OF ESOPS

Contribution Limits

It is often claimed that an important tax advantage of an ESOP is that the corporation can make tax-deductible contributions to fund it. This advantage, however, is not unique to an ESOP. Contributions to other pension plans are also tax deductible. In fact, so is straight salary.

Because employees can earn the before-tax rate of return on assets invested in a pension plan, it is generally tax-advantageous to provide at least a portion of compensation in the form of a pension.[13] An ESOP might be more tax-advantageous than other types of pension plans if the corporation can make more generous contributions to an ESOP than to these alternative pension plans. But this is generally not the case. ESOP contributions are limited, as are other defined-contribution plans, to twenty-five percent of compensation.[14]

As a tax-qualified pension plan, an ESOP cannot discriminate in favor of highly compensated employees.[15] Therefore, it is difficult for senior management to control a large fraction of the shares of an ESOP. Even if the ESOP owns the entire company (as is true of AVIS Corp.), senior management might find it difficult to control a large fraction of the company's stock.[16]

The 1986 Tax Act requires that employee participants in an ESOP be 100 percent-vested at the end of five years (cliff-vesting) or at least at the rate of 20 percent for each year of employment after two years of employment with the firm. A potential nontax cost of these vesting requirements is that with employee turnover, the remaining employees of the firm might receive an unintended benefit. Indeed, remaining employees might have an incentive to promote employee turnover for this reason. An employee can factor expected turnover into his calculations of the amount of current compensation that he is willing to forgo for these expected future benefits. Because of both risk aversion and imperfect information, however, he might be willing to give up far less in current compensation than the cost of these benefits to the employer despite their tax-favored treatment.

Given these antidiscrimination funding requirements, many ESOPs are funded with contribution percentages far less than the allowable 25 percent of compensation. For example, Marsh and McAllister (1981) indicate that in over 80 percent of the ESOP plans in firms with over 500 employees, contributions to the ESOP amount to 10 percent or less of compensation. In a more recent study, Conte and Svejnar (1989) find that ESOP contributions average 10 percent of salary and wages.

The primary reason that these contributions are modest relative to contribution limits, despite the tax advantage of increasing contributions and reducing salary, is that the benefits are not valued highly by lower-level employees. The main reason is that they have a relatively strong preference for current over future consumption; they do not wish to save 25 percent of their compensation to secure future pension benefits, particularly young employees. If the firm did contribute a large fraction of their compensation into an ESOP, such employees would be forced to borrow on personal account each year to meet their current consumption needs. Given the deadweight costs of originating and administering such a loan, a lending institution would require that the borrowing rate substantially exceed its lending rate, even if the lender took into account the fact that an employee will realize a future pension benefit that could be used to pay off the loan.

Note that it is not possible to secure a loan with the future proceeds of a pension benefit without disqualifying the pension plan. Moreover, interest incurred on debt to finance personal consumption may be nondeductible. Given these costs, many employees could not borrow at all, and others might feel that they are still better off with current salary than with deferred ESOP income. Although the corporation could still make pension contributions for these employees, a competitive labor market might force the firm to supplement employee compensation if it is to retain the services of such employees. This extra cost constrains the level of ESOP funding.

Prior to the 1986 Tax Act, the contribution limits were more generous for a defined-benefit pension plan than for an ESOP. Generally, a defined-benefit pension plan provides the participant with a retirement benefit that depends on the level of final salary and/or the number of years of service. Various funding rules allow the corporation to accelerate the funding of its defined-benefit pension fund. This is not possible with a defined-contribution plan.

One motivation for overfunding a pension plan is that it enables the corporate sponsor to earn the before-tax rate of return on its investment. The corporation can reduce funding in later years to realize the benefit of overfunding. With the 1986 and 1988 Tax Acts, it became less desirable as well as more difficult to overfund defined-benefit pension plans. Moreover, it now seems more likely that marginal tax rates will increase than decrease. This further reduces the incentive to overfund. All else equal, it is preferable to fund the pension plan when tax rates are high. As a result, defined-contribution pension plans have become more competitive with defined-benefit pension plans. This might be another reason why firms have established ESOPs.

Some of the advantage of tax-free accumulation in an ESOP is lost, however, since it is necessary for an ESOP to hold at least 50 percent of its assets in its company's stock, and common stock is not the most tax-favored security to hold in a pension fund. This may have been particularly so prior to the 1986 Tax Act. At that time, shares might have borne a high implicit tax as we discussed earlier. That is, the before-tax rate of return on shares on a risk-adjusted basis might have been far below the risk-adjusted returns on fully taxable bonds.

With the 1986 Tax Act, 100 percent of realized capital gains became taxable. In addition, the corporate dividend-received deduction was reduced from 85 percent to 80 percent (and reduced further to 70 percent in many circumstances following passage of the 1987 Act). As a result, the implicit tax on shares is likely to have fallen and the required risk-adjusted before-tax rate on shares is likely to have increased. This generally means that the tax penalty for holding company stock in the pension plan has become smaller. This is another reason that ESOPs might have become more popular after the 1986 Tax Act. Moreover, contribution limits and antidiscrimination rules became more uniform across different types of pension plans. Because these rules often represent binding constraints, many corporations have substituted defined-contribution plans for their defined-benefit plans. Defined-contribution plans are simpler, less costly to operate, and less vulnerable to attack by the firm's many constituents.

The 1986 Tax Act imposed an excise tax of 10 percent on the excess assets of a terminated defined-benefit pension plan. This rate was increased to 15 percent with the 1988 Tax Act. Prior to 1989, however, corporations were allowed to transfer such excess assets to an ESOP without paying this excise tax. Merrill Lynch, for example, established an ESOP on the termination of its defined-benefit pension plan in 1988.[17]

Risk-Sharing Considerations

ESOPs provide a form of employee ownership in the corporation. This is an important reason why ESOPs have been championed by such members of Congress as retired Senator Long. Employee stock ownership is presumed to align the interests of the employee more closely with the overall goals of the shareholders, relative to a pure salary contract. AVIS, which is 100 percent owned by an ESOP, emphasizes employee ownership in advertisements. By implication, customers are meant to feel that AVIS's employee-owners are working harder to meet their needs.[18]

While employee ownership of shares may succeed in promoting a commonality of interests between employees and owners relative to straight salary contracts, it might be more efficient to provide these incentives in alternative ways. Where employees are risk-averse relative to shareholders, efficient risk sharing requires that employees bear little risk of change in the value of the firm. But where their activities affect the value of the firm, and these actions are unobservable to shareholders except at prohibitive cost, it is desirable to require employees to bear some risk of changes in the value of the firm for incentive reasons. Risk-averse employees will require additional compensation, however, if they are exposed to risk that is beyond their control. Efficient incentive contracting, therefore, requires a judicious trading off of risk sharing and incentives.[19]

It is useful to think of stock prices as an indirect monitor of employee inputs. The value of the firm can be viewed as being determined jointly by employee actions and actions chosen by others such as competitors, customers, and nature (that is, random factors). Oftentimes it is possible to devise accounting measures of performance (e.g., divisional profits or physical output measures) that serve as less "noisy" indirect monitors of employee inputs. The reliance on such measures through incentive compensation arrangements is often a more efficient way (relative to stock-market-value-based measures) to align the interests of employees with those of shareholders. More generally, both types of measures (stock-based and accounting-based) contain information that is useful in drawing inferences about the effectiveness of employee performance, but stock-based measures are likely to prove far more "informative" with respect to senior management performance than with respect to lower-level employees.[20] As a consequence, the implementation of an ESOP may exact a cost along the incentive contracting dimension.

Weirton Steel's 100 percent employee-owned ESOP decided to take Weirton public again after a successful revitalization of the company. Part of the reason for the sale of company stock was that many of the vested employees in the ESOP did not want to risk undertaking a $500 million expansion of the firm's steel-producing capacity. They preferred a safer position.[21]

It is interesting to note that employee stock ownership was quite common in the 1920s (Patard, 1985). But due to the market crash begun in 1929, 90 percent of the stock ownership plans in place before the crash were discontinued by the mid–1930s. Those not terminated restricted participation exclusively to highly-paid employees. This evidence suggests that risk-sharing considerations are very important.

The tax rules require that employers allow employees to diversify their holdings at the later of age 55 and 10 years of employment. In the first four years following the passage of this milestone, employees must be permitted to diversify up to 25 percent of their holdings, and in the fifth year they can invest up to 50 percent of their holdings in nonemployer securities.

If employees receive nontraded company stock when they retire or leave the company, they have the right to put the stock back to the company for cash. Depending on the demographics, it might be very costly for the corporation to redeem these shares. Additional funds might have to be raised at a time when it is very costly to do so. Moreover, the release of shares to the employees of a private company might force the corporation to comply with Securities and Exchange Commission reporting requirements. (The threshold is 500 shareholders.) This is also costly.

Prior to the 1987 Tax Act, many ESOP sponsors provided their employees with a defined-benefit pension plan offset. Examples include Ashland Oil, Bank of New York, and Hartmarx.[22] In these arrangements, the defined-benefit plan might guarantee employees a retirement benefit of say 50 percent of their terminal salary during each year of retirement, but distributions to employees would be made from the defined-benefit plan only if the ESOP failed to provide at least that same level of benefits. The defined-benefit promise serves as a guaranteed floor. This reduces the employee's risk by essentially providing the employee with a put option. Note that shielding employees from risk also means sacrificing incentives. The 1987 Tax Act restricted the use of these defined-benefit-offset provisions.

Firms have discovered other means to reduce the employee's risk of holding company stock in an ESOP. The ESOP can invest up to 50 percent of its assets in other than company stock.[23] The ESOP can also be supplemented with other types of compensation plans to reduce risk. For example, an ESOP might be combined with another defined-contribution plan invested entirely in bonds.

Many firms have started to fund the ESOP with convertible voting preferred stock.[24] Holding preferred shares is generally less risky than holding the company's common stock in the ESOP. Given its superior dividend yield, the preferred will tend to sell at a premium over the common (if convertible into at least one share of common) and retain more of its value than the common stock if the value of the company should fall. If the preferred issue represented a substantial majority of the company's stock, however, it would have little protection in the event that the company does poorly.

Moreover, some ESOPs provide employees with a put option. That is, if the preferred stock happens to be selling below the conversion price when the employee retires or leaves the firm, the employee can put the stock back to the company for the conversion price. This put option is valuable to employees and protects them against the risk of a decline in the price of the common stock.

In summary, an ESOP provides a pension savings alternative to more conventional tax-qualified pension funds, one that provides employees with an ownership interest in the firm. Employee ownership might lead the firm's "productivity" to improve as employees' interests become better aligned with the firm's other shareholders. But such compensation arrangements may be at the expense of other more efficient forms (ignoring taxes), both for risk-sharing and incentive reasons.

Moreover, there can be severe nontax costs if an ESOP must refinance to repurchase shares from departing employees. Shares that are initially contributed to the trust must eventually be cashed out, and high transaction costs might be incurred to accomplish this task.

With these nontax costs and benefits of establishing an ESOP in mind, let us turn next to the tax benefits. We discuss primarily the tax advantages of a leveraged ESOP and the tax deductibility of dividends on ESOP shares.

A CLOSER LOOK AT TAX ADVANTAGES OF AN ESOP

Prior to the 1986 Tax Act there were two basic types of ESOPs: a tax deduction ESOP (where contributions to the trust give rise to tax deductions) and a tax credit ESOP (where contributions to the trust give rise to tax credits). The tax credit ESOP was eliminated with the 1986 Tax Act. The 1984 Tax Act added significant tax incentives to encourage ESOPs. The 1984 Tax Act provided that (1) shareholders in a closely held company could obtain a tax-free rollover on the sale of their shares to an ESOP if it attained at least 30 percent ownership of the company and if the seller purchased qualified replacement securities such as corporate bonds; (2) the corporation could receive a deduction for dividends paid on ESOP stock, provided that the dividends were paid out currently to employees; and (3) a bank, insurance company, or other commercial lender was permitted to exclude from income 50 percent of the interest received on loans to ESOP sponsors, provided that the proceeds of the loan were used to finance the acquisition of employer stock for the ESOP.

The 1986 Tax Act added to these benefits. The 1986 Tax Act provided (1) an estate tax exclusion for 50 percent of the proceeds of certain sales of company stock to an ESOP; (2) an expansion of the corporate dividend deduction to include dividends used to repay principal or interest on the loan used to acquire employer securities; (3) a provision allowing mutual funds to be added to the list of lenders eligible to receive the partial interest exclusion on loans to acquire employer securities; and (4) an exemption from the 10 percent excise tax on reversions from defined-benefit pension plans that are transferred to an ESOP before 1989. The Act repealed the payroll-based ESOP tax credit and required that certain employees be allowed to diversify their accounts.

The Fifty Percent Interest Exclusion
Under Code Sec. 133, banks, insurance companies, or regulated investment companies may exclude from gross income 50 percent of the interest that they receive on a loan used to buy company stock for an ESOP. There are three types of loans. These include (1) an immediate allocation loan, (2) a leveraged-ESOP loan, and (3) a back-to-back leveraged-ESOP loan. An immediate allocation loan is a loan to the company sponsoring the ESOP. The other two loans are effectively loans to the ESOP itself.

In an immediate allocation loan, the company borrows an amount equal to one year's contribution to an ESOP and transfers qualifying employer securities to the ESOP. The loan, including any period of refinancing, cannot ι ·tend beyond a seven-year term. The transferred securities must be alloc.ted to the individual accounts of employees within one year of the date of the loan (hence the term "immediate allocation").

The immediate allocation loan provides an opportunity for tax arbitrage in appropriate circumstances. To illustrate this, note that if lending markets are competitive and if there are no special costs associated with ESOP loans, the risk-adjusted before-tax rate of return on the loan, R_I, will be given by the following relation:

$$R_I(1 - .5t_c) = R_b(1 - t_c)$$

or $$R_I = R_b(1 - t_c)/(1 - .5t_c),$$

where t_c = corporate marginal tax rate;
R_b = the before-tax risk-adjusted return on fully taxable bonds; and
R_I = the required before-tax rate of return on the ESOP loan.

So if corporate marginal tax rates are 34 percent, this implies that the rate of interest on the immediate allocation loan will be 79.5 percent of the fully taxable rate.[25] Empirical evidence suggests that ESOP loan rates are set between 80 percent and 90 percent of the fully taxable rate, with securitized loans priced at roughly 75 percent of the prime rate.[26]

Assume for the moment that the corporation already has an ESOP and has determined the magnitude of this year's required contribution of stock. If the firm were to finance the contribution to the ESOP with an immediate allocation loan, the corporation's after-tax interest cost would be $R_I(1 - t_c)$ or approximately 80 percent of the after-tax cost of an ordinary loan for a 34 percent corporation that captures most of the tax benefits of the 50 percent interest exclusion via an interest rate reduction. If the corporation were otherwise planning to repurchase its stock using its internal cash flow, it would be tax-advantageous to use the proceeds of the immediate allocation loan to buy shares in the open market to contribute to the ESOP and use its internal cash flow to pay back some company debt.

Moreover, if the company currently contributes stock to a defined-contribution pension plan *other* than an ESOP, it would be tax-advantageous for the company to switch to an ESOP. The seven-year immediate allocation loan is quite valuable. For example, if the before-tax bond rate is equal to 10 percent, the immediate allocation loan would have a before-tax rate of interest of 8 percent and an after-tax rate of interest of 5.28 percent (or 8 percent(1 − 34 percent)). If the corporation's ordinary borrowing rate is 10 percent, its after-tax cost is 6.6 percent. The immediate allocation loan offers an after-tax savings of 1.32 percent per year for a maximum of seven years. The present value of this benefit at a discount rate of 6.6 percent is 7.3 percent of the principal amount of the loan.[27]

While the immediate allocation loan is a loan for only one year's contribution to the ESOP, it is also possible for the ESOP to borrow to acquire stock that will fund the contributions to the pension fund for many years. This is called a leveraged ESOP. The ESOP borrows enough such that the loan proceeds can buy sufficient stock to fund, say, the next fifteen annual contributions. As with immediate allocation loans, qualified lenders can exclude from taxable income 50 percent of the interest received on the leveraged ESOP loan.

If a leveraged ESOP borrows and buys company stock, the stock is placed in a so-called "suspense account." Each year as the corporation makes tax-deductible cash contributions to its ESOP, stock is released from the suspense account and allocated to the accounts of the participants. The contribution is then used to pay down the loan. The corporation can deduct up to 25 percent of compensation each year, the same as for an unleveraged ESOP. It also can deduct the interest payments that it contributes to the ESOP to pay the interest on the ESOP loan. Also any dividends that are paid on the stock allocated to the participants or on the unallocated shares held in the suspense account can be used to pay down the loan. These dividends are tax deductible to the corporation.

It is often claimed that a leveraged ESOP is tax-advantageous because the corporation can make tax-deductible principal repayments on its ESOP loans. As we have already noted, however, all compensation payments are tax-deductible to the corporation. However, the 50 percent exclusion of interest on the loan and the deductibility of certain dividends *are* tax-advantageous. These options are not available with other plans.

It is harder to quantify whether the corporation should use an immediate allocation loan or a leveraged-ESOP structure. The term of the leveraged-ESOP loan can extend for as many years as the company wishes to precommit to contribute stock to its ESOP.[28] It must, however, pay down the ESOP loan uniformly over its life. The immediate allocation loan can only extend for a period of seven years. But it can be a term loan in which all principal is repaid at maturity. Each year the corporation can issue another immediate allocation loan to fund that year's contribution to its ESOP. Although a leveraged ESOP loan is initially a much larger loan than an immediate allocation loan, the size of the loan falls each year as the principal on the note is reduced.

Another advantage of immediate allocation loans over leveraged ESOP loans is that where share prices are increasing over time, immediate allocation loans yield larger tax deductions for a given cost of buying shares deposited into the ESOP. The reason for this is that in a leveraged ESOP, tax deductions are based on the value of the stock at the time the shares are first acquired, whereas in the immediate allocation plan, the deductions are based on share prices at the time the shares are allocated to participant accounts.[29] Depending on the length and size of the ESOP program, the present value of the tax benefits could be greater with an immediate allocation loan than with a leveraged-ESOP loan.

If future legislation were to limit the tax benefits of ESOP programs, the long-term loan might prove more or less attractive than the immediate allocation loan depending upon the particular "grandfather" provisions included in the legislation. It is interesting to note that many of the ESOP loans are written with provisions that guarantee the lender a benchmark after-tax rate of return that floats with the return on a taxable loan of comparable risk (e.g., Treasury bill plus some fixed number of basis points). The rate of interest on the loan changes if statutory tax rates change or if the percentage of interest that is tax-exempt were to change. The corporation could be at a definite disadvantage if Congress were to limit tax-deductible contributions to defined-contribution plans and, as a result, prevent the corporation from making tax-deductible contributions to its pension plan of sufficient size to pay down the loan.

The back-to-back loan is very similar to the leveraged ESOP loan. In this case, the corporation borrows to purchase company stock and relends the same amount to its ESOP. The ESOP buys the company's stock with the proceeds. There are two separate loans, one from the qualifying institution to the corporation, and one from the corporation to the ESOP trust. To qualify for the same tax treatment as the leveraged-ESOP loan, the repayment schedule and the interest rate must be essentially identical. If not, the back-to-back loan is limited to a term of seven years. Moreover, leveraged-ESOP loans cannot be accelerated in the case of a default. As a result, many lenders prefer back-to-back loans. Also, the lender might feel more secure dealing with a corporation than with a trustee pension plan. A pension plan never borrows except to finance a leveraged ESOP. The body of law concerning the property rights of the parties to leveraged-ESOP transactions is not well established.

The leveraged-ESOP structure has been used in a number of leveraged-buyout transactions. It has also been used to accomplish such corporate finance objectives as (1) implementing a share repurchase program, (2) selling a division to employees, (3) placing a large block of the company's stock in employee (friendly) hands, and (4) taking a company private. However, there are several problems with this structure. The company must project future employee contributions. Overestimating the required payments would cause the employer to borrow an amount in excess of the actual annual requirements. Prepaying this excess amount of debt would result in the allocation of shares to the participants' accounts. Employees could benefit at the expense of the other shareholders.

The Deduction of Dividend Payments

Under Code Sec. 404(k), the corporation can deduct dividends to an ESOP if (1) the dividends are paid in cash directly to ESOP participants, (2) the dividends are paid to the ESOP and it distributes them to participants within 90 days of the close of the plan year, or (3) the dividends on ESOP stock (whether in the suspense account or allocated to participants) are used to make payments on an ESOP loan as described in Code Sec. 404(a)(9). The ability to take a deduction for dividends used to make payments on an ESOP loan was introduced by the 1986 Tax Act.

The deductibility of dividends eliminates the entity-level tax on part of the corporate income. In the extreme, if all the shares of a corporation were owned by its employees, and the corporation paid out tax-deductible dividends equal to its predividend taxable income, all of the corporation's income would be taxed only once at the individual shareholder level. It is not entirely clear, however, that this should be taken too literally. The 1984 Act contained a provision empowering the Treasury to disallow dividend deductions to the extent they are deemed to "contribute to tax avoidance." Presumably this would be invoked if profitable businesses sought to distribute all profits as tax-deductible dividends. On the other hand, the provision may simply be a "paper tiger."

To see that dividends which are deductible to the corporation and paid on ESOP shares to participants convert the corporate tax to a single level of taxation under most circumstances, assume that the corporation is currently contributing $10 million to an ESOP at the end of each year. Further assume that this is less than the maximum contribution permitted of 25 percent of compensation.[30] Assume that the employer pays a dividend of $3 million at year end on the ESOP shares and that this dividend is paid directly to the participants. Now suppose the corporation alters its policy by contributing $13 million to the ESOP instead of the usual $10 million and by reducing employee salary by $3 million. As a result, while salary is reduced by $3 million, employees receive $3 million in dividends from the ESOP. Employee pension accounts grow in value by the return on the pension assets less $3 million distributed as a dividend, but the corporation contributes an additional $3 million to the ESOP. So the accumulation in employee ESOP accounts, as well as their current compensation (salary plus dividends), is unaffected by this change in policy. From the corporation's viewpoint, the before-tax cash outflows are also exactly the same whether the corporation contributes to a qualified stock-bonus plan and pays a dividend on these shares or it contributes to an ESOP.

For example, assume that employee salaries, before the ESOP plan was adopted, totaled $50 million. If $10 million was also contributed to a stock bonus plan and $3 million in dividends were paid, the total pretax cash outflows would be $63 million. Under the ESOP plan, with dividends paid currently to employees, cash outflows would be $47 million in salary, $13 million in contribution to the ESOP, and $3 million in dividends on the ESOP shares. The total of $63 million is exactly the same as if the corporation contributed to a stock-bonus plan. After tax, however, the corporation is better off because it secures a tax deduction for $3 million of dividends. So if corporate tax rates are 34 percent, the corporation can eliminate just over $1 million in tax per year from the dividends paid to employees through securities that they hold in their ESOP accounts.[31] In effect, as employees accumulate securities in their ESOP accounts, they receive tax-deductible dividends from the corporation that convert income that would have been taxed at the corporate level, and then again at the personal level, to income that is taxed only once at the personal level.

Notice, however, that this plan works only if employees are not up against the 25 percent-of-compensation contribution limits. If the corporation is already funding contributions to an ESOP to the maximum allowed under the tax rules, it could not increase its funding and reduce current compensation as assumed in the analysis above unless a leveraged ESOP structure is used and dividends are used to pay down ESOP loans.

Corporate deductions can also be secured when dividends are used to make payments on an ESOP loan. But, contrary to popular belief, there is no tax advantage to using dividends to make payments on a leveraged loan. To see this, note that to secure a tax deduction for the dividends, participants must be allocated shares in the ESOP equal in dollar value to the dividends used to pay down the loan. Since employees are allocated shares equal to their share of the dividends, the firm should be able to cut back other pension contributions in the same amount, leaving employees unaffected. As a result, the corporation's taxable income is also unaffected, so the deductibility of dividends does not reduce the corporate-level tax in this case.

The one case in which dividend deductibility on ESOP loans is advantageous is where employees want to add to their pension savings beyond the 25 percent-of-compensation limits. They are permitted to exceed the limits by using dividends to make payments on the ESOP loan. On the other hand, except in small, privately held corporations, it is very uncommon that employees wish to invest so heavily in pension savings, especially in a plan that is so poorly diversified.

ESOPs Financed with Equity Providing Dividend Pass-Through versus Debt-Financed Pension Plans Investing in Debt Securities

In the preceding discussion, we demonstrated that if for nontax reasons employee stock were held in the pension fund, an ESOP could profitably be used to effect tax savings. In this section we demonstrate that, ignoring the advantage of the 50 percent interest exemption on qualified ESOP loans, as well as other less important special tax features, ESOPs are really dominated by other pension funds that avoid investing in employer equity securities. We further argue that in many relevant cases, the interest rate subsidy resulting from the 50 percent exclusion of interest income roughly compensates for the tax *disadvantage* of ESOPs. So, in the end, whether ESOPs are desirable, particularly for publicly traded companies, depends largely on the nontax benefits of employee ownership of employer shares.

To establish that ESOPs with dividend pass-through to employees are weakly dominated by debt-financed defined-contribution pension plans, we proceed in stages. We begin by analyzing the after-tax cash flows to employees and employers when \$1 is contributed into a pension plan, financed by debt bearing interest at rate R_b. The pension plan in turn invests in interest-bearing securities yielding rate R_b per year. The tax rates of the employer and the employee are t_c and t_p, respectively.

Case I:
Debt-financed Pension Fund

	Time Period		
	Today (time 0)	Annually Through Retirement	At Retirement (n years)
Cash Flow to:			
Employer	$+t_c$	$-R_b(1-t_c)$	-1
Employee	0	0	$+(1+R_b)^n(1-t_p)$

At time 0, the employer borrows \$1 and deposits it into the pension plan, a net cash flow of \$0. A tax deduction of \$1 for the contribution to the pension fund, however, yields a tax savings of t_c for the employer, so total cash flow is $+t_c$. Each year thereafter, through retirement, the employer pays out interest of R_b, which is tax deductible at rate t_c. Finally, at retirement, in n years, the employer repays the \$1 principal amount of the loan and the employee cashes out the pension. By this time, the pension assets have grown in value to $(1 + R_b)^n$, and the employee is taxed on this amount at rate t_p.

Next, compare these cash flows to those that result from the employer forming an ESOP, financing the $1 contribution to the trust with a preferred stock paying a dividend of R_b per period. Dividends are reinvested in the trust rather than paid out each year to the employee.

Case II:
Preferred Stock-Financed ESOP with Dividends
Reinvested in the Pension Plan

	Time Period		
	Today (time 0)	Annually Through Retirement	At Retirement (n years)
Cash Flow to:			
Employer	$+t_c$	$-R_b$	-1
Employee	0	0	$+(1 + R_b)^n (1 - t_p)$

Except for the annual cash outflow for the employer to service the security issued to fund the pension plan, cash flows are identical to those for the debt-financed pension fund. Here, however, the dividend payments are nondeductible, so while the employee is indifferent across the alternatives, the employer is worse off by $R_b t_c$ per period. Note that $R_b t_c$ is simply the tax shield from interest deductibility available in Case I but not Case II.

Finally, consider the case of an ESOP financed with employer preferred stock, but where these dividends are paid out to the employee each period.

Case III:
Preferred Stock-Financed ESOP with Dividends Passed
Through to Employees

	Time Period		
	Today (time 0)	Annually Through Retirement	At Retirement (n years)
Cash Flow to:			
Employer	$+t_c$	$-R_b(1 - t_c)$	-1
Employee	0	$+R_b(1 - t_p)$	$+1 - t_p$

Note that while the cash flows to the employer in this case coincide with those in Case I (debt-financed pension plan), those for the employee are not directly comparable since both interim and terminal cash flows are different. To make them comparable, suppose the employer reduces the employee's salary by R_b per period, contributing this amount to a non-ESOP pension plan that earns interest at rate R_b per period. In this case, the interim cash flows to the employee will be $0, just as in Case I.

To see how the ESOP with dividend pass-through compares with a debt-financed pension, then, we need only compare the terminal after-tax cash flow to the employee in this case with that in Case I (since all other cash flows to both parties now coincide). The supplementary pension plan for the employee accumulates to the future value of an annuity of R_b dollars for n periods with interest at rate R_b per period. This is equal to:

$$R_b [(1 + R_b)^n - 1] / R_b \text{ or } (1 + R_b)^n - 1$$

This is fully taxable at rate t_p, so the after-tax amount is:

$$(1 + R_b)^n (1 - t_p) - (1 - t_p)$$

We can now add this supplementary pension amount to the $1 - t_p$ available from the ESOP, and we are left with:

$$(1 + R_b)^n (1 - t_p)$$

This is exactly the same terminal amount the employee receives in Case I, the debt-financed pension plan.

While a comparison of Cases I and III makes it appear as though the ESOP (with dividend pass-through) is equivalent to the debt-financed non-ESOP pension plan, this is only because we have allowed the ESOP to invest in preferred shares that have no equity-like features to them. That is, the dividend yield is the full interest rate, and there is no capital gain component to it. But in fact, the ESOP assets must be invested primarily (that is, at least 50 percent) in employer common stock or convertible preferred stock, and these securities almost always have an expected capital appreciation component.[32]

Case II can be viewed as a case in which the ESOP is financed with nondividend-paying common stock. The interim cash outflow of R_b can be interpreted as the nondeductible sinking fund contribution required to cover the appreciation in the share of stock that the employer will have to repurchase from the employee at time n.

More typically, the employer securities contributed to the ESOP will have a dividend yield somewhere in between those for Cases II and III. In such circumstances, the employer will be worse off, relative to a non-ESOP pension plan, by the value of a tax deduction on the difference between the current yield on the ESOP securities and the interest rate on debt. In this light, one might view the availability of the tax exemption to qualified ESOP lenders of half the interest income on ESOP loans as a way of neutralizing the disadvantage demonstrated above. The analysis also helps to explain why high dividend-yielding convertible preferred stocks have become so popular as an investment in ESOPs.[33]

If the 50 percent interest income exemption roughly compensates for the reduced deductibility of the employer cost to service the securities issued to fund the ESOP, then the differences between ESOPs and other pension plans become restricted largely to the nontax dimension. In particular, with more employer securities in the ESOP, work incentives are clearly affected, and voting control is clearly enhanced, thereby providing a superior takeover defense (or more pejoratively, enhanced management entrenchment).

EVIDENCE ON THE GROWING IMPORTANCE OF ESOPS IN THE U.S. ECONOMY

It is unfortunate that the most complete survey available of the prominent features of ESOPs goes only through 1984.[34] The Deficit Reduction Act of 1984 and the Tax Reform Act of 1986 had dramatic effects on incentives to utilize these trusts to take advantage of the tax-favored leveraging opportunities and dividend deductibility. Table 18–1 reveals that at year-end 1988, there were 9,500 ESOPs in existence covering 9.5 million workers. The number of new plans established in 1985 and 1986 (591 per year) was 19 percent higher than the average over the six years ending in 1984. And the number of new plans established in 1987 and 1988 (727 per year) was 27 percent higher than 1985 and 1986. Moreover, an estimated 500 additional plans were established in the first four months of 1989 alone.

The U.S. General Accounting Office estimates that of the 6,904 ESOPs at year-end 1984, only 4174 were still active. Approximately 90 percent of these plans were tax-credit ESOPs. Total assets in ESOPs at year-end

TABLE 18–1
Growth in the Number of ESOP Plans and Number of Employees Covered

Year	Number of Plans [a]	Number of Employees Covered [a]
1978	4,028	2,800,000
1984	6,904	6,576,000
1986	8,046	7,800,000
1988	9,500	9,500,000[b]
Average Increase per Year:		
1978-84	479	679,000
1984-86	571	612,000
1986-88	777	850,000

[a]Source: National Center for Employee Ownership (Oakland, CA)
[b]Note that this exceeds 10% of the nation's labor force.

1984 were $19 billion, of which $15 billion were in tax-credit ESOPs ($2,300 per covered employee) and $4 billion were in other ESOPs ($5,700 per covered employee).

Although it was the 1984 Tax Act that introduced the interest income exemption for qualified ESOP loans and deductibility of dividends paid out to employees, ESOP activity accelerated more quickly following the 1986 Act. The 1986 Act contained a number of ESOP and non-ESOP provisions that affected the desirability of ESOPs, to which we alluded earlier.

Since 1986, leveraged ESOPs in particular have exploded in economic significance. According to the National Center for Employer Ownership, new ESOP borrowings grew from $1.2 billion in 1986 to $5.5 billion in 1987 and $6.4 billion in 1988. In addition, based on our analysis of disclosures available through the Dow Jones News Retrieval Service, plans to undertake more than $9 billion of ESOP borrowings were announced during 1989 through May 10 alone![35] It is perhaps not surprising, therefore, that on June 6, 1989, Dan Rostenkowski, as chairman of the House Ways and Means Committee, introduced legislation to repeal the 50 percent interest exemption on ESOP loans. While this proposal is prompted by concerns over revenue losses to the U.S. Treasury, our analysis suggests that this concern may be misplaced. We have argued that takeover defense considerations are likely to have dominated. It is interesting to note that another batch of new ESOPs were hurriedly introduced by dozens of companies following the Rostenkowski proposal in an attempt to beat the new effective date for any adverse tax changes that might result from the passage of legislation.[36]

SUMMARY

An ESOP is an interesting organizational vehicle. Its main advantages over other forms of compensation are that it allows the corporation to obtain a below-market-rate-of-interest loan and that dividends on common stock are tax deductible if they are paid to ESOP participants. In the limit (100 percent employee ownership), the corporate tax theoretically can be eliminated, although as a practical matter, gutting the corporate tax is impossible even with 100 percent employee ownership. And depending upon the circumstances, another great cost or benefit is its effectiveness as a defensive weapon. This is a cost when entrenchment allows existing management to secure private gain at the expense of shareholders and when a transfer of control over managerial decision rights to a more efficient group is prevented. It is a benefit, however, to the extent such protection from an outside bid promotes investment by employees in firm-specific capital that improves employee performance. Another important disadvantage of an ESOP is possible distortions in incentive compensation arrangements.

As if so often the case in public policy debates, the analysis to date of tax and nontax factors in the use of ESOPs has failed to consider the alternative institutional arrangements that are displaced by ESOPs. We have attempted to repair that omission here, and in so doing, we find ESOPs lacking in magic for their corporate sponsors along both tax and incentive dimensions, except perhaps in closely held businesses. With these usual suspects rounded up, we are left with the creation of impediments to changes in corporate control as the prime motivation for ESOPs.

Notes

1. *Pensions and Investment Age Magazine,* July 24, 1989, and Blasi (1988).
2. According to *The Wall Street Journal* (4/5/89), 179,000 companies are incorporated in Delaware, including 56 percent of the Fortune 500 and 45 percent of New York Stock Exchange companies.
3. The three-year waiting period also does not apply if the board of directors and two-thirds of the disinterested stockholders vote in favor of the merger.
4. Bader and Hourihan (1989b).
5. Examples include Ralston Purina, Boise Cascade, and Whitman. (*Business Week,* May 15, 1989).
6. This is not to say that the bargain is one-sided. It may be that the corporation contributes more to the ESOP than the employee gives up in future health-care protection to compensate the employee for bearing the risk of unexpected changes in the cost of health care. On the other hand, employees might manage health care costs more efficiently when they are responsible for the costs.
7. See Stiglitz (1973), Miller (1977), Auerbach (1983), and Scholes and Wolfson (1987, 1990).
8. Jensen (1986).
9. Jensen (1989).
10. *Federal Income Tax Aspects of Corporate Financial Structures* (Joint Committee on Taxation), January 18, 1989, Table I-A, I-B on pp. 8-9.
11. This ignores any corporate "alternative minimum tax" that may be assessed.
12. See Scholes and Wolfson (1989) for further discussion of these issues.
13. If the before-tax rate of interest is R_b and the employee's marginal tax rate today is t_{po} and on retirement in n years is t_{pn}, then for each \$1 of after-tax income contributed to the pension fund the employee realizes a return of:

$$\frac{\$1}{(1 - t_{po})} \quad (1 + R_b)^n (1 - t_{pn}).$$

   If the employee's marginal tax rate is expected to remain constant, she would prefer pension over salary if the before-tax rates of return on assets invested in the pension plan were greater than the after-tax rates of return from investing outside the pension plan. Even if the before-tax rates of return were greater in the pension plan, the employee might prefer to invest outside the pension plan if she expected her marginal tax rate to increase in the future or if she had particularly strong demand for current consumption and her borrowing rate was high.
14. An ESOP is defined in Code Section 4975 as a stock bonus plan (where contributions may be discretionary or contingent on measures of performance, like company profits), or as a combination stock bonus plan and money purchase pension plan (where contributions are neither discretionary nor conditioned on

performance measures). If the ESOP is set up as a stock-bonus plan only, annual contributions are limited to 15 percent of employee compensation. ESOPs that are a combination of stock bonus and money purchase pension plans face annual contribution limits equal to 25 percent of employee compensation.

This amount cannot exceed $30,000 for any employee and only up to $200,000 of compensation is taken into account in determining the percentage allocation to an employee. This $30,000 limit will increase over time with inflation adjustments. That is, the maximum contribution must be less than 25 percent of $90,000, indexed to inflation after 1986 once this amount exceeds $30,000. In some cases employees can contribute more to an ESOP than to other defined-contribution programs. If less than one third of the employees participating in the ESOP are highly compensated, the limits can be increased. It is unlikely, however, that lowly-compensated employees would want to contribute more than 25 percent of their salary to a defined-contribution plan due to a desire for current consumption.

15. Indeed, because ESOPs cannot be integrated with social security benefits, while other plans can be, ESOPs face tougher antidiscrimination rules.

16. At least 70 percent of ESOP participants must be non-highly compensated employees. The 1986 Tax Act defines "highly compensated employees" as those who own 5 percent or more of the company stock, those who earn more than $75,000 in compensation from the company, those who earn over $50,000 and are in the top 20 percent of employee compensation in the corporation, and officers whose compensation exceeds 150 percent of the contribution limit specified in the Code ($45,000 as of January 1, 1987, or 1.5 × $30,000). Union employees can be excluded from the ESOP (and typically are if the company and the union bargain over contract provisions such as salary, health, and retirement programs).

17. In addition, Figgie International, Transco Energy, ENRON, and Ashland Oil terminated defined-benefit pension plans and transferred the surplus to a company-sponsored ESOP.

18. Avis claims that its customer complaints have dropped by 40 percent since its ESOP was formed. It also claims that its costs are now well below those of Hertz, its competitor, although Hertz's costs used to be lower. There is conflicting evidence, however, as to whether ESOP plan adoptions are associated with increased "productivity." For a discussion of the evidence, see Blasi (1988), Conte and Svejnar (1989), and Cooper (1989).

19. Holmstrom (1978) provides a particularly clear statement of the problem, as well as its solution.

20. See Lambert and Larcker (1987) for an analysis of stock-based versus accounting-based measures of performance in incentive contracting.

21. *Business Week,* January 23, 1989.

22. See *Forbes* (1986).

23. In a comprehensive survey conducted by the U.S. General Accounting Office in 1986, however, four-fifths of ESOPs invested 75 percent or more of their assets in sponsoring company stock.

24. Our analysis of ESOP announcements in the first four months of 1989 from the Dow Jones New Retrieval Service indicates that more than half of all new securities acquired by ESOPs are employer convertible preferred stocks.

25. Insurance companies are required to include 15 percent of any tax-exempt interest that they receive in taxable income. As a result, the insurance company would require a rate of interest that is 82 percent of the fully taxable rate (or R_I $= .66R_b / (1 - 1.15 \times .5 \times .34)$). See Bader and Hourihan (1989a). Mutual funds can create dual-class ownership, where one class receives the partially tax-exempt interest and other shareholders receive fully taxable interest. As a result, corporations with a 34 percent marginal tax rate or high marginal-tax-rate qualified noncorporate taxpayers might be the marginal holders of the tax-exempt piece.

26. See Kaplan (1989), Merrill Lynch (1988), Shearman and Sterling (1989), and Shackleford (1988). Care must be exercised in gathering evidence on these rates. Because of the 50 percent exclusion, it pays to set a high rate on an ESOP loan and a lower rate on fully taxable loans. The tax laws impose restraints on this, but there is still room to set rates opportunistically. To test this, loans should be separated into two piles: those where the lender has no other business dealings with the buyer and those where the lender also engages in non-ESOP transactions with the borrower. Care must also be exercised to determine the correct risk adjustment to be made in comparing interest rates across loans.

27. The government also subsidizes any deadweight costs that are uniquely incurred to underwrite the ESOP loan. The lender deducts its costs to process and underwrite the loan while the borrower pays less than 100 percent of the these costs through the interest break. Further, the 50 percent interest exclusion encourages the bundling of other services with the loan to secure a 50 percent income exclusion on revenues generated from these other services.

28. Although the term of the ESOP debt is limited by the number of years to which the employer will commit to making ESOP contributions, the maturity of the loan is restricted to 10 years if the employer uses the "principal method" of allocation to release shares from the suspense account. Generally, the proportional method is used, wherein shares are released from the suspense account in proportion to interest and principal that is paid on the loan.

29. See Freiman (1989) for a more extensive analysis of this issue.

30. As discussed earlier, very few plans actually face binding constraints on the contribution limit. This is particularly so for public companies.

31. Moreover, the firm and certain employees can avoid paying some social security taxes on their reduced salary.

32. The preferred stock must be convertible into the common stock of the company

at a "reasonable" conversion price, which has not yet been clearly defined. The firm must not be permitted to call the preferred, or if it can, the preferred must be convertible prior to the call. It must be convertible into a readily tradeable stock if traded on a securities market. If no such stock exists, the preferred must be convertible into the issue that contains the most voting and dividend rights among all outstanding shares. This last condition might be difficult to satisfy in certain cases. For example, if an ESOP is formed in conjunction with a leveraged buyout, the structure of the leveraged buyout might be such that it is difficult to know which security has the greatest voting and dividend rights.

33. Other reasons for the popularity of high dividend-yielding convertible preferred stock include (1) reduced investment risk for employees, although this presumably comes at the expense of reduced incentives, and (2) leveraging of voting rights in presumably friendly hands (a defense weapon).

34. United States General Accounting Office (1986).

35. We are grateful to Karen Wruck for assistance in securing these announcement data.

36. *Pensions and Investment Age Magazine*, July 24, 1989.

References

Auerbach, A. J. (September 1983). Taxation, Corporate Financial Policy and the Cost of Capital, Taxation, Corporate Financial Policy and the Cost of Capital. *Journal of Economic Literature, 21,* 905-40.

Bader, L. N., and Hourihan, J. A. (March 1989a). *The Investor's Guide to ESOP Loans.* New York: Salomon Brothers.

Bader, L. N., and Hourihan, J. A. (May 1989b). *Financial Executives Guide to ESOPs: 1989 Update.* New York: Salomon Brothers.

Blasi, J. R. (March 1988). *Employee Ownership: Revolution or Ripoff?* New York: Ballinger.

Conte, M. A., and Svejnar, J. (March 1989). The performance effects of employee ownership plans. Brookings Institution working paper.

Cooper, J. E. (March 1989). Employee stock ownership plans and economic efficiency. Harvard University working paper.

Forbes, D. (November 1986). The Controversial ESOP Pension. *Dun's Business Month,* pp. 40-1.

Freiman, H. A. (June 1989). *Understanding Leveraged ESOP Economics.* New York: Fidelity Management Trust Company.

Holmstrom, B. (Spring 1978,). Moral Hazard and Observability. *Bell Journal of Economics,* 74-91.

Jensen, M. C. (May 1986). The Agency Cost of Free Cash Flow: Corporate Finance and Takeovers. *American Economic Review, 76,* No. 2.

Jensen, M. C. (January 1989). Capital markets, organizational innovation, and restructuring. Harvard Business School working paper.

Kaplan, S. (1989). ESOP Notes, personal correspondence, dated March 31, 1989.

Lambert, R. A. and Larcker, D. F. (1987). An Analysis of the Use of Accounting and Market Measures of Performance in Executive Compensation Contracts. *Journal of Accounting Research (Supplement)*, pp. 85-125.

Marsh, T. R. and McAllister, D. E. (Spring 1981). ESOPs Tables: A Survey of Companies with Employee Stock Ownership Plans. *Journal of Corporation Law*, pp. 551-623.

Merrill Lynch. (October 1988). Employee Stock Ownership Plans.

Miller, M. H. (May 1977). Debt and Taxes. *Journal of Finance, 32*, pp. 261-75.

Patard, R. J. (1985). Employee stock ownership in the 1970s. *Employee Ownership—A Reader*. National Center for Employee Ownership, p. 58.

Scholes, M. S. and Wolfson, M. A. (1988). *The Cost of Capital and Changes in Tax Regimes, in Uneasy Compromise: Problems of a Hybrid Income-consumption Tax.* (Aaron, Galper and Pechman, eds.) Brookings Institution, pp. 157-94.

Scholes, M. S. and Wolfson, M. A. (1989). *Converting Corporations to Partnerships through Leverage: Theoretical and Practical Impediments, in Taxes and Corporate Restructurings.* (John B. Shoven, ed.) Brookings Institution.

Scholes, M. S. and Wolfson, M. A. (1990). *Taxes and Business Strategy: A Global Planning Approach.* Engelwood Cliffs, NJ: Prentice Hall.

Shackleford, D. A. (August 1988). *The Tax Incidence of the Interest Income Exclusion in Leveraged Employee Stock Ownership Plans.* University of Michigan working paper.

Shearman and Sterling. (January 1989). *ESOPs: What They Are and How They Work.*

Stiglitz, J. E. (1973). Taxation, Corporate Financial Policy, and the Cost of Capital. *Journal of Public Economics, 2*, 1-34.

U.S. Government Accounting Office. (February 1986). *Employee Stock Ownership Plans.* GAO-PEMD-86-4BR.

CHAPTER 19

THE RECORD OF LBO PERFORMANCE

William F. Long
David J. Ravenscraft

INTRODUCTION

As the number and size of leveraged buyouts increased over the last decade, so did the amount of research into LBO phenomena.   Most of this research focused on the prebuyout characteristics of the LBO firm and its industry, or the impact of LBOs on the prebuyout shareholders and bondholders. Because of the nature of going private transactions, only a few studies attempted to assess the postbuyout performance of LBO firms.

The most recent entry into the postbuyout research field is a paper released by Kohlberg Kravis Roberts & Co. (KKR), entitled, "Presentation on Leveraged Buy-Outs." The paper was based largely on an empirical study of 17 LBOs performed by KKR in which it still had an equity stake as of January 1989.[1] On May 25, 1989, at a hearing before the

William F. Long is Guest Scholar, Brookings Institution, Washington, D.C., and independent economic consultant. He holds a Ph.D., 1970, from the University of California, Berkeley.

David J. Ravenscraft is Associate Professor of Finance at the University of North Carolina (Ph.D. from Northwestern).

The views presented in this paper are the authors', and do not necessarily reflect those of the Brookings Institution. We would like to thank Bob Eisenbeis, Mike Scherer, Ivan Bull, and participants at a Brookings seminar for helpful comments on earlier drafts. Bob Eisenbeis collaborated on the proposal discussed in the "LBO Performance: A Proposal," page 530.

House Subcommittee on Telecommunications and Finance, Emil M. Sunley of Deloitte Haskins & Sells presented some retabulations of the data used in the KKR study. For our analysis of those retabulations, see appendix (page 540, this volume).

This chapter reviews the main KKR findings and compares these findings to other analyses of postbuyout performance.[2] These other studies include two papers presented at last year's Salomon Brothers Center conference on management buyouts by Kaplan (1989) and Bull (1989), a study of LBOs that return to the public sector via initial public offerings (IPOs) by Muscarella and Vetsuypens (1989), a study of largely publicly reporting LBOs by Smith (1989), and a National Science Foundation study (1989) analyzing the impact of restructurings on R&D expenditures. The KKR study stands out from the others in some very important ways. It discloses the identities of the companies in the sample and it provides year-by-year aggregate data for the seven-year company histories. Without those disclosures, we could not have conducted the extensive review reported below.

We conclude that some of the KKR findings, particularly in regard to employment, capital spending, and R&D, are inconsistent with other work. At least part of this difference can be traced to methodological problems in the KKR paper. Furthermore, we conclude that weaknesses in the methods used in *all* the current research, together with a number of still unanswered questions, suggest the need for further research. We summarize a proposal we have developed for pursuing this additional research.

COMPARISON OF KKR FINDINGS WITH OTHER POST-LBO RESULTS

Table 19–1 contains a convenient comparison of the numerical findings from the six studies that have investigated post-LBO performance.[3] Two observations are evident from this table. First, the size of KKR's sample is in line with the small samples used in other studies. Second, the KKR findings often contradict the results of other work. The KKR study finds increases in employment, R&D, and capital expenditures, whereas the other studies find no change or a decrease in these variables. This section explores these differences by presenting each of the KKR study's seven major findings (p. 2–1) and comparing them to results of the other studies. The last subsection discusses two key variables contained in other studies, but omitted from the KKR analysis.

TABLE 19–1
Results from Post-LBO Studies[a]

Variable	KKR[b]	Kaplan[c]	Bull[d]	Smith[e]	M&V[f]	NSF[g]
Sample size	17	19	25		35	8
Employment	13%	0.0%		−17%	−0.6%	
Employment - Ind. Adj.		−15.3%				
R&D	15%			-		−12.8%
Capital Expense	1.9%	−0.63%	−21.9%	-		
Capital Expense - Ind. Adj.		−2.9%	−24.7%			
Sales		17.4%	20.2%	20.4%	9.4%	
Sales - Ind. Adj.		−8.3%	6.5%			
Operating Income/Sales		2.60%	0.0%	0.0%	26.2%	
Operating Income/Sales - Ind. Adj.		2.43%	48.0%			
Return to LBO equity	35–40%	113%				

[a]Given the different methodologies to the various studies, this table should be taken only as suggestive of the differences in results among the studies. Employment, capital expenditures, R&D, and operating income/sales represent the difference between pre- and post-LBO values, except for NSF R&D which is the difference between 1986 and 1987 R&D for the 8 LBO, buyback, and other nonmerger restructuring firms.

[b]Results are taken from the summary discussion or from charts for each variable. They are based on the changes over the seven years from three years prior to the buyout to three years after the buyout.

[c]Capital expenditures, sales, and operating income/sales results are taken from Table 4.2 in Kaplan (1988). They represent the median standardized change between the year prior to the buyout and two years after the buyout. The employment numbers are based on 33 observations. They appear in Table 6.1 and represent the median standardized change between the year prior to the buyout and one to four years after the buyout, depending on data availability. The equity return data are based on 21 observations. They are drawn from Table 7.1, and are measured as the median return from the buyout completion date to the date of IPO or sale. These returns decline to 26.1 percent when adjusted for leverage and changes in the S&P 500.

[d]Data are taken from Tables 3, 5, and 7 in Bull (1989) and represent the change in the median value between the two years before and two years after the buyout. The unadjusted operating income/sales number is not presented in the report; it is taken from the statement that no significant change in operating income/sales occurred (p. 18). Almost one half of the observations are LBOs of a division of a company.

[e]Employment, sales, and operating income are taken from Tables 9, 8, and footnote 35, respectively. The sample size is not given because the two-year or more post-LBO sample varies between 29 and 3 observations. The table contains only the sign (negative in all cases) for R&D and capital spending because Smith presents data only the ratio of R&D/sales and capital/sales. Smith did find post-LBO increases in cash flow divided by sales, but no (operating income + depreciation)/sales.

[f]Results are taken from Table 6 in Muscarella and Vetsuypens (1989). With the exception of the equity value, they represent the median rate of change between the LBO and the subsequent IPO. The employment change is based on only 26 observations, while the return to LBO equity is based on 58 observations. The equity data are presented in Table 10. Divisional LBOs represent over half of the observations. KKR was involved in 8 of the LBOs.

[g]Sample includes "companies involved in leveraged buyouts, buybacks, or major restructurings (to avoid becoming targets of takeovers)" (NSF, 1989), p. 2. Other R&D performing companies increased R&D by 5.4 percent over the same period.

LBOs Increase Employment

Average annual employment for the 17 KKR companies after the buyout was 13 percent higher than average annual employment before the buyout.[4] Kaplan (1988), Smith (1989), and Muscarella and Vetsuypens (M&V) (1989) also analyzed employment effects of LBOs. None of these studies confirms this employment growth. Kaplan found almost no change in employment, M&V found a slight decline in employment, and Smith found a sharp decline in employment, but no change in employment divided by sales. Kaplan further demonstrates that employment was increasing in the LBOs' industries. If the LBO firm's employment growth is compared to that of its industry, relative employment declines by 15.3 percent. Therefore, to accurately assess the change in employment, the KKR and M&V studies should have controlled for industry growth.[5] Based on Kaplan's study, industry controls would probably substantially reduce the employment growth numbers for the KKR and M&V studies.

LBOs Increase Research and Development Expenditures

According to the KKR study, post-LBO R&D expenditures were 15 percent higher than pre-LBO expenditures for the 17 KKR companies combined. In a recent response to a request from Congress, the National Science Foundation (NSF) (1989) presents conflicting data. While the NSF study did not compare R&D expenditures before and after the LBO, it did demonstrate that R&D declined between 1986 and 1987 by 12.8 percent for the 8 out of 200 leading U.S. R&D performing companies which had undergone LBO, buy-back, or other nonmerger restructuring. Not all of the 8 firms are LBOs,[6] but, according to NSF's response, "each of these firms had a significant reduction in R&D spending." The 176 firms that were not involved in mergers, LBOs or other restructurings increased their R&D by 5.4 percent. The NSF study adjusted for inflation whereas the KKR study did not. Neither study controlled for changes in industry R&D.

Smith provides conflicting evidence. She finds significant declines in R&D/sales for the seven firms with available data. However, she cautions that "the generalization of these results is highly questionable because of the likely immateriality of R&D expenditures of nondisclosers" (page 39).

LBOs Yield Higher Taxes to the Federal Government

KKR, Kaplan, Bull, and Smith all confirm that the taxes paid by the LBO firm are virtually eliminated after the buyout. Kaplan concludes that "Potential tax benefits generated by the buyouts are large, ranging from 31 percent to 135 percent of the premium paid to prebuyout shareholders" [Kaplan (1989), p. 21]. While taxes clearly play a role in explaining LBO premiums, the large potential range (31–135 percent) of this role indicates the complexity in accurately assessing tax effects. LBOs also create wealth for shareholders, LBO investors, and bondholders (at least in terms of interest received), and taxes paid on this wealth result in increased government revenue. KKR shows that the capital gains tax paid by shareholders and investors and interest income tax paid by debt holders more than compensate for the tax reductions that the LBO firm receives. The net result was an increase in taxes paid of $2.9 billion dollars. This finding requires assumptions concerning: (1) the distribution of shareholders and bondholders among individuals, banks, corporations, and tax-exempt organizations at the time of the LBO, (2) the average basis of stock purchased by LBO shareholders, (3) the relevant marginal rates of each group, and (4) the absence of transfers from bondholders, employees, suppliers, and communities to shareholders, since these losses would off-set shareholder gains.

LBOs Keep Capital Spending Strong

The KKR study finds that capital spending increases from an average of $1,054 million in the three years preceding the LBO to $1,264 in the third year after the LBOs for more than a 14 percent increase. However, capital spending was lower than the pre-LBO average in the year of the LBO and the subsequent two years, so that the average for the three postbuyout years is $1,121 million, an increase of 1.9 percent. The lower capital expenditures in the first two years are consistent with both Kaplan's and Bull's results. They find declines in capital spending of 0.6 percent and 21.9 percent and industry adjusted declines of 2.9 percent and 24.7 percent between one year before the LBO and two years after the LBO. Smith's study adds further evidence, showing a significant decline in capital spending/sales, both with and without industry controls.

A key issue, for capital spending, R&D and employment, is whether the cutbacks eliminate unproductive expenditures, or whether they signal increased myopia on the part of the LBO management The answer to this question requires data on the long-run performance and the long-run competitive position of the LBO firm.

LBOs Adequately Handle Negative Events Such as Economic Downturns

In the early 1980s the U.S. experienced one of the worst postwar recessions. The 13 buyouts arranged by KKR before or during this recession survived the recession. The KKR study notes: "these buy-outs retired all debt on time and collectively provided the equity investors an annual compounded rate of return of approximately 35 percent" (p. 4–2). KKR also provides a two-page case study on Houdaille, an LBO which overcame a number of difficulties caused in part by the early '80s recession. Thus, limited historical evidence suggests that at least buyouts arranged by KKR can survive a recession. Buyouts have changed dramatically, however, since the late '70s/early '80s. The size of LBO firms has increased, and LBOs have expanded into new industries. Perhaps most important, the competition in the market for corporate control has increased in the 1980s. Competition in bidding can lead to the winner's curse in which the bidder with the most optimistic projections wins the target firm. For example, a firm predicting economic growth will be able to outbid another firm predicting a recession, all else equal. While all firms build a margin of error into their forecasts, competition can serve to reduce that margin. In light of these possible changes, the application of KKR's early experience to a future recession must be done with caution. Moreover, as the Revco LBO indicated, LBO bankruptcies occur even in nonrecessionary periods.

LBOs Are Not Run with a View to Quarter-to-Quarter Earnings

This finding is difficult to verify with concrete numbers and is therefore based on KKR's experience. Bull's interviews with institutional investors, LBO managers, and LBO deal-makers supports this view. Case studies of five divisional LBOs by Ravenscraft and Scherer (1987) provide some contradictory evidence. They conclude that "most of the interviewees who had made such (R&D) cuts expressed unease and hope that, once their debt burdens became lighter through repayments, they would be able to invest more in future-building activities" (p. 155).

LBOs Yield High Returns to Investors

All relevant studies show substantial returns to equity investors in the LBOs. KKR's estimated return appears conservative relative to estimates provided by Kaplan and M&V. Assuming these returns are correctly calculated, the critical questions are: What are the sources of these high returns, and how can significantly above-average returns persist for over a decade in a competitive corporate control market?

Omitted Performance Variables

The KKR study makes repeated references to the positive impact of LBOs on efficiency. Such improvements should show up in increases to operating income/sales, and, perhaps, sales. Unlike Kaplan, Bull, Smith, and M&V, the KKR study does not present any evidence on these two variables. Kaplan, Bull, Smith, and M&V all find improvements in sales. Kaplan finds that the LBOs' sales are not growing as fast as their industries' sales, implying a decline in market share. Bull's data yield the opposite result.

Improvements in profits/sales are found by Kaplan and M&V, but not by Bull and Smith. In Bull's sample, the industry profit rate was declining, so the LBO's profit rate, which was unchanged, looked good by comparison. Smith finds an increase in operating cash flow/sales, where operating cash flow is defined as "the net increase in cash and marketable securities arising from 'normal' operations, without considering royalty, dividend, or interest income, or gains/losses from the sale of PPE, extraordinary items, or payments of interest or dividends" (p. 13). The cash flow gains stem from a decrease in the inventory holding period and the receivables collection period and not a reduction in "discretionary expenditures." Since the gains are in accrual accounting items, it is not surprising that she finds gains in cash flow and not operating income. The studies that show improvements in operating profits do not identify the sources of the gains. Are they due to real efficiencies, or are they the result of cutbacks that will hurt long-run profits?

METHODOLOGICAL ISSUES

The preceding section suggested some substantial differences in the results of post-LBO studies. This section focuses on methodology as a potential source for these differences.

Sample Characteristics

By far the biggest concern about the post-LBO research is the small, potentially biased samples. According to Mergers and Acquisitions, there were 1,473 LBOs between 1983 and the second quarter of 1988. Eighteen percent of these were "going private," 68 percent were divestitures and 16 percent were "private market" LBOs.[7] By comparison, the sample sizes given in Table 19–1 are quite small, less than 3 percent of the total number of LBOs. M&V's 35 observation sample is probably the least representative, focusing on only LBOs that succeed through subsequent IPOs. Kaplan's and Smith's samples suffer from a similar bias. For samples for which data on the second postbuyout year were available, IPO, sale, or releveraged companies represented 13 of the 19 companies in Kaplan's sample, and 29 out of 58 companies in Smith's total sample. Furthermore, Kaplan provides some evidence for the existence of a "success" bias, since the 13 resale companies displayed greater operating income, capital expenditure, and employment gains (or lower losses) than the 6 nonresale companies. Smith runs a number of tests to demonstrate the lack of bias in her sample. In one test, she fails to find any significant difference between IPO companies and the rest of her sample. Since Smith and Kaplan employ similar data collection techniques and cover similar periods, there must be a substantial overlap in their samples. Thus, it is unclear why they reach different conclusions on sampling bias and other issues where they perform similar tests.

Bull's sample comes from confidential data provided by six institutional investors. It includes quite distinct LBO types, including 8 full company going private LBOs, 11 divisional LBOs, and 6 LBOs of private companies. While this diversity makes the sample more representative, it also raises the possibility that one group, that is, divisional LBOs, may dominate the results. Ideally, we would want separate statistics on each distinct LBO type. One critical problem with small samples is that they preclude statistically meaningful sample divisions.

The KKR study includes all LBOs it performed in which it still had an equity stake as of January 1989. Interpreted as a sample of all LBOs, it is small; only the NSF R&D study's sample of eight LBO and other nonmerger restructurings is smaller. The KKR sample does not appear, however, to suffer from the same biases as the Kaplan, Smith and M&V studies. Still, the KKR LBOs may not be typical. They are, in fact, much larger than the average LBO by a substantial margin. The admittedly crude estimates contained in Table 19–2 suggest that the average 1988 sales value for the KKR companies was about $2.5 billion and the median sales was $1.0 billion. According to a 1984 Fortune article, the KKR companies may also be more diversified.[8] Both size and diversification have been found to be important factors in determining employment, capital spending, R&D, and firm efficiency. Size and diversification also increase the firm's ability to reduce debt through divestiture. Finally, the generality of the KKR study's finding is limited by the fact that all the LBOs were arranged by KKR. Since KKR is one of most experienced leaders in the LBO field, their firms may fare better than the norm. In any case, policies and practices clearly differ among LBO investors and KKR's focus on its own firms may limit the generality of the findings.

The Number of Post-LBO Data Years

It takes time for the full effects of an LBO's success or failure to materialize. Thus, the longer the post-LBO data period, the better. Long time periods, however, would preclude an analysis of many recent LBOs for which sufficient post-LBO data are unavailable. Balancing this trade-off is difficult. Data constraints limited Kaplan, Smith and Bull to at most two post-LBO years. The M&V study contains post-LBO data for an average of three years but with a range of four months to eight years.

The KKR study appears to be reporting data on the postbuyout years one through three for "All KKR Companies." However, this raises a potentially serious problem. For 7 of the 17 companies, the LBO occurred in 1986 or later. Obviously, three years of post-LBO data are not available for these seven companies. The KKR study used projected data for those companies and years for which it did not have actual data.[9]

From a technical standpoint, the use of projections in a study which attempts to examine post-LBO performance is questionable. KKR's projections, whatever their basis, specifically estimate the variables under study in the report—employment, capital spending, R&D, taxes, and debt—thus confusing actual and expected perfor-

TABLE 19–2
KKR Sample Companies—Estimates of Sales and Employment

	Buyout Year	Source[a]	Revenues ($ millions)	Number of Employees
A. Buyout occurring in 1985 or earlier				
A. J. Industries	77	S&P	98	1,400
Fred Meyer	81	S&P	1,850	16,000
Houdaille Industries	79	S&P	300	5,000
L. B. Foster Co.	77	S&P	211	571
M&T	85	D&B[b]	50	3
Malone & Hyde	84	S&P	3,000	8,010
Marley Co.	81	S&P	531	5,200
Motel 6	85	S&P	297	8,000
Pace Industries	84	S&P	2,000	19,300
Pacific Realty Trust	83	S&P[c]	3	24
Totals			8,340	63,508
Means			834	6,351
B. Buyout occurring in 1986 or later				
Beatrice Companies	86	D&B	4,010	19,700
Duracell	88	S&P	1,000	9,200
Jim Walter Corporation	87	D&B	2,180	17,700
Owens-Illinois	87	S&P	3,670	44,048
Safeway STores	86	S&P	18,300	124,000
Seaman Furniture Company	87	S&P	275	1,350
Stop & Shop Companies	88	S&P	4,340	48,000
Totals			33,775	233,998
Means			4,825	37,714
Ratio of means - B : A			5.79	5.94
Grand Totals			42,115	297,506
Means			2,477	17,500

[a]S&P = *Standard & Poor's Register of Corporations, 1989;* D&B = *Dun & Bradstreet Million Dollar Directory, 1989.*
[b]Company not in either of the main sources. The data are from *Dun & Bradstreet Million Dollar Directory, 1988,* and may be very inaccurate.
[c]Company not in either of the main sources. The data are from *Standard & Poor's Register of Corporations, 1988,* and may be very inaccurate.

mance. Both Kaplan and Bull found that LBO projections were overly optimistic.

The use of projections is potentially serious because the seven LBOs occurring in the post–1985 period are almost six times as large as the other companies. Table 19–2 shows that average sales for the "1985 or before" subsample of 10 companies were $834 million, versus $4,825 million for the "1986 and after" companies. The number of employees in the two samples were 6,351 for the pre–1986 sample and 37,714 for the post–1985 sample.

Since the KKR study simply sums the employment, capital expenditures, R&D, and other variables for the 17 companies without the use of ratios, the differences in average sizes become critical. In practical terms, the performance of these variables is driven by the projected data of the seven post–1985 LBOs. This is particularly true for the third post-LBO year, since post–1985 companies account for over 75 percent of the data in that year.

Changes in Company Structure

A major restructuring of firms including divestitures, and in some cases acquisitions, often follows an LBO. These changes make it difficult to compare pre-/post-LBO company characteristics. Bull addressed this problem by deleting firms which underwent a major restructuring. That may have introduced additional sampling bias if restructuring is related to the items of interest. Kaplan controls for restructuring "by repeating the analyses for the subset of MBOs that restate prebuyout financial statements for the divestitures or do not have postbuyout divestitures and acquisitions" [Kaplan (1988), p. 26]. Smith splits her sample into subsamples of firms with and without asset sales. While Kaplan does not find many differences between the samples with and without restructuring, Smith provides evidence that the restructured sample is less reliable. M&V and NSF do not address the restructuring issue.

The KKR study's solution was to revise the pre-LBO data, eliminating data for subsequently divested units. While this procedure is probably superior to the Kaplan, Bull, or Smith approach, some details are needed on how the pre-LBO data were adjusted. In particular, how important were the dual problems of common cost allocation and transfer pricing and how were they addressed?

The KKR study's handling of acquisitions was much less satisfactory. The study states: "Operations that were acquired by the companies are included in the data from the date of acquisition" (p. 3–1). The impact of including acquisitions is to bias the conclusions toward positive changes, since the acquired companies' data are included in the post-LBO, but not the pre-LBO, data. This bias is potentially serious because Owens-Illinois, Motel 6, Houdaille Industries, L. B. Foster, Fred Meyer, Malone &

Hyde, and U.S. Natural Resources all made significant acquisitions (p. 4–5). The acquisition of Brockway by Owens-Illinois is particularly important since, in 1986, it had sales of about one billion dollars, employment of about 12,000, capital expenditures of about $37 million, and a sizeable R&D program. Why the authors decided to exclude divestitures and include acquisitions is a puzzle. In any case, the data should be reestimated with acquisitions excluded, or with the acquired companies' data added in the pre-LBO period.

Levels versus Ratios

All post-LBO studies employ some variables measured as levels instead of ratios, that is, capital expenditures instead of capital expenditures/sales or capital expenditures/employees. Which measurement is appropriate depends on the question posed. Ratios, however, have a number of inherent advantages, including implicit adjustment for firm growth, large firm dominance, and inflation (assuming the price indexes for the numerator and denominator are similar). When levels are used, these issues must be handled carefully.

The importance of the ratio versus level issue can be seen in the KKR study data. For R&D, capital expenditures, and employment, the three year pre-LBO averages were $94 million, $1,117 million, and 264 thousand workers, respectively. The post-LBO three year averages for these three variables were $106 million, $1,121 million, and 302 thousand workers. In terms of levels, there was an increase in all three variables, although the change in capital expenditures is relatively small. If instead the ratios of R&D/employee and capital expenditures/employee are used, thus adjusting for firm growth, part of which stems from acquisitions, the two relative measures decline. R&D per employee drops from $360 to $350 and capital expenditures per employee drops from $4,236 to $3,708.[10]

Hidden in even these numbers is the potential dominance of changes in a few large firms. For example, the crude numbers in Table 19–2 suggest that Safeway accounts for roughly 40 percent of the total sample employment. Suppose, to illustrate with an extreme case, Safeway had increased employment by 15 percent and each of the other 16 firms had cut employment by 10 percent; the KKR study would have concluded that LBOs increase employment. If the KKR sample were in fact the whole population of LBOs, then perhaps this aggregation technique would make sense. However, if we are trying to make inferences from a small sample concerning general LBO tendencies, it makes little sense to let a few observations dictate the conclusion. Safeway may reflect a special case, not the general rule. The NSF study aggregates data in a manner similar to KKR's. Since NSF finds declines for all 8 LBO, buyback, and other nonmerger restructurings, the method of aggregation is less important for their data. Kaplan and Bull address the aggregation issue by taking the mean of the percentage changes for each firm; M&V do so by taking the median rate of change. For the illustration given above, Kaplan's approach would add 16 firms times −10 percent and 1 firm times 15 percent for an average percentage decline in employment of 8.6 percent.

Adjustment for Industry Values

Kaplan, Smith, and Bull compare the performance of the LBO firm to its industry.[11] As discussed in the section above comparing KKR findings with other post-LBO results and illustrated in Table 19–1, the industry controls are critical in a number of cases, including employment, sales, and profits. Therefore, it is important to separate LBO-related changes from changes in the LBO firm's industry. Industry controls should be added to the NSF, M&V, and KKR studies. NSF and M&V compared their results to economywide changes. The KKR study should adjust for the level of inflation, which has averaged 5 percent over the 1977–87 period, and real growth, which for employment has averaged about 2.2 percent over the same period.[12] Next to the U.S. average inflation and real growth numbers, the KKR study's growth rates may not seem so exceptional.

Usage of Data from the LBO Year

The KKR study typically includes data for the LBO year in the pre-LBO calculations, arguing that these decisions are committed prior to the LBO. All other researchers avoid this practice. As Bull notes, "The year of the buyout is excluded from comparisons because it frequently includes recognition of a number of atypical events which distort comparisons" (p. 6).

Excluding the LBO year from the KKR analysis does change some of the results. For example, the study concludes, "average capital spending increased 1.9 percent after the LBO versus prior to the LBO" (p. 7–2).

That percentage increase is based on an average of $1,101 million pre-LBO and $1,122 million post-LBO. The $1,101 value is the average of the years (–3, –2, –1, and 0). If the LBO year is removed from the calculation, the average for the pre-LBO period is $1,117 million, indistinguishable from the post-LBO value.

LBO PERFORMANCE: A RESEARCH PROPOSAL

Some of the methodological problems discussed in the last section can be addressed by a more careful employment of currently available data. However, some of the most serious problems faced by all studies stem from data constraints that cannot be solved with existing data. The small and potentially biased sample size, together with limited information on each LBO, seriously impairs our confidence in the accuracy and generality of the current post-LBO studies. Major strides in our understanding of LBOs will come only when current data constraints are lifted. With improved data we can also begin to ask a richer set of questions, focusing on the critical factors which enable an LBO to change performance. Most of the current research has struggled merely to describe a change in performance. Research needs to move beyond this and towards an understanding of how, why, and under what conditions LBOs affect performance. This section describes a research proposal for correcting previous methodological problems and for addressing additional LBO-related issues.[13]

Solutions to Methodological Problems

Three confidential data sources, the Quarterly Financial Report (QFR), the Census and Annual Survey of Manufactures, and an annual survey by the National Science Foundation (NSF), contain rich sources of information that can be employed to remove many of the current post-LBO data constraints. The Census Bureau collects the information for all three sources, and the latter two have been combined in the Longitudinal Research Data (LRD) file by the Bureau's Center for Economic Studies (CES). The authors have been granted access to these data sources, subject to confidentiality restrictions and adequate project funding.

The QFR series provides a quarterly income statement and balance sheet on all firms—public and private—with more than $25 million in assets and a large scientific sample of firms under $25 million. By the mid–1980s 4,000 to

5,000 firms with assets of $25 million or more were providing data every quarter to the QFR, and another 12,000 to 16,000 smaller firms were submitting data for some years. The reporting firms also explain in their report any change in name, state, and date of incorporation, and explicitly report structural changes, such as: organization as a completely new business, change in corporate title, formation as a successor company to another company, sale of assets, merger, discontinuation of business, and legal dissolution.

The LRD file contains Census and Annual Survey data on manufacturing establishments (plants) of companies. Detailed, separate data are filed by a company for each of its establishments that meet the reporting requirement. For census years, these data contain essentially the universe of all but the very smallest manufacturing establishments. In noncensus years, the LRD file contains data on all manufacturing establishments with over 250 employees and a large scientific sampling of smaller manufacturing establishments. In 1985, roughly 56,000 establishments reported to the Annual Survey.

With the corporate status changes reported to the QFR and a list of all LBOs reported by *Mergers and Acquisitions*, a very large sample of LBOs can be identified. Through a careful matching of the public LBO data, the final LBO sample should maintain the properties of the QFR and LRD files, that is, the near universe of large firms and a scientific sample of smaller firms. As indicated, a large, representative, unbiased sample is the first requirement for obtaining accurate post-LBO performance measures and for testing richer LBO hypotheses. However, other methodological problems must also be addressed, including the number of postbuyout years, changes in company structure, and industry controls.

Computerized files for the QFR data exist from 1974 to 1988. For the LRD data, they exist from 1972 to 1987. Thus, for all but the most recent LBOs, two or more years of post-LBO data are available. This time series of data also allows the exploration of two issues ignored by other researchers. First, has the performance of LBOs changed over time? For example, has a decade of experience led to better LBOs, or has dramatically increased activity led towards more marginal LBO candidates? Second, what does the lag structure of the return to LBOs look like? Specifically, does performance improve in the first post-LBO year or does it take time for the LBO changes to take effect? Does the improved performance dissipate as the debt gets reduced or after the firm returns to the public sector?

Use of post-LBO data for one, two, or three years limits research findings, and results in an incomplete picture of LBO performance. And, when absolute measures are used instead of relatives, much greater weight is given to the more recent, larger LBOs. The average "life cycle" for an LBO restructuring may be more like five to seven years in length, and is certainly greater than three. For the earliest 100–200 LBOs in the file, we expect to be able to capture the full cycle for each firm, and assess its performance at the end of the cycle. That will give us a picture of the long-run effects for those LBOs, so we will have a basis for reaching conclusions about whether LBOs have a positive effect on the economy.

Many LBOs refocus the firm by selling off divisions, which also helps to pare down the debt. Dramatic changes in the corporation's business unit portfolio can impair pre/post comparisons made at the whole company level. This problem is readily addressed, for manufacturing firms, by the use of establishment data in the LRD file. Because of the disaggregated nature of the LRD data, a continuous time series of plant data exists whether the establishment remains with the restructured firm or is sold off to a new or existing company. Almost no analysis has been done on the postdivestiture performance of LBO sell-offs, even though this information is needed to completely understand the impact of LBOs. For both manufacturing and nonmanufacturing firms, the QFR data provide information if the sold-off unit remains independent and has assets of $25 million or more.

A final methodological issue that needs addressing is industry controls. As Table 19–1 shows, LBO performance can look quite different when it is compared to industry changes over the same period. For manufacturing firms, the Census and Annual Survey industry aggregates provide an accurate picture of industry performance. For nonmanufacturing, the QFR industry totals can be employed, although the nonmanufacturing industries are broadly defined and require that a firm be classified into its primary industry only.

Key Unanswered LBO Issues

With a combination of the confidential Census data and public sources, the major results presented in Table 19–1 can be replicated with a sample that is relatively free of bias and 10 to 50 times as large as those of previous work. Our goal, however, is to go well beyond replication of existing work. This sections outlines four key areas that we plan to address.[14]

Theories of LBO Value Creation

There are two critical issues concerning value creation. First, do the positive returns to prebuyout shareholders and postbuyout investors stem from real improvements in company performance or from other factors such as undervalued assets, unrealistic expectations or transfers from bondholders, employees, or government? Second, what factors determine the LBO's ability to enhance company performance? Following Kaplan's methodology, evidence on the first issue can be obtained by regressing changes in company performance and proxies for the other factors on the pre-LBO shareholder and post-LBO investor returns.[15] However, a primary focus of the study will be on the second issue.

There are at least four critical components of LBOs which can be linked to improved performance. First, an LBO increases leverage, which reduces management's ability to waste "free cash flows" [cash flows over and above current positive net present value projects, Jensen (1986)] and reduces the shareholder free rider problem by dramatically decreasing the number of interested outside parties who need to oversee the company's operations. Second, LBOs often convert a public company into a private one, eliminating the cost and constraints of public ownership. In some cases, however, publicly held debt still forces the company to report 10Ks and 10Qs.[16] Third, management participation generally increases as a result of the buyout. This helps eliminate the agency problem that arises from a separation of ownership and control. In a few LBOs, the presumably inefficient management is also replaced. Fourth, LBOs often result in a much simpler corporate structure. This is especially true for divisional LBOs in which the division is freed from a large corporate bureaucracy. Corporate structure is also simplified and refocused when significant divestiture activity accompanies the LBO. The key is to isolate each of these individual factors.

To illustrate a potential method for identifying the role of each factor, consider the following linear regression:

$$CHPERF = \beta_0 + \beta_1 * CHLEV + \beta_2 * CHEQUITY + \beta_3 * CHMNG + \beta_4 * PUBLIC + \beta_5 * PRIVATE + \beta_6 * REPORT + \beta_7 * DIVISION + \beta_8 * DIVEST + \varepsilon.$$

CHPERF, CHLEV, and CHEQUITY represent the prepost change in performance, leverage and equity ownership of senior management, respectively. Performance can be measured in terms of operating income/sales, cash flow, productivity, sales, or market share.[17] The other six variables are dummy variables with a value of 1 if: there is a change in senior management (CHMNG), the LBO firm remains public (PUBLIC), the LBO firm was a private firm to begin with (PRIVATE), the LBO firm goes private but still files 10K reports (REPORT), the LBO involved a division of the company (DIVISION), a significant part (10 percent) of the LBO firm was subsequently divested (DIVEST).[18]

The Jensen free cash flow hypothesis would predict a positive coefficient on β_1. Agency theory would predict a positive coefficient on β_2. The coefficient of CHMNG, β_3, should be positive according to the inefficient management hypothesis. The coefficients, β_4, β_5, and β_6, should be negative, since they represent cases where the benefits of going private are not fully realized. Finally, if simplifying corporate structure corrects ill-conceived diversification, as studies of merger activity by Ravenscraft and Scherer (1987) and studies of common cost and diversification by Long, et al. (1982) suggest, then β_7 and β_8 should be positive.

Smith analyzed an equation similar to the one proposed here. Specifically, she regressed the change in operating cash flow/assets variable on changes in leverage and equity ownership, the first two variables in our equation. Her change in equity ownership variable was even more detailed, containing separate variables for officers, outside directors, and other major holders. Her results are very encouraging especially given her small sample and limited time series. She found that all four variables were positive and statistically significant in the sample without assets sales. She interprets this evidence as supporting agency theory and Jensen's free cash flow hypothesis.

The above model can be extended in a number of ways. One is to include interaction terms, to test for the effects of two of the variables in combination. An example would be the term CHLEV*CHEQUITY, to test the hypothesis that it takes both high leverage and significant management equity ownership to improve efficiency. Another promising extension would be to include a number of other financial, business and industry factors that might influence LBO performance. For example, the KKR study lists "criteria for selecting companies for acquisition" (p. 5–2). Many of these could be quantified and related to the ex post performance of the LBO.

Impact of Macroeconomic Conditions on LBOs

Post-LBO investor returns appear to be substantially above normal, as illustrated in Table 19–1. One explanation of high returns is increased risk. An obvious potential source of increased LBO risk stems from the dangers of high leverage in a recession. How to appraise this risk in advance of a serious recession is, however, difficult.

One approach would employ available macroeconomic modeling techniques to project the performance of LBO firms if there is a deterioration in the economy. Most firms surely appraise alternative macroeconomic scenarios before making an LBO. However, independent confirmation for a large sample of LBOs of the accuracy of these projections and the extent of downside protection incorporated into the bid is needed. The firm, establishment and industry time series data available in the Census would provide a solid, consistent foundation for these forecasts. The QFR file also contains separate data for commercial loan debt and commercial bond debt, which can be used to further refine the macroeconomic models. A second approach would look at the limited historical experience available—the early 1980s recession. This approach was employed by KKR and is subject to the criticisms discussed in the second section above. Our project would expand the KKR sample and compare each LBO's performance to other firms in its industry.

A related issue of considerable current interest is the impact of a recession on financial institutions which hold LBO and other high-yield debt. Key questions in this regard are: How susceptible are LBO cash flows to an economic downturn? How much of the high-yield debt risk can be diversified by holding LBOs in different industries? And how extensive and concentrated are financial institution holdings of high-yield debt? Some evidence on these questions can be obtained by evaluating portfolios of LBOs under different macroeconomic conditions. More exact answers require detailed information on the high-yield debt holdings by financial institutions. Such data exist or are being collected, and we are pursuing the possibility of linking the information with the Census data.

Selectivity Bias
As discussed in the preceding section, current research into LBOs suffers from a potential selectivity bias. To evaluate current research and the potential for using public data for future research, a better understanding of the nature of this bias is useful. The specific questions to be addressed are:

- Are IPO companies representative of all LBOs?
- Do post-LBO data differ for private companies holding public debt?

- Are post-LBO data affected by company size and diversification?
- How is the LBO performance influenced by the financial advisor?

These questions could be studied by dividing the sample into different classifications or by adding the relevant variables to the regression equation discussed above.

The Impact of LBOs on Other Important Variables

The Census files contain data that will provide additional details on a number of important issues, including the impact of LBOs on workers and R&D. Workers are divided into production and nonproduction employees. If LBOs mainly reduce unnecessary overhead, then nonproduction employment should decline relative to production employment. Number of employees is only part of the employment picture, of course, since wages are equally important. No study investigates the impact of LBOs on compensation per employee or total wages, two data items that can be computed with Census data. With respect to R&D, the LRD file provides more detailed and consistently defined data than are generally publicly available. We can separately identify the impact of LBOs on basic research, company financed R&D, and government funded R&D.

SUMMARY AND CONCLUSION

A recent study by KKR concluded that LBOs: "increase employment, increase research and development, yield higher taxes to the federal government, keep capital spending strong, are able adequately to handle negative events such as economic downturns, are not run with a view to quarter to quarter earnings and yield high returns to investors." We argue that methodological problems in the KKR study, together with conflicting results from other post-LBO performance research, suggests that the KKR conclusions are premature. According to other post-LBO research, LBOs reduce employment (especially relative to the industries in which they operate), decrease R&D, and reduce capital spending. The KKR findings on employment, R&D, and capital spending might be reversed if the study had: used actual instead of projected data, omitted acquisitions from the post-LBO data, used ratios instead of levels, adjusted for growth in the LBO's industry (or adjusted for U. S. economy inflation and real growth), and omitted the LBO year from the pre-LBO data. The one KKR result that is verified by other post-LBO research is that LBOs yield high returns to investors, but these other studies are biased towards successful LBOs. In addition to the KKR findings, other researchers have generally observed increases in operating income/sales or operating cash flow/sales as a result of the LBO.

Despite some apparent differences in results, post-LBO studies, with the exception of the NSF congressional response, draw fairly favorable conclusions regarding overall LBO performance. This paper does not find that such a conclusion is incorrect. It does demonstrate that drawbacks in existing research severely limit the confidence that should be placed in any conclusion, whether positive or negative, especially with respect to long-run performance. Post-LBO research has been plagued with data constraints, including small, potentially biased samples and problems in adjusting for changes in corporate structure. Furthermore, it has provided little or no evidence on how improvements in performance are obtained and whether these improvements are sustained in the longer run. Evidence is also sparse on LBO performance in a recession and the repercussions of poor LBO performance on the banking and other financial industries.

We have attempted to go beyond simply criticizing existing work. Our proposed study is designed to obtain a large, representative time series of post-LBO data, and to address a number of key LBO issues, several of which have not yet been explored. With this study, we intend to provide some solid answers on how, why, and under what circumstances LBOs improve performance, and on the implications of LBO performance for the general corporate governance issues of level of indebtedness, management participation in ownership, diversification, and constraints imposed by public ownership of equity.

Notes

1. The data for the study were tabulated by Deloitte Haskins & Sells. An abbreviated version of this paper appeared in the *Journal of Applied Corporate Finance,* spring 1989.
2. The chapter's emphasis on the KKR study was requested by the conference chairman.
3. For some details on the composition of the sample and methodology used in each study, see the third section of this chapter below.
4. The 13 percent number is not actually given in the text. It was calculated by finding average employment for years –3, –2, –1, and 0 for the pre-LBO period, and average employment for years +1, +2, and +3 for the post-LBO period, and then determining the percentage increase.

5. Smith employs industry controls for the employee/sales variable, but not for the employment level variable.
6. It is worth noting in this context that the definition of the term *LBO* differs across researchers and reporters. For example, some include "public LBOs"—companies that restructure through a substantial exchange of equity for debt, but remain public. Others focus only on the management buyouts (MBOs) in which pre-LBO senior management participates in the buyout. In our view, it is important to employ a broad definition in order to fully understand the causes and consequences of LBOs.
7. Source, *Mergers & Acquisitions,* November/December 1988, p. 50.
8. Irwin Ross, "How the Champs Do Leveraged Buyouts," *Fortune,* January 23, 1984, pp. 70–78.
9. This was confirmed in a phone conversation with a representative of KKR. Each of the companies which did not have actual data used its most recent business plan as a source for data for the study.
10. These calculations use years –3, –2, and –1 for the pre-LBO period. If the LBO year is also used, the averages for R&D, capital expenditures, and employment are $92 million, $1,101 million, and 267,000 employees, respectively. R&D per employee is $345, and capital expenditures per employee is $4,128.
11. The industry adjustments are, however, somewhat crude. They are based on Compustat's primary industry classification. Most firms are engaged in several different lines of business, so it is inaccurate to use only a single industry control.
12. See the *1988 Economic Report to the President.* Inflation was measured as the average change in the producer price index for finished goods.
13. Drafted by the two authors of this chapter and a colleague, Robert Eisenbeis. Currently, finding adequate funding is the only remaining major roadblock to executing our proposal.
14. We would like to thank Mike Scherer for some seminal thoughts on the issues discussed in this section.
15. Kaplan concludes that taxes play a key role in explaining prebuyout shareholder returns, and that postbuyout improvements in operating income/sales play a key role in explaining postbuyout investor returns. M&V also provide support for the second finding.
16. The cost of public ownership does not refer simply to the reporting costs of 10Ks and annual reports. The broader issue is, do LBOs eliminate the "need to be concerned with short-term movements in stock price" and "the reluctance to make tough decisions because of the fear that the public market may react negatively" [KKR (1989b), p. 68].
17. The latter measure may be especially useful, since increases in market share may reflect a long-run building strategy, whereas declines in market share may reflect a cash flow strategy.

18. M&V begin to explore some of these questions with a simple bivariate correlation analysis. They find superior performance for divisional LBOs, LBOs that increase managerial incentives, and LBOs that stay private for more than 29 months.

References

Bull, Ivan. (1989). "Management Performance in Leveraged Buyouts: An Empirical Analysis," in (Yakov Amihud, ed.) *Leveraged Management Buyouts*. Homewood, IL: Dow Jones-Irwin

Jensen, Michael C. (May 1986). "Agency Costs of Free Cash Flow, Corporate Finance and Takeovers," *American Economic Review*, pp. 323–29.

Kaplan, Steven. (May 1988). "Sources of Value in Management Buyouts," Harvard University Ph.D. thesis.

Kaplan, Steven. (1989). "A Summary of Sources of Value in Management Buyouts," in (Yakov Amihud, ed.) *Leveraged Management Buyouts*. Homewood, IL: Dow Jones-Irwin.

Kohlberg Kravis Roberts & Co. (January 1989a) "Presentation on Leveraged Buyouts." Manuscript.

Kohlberg Kravis Roberts & Co. (with Deloitte Haskins & Sells). (spring 1989b). "Leveraged Buyouts," *Journal of Applied Corporate Finance*, vol. 2, no. 1, pp. 64–70.

Long, William F., David F. Lean, David J Ravenscraft, and Curtis L. Wagner III. (September 1982). "Benefits and Costs of the Federal Trade Commission's Line of Business Program—Volume I: Staff Analysis," *Bureau of Economics Staff Report to the Federal Trade Commission*.

Muscarella, Chris J., and Michael R. Vetsuypens. (January 1989). "Efficiency and Organizational Structure: A Study of Reverse LBO's." Manuscript.

National Science Foundation. (February 1989) "An Assessment of the Impact of Recent Leveraged Buyouts and Other Restructurings on Industrial Research and Development Expenditures." Prepared for the Subcommittee on Telecommunications and Finance, House Committee on Energy and Commerce.

Ravenscraft, David J., and F. M. Scherer. (1987). *Mergers, Sell-offs, and Economic Efficiency*. Washington, DC: Brookings Institution.

Smith, Abbie. (January 1989). "Corporate Ownership Structure and Performance: The Case of Management Buyouts," University of Chicago manuscript.

Sunley, Emil M. (May 25, 1989). "Summary Statement of Emil M. Sunley, Deloitte Haskins & Sells, on the Study of KKR Leveraged Buy-outs." Presented before the Subcommittee on Telecommunications and Finance of

APPENDIX TO CHAPTER 19

KKR RETABULATIONS OF EMILE M. SUNLEY

On May 25, 1989, at a hearing before the House Subcommittee on Telecommunications and Finance, Emil M. Sunley of Deloitte Haskins & Sells commented on this paper's review of the KKR study. In an addendum to his testimony, he presented two sets of retabulations of data used in the original KKR study. This appendix briefly analyzes the results of the retabulations.

The KKR addendum adjusts the historical capital spending and R&D data for inflation using the Implicit Deflator for Nonresidential Fixed Investment (Structures and Equipment) for capital spending and the GNP deflator for R&D. Using the consistent standard of averaging the three pre-LBO years and three post-LBO years, the new data exhibits a decline in both capital spending and R&D. The average pre-LBO level of capital spending in millions of 1987 dollars is $1,168. The average post-LBO level of capital spending is $1,104 or a 5 percent decline in capital spending. The comparable numbers for R&D spending are $103 pre-LBO and $101 post-LBO or a 2 percent decline. This one adjustment brings at least the direction of change in line with other research.

In a second retabulation, the KKR addendum presents data omitting the seven companies for which projected data were used. The noninflation adjusted post-LBO increases in employment, capital spending, and R&D appear to be even stronger for the 10 pre-1986 companies than for the 17 companies as a whole. Comparable inflation adjusted figures are not given even though inflation was significantly higher in the late '70s and early '80s. Employment increases from an average of 52 thousand over the three pre-LBO years to an average of 65 thousand in the three post-LBO years. Capital spending increases from $265 million to $311 million and R&D increases from $4.9 million to $8.3 million over the same period. This appears to demonstrate that projections were not driving the overall results. However, because of the other methodological problems in the study, it is difficult to compare the total and pre-1986 sample.

Consider the R&D data for the 10 companies. The 70 percent increase in post-LBO R&D can only be described as phenomenal. Such growth is rare for even quickly growing high-tech companies which are not, according to KKR, typical candidates for LBOs. This sharp R&D rise most likely results from the failure to correct the tabulations for acquisitions or other factors highlighted in our original analysis.

According to KKR, 5 of the 10 companies had substantial acquisitions after the LBO. Any sizeable acquisition could explain a significant part of the observed increase in R&D. To illustrate, take Houdaille Industries acquisition of John Crane, Inc.

Though John Crane was a private company, Standard & Poor's and Dun & Bradstreet estimate that its sales were between $100 and $150 million and employment between 1,800 and 2,550 employees. According to NSF data, the 1981 and 1982 R&D to sales ratios for the industries in which John Crane operated ranged from 1.9 percent to 2.5 percent. Assuming that John Crane's R&D expenditures were typical of its industry peers, its R&D would be between $1.9 and $3.8 million. Thus, the acquisition of John Crane could explain between 55 and 100 percent of the post-LBO R&D increase.

The KKR study consistently confuses acquisitions with real economic growth. Unless synergies are created, no new productive resources are brought into the industry through acquisition. John Crane's R&D expenditures would have existed whether Houdaille acquired them or not. To illustrate this point, consider an LBO that lays off 400 employees and then buys a company with an existing employment of 500. The KKR study's logic would lead to the conclusion that the LBO had created 100 jobs. The real effect is that 400 people who had been working no longer are working.

The congressional statement by Sunley concluded with "the answers found for KKR companies contradict much of the 'conventional wisdom' about LBOs" (page 13). Unfortunately, they also contradict most of the related evidence in other LBO studies. By comparing the methodology of current post-LBO research, we have uncovered some potential explanations for the discrepancies in current research. The KKR addendum has increased our knowledge by permitting us to explore two of the methodological problems in the original KKR study. It has not changed our original conclusions about the probable post-LBO performance of the KKR LBOs.

CHAPTER 20

TO WHAT EXTENT DO CORPORATIONS FACE DOUBLE TAXATION: COMMENTS ON CHAPTER 18

Alan J. Auerbach

In the 1960s, economists thought they understood the effects of the corporation income tax, as a second level of taxation of the capital income originating in the corporate sector. Since then, we have become increasingly sophisticated in our recognition of the incentives caused by the interactions of corporate and personal taxes, but with this sophistication has come an end to that blissful state of clear understanding. The chapter by Scholes and Wolfson provides ample evidence of these twin developments. Combining careful reasoning with an appreciation of the nuances of the tax code, the authors question whether corporate income really is subject to double taxation and discuss in considerable depth one key method of avoiding double taxation, the Employee Stock Ownership Plan (ESOP).

Scholes and Wolfson make a number of important points. In my comments, I will try to elucidate and evaluate what I see as the chapter's main themes.

1. *For new investments yielding a normal rate of return, the Tax Reform Act of 1986 favors debt over equity more than in the past.*

There is little question that the Economic Recovery Tax Act of 1981

Alan J. Auerbach, Ph.D. Harvard, is Professor of Economics and Chairman of the Department at the University of Pennsylvania.

did so, reducing marginal tax rates on all individuals and thereby reducing for everyone the personal tax advantage of partially taxed equity over fully taxed debt. The effects of the 1986 Act are more complicated, however, because the further reduction in personal taxes was accompanied by an increase in capital gains taxes and a reduction in the corporate tax rate. The increase in capital gains taxes also make debt more attractive, but the corporate rate reduction works in the opposite direction. It is clear now that no one can have an absolute tax preference for equity over debt, since the maximum single tax on interest income, 33 percent, is below the minimum tax on equity income, the corporate level 34 percent tax rate. But equity may be found in the portfolios of low bracket investors, such as pension funds, for whom equity has never been tax favored. For such investors, the 1986 Act increased the attractiveness of equity through the corporate rate reduction. It is not transparent to me that the net impact on the demand for equity should have declined as a result of these provisions of the 1986 Act.

2. *One must distinguish between the incentives for new enterprises to issue debt to finance marginal investments from incentives to refinance existing cash flows by restructuring. For existing equity flows, the corporate double tax is less avoidable and hence more likely to be capitalized.*

Let us posit that there is a tax advantage to issuing debt instead of equity to finance a new project that yields a normal rate of return. If there is additional value to the enterprise, this value cannot be financed by debt without the payment of additional individual taxes. This value could come from inframarginal rents to new projects or quasi-rents to existing projects. In either case, however, the firm must subject its owners to immediate personal taxes to replace debt with equity. This reduces the tax advantage to debt.

Consider a simple example of an equity position in which the investor has a zero basis for tax purposes. Then, if the corporation borrows to repurchase equity or pay a dividend, the investor pays a tax on the entire distribution now, instead of in the future. If the corporation invests at the same after-tax rate as the investor, then the personal tax today just equals in present value the personal tax forgone in the future, and the investor is indifferent with respect to the decision. In reality, there are many complications that must be considered, but the basic message is an important one, that to a certain extent the double taxation of equity earnings is inescapable. This has an important corollary implication, that the inescapable double taxes should be capitalized into corporate values, reducing the effective tax rate on marginal investment financed by retained earnings.

This general point is not a new one, but its implications in the current economic environment are important. In particular, with the increase in capital gains taxes in 1986, it is difficult to explain the vast degree of restructuring activity that has occurred as being caused by *changes* in the tax treatment of debt and equity. Moreover, to the extent that restructuring is associated with changes in ownership, the 1986 Act's repeal of the General Utilities doctrine, increase in the corporate capital gains tax rate, and reduction in the acceleration of depreciation allowances all work against restructuring.

A second important implication of the unavoidability and capitalization of the double tax on corporate earnings is that attempts to reduce the double taxation of corporate earnings should focus on new equity issues. Providing relief for all returns to equity would provide considerable windfalls without necessarily affecting the cost of capital very much.

3. *There are other ways than borrowing to reduce corporate taxes. One that has grown in popularity is the ESOP. But it is not clear that the growth in ESOPs is the result of tax factors.*

Since so much of the current policy focus is on borrowing, Scholes and Wolfson point out that the corporate tax can be avoided in other ways. They focus in great detail on the ESOP because it has grown so much in popularity. Here, once again, the message is not a simple one. ESOPs do convey tax benefits, but these must be measured against the benefits accruing to other, related devices, such as the funding of regular employee pension plans. Compared to the regular pension plan, the ESOP has the advantage of a special tax subsidy to those lending to it plus the ability of the parent corporation to deduct dividends paid to the ESOP in certain cases. On the other hand, the ESOP has the tax disadvantage that it must invest at least half its funds in the equity of the parent corporation, while debt is the asset of choice for a nontaxable entity. From a tax perspective alone, the advantage of the ESOP over the qualified pension plan is unclear. Moreover, the other economic effects are also unclear.

Giving workers more of a share in their company gives them greater work incentives, but also worsens the allocation of risk. In the case of leveraged buyouts, it is often argued that the increase in share prices results from a move toward greater incentives, away from more efficient distribution of risk: Managers produce more due to the added incentives conveyed by having a large stake in the company that they must be compensated for having so much of their wealth tied up in a single asset. I find this argument much more plausible for a CEO in an LBO than a production worker in an ESOP. Regardless of his effort, the worker's impact on the value of *his share* of the ESOP is negligible.

Why, then, are ESOPs growing? One credible explanation the authors give is their usefulness in takeover defenses, making it harder for raiders to acquire voting control of a target company's stock. In this sense, the ESOP substitutes for debt in two distinct ways in reducing the double taxation of equity: as an alternative device for achieving reduced taxation, and as a way of thwarting debt-financed acquisitions. It is hard to believe that the current incentives associated with the establishment of ESOPs cause them to be used appropriately, from a social perspective.

4. *Conclusions: Where do we go from here?*

Scholes and Wolfson show that debt can only eliminate part of the corporate tax, and that it is not the only way to do so. One obvious implication is that tax policy initiatives should not focus on debt alone, and certainly not on particular kinds of debt. This is an important conclusion, given the current legislative climate, and is simply reinforced by the increasing difficulty of distinguishing debt from equity. There may be a tax advantage to debt, but it does not lie behind the recent *surge* in takeovers. One should not address the imbalances simply to curb takeovers.

CHAPTER 21

LBO PERFORMANCE: COMMENTS ON CHAPTER 19

Kenneth Lehn

Long and Ravenscraft apparently have three objectives in their paper: (1) to critique the recent study of leveraged buyouts (LBOs) by Kohlberg Kravis Roberts (KKR), (2) to survey the literature on the effects of LBOs on performance, and (3) to propose a study of LBOs that purportedly will improve upon existing studies. Although they raise some valid methodological points, their paper suffers from a preoccupation with the KKR study, an incomplete discussion of both the theoretical and empirical research on post-LBO performance, and a poorly specified model in their research proposal. Each of these criticisms is discussed in turn.

PREOCCUPATION WITH THE KKR STUDY

Long and Ravenscraft correctly criticize the methodology employed in the KKR study. Most valid are their criticisms of KKR's pooling of actual performance data with projected performance data, and KKR's asymmetric treatment of post-LBO acquisitions and divestitures. Notwithstanding the merits of some of their criticisms, however, Long and

Kenneth Lehn is Chief Economist, U.S. Securities and Exchange Commission. The views expressed herein are those of the author and do not necessarily reflect the views of the Commission or the author's colleagues on the Staff of the Commission.

547

Ravenscraft's preoccupation with the KKR study is inappropriate for a paper that attempts to be a scholarly piece on LBOs. Since KKR's business is doing LBOs, not conducting scholarly studies of LBOs, its study should not be elevated to the central role it plays in this paper.

INCOMPLETE SURVEY OF THE LITERATURE

Long and Ravenscraft critique the existing literature on the effects of LBOs on numerous variables, including profitability, corporate taxes, tax revenue, employment, research and development, and capital expenditures. Their survey ignores several studies that directly examine some of these issues.

For example, Smith (1989) examines 58 management buyouts (MBOs) during 1977-1986, and, similar to Kaplan (1988), Bull (1988), and Muscarella and Vetsuypens (1989), concludes that several pretax measures of operating profits, adjusted for industry trends, increase significantly following MBOs.[1] Smith finds that at least part of the increase in post-MBO profitability derives from a reduction in the amount of resources tied up in working capital; specifically, she finds evidence of a reduction in both the inventory holding period and the accounts receivable collection period. Smith concludes that the increase in post-MBO profitability does not derive from a reduction in discretionary expenditures (e.g., maintenance and repairs, advertising, research and development). For example, only 5 of the 58 companies in her sample reported material expenditures on research and development prior to their respective MBOs, suggesting that cutbacks in R&D are not an important source of the increase in post-MBO profits. Finally, although she finds a significant reduction in capital expenditures following the MBOs, she concludes that this reduction does not account for the post-MBO increase in operating profits, since capital expenditures are not an operating expense. This study is well-executed and insightful, and warrants inclusion in any serious survey of the literature on LBOs.

Long and Ravenscraft also neglect two scholarly studies concerning the tax consequences of LBOs. Schipper and Smith (1988) carefully examine the effect of LBOs on corporate tax payments for a sample of 93 LBOs during 1982-1986, and, like Kaplan and Bull, conclude that tax savings associated with these transactions are an important source of LBO premiums.[2] Contrary to Long and Ravenscraft's assertion that no such study exists, Jensen, Kaplan, and Stiglin (1989) estimate the effect of 48 LBOs during 1979-1985 on tax revenues and find that, on average, LBO transactions increase federal tax revenues by $59.4 million in the year following the LBO, and $110 million on a present value basis.[3]

In addition to neglecting other scholarly studies on post-LBO performance, Long and Ravenscraft's survey fails to place the existing empirical evidence in a theoretical context. For example, how do the authors interpret the existing evidence concerning the effects of LBOs on capital expenditures? Do reductions in these expenditures reflect elimination of wasteful projects, *à la* Jensen's free cash flow theory? Or, as many critics of LBOs believe, do they represent reductions in socially valuable projects? How would Long and Ravenscraft attempt to distinguish between these competing views?

Similarly, how do Long and Ravenscraft interpret the evidence on the employment effects of LBOs? They correctly note that because existing studies examine the effect of LBOs on the number of employees only, and not on wages and compensation, the studies are premature in concluding that LBOs "do not transfer wealth from workers to investors."[4] However, even if evidence showed that wages and compensation are cut, on average, following LBOs, would that establish that LBOs *per se* work to the detriment of employees? Or would it mean that the economics of the industries in which LBOs occur require cutbacks, and that LBOs are simply a manifestation of these industry conditions? In addition, it is difficult to test the general proposition that LBOs redistribute wealth from workers to investors, since these are not separate, monolithic groups. Many workers, of course, are beneficiaries of public and private pension plans that have been major recipients of LBO premiums.

POORLY DESIGNED MODEL IN RESEARCH PROPOSAL

Despite some weaknesses in their critique of the existing literature on LBOs, Long and Ravenscraft make several valid methodological points. Most importantly, the relatively sparse amount of publicly available, post-LBO data requires researchers to confine their studies to small sample sizes. In addition, these samples also may not be representative of all LBOs, since many firms in these samples are companies that have gone public following their respective LBOs. Long and Ravenscraft have proposed to rectify this problem by examining a rich database maintained by the Census Bureau's Center for Economic Studies. Careful examination of these data will shed a great deal of empirical light on the effects of LBOs, and Long and Ravenscraft should be encouraged to explore this project. It should be noted that Professor Lichtenberg of Columbia University has nearly completed a very similar analysis of the Census Bureau's data.

Although the Census Bureau's database should answer numerous questions about LBOs, I am wary of the model that Long and Ravenscraft wish to test. In short, they propose to estimate the pre-post change in the ratio of operating income to sales as a function of a number of variables, including the pre-post change in leverage, the pre-post change in equity ownership by management, a dummy variable for whether or not there was a change in senior management, and several other variables describing the public status of the companies before and after the LBOs, and organizational changes associated with the LBOs. The model attempts to test four theories of LBO value creation, but I am not convinced that this model actually tests any of these theories. Most importantly, their independent variables presumably are endogenously determined in ways that maximize firm value. Accordingly, even if all of the theories are valid, it is unlikely that significant relationships between the independent variables and the dependent variable would be detected empirically.

The first theory that Long and Ravenscraft attempt to test is Jensen's free cash flow theory. Long and Ravenscraft argue that Jensen's theory predicts a direct relationship between change in leverage and change in operating income following LBOs. However, for several reasons, Jensen's theory would seem to predict no such relationship. First, firms presumably choose post-LBO capital structures and organizational forms that maximize firm value. Since the advantages of additional leverage vary from firm to firm, if each firm chooses the optimal amount of leverage, no significant relationship will exist between change in leverage and change in operating income. Put differently, if a direct relationship between these two variables did exist, would the implication be that some firms forwent higher profits because they did not increase leverage enough?

There is an additional reason why the Jensen hypothesis may not predict a significant relationship between change in leverage and change in operating income. The Jensen hypothesis states that leverage mitigates agency problems by committing management to pay out excess cash flow. Suppose that the XYZ Corporation presently is generating a large amount of free cash flow, and it is expected to continue to generate equivalent amounts. Assume that the company has not yet "squandered" free cash flow on value-reducing projects, but that the market expects it to. The stock price of the company will then be lower than it otherwise could be, and a profitable LBO could be consummated. However, since the Jensen hypothesis states that value is created by committing management to pay out free cash flow, the hypothesis does not require an increase in operating profits. Hence, an insignificant relationship between change in leverage and change in the operating income to sales ratio is not inconsistent with the free cash flow theory.

The proposed test of Jensen's hypothesis also is confounded in another way. Leverage may create value by providing managers with strong incentives to undo previously unproductive uses of free cash flow (e.g., selling off assets that were previously acquired in value-reducing transactions); hence, one might expect that change in leverage is associated with the value of post-LBO asset sales. However, pre-post comparisons are difficult when significant asset sales accompany LBOs, for reasons discussed by Long and Ravenscraft. For example, suppose that prior to an LBO, a tire company with an operating income/sales of 0.10 had used free cash flow unproductively by acquiring an oil company, which after its acquisition, had a corresponding ratio of 0.20. Assuming that the tire and oil operations each accounted for 50 percent of the firm's operations, the firm's pre-LBO operating income/sales ratio would be 0.15. If following, the LBO, the company sold the oil assets, its operating income/sales would decline to 0.10, despite the fact that value may well have been created by the asset sale. Since operating income excludes proceeds from asset sales, the data would reveal a decline in the firm's overall operating income/sales, and no change in the profit rate of the retained operations.

Long and Ravenscraft also state that agency theory predicts a direct relationship between the change in the percentage of equity held by management and the change in the ratio of operating income to sales. This test also is problematic. Again, presumably the change in the equity ownership of senior management is endogenous to value maximization, suggesting no observable relationship between these two variables. Furthermore, even in the rare cases where managers own relatively little equity following LBOs, the equity typically is tightly held by an outside specialist who monitors the firm's activities closely (e.g., a KKR). It seems that ownership concentration, as well as equity ownership by management, is critical in any test of agency theory.

The other theories that Long and Ravenscraft propose to test are either incapable of being tested in their proposed model, or are of second-order importance. The theory that LBOs create value by allowing firms to escape the costs of public regulation may be relevant in explaining LBOs of small firms, but since these costs have a large fixed cost component, it is unreasonable to think that they are important in explaining large transactions, such as Safeway, Beatrice, and RJR Nabisco. Hence, it is heroic to believe that variables describing the public/private status of these firms will be correlated with the change in profit rates.

Long and Ravenscraft's proposed model also attempts to test the "inefficient manager" hypothesis by including a dummy variable for whether or not there was a change in senior management following the LBO. This test is weak, since managers presumably will be replaced only when it is profitable to do so; hence, in equilibrium, no significant relationship is expected between this variable and change in operating income/sales. Two independent variables describing the change in organizational structure are included as independent variables to test the effect that simplified structures have on operating income/sales. As with most of the other independent variables, the authors need to endogenize the choice of organizational structure before examining its effect on profitability.

Finally, Long and Ravenscraft also propose to examine the likely impact of a recession on the performance of LBO firms, by employing available macroeconomic models. Bernanke and Campbell (1988) have conducted a similar analysis, and not surprisingly, predict a significant increase in default rates in the event of a recession. Formal macroeconomic modeling, however, may neglect contractual means that exist to mitigate the effects of a recession on LBO firms, including interest rate caps, options to defer interest payments, and overlapping ownership of the subordinated debt and equity in these companies, all of which reduce the expected bankruptcy costs.

Notes

1. Abbie Smith, "Corporate Ownership Structure and Performance: The Case of Management Buyouts," University of Chicago manuscript, (January 1989).
2. Katherine Schipper and Abbie Smith, "Corporate Income Tax Effects and Management Buyouts," University of Chicago manuscript, (June 1988).
3. Michael C. Jensen, Steven Kaplan, and Laura Stiglin, "Effects of LBOs on Tax Revenues of the U.S. Treasury," Division of Research, Graduate School of Business Administration, Harvard University, (February 6, 1989).

4. The SEC's Office of Economic Analysis presently is conducting a survey of more than 150 companies that bought assets from companies that did an LBO during 1980–1988. Among the questions that these companies have been asked are the number of employees before and after the asset sales, and the total wages and compensation of employees before and after the asset sales.

CHAPTER 22

LBO PERFORMANCE: COMMENTS ON CHAPTER 19

Roberta Romano

The Wall Street Journal (WSJ) has provided us with an account of William Long and David Ravenscraft's (L&R) paper on LBO performance, an account which is not fully consistent with at least my reading of what is in their paper. The principal point that I wish to make in my comment on L&R's paper therefore concerns the misimpression that can be conveyed by scholarship filtered through press coverage. There is also a self-evident corollary, the researchers' need for care in crafting their study. When the most sophisticated business newspaper's coverage draws an implication from research that ought not to be made, we have to worry—especially in the context of a politically charged subject such as LBOs.

The WSJ suggests that L&R's critique of a study of LBO performance by Kohlberg Kravis Roberts & Company (KKR) shows that LBOs are harmful for the economy.[1] Yet when I read L&R's paper, I found no evidence to support such a conclusion. L&R make some careful and very good criticisms of KKR's study, but they provide no original data on this issue. Instead, they propose to obtain new data, which could improve the quality of decision-making.

How could the confusion over the policy implication of L&R's paper arise? We all have our anecdotes of inaccurate newspaper quotes, but some of the blame must be shouldered by researchers for not underscoring

Roberta Romano is Professor of Law at the Yale Law School and at the School of Organization and Management. She received her J.D. from Yale.

the limits of their analysis, especially when it is likely to be reported in the press. The need for care should be painfully obvious in a context of researchers providing a paper to members of Congress contemplating the regulation of LBOs. I am therefore going to discuss L&R's paper from this perspective, of how a reader could arrive at an incorrect conclusion concerning the import of the paper, rather than review the criticisms that L&R make of the KKR study or their research proposal.

We are all guided by our priors when evaluating empirical research (as good Baysians we should be). So I wish to make clear at the outset my priors, which are informed by my reading of the academic literature on LBOs quite apart from KKR's study: I am hard-pressed to reject the notion that LBOs are efficiency enhancing. In addition, I find it improbable that the KKRs, Forstmann Littles, and other investment banks in the LBO market would pay out large premia and invest in LBOs if profits were not to be had post-buyout. I further doubt whether we will find wealth transfers to be the major explanation of the documented gains to pre- and post-buyout shareholders. The studies of effects on bondholders do not document losses anywhere near the size of shareholder gains; some find no losses at all (e.g., Marais, Schipper, and Smith). This asymmetry is also true concerning transfers from the U.S. fisc: Jensen, Kaplan, and Stiglin estimate, what L&R call for, that on net, tax payments increase in an LBO. And we've just heard Myron Scholes and Mark Wolfson argue that, to the extent LBOs are positive net present value transactions, the LBO debt shield cannot eliminate taxes on those returns. Moreover, as far as I am aware, there is no systematic data on the effect of LBOs on the wealth of the remaining transfer candidate, labor.

L&R do not discuss these wealth transfer issues and never explicitly state that they believe that wealth transfers are the source of LBO gains. Yet the WSJ conveyed, at least to me, the impression that L&R would favor such an explanation. I will try to identify how a cursory reading of L&R's paper creates such an impression, and why, in my opinion, they ought to be far more explicit concerning the policy implication (or lack thereof) of their critique.

Data Comparisons. L&R emphasize that contrary to KKR's finding, all other studies find reductions in research and development (R&D) expenditures, capital expenditures, and employment levels after an LBO. However, the National Science Foundation (NSF) study they use to question KKR on R&D expenditures suffers from similarly serious flaws of an extremely small sample, not all of which are LBOs, and noncomparable or limitedly comparable pre- and post-buyout years. A further complication in understanding the R&D data is that both Kaplan and Smith find that most firms in their LBO samples engaged in no reportable R&D expenditures. Yet L&R treat the NSF's data as more reliable or correct than KKR's without explanation. L&R's treatment of this data may be plausible because they find other data in KKR to be at odds with the literature, but L&R do not elaborate their reasoning. They are content with simply pointing out the discrepancy to question the validity of KKR's study and, by implication, its conclusions. Similarly, there are ambiguities in the employment level comparisons L&R provide. Kaplan's data show an increase in employment levels post-LBO but a decline in employment levels when compared to industry levels. L&R stress that industry-adjusted comparisons are more useful and therefore emphasize Kaplan's finding of a decrease. But the industry-controlled employment level decline in Kaplan's sample was not statistically significant whereas the employment level increase post-LBO was (Jensen 1989, note 14). It is not surprising that the WSJ, unaware of these qualifications to aid in interpreting the significance of the comparisons, viewed L&R's analysis as indicative of errors in KKR's research and conclusions.

Moreover, the key qualification missing from L&R's discussion of the data, which could have mitigated the WSJ's confusion over the significance of L&R's critique, is the recognition that there is no basis for assuming or concluding that a reduction in R&D or capital expenditures is necessarily a bad thing. Jensen's free cash flow theory (Jensen, 1986; 1988), to which L&R refer as a potential explanation for LBO gains, suggests that these types of expenditures *should* be reduced for takeover targets, that firms are prime subjects for restructuring when they have been engaged in R&D and capital expenditure programs that have negative net present values. I am sure that L&R would agree that their comparison is not intended as a normative objection to LBOs, but their silence can very easily be misconstrued. The reader's natural inference is to assume that the import of L&R's pointing out the disparity in KKR's findings is to undermine KKR's conclusion.

This concern over unqualified use of comparative data is highlighted when we consider L&R's quite different treatment of data that are consistent across all other studies but not included in the KKR study, the increased profitability of LBO firms and the high returns obtained by investors. In contrast to their unqualified discussion of the changes in other variables studied, when discussing the uniform finding of increased profitability,

L&R add a caveat that we do not know if the profitability measures indicate real efficiency gains or mask something else. (This statement is perhaps the source of the WSJ's gleaning of a wealth transfer LBO theme earlier noted.) L&R further imply that the high investor returns might not be correctly calculated by using a phrase that is not employed (but could be) when they discuss other data in the existing research on LBOs, "*assuming the returns are correctly calculated*" (emphasis added).

I would suggest a more cautious caveat is in order, one which provides a different gloss on the import of the data for evaluating the LBO phenomenon. The overwhelming evidence on sources of gains and transfers referred to earlier suggests that the more important question for further study is not whether there are efficiency gains from LBOs, but to what extent the gains would have occurred without the LBO, or to put it another way, what proportion are due to the new managerial incentives created by the LBO structure? Framing the issue more carefully in this way would result in a reader's being less likely to jump to overbroad conclusions. It is therefore unfortunate that L&R qualify only their discussion of profitability and returns and in the way they do so, if their point is that we need more data on LBOs before deciding whether or not to regulate, instead of the objective that the WSJ inferred from their presentation of the data, that LBOs should be restricted.

Methodological Issues. L&R rightfully criticize KKR for using projections to provide multiyear post-buyout results, and the lack of clear labelling thereof. But L&R could go further and note the problematic use of simple extrapolations from the past, comparing pre- and post-LBO performance, to draw lessons for public policy. The crucial information for *normative* evaluation is not simply postbuyout versus pre-buyout statistics, but post-buyout statistics versus a "counterfactual," what would have happened to the firm without the restructuring. For instance, if employment levels or R&D expenditures would have been reduced even more if no buyout had occurred, the policy ramifications are quite different from those based on an assumption that pre-buyout levels would have been maintained. This is, indeed, one of the reasons why L&R are interested in examining level variables that are industry-controlled. My point is not to require impossible empirical research; rather, it is to highlight the need for greater care in interpretation of data. By failing to make the subtleties of data extrapolation clear, L&R allow their criticism of KKR for finding increasing rather than decreasing expenditure and employment levels to be easily misconstrued as implying a criticism of LBOs.

The discussion of another methodological issue less closely related to the data comparisons could also encourage use of L&R's work as an attack on LBOs. For instance, L&R suggest that other researchers' studies have an unacknowledged sample selection bias in the direction of successful LBOs, because they were limited to LBOs with public documentation post-buyout, which is generated by public offerings or sales resulting in SEC filings. A conscientious reporter or legislator could readily infer from this point, an attack on LBOs. However, the direction of the selection bias is far from obvious. The public offerings in question are frequently debt issues, and the more troubled LBO firms are likely to be those that resort to additional public debt offerings and hence appear in the studies' samples, while the more successful LBO firms may be reducing their debt load and not reporting their results publicly. Further, to the extent that L&R assert that KKR's study does not suffer from such selection bias, and consists of LBOs quite different from the average, it makes it more difficult to understand why they engaged in the effort of highlighting disparities between KKR and other studies (if they are not comparable), unless the point was to discredit not only KKR but LBOs in general (or to obtain Congress's attention). I do not think that this is L&R's aim, but legislators with an axe to grind can use L&R's paper more freely for their own purposes by being able to rely on their specific criticisms without having to cope with their overall inconsistencies.

Research Proposal. Finally, L&R's construction of a research proposal also provides an instance where a possibly undesired impression is created. In specifying how they propose to investigate if the high returns to investors in an LBO are due to high risk, L&R plan to investigate the effects on LBO firms of a recession. This is most certainly useful information, but it is not the only, or most interesting, indicia of risk (except to certain politicians out to restrict LBOs a priori). L&R could examine risk measures more directly related to management's incentives, as management typically receives a very large share of the returns post-buyout and bears great risk. They could investigate, for example, rates of management turnover after LBOs, as well as actual buyout failures. Anecdotal evidence suggests that when an LBO firm runs into difficulty the CEO is fired and that the risk of termination for the LBO firm manager is far greater than that for the CEO of a publicly held corporation. The provision of systematic evidence on this issue would greatly clarify the risk-return trade-off in LBOs, without catering only to the bugaboo of certain legislators.

L&R's primary conclusion is that KKR's claim concerning the benefits from LBOs is premature. This conclusion does not mean that additional research will demonstrate that KKR's claim is wrong, as the WSJ suggests—KKR could as well be right. This point was made explicit in the version of the paper presented at the Conference (although not that distributed to Congress and the press) and I think it is a very important change. When not made explicit, the subtext is that premature implies wrong, rather than agnosticism. The valid criticisms of KKR in L&R's paper are then overwhelmed by the bottom line story—the WSJ's inference—that KKR is wrong on LBOs. And this is what I find troubling with the L&R paper (and the circumstances of its advance publicity). Research in this area is quick to be claimed, and distorted for partisan purposes by all sides.

As scholars we share a commitment to the truth: Unlike KKR, we do not have a material interest in the outcome of congressional deliberations on regulatory matters. The public and officeholders know this and rely on the credibility of our work. Integral to our calling is a responsibility to make sure that the media and Congress properly understand the limits and implications of our research. We should diligently make clear when we are making behavioral claims and when we are making normative ones. While L&R are to be commended for their useful critique of the KKR study,[2] a more cautiously crafted paper would have provided greater service to the cause of improving the quality of public decision-making.

Notes

1. "A study by [L&R] blasts a ballyhooed study of leveraged buyouts by [KKR], criticizing its methodology and challenging its pro-takeover conclusions" (Ricks).
2. I hope it is clear from my remarks that, in my judgment, Ken Lehn is correct in noting that L&R's preoccupation with KKR's study as opposed to the academic literature is seriously misplaced.

References

Jensen, M. (1986). "The Agency Costs of Free Cash Flow: Corporate Finance and Takeovers," *American Economic Review, 76,* 323.
Jensen, M. (1988). "Takeovers: Their Causes and Consequences," *Journal of Economic Perspectives, 2,* 21.
Jensen, M. (1989). "Active Investors, LBOs, and the Privatization of Bankruptcy," Harvard Business School unpublished manuscript.

Jensen, M., Kaplan, S., and Stiglin, L. (1989). "Effects of LBOs on Tax Revenues of the U.S. Treasury," *Tax Notes, 42,* 727.

Kaplan, S. (1988). "Sources of Value in Management Buyouts," unpublished doctoral dissertation, Harvard University.

Marais, L., Schipper, K., and Smith, A. "Wealth Effects of Going Private for Senior Securities," *Journal of Financial Economics* (forthcoming).

Ricks, T. (May 10, 1989). "Two Scholars Blast KKR Buy-out Study that Reached Pro-Takeover Conclusions," *The Wall Street Journal.*

Smith, Abbie. (1989). "Corporate Ownership Structure and Performance: The Case of Management Buyouts," University of Chicago Graduate School of Business School unpublished manuscript.

CHAPTER 23

COMMENTS ON CORPORATE RESTRUCTURING AND FINANCIAL ANALYSIS

Kose John

INTRODUCTION

During most of this conference I have heard views being taken from the perspectives of law and economics on the pros and cons of regulating aspects of corporate restructuring. Instead of joining this debate on whether to regulate or what regulation is appropriate, I want to examine corporate restructuring from the perspective of the theory of modern corporate finance. In the 1980s corporate restructuring has been a major activity on the corporate scene in the U.S. and abroad. There has been a number of interesting events and phenomena in these areas of takeovers, mergers, spin-offs, LBOs, MBOs, and going-private transactions. Most of us would readily concede that these events of corporate restructuring are a major part of modern corporate finance. And yet, in discussions of corporate restructuring, often one hears ill-formed new theories, ad hoc explanations, or ex post rationalizations rather than a careful analysis within the existing framework of the theory of corporate finance and its extensions. The papers at this conference were no exceptions. Is it because the evidence

Kose John is a Professor of Finance and Yamaichi Faculty Fellow at the Stern School of Business, New York University. He holds a Ph.D. in Business Administration from the University of Florida, Gainesville, Florida.

on corporate restructuring does not square with the existing paradigms of corporate finance? Do we need new paradigms to structure our thinking on issues of corporate restructuring?

Within the limited scope of these comments, I want to examine the empirical evidence on a specific form of corporate restructuring, that is, leveraged management buyouts within the framework of the established paradigms of corporate finance. See also John (1989).

THE CASE OF MBOs

In management buyouts (MBOs) a group of investors (including members of the management of the target company) forms a shell holding corporation (whose equity is privately held) to acquire the target company. Subsequent to the acquisition the newly formed company goes private. The acquisition itself is financed by very high levels of debt, ranging from 6 to 12 times the value of equity (Shleifer and Vishny, 1988).

The available evidence on MBOs indicates impressive average profitability for these restructurings. An MBO announcement elicits significant increases in stock prices (above 20 percent excess returns). The buyout investors offer premiums of about 50 percent of the pre-offer prices to take the company private and then earn additional premiums for themselves when the firm goes public again [see, e.g., Amihud (1989)]. The commonly mentioned sources of this value increase for shareholders in MBOs are (1) tax shields, (2) incentive effects, (3) wealth transfers from other stakeholders, and (4) possible private information held by management and buyout investors. The available evidence [e.g., see Bull (1989) and Kaplan (1989)] seems to favor the value creation views over the value transfer views. Kaplan (1989) concludes that the total returns created by the buyouts for public shareholders and post-buyout investors have been large, approximately 80 percent above the market return. Tax benefits and operating improvements seem to be the major components of this additional value.

CORPORATE FINANCE

The capital structure theories in corporate finance, address most closely issues of optimality of this highly levered going private restructurings.

Here we can turn to the discussion in a standard textbook for the dominant themes [see, e.g., Brealey and Myers (1988), pp. 408–37]. As shown in Modigliani and Miller (1963), the preferential treatment of debt by the taxing authority gives levered firm, additional value in the form of tax shields from debt. Of course, as Miller (1977) argues, this advantage of debt has to be adjusted for any adverse treatment of debt in personal taxation. The net tax advantage of debt could be an important factor in determining the mode of corporate financing. There are offsetting costs of debt finance, e.g., bankruptcy costs and agency costs of debt, which may depend on the characteristics of the assets. The trade-off may produce optimal debt levels, usually below 60 percent for publicly traded firms. For most corporations the debt ratio is less than 50 percent [see, e.g., Ross and Westerfield (1988), pp. 379–82].

Now the evidence on the impressive profitability of MBOs raises several questions within the conventional framework of our capital structure theory. The extraordinarily high returns seem to call into question the optimality of the debt levels of most of the existing corporations. If the high degrees of leverage achieved in MBOs are the optimal ones, should the existing firms simply undergo restructuring of capital through leveraged repurchases and so on until these high leverage levels are attained? Clearly the tax advantages which seem to be an important component of the profitability in MBOs are also available to other ongoing publicly traded firms. Recent developments in finance in the form of junk bonds (designed and marketed as such) and "strip financing" have made it easier to achieve high leverage levels.

A related puzzling aspect of the evidence is the significant highly positive effect on stock prices of MBO announcements [the average cumulative excess return within days around the announcement is about 20 percent, see Amihud (1988), pp. 5–10]. If such high leverage levels are recognized to be optimal, such that it is common knowledge that the firm has unutilized debt capacity, then the value of potential tax shields should be incorporated in the prices prior to the actual announcement of the MBO. Around the announcement itself there should not be a significant price effect.

The common wisdom as to why we do not observe extremely high leverage levels has been the direct and indirect bankruptcy costs of risky debt as well as the distortions in investment incentives it causes, such as underinvestment and risk shifting. Why are these debt-related costs less important in the setting of MBOs? Maybe under the particular organizational and ownership structure of an MBO these debt-related costs are lower and the contracts between borrowers and lenders are designed to lower agency costs. But these contracts are available to public corporations as well.

OWNERSHIP AND INCENTIVES

Maybe a crucial aspect of the viability of high levels of debt in an MBO is the incentive effects on managers when they have substantial stock ownership in the firm. These incentive effects may work through two channels. One mechanism is illustrated by Grossman and Hart (1984). Here debt acts as a precommitment device. By forgoing private benefits of control in the event of bankruptcy, the managers are bonding themselves to pursue high levels of investments, even though investment is not easily monitored by outsiders. Here a high degree of ownership by managers may mean very valuable private benefits and consequently stronger bonding effect. Another mechanism may be that if management's wealth is as undiversified as it is in the MBO setting, they are exposed to a large fraction of the total risk of the firm (not just the systematic risk). This may serve to align their incentives closely with that of debtholders, off-setting the usual risk-shifting incentives of risky debt.

It may be more costly for a publicly held firm to achieve the high degree of management stock ownership as in the case of an MBO and therefore the high degree of leverage of an MBO. It is well-documented that the debt ratios after an MBO are much higher than those pre-MBO and those of public corporations in general, Kim and Sorensen (1986) and Amihud, Lev, and Travlos (1988) present some additional evidence that firms with greater stock ownership of insiders have more debt than those with diffuse stock ownership. However, linking manager's incentives closely with the firm's stock value, as is the case in MBOs, can be accomplished in public corporations by appropriately designed managerial compensation contracts. If there is a failure in the compensation contracts in the public corporations, a raider can take over the firm and restructure the contracts, without necessarily going private.

If the value of the concentration of ownership is the value of increased control, this can be achieved even in public corporations by having the insiders hold a substantial control (say, exceeding 50 percent of the voting power). Such large shareholders will also have the incentives to monitor the management better than dispersed public shareholders. However, we find that highly concentrated ownership is rare among public firms in spite of its apparent value as an organizational structure. Moreover, if the crucial ingredient of value gains from an MBO either from the high-debt tax shield or improved incentives is the concentrated management ownership than why do we find straight leveraged buyouts (as opposed to MBOs)?

CONCLUDING REMARKS

Examining the evidence on the value gains from MBOs makes one wonder whether the conventional capital structures are optimal for the majority of existing corporations. A second question is whether these gains could be attained without going private, by appropriate recapitalization and design of managerial and debt contracts. This question is important because of the high cost of reduced liquidity when firms go private [see Amihud and Mendelson (1986)]. The lower the liquidity of a financial asset the higher its required rate of return, controlling for risk, such that the price of the illiquid restricted (or letter) stock is about 25 percent to 30 percent below the price of the publicly traded stock. Whether the unique benefits of going private can offset this cost is an important question [see also Amihud (1989), pp. 24–25].

In conclusion it seems apparent that control and ownership structure are important ingredients of value gains from MBOs. However these going-private transactions with high leverage and high concentration of ownership do not seem to be right for all firms, at all times. Perhaps dynamic models of corporate financing with possible life-cycle effects may shed light on these phenomena where going private and then going public, both, seem to create value.

References

Amihud, Y. (1989). Leverage Management Buyouts and Shareholders' Wealth. In Y. Amihud (ed.), *Leveraged Management Buyout* (Chapter 1). Homewood, IL: Dow Jones-Irwin.

Amihud, Y., Lev, B. and Travlos, N. (1988). Corporate Control and the Choice of Investment Financing. New York University working paper.

Amihud, Y. and Mendelson, H. (December 1986). Asset Pricing and the Bid-Ask Spread. *Journal of Financial Economics,* 223–46.

Brealey, R., and Myers, S. (1988). *Principles of Corporate Finance* (Third Edition). New York: McGraw-Hill.

Bull, I. (1989). Management Performance in Leveraged Buyouts: An Empirical Analysis. In Y. Amihud (ed.), *Leveraged Management Buyout* s(Chapter 3). Homewood, IL: Dow Jones-Irwin.

Grossman, S., and Hart, O. (1984). Corporate Financial Structures and Managerial Incentives. In J. McCall, (ed.), *The Economics of Information and Uncertainty.* Chicago: University of Chicago Press.

John, K. (1989). Motivations for Going Private. New York University working paper.

Kaplan, S. N. (1989). Sources of Value in Management Buyouts. In Y. Amihud (ed.), *Leveraged Management Buyouts* (Chapter 4). Homewood, IL: Dow Jones-Irwin.

Kim, W.S., and Sorensen, E. H. (1977). Debt and Taxes. *Journal of Finance 32,* 2, 261–75.

Modigliani, F., and Miller, M. (1963). Corporate Income Taxes and the Cost of Capital: A Correction. *American Economic Review 53,* 3, 433–43.

Ross, S.A., and Westerfield, R. W. (1988). *Corporate Finance.* St. Louis: Time Mirror-Mosbey College Publishing.

Shleifer, A., and Vishny, R. W. (1988). Management Buyouts as a Response to Market Pressure. In A. Auerbach (ed.), *Mergers and Acquisitions.* Chicago: University of Chicago Press.

CHAPTER 24

ROUNDTABLE DISCUSSION

*Lawrence Summers, Frank E. Richardson III,
Gordon F. Wolf, Jeffrey L. Berenson,
Alan Auerbach, Kose John*

MERTON H. MILLER, MODERATOR

We are now in our windup session. The organizers have arranged a provocative panel consisting of three practitioners and two people who come from, what I would call, the real world which is academia. One of them is Larry Summers of Harvard University, a man who has written extensively on these topics

Merton H. Miller is Robert R. McCormick Distinguished Service Professor of Finance at the Graduate School of Business (GSB), University of Chicago. He received his Ph.D. from Johns Hopkins University in 1952.

Lawrence H. Summers is the Nathaniel Ropes Professor of Political Economy at Harvard University, where he specializes in macroeconomics and the economics of taxation. He holds a Ph.D. from Harvard.

Frank E. Richardson III is President of Wesray Capital Corporation and Director of several corporations including Avis, Inc., Wilson Sporting Goods Co., and Avis Europe Limited. Mr. Richardson has a J.D. from Harvard Law School.

Gordon F. Wolf is Director and President of Golodetz Trading Corporation; Operating Principal of the Fund; and the President of Primary Capital Management I, Inc. He received is J.D. and M.B.A. degrees from Rutgers University.

Jeffrey L. Berenson is currently the Co-Director of the Merchanty Banking Group at Merrill Lynch Capital Markets. His B.A. degree was earned at Princeton, 1972.

Alan J. Auerbach, Ph.D. Harvard, is Professor of Economics and Chairman of the Department at the University of Pennsylvania.

Kose John is a Professor of Finance and Yamaichi Faculty Fellow at the Stern School of Business, New York University. He holds a Ph.D. in Business Administration from University of Florida, Gainesville, Florida.

including one recent and extremely provocative paper on wealth transfers in takeovers. It was so provocative, I am told, that it reduced even Mike Jensen to just silent rage and—you had to be there, as they say. Another academic speaker is Kose John of New York University. Of the three practitioners, one is Frank Richardson, President of Wesray Capital Corporation, one of the early pioneers in LBO-takeover work. Another is Gordon Wolf, an investment banker and mutual fund manager. The third is Jeffrey Berenson of Merrill Lynch, another corporation that some of you may have heard of and that among its many other activities does a certain amount of work in this area. And the last speaker, Kose, is an all-around theorist, particularly expert, among other things, on signaling theory, a subtle branch of economic theory that has become something of an Indian specialty in economics. Apparently it takes the traditional 5,000 years of civilization in order to see the subtleties of some of these models.

Now our format will be something like this: We will let each of the speakers have a few minutes to state a theme or some several themes. We will take them in turn, in the order that I introduced them, and then let them have at each other for a while and then we will turn it over for general, free-for-all discussion. Not just simply on the subject of this particular panel but on anything in connection with this conference that anyone would care to ask anybody else.

Larry, let me hand the platform over to you.

LAWRENCE SUMMERS

I will make a few observations on broad policy issues associated with leveraged buyouts. Let me begin with this one. There is no question that the world is better off with leveraged buyouts than without. There is no question that on balance LBOs are a good thing that have created value and increased efficiency. That observation while correct, it seems to me, is virtually irrelevant to the question of whether some policy should be instituted that would in some way scale back leveraged buyouts. Proposals for policy changes are not proposals that will eliminate these transactions entirely. They are proposals for policies that would scale them back in some way; that would restrict some or all in some way. The observation that energy consumption makes a tremendous contribution to the economy in no way would belay the case for some measure directed at increasing energy conservation. In just the same way the observation that overall LBOs are desirable is essentially irrelevant to the question of whether policies that would scale them back in some way at the margin would be in some way desirable. I think when we focus on whether they are good or bad that is really the wrong question. The right question is are the marginal ones good or are the marginal ones bad?

Let me comment on four aspects of evidence that are brought to bear, one way or other, on the question as to whether they are desirable. First, I think skepticism is warranted about any conclusion about a recent and on-going phenomena. I want to quote from the business press. One prominent business magazine gushed: "These new entrepreneurs are infusing new energy into American business. While some condemn their use of debt and their financial machinations, the fact is they are making money and that is what Wall Street loves." Another business publication reviewing the events of a crucial year wrote: "the changes that seem most in evidence this year have to do with far greater sophistication of business thought and practice. These involve persistent reexamination of the assump-tions underlying corporate policies and a willingness to consider alternatives, sometimes radically different ways, of solving problems and making money." One of the leaders of the new movement wrote a warning against possible change: "Let us remember that bad cases make bad law and the precedents that might be economic milestones in the country's future economic progress can easily become, under uninformed theoretical populist attack on business, economic millstones on our nation's economic progress for decades ahead. We must apply experience and realism to under-standing economic and business trends. We must not lose sight of the fact that competition presupposes losers in the market place as well as winners. This is the enterprise system."

Everything I just quoted was written in 1968 about the rise of conglom-erate movement.

And I could go on. I could find business and academic acolytes singing the praises of conglomerates noting the improvements of performance that had taken place in the succeeding several years following the conglomerate surge. And today we learn that that institution is a disaster. I am not saying that 10 years from now we will reach the same conclusion with respect to LBOs only that a certain skepticism is called for. We have seen this kind of enthusiasm about innovation before.

Second, the tax argument that these transactions are good for the Treasury, for they raise revenue and therefore are not subsidized, is simply an analytic error. The argument was made for many years that the oil industry in the United States was tax subsidized. If it was true, that argument would hardly be refuted by evidence suggesting that the oil industry in total paid a positive amount of tax. In just the same way the argument that LBOs are tax subsidized is hardly refuted by the observation that a transaction that is said to create $12 billion in efficiency gains also results in some gain to the federal treasury. The right question to ask is: If one envisions a transaction where there were no efficiency gains, would the treasury be better off in such transaction? That is the correct way to assess whether a transaction is tax subsidized, not just to claim revenues from the efficiency gain which we assume to exist. If one does that calculation, there is no question, given that corporations deduct interest at 34 percent and that people pay in taxes on interest at an average rate of 7 percent, that these transactions are surely subsidized by the tax system. It is also true that when people are willing to pay $12 billion more for a company than it was selling for before, that one cannot explain anything like the whole premium by tax effect; and so it is likely that these transactions would go through—most of them—without the benefit of tax subsidy. Whether the *marginal* one would go through without the tax subsidy is much more questionable.

Observation three: There is a problem in interpreting all of this evidence on post-buyout performance. There are essentially two strands of the criticism of LBOs. They go in opposite directions. One is that they cut back on everything and scale back on what the company does. The other is that the managers steal the company. Reading press reports, of which I have no direct knowledge of what the actual facts of the situation are, one reads that in the RJR Nabisco deal, efforts were made by the two bidding factions to get together and agree on a common bid.

I think it is fair to say that these efforts might have succeeded. And if these efforts had succeeded, shareholders at RJR Nabisco would have received rather less than they in fact received. And one can be reasonably confident that in some substantial number of cases, efforts to assure that there be only one bid, do succeed. To that extent there will be some element of buying companies that are undervalued, by people who have special information that points to their being undervalued. If that is true, then there is every reason to expect that in the aftermath of such an event one will see spectacular performance, and one will see abnormally good performance. To the extent that one observes a sample to take the extreme negative case of some companies that are being stolen at too low a price and some companies that are being liquidated, one might expect to see no difference between the on-average performance after the LBO and what took place beforehand. It would hardly be appropriate to conclude from that that the institution was a wholly benign one. Again, I think the evidence we have is rather badly oversold.

Last observation: What does this say about economic policy? Less, I think, than it might seem because we have not been successful in crafting a very satisfactory solution that would not have highly adverse consequences. I do think there is a need to examine very closely tax provisions in this area, and I have the suspicion (though I can't identify the means) that appropriate tax reforms would eliminate some marginal undesirable, heavily subsidized LBOs without interfering with a great deal of economic activity that is efficiency enhancing. At the same time I think strengthening the role of outside directors to protect shareholders from the possibility of companies being taken away inappropriately is a second area where scrutiny is appropriate. And above all else I think a healthy skepticism and need for continuing scrutiny is what is suggested by our experience with conglomerates.

FRANK E. RICHARDSON

I have been fortunate in that I have been able to observe firsthand most of the buyouts that Wesray has organized (about 36 buyouts) and we have sponsored two other affiliated groups who among them have organized about 8 buyouts. Having a ringside seat at this phenomenon I am heavily influenced by what I have observed empirically as opposed to arriving at generalizations based on aggregate data or statistical tests on all the buyouts.

Yet the first thing that really strikes me is that our language, our semantics, is really hindering the dialogue because those of us who have been through these deals are constantly saying to each other you really cannot generalize because each deal is different depending on the product, the size, the capital structure, the management context. I think this is particularly important to emphasize in the congressional dialogue going on in Washington now because the term *leverage buyout* is being applied to two kinds of transactions, which to me are different as night and day: (1) The old classic bootstrap which was really a divestment or divestiture of a fairly simple business. (2) The other is the going private of a public multi-product companies.

KKR's original deals were, as you all know, done at Bear Stearns. When they set out to raise their first fund, there were about 10 deals which they showed as their track record. All of these deals were single product companies, most of them bought as divestitures from public companies; a couple of them were entrepreneurial family companies purchased through a fairly high degree of leverage. About 7 out of 10 were extremely successful. Wesray just by kind of historical development of our policy has stuck to deals very similar to that. For example, Gibson, a third-tier subsidiary of RCA, was a greeting card company owned by C.I.T., which in turn was a finance company owned by RCA. Probably the largest deal of this type that I am aware of was Duracel—a divestiture of Dart which was a KKR deal but that is a single-line company even though they paid a $1.8 billion for it. I know because we were competing bidder. We dropped out at $1.4 billion. We thought that was far too much risk. That deal is far exceeding their maximum management projections and the deal is going to work just fine.

I would contrast these deals to what's emerged recently and what's caused all the attention: the going private transaction of a public company, almost always a multiproduct company like RJR or Beatrice, which are to me totally different transactions from what I call *leveraged buyouts*—except that we happen to use the same name. In doing those latter deals, there is a totally different kind of risk being taken. There is a very rapid escalation of a bust-up value—that is, the value of each of the pieces standing alone—and then because it is done in a public context, decisions have to be made quickly, usually in an auction-type mode, and people are really betting on what the breakup value is.

In the old-fashioned KKR or Wesray type deals of which many still are being done, the risk profile is totally different. The group putting the deal together has the opportunity to focus in depth on the product line and the management so that the projections of that one kind of business amount a totally different kind of assessment—an ability to predict more securely what the future will hold. I think that much of the outrage and concern relates more to Beatrice and RJR deals where it's clear that people are kind of winging it and the company is going to be radically changed. Of course, jobs will be lost. Any consideration of tax regulations or legal fairness should focus on the fact that you are dealing with two different beasts. Consider what happens to a Wilson Sporting Goods which was one of our extremely successful transaction. Wilson belonged to Pepsi for about 20 years, they had about 12 different presidents; they were all guys who were being trained how to put sugar water with caramel coloring in the cans and sell it to people and they were sent out to run a tennis racket and a golf ball company and none of them succeeded. After it was purchased in a highly leveraged format, Wilson's operating earnings went from minus $18 million to plus $45 million in a three-year period. Something happened there different from just changing management techniques. A radical change occurred. It would be hard to say that for some reason those transactions are wrong or bad or poor for the economy, but it is not something that can be statistically analyzcd.

My final point is that (case) law in this country is that all public companies being sold have to be auctioned off. And I just read the Macmillan case and you see the incredible machinations that that management went through to avoid the effects of that auction process. Auctions have changed the way in which companies are being sold, and it is causing some very, very high prices to be paid. I do not like going through auctions because a tremendous amount of time is wasted and the whole due-diligence function is circumvented. But the Supreme Court of Delaware is forcing companies be sold through auction and this process maybe giving rise to some of the very problems that people are talking about, namely, the potential failures.

GORDON F. WOLF

I come from the M&A side of the business. Speaking of value additivity of restructuring, it is the greatest thing in the world for us to keep restructuring portfolios because it generates all the fees that make investment bankers rich. The approach that I take in analyzing restructuring is that the corporation really is nothing more than the sum of the strategic business units that it is composed of. And the corporate body, the shares that trade, is really a vessel to hold this group of strategic business units. Maximizing shareholder wealth is simply the continual restructuring of that portfolio much the way an investor would restructure his own stock portfolio by making the decision of whether sell the shares and buy others or retain them, according to which combination maximizes total returns to the portfolio.

One of the problems in utilizing this model is that the accounting standards that we now have and that we have been used to really do not provide us, the outside investors, with the data needed to evaluate that portfolio of strategic business units prior to a restructuring as to what the "true" value of the corporation is. This is true even if it were correct to ignore taxes, and more fundamental issues such as whether the discounted cash flow model is most appropriate. The primary goal of management is to take that optimal composition of strategic business units (SBUs) and run it to maximize shareholder value.

What does this mean in a corporate control-restructuring scenario? We are involved in one in which a target company had five SBUs of which two were low growth, high cash flow, mature businesses. And they were performing at a rate lower than that set by the target management for the entire corporation. The target was trading about 7.5 times net which is a relatively low multiple. An outside group of investors identified the two SBUs as ripe for divestiture. We were engaged to help the outside investor group develop a plan. We did so, and then we approached management to see if we could obtain more information. We came up with good ideas what to do with these strategic business units but were turned down. Then the company decided that this was not such a bad idea after all. They split the company into five separate corporations in anticipation of divesting the two strategic business units. They did so and from the proceeds of divestiture they bought back 40 percent of the outstanding shares which had the effect of increasing earnings per share of the corporate business units that remained. A corporate control transaction developed when my investors, still dissatisfied with the share price, launched a tender offer at about 40 percent over the new market price. Then looking at the strategic business units that were left, another investor came in and bid somewhere in excess of 50 percent above where my investors had tended. The result was that the stock which when we started was $40 went to $80 and finally was acquired at $140 a share.

The conclusion I have come to from this and other cases is that, for a more efficient valuation of corporations as a whole, we need to have substantially better access to the data that support the strategic business unit provided on a regular basis so that we as investors can make periodic calculations and decisions as to how well management is managing its own portfolio. The defensive benefit is that the stock price should react and be substantially higher than it otherwise would be, knowing that the private value of those strategic business units might be greater than the sum of its parts.

JEFFREY L. BERENSON

Merrill Lynch as an institution and to an extent me personally has been involved in something like $50–$60 billion in transaction value buyouts in the last decade. So we had an opportunity both as a principal and as an agent to form views that have some relevance to this whole dialogue. Let me concentrate on the couple of issues that I view as more practical than academic. From my perspective as an M&A practitioner, on the question of value of LBOs there are two things that buyout phenomena have done which have been and will continue to be important to the way U.S. corporations do business.

1. LBOs have transferred ownership into the hands of management and changed the history of the way corporate managers in America have been compensated over the last 20 or 30 years. This demonstrates that a

premium historically had been typically put on being big, not on being profitable and not on creating wealth.

2. Much to the dismay of most corporate managers in America, the buyout phenomena has created a marketplace for corporations that is significantly more expanded than it was; it puts people under pressure to perform. Somebody made a comment here earlier about managers stealing companies. There seems to be a lot of skepticism still about the ability of people to do deals in a way that is somehow unfair based on the notion of an inside track. In my experience this is utter nonsense. This market is infinitely more efficient than any market I have been exposed to and I have done a lot of business outside the United States. I think you would be hard-pressed to find good evidence which would suggest that you can steal a company. RJR was mentioned as such a case, and the proof is in the pudding. The fact of the matter is that the KKR and Shearson did not get together, and that KKR acquired a company for prices that were generally viewed as being quite rich.

On the issue of regulations, I would just suggest to you that trying to regulate this business is quite dangerous. It is very easy to sit around and pick on things like deductibility of interest, to define what is debt and what is equity, but once you start that there is no stop to it. There is great danger in amending the tax code to deal with whatever the abuses of LBO phenomena one might feel exist.

Finally are LBOs good or bad? I think it is too early to tell in general. Thus far I would say they have been good. I think we have to go through a recession. I think that the market will take care of the marginal credits. I think the thing that we should focus on is whether the phenomena on balance create benefits to the economy.

KOSE JOHN

Yesterday and today we heard primarily two kinds of things. One considers professional, legal, or economic policy issues, and the other takes bits and pieces, trying to explain what is going on in the corporate restructuring area. You always get the feeling that they are respectively either ad hoc rationalizations or little bits which explain only one aspect of corporate restructuring. As one who thinks of himself as working in corporate finance I kept asking myself, "how do these things—major events in the restructuring of corporations—square with the what we usually think of as the broad paradigms in corporate finance." I thought this was a good time to ask these questions because Mert Miller is sitting by my side.

One of the things in finance, that the corporate finance people spend lot of time on, is the issue of whether there is an optimal debt equity structure. Take the case of management buyouts where the buyout person pays a high premium for an existing corporation, premiums up to 50 percent, takes the firm private, and is still able to garner for himself substantial returns on his equity. As was pointed out in several studies, there seems to be a large amount of value created for the person involved, partly to the equity holders and partly to the person who is doing the buyouts. Now, considering conventional corporate finance, if it is suggested that these highly leveraged transactions seem to generate value, then the question is, what about the usual thing said about the optimality of the capital structure? The usual notion, as we all know, is that some amount of debt is good because we get the tax shields which add value to the corporation provided of course, that the personal tax situation on debt versus equity income does not overturn the corporate tax deductibility of debt. For whatever reason, whether it is the tax shields or not, if these high leveraged transactions are in some sense optimal in creating all this new value, then the natural question is, can public corporations generate this value by recapitalizing themselves? There are many avenues available to corporations to achieve a high degree of leverage and increase in values.

The second issue then is: "Is going private an essential part of it?" Can an ongoing corporation without going private generate the same kind of value by recapitalizing themselves, by achieving a high degree of debt? One of the things that has been brought out several times is that there have been a lot of changes in the tax structure which seem to indicate that the value of leverage as a means of achieving tax shelters has, if anything, gone up. These changes have been in the corporate tax structure as well as the personal tax structure. Second are the improvements made in the packaging the reorganization and the marketing of junk bonds made it easier, at least from the point of view of transaction costs, to achieve a high degree of leverage?

Then a natural question is why don't you find most firms doing it? Now, of course, a comeback would be well it is not so simple; the usual corporate finance paradigms would say, there are all these varied associated costs of leverage like bankruptcy costs/agency costs, both direct and indirect. You tend to monkey around with impacts on investment policies resulting from this high degree of debt. Then maybe there is something in the specifics of the contracts between lenders and borrowers in these highly leveraged transactions which make it such that these agency costs of debt are lower. Then, of course, this contracting out is available to public corporations also. Maybe you could alter the contracting of the debt and in fact lower the agency costs without necessarily going to a going private situation.

The issue is that the change in the organizational structure and the ownership structure is a crucial part of the outcome. In other words, the debt is not viable unless you leave a manager who wants a substantial fraction of the firm. Then the immediate retort is, that either through management contract or through reorganizing firms where the managers hold large fractions of the firm maybe you could attain some of this. But if you go back and look at public corporations, you do not see large fractions of ownership by management. Maybe then we should then follow what Sandy Grossman said yesterday and simply say: "Well, this highly leveraged state with high concentration of ownership is not for all firms at all times." Maybe there is a life cycle theory of firms. Where firms start out as entrepreneurial firms, then the entrepreneur later disappears from the scene. When there is deviation from the idealized state, what is involved is resetting by these LBOs. But again, then you ask, well, why do you allow the deviations for such a long time before you reset.

These are just a few of questions I wanted to raise about LBOs in the context of the classical corporate finance framework. These are things we all need to think about.

MODERATOR

Thank you very much. I gather we are getting into real conflict here. It is not about LBOs but academics versus practitioners. But anyway, let the panelists have at each other. Let's proceed in the order in which they started.

Larry, what is your reaction to this?

PANEL DISCUSSION

Lawrence Summers
Framers of the Constitution recognized that war was too important to leave to generals, even though it was only those who in the military who had recent experience with the battlefield. And I feel the same way about the suggestion I think actually explicit in the previous two commentators' views that one can really only learn from experience by being beneficially involved in these experiences. Perhaps it is true, that companies are never stolen....

I confess that when I hear the argument made that auctions are unde-

sirable because they result in the payment of excessive prices, I understand that kind of logic. We face lot of competition to get first-rate
economics graduate students to come to school. On our small economic
scale we saw that some people started giving larger stipends above normal scholarships. They put pressure on other people. People who have
put pressure on them complained and thought it was really much better
for everybody get together and offer low fellowships and then the students
would not have any other place to go, and the money would not be wasted
on the students. Some think we pay excessive prices for students and they
have a point. Yes, and it seems to me that the character of this suggestion
that auctions are in some sense dangerous is exactly of that kind. The
argument is made, well, look, KKR and Shearson did not get together and
that proves that competition really works. Maybe, and I hasten to say that
I have no direct knowledge of any kind. Maybe it is the case that every
time when there is an effort made to get together it never works and there
are always two people bitterly competing to the end; and somehow even
though there are two people always bitterly competing to the end, it's just
worked out that the person who paid the price, paid the right price and
realized an average gain of 50 percent over the succeeding year. I guess
that's possible. I guess another possibility is that the competition was not
quite as severe as all that; that that was the reason why there was some
premium seems a little more likely to me.

The panelists were at pains to stress that all deals were different and one
cannot generalize. I think there clearly is a difference between the spinoffs and
between going private deals, but if all deals are different and they really are so
wildly different, I imagine there must be some types of deals that are not in the
public interest, and that they ought to be restricted a little bit. I would be
interested getting their thoughts about which of the deals are restrictive, suggesting
that perhaps we need to tighten regulation in some way or other. For example,
reduce tax breaks for them.

Moderator
That is a kind of what I would call a Summers talk.

Kose John
I just want to ask a question instead of making of this an academic versus a
practitioners thing. Larry, I did not quite understand, your benchmark for
knowing whether or not a particular tax regime will give more or less taxes. It
is to ask the question what taxes would the firm have paid in the new regime

if, in fact, the firm's cash flows remain the same? I do not see why that is a proper benchmark because if in fact the tax regime is changing the incentives, and in fact is creating more cash flow, then it should be a factor to see whether there will be *new* taxes paid under the transformed cash flow system, not really with the respect to cash flow which was in place under the old regime.

Lawrence Summers

Suppose I can go to work doing two things: I can go to work working honestly in which case I will pay 30 percent of my income in tax (lots of laughter) or I can go to work in a less licit sector in which case I will pay 10 percent of my income in tax. Now it seems to me it will be sensible to argue that there was a sense in which work in the illicit sector was being subsidized by virtue of the fact that it had lower tax rate, and you would expect to see excessive effort going to work in the untaxed sector.... Then somebody came along and did a study. And said, look, all the people who were not working before, who instead went to work in the illicit sector, are now paying 10 percent of their income in the taxes. That would hardly be an argument that that illicit sector was being subsidized.

The point is, of course, when you create income you are supposed to pay taxes. The question is whether across different ways of earning income some of them involve paying less taxes than others on the same amount of income. The argument that LBOs are subsidized is exactly that.

Kose John

But what if the taxes are creating incentives for you to create the new wealth? Let's say the taxes are creating the new incentives for you who know how to create a new product or to create this additional income. The taxes have something to do with the incentives in the "new" regime.

Lawrence Summers

That is my point. There are tax benefits to these transactions clearly, but nonetheless income is taxed; so this process does create a huge amount of income and thus create extra taxes—but there are tax benefits. This means, and this is the relevant criteria, that if the transaction were purely neutral on other grounds it would be driven to take place by the tax benefits. Now in fact many of these transactions are not purely neutral on other grounds so they would take place with or without the tax benefits and the tax benefits primarily affect the distribution.

Frank, what do you think?

Frank Richardson

Well, I really did not hear Larry say anything that I feel I need to respond to. First, I did not know we were supposed to have a confrontation with academics. I feel I owe a great deal of what got me here to academics and up to this meeting I wanted to think I was completely at peace with them. I am glad that the academics have the ability to take an accurate overview, as I said I am having a lot of trouble doing so. If there is going to be regulation it is nice to know that there are people who can draw generalizations about this activity. I think, we are all moving almost faster than we can adapt or think. Whatever we do has to take into account what other countries are doing vis-à-vis the U.S. in takeovers. We should not do as the English did, enact tax policy that penalizes the English and benefits everybody else.

Jeffrey Berenson

In response to some of your articulate barbs, Larry, I would say the following: To me it is not good enough to say I think I smell a rat. I think you have to show me where the rat is. As to the question of fairness, procedural fairness, I stand by what I said, I think that this business is procedurally quite fair. Sometimes almost too fair. I do not think that you can criticize the LBO business because somebody earns a 50 percent rate of return. You really have to look into what generates that rate of return; and I may not be smart enough, and others may be. But I cannot tell you where the economy is going; I cannot tell you how multiples will expand; I cannot tell what is going to happen to interest rates. And those are all essential elements in determining rates of return. Part of the risk in LBO operations is that you guess wrong. I cannot define a good deal or a bad deal except in retrospect. I would encourage you to bear that in mind if you think about interventionist policy with respect to the LBO business because it carries some real dangers with it.

Alan Auerbach

I think that Kose was right in pointing out the difference between changes in behavior that are considered as efficiency gains and changes of behavior that are associated with taxes.

Frank Richardson

Giving the manager who is responsible for making the results happen a significant direct equity stake now changes the way people behave, as long as it is properly structured. It really does. They spend more time on it. In the shower they think how to improve efficiency. Instead of playing golf on Friday afternoons, they work Saturday mornings, cheerfully, willingly. And for some reason it is different from bonus stock appreciation rights or stock options; usually, that is, the potential rewards are enough to create what you might call an estate. That is part of it but I think there is another much more important part which is that, where it works, there is a different atmosphere created. We are really getting rid of supervision by the so-called corporate group in the central office, which creates a dynamic that frustrates initiative. When you get rid of that and have him report solely to his own board of directors and have personal relationships with his officers...a difference in morale and spirit occurs.

INDEX

APPENDIX A
PRINCIPAL COURT CASES[†]

[†]For full citation see chapter footnotes.

APPENDIX B
FIGURES

APPENDIX C
TABLES

CONTRIBUTORS

Kevin G. Abrams is an associate with Richards, Layton & Finger. Mr. Abrams is a contributor to three chapters on corporate law contained in *The Delaware Law of Corporations and Business Organizations* and has co-authored numerous articles on various aspects of corporate law in numerous publications.

William T. Allen is Chancellor (presiding judge) of the Delaware Court of Chancery, which is a nonjury trial court that in effect is the nation's only specialized court of corporation law. Chancellor Allen has written a large number of opinions construing the requisites and operation of the "business judgment rule," and treating the obligations of boards of directors in takeover environments including most recently: *City Capital Associates Limited v. Interco Inc.*, 551 A.2d 787 (Del. Ch. 1988); In *Re RJR Nabisco, Inc. Shareholders Litigation*, C.A. No. 10389 (Del. Ch. January 31, 1989); *Paramount Communications Inc. v. Time Incorporated and Warner Communications*, Del. Ch., C.A. No. 10866 (July 14, 1989). Before assuming his current office in June 1985, Chancellor Allen practiced corporation and banking law in a Wilmington, Delaware, firm. He holds degrees from New York University (B.S., 1969) and the University of Texas (J.D., 1972).

Yakov Amihud is currently Visiting Professor at New York University, Leonard N. Stern School of Business from the Faculty of Management, Tel Aviv University. Teaching and research interests include corporate finance and securities market microstructure. Editor of *Market Making and the Changing Structure of the Securities Industry* (with T. Ho and R. Schwartz), and of *Leveraged Management Buyouts* (BUSINESS ONE IRWIN), he has published numerous articles on the effects of ownership structure and control in firms on corporate policies and on asset liquidity or expected returns; the securities markets' trading mechanisms impacts on price behavior; and market-making and dealership in securities markets.

Alan J. Auerbach, Ph.D. Harvard, is Professor of Economics and Chairman of the Department at the University of Pennsylvania. Dr. Auerbach's research and teaching focuses on Public Finance, especially issues of saving, investment, and capital income taxation. His publications include numerous articles in scholarly journals plus several books, including *The Taxation of Capital Income* and *Dynamic Fiscal Policy*.

Jeffrey L. Berenson is currently the Co-Director of the Merchant Banking Group at Merrill Lynch Capital Markets. His B.A. degree was earned at Princeton, 1972.

James L. Bicksler, who holds a Ph.D. Finance from the Stern School of Business, NYU, is a Professor of Finance at Rutgers University—Graduate School of Management. He has published in numerous professional journals including the *Journal of Finance, Journal of Financial Economics, Journal of Quantitative and Financial Analysis* and the *American Economic Review* and has edited several books in corporate finance, capital markets, and portfolio analysis. Dr. Bickslerhas consulted and testified on a variety of issues in financial economics, including several cases involving corporate governance and the market for corporate control.

Dennis J. Block, of Weil, Gotshal & Manges, is a corporate counselor and litigator who specializes in mergers and acquisitions and corporate and securities litigation. He is the co-author of *The Business Judgment Rule: Fiduciary Duties of Corporate Directors and Officers* (3d ed. 1989 & Supp. 1990) and co-author of "Securities Litigation—An Overview," published in *Securities Law Techniques* (A. Sommer, ed., 1985), co-author of a monthly column in the *New York Law Journal,* co-ediotr of *The Corporate Counsellor's DeskBook* (3d ed. 1990), and a member of the editorial boards of several legal publications. Mr. Block is a graduate of Brooklyn Law School and, before entering private practice, was a Branch Chief of Enforcement at the New York Regional office of the Securities and Exchange Commission.

Michael Bradley is the Everett E. Berg Professor of Business Administration, Professor of Finance, and Professor of Law at The University of Michigan. Professor Bradley received his Ph.D. in economics and finance from the University of Chicago in 1979. His research efforts have centered around the law and economics of corporate governance issues, with particular emphasis on the theory and evidence on corporate takeovers by tender offer, i.e., "hostile" takeovers. His work has been published in many financial economics journals and in law reviews.

Moshe Burnovski earned his Ph.D. from Tel Aviv University where he is on the Faculty of Management. His interests include corporate law, antitrust theories and regulation of intellectual property rights.

Andrew H. Chen is Distinguished Professor of Finance, Edwin L. Cox School of Business, Southern Methodist University. Professor Chen holds a Ph.D. degree from the University of California, Berkeley. He has authored and co-authored more than forty papers in academic and professional publications primarily in corporate finance. He has been consultant to law firms, banks, government agencies, and corporations, and expert witness in many rate cases. He has also been editor of several journals in economics and finance.

John C. Coffee, Jr., is the Adolf A. Berle Professor of Law at Columbia Law School. He is reporter to the American Law Institute in its efforts to draft new standards for corporate governance, and is co-author of a casebook on corporation law and a textbook on business organization and finance. Professor Coffee formerly practiced corporate law in New York with Cravath, Swaine & Moore.

James H. Evans, retired Chairman of the Board of Union Pacific Corp. (1977–1985), is currently Director of Citicorp, General Motors Corp., and Metropolitan Life Insurance Co. He is a graduate of Centre College and the University of Chicago Law School.

David L. Finger is an associate with Richards, Layton & Finger in Wilmington, Delaware.

Jesse A. Finkelstein is a member of Richards, Layton & Finger. He is a co-author of the five-volume treatise entitled *The Delaware Law of Corporations and Business Organizations* and is a co-author of *Meetings of Stockholders*. Mr. Finkelstein has authored numerous articles on various aspects of corporate law in legal and securities journals and reviews.

Blaine V. Fogg, Partner, concentrates in corporate law at Skadden, Artps, Slate, Meagher & Flom. He holds the J.D., Harvard University, 1965. He has considerable experience in mergers and acquisitions, tender offers, leveraged buyouts and recapitalizations, and joint ventures, and has represented many clients in a wide variety of transactions, including the buying group in the 1988 leveraged buyout of The Grand Union Company. Mr. Fogg co-authored a major treatise on the Hart-Scott-Rodino Antitrust Improvement Act of 1989, and he has authored various articles on tender offers and defensive tactics.

Ronald J. Gilson, a J.D. from Yale Law School, is Professor of Law at Stanford Law School, a Visiting Scholar at the Hoover Institution, and counsel to the San Francisco firm of Marron, Reid & Sheehy. He is a Reporter of the American Law Institute's Corporate Governance Project (with special responsibility for standards governing transactions in control), and Director of the Law and Business Program at Stanford Law School. Professor Gilson has written extensively in the area of corporate acquisitions, including *The Law and Finance of Corporate Acquisitions* (Foundation Press, 1986) with 1987 and 1988 Supplements and many recent *Law Journal* articles concerning corporate acquisitions.

Leo Herzel is a partner at Mayer, Brown & Platt. His specialty is corporate and securities law, which he teaches at the University of Chicago Law School. He writes frequently for legal and business periodicals, and on a regular basis for the *London Financial Times*. He is a director of Brunswick Corporation.

Isaac M. Jaroslawicz is an associate with the Business & Securities Litigation Department of Weil, Gotshal & Manges, after a 15-year career on Wall Street. Mr. Jaroslawicz graduated *magna cum laude* from the Benjamin N. Cardozo School of Law, and was a 1988 Regional Champion in both the ABA National Trial Competition and the ABA National Moot Court Competition. He was also a member of both the Law Review and Moot Court Board, and interned as a student clerk to the Hon. Robert W. Sweet, U.S. District Judge for the Southern District of New York.

Kose John is a Professor of Finance and Yamaichi Faculty Fellow at the Stern School of Business, New York University. He holds the Ph.D. in Business Administration from University of Florida, Gainesville, Florida. He has published articles on options, capital market theory and corporate finance in the leading journals in economics and finance. His current research interests include design and valuation of optimal financing contracts and corporate securities. He currently serves on the Editorial Board of several journals of finance and economics.

Kenneth M. Lehn is Chief Economist, U.S. Securities and Exchange Commission, June 1987 to present, on leave from Washington University from which he received the Ph.D. in 1981. He has published many recent journal articles on takeovers, his latest in the 1989 *Journal of Finance* on "Going Private."

William F. Long is Guest Scholar, Brookings Institution, Washington, D.C., and independent economic consultant. He holds a Ph.D., 1970 from the University of California, Berkeley. Past positions: manager, Line of Business Program, Federal Trade Commission, 1974–1986; Assistant Professor, Economics, Cornell University, 1967–1971.

Merton H. Miller is Robert R. McCormick Distinguished Service Professor of Finance at the Graduate School of Business (GSB), University of Chicago. He received his Ph.D. from Johns Hopkins University in 1952. Miller has written extensively on a variety of topics in economics and finance. Along with Franco Modigliani of M.I.T., he developed the much cited "M&M Theorems" on capital structure and dividend policy that are the foundations of the theory of corporate finance. Professor Miller is the author of several books, including *The Theory of Finance* (with Eugene F. Fama; Holt, Rinehart, and Winston, 1972). Miller recently served as chairman of a special panel appointed by the Chicago Mercantile Exchange to examine the role of futures markets in the Crash of October 1987.

Ira M. Millstein is a senior partner with Weil, Gotshal & Manges, New York City. He is a graduate of Columbia University School of Law (1949). Mr. Millstein writes and lectures on antitrust, government regulation, and corporate governance matters. He is co-author of *The Limits of Corporate Power* (Macmillan 1981) and co-editor of *The Impact of the Modern Corporation* (Columbia University Press, 1984).

Theodore N. Mirvis is a partner in the law firm of Wachtell, Lipton, Rosen & Katz. Mr. Mirvis received his J.D. degree from Harvard Law School in 1976.

The Honorable **Andrew G.T. Moore II** has been Justice of the Delaware Supreme Court since 1982. From 1964 to 1982, Justice Moore practiced law in Wilmington, Delaware, primarily in the field of corporate litigation as a Partner of the firm of Connolly, Bove & Lodge. His J.D. degree was from Tulane University. As a member of the Delaware Supreme Court, Justice Moore has authored many corporate opinions of national interest, including the following cases: *Macmillan, Newmont Mining, Revlon, Inc.,* and *Unocal.* Justice Moore is an adjunct professor of law at Delaware Law School, where he teaches a seminar in advanced corporation law.

Stephen A. Radin practices law with the firm of Weil, Gotshal & Manges in New York. He is a graduate of Columbia Law School, where he was named a Harlan Fiske Stone Scholar. Mr. Radin is co-author of *The Business Judgment Rule: Fiduciary Duties of Corporate Directors* (Prentice-Hall, 3d ed. 1989 & Supp. 1990), and the author or co-author of numerous articles and continuing legal education materials on corporate governance, the business judgment rule, corporate takeovers, corporate litigation, and D&O insurance. He is also an Adjunct Professor at Fordham University Graduate School of Business Administration.

David J. Ravenscraft is Associate Professor of Finance at the University of North Carolina (Ph.D. from Northwestern). Dr. Ravenscraft's current research deals with a variety of issues in finance, economics, and strategy including: mergers, takeovers, leveraged buyouts, and sell-offs. He has written over a dozen articles in the merger area and recently completed a book entitled *Mergers, Sell-Offs & Economic Efficiency* (Brookings Institution), co-authored with F. M. Scherer. Prior to joining the UNC's faculty in 1987, he was a research economist for the Federal Trade Commission's Line of Business Program.

Frank E. Richardson III is President of Wesray Capital Corporation and Director of several corporations including Avis, Inc., Wilson Sporting Goods Co., and Avis Europe Limited. Mr. Richardson has a J.D. from Harvard Law School.

William D. Rifkin (A.B. degree Stanford and M.B.A. Harvard) is a Managing Director of Salomon Brothers Inc. and Co-Head of the Merger and Acquisition (M&A) Group. He has been part of a team representing Norton Simon Inc. when acquired by Esmark, Inc.; Esmark, Inc. when acquired by Beatrice Companies; the Seagram Company Ltd. when it acquired Tropicana Products, and many other M&A activities.

Roberta Romano is Professor of Law at the Yale Law School and at the School of Organization and Management. She is coeditor of the *Journal of Law, Economics, and Organization,* and a member of the executive council of the American Law School Association section on business associations. She received her J.D. from Yale. Her research has focused on state competition for corporate charters, the political economy of takeover laws, and directors' liability to shareholders.

Lowell E. Sachnoff is a senior partner in the firm of Sachnoff & Weaver, Ltd. He is a graduate of Harvard Law School. His practice is concentrated in the area of corporate and securities law and litigation in these areas, including securities litigation and corporate takeover matters.

Cindy A. Schipani is an Assistant Professor of Business Law at The University of Michigan. She received her J.D. at the University of Chicago Law School in 1982. Before joining the faculty of the University of Michigan in 1986, Professor Schipani was a law clerk to Michigan Supreme Court Justice Charles L. Levin and an associate at Mayer, Brown & Platt in Chicago and Dickinson, Wright, Moon, Van Dusen & Freeman in Detroit. Her research efforts include corporate governance issues and issues related to financial institutions and fiduciary duties in the takeover context.

Myron Scholes is currently a Senior Advisor at Salomon Brothers, Inc., on leave from Stanford University Graduate School of Business, where he is the Frank E. Buck Professor; and the Hoover Research Institute, where he is a Senior Researcher, and from the School of Law. Scholes, best known for his seminal work in options analysis with Fischer Black, has published numerous important journal articles in the fields of the capital asset pricing model and dividend policy, and taxation analysis and its impacts. Professor Scholes is President-Elect of the American Finance Association.

Lemma W. Senbet is Albright Professor of Finance, University of Wisconsin-Madison. He has many widely cited publications in the areas of corporate finance, international finance, and agency relationships. Articles have appeared in such journals as *Journal of Finance, Journal of Business* and *Journal of Financial and*

Quantitative Analysis. He is Associate Editor for nine professional journals and co-author of a book, *Agency Problems and Financial Contracting.*

Stuart L. Shapiro, Partner, Skadden, Arps, Slate, Meagher & Flom (J.D., Georgetown University, 1969). He concentrates in securities, corporate and takeover litigation, and merger and acquisition strategic advice. He represents corporations, individuals, and investment banks and has been engaged in this area of practice since 1970. Mr. Shapiro's takeover cases have included *Household International v. Moran, Revlon v. MacAndrews & Forbes,* and *Campeau v. Federated Department Stores.*

Lawrence H. Summers is the Nathaniel Ropes Professor of Political Economy at Harvard University where he specializes in macroeconomics and the economics of taxation. He holds a Ph.D. from Harvard. Two books, *The Asset Price Approach to Capital Taxation* and *Understanding Unemployment*, were published in 1989. He has published widely in the scholarly journals. Summers has served as a consultant to the Department of Labor and the Treasury in the United States as well as to the governments of Jamaica, Indonesia, and Mexico, and to a number of major U.S. corporations. He is the editor of *The Quarterly Journal of Economics*, a member of the Brookings Panel of Economic Activity, and a Research Associate of the National Bureau of Economic Research.

Elliott J. Weiss has an LL.B. degree from Yale and is currently Professor at Benjamin N. Cordozo School of Law, Yeshiva University. Previously he was Executive Director, Investor Responsibility Center, Washington, D.C., from 1972 to 1976; Assistant Director and Legal Advisor at the U.S. Agency for International Development from 1967 to 1972 and Associate at Paul, Weiss, Rifkind, Wharton & Garrison, New York, from 1965 to 1967. He has many scholarly articles in law journals on takeovers and disclosure and a book in progress, *Effective Boards of Directors: The Key to Corporate Accountability* (with H. M. Williams).

Gordon F. Wolf is Director and President of Golodetz Trading Corporation. He is the Operating Principal of the Fund and the President of Primary Capital Management I, Inc. He received J.D. and M.B.A. degrees from Rutgers University and a B.A. from Colgate University.

Mark A. Wolfson is Joseph McDonald Professor at Stanford University. He has a Ph.D. degree from the University of Texas. He is a Research Associate of the National Bureau of Economic Research and is on the editorial board of several accounting and financial journals. And he has dozens of publications and working papers in the areas of taxes, accounting, disclosures, and in corporate finance overall.